THE JAVA 1.1 Programmer's Reference

VENTANA

THE JAVA 1.1 Programmer's Reference

Daniel I. Joshi & Pavel A. Vorobiev, Ph.D.

The Java 1.1 Programmer's Reference

Library of Congress Cataloging-in-Publication Data

Joshi, Daniel I.
The Java 1.1 Programmer's Reference/Daniel Joshi. — 1st ed.
p. cm.
ISBN 1-56604-687-4
1. Java (Computer language) I. Title
QA76.73.J38J672 1997
005.13'3—dc21 97-16176
CIP

First Edition 9 8 7 6 5 4 3 2 1

Printed in the United States of America

Ventana Communications Group
P.O. Box 13964
Research Triangle Park, NC 27709-3964
919.544.9404
FAX 919.544.9472
http://www.vmedia.com

Ventana Communications Group is a division of International Thomson Publishing.

President
Michael E. Moran

Vice President of Content Development
Karen A. Bluestein

Director of Acquisitions and Development
Robert Kern

Editorial Operations Manager
Kerry L. B. Foster

Production Manager
John Cotterman

Art Director
Marcia Webb

Brand Manager
Jamie Jaeger Fiocco

Creative Services Manager
Diane Lennox

Acquisitions Editor
Neweleen A. Trebnik

Project Editor
Jennifer J. Rowe

Development Editor
Michelle Corbin Nichols

Copy Editor
Norma Emory

CD-ROM Specialist
Ginny Phelps

Technical Reviewer
Richard Jessup

Desktop Publisher
Jaimie Livingston

Proofreader
Tom Collins

Interior Designer
Patrick Berry

Cover Illustrator
Lisa Gill

About the Authors

Daniel I. Joshi is founder of Joshi Publishing & Marketing LLC, a Java consulting company for the media industry (www.joshipublishing.com). He continues to work as a developer in various programming languages for several Fortune 500 companies. Daniel has been working with Java since its early days.

As a veteran Java writer, he is the leading author for Ventana's *Migrating from Java 1.0 to 1.1, The Comprehensive Guide to the JDBC SQL API, The Comprehensive Guide to Visual J++*, and Sam's *Teach Yourself Java in Café in 21 Days*. Daniel also contributed to the *Java Developer's Reference* and *Web Programming Unleashed* (both Sams). As a speaker, Daniel frequently hosts cyber-conferences on Java and Java-related technologies.

Pavel A. Vorobiev is a doctoral graduate in both Physics and Mathematics. Since his migration from science to software development, he has developed several large and sophisticated projects in C++, and currently works as a senior C++ and Java developer for RCC Consultants, Inc.

Pavel started his career in Java publishing as a technical editor for *The Comprehensive Guide to Visual J++* and *The Comprehensive Guide to the JDBC SQL API*. Pavel is also coauthor of *Migrating from Java 1.0 to Java 1.1*.

Acknowledgments

I would like to acknowledge Neweleen Trebnik for her support (as always) through the entire process. To Michelle Nichols for working very hard with me to set the standards used in this book, and to Jennifer Rowe for helping implement them. I would also like to acknowledge Richard Jessup and Norma Emory for their meticulous reviews of this book. And, last, but not least, I would like to thank Pavel Vorobiev for helping me make this book a reality in such a short time.

—D. I. J.

I would like to thank my wife Marina for all the encouragement, love, and support she gave me throughout the process of writing this book. I would also like to thank my partner, Dan Joshi, for providing such an excellent work environment.

—P. A. V.

Contents

	JumpTable	xiii
	Introduction	xxxiii
Chapter 1	The java.applet Package	1
Chapter 2	The java.awt Package	11
Chapter 3	The java.awt.datatransfer Package	137
Chapter 4	The java.awt.event Package	147
Chapter 5	The java.awt.image Package	185
Chapter 6	The java.awt.peer Package	205
Chapter 7	The java.beans Package	221
Chapter 8	The java.io Package	255
Chapter 9	The java.lang Package	343
Chapter 10	The java.lang.reflect Package	425
Chapter 11	The java.math Package	439
Chapter 12	The java.net Package	447
Chapter 13	The java.rmi Package	489
Chapter 14	The java.rmi.dgc Package	509
Chapter 15	The java.rmi.registry Package	515
Chapter 16	The java.rmi.server Package	521

Chapter 17 **The java.security Package** 545
Chapter 18 **The java.security.acl Package** 581
Chapter 19 **The java.security.interfaces Package** 591
Chapter 20 **The java.sql Package** 597
Chapter 21 **The java.text Package** 629
Chapter 22 **The java.util Package** 663
Chapter 23 **The java.util.zip Package** 705
Chapter 24 **The sun.tools.debug Package** 733
Chapter 25 **The sunw.io Package** 759
Chapter 26 **The sunw.util Package** 761

Appendix A **About the Companion CD-ROM** 765
Glossary 769

Jump Table

The following jump table is an alphabetical listing of all the entries in this book, and is provided as an aid in locating information about a particular Java class when all you know is the class name.

Class	Type	Package	Relevent to	Page
AbstractMethodError	Class	java.lang		344
AccessException	Class	java.rmi	Java 1.1, RMI	490
Acl	Interface	java.security.acl	Java 1.1, Security	582
AclEntry	Interface	java.security.acl	Java 1.1, Security	583
AclNotFoundException	Class	java.security.acl	Java 1.1, Security	585
ActionEvent	Class	java.awt.event	Java 1.1	148
ActionListener	Interface	java.awt.event	Java 1.1	149
Adjustable	Interface	java.awt	Java 1.1	12
AdjustmentEvent	Class	java.awt.event	Java 1.1	150
AdjustmentListener	Interface	java.awt.event	Java 1.1	151
Adler32	Class	java.util.zip	Java 1.1	706
AlreadyBoundException	Class	java.rmi	Java 1.1, RMI	490
Applet	Class	java.applet		2
AppletContext	Interface	java.applet		5
AppletStub	Interface	java.applet		7
AreaAveragingScaleFilter	Class	java.awt.image	Java 1.1	186
ArithmeticException	Class	java.lang		344
Array	Class	java.lang.reflect	Java 1.1, Reflection	426
ArrayIndexOutOfBoundsException	Class	java.lang		345
ArrayStoreException	Class	java.lang		346
AudioClip	Interface	java.applet		8
AWTError	Class	java.awt		13
AWTEvent	Class	java.awt	Java 1.1	14
AWTEventMulticaster	Class	java.awt	Java 1.1	16
AWTException	Class	java.awt		19
BeanDescriptor	Class	java.beans	Java 1.1, Java Beans	222
BeanInfo	Interface	java.beans	Java 1.1, Java Beans	223
Beans	Class	java.beans	Java 1.1, Java Beans	224
BigDecimal	Class	java.math	Java 1.1, JDBC	440
BigInteger	Class	java.math	Java 1.1	444

Class	Type	Package	Relevent to	Page
BindException	Class	java.net	Java 1.1	448
BitSet	Class	java.util		664
Boolean	Class	java.lang		347
BorderLayout	Class	java.awt		20
BreakIterator	Class	java.text	Java 1.1, Internationalization	630
BufferedInputStream	Class	java.io		256
BufferedOutputStream	Class	java.io		258
BufferedReader	Class	java.io	Java 1.1, Internationalization	259
BufferedWriter	Class	java.io	Java 1.1, Internationalization	260
Button	Class	java.awt		22
ButtonPeer	Interface	java.awt.peer		206
Byte	Class	java.lang	Java 1.1	348
ByteArrayInputStream	Class	java.io		262
ByteArrayOutputStream	Class	java.io		263
Calendar	Class	java.util	Java 1.1, Internationalization	665
CallableStatement	Interface	java.sql	Java 1.1, JDBC	598
Canvas	Class	java.awt		24
CanvasPeer	Interface	java.awt.peer		206
CardLayout	Class	java.awt		26
Certificate	Interface	java.security	Security, Java 1.1	546
Character	Class	java.lang		350
CharacterIterator	Interface	java.text	Java 1.1, Internationalization	633
CharArrayReader	Class	java.io	Java 1.1, Internationalization	265
CharArrayWriter	Class	java.io	Java 1.1, Internationalization	266
CharConversionException	Class	java.io	Java 1.1, Internationalization	268
Checkbox	Class	java.awt		29
CheckboxGroup	Class	java.awt		32
CheckboxMenuItem	Class	java.awt		34
CheckboxMenuItemPeer	Interface	java.awt.peer		206
CheckboxPeer	Interface	java.awt.peer		207

Class	Type	Package	Relevent to	Page
CheckedInputStream	Class	java.util.zip	Java 1.1	707
CheckedOutputStream	Class	java.util.zip	Java 1.1	708
Checksum	Interface	java.util.zip	Java 1.1	710
Choice	Class	java.awt		36
ChoiceFormat	Class	java.text	Java 1.1, Internationalization	634
ChoicePeer	Interface	java.awt.peer		207
Class	Class	java.lang	Reflection	352
ClassCastException	Class	java.lang		355
ClassCircularityError	Class	java.lang		356
ClassFormatError	Class	java.lang		356
ClassLoader	Class	java.lang		357
ClassNotFoundException	Class	java.lang		359
Clipboard	Class	java.awt.datatransfer	Java 1.1	138
ClipboardOwner	Interface	java.awt.datatransfer	Java 1.1	141
Cloneable	Interface	java.lang		359
CloneNotSupportedException	Class	java.lang		360
CollationElementIterator	Class	java.text	Java 1.1, Internationalization	636
CollationKey	Class	java.text	Java 1.1, Internationalization	638
Collator	Class	java.text	Java 1.1, Internationalization	640
Color	Class	java.awt		38
ColorModel	Class	java.awt.image		186
Compiler	Class	java.lang		361
Component	Class	java.awt		40
ComponentAdapter	Class	java.awt.event	Java 1.1	151
ComponentEvent	Class	java.awt.event	Java 1.1	153
ComponentListener	Interface	java.awt.event	Java 1.1	154
ComponentPeer	Interface	java.awt.peer		208
ConnectException	Class	java.net	Java 1.1	449
ConnectException	Class	java.rmi	Java 1.1, RMI	491
ConnectIOException	Class	java.rmi	Java 1.1, RMI	492

Class	Type	Package	Relevent to	Page
Connection	Interface	java.sql	Java 1.1, JDBC	601
Constructor	Class	java.lang.reflect	Java 1.1, Reflection	428
Container	Class	java.awt		45
ContainerAdapter	Class	java.awt.event	Java 1.1	155
ContainerEvent	Class	java.awt.event	Java 1.1	156
ContainerListener	Interface	java.awt.event	Java 1.1	157
ContainerPeer	Interface	java.awt.peer		209
ContentHandler	Class	java.net		450
ContentHandlerFactory	Interface	java.net		452
CRC32	Class	java.util.zip	Java 1.1	711
CropImageFilter	Class	java.awt.image		187
Cursor	Class	java.awt	Java 1.1	48
Customizer	Interface	java.beans	Java 1.1, Java Beans	225
DatabaseMetaData	Interface	java.sql	Java 1.1, JDBC	603
DataFlavor	Class	java.awt.datatransfer	Java 1.1	142
DataFormatException	Class	java.util.zip	Java 1.1	712
DatagramPacket	Class	java.net		453
DatagramSocket	Class	java.net		454
DatagramSocketImpl	Class	java.net	Java 1.1	458
DataInput	Interface	java.io		268
DataInputStream	Class	java.io		269
DataOutput	Interface	java.io		271
DataOutputStream	Class	java.io		272
DataTruncation	Class	java.sql	Java 1.1, JDBC	608
Date	Class	java.sql	Java 1.1, JDBC	609
Date	Class	java.util		668
DateFormat	Class	java.text	Java 1.1, Internationalization	642
DateFormatSymbols	Class	java.text	Java 1.1, Internationalization	645
DebuggerCallback	Interface	sun.tools.debug	Java 1.1	734
DecimalFormat	Class	java.text	Java 1.1, Internationalization	646

Class	Type	Package	Relevent to	Page
DecimalFormatSymbols	Class	java.text	Java 1.1, Internationalization	648
Deflater	Class	java.util.zip	Java 1.1	712
DeflaterOutputStream	Class	java.util.zip	Java 1.1	715
DGC	Interface	java.rmi.dgc	RMI, Java 1.1	510
Dialog	Class	java.awt		49
DialogPeer	Interface	java.awt.peer		210
Dictionary	Class	java.util		671
DigestException	Class	java.security	Security, Java 1.1	547
DigestInputStream	Class	java.security	Security, Java 1.1	548
DigestOutputStream	Class	java.security	Security, Java 1.1	550
Dimension	Class	java.awt		51
DirectColorModel	Class	java.awt.image		188
Double	Class	java.lang		362
Driver	Interface	java.sql	Java 1.1, JDBC	611
DriverManager	Class	java.sql	Java 1.1, JDBC	612
DriverPropertyInfo	Class	java.sql	Java 1.1, JDBC	613
DSAKey	Interface	java.security.interfaces		592
DSAKeyPairGenerator	Interface	java.security.interfaces		592
DSAParams	Interface	java.security.interfaces		593
DSAPrivateKey	Interface	java.security.interfaces		594
DSAPublicKey	Interface	java.security.interfaces		594
EmptyStackException	Class	java.util		672
Enumeration	Interface	java.util		673
EOFException	Class	java.io		274
Error	Class	java.lang		363
Event	Class	java.awt		52
EventListener	Interface	java.util	Java 1.1	674
EventListener	Interface	sunw.util	Java 1.1, Java Beans	762
EventObject	Class	java.util	Java 1.1	674
EventObject	Class	sunw.util	Java 1.1, Java Beans	762

Class	Type	Package	Relevent to	Page
EventQueue	Class	java.awt	Java 1.1	56
EventSetDescriptor	Class	java.beans	Java 1.1, Java Beans	229
Exception	Class	java.lang		364
ExceptionInInitializerError	Class	java.lang	Java 1.1	365
ExportException	Class	java.rmi.server	RMI, Java 1.1	522
Externalizable	Interface	java.io	Java 1.1, Object Serialization	274
FeatureDescriptor	Class	java.beans	Java 1.1, Java Beans	231
Field	Class	java.lang.reflect	Java 1.1, Reflection	430
FieldPosition	Class	java.text	Java 1.1, Internationalization	650
File	Class	java.io		276
FileDescriptor	Class	java.io		278
FileDialog	Class	java.awt		57
FileDialogPeer	Interface	java.awt.peer		210
FileInputStream	Class	java.io		279
FilenameFilter	Interface	java.io		280
FileNameMap	Interface	java.net	Java 1.1	459
FileNotFoundException	Class	java.io		282
FileOutputStream	Class	java.io		282
FileReader	Class	java.io	Java 1.1, Internationalization	283
FileWriter	Class	java.io	Java 1.1, Internationalization	284
FilteredImageSource	Class	java.awt.image		189
FilterInputStream	Class	java.io		285
FilterOutputStream	Class	java.io		286
FilterReader	Class	java.io	Java 1.1, Internationalization	288
FilterWriter	Class	java.io	Java 1.1, Internationalization	289
Float	Class	java.lang		366
FlowLayout	Class	java.awt		60
FocusAdapter	Class	java.awt.event	Java 1.1	158
FocusEvent	Class	java.awt.event	Java 1.1	160
FocusListener	Interface	java.awt.event	Java 1.1	161

Class	Type	Package	Relevent to	Page
Font	Class	java.awt		61
FontMetrics	Class	java.awt		64
FontPeer	Interface	java.awt.peer	Java 1.1,	211
Format	Class	java.text	Java 1.1, Internationalization	651
Frame	Class	java.awt		66
FramePeer	Interface	java.awt.peer		211
Graphics	Class	java.awt		68
GregorianCalendar	Class	java.util	Java 1.1, Internationalization	675
GridBagConstraints	Class	java.awt		71
GridBagLayout	Class	java.awt		73
GridLayout	Class	java.awt		76
Group	Interface	java.security.acl	Java 1.1, Security	585
GZIPInputStream	Class	java.util.zip	Java 1.1	716
GZIPOutputStream	Class	java.util.zip	Java 1.1	717
Hashtable	Class	java.util		678
HttpURLConnection	Class	java.net	Java 1.1	460
Identity	Class	java.security	Security, Java 1.1	552
IdentityScope	Class	java.security	Security, Java 1.1	554
IllegalAccessError	Class	java.lang		368
IllegalAccessException	Class	java.lang		369
IllegalArgumentException	Class	java.lang		370
IllegalComponentStateException	Class	java.awt	Java 1.1	77
IllegalMonitorStateException	Class	java.lang		371
IllegalStateException	Class	java.lang	Java 1.1	372
IllegalThreadStateException	Class	java.lang		373
Image	Class	java.awt		78
ImageConsumer	Interface	java.awt.image		189
ImageFilter	Class	java.awt.image		190
ImageObserver	Interface	java.awt.image		194
ImageProducer	Interface	java.awt.image		194

Class	Type	Package	Relevent to	Page
IncompatibleClassChangeError	Class	java.lang		374
IndexColorModel	Class	java.awt.image		195
IndexedPropertyDescriptor	Class	java.beans	Java 1.1, Java Beans	232
IndexOutOfBoundsException	Class	java.lang		375
InetAddress	Class	java.net		463
Inflater	Class	java.util.zip	Java 1.1	719
InflaterInputStream	Class	java.util.zip	Java 1.1	721
InputEvent	Class	java.awt.event	Java 1.1	162
InputStream	Class	java.io		291
InputStreamReader	Class	java.io	Java 1.1, Internationalization	292
Insets	Class	java.awt		81
InstantiationError	Class	java.lang		376
InstantiationException	Class	java.lang		376
Integer	Class	java.lang		377
InternalError	Class	java.lang		379
InterruptedException	Class	java.lang		379
InterruptedIOException	Class	java.io		293
IntrospectionException	Class	java.beans	Java 1.1, Java Beans	234
Introspector	Class	java.beans	Java 1.1, Java Beans	234
InvalidClassException	Class	java.io	Java 1.1, Object Serialization	294
InvalidKeyException	Class	java.security	Security, Java 1.1	556
InvalidObjectException	Class	java.io	Java 1.1, Object Serialization	295
InvalidParameterException	Class	java.security	Security, Java 1.1	556
InvocationTargetException	Class	java.lang.reflect	Java 1.1, Reflection	432
IOException	Class	java.io		295
ItemEvent	Class	java.awt.event	Java 1.1	163
ItemListener	Interface	java.awt.event	Java 1.1	164
ItemSelectable	Interface	java.awt	Java 1.1	82
Key	Interface	java.security	Security, Java 1.1	557
KeyAdapter	Class	java.awt.event		165

Class	Type	Package	Relevent to	Page
KeyEvent	Class	java.awt.event	Java 1.1	165
KeyException	Class	java.security	Security, Java 1.1	558
KeyListener	Interface	java.awt.event	Java 1.1	169
KeyManagementException	Class	java.security	Security, Java 1.1	559
KeyPair	Class	java.security	Security, Java 1.1	559
KeyPairGenerator	Class	java.security	Security, Java 1.1	560
Label	Class	java.awt		83
LabelPeer	Interface	java.awt.peer		212
LastOwnerException	Class	java.security.acl	Java 1.1, Security	586
LayoutManager	Interface	java.awt		84
LayoutManager2	Interface	java.awt	Java 1.1	86
Lease	Class	java.rmi.dgc	RMI, Java 1.1	511
LightweightPeer	Interface	java.awt.peer	Java 1.1,	212
LineNumberInputStream	Class	java.io	Java 1.1	296
LineNumberReader	Class	java.io	Java 1.1, Internationalization	297
LinkageError	Class	java.lang		380
List	Class	java.awt		87
ListPeer	Interface	java.awt.peer		213
ListResourceBundle	Class	java.util	Java 1.1, Internationalization	681
LoaderHandler	Interface	java.rmi.server	RMI, Java 1.1	522
Locale	Class	java.util	Java 1.1, Internationalization	682
LocateRegistry	Class	java.rmi.registry	RMI, Java 1.1	516
LogStream	Class	java.rmi.server	RMI, Java 1.1	524
Long	Class	java.lang		381
MalformedURLException	Class	java.net		464
MarshalException	Class	java.rmi	Java 1.1, RMI	493
Math	Class	java.lang		382
MediaTracker	Class	java.awt		91
Member	Interface	java.lang.reflect	Java 1.1, Reflection	433
MemoryImageSource	Class	java.awt.image		197

Class	Type	Package	Relevent to	Page
Menu	Class	java.awt		92
MenuBar	Class	java.awt		97
MenuBarPeer	Interface	java.awt.peer		213
MenuComponent	Class	java.awt		98
MenuComponentPeer	Interface	java.awt.peer		214
MenuContainer	Interface	java.awt		100
MenuItem	Class	java.awt	Java 1.1	100
MenuItemPeer	Interface	java.awt.peer		214
MenuPeer	Interface	java.awt.peer		215
MenuShortcut	Class	java.awt	Java 1.1	102
MessageDigest	Class	java.security	Security, Java 1.1	562
MessageFormat	Class	java.text	Java 1.1, Internationalization	652
Method	Class	java.lang.reflect	Java 1.1, Reflection	434
MethodDescriptor	Class	java.beans	Java 1.1, Java Beans	235
MissingResourceException	Class	java.util	Java 1.1, Internationalization	684
Modifier	Class	java.lang.reflect	Java 1.1, Reflection	436
MouseAdapter	Class	java.awt.event	Java 1.1	170
MouseEvent	Class	java.awt.event	Java 1.1	171
MouseListener	Interface	java.awt.event	Java 1.1	172
MouseMotionAdapter	Class	java.awt.event	Java 1.1	173
MouseMotionListener	Interface	java.awt.event	Java 1.1	176
MulticastSocket	Class	java.net	Java 1.1	465
Naming	Class	java.rmi	Java 1.1, RMI	494
NegativeArraySizeException	Class	java.lang		384
NoClassDefFoundError	Class	java.lang		385
NoRouteToHostException	Class	java.net	Java 1.1	466
NoSessionException	Class	sun.tools.debug	Java 1.1	734
NoSuchAlgorithmException	Class	java.security	Security, Java 1.1	564
NoSuchElementException	Class	java.util		685
NoSuchFieldError	Class	java.lang		386

Class	Type	Package	Relevent to	Page
NoSuchFieldException	Class	java.lang	Java 1.1	386
NoSuchLineNumberException	Class	sun.tools.debug	Java 1.1	735
NoSuchMethodError	Class	java.lang		387
NoSuchMethodException	Class	java.lang		388
NoSuchObjectException	Class	java.rmi	Java 1.1, RMI	495
NoSuchProviderException	Class	java.security	Security, Java 1.1	565
NotActiveException	Class	java.io	Java 1.1, Object Serialization	299
NotBoundException	Class	java.rmi	Java 1.1, RMI	496
NotOwnerException	Class	java.security.acl	Java 1.1, Security	588
NotSerializableException	Class	java.io	Java 1.1, Object Serialization	299
NullPointerException	Class	java.lang		388
Number	Class	java.lang		389
NumberFormat	Class	java.text	Java 1.1, Internationalization	654
NumberFormatException	Class	java.lang		390
Object	Class	java.lang		391
ObjectInput	Interface	java.io	Java 1.1, Object Serialization	300
ObjectInputStream	Class	java.io	Java 1.1, Object Serialization	301
ObjectInputValidation	Interface	java.io	Java 1.1, Object Serialization	303
ObjectOutput	Interface	java.io	Java 1.1, Object Serialization	305
ObjectOutputStream	Class	java.io	Java 1.1, Object Serialization	306
ObjectStreamClass	Class	java.io	Java 1.1, Object Serialization	308
ObjectStreamException	Class	java.io	Java 1.1, Object Serialization	309
ObjID	Class	java.rmi.server	RMI, Java 1.1	525
Observable	Class	java.util		686
Observer	Interface	java.util		687
Operation	Class	java.rmi.server	RMI, Java 1.1	526
OptionalDataException	Class	java.io	Java 1.1, Object Serialization	310
OutOfMemoryError	Class	java.lang		393
OutputStream	Class	java.io		312
OutputStreamWriter	Class	java.io	Java 1.1, Internationalization	313

Class	Type	Package	Relevent to	Page
Owner	Interface	java.security.acl	Java 1.1, Security	588
PaintEvent	Class	java.awt.event	Java 1.1	177
Panel	Class	java.awt		102
PanelPeer	Interface	java.awt.peer		215
ParameterDescriptor	Class	java.beans	Java 1.1, Java Beans	237
ParseException	Class	java.text	Java 1.1, Internationalization	656
ParsePosition	Class	java.text	Java 1.1, Internationalization	657
Permission	Interface	java.security.acl	Java 1.1, Security	589
PipedInputStream	Class	java.io		314
PipedOutputStream	Class	java.io		316
PipedReader	Class	java.io	Java 1.1, Internationalization	317
PipedWriter	Class	java.io	Java 1.1, Internationalization	318
PixelGrabber	Class	java.awt.image		199
Point	Class	java.awt		104
Polygon	Class	java.awt		105
PopupMenu	Class	java.awt	Java 1.1	108
PopupMenuPeer	Interface	java.awt.peer	Java 1.1,	216
PreparedStatement	Interface	java.sql	Java 1.1, JDBC	614
Principal	Interface	java.security	Security, Java 1.1	566
PrintGraphics	Interface	java.awt	Java 1.1	110
PrintJob	Class	java.awt	Java 1.1	110
PrintStream	Class	java.io		319
PrintWriter	Class	java.io	Java 1.1, Internationalization	320
PrivateKey	Interface	java.security	Security, Java 1.1	567
Process	Class	java.lang		394
Properties	Class	java.util		688
PropertyChangeEvent	Class	java.beans	Java 1.1, Java Beans	238
PropertyChangeListener	Interface	java.beans	Java 1.1, Java Beans	239
PropertyChangeSupport	Class	java.beans	Java 1.1, Java Beans	240
PropertyDescriptor	Class	java.beans	Java 1.1, Java Beans	241

Class	Type	Package	Relevent to	Page
PropertyEditor	Interface	java.beans	Java 1.1, Java Beans	243
PropertyEditorManager	Class	java.beans	Java 1.1, Java Beans	244
PropertyEditorSupport	Class	java.beans	Java 1.1, Java Beans	245
PropertyResourceBundle	Class	java.util	Java 1.1, Internationalization	690
PropertyVetoException	Class	java.beans	Java 1.1, Java Beans	248
ProtocolException	Class	java.net		468
Provider	Class	java.security	Security, Java 1.1	568
ProviderException	Class	java.security	Security, Java 1.1	569
PublicKey	Interface	java.security	Security, Java 1.1	570
PushbackInputStream	Class	java.io		322
PushbackReader	Class	java.io	Java 1.1, Internationalization	323
Random	Class	java.util		691
RandomAccessFile	Class	java.io		325
Reader	Class	java.io	Java 1.1, Internationalization	327
Rectangle	Class	java.awt		113
Registry	Interface	java.rmi.registry	RMI, Java 1.1	517
RegistryHandler	Interface	java.rmi.registry	RMI, Java 1.1	519
Remote	Interface	java.rmi	Java 1.1, RMI	497
RemoteArray	Class	sun.tools.debug		736
RemoteBoolean	Class	sun.tools.debug		737
RemoteByte	Class	sun.tools.debug		738
RemoteCall	Interface	java.rmi.server	RMI, Java 1.1	527
RemoteChar	Class	sun.tools.debug		739
RemoteClass	Class	sun.tools.debug		740
RemoteDebugger	Class	sun.tools.debug		742
RemoteDouble	Class	sun.tools.debug		743
RemoteException	Class	java.rmi	Java 1.1, RMI	497
RemoteField	Class	sun.tools.debug		744
RemoteFloat	Class	sun.tools.debug		745
RemoteInt	Class	sun.tools.debug		746

Class	Type	Package	Relevent to	Page
RemoteLong	Class	sun.tools.debug		747
RemoteObject	Class	java.rmi.server	RMI, Java 1.1	528
RemoteObject	Class	sun.tools.debug		747
RemoteRef	Interface	java.rmi.server	RMI, Java 1.1	529
RemoteServer	Class	java.rmi.server	RMI, Java 1.1	531
RemoteShort	Class	sun.tools.debug		749
RemoteStackFrame	Class	sun.tools.debug		750
RemoteStackVariable	Class	sun.tools.debug		752
RemoteString	Class	sun.tools.debug		753
RemoteStub	Class	java.rmi.server	RMI, Java 1.1	532
RemoteThread	Class	sun.tools.debug		754
RemoteThreadGroup	Class	sun.tools.debug		755
RemoteValue	Class	sun.tools.debug		756
ReplicateScaleFilter	Class	java.awt.image	Java 1.1	203
ResourceBundle	Class	java.util	Java 1.1, Internationalization	693
ResultSet	Interface	java.sql	Java 1.1, JDBC	616
ResultSetMetaData	Interface	java.sql	Java 1.1, JDBC	619
RGBImageFilter	Class	java.awt.image		202
RMIClassLoader	Class	java.rmi.server	RMI, Java 1.1	533
RMIFailureHandler	Interface	java.rmi.server	RMI, Java 1.1	534
RMISecurityException	Class	java.rmi	Java 1.1, RMI	499
RMISecurityManager	Class	java.rmi	Java 1.1, RMI	500
RMISocketFactory	Class	java.rmi.server	RMI, Java 1.1	535
RuleBasedCollator	Class	java.text	Java 1.1, Internationalization	658
Runnable	Interface	java.lang		396
Runtime	Class	java.lang		397
RuntimeException	Class	java.lang		398
Scrollbar	Class	java.awt		116
ScrollbarPeer	Interface	java.awt.peer		216
ScrollPane	Class	java.awt	Java 1.1	119

Class	Type	Package	Relevent to	Page
ScrollPanePeer	Interface	java.awt.peer	Java 1.1,	217
SecureRandom	Class	java.security	Security, Java 1.1	570
Security	Class	java.security	Security, Java 1.1	572
SecurityException	Class	java.lang		399
SecurityManager	Class	java.lang		399
SequenceInputStream	Class	java.io		329
Serializable	Interface	java.io	Java 1.1, Object Serialization	330
Serializable	Interface	sunw.io	Java 1.1, Java Beans	760
ServerCloneException	Class	java.rmi.server	RMI, Java 1.1	536
ServerError	Class	java.rmi	Java 1.1, RMI	502
ServerException	Class	java.rmi	Java 1.1, RMI	502
ServerNotActiveException	Class	java.rmi.server	RMI, Java 1.1	536
ServerRef	Interface	java.rmi.server	RMI, Java 1.1	537
ServerRuntimeException	Class	java.rmi	Java 1.1, RMI	504
ServerSocket	Class	java.net		469
Shape	Interface	java.awt	Java 1.1	122
Short	Class	java.lang	Java 1.1	402
Signature	Class	java.security	Security, Java 1.1	573
SignatureException	Class	java.security	Security, Java 1.1	578
Signer	Class	java.security	Security, Java 1.1	578
SimpleBeanInfo	Class	java.beans	Java 1.1, Java Beans	248
SimpleDateFormat	Class	java.text	Java 1.1, Internationalization	659
SimpleTimeZone	Class	java.util	Java 1.1, Internationalization	694
Skeleton	Interface	java.rmi.server	RMI, Java 1.1	538
SkeletonMismatchException	Class	java.rmi.server	RMI, Java 1.1	540
SkeletonNotFoundException	Class	java.rmi.server	RMI, Java 1.1	540
Socket	Class	java.net		472
SocketException	Class	java.net		476
SocketImpl	Class	java.net		476
SocketImplFactory	Interface	java.net		478

Class	Type	Package	Relevent to	Page
SocketSecurityException	Class	java.rmi.server	RMI, Java 1.1	541
SQLException	Class	java.sql	Java 1.1, JDBC	620
SQLWarning	Class	java.sql	Java 1.1, JDBC	622
Stack	Class	java.util		695
StackFrame	Class	sun.tools.debug		757
StackOverflowError	Class	java.lang		404
Statement	Interface	java.sql	Java 1.1, JDBC	623
StreamCorruptedException	Class	java.io	Java 1.1, Object Serialization	331
StreamTokenizer	Class	java.io		331
String	Class	java.lang		404
StringBuffer	Class	java.lang		408
StringBufferInputStream	Class	java.io		334
StringCharacterIterator	Class	java.text	Java 1.1, Internationalization	660
StringIndexOutOfBoundsException	Class	java.lang		411
StringReader	Class	java.io	Java 1.1, Internationalization	335
StringSelection	Class	java.awt.datatransfer	Java 1.1	143
StringTokenizer	Class	java.util		697
StringWriter	Class	java.io	Java 1.1, Internationalization	336
StubNotFoundException	Class	java.rmi	Java 1.1, RMI	505
SyncFailedException	Class	java.io	Java 1.1	337
System	Class	java.lang		411
SystemColor	Class	java.awt	Java 1.1	123
TextArea	Class	java.awt		126
TextAreaPeer	Interface	java.awt.peer		217
TextComponent	Class	java.awt		130
TextComponentPeer	Interface	java.awt.peer		218
TextEvent	Class	java.awt.event	Java 1.1	178
TextField	Class	java.awt		131
TextFieldPeer	Interface	java.awt.peer		219
TextListener	Interface	java.awt.event		179

Class	Type	Package	Relevent to	Page
Thread	Class	java.lang		413
ThreadDeath	Class	java.lang		417
ThreadGroup	Class	java.lang		418
Throwable	Class	java.lang		419
Time	Class	java.sql	Java 1.1, JDBC	625
Timestamp	Class	java.sql	Java 1.1, JDBC	626
TimeZone	Class	java.util	Java 1.1, Internationalization	700
Toolkit	Class	java.awt		132
TooManyListenersException	Class	java.util	Java 1.1, Internationalization	701
Transferable	Interface	java.awt.datatransfer	Java 1.1	144
Types	Class	java.sql	Java 1.1, JDBC	627
UID	Class	java.rmi.server	RMI, Java 1.1	542
UnexpectedException	Class	java.rmi	Java 1.1, RMI	506
UnicastRemoteObject	Class	java.rmi.server	RMI, Java 1.1	543
UnknownError	Class	java.lang		420
UnknownHostException	Class	java.net		478
UnknownHostException	Class	java.rmi	Java 1.1, RMI	507
UnknownServiceException	Class	java.net		479
UnmarshalException	Class	java.rmi	Java 1.1, RMI	508
Unreferenced	Interface	java.rmi.server	RMI, Java 1.1	544
UnsatisfiedLinkError	Class	java.lang		421
UnsupportedEncodingException	Class	java.io	Java 1.1, Internationalization	337
UnsupportedFlavorException	Class	java.awt.datatransfer	Java 1.1	145
URL	Class	java.net		480
URLConnection	Class	java.net		483
URLEncoder	Class	java.net		485
URLStreamHandler	Class	java.net		486
URLStreamHandlerFactory	Interface	java.net		487
UTFDataFormatException	Class	java.io		338
Vector	Class	java.util		702

Class	Type	Package	Relevent to	Page
VerifyError	Class	java.lang		422
VetoableChangeListener	Interface	java.beans	Java 1.1, Java Beans	249
VetoableChangeSupport	Class	java.beans	Java 1.1, Java Beans	250
VirtualMachineError	Class	java.lang		422
Visibility	Interface	java.beans	Java 1.1, Java Beans	253
VMID	Class	java.rmi.dgc	RMI, Java 1.1	512
Void	Class	java.lang	Java 1.1, Reflection	423
Window	Class	java.awt		135
WindowAdapter	Class	java.awt.event	Java 1.1	181
WindowEvent	Class	java.awt.event	Java 1.1	182
WindowListener	Interface	java.awt.event	Java 1.1	183
WindowPeer	Interface	java.awt.peer		219
WriteAbortedException	Class	java.io	Java 1.1, Object Serialization	339
Writer	Class	java.io	Java 1.1, Internationalization	340
ZipEntry	Class	java.util.zip	Java 1.1	722
ZipException	Class	java.util.zip	Java 1.1	724
ZipFile	Class	java.util.zip	Java 1.1	724
ZipInputStream	Class	java.util.zip	Java 1.1	726
ZipOutputStream	Class	java.util.zip	Java 1.1	730

Introduction

The Java 1.1 Programmer's Reference is written by Java programmers for Java programmers. It is designed with the mind-set that the reader will not just read through the book but will actually use it while working in Java.

We think *The Java 1.1 Programmer's Reference* is different from typical big volume Java books in that two authors worked together to generate all the material for this book. We did not gather a team, each of whom contributed a chapter using his or her own style and advice. That sort of collaboration can result in a collection of splintered essays. As you will see, despite its size, *The Java 1.1 Programmer's Reference* is fluid and useful from beginning to end.

This book has been designed to supplement the documentation available online at JavaSoft http://www.javasoft.com. Most of the reference books we've seen are basically a rehash of what is already available online without really adding anything. However, when we began formulating the contents of this book, we started by looking at what JavaSoft's online documentation didn't cover.

The first thing that we agreed upon was the need for examples. As developers, we know that studying code often can be the most effective way to appreciate what is going on. We had initially thought to create an example for every class. However, we soon realized that was not realistic. Some classes are not designed to be used in a direct fashion, and the examples that were created usually were too simplistic if they demonstrated just one class. So you will notice selectively designed larger examples that use several related classes and do something useful. This is extremely important because these examples go beyond just showing you what a given class is to actually express how the class works and interacts with other classes.

We also noticed that the online documentation has thoroughly detailed every member of a given class with banal definitions. Because of this, we have not included definitions; instead, you will find an alphabetical list of all members of a given class for quick reference.

Note

Each class does contain a definition to ensure that readers who do not have JavaSoft's online documentation handy can still use this book.

Every now and then, a class in the online documentation will have a "See Also" section listing other classes that relate to the current one. We found this to be very useful but noticed these cross-references were quite scarce in the online documentation. As a result, we made sure that each entry in this book contains a list of related classes that you can go to for more information.

In summary, we have tried to tailor this book around the online documentation, focusing our efforts on its visible gaps. Some of this tailoring is easy to spot; others are not as obvious as you read but will prove quite productive as you work.

How This Book Is Organized

The Java 1.1 Programmer's Reference covers every single public class in Java 1.1, including interfaces and exceptions. All of these classes have been documented using the following format:

- **Icons.** Relevant icons appear at the beginning of each class. Icons have been used to denote Java 1.1 and its various features including Java Database Connectivity (JDBC), Remote Method Invocation (RMI), object serialization, Java beans, and reflection.
- **Definition.** This section can be a sentence or several paragraphs describing what the class is. The purpose of this section is twofold: First, it is here to facilitate a more complete, concise, and/or readable definition than what is available online at JavaSoft. Second, it has been added for those who might not have the online documentation handy. This way the book can remain self-sufficient.
- **Syntax & Usage.** In this section is the real meat. This section can span several pages and include examples with corresponding analyses, references to other examples, discussions of usage, warnings, tips, tricks, and much more.
- **Fields.** There's an alphabetical list of the fields for the given class, including their type and modifiers.
- **Constructors.** You'll find an alphabetical list of the constructors for the given class, including parameters.

- **Methods.** There's an alphabetical list of the methods for the given class, including parameters and a return type.
- **See Also**. This list of related classes includes those that the current class extends and interface(s) that it implements. Also listed are classes mentioned in the text and any other relevant classes. A reference to an entire package is denoted using standard Java syntax (i.e., appending an asterisk to the package name).

Conventions Used in This Book

As with any book that deals with a programming language, a set of conventions, formatting, and verbiage has to be chosen for this one. Obviously, most of its conventions are generic to the Java community. However, some conventions have been coined for a particular technology new to 1.1 and therefore have been defined in the chapter discussing that technology. Several conventions that may be ambiguous or simply nonstandard in the Java community are defined here.

Note

This book includes a glossary of definitions of key Java vocabulary terms, complete with cross-references and references back to classes in the book. If you come across a term you don't understand, be sure to check the glossary.

Conventional Vocabulary

The following terms used in this book may need clarifying:

- **appletcation.** This is a nonstandard term used for Java programs that can be executed as either a Java applet or application (depending on where they are executed from).
- **component.** We have used the term *component* in place of the Abstract Window Toolkit's term *widget*. Since all AWT widgets extend from the java.awt.Component class, it seemed more logical to call them components.
- **parameter.** Arguments for a given method or constructor are referred to as parameters.
- **pseudoexample.** Any time you see this term, it means that the code to which it refers is syntactically correct but would not compile (or it would compile but when executed would not produce the desired result). Pseudoexamples are code snippets used for illustration purposes only.

- **runnable example.** The term *runnable* is meant to let you know that the referenced code is meant to be compiled and executed in Java.
- **user.** A *user* is anyone executing a given Java program: a programmer testing code or simply a person using a Java program.

Conventional Formatting

This book has tried to reconcile all potentially ambiguous situations with the following formatting:

- Java keywords and reserved words appear in **boldface type**. This helps to avoid ambiguous statements such as this: "This for loop goes through for the duration of the loop." To the untrained eye, the keyword **for** makes this sentence confusing. Boldfacing the keyword clarifies the sentence's meaning: "This **for** loop goes through for the duration of the loop."
- In the snippets of code, you will notice some comments are italicized. This is to tell you that the comment in the code is an instruction of what to do or where you should place your own code. For example:

  ```
  for (x = 0; x < 5; x++) {
     //Body of the loop
  }
  ```

  The comment *Body of the loop* tells you that, if this were real, the body of the loop would be contained there.
- All method names in this book end with open-and-close parentheses: for example, setState().
- The new features released with the Java Development Kit (JDK) 1.1 are loosely referred to in this book as Java 1.1, the JDK 1.1, or just 1.1.

Feedback

If you have a tip, trick, example, or anything else that you think would be a good addition or if you wish to send us feedback about what you liked/disliked about this book, please e-mail us at the following address:

feedback@joshipublishing.com

Note, we may not be able to reply to each individual message.

Online Updates

Ventana provides an excellent way to keep the information in the book up-to-date: online updates. You can access this valuable resource via Ventana's World Wide Web site at http://www.vmedia.com/updates.html. Once there, you'll find updated material relevant to *The Java 1.1 Programmer's Reference.*

Let's Get Started!

Despite all of the published books, online documentation, and other resources available, there still appear to be several fundamental holes. This is probably because Java is growing exponentially and with this growth comes a lot of hype, sometimes making it hard to tell fact from fiction. We hope that this book will help you, the task-oriented Java programmer, fill some of these gaps and better accomplish your tasks.

Daniel I. Joshi
Pavel A. Vorobiev, Ph.D.

1 The java.applet Package

The java.applet package is a small package that defines the necessary functionality for Java applets. The key class, Applet, is the parent class to all Java programs to be executed as applets.

Class Applet

public synchronized java.applet.Applet extends java.awt.Panel

The Applet class is the key class for your Java program to extend in order to be considered a Java applet, that is, to be embedded inside a browser and executed by any Java-capable browser on the Internet. Once you have extended the Applet class, you need to design your applet around the life-cycle methods (init(), start(), stop(), destroy()).

The primary advantage of using a Java applet is that it can be ported to the Internet and embedded in a Web page with the <APPLET> tag, or by using the applet viewer that comes with the JDK. On the other hand, because of the extreme exposure of the Internet, applets have been severely restricted in what they can do.

Java 1.1 Tip

With the addition of the new security application programming interface (API) to Java 1.1, you can bypass some of the restrictions imposed on Java applets. For example, Java Development Kit (JDK) 1.1 applets can be granted a "trusted" status; their authenticity is verified via a digital signature and accompanying certificate for the public key (via an X.509 certificate).

The Applet class itself extends from java.awt.Panel. Thus, it inherits a default panel making it easier to design a Graphical User Interface (GUI) in Java.

Syntax & Usage

To use the Applet class, you must subclass it and then override the life-cycle methods to give it functionality. The following is a breakdown of Applet life-cycle methods:

- **init().** In this method, you include any of the applet's initialization, including loading images and environmental parameters. If you are using threads, this is usually the best place to start them. This method is called exactly once during the applet's life cycle: when the applet is first loaded.

Note

The init() method is overridden in practically all applets.

- **start().** This method is used to initialize anything an applet does after suspension, for instance, to restart an applet's threads. This method may be called more than once.

- **stop().** Override this method if you need to stop an applet's execution before quitting the applet or in temporary situations in which the applet may be paused, for instance, in stopping an applet's thread(s). This method may be called more than once.
- **destroy().** Override this method to destroy an applet's threads and free associated resources (e.g., close files, etc.). This method is called exactly once in the applet's life cycle: at the very end when the applet is closed.

A Java applet's panel behaves differently based on where you run it. The following is a list of potential scenarios from which your applet could be loaded and how your applet responds to each one:

- **Internet browser**. The applet is located inside an HTML document's window using the <APPLET> tag. Its size must be specified in the HTML file's <APPLET> tag. Then it is loaded along with the HTML document whenever someone visits the site.
- **Applet viewer.** The JDK's appletviewer.exe is very similar to the browser discussed previously, except that it looks for and loads only the <APPLET> tag in the HTML document. When executing your Java applet, it creates a special Frame for the applet with a list of specific menu commands.
- **Application.** You also can run it as a Java application under java.exe. You must explicitly create a Frame for the applet in a static main() method or in the applet's constructor and place the applet's panel into that Frame. You also must explicitly resize that Frame.

Note

If you run your applet locally as an application, it is not subject to the sandbox security restrictions that normally are imposed.

The Applet class also provides other useful functionality. To start off, you can use it to load images and audio clips. Consider the following:

```
Image myImage = getImage(
   getDocumentBase()+"/images", "Globe.gif");
AudioClip myClip = getAudioClip(
   getDocumentBase()+"/audio", "Ding.au");
```

Method getDocumentBase() is used here to get the location—file directory or URL address—of the document in which the applet is embedded.

Class Applet also is used to handle parameters passed from the <APPLET> tag in an HTML file. For example:

```
Class myApplet extends Applet
{
   String m_sPar = "undefined";
<Codefinal String PARAM = "Param1";
```

```
    public void init()
    {
        String param = getParameter(PARAM1);
        if (param != null)
            m_sPar = param;
    }
}
```

> **Tip**
>
> *It is always a good idea to check whether you received a value for a parameter or it is undefined. This is exemplified in this snippet with an if conditional.*

You also can override the getParameterInfo() method to provide information from other programs about parameters your applet would accept:

```
public String[][] getParameterInfo() {
    return new String[][] {
{"BACKGROUND", "Color", "background color"},
{"MAX_LINES",  "int",  "num. of text lines"}
    };
}
```

Finally, you could provide information about author, version, and copyright of your applet by overriding the getAppletInfo() method, as follows:

```
public String getAppletInfo()
{
    return "Name: myApplet\r\n" +
        "Version: 1.00\r\n" +
        "Copyright: The Best Software";
}
```

Fields None

Constructors

Modifiers	Constructor
public	Applet()

Methods

Modifiers	Return Type	Method
public	void	destroy()
public	AppletContext	getAppletContext()
public	String	getAppletInfo()
public	AudioClip	getAudioClip(URL)
public	AudioClip	getAudioClip(URL, String)
public	URL	getCodeBase()
public	URL	getDocumentBase()
public	Image	getImage(URL)
public	Image	getImage(URL, String)
public	Locale	getLocale()
public	String	getParameter(String)
public	String[][]	getParameterInfo()
public	void	init()
public	boolean	isActive()
public	void	play(URL)
public	void	play(URL, String)
public	void	resize(Dimension)
public	void	resize(int, int)
public final	void	setStub(AppletStub)
public	void	showStatus(String)
public	void	start()
public	void	stop()

See Also java.applet.AppletContext • java.applet.AppletStub • java.awt.Panel • java.lang.Runnable • java.lang.Thread

Interface AppletContext

public abstract synchronized interface java.applet.AppletContext

This is an interface that allows you to interact with your applet's environment (hereinafter referred to as its host). If your host is an Internet browser (and not the JDK's applet viewer, which has limited browsing capabilities), you can use AppletContext for a variety of functions.

The AppletContext interface allows you to load external files (such as audio clips or images), to send messages to the host's status bar using the showStatus() method, and to load HTML documents to the host using showDocument().

Note

Because AppletContext is an interface, it does not have any constructors. So in order to use it, you must call the method getAppletContext() from the java.applet.Applet class. This will retrieve an instance of the applet context for this applet.

Finally, AppletContext also is used to locate other applets that may be running using the getApplet() or getApplets() method.

Syntax & Usage

The following is an example in which you access an applet's environment to display a message in its browser's status bar using showStatus(). After that, showDocument() is used to load the HTML file determined by the URL address:

```
class myApplet extends Applet
{
..
AppletContext appl = getAppletContext();
appl.showStatus(
   "Please read my ReadMe.html");
try
{
appl.showDocument(new URL(
"http://www.myURL.com/ReadMe.html"));
}
catch (MalformedURLException e)
   {}
}
```

Note

This method may be ignored if the application accessing the applet is not a Web browser.

This example shows how to print the list of all applets running simultaneously:

```
class myApplet extends Applet
{
..
AppletContext appl = getAppletContext();
Enumeration en = appl.getApplets();
while (en.hasMoreElements())
   System.out.println(en.nextElement().
      toString());
}
```

Fields None

Methods

Modifiers	Return Type	Method
public abstract	Applet	getApplet(String)
public abstract	Enumeration	getApplets()
public abstract	AudioClip	getAudioClip(URL)
public abstract	Image	getImage(URL)
public abstract	void	showDocument(URL)
public abstract	void	showDocument(URL, String)
public abstract	void	showStatus(String)

See Also java.applet.Applet • java.applet.AudioClip • java.applet.AppletStub • java.awt.image

Interface AppletStub

public abstract synchronized interface java.applet.AppletStub

This interface is used internally—when an applet is loaded, a stub is appended to it by making an internal call to the setStub() method—and acts as an interface between the browser (or the applet viewer) and the applet that is executing.

Syntax & Usage You cannot access any default implementation of this interface. The only way to use this interface is to develop your own implementation of AppletStub.

Fields None

Methods

Modifiers	Return Type	Method
public abstract	void	appletResize(int, int)
public abstract	AppletContext	getAppletContext()
public abstract	URL	getCodeBase()
public abstract	URL	getDocumentBase()
public abstract	String	getParameter(String)
public abstract	boolean	isActive()

See Also java.applet.Applet • java.applet.AppletContext

Interface AudioClip

public abstract synchronized interface java.applet.AudioClip

This interface is used to define the methods needed to use an audio clip in Java.

Syntax & Usage

Specifically, you can retrieve an object implementing this interface (which you can use to play sound clips in your applet) by calling the getAudioClip() method from either the AppletContext or Applet classes.

The following example shows the usage of the AudioClip interface:

```
class myApplet extends Applet
{
AudioClip m_clip;

public myApplet()
{
try
{
   m_clip = getAudioClip(new URL(
   "http://www.myURL.com/myClip.au"));
}
catch (Exception e)
{
   m_clip = null;
}
if (m_clip != null)
   m_clip.loop();
}

public void finalize()
{
if (m_clip != null)
   m_clip.stop();
}
}
```

First, you need to get an instance of AudioClip using the java.Applet.getAudioClip() method. For that, you need to specify a URL location and catch possible exceptions. If the clip is loaded, it starts to play repeatedly (endlessly) using the loop() method. Alternatively, you can use the play() method to play this clip once only.

Last, when the applet is destroyed and the finalize() method is invoked, AudioClip will be stopped by invoking stop() method.

Fields None

Methods

Modifiers	Return Type	Method
public abstract	void	loop()
public abstract	void	play()
public abstract	void	stop()

See Also java.applet.Applet
java.applet.AppletContext

The java.awt Package

2

The java.awt is a very large package that comprises the functionality to design your graphical user interface (GUI). It contains Java components (a.k.a. *widgets*), containers, and its layout.

This package, commonly referred to as the Abstract Window Toolkit (AWT), is revolutionary in GUI design because it allows you to program a GUI that is portable across all platforms that are Java-supported. However, such versatility did not come without compromises: The AWT lacks many of the very basic characteristics in modern GUI designs. Also, since each platform displays GUI objects differently, layouts must be used to automatically handle these idiosyncrasies.

Interface Adjustable

public abstract synchronized interface java.awt.Adjustable

The Adjustable interface is used for objects with values that can be changed (i.e., adjusted) inside a specified range.

Tip

The Adjustable interface is used with ScrollPane and Scrollbar objects for specifying various adjustable values for its horizontal and/or vertical scrollbars.

Syntax & Usage Please see examples under "Class ScrollPane" and "Class Scrollbar" later in this chapter.

Fields

Modifiers	Type	Field
public static final	int	HORIZONTAL
public static final	int	VERTICAL

Constructors None

Methods

Modifiers	Return Type	Method
public abstract	void	addAdjustmentListener(AdjustmentListener)
public abstract	int	getBlockIncrement()
public abstract	int	getMaximum()
public abstract	int	getMinimum()
public abstract	int	getOrientation()
public abstract	int	getUnitIncrement()
public abstract	int	getValue()
public abstract	int	getVisibleAmount()
public abstract	void	removeAdjustmentListener(AdjustmentListener)
public abstract	void	setBlockIncrement(int)
public abstract	void	setMaximum(int)
public abstract	void	setMinimum(int)

Modifiers	Return Type	Method
public abstract	void	setUnitIncrement(int)
public abstract	void	setValue(int)
public abstract	void	setVisibleAmount(int)

See Also java.awt.Scrollbar • java.awt.ScrollPane

Class AWTError

public synchronized java.awt.AWTError extends java.lang.Error

This class is used when there is an AWT-based error. Note that even though this class is not derived from java.lang.Exception, it can be caught.

Syntax & Usage AWTError contains only one public member, which is its constructor. The constructor takes one string parameter to be used as an error message. Specifically, this error is thrown by the getDefaultToolkit() method from the Toolkit class if the default toolkit is not found or could not be instantiated.

The following shows an example of how you would catch the AWTError when using the getDefaultToolkit() method:

```
Toolkit defToolkit;
try
{
   defToolkit = Toolkit.getDefaultToolkit();
}
catch(AWTError e)
{
   defToolkit = null;
}
```

Fields None

Constructors

Modifiers	Constructor
public	AWTError(String)

Methods None

See Also java.awt.Toolkit • java.lang.Error • java.lang.Throwable

Class AWTEvent

public abstract synchronized java.awt.AWTEvent extends java.util.EventObject

AWTEvent defines a set of event masks that categorizes events, thus any component-based classes that wish to receive events use the enablesEvent() method to specify the appropriate event mask.

Note

If you register a listener to a component, the event mask is automatically specified internally.

Syntax & Usage

This class represents the root class for all AWT-based events. AWTEvent subclasses are listed as follows:

- ActionEvent
- AdjustmentEvent
- ComponentEvent
- ContainerEvent (extends ComponentEvent)
- FocusEvent (extends ComponentEvent)
- InputEvent (extends ComponentEvent)
- ItemEvent
- KeyEvent (extends InputEvent)
- MouseEvent (extends InputEvent)
- PaintEvent
- TextEvent
- WindowEvent

Note

The AWTEvent subclasses replace the single java.lang.Event object used in Java 1.0.

The following is a simple example that shows how to use the enablesEvent() method and invoke the AWTEvent class:

```
class myCanvas extends Canvas
{
   public myCanvas()
   {
      enableEvents(AWTEvent.FOCUS_EVENT_MASK);
   }

   public void processEvent(AWTEvent ev)
   {
      switch (ev.getId())
      {
      case FocusEvent.FOCUS_GAINED:
         setBackground(Color.red);
         break;
      case FocusEvent.FOCUS_LOST:
         setBackground(Color.blue);
         break;
      }
      super.processEvent(ev);
   }
}
```

As soon as you've specified AWTEvent.FOCUS_EVENT_MASK in the enablesEvent() method, this Canvas will receive focus events. So now you can override the processEvent(AWTEvent ev) method and process these events. The preceding code processes the events by changing the background color.

Fields

Modifiers	Type	Field
public static final	long	ACTION_EVENT_MASK
public static final	long	ADJUSTMENT_EVENT_MASK
public static final	long	COMPONENT_EVENT_MASK
protected	boolean	consumed
public static final	long	CONTAINER_EVENT_MASK
public static final	long	FOCUS_EVENT_MASK
protected	int	id
public static final	long	ITEM_EVENT_MASK
public static final	long	KEY_EVENT_MASK
public static final	long	MOUSE_EVENT_MASK
public static final	long	MOUSE_MOTION_EVENT_MASK
public static final	int	RESERVED_ID_MAX
public static final	long	TEXT_EVENT_MASK
public static final	long	WINDOW_EVENT_MASK

Constructors

Modifiers	Constructor
public	AWTEvent(Event)
public	AWTEvent(Object, int)

Methods

Modifiers	Return Type	Method
protected	void	consume()
public	int	getID()
protected	boolean	isConsumed()
public	String	paramString()
public	String	toString()

See Also java.awt.Component • java.awt.event.ActionEvent • java.awt.event.AdjustmentEvent • java.awt.event.ComponentEvent • java.awt.event.ContainerEvent • java.awt.event.FocusEvent • java.awt.event.InputEvent • java.awt.event.ItemEvent • java.awt.event.KeyEvent • java.awt.event.MouseEvent • java.awt.event.PaintEvent • java.awt.event.TextEvent • java.awt.event.WindowEvent • java.util.EventListener • java.util.EventObject

Class AWTEventMulticaster

public synchronized java.awt.AWTEventMulticaster extends java.lang.Object implements java.awt.event.ComponentListener, ContainerListener, FocusListener, KeyListener, MouseListener, MouseMotionListener, WindowListener, ActionListener, ItemListener, AdjustmentListener, TextListener

This class manages event listeners and delegates events to the appropriate listener (or listeners) in its chain (those that have registered themselves to the component responsible for the event).

Syntax & Usage Using this class, one event can be passed to more than one listener. It does not facilitate any constructor. Instead, it provides a set of overloaded add() methods, allowing you to create chains of ActionListeners, AdjustmentListeners, and so on. So every time a new event is fired into such a chain, it is delivered to all listeners in the chain.

The following example shows a subclass of Button, which can accept new action listeners by using the addListener() method or can remove action listeners using removeListener().

The add() methods from the AWTEventMulticaster take two parameters of the same type, in this case ActionListener. If the first listener is **null**, it returns the second listener; if the second listener is **null**, it returns the first. So the listener chain can be started. If neither the first nor the second parameter is **null**, then it creates and returns a new AWTEventMulticaster instance that links both listeners to the chain:

```
class myButton extends Button
{
  ActionListener m_MultiListener = null;

  public void addListener(
    ActionListener lstn)
  {
    m_MultiListener = AWTEventMulticaster.
      add(m_MultiListener, lstn);
  }

  public void removeListener(
    ActionListener lstn)
  {
    m_MultiListener = AWTEventMulticaster.
      remove(m_MultiListener, lstn);
  }

  public void processActionEvent(
    ActionEvent evt)
  {
    if (m_MultiListener != null)
      m_MultiListener.
      actionPerformed(evt);
  }
}
```

If an action event occurs and the processActionEvent() method is invoked, the action event is delivered to all registered listeners.

Fields

Modifiers	Type	Field
protected	EventListener	a
protected	EventListener	b

Constructors

Modifiers	Constructor
protected	AWTEventMulticaster(EventListener, EventListener)

Methods

Modifiers	Return Type	Method
public	void	actionPerformed(ActionEvent)
public static	ActionListener	add(ActionListener, ActionListener)
public static	AdjustmentListener	add(AdjustmentListener, AdjustmentListener)
public static	ComponentListener	add(ComponentListener, ComponentListener)
public static	ContainerListener	add(ContainerListener, ContainerListener)
public static	FocusListener	add(FocusListener, FocusListener)
public static	ItemListener	add(ItemListener, ItemListener)
public static	KeyListener	add(KeyListener, KeyListener)
public static	MouseListener	add(MouseListener, MouseListener)
public static	MouseMotionListener	add(MouseMotionListener, MouseMotionListener)
public static	TextListener	add(TextListener, TextListener)
public static	WindowListener	add(WindowListener, WindowListener)
protected static	EventListener	addInternal(EventListener, EventListener)
public	void	adjustmentValueChanged(AdjustmentEvent)
public	void	componentAdded(ContainerEvent)
public	void	componentHidden(ComponentEvent)
public	void	componentMoved(ComponentEvent)
public	void	componentRemoved(ContainerEvent)
public	void	componentResized(ComponentEvent)
public	void	componentShown(ComponentEvent)
public	void	focusGained(FocusEvent)
public	void	focusLost(FocusEvent)
public	void	itemStateChanged(ItemEvent)
public	void	keyPressed(KeyEvent)
public	void	keyReleased(KeyEvent)
public	void	keyTyped(KeyEvent)
public	void	mouseClicked(MouseEvent)
public	void	mouseDragged(MouseEvent)
public	void	mouseEntered(MouseEvent)
public	void	mouseExited(MouseEvent)
public	void	mouseExited(MouseEvent)
public	void	mouseMoved(MouseEvent)
public	void	mousePressed(MouseEvent)
public	void	mouseReleased(MouseEvent)
public static	ActionListener	remove(ActionListener, ActionListener)
public static	AdjustmentListener	remove(AdjustmentListener, AdjustmentListener)
public static	ComponentListener	remove(ComponentListener, ComponentListener)
public static	ContainerListener	remove(ContainerListener, ContainerListener)

Modifiers	Return Type	Method
protected	EventListener	remove(EventListener)
public static	FocusListener	remove(FocusListener, FocusListener)
public static	ItemListener	remove(ItemListener, ItemListener)
public static	KeyListener	remove(KeyListener, KeyListener)
public static	MouseListener	remove(MouseListener, MouseListener)
public static	MouseMotionListener	remove(MouseMotionListener, MouseMotionListener)
public static	TextListener	remove(TextListener, TextListener)
public static	WindowListener	remove(WindowListener, WindowListener)
protected static	EventListener	removeInternal(EventListener, EventListener)
protected	void	saveInternal(ObjectOutputStream, String)
public	void	textValueChanged(TextEvent)
public	void	windowActivated(WindowEvent)
public	void	windowClosed(WindowEvent)
public	void	windowClosing(WindowEvent)
public	void	windowDeactivated(WindowEvent)
public	void	windowDeiconified(WindowEvent)
public	void	windowIconified(WindowEvent)
public	void	windowOpened(WindowEvent)

See Also java.awt.Component • java.awt.event.ActionListener • java.awt.event.AdjustmentListener • java.awt.event.ComponentListener • java.awt.event.ContainerListener • java.awt.event.FocusListener • java.awt.event.ItemListener • java.awt.event.KeyListener • java.awt.event.MouseListener • java.awt.event.MouseMotionListener • java.awt.event.TextListener • java.awt.event.WindowListener

Class AWTException

public synchronized java.awt.AWTException extends java.lang.Exception

The AWTException class is thrown anytime an AWT-based exception occurs.

Syntax & Usage This exception is not thrown directly by any of the AWT methods and is not extended by any other exception. At this stage of Java 1.1 development, it is not clear how you can use this exception. It's probably reserved for future use.

Fields None

Constructors

Modifiers	Constructor
public	AWTException(String)

Methods None

See Also java.lang.Exception • java.lang.Throwable

Class BorderLayout

public synchronized java.awt.BorderLayout extends java.lang.Object implements java.awt.LayoutManager2, java.io.Serializable

BorderLayout is a layout used for formatting components in a container. Using an overridden add() method, you specify where you want the components to load, using the following directional strings: North, South, East, West, and Center. A component specified with one of the previously listed directional strings will be loaded in the corresponding edge of its container.

Note

If you add a component to a container using BorderLayout without specifying anything, BorderLayout automatically displays the component centered.

Syntax & Usage

The following example uses BorderLayout to add five buttons to the top, bottom, left, right, and center of an applet's panel:

```
public class myApplet extends Applet
{

   public void init()
   {
      setLayout(new BorderLayout(20, 10));
      add(new Button("North"), "North");
      add(new Button("South"), "South");
      add(new Button("East"), "East");
      add(new Button("West"), "West");
      add(new Button("Center"), "Center");
   }
}
```

This example uses the constructor for BorderLayout, which lets you specify a horizontal gap of 20 and a vertical gap of 10 pixels (see Figure 2-1).

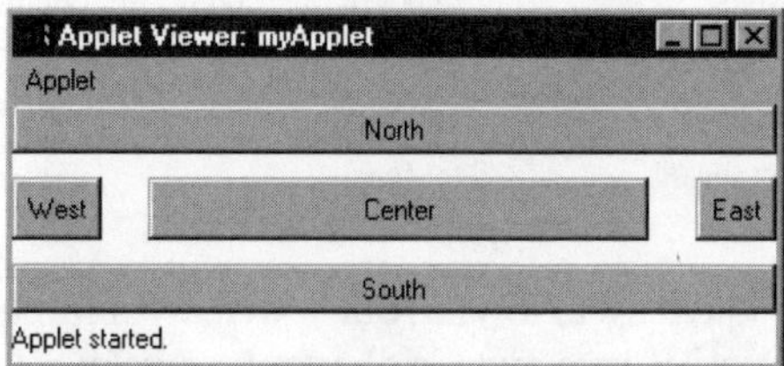

Figure 2-1: BorderLayout.

One method in the BorderLayout class has been deprecated in the JDK 1.1.

Deprecated Method	Replaced by
addLayoutComponent(String, Component)	addLayoutComponent(Component, Object)

Fields

Modifiers	Type	Field
public static final	String	CENTER
public static final	String	EAST
public static final	String	NORTH
public static final	String	SOUTH
public static final	String	WEST

Constructors

Modifiers	Constructor
public	BorderLayout()
public	BorderLayout(int, int)

Methods

Modifiers	Return Type	Method
public	void	addLayoutComponent(Component, Object)
public	void	addLayoutComponent(String, Component)
public	int	getHgap()
public	float	getLayoutAlignmentX(Container)
public	float	getLayoutAlignmentY(Container)
public	int	getVgap()
public	void	invalidateLayout(Container)
public	void	layoutContainer(Container)
public	Dimension	maximumLayoutSize(Container)
public	Dimension	minimumLayoutSize(Container)

Modifiers	Return Type	Method
public	Dimension	preferredLayoutSize(Container)
public	void	removeLayoutComponent(Component)
public	void	setHgap(int)
public	void	setVgap(int)
public	String	toString()

See Also java.awt.CardLayout • java.awt.FlowLayout • java.awt.Frame • java.awt.GridBagLayout • java.awt.GridLayout • java.awt.LayoutManager2 • java.awt.Panel • java.io.Serializable • java.lang.Object

Class Button

public synchronized java.awt.Button extends java.awt.Component

The Button class is a GUI component that represents nothing more than a box that looks like a button. When clicked, it sends a message to its owner, which can execute a block of code in response.

When instantiating a button, you can specify a string to be used as its label.

Syntax & Usage The following example creates a Button object with the caption Sample Button and adds it to an applet's panel. This example also implements the ActionListener interface to be responsive if a user clicks on the button:

```
public class ButtonTest extends Applet
{
   static final int cmdCmdID = 1;
   Button m_Button;

   public void init()
   {
      m_Button = new Button("Sample Button");
      m_Button.addActionListener(
         new ButtonAdapter(cmdCmdID));
      add(m_Button);
   }

   protected void makeAction(int commandID)
   {
      switch (commandID)
      {
      case cmdCmdID:
```

```
    // Process Sample Button notification
      break;
    }
  }

  // Action adapter
  class ButtonAdapter implements
    ActionListener
  {
    private int m_commandID;

    ButtonAdapter(int commandID)
    {
      m_commandID = commandID;
    }

    public void actionPerformed(
      ActionEvent e)
    {
      makeAction(m_commandID);
    }

  }

}
```

The constant cmdCmdID (declared as a **static final int**) is used to create the ButtonAdapter object for this button.

Class ButtonAdapter is defined as an inner class and implements the ActionListener interface. It takes and holds an int variable as an identifier for m_Button, which is being listened to. When an action event originating from m_Button occurs, ButtonAdapter calls the makeAction() method specifying the identifier for the event. In turn, the makeAction() method reconciles the notifying component, using the passed identifier, and responds accordingly (see Figure 2-2).

Tip

This scheme of notification is recommended in the JDK 1.1 for processing ActionEvents.

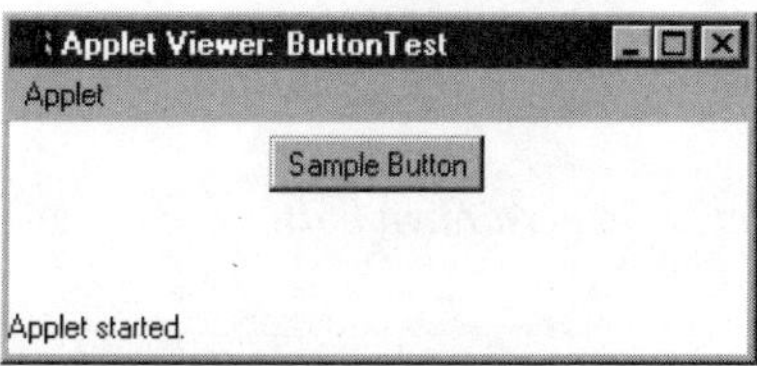

Figure 2-2: A button.

Fields None

Constructors

Modifiers	Constructor
public	Button()
public	Button(String)

Methods

Modifiers	Return Type	Method
public	void	addActionListener(ActionListener)
public	void	addNotify()
public	String	getActionCommand()
public	String	getLabel()
protected	String	paramString()
protected	void	processActionEvent(ActionEvent)
protected	void	processEvent(AWTEvent)
public	void	removeActionListener(ActionListener)
public	void	setActionCommand(String)
public synchronized	void	setLabel(String)

See Also java.awt.Canvas • java.awt.Checkbox • java.awt.CheckboxGroup • java.awt.Choice • java.awt.Component • java.awt.Label • java.awt.List • java.awt.Scrollbar • java.awt.TextArea • java.awt.TextComponent • java.awt.TextField • java.awt.event.ActionListener

Class Canvas

public synchronized java.awt.Canvas extends java.awt.Component

Canvas is a component with little built-in functionality; however, it can be subclassed to draw images. To draw images (graphics) using the Canvas class, you must implement the paint() method.

Also, Canvas—like any object derived from the java.awt.Component class—can receive mouse and keyboard input, so it can be very useful in defining new and custom components.

Note

Canvas is similar to owner-drawn buttons in the Windows Software Development Kit (SDK).

Syntax & Usage The following example subclasses Canvas to get a two-state picture button. If a user clicks his or her mouse in the component's BitmapBtn, it will trigger a picture to be loaded. This is controlled by the internal variable boolean m_bState used to specify the state of the component. Other classes can obtain the current state of control using the public boolean getState() method.

```
public class BitmapBtn extends Canvas
   implements MouseListener
{
   protected boolean m_bState;
   Image m_Image1;  // for state true
   Image m_Image2;  // for state false

   // Constructor
   public BitmapBtn(boolean bState,
      Image img1, Image img2)
   {
      m_bState = bState;
      m_Image1 = img1;
      m_Image2 = img2;
      addMouseListener(this);
   }

   // Get button's state
   public boolean getState()
   {
      return m_bState;
   }

   public void mousePressed(MouseEvent e)
   {
      m_bState = !m_bState;
      repaint();
   }

   public void mouseClicked(MouseEvent e) {}
   public void mouseEntered(MouseEvent e) {}
   public void mouseExited(MouseEvent e) {}
   public void mouseReleased(MouseEvent e) {}

   //  Draw current image
   public void paint(Graphics g)
   {
      if (m_bState)
         g.drawImage(m_Image1, 0, 0, null);
      else
         g.drawImage(m_Image2, 0, 0, null);
   }
}
```

The BitmapBtn class provides one constructor that takes a boolean variable as the initial control's state and two Images: 1 for state true and 2 for state false.

To process mouse input, the BitmapBtn class implements the MouseListener interface. But only the mousePressed() method has functionality. The mousePressed() method triggers control's state and forces it to repaint.

Like all subclasses of Canvas, the BitmapBtn class implements the paint() method. Depending on the control's state, this method draws one of two images stored in BitmapBtn.

Note

If you want to execute the above example as an application, be sure to add main().

See also the example under "Class SystemColor," later in this chapter.

Fields None

Constructors

Modifiers	Constructor
public	Canvas()

Methods

Modifiers	Return Type	Method
public	void	addNotify()
public	void	paint(Graphics)

See Also java.awt.Button • java.awt.Checkbox • java.awt.CheckboxGroup • java.awt.Choice • java.awt.Component • java.awt.Label • java.awt.List • java.awt.Scrollbar • java.awt.TextArea • java.awt.TextComponent • java.awt.TextField • java.awt.event.MouseListener

Class CardLayout

public synchronized java.awt.CardLayout extends java.lang.Object implements java.awt.LayoutManager2, java.awt.Serializable

CardLayout is a layout. It is unique because it does not show all of the GUI components on the screen at any one time. An easy way to understand CardLayout is to think of a stack of cards in which only one is on top at any one time. However, the other components reside underneath and can be brought to the top.

Syntax & Usage

CardLayout can be useful, for instance, to create tabbed dialogs that instantly change in appearance based on user input. When adding components to CardLayout using the add() method, you must specify two parameters: The first parameter is a String used to uniquely identify the component and the second parameter is the component itself.

The following example demonstrates CardLayout by creating a panel that contains three different labels, with only one label displayed at any one time. The example also contains two buttons—Next and Previous—that let you navigate between the labels:

> **Note**
>
> *In real-world situations, the best candidates for this scenario would be several sub-Panels, each of which could hold a set of components and be displayed one at a time based on the user's input.*

```
public class myApplet extends Applet
{
   static final int cmdNextID = 1;
   static final int cmdPrevID = 2;

   Panel tabPanel;
   CardLayout layout;

   public void init()
   {
      Button btNext = new Button("Next");
      btNext.addActionListener(new
         ButtonAdapter(cmdNextID));
      add(btNext);
      Button btPrev = new Button("Previous");
      btPrev.addActionListener(new
         ButtonAdapter(cmdPrevID));
      add(btPrev);

      tabPanel = new Panel();
      tabPanel.resize(150, 100);
      layout = new CardLayout();
      tabPanel.setLayout(layout);
      tabPanel.add("1", new Label(
         "1-st component"));
      tabPanel.add("2", new Label(
         "2-nd component"));
      tabPanel.add("3", new Label(
         "3-rd component"));
      add(tabPanel);
   }
```

```
    protected void makeAction(int commandID)
    {
        switch (commandID)
        {
        case cmdNextID:
            layout.next(tabPanel);
            break;
        case cmdPrevID:
            layout.previous(tabPanel);
            break;
        }
    }
}
```

The panel tabPanel uses CardLayout as its layout. Three components are added to tabPanel and appear one at a time. In this simple example, the components are labels.

Two buttons labeled Next and Previous are used to manage the components in CardLayout. To make these buttons responsive, you use the ButtonAdapter class described in the example for class Button.

The makeAction() method is invoked when a button is pressed. This method calls next() and previous() methods of the CardLayout object. You also can use the first() and last() methods to jump to the top of the stack or to the bottom of the stack, respectively. Figure 2-3 shows the previous example in action.

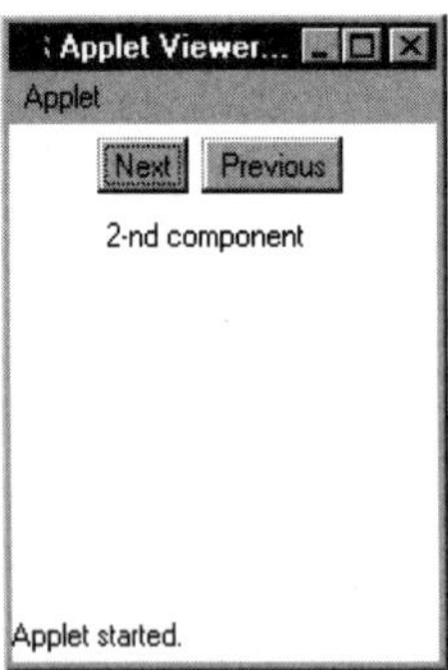

Figure 2-3: CardLayout.

One method in the CardLayout class has been deprecated in the JDK 1.1.

Deprecated Method	Replaced by
addLayoutComponent(String, Component)	AddLayoutComponent(Component, Object)

Fields None

Constructors

Modifiers	Constructor
public	CardLayout()
public	CardLayout(int, int)

Methods

Modifiers	Return Type	Method
public	void	addLayoutComponent(Component, Object)
public	void	addLayoutComponent(String, Component)
public	void	first(Container)
public	int	getHgap()
public	float	getLayoutAlignmentX(Container)
public	float	getLayoutAlignmentY(Container)
public	int	getVgap()
public	void	invalidateLayout(Container)
public	void	last(Container)
public	void	layoutContainer(Container)
public	Dimension	maximumLayoutSize(Container)
public	Dimension	minimumLayoutSize(Container)
public	void	next(Container)
public	Dimension	preferredLayoutSize(Container)
public	void	previous(Container)
public	void	removeLayoutComponent(Component)
public	void	setHgap(int)
public	void	setVgap(int)
public	void	show(Container, String)
public	String	toString()

See Also java.awt.BorderLayout • java.awt.FlowLayout • java.awt.GridBagLayout • java.awt.GridLayout • java.awt.LayoutManager2 • java.io.Serializable • java.lang.Object

Class Checkbox

public synchronized java.awt.Checkbox extends java.awt.Component implements java.awt.ItemSelectable

A Checkbox is a GUI component. Checkboxes can stand alone or be grouped into CheckboxGroups. In the first case, checkboxes can be used for single selection (true/false, yes/no). Grouped checkboxes may be used for multiple selection and will be considered with the CheckboxGroup class.

Syntax & Usage Checkboxes can be set to a state of either **true** or **false** for a given option. Usually, checkboxes are best suited for a particular user preference, as they provide an option for the user to toggle on or off. The following example demonstrates stand-alone checkboxes:

```
public class myApplet extends Applet
{
   static final int chkUseID = 1;
   Checkbox chkUse;
   Checkbox chkPrj;
   Checkbox chkView;

   public void init()
   {
      chkUse = new Checkbox(
         "Use toolbars", true);
      chkUse.addItemListener(new
         ItemAdapter(chkUseID));
      add(chkUse);
      chkPrj = new Checkbox("Project toolbar");
      add(chkPrj);
      chkView = new Checkbox("View toolbar");
      add(chkView);
   }

   protected void makeAction(int itemID)
   {
      switch (itemID)
      {
      case chkUseID:
         if (chkUse.getState())
         {
            chkPrj.enable(true);
            chkView.enable(true);
         }
         else
         {
            chkPrj.setState(false);
            chkPrj.enable(false);
            chkView.setState(false);
            chkView.enable(false);
         }
         break;
      }
   }
```

```
    class ItemAdapter implements ItemListener
    {
      // Holds item's ID
      private int m_itemID

      ItemAdapter(int itemID)
      {
        m_itemID = itemID;
      }

      public void itemStateChanged(ItemEvent e)
      {
        makeAction(m_itemID);
      }
    }

}
```

This applet uses three checkboxes, labeled Use Toolbars, Project Toolbar, and View Toolbar. The first one is constructed with the true state; the others are false by default. To process notification from checkboxes, you can use the ItemListener interface. This implementation calls the makeAction() method with a proper ID when the state of one of the checkboxes changes.

Note

ItemListener is similar to the ActionListener interface described in the Button class.

The makeAction() method will act depending on the current state of Checkbox chkUse. If it is checked, then the method enables the two other checkboxes. If chkUse is unchecked, it sets the two other checkboxes to **false** and disables them (see Figure 2-4).

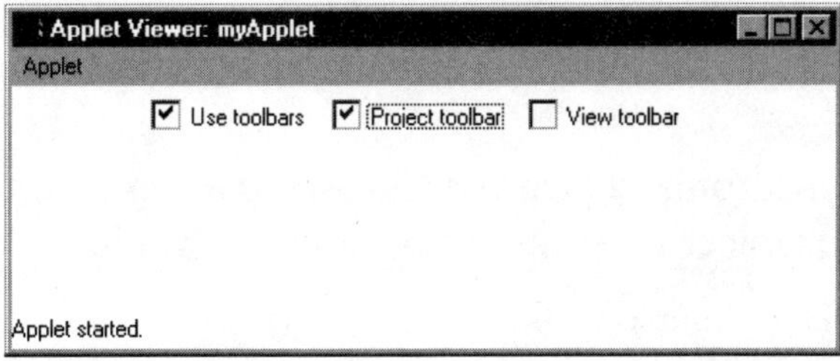

Figure 2-4: Checkboxes.

Fields None

Constructors

Modifiers	Constructor
public	Checkbox()
public	Checkbox(String)
public	Checkbox(String, boolean)
public	Checkbox(String, boolean, CheckboxGroup)
public	Checkbox(String, CheckboxGroup, boolean)

Methods

Modifiers	Return Type	Method
public	void	addItemListener(ItemListener)
public	void	addNotify()
public	CheckboxGroup	getCheckboxGroup()
public	String	getLabel()
public	Object[]	getSelectedObjects()
public	boolean	getState()
protected	String	paramString()
protected	void	processEvent(AWTEvent)
protected	void	processItemEvent(ItemEvent)
public	void	removeItemListener(ItemListener)
public	void	setCheckboxGroup(CheckboxGroup)
public synchronized	void	setLabel(String)
public	void	setState(boolean)

See Also java.awt.Button • java.awt.Canvas • java.awt.CheckboxGroup • java.awt.Choice • java.awt.Component • java.awt.ItemSelectable • java.awt.Label • java.awt.List • java.awt.Scrollbar • java.awt.TextArea • java.awt.TextComponent • java.awt.TextField • java.awt.event.ItemListener

Class CheckboxGroup

public synchronized java.awt.CheckboxGroup extends java.lang.Object implements java.io.Serializable

The CheckboxGroup class is a GUI component used to organize a collection of checkboxes into a group. The CheckboxGroup class allows you to group several checkboxes, yet have only one checkbox with the ability to be true (i.e., checked) at any one time.

Syntax & Usage The following applet demonstrates how to use a CheckboxGroup:

```
public class myApplet extends Applet
{
   public void init()
   {
      CheckboxGroup chkGroup = new
         CheckboxGroup();
      Checkbox chkRed   = new Checkbox(
         "Red", chkGroup, true);
      add(chkRed);
      Checkbox chkBlue  = new Checkbox(
         "Blue", chkGroup, false);
      add(chkBlue);
      Checkbox chkGreen = new Checkbox(
         "Green", chkGroup, false);
      add(chkGreen);
      Checkbox chkWhite = new Checkbox(
         "White", chkGroup, false);
      add(chkWhite);
      chkGroup.setSelectedCheckbox(chkWhite);
   }
}
```

This example uses four checkboxes, labeled Red, Blue, Green, and White. They are constructed using the CheckboxGroup chkGroup container. You need to explicitly specify the initial state of the checkboxes when you use this constructor; however, the setSelectedCheckbox() method used later supersedes this initial selection and selects the chkWhite Checkbox (see Figure 2-5).

Tip

You can use the ItemListener interface to process any notification from checkboxes grouped in CheckboxGroup.

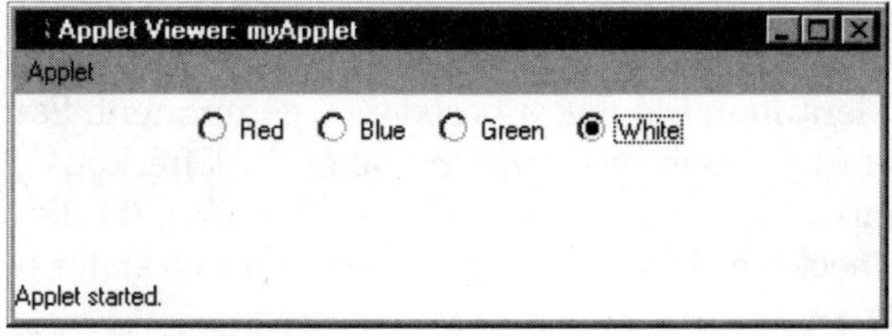

Figure 2-5: CheckboxGroup.

Some methods in the CheckboxGroup class have been deprecated in the JDK 1.1.

Deprecated Method	Replaced by
Checkbox getCurrent()	Checkbox getSelectedCheckbox()
void setCurrent(Checkbox box)	void setSelectedCheckbox(Checkbox box)

Fields None

Constructors

Modifiers	Constructor
public	CheckboxGroup()

Methods

Modifiers	Return Type	Method
public	Checkbox	getCurrent()
public	Checkbox	getSelectedCheckbox()
public synchronized	void	setCurrent(Checkbox)
public synchronized	void	setSelectedCheckbox(Checkbox)
public	String	toString()

See Also java.awt.Button • java.awt.Canvas • java.awt.Checkbox • java.awt.Choice • java.awt.Component • java.awt.Label • java.awt.List • java.awt.Scrollbar • java.awt.TextArea • java.awt.TextComponent • java.awt.TextField • java.awt.event.ItemListener • java.io.Serializable • java.lang.Object

Class CheckboxMenuItem

public synchronized java.awt.CheckboxMenuItem extends java.awt.MenuItem implements java.awt.ItemSelectable

A CheckboxMenuItem is a menu-based GUI component. Essentially, a CheckboxMenuItem is very similar to that of the Checkbox class except that it is attached to and displayed in a menu. Otherwise, it follows the same format as a Checkbox, in that it toggles between two states of either on or off, as **true** and **false**.

Syntax & Usage The following applet example demonstrates how to use CheckboxMenuItem:

```
public class myApplet extends Applet
{
   public void init()
   {
```

```
        Frame frame = new
        Frame("CheckboxMenuItem");
        frame.setSize(200, 100);

        Menu mColor = new Menu("Color");
        CheckboxMenuItem mRed = new
          CheckboxMenuItem("Red", true);
        mColor.add(mRed);
        CheckboxMenuItem mBlue = new
          CheckboxMenuItem("Blue", false);
        mColor.add(mBlue);
        CheckboxMenuItem mGreen = new
          CheckboxMenuItem("Green", false);
        mColor.add(mGreen);
        CheckboxMenuItem mWhite = new
          CheckboxMenuItem("White", false);
        mColor.add(mWhite);
        MenuBar mBar = new MenuBar();
        mBar.add(mColor);

        frame.setMenuBar(mBar);
        frame.setVisible(true);
    }
}
```

This example constructs a sample frame to hold the menu. Then it creates Menu mColor to hold the menu items and four CheckboxMenuItems, labeled Red, Blue, Green, and White. The first one is checked initially, while the others are specified to be unchecked initially.

When creating a CheckboxMenuItem object, you can indicate whether you want it to be checked initially by using setState().

MenuBar mBar, which is added to the frame using setMenuBar(), holds Menu mColor (see Figure 2-6).

Tip

You can use the ItemListener interface to process notification from CheckboxMenuItem.

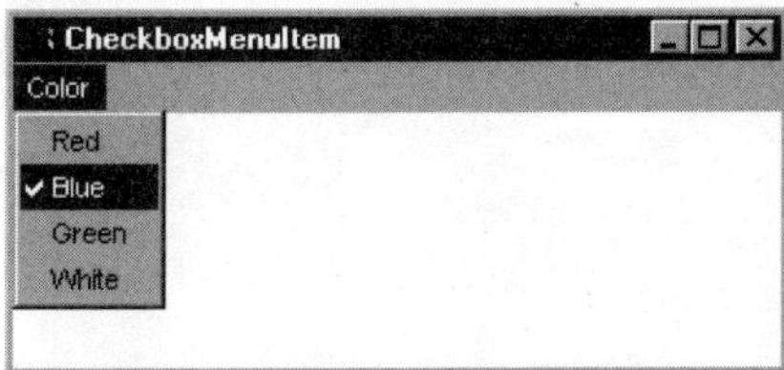

Figure 2-6: CheckboxMenuItem.

Fields None

Constructors

Modifiers	Constructor
public	CheckboxMenuItem()
public	CheckboxMenuItem(String)
public	CheckboxMenuItem(String, boolean)

Methods

Modifiers	Return Type	Method
public	void	addItemListener(ItemListener)
public	void	addNotify()
public synchronized	Object[]	getSelectedObjects()
public	boolean	getState()
public	String	paramString()
protected	void	processEvent(AWTEvent)
protected	void	processItemEvent(ItemEvent)
public	void	removeItemListener(ItemListener)
public synchronized	void	setState(boolean)

See Also java.awt.Checkbox • java.awt.Frame • java.awt.ItemSelectable • java.awt.Menu • java.awt.MenuBar • java.awt.MenuItem • java.awt.PopupMenu

Class Choice

public synchronized java.awt.Choice extends java.awt.Component implements java.awt.ItemSelectable

The Choice class is a GUI component that allows you to create a drop-down list of items for the user to choose from. It does not take up much space on the screen because the list can stay hidden when it is not being used.

Syntax & Usage The following applet example demonstrates using Choice:

```
public class myApplet extends Applet
{
   public void init()
   {
```

```
        Choice mColor = new Choice();
        mColor.addItem("Red");
        mColor.addItem("Blue");
        mColor.addItem("Green");
        mColor.addItem("White");
        mColor.remove("Red");
        mColor.select("Blue");
        add(mColor);
    }
}
```

This example creates Choice mColor. Four strings, labeled Red, Blue, Green, and White, have been added, using the addItem() method. To demonstrate using a Choice object, the Red item is removed using the remove() method, and the Blue item is selected using the select() method (see Figure 2-7).

Tip

You can use the ItemListener interface to process notification from Choice.

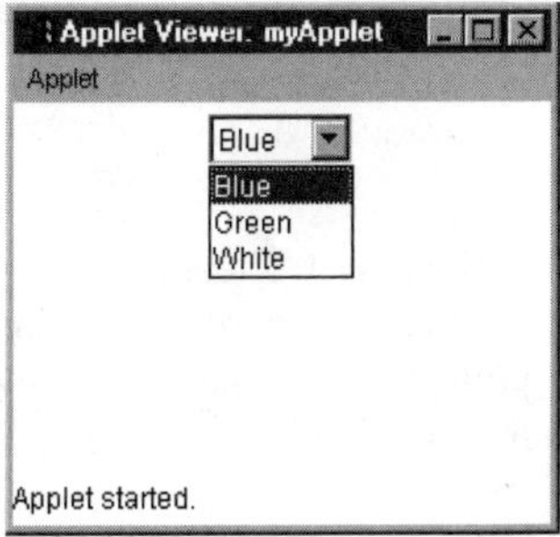

Figure 2-7: Choice.

One method in the Choice class has been deprecated in the JDK 1.1.

Deprecated Method	Replaced by
int countItems()	int getItemCount()

Fields None

Constructors

Modifiers	Constructor
public	Choice()

Methods

Modifiers	Return Type	Method
public synchronized	void	add(String)
public synchronized	void	addItem(String)
public	void	addItemListener(ItemListener)
public	void	addNotify()
public	int	countItems()
public	String	getItem(int)
public	int	getItemCount()
public	int	getSelectedIndex()
public synchronized	String	getSelectedItem()
public synchronized	Object[]	getSelectedObjects()
public synchronized	void	insert(String, int)
protected	String	paramString()
protected	void	processEvent(AWTEvent)
protected	void	processItemEvent(ItemEvent)
public synchronized	void	remove(int)
public synchronized	void	remove(String)
public synchronized	void	removeAll()
public	void	removeItemListener(ItemListener)
public synchronized	void	select(int)
public synchronized	void	select(String)

See Also java.awt.Button • java.awt.Canvas • java.awt.Checkbox • java.awt.CheckboxGroup • java.awt.Component • java.awt.ItemSelectable • java.awt.Label • java.awt.List • java.awt.Scrollbar • java.awt.TextArea • java.awt.TextComponent • java.awt.TextField

Class Color

public synchronized java.awt.Color extends java.lang.Object implements java.io.Serializable

The Color class provides an encapsulated version of Red-Green-Blue (RGB) based colors for Java. You use Color objects to specify colors in your programs.

Syntax & Usage Usually, you use the Color class to specify colors in text and graphics that are drawn on your applet pane or in a Canvas subclass using the paint() method.

Tip

You can use lighter() or darker() to change the brightness of a Color object.

This class lets you specify specific RGB values, or you can specify a basic color using one of its fields, depending on how precise you want to be.

The following code snippet demonstrates using Color. It takes Color.yellow; extracts its components by using the getRed(), getGreen(), and getBlue() methods; and then prints the results:

```
Color mColor = Color.yellow;
int nRed = mColor.getRed();
int nGreen = mColor.getGreen();
int nBlue = mColor.getBlue();
System.out.println("Red:"+nRed+
   "  Green:"+nGreen+"  Blue:"+nBlue);
```

See also the example for "Class Graphics," later in this chapter.

Fields

Modifiers	Type	Field
public static final	Color	black
public static final	Color	blue
public static final	Color	cyan
public static final	Color	darkGray
public static final	Color	gray
public static final	Color	green
public static final	Color	lightGray
public static final	Color	magenta
public static final	Color	orange
public static final	Color	pink
public static final	Color	red
public static final	Color	white
public static final	Color	yellow

Constructors

Modifiers	Constructor
public	Color(float, float, float)
public	Color(int)
public	Color(int, int, int)

Methods

Modifiers	Return Type	Method
public	Color	brighter()
public	Color	darker()
public static	Color	decode(String)
public	boolean	equals(Object)
public	int	getBlue()
public static	Color	getColor(String)
public static	Color	getColor(String, Color)
public static	Color	getColor(String, int)
public	int	getGreen()
public static	Color	getHSBColor(float, float, float)
public	int	getRed()
public	int	getRGB()
public	int	hashCode()
public static	int	HSBtoRGB(float, float, float)
public static	float[]	RGBtoHSB(int, int, int, float[])
public	String	toString()

See Also java.awt.Canvas • java.awt.Component • java.io.Serializable • Java.lang.Object

Class Component

public abstract synchronized java.awt.Component extends java.lang.Object implements java.awt.image.ImageObserver, java.awt.MenuContainer, java.io.Serializable

The Component class is an **abstract** class from which all AWT components are extended (this includes the **abstract** Container class and its subclasses, such as Panel). It defines the basic functionality used by AWT components (Button, Checkbox, CheckboxGroup, Choice, TextArea, TextField, and so on).

Syntax & Usage Component is itself an **abstract** class. Thus, you cannot directly instantiate it. However, you can benefit from its functionality by instantiating its subclasses. Please see the examples for the component-derived classes listed under "See Also," later in this entry.

Some methods in the Component class have been deprecated in the JDK 1.1 and are listed in the following table.

Deprecated Method	Replaced By
Boolean action(Event, Object)	Use ActionListener to process action events
Rectangle bounds()	Rectangle getBounds()
Void deliverEvent(Event e)	DispatchEvent(AWTEvent e)
Void disable()	void setEnabled(false)
Void enable()	void setEnabled(false)
Void enable(boolean)	void setEnabled(boolean)
ComponentPeer getPeer()	In the JDK 1.1 programs should not directly manipulate peers
Boolean gotFocus(Event, Object)	processFocusEvent(FocusEvent)
Boolean handleEvent(Event evt)	processEvent(AWTEvent)
Void hide()	void setVisible(false)
Boolean inside(int, int)	boolean contains(int, int)
Boolean keyDown(Event, int)	processKeyEvent(KeyEvent)
Boolean keyUp(Event, int)	processKeyEvent(KeyEvent)
Void layout()	void doLayout()
Component locate(int, int)	Component getComponentAt(int, int)
Point location()	Point getLocation()
Boolean lostFocus(Event, Object)	processFocusEvent(FocusEvent)
Dimension minimumSize()	Dimension getMinimumSize()
Boolean mouseDown(Event, int, int)	processMouseEvent(MouseEvent)
Boolean mouseDrag(Event, int, int)	processMouseMotionEvent(MouseEvent)
Boolean mouseMove(Event, int, int)	processMouseMotionEvent(MouseEvent)
Boolean mouseEnter(Event, int, int)	processMouseEvent(MouseEvent)
Boolean mouseExit(Event, int, int)	processMouseEvent(MouseEvent)
Boolean mouseUp(Event, int, int)	processMouseEvent(MouseEvent)
Void move(int, int)	void setLocation(int, int)
Void nextFocus()	void transferFocus()
Boolean postEvent(Event)	dispatchEvent(AWTEvent)
Dimension preferredSize()	Dimension getPreferredSize()
Void reshape(int, int, int, int)	void setBounds(int, int, int, int)
Void resize(int, int)	void setSize(int, int)
Void resize(Dimension)	void setSize(Dimension)
Void show()	void setVisible(true)
Void show(boolean)	void setVisible(boolean)
Dimension size()	Dimension getSize()

Fields

Modifiers	Type	Field
public static final	float	BOTTOM_ALIGNMENT
public static final	float	CENTER_ALIGNMENT
public static final	float	LEFT_ALIGNMENT
protected	Locale	locale
public static final	float	RIGHT_ALIGNMENT
public static final	float	TOP_ALIGNMENT

Constructors

Modifiers	Constructor
protected	Component()

Methods

Modifiers	Return Type	Method
public	boolean	action(Event, Object)
public synchronized	void	add(PopupMenu)
public synchronized	void	addComponentListener(ComponentListener)
public synchronized	void	addFocusListener(FocusListener)
public synchronized	void	addKeyListener(KeyListener)
public synchronized	void	addMouseListener(MouseListener)
public synchronized	void	addMouseMotionListener(MouseMotionListener)
public	void	addNotify()
public	Rectangle	bounds()
public	int	checkImage(Image, ImageObserver)
public	int	checkImage(Image, int, int, ImageObserver)
public	boolean	contains(int, int)
public	boolean	contains(Point)
public	Image	createImage(ImageProducer)
public	Image	createImage(int, int)
public	void	deliverEvent(Event)
public	void	disable()
protected final	void	disableEvents(long)
public final	void	dispatchEvent(AWTEvent)
public	void	doLayout()
public	void	enable()
public	void	enable(boolean)
protected final	void	enableEvents(long)
public	float	getAlignmentX()
public	float	getAlignmentY()
public	Color	getBackground()
public	Rectangle	getBounds()

Modifiers	Return Type	Method
public	ColorModel	getColorModel()
public	Component	getComponentAt(int, int)
public	Component	getComponentAt(Point)
public	Cursor	getCursor()
public	Font	getFont()
public	FontMetrics	getFontMetrics(Font)
public	Color	getForeground()
public	Graphics	getGraphics()
public	Locale	getLocale()
public	Point	getLocation()
public	Point	getLocationOnScreen()
public	Dimension	getMaximumSize()
public	Dimension	getMinimumSize()
public	String	getName()
public	Container	getParent()
public	ComponentPeer	getPeer()
public	Dimension	getPreferredSize()
public	Dimension	getSize()
public	Toolkit	getToolkit()
public final	Object	getTreeLock()
public	boolean	gotFocus(Event, Object)
public	boolean	handleEvent(Event)
public	void	hide()
public	boolean	imageUpdate(Image, int, int, int, int, int)
public	boolean	inside(int, int)
public	void	invalidate()
public	boolean	isEnabled()
public	boolean	isFocusTraversable()
public	boolean	isShowing()
public	boolean	isValid()
public	boolean	isVisible()
public	boolean	keyDown(Event, int)
public	boolean	keyUp(Event, int)
public	void	layout()
public	void	list()
public	void	list(PrintStream)
public	void	list(PrintStream, int)
public	void	list(PrintWriter)
public	void	list(PrintWriter, int)

Modifiers	Return Type	Method
public	Component	locate(int, int)
public	Point	location()
public	boolean	lostFocus(Event, Object)
public	Dimension	minimumSize()
public	boolean	mouseDown(Event, int, int)
public	boolean	mouseDrag(Event, int, int)
public	boolean	mouseEnter(Event, int, int)
public	boolean	mouseExit(Event, int, int)
public	boolean	mouseMove(Event, int, int)
public	boolean	mouseUp(Event, int, int)
public	void	move(int, int)
public	void	nextFocus()
public	void	paint(Graphics)
public	void	paintAll(Graphics)
protected	String	paramString()
public	boolean	postEvent(Event)
public	Dimension	preferredSize()
public	boolean	prepareImage(Image, ImageObserver)
public	boolean	prepareImage(Image, int, int, ImageObserver)
public	void	print(Graphics)
public	void	printAll(Graphics)
protected	void	processComponentEvent(ComponentEvent)
protected	void	processEvent(AWTEvent)
protected	void	processFocusEvent(FocusEvent)
protected	void	processKeyEvent(KeyEvent)
protected	void	processMouseEvent(MouseEvent)
protected	void	processMouseMotionEvent(MouseEvent)
public synchronized	void	remove(MenuComponent)
public synchronized	void	removeComponentListener(ComponentListener)
public synchronized	void	removeFocusListener(FocusListener)
public synchronized	void	removeKeyListener(KeyListener)
public synchronized	void	removeMouseListener(MouseListener)
public synchronized	void	removeMouseMotionListener(MouseMotionListener)
public	void	removeNotify()
public	void	repaint()
public	void	repaint(int, int, int, int)
public	void	repaint(long)
public	void	repaint(long, int, int, int, int)
public	void	requestFocus()
public	void	reshape(int, int, int, int)

Modifiers	Return Type	Method
public	void	resize(Dimension)
public	void	resize(int, int)
public	void	setBackground(Color)
public	void	setBounds(int, int, int, int)
public	void	setBounds(Rectangle)
public synchronized	void	setCursor(Cursor)
public	void	setEnabled(boolean)
public synchronized	void	setFont(Font)
public	void	setForeground(Color)
public	void	setLocale(Locale)
public	void	setLocation(int, int)
public	void	setLocation(Point)
public	void	setName(String)
public	void	setSize(Dimension)
public	void	setSize(int, int)
public	void	setVisible(boolean)
public	void	show()
public	void	show(boolean)
public	Dimension	size()
public	String	toString()
public	void	transferFocus()
public	void	update(Graphics)
public	void	validate()

See Also java.awt.Button • java.awt.Canvas • java.awt.Checkbox • java.awt.CheckboxGroup • java.awt.Choice • java.awt.Container • java.awt.ImageObserver • java.awt.ItemSelectable • java.awt.Label • java.awt.List • java.awt.MenuContainer • java.awt.Scrollbar • java.awt.TextArea • java.awt.TextComponent • java.awt.TextField • java.io.Serializable • java.lang.Object

Class Container

public abstract synchronized java.awt.Container extends java.awt.Component

The Container class extends the Component class. Container represents an **abstract** class from which all containers, including Panel, Frame, and Dialog, are derived.

Syntax & Usage

Container is itself an **abstract** class. Thus, you cannot directly instantiate it. However, you can benefit from its functionality by instantiating its subclasses. A Container contains the basic functionality used by its subclasses to design a container with which to house components and become the holding tank for a Java program's GUI. This includes the ability to specify and use a layout manager, as well as to keep an active list and order of components (e.g., buttons) that can be added to or removed from it.

Please see the examples for the component-derived classes listed under "See Also," later in this section.

Some methods in the Container class have been deprecated in the JDK 1.1.

Deprecated Method	Replaced by
int countComponents()	int getComponentCount()
Void deliverEvent(Event e)	dispatchEvent(AWTEvent e)
Insets insets()	Insets getInsets()
void layout()	void doLayout()
Component locate(int, int)	Component getComponentAt(int, int)
Dimension minimumSize()	Dimension getMinimumSize()

Fields None

Constructors

Modifiers	Constructor
protected	Container()

Methods

Modifiers	Return Type	Method
public	Component	add(Component)
public	Component	add(Component, int)
public	void	add(Component, Object)
public	void	add(Component, Object, int)
public	Component	add(String, Component)
public	void	addContainerListener(ContainerListener)
protected	void	addImpl(Component, Object, int)
public	void	addNotify()
public	int	countComponents()
public	void	deliverEvent(Event)
public	void	doLayout()

Modifiers	Return Type	Method
public	float	getAlignmentY()
public	Component	getComponent(int)
public	Component	getComponentAt(int, int)
public	Component	getComponentAt(Point)
public	int	getComponentCount()
public	Component[]	getComponents()
public	Insets	getInsets()
public	LayoutManager	getLayout()
public	Dimension	getMaximumSize()
public	Dimension	getMinimumSize()
public	Dimension	getPreferredSize()
public	Insets	insets()
public	void	invalidate()
public	boolean	isAncestorOf(Component)
public	void	layout()
public	void	list(PrintStream, int)
public	void	list(PrintWriter, int)
public	Component	locate(int, int)
public	Dimension	minimumSize()
public	void	paint(Graphics)
public	void	paintComponents(Graphics)
protected	String	paramString()
public	Dimension	preferredSize()
public	void	print(Graphics)
public	void	printComponents(Graphics)
protected	void	processContainerEvent(ContainerEvent)
protected	void	processEvent(AWTEvent)
public	void	remove(Component)
public	void	remove(int)
public	void	removeAll()
public	void	removeContainerListener(ContainerListener)
public	void	removeNotify()
public	void	setLayout(LayoutManager)
public	void	validate()
protected	void	validateTree()

See Also java.awt.Component • java.awt.Dialog • java.awt.Frame • java.awt.Panel

Class Cursor

public synchronized java.awt.Cursor extends java.lang.Object implements java.io.Serializable

This class represents an encapsulation of the various bitmap-based mouse cursors. Using setCursor() from the Component class, you can determine which cursor displays.

Syntax & Usage

The following example demonstrates the functionality of the Cursor class. It creates a sample Frame object. Then, it takes the system cursor, using the getPredefinedCursor() method and specifying the Cursor.CROSSHAIR_CURSOR constant as the cursor image that you wish to use. The cursor is then assigned to the frame using the Component.setCursor() method:

```
Frame frame = new Frame("Cursor");
frame.setSize(200, 100);
frame.setVisible(true);
Cursor mCursor = Cursor.getPredefinedCursor(
   Cursor.CROSSHAIR_CURSOR);
if (mCursor != null)
   frame.setCursor(mCursor);
```

When the mouse pointer moves over the frame for this example, the mouse cursor will be in the form of crossed hairs.

Fields

Modifiers	Type	Field
public static final	int	CROSSHAIR_CURSOR
public static final	int	DEFAULT_CURSOR
public static final	int	E_RESIZE_CURSOR
public static final	int	HAND_CURSOR
public static final	int	MOVE_CURSOR
public static final	int	NE_RESIZE_CURSOR
public static final	int	NW_RESIZE_CURSOR
public static final	int	N_RESIZE_CURSOR
protected static	Cursor[]	predefined
public static final	int	SE_RESIZE_CURSOR
public static final	int	SW_RESIZE_CURSOR

Modifiers	Return Type	Method
public static final	int	S_RESIZE_CURSOR
public static final	int	TEXT_CURSOR
public static final	int	WAIT_CURSOR
public static final	int	W_RESIZE_CURSOR

Constructors

Modifiers	Constructor
public	Cursor(int)

Methods

Modifiers	Return Type	Method
public static	Cursor	getDefaultCursor()
public static	Cursor	getPredefinedCursor(int)
public	int	getType()

See Also java.awt.Component • java.awt.Frame • java.io.Serializable • java.lang.Object

Class Dialog

public synchronized java.awt.Dialog extends java.awt.Window

The Dialog class represents a tool that you can use to create dialog boxes. Dialogs are temporary windows that display an important message or perform specific tasks in your Java program.

Syntax & Usage You can specify your Dialog object to be modal, meaning that the user must respond to it before continuing.

Note

The default layout for Dialog objects is BorderLayout.

Tip

*Whenever you construct a Dialog object, you must attach it to a Frame (you cannot pass **null** as a parent Frame object in the Dialog's constructor). In light of this, there is no default Dialog constructor.*

The following example demonstrates using Dialog. Notice that it creates a Frame object as the parent for the sample Dialog object:

```
Frame frame = new Frame("Parent");
Dialog dialog = new Dialog(frame, "Dialog");
dialog.setSize(120, 120);
dialog.setBackground(Color.lightGray);
dialog.setLayout(new FlowLayout());
dialog.add(new Label("Are you sure ?"));
dialog.add(new Button("Yes"));
dialog.add(new Button("No"));
dialog.setResizable(false);
dialog.show();
```

After constructing the frame, the example constructs a modal Dialog object called Dialog, specifying Frame as the parent frame. It also sets the dialog's size to (120, 120) and the background color to light gray. Following that, the dialog specifies FlowLayout to manage the following components that are added to Dialog: one label and two buttons labeled Yes and No, respectively. Last, the resizable property for Dialog is set to false, and the dialog is displayed using the show() method (see Figure 2-8).

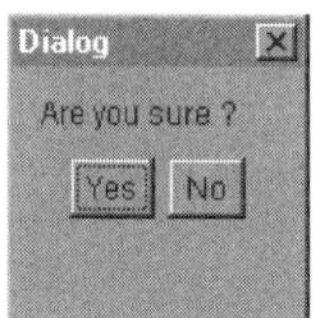

Figure 2-8: Dialog.

Tip

You can use java.awt.event.WindowListener to process notification from Dialog's window.

Tip

If you want to create the above dialog to load from a Java applet, all you need to do is specify the main applet class as the parent class in the Dialog's constructor. You can do this because the main applet class is a java.applet.Applet subclass, which in turn is a Panel subclass.

Fields None

Constructors

Modifiers	Constructor
public	Dialog(Frame)
public	Dialog(Frame, boolean)
public	Dialog(Frame, String)
public	Dialog(Frame, String, boolean)

Methods

Modifiers	Return Type	Method
public	void	addNotify()
public	String	getTitle()
public	boolean	isModal()
public	boolean	isResizable()
protected	String	paramString()
public	void	setModal(boolean)
public synchronized	void	setResizable(boolean)
public synchronized	void	setTitle(String)
public	void	show()

See Also java.applet.Applet • java.awt.Component • java.awt.Frame • java.awt.Panel • java.awt.Window • java.awt.event.WindowListener

Class Dimension

public synchronized java.awt.Dimension extends java.lang.Object implements java.io.Serializable

The Dimension object is used to encapsulate the width and height of something in Java.

Syntax & Usage This class is usually very useful for drawing objects using the java.awt.Graphics class. The following example demonstrates the usage of Dimension:

```
Button btn = new Button("Yes");
add(btn);
Dimension size = btn.getPreferredSize();
int w = size.width*2;
int h = size.height*2;
Dimension newSize = Dimension(w, h);
btn.setSize(newSize);
```

A Dimension object called size is created using the getPreferredSize() method from the Button class. This size object contains the dimensions for the sample Button object (btn). Then, using the ints w and h, you hold twice the value for the width and height of the button, based on the size.width and size.height fields, respectively.

Finally, construct a new Dimension object called newSize with w and h as the width and height of the Dimension object (remember that they are double the values attained from the first Dimension object size). Then, using newSize, you specify the new size for btn, which effectively doubles the size of the button.

Fields

Modifiers	Type	Field
public	int	height
public	int	width

Constructors

Modifiers	Constructor
public	Dimension()
public	Dimension(Dimension)
public	Dimension(int, int)

Methods

Modifiers	Return Type	Method
public	boolean	equals(Object)
public	Dimension	getSize()
public	void	setSize(Dimension)
public	void	setSize(int, int)
public	String	toString()

See Also java.awt.Graphics • java.awt.Rectangle • java.io.Serializable • java.lang.Object

Class Event

public synchronized java.awt.Event extends java.lang.Object implements java.io.Serializable

The Event class represents an object encapsulation of a GUI-initiated event. When an Event object is instantiated, it is given a unique ID (based on what type of event it is).

EventObject

The class java.awt.Event has been replaced in Java 1.1 by an entire hierarchy of classes that extends from java.util.EventObject. Basically, there are two groups in the EventObject hierarchy:

- **Low-level or detail-oriented types of events.** These include java.awt.event.ComponentEvent, FocusEvent, InputEvent, KeyEvent, MouseEvent, ContainerEvent, and WindowEvent.
- **A higher-level group called semantic events.** These include java.awt.event.ActionEvent, AdjustmentEvent, ItemEvent, and TextEvent.

This hierarchy provides greater versatility than one Event class in which events can be distinguished only by their IDs. Also, notice that one of the new event classes can represent a group of related events, for example, the MouseEvent object can be used to represent mouseUp(), mouseDown(), mouseMove(), and so on.

Syntax & Usage Use of the old-style event model is not recommended in the JDK 1.1. Please see examples of a new event-delegation model in the java.awt.event package.

Fields

Modifiers	Type	Field
public static final	int	ACTION_EVENT
public static final	int	ALT_MASK
public	Object	arg
public static final	int	BACK_SPACE
public static final	int	CAPS_LOCK
public	int	clickCount
public static final	int	CTRL_MASK
public static final	int	DELETE
public static final	int	DOWN
public static final	int	END
public static final	int	ENTER
public static final	int	ESCAPE
public	Event	evt
public static final	int	F1
public static final	int	F10
public static final	int	F11
public static final	int	F12
public static final	int	F2
public static final	int	F3
public static final	int	F4
public static final	int	F5

Modifiers	Type	Field
public static final	int	F6
public static final	int	F7
public static final	int	F8
public static final	int	F9
public static final	int	GOT_FOCUS
public static final	int	HOME
public	int	id
public static final	int	INSERT
public	int	key
public static final	int	KEY_ACTION
public static final	int	KEY_ACTION_RELEASE
public static final	int	KEY_PRESS
public static final	int	KEY_RELEASE
public static final	int	LEFT
public static final	int	LIST_DESELECT
public static final	int	LIST_SELECT
public static final	int	LOAD_FILE
public static final	int	LOST_FOCUS
public static final	int	META_MASK
public	int	modifiers
public static final	int	MOUSE_DOWN
public static final	int	MOUSE_DRAG
public static final	int	MOUSE_ENTER
public static final	int	MOUSE_EXIT
public static final	int	MOUSE_MOVE
public static final	int	MOUSE_UP
public static final	int	NUM_LOCK
public static final	int	PAUSE
public static final	int	PGDN
public static final	int	PGUP
public static final	int	PRINT_SCREEN
public static final	int	RIGHT
public static final	int	SAVE_FILE
public static final	int	SCROLL_ABSOLUTE
public static final	int	SCROLL_BEGIN
public static final	int	SCROLL_END
public static final	int	SCROLL_LINE_DOWN
public static final	int	SCROLL_LINE_UP

Modifiers	Type	Field
public static final	int	SCROLL_LOCK
public static final	int	SCROLL_PAGE_DOWN
public static final	int	SCROLL_PAGE_UP
public static final	int	SHIFT_MASK
public static final	int	TAB
public	Object	target
public static final	int	UP
public	long	when
public static final	int	WINDOW_DEICONIFY
public static final	int	WINDOW_DESTROY
public static final	int	WINDOW_EXPOSE
public static final	int	WINDOW_ICONIFY
public static final	int	WINDOW_MOVED
public	int	x
public	int	y

Constructors

Modifiers	Constructor
public	Event(Object, int, Object)
public	Event(Object, long, int, int, int, int, int)
public	Event(Object, long, int, int, int, int, int, Object)

Methods

Modifiers	Return Type	Method
public	boolean	controlDown()
public	boolean	metaDown()
protected	String	paramString()
public	boolean	shiftDown()
public	String	toString()
public	void	translate(int, int)

See Also java.awt.event.ActionEvent • java.awt.event.AdjustmentEvent • java.awt.event.ComponentEvent • java.awt.event.ContainerEvent • java.awt.event.FocusEvent • java.awt.event.InputEvent • java.awt.event.ItemEvent • java.awt.event.KeyEvent • java.awt.event.MouseEvent • java.awt.event.TextEvent • java.awt.event.WindowEvent • java.io.Serializable • java.lang.Object • java.util.EventObject

Class EventQueue

public synchronized java.awt.EventQueue extends java.lang.Object

All GUI-based platforms in Java use an event queue, which is responsible for managing and coordinating all Java components, including their interactions with the user and among themselves. For instance, every keystroke on the keyboard and/or mouse click generates an event that gets posted in the event queue. A Java component then picks out those events that originate from itself and process them (please see Chapter 4, "The java.awt.event Package," for details).

Syntax & Usage

In Java 1.0, the event queue is hidden from programmers and not available for use in Java applications. However, Java 1.1 has changed this with the addition of the EventQueue class, which is responsible for queuing events in Java. This class enables you to use events more efficiently. For instance, you can implement an EventQueue to compress a sequence of events into one.

> **Note**
>
> *You need to use a trusted (signed) applet or Java application to get access to the EventQueue class.*

The following example demonstrates the usage of EventQueue:

```
Frame frame = new Frame("EventQueue");
frame.setSize(200, 100);
frame.setVisible(true);

Toolkit toolkit = frame.getToolkit();
EventQueue sysQueue =
   toolkit.getSystemEventQueue();
AWTEvent ev = null;
while (ev == null)
   ev = sysQueue.peekEvent(
      ComponentEvent.COMPONENT_RESIZED);
System.out.println("Resize event: "
   +ev.toString());
```

In the above example, you create a simple Frame object that you'll use to generate events. Using the Frame object, you can get a reference to the Toolkit object and a reference to the system event queue using the getSystemEventQueue() method from the Toolkit class. As soon as you have a reference to the system event queue, you can peek at the events in the queue using the peekEvent() method. Specifically, in the previous code, the peekEvent() method is located inside the **while** loop to peek at resizing events that are occurring in the sample Frame. Once this resizing event occurs, the loop ends and the program prints the event's information to the standard output.

Tip

If you attempt to use the EventQueue class from an untrusted applet, Java will raise a security exception. Instead, use a trusted (signed) applet or Java application.

Fields None

Constructors

Modifiers	Constructor
public	EventQueue()

Methods

Modifiers	Return Type	Method
public synchronized	AWTEvent	getNextEvent()
public synchronized	AWTEvent	peekEvent()
public synchronized	AWTEvent	peekEvent(int)
public synchronized	void	postEvent(AWTEvent)

See Also java.awt.event.KeyEvent • java.awt.event.MouseEvent • java.awt.event.TextEvent. • java.awt.event.WindowEvent • java.lang.Object • java.util.EventObject

Class FileDialog

public synchronized java.awt.FileDialog extends java.awt.Dialog

The FileDialog class links to the set of system dialogs that are part of the user's Operating System (OS).

Syntax & Usage In Windows 95 and NT, the two system dialogs you can interact with are the Open dialog (Figure 2-9) and the Save As dialog (Figure 2-10).

Note

If you used FileDialog on a Mac- or UNIX-based platform, you would see different dialogs based on their respective set of system dialogs.

Figure 2-9: Open dialog in Windows 95/NT.

Figure 2-10: Save As dialog in Windows 95/NT.

Note

FileDialogs are always modal.

The advantage of using a system-based dialog is that it changes with each platform, but the functionality is essentially the same. This lets the user spend less time trying to understand a new interface and more time being productive with your Java program.

The following example demonstrates the usage of the FileDialog class:

```
Frame frame = new Frame("Sample Frame");
FileDialog OpenDlg = new FileDialog(frame,
  "Open Archive File", FileDialog.LOAD);
OpenDlg.setFile("*.jar;*.zip");
OpenDlg.show();
```

```
String sFileName = OpenDlg.getFile();
if (sFileName == null)
   System.out.println(
      "No file has been selected");
else
   System.out.println("File "+sFileName+
      " has been selected");
```

To construct a FileDialog object, you need a reference to a constructed Frame object. Then you can construct a FileDialog specifying the dialog's title and type (LOAD in this case). The method setFile() is used to set the initial selection in the FileDialog object, and the show() method is invoked to display the dialog.

After the FileDialog dialog is finished, you use the getFile() method to retrieve the filename selected by the user. If the resulting string is **null**, then that means the user made no selection.

Fields

Modifiers	Type	Field
public static final	int	LOAD
public static final	int	SAVE

Constructors

Modifiers	Constructor
public	FileDialog(Frame)
public	FileDialog(Frame, String)
public	FileDialog(Frame, String, int)

Methods

Modifiers	Return Type	Method
public	void	addNotify()
public	String	getDirectory()
public	String	getFile()
public	FilenameFilter	getFilenameFilter()
public	int	getMode()
protected	String	paramString()
public synchronized	void	setDirectory(String)
public synchronized	void	setFile(String)
public synchronized	void	setFilenameFilter(FilenameFilter)
public	void	setMode(int)

See Also java.awt.Dialog • java.awt.Frame

Class FlowLayout

public synchronized java.awt.FlowLayout extends java.lang.Object implements java.awt.LayoutManager, java.io.Serializable

FlowLayout is one of the easiest layout managers to use. Its logic is based on the fact that as components are displayed, the container moves left to right, laying out each component, until it comes to the border of the container. Then it continues on the next line—similar to that of a typewriter.

Syntax & Usage

The following example demonstrates the use of the FlowLayout class:

```
FlowLayout layout = new
  FlowLayout(FlowLayout.RIGHT);
layout.setVgap(20);
layout.setHgap(20);
setLayout(layout);
add(new Button("One"));
add(new Button("Two"));
add(new Button("Three"));
add(new Button("Four"));
```

First you construct a new FlowLayout object specifying right alignment. Then you call the methods setVgap() and setHgap() that are used to set the vertical and horizontal gaps to be used by the FlowLayout object (you could have alternatively specified these values in the constructor). Finally, you set the constructed FlowLayout object as the current layout manager, thus specifying all components added to this container will be managed by FlowLayout (see Figure 2-11).

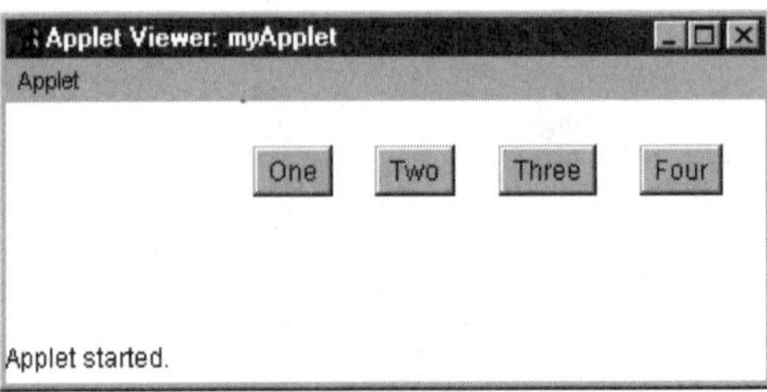

Figure 2-11: FlowLayout.

Fields

Modifiers	Type	Field
public static final	int	CENTER
public static final	int	LEFT
public static final	int	RIGHT

Constructors

Modifiers	Constructor
public	FlowLayout()
public	FlowLayout(int)
public	FlowLayout(int, int, int)

Methods

Modifiers	Return Type	Method
public	void	addLayoutComponent(String, Component)
public	int	getAlignment()
public	int	getHgap()
public	int	getVgap()
public	void	layoutContainer(Container)
public	Dimension	minimumLayoutSize(Container)
public	Dimension	preferredLayoutSize(Container)
public	void	removeLayoutComponent(Component)
public	void	setAlignment(int)
public	void	setHgap(int)
public	void	setVgap(int)
public	String	toString()

See Also java.awt.BorderLayout • java.awt.CardLayout • java.awt.Component • java.awt.Container • java.awt.GridBagLayout • java.awt.GridLayout • java.awt.LayoutManager • java.io.Serializable • java.lang.Object

Class Font

public synchronized java.awt.Font extends java.lang.Object implements java.io.Serializable

The Font class represents an object that describes a font with specific attributes in your Java program.

Syntax & Usage Font objects are often used in Java programs in conjunction with the paint() method, letting you specify a font with a specific size, type, and attributes (bold, etc.) for text displayed in your applet's pane. This is done using the setFont() class in the Graphics class. You also can specify fonts if you are drawing things inside a Frame or in a subclassed Canvas object.

The Font class currently supports the following five fonts:

- Courier
- Dialog
- Helvetica
- Symbol
- TimesRoman

The Font class supports the following three styles that are specified in its constructor using the appropriate fields in the Font class:

- Font.BOLD
- Font.ITALIC
- Font.PLAIN

> **Note**
>
> *The Font class does not support underline or strikethrough.*

You can combine more than one attribute into a single value by using two styles. For instance, Font.BOLD + Font.ITALIC creates a font with both bold and italic attributes.

The following example demonstrates the usage of the Font class in the paint() method:

```
public void paint(Graphics g)
{
   Font fnt = new Font("TimesRoman",
      Font.PLAIN, 24);
   g.setFont(fnt);
   String str = fnt.getName()+
      " ("+fnt.getFamily()+"), "+
      fnt.getSize()+" "+
      (fnt.isBold() ? "Bold " : "")+
      (fnt.isItalic() ? "Italic " : "")+
      (fnt.isPlain() ? "Plain " : "");
   g.drawString(str, 20, 20);
}
```

In this example, you first create a new TimesRoman Font object, specifying the style to be PLAIN and the size to be 24 points. This font is set to the current Graphics object by using the Graphics.setFont() method. Then the example creates a string containing the full description of the current Font, using the getName(), getFamily(), getSize(), isBold(), isItalic(), and isPlain() methods from the Font class. Finally, the string resulting from all these method calls is displayed, using the drawString() method (see Figure 2-12).

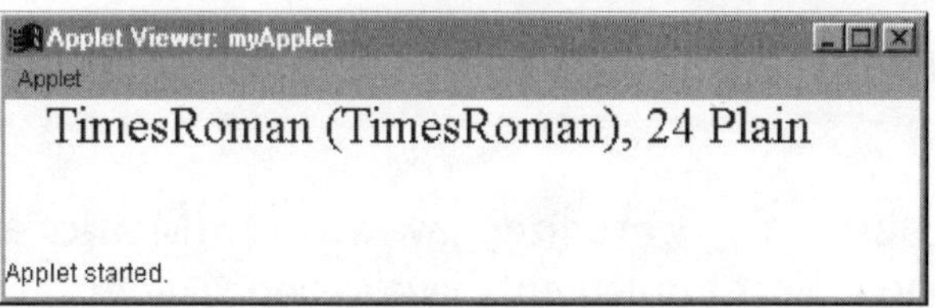

Figure 2-12: Font.

Fields

Modifiers	Type	Field
public static final	int	BOLD
public static final	int	ITALIC
protected	String	name
public static final	int	PLAIN
protected	int	size
protected	int	style

Constructors

Modifiers	Constructor
public	Font(String, int, int)

Methods

Modifiers	Return Type	Method
public static	Font	decode(String)
public	boolean	equals(Object)
public	String	getFamily()
public static	Font	getFont(String)
public static	Font	getFont(String, Font)
public	String	getName()
public	FontPeer	getPeer()
public	int	getSize()
public	int	getStyle()
public	int	hashCode()
public	boolean	isBold()
public	boolean	isItalic()
public	boolean	isPlain()
public	String	toString()

See Also java.awt.Canvas. • java.awt.FontMetrics • java.awt.Frame • java.awt.Graphics • java.io.Serializable • java.lang.Object

Class FontMetrics

public abstract synchronized java.awt.FontMetrics extends java.lang.Object implements java.io.Serializable

The FontMetrics class is used to get information about a specified Font object. Specifically, you can get information on the dimensions, string width, ascent, descent, and any other metrics about the font.

Syntax & Usage

The following are details for some useful functions in the FontMetrics class:

- **int getAscent().** This returns the font ascent (i.e., the distance from the baseline to the top of most alphanumeric characters).
- **int getDescent().** Use this to return the font descent (i.e., the distance from the baseline to the bottom of most alphanumeric characters).
- **int getLeading().** This command returns the font leading (i.e., the amount of space to be reserved between the descent of one line of text and the ascent of the next line).
- **int getHeight().** This returns the standard height of a line of text in this font (i.e., the sum of the three previous components).

The following example demonstrates the usage of the FontMetrics class to draw an arbitrary line of text—"Hello, World!"—precisely in the middle of a rectangle:

```
public void paint(Graphics g)
{
   Rectangle rc = new Rectangle(10,
      10, 200, 50);
   g.drawRect(rc.x, rc.y, rc.width,
      rc.height);
   String str = "Hello, World!";
   Font fnt = new Font("TimesRoman",
      Font.PLAIN, 24);
   g.setFont(fnt);
   FontMetrics fm = g.getFontMetrics();
   int x = rc.x + (rc.width -
      fm.stringWidth(str))/2;
   int y = rc.y + (rc.height +
      fm.getAscent() - fm.getDescent())/2;
   g.drawString(str, x, y);
}
```

The paint() method creates a Rectangle object and draws it, using the drawRect() method from the Graphics class. The code following that constructs a Font object (fnt) and sets it as the current font to be used for this

Graphics object using the setFont() method from the Graphics class. Now that you have a font defined and specified for this Graphics object, you can create a FontMetrics object that will reflect the Font properties used in this Graphics object.

The goal here is to calculate the x and y positions to draw a string in the exact middle of the rectangle. The x position is calculated using the stringWidth() method that retrieves the width of the specified string. The y position is calculated using the distance from the rectangle's top to the baseline (ascent + descent), thereby centering it in the rectangle. Finally, you draw the string at the calculated position using the drawString() method (see Figure 2-13).

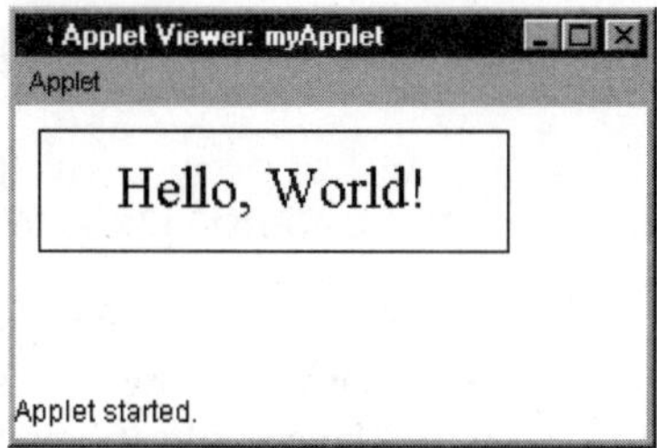

Figure 2-13: FontMetrics.

Fields

Modifiers	Type	Field
protected	Font	font

Constructors

Modifiers	Constructor
protected	FontMetrics(Font)

Methods

Modifiers	Return Type	Method
public	int	bytesWidth(byte[], int, int)
public	int	charsWidth(char[], int, int)
public	int	charWidth(char)
public	int	charWidth(int)
public	int	getAscent()
public	int	getDescent()
public	Font	getFont()
public	int	getHeight()
public	int	getLeading()
public	int	getMaxAdvance()
public	int	getMaxAscent()

Modifiers	Return Type	Method
public	int	getMaxDecent()
public	int	getMaxDescent()
public	int[]	getWidths()
public	int	stringWidth(String)
public	String	toString()

See Also java.awt.Font • java.awt.Graphics • java.io.Serializable • java.lang.Object

Class Frame

public synchronized java.awt.Frame extends java.awt.Window implements java.awt.MenuContainer

The Frame class comes from the **abstract** class Window that is the primary window in any and all of your GUI-based Java applications. Frames include a top-level window, a title, and a border that you can customize or disable.

Tip

You do not need to use the Frame class when building applets, because their hosting environment (e.g., a browser or the applet viewer) creates one for it, usually by using its own frame for the applet's.

Syntax & Usage The following example demonstrates the usage of the Frame class:

```
Frame frame = new Frame("Sample Frame");
frame.setBounds(150, 50, 220, 120);
frame.setBackground(Color.lightGray);
frame.setLayout(new FlowLayout());
frame.add(new Label(
   "This is a Sample Frame"));
frame.add(new Button("OK"));
frame.setResizable(false);
frame.setVisible(true);
```

Here, a new Frame object with the title 'Sample Frame' is created. Then the program sets the position and size for the new frame using the setBounds() method. The frame's background color is specified using the setBackground() method. After that, you specify FlowLayout to be the layout manager for this frame and add two components to the Frame. Finally, you set the resizable property to false (the default is true) and display the frame using the setVisible(true) method (using setVisible() to show the frame is a required step for any frame you wish to have displayed). This example is shown in Figure 2-14.

Note

You can use the WindowListener interface to process WindowEvents from Frame (please see the example for that interface in Chapter 4, "The java.awt.event Package").

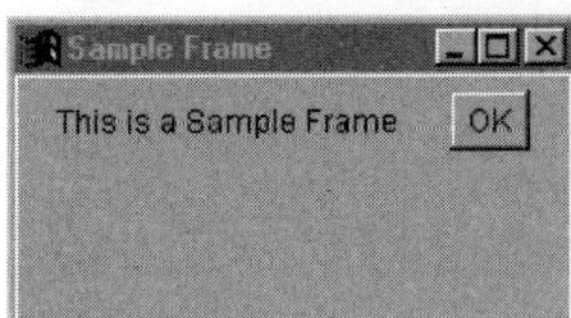

Figure 2-14: Frame.

Two methods in the Frame class have been deprecated in the JDK 1.1.

Deprecated Method	Replaced by
int getCursorType()	Cursor Component.getCursor()
void setCursor(int)	void Component.setCursor(Cursor).

Fields

Modifiers	Type	Field
public static final	int	CROSSHAIR_CURSOR
public static final	int	DEFAULT_CURSOR
public static final	int	E_RESIZE_CURSOR
public static final	int	HAND_CURSOR
public static final	int	MOVE_CURSOR
public static final	int	NE_RESIZE_CURSOR
public static final	int	NW_RESIZE_CURSOR
public static final	int	N_RESIZE_CURSOR
public static final	int	SE_RESIZE_CURSOR
public static final	int	SW_RESIZE_CURSOR
public static final	int	S_RESIZE_CURSOR
public static final	int	TEXT_CURSOR
public static final	int	WAIT_CURSOR
public static final	int	W_RESIZE_CURSOR

Constructors

Modifiers	Constructor
public	Frame()
public	Frame(String)

Methods

Modifiers	Return Type	Method
public	void	addNotify()
public synchronized	void	dispose()
public	int	getCursorType()
public	Image	getIconImage()
public	MenuBar	getMenuBar()
public	String	getTitle()
public	boolean	isResizable()
protected	String	paramString()
public synchronized	void	remove(MenuComponent)
public synchronized	void	setCursor(int)
public synchronized	void	setIconImage(Image)
public synchronized	void	setMenuBar(MenuBar)
public synchronized	void	setResizable(boolean)
public synchronized	void	setTitle(String)

See Also java.awt.Dialog • java.awt.MenuBar • java.awt.MenuContainer • java.awt.MenuItem • java.awt.Window • java.awt.event.WindowListener

Class Graphics

public abstract synchronized java.awt.Graphics extends java.lang.Object

The Graphics class contains a plethora of **public** methods that are at your disposal to draw just about every kind of text or object. Included in the Graphics class is the ability to create lines, rectangles, polygons with any number of sides, arcs, and, of course, all kinds of text.

The Graphics class, as you already know, comes from the AWT package, which also is responsible for building GUIs in Java. The Graphics class works intimately with the paint() method.

Syntax & Usage The recommended way to use the Graphics class is to implement all your painting in the paint() method. You can obtain its Graphics object by calling the getGraphics() method from the Component class anywhere in your program, but your painting will not be updated until your component needs to be repainted by the system (as a result of minimizing the window, for example).

Tip

The Graphics class needs to be imported at the beginning of your Java program before it can be used:

```
import java.awt.*;
```

The following example uses Graphics to fill a circle by colors defined in the Color class:

```
public void paint(Graphics g)
{
  Color colors[] = { Color.black, Color.blue,
    Color.cyan, Color.darkGray, Color.gray,
    Color.green, Color.lightGray,
    Color.magenta, Color.orange, Color.pink,
    Color.red, Color.white, Color.yellow };
  int nStep = (int)Math.ceil(
    360.0 / colors.length);
  int x = 20, y = 20,
    width = 100, height = 100;
  g.drawOval(x, y, width, height);
  for (int k=0; k<colors.length; k++)
  {
    g.setColor(colors[k]);
    g.fillArc(x, y, width, height,
      k*nStep, nStep);
  }
}
```

This example starts off by forming an array of all colors defined in the Color class as static variables. Then it calculates the angle step by dividing 360 degrees on the length of that array. Variables x, y, width, and height are used to bind the rectangle for painting the circle. Finally, in a **for** loop, the program sets colors from the array using the setColor() method and fills the arc using the fillArc() method (see Figure 2-15).

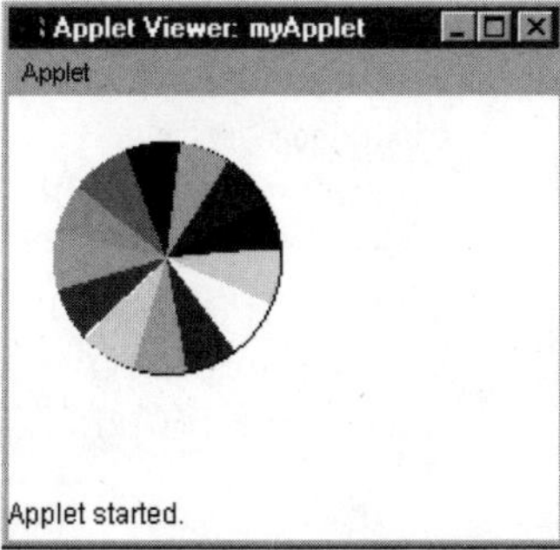

Figure 2-15: Graphics.

One method in the Graphics class has been deprecated in the JDK 1.1.

Deprecated Method	Replaced by
Rectangle getClipRect()	Rectangle getClipBounds()

Fields None

Constructors

Modifiers	Constructor
protected	Graphics()

Methods

Modifiers	Return Type	Method
public abstract	void	clearRect(int, int, int, int)
public abstract	void	clipRect(int, int, int, int)
public abstract	void	copyArea(int, int, int, int, int, int)
public abstract	Graphics	create()
public	Graphics	create(int, int, int, int)
public abstract	void	dispose()
public	void	draw3DRect(int, int, int, int, boolean)
public abstract	void	drawArc(int, int, int, int, int, int)
public	void	drawBytes(byte[], int, int, int, int)
public	void	drawChars(char[], int, int, int, int)
public abstract	boolean	drawImage(Image, int, int, Color, ImageObserver)
public abstract	boolean	drawImage(Image, int, int, ImageObserver)
public abstract	boolean	drawImage(Image, int, int, int, int, Color, ImageObserver)
public abstract	boolean	drawImage(Image, int, int, int, int, ImageObserver)
public abstract	boolean	drawImage(Image, int, int, int, int, int, int, int, int, Color, ImageObserver)
public abstract	boolean	drawImage(Image, int, int, int, int, int, int, int, int, ImageObserver)
public abstract	void	drawLine(int, int, int, int)
public abstract	void	drawOval(int, int, int, int)
public abstract	void	drawPolygon(int[], int[], int)
public	void	drawPolygon(Polygon)
public abstract	void	drawPolyline(int[], int[], int)
public	void	drawRect(int, int, int, int)
public abstract	void	drawRoundRect(int, int, int, int, int, int)
public abstract	void	drawString(String, int, int)
public	void	fill3DRect(int, int, int, int, boolean)

Modifiers	Return Type	Method
public abstract	void	fillArc(int, int, int, int, int, int)
public abstract	void	fillOval(int, int, int, int)
public abstract	void	fillPolygon(int[], int[], int)
public	void	fillPolygon(Polygon)
public abstract	void	fillRect(int, int, int, int)
public abstract	void	fillRoundRect(int, int, int, int, int, int)
public	void	finalize()
public abstract	Shape	getClip()
public abstract	Rectangle	getClipBounds()
public	Rectangle	getClipRect()
public abstract	Color	getColor()
public abstract	Font	getFont()
public	FontMetrics	getFontMetrics()
public abstract	FontMetrics	getFontMetrics(Font)
public abstract	void	setClip(int, int, int, int)
public abstract	void	setClip(Shape)
public abstract	void	setColor(Color)
public abstract	void	setFont(Font)
public abstract	void	setPaintMode()
public abstract	void	setXORMode(Color)
public	String	toString()
public abstract	void	translate(int, int)

See Also java.applet.Applet • java.awt.Color • java.awt.Font • java.awt.FontMetrics • java.lang.Object

Class GridBagConstraints

public synchronized java.awt.GridBagConstraints extends java.lang.Object implements java.lang.Cloneable, java.io.Serializable

This class works intimately with the GridBagLayout layout class. It holds the structure of data, specifying how components are to be laid out using GridBagLayout based on the following: the relative size, the position of each new component, and any other related information. An instance of this class works as a container for information to be passed to GridBagLayout.

Syntax & Usage Please see the example under "Class GridBagLayout," which follows.

Fields

Modifiers	Type	Field
public	int	anchor
public static final	int	BOTH
public static final	int	CENTER
public static final	int	EAST
public	int	fill
public	int	gridheight
public	int	gridwidth
public	int	gridx
public	int	gridy
public static final	int	HORIZONTAL
public	Insets	insets
public	int	ipadx
public	int	ipady
public static final	int	NONE
public static final	int	NORTH
public static final	int	NORTHEAST
public static final	int	NORTHWEST
public static final	int	RELATIVE
public static final	int	REMAINDER
public static final	int	SOUTH
public static final	int	SOUTHEAST
public static final	int	SOUTHWEST
public static final	int	VERTICAL
public	double	weightx
public	double	weighty
public static final	int	WEST

Constructors

Modifiers	Constructor
public	GridBagConstraints()

Methods

Modifiers	Return Type	Method
public	Object	clone()

See Also java.awt.BorderLayout • java.awt.CardLayout • java.awt.FlowLayout • java.awt.GridBagLayout • java.awt.GridLayout • java.io.Serializable • java.lang.Cloneable • java.lang.Object

Class GridBagLayout

public synchronized java.awt.GridBagLayout extends java.lang.Object implements java.awt.LayoutManager2, java.io.Serializable

The GridBagLayout class is a layout that aligns components vertically and horizontally, without requiring that the components be the same size. This is done through the use of a flexible grid that can vary in size and have a component occupy more than one cell.

Syntax & Usage With GridBagLayout, you specify how each component lays out using an instance of GrigBagConstraints.

Tip

GridBagLayout is probably the most versatile of all the layouts available in the AWT. However, it is also the most complex. For a simpler version of the GridBagLayout class, use the GridLayout class instead. Or, for more information on GridBagLayout, consult the Java API spec.

The following example demonstrates the usage of the GridBagLayout and GridBagConstraints classes.

GridBagLayout manages the placing of new components similar to how bricks are organized on a wall. You specify the size and relative (or absolute) position of each 'brick' in an instance of the GridBagLayout class.

```
GridBagLayout m_layout;
GridBagConstraints m_constr;

public void init()
{
  m_layout = new GridBagLayout();
  m_constr = new GridBagConstraints();
  m_constr.weightx = 100;
  m_constr.weighty = 100;
  setLayout(m_layout);

  addToGreed(new Label("First name:"), 0, 0, 1, 1);
  addToGreed(new TextField(15), 1, 0, 1, 1);
  addToGreed(new Label("Last name:"), 0, 1, 1, 1);
  addToGreed(new TextField(15), 1, 1, 1, 1);
  addToGreed(new Label("Telephone:"), 0, 2, 1, 1);
```

```
        addToGreed(new TextField(15), 1, 2, 1, 1);
        addToGreed(new Button("Add new record"), 0, 3, 1, 1);
        addToGreed(new Button("Delete record"), 1, 3, 1, 1);
        addToGreed(new List(6, false), 0, 4, 2, 3);
    }

    protected void addToGreed(Component comp,
        int x, int y, int w, int h)
    {
        m_constr.gridx = x;
        m_constr.gridy = y;
        m_constr.gridwidth = w;
        m_constr.gridheight = h;
        m_constr.fill = GridBagConstraints.BOTH;
        m_layout.setConstraints(comp, m_constr);
        add(comp);
    }
```

The first thing you do here is declare the GridBagLayout object m_layout and the GridBagConstraints object m_constr. Following that, in the init() method, you construct these objects and set m_layout as the current layout manager. The fields GridBagConstraints.weightx and GridBagConstraints.weighty are set to 100 to have the components occupy the entire area. Then the example creates several components and adds them to the applet's panel, using the addToGreed() method defined earlier.

The addToGreed() method fills GridBagConstraints fields with x, y coordinates and width, height values for the component to be added. The GridBagConstraints.fill field is set to BOTH, letting you resize the component both horizontally and vertically. Once you have specified everything just mentioned for the component, you can use the add() method to add the component (see Figure 2-16).

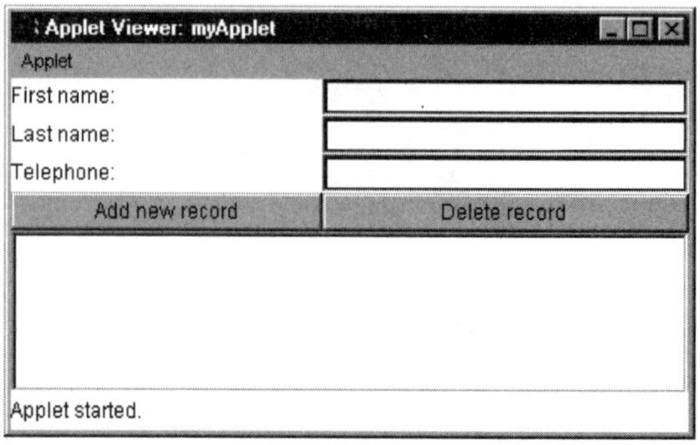

Figure 2-16: GridBagLayout and GridBagConstraints.

Fields

Modifiers	Type	Field
public	double[]	columnWeights
public	int[]	columnWidths
protected	Hashtable	comptable
protected	GridBagConstraints	defaultConstraints
protected	GridBagLayoutInfo	layoutInfo
protected static final	int	MAXGRIDSIZE
protected static final	int	MINSIZE
protected static final	int	PREFERREDSIZE
public	int[]	rowHeights
public	double[]	rowWeights

Constructors

Modifiers	Constructor
public	GridBagLayout()

Methods

Modifiers	Return Type	Method
public	void	addLayoutComponent(Component, Object)
public	void	addLayoutComponent(String, Component)
protected	void	AdjustForGravity(GridBagConstraints, Rectangle)
protected	void	ArrangeGrid(Container)
public	GridBagConstraints	getConstraints(Component)
public	float	getLayoutAlignmentX(Container)
public	float	getLayoutAlignmentY(Container)
public	int [][]	getLayoutDimensions()
protected	GridBagLayoutInfo	GetLayoutInfo(Container, int)
public	Point	getLayoutOrigin()
public	double [][]	getLayoutWeights()
protected	Dimension	GetMinSize(Container, GridBagLayoutInfo)
public	void	invalidateLayout(Container)
public	void	layoutContainer(Container)
public	Point	location(int, int)
protected	GridBagConstraints	lookupConstraints(Component)
public	Dimension	maximumLayoutSize(Container)
public	Dimension	minimumLayoutSize(Container)
public	Dimension	preferredLayoutSize(Container)
public	void	removeLayoutComponent(Component)
public	void	setConstraints(Component, GridBagConstraints)
public	String	toString()

See Also java.awt.BorderLayout • java.awt.CardLayout • java.awt.FlowLayout • java.awt.GridBagConstraints • java.awt.GridLayout • java.awt.LayoutManager2 • java.io.Serializable • java.lang.Object

Class GridLayout

public synchronized java.awt.GridLayout extends java.lang.Object implements java.awt.LayoutManager, java.io.Serializable

The GridLayout class gives you the ability to lay out components in a grid. When you construct a GridLayout, you specify rows and columns to allocate locations for your UI components. For instance, you can build a GridLayout that has two components on each row for two rows.

Syntax & Usage

The following example demonstrates the usage of the GridLayout class:

```
public void init()
{
   setLayout(new GridLayout(4, 2, 20, 10));
   add(new Label("First name:"));
   add(new TextField(15));
   add(new Label("Last name:"));
   add(new TextField(15));
   add(new Label("Telephone:"));
   add(new TextField(15));
   add(new Button("Add new record"));
   add(new Button("Delete record"));
}
```

You first construct a GridLayout object specifying four rows, two columns, a 20-pixel horizontal gap, and a 10-pixel vertical gap. Then you add the same components (save the List component because it requires more space than the other components) that were added in the example for the GridBagLayout class. However, rather than giving precise coordinates, GridLayout will place them in a 4 X 2 table with equal sizes for all cells (see Figure 2-17).

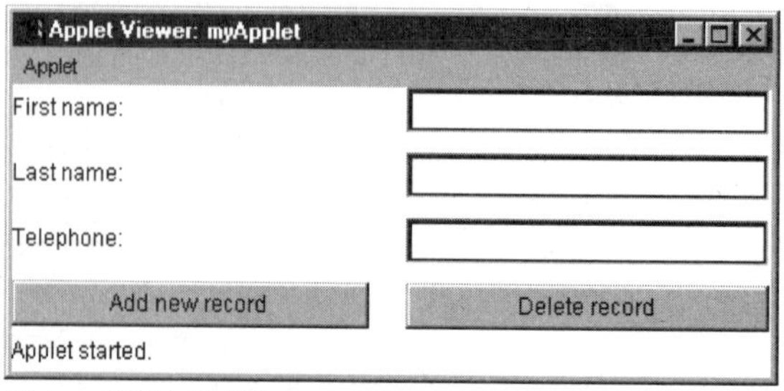

Figure 2-17: GridLayout.

Fields None

Constructors

Modifiers	Constructor
public	GridLayout()
public	GridLayout(int, int)
public	GridLayout(int, int, int, int)

Methods

Modifiers	Return Type	Method
public	void	addLayoutComponent(String, Component)
public	int	getColumns()
public	int	getHgap()
public	int	getRows()
public	int	getVgap()
public	void	layoutContainer(Container)
public	Dimension	minimumLayoutSize(Container)
public	Dimension	preferredLayoutSize(Container)
public	void	removeLayoutComponent(Component)
public	void	setColumns(int)
public	void	setHgap(int)
public	void	setRows(int)
public	void	setVgap(int)
public	String	toString()

See Also java.awt.BorderLayout • java.awt.CardLayout • java.awt.FlowLayout • java.awt.GridBagLayout • java.awt.LayoutManager • java.awt.LayoutManager2 • java.io.Serializable • java.lang.Object

Class IllegalComponentStateException

public synchronized java.awt.IllegalComponentStateException extends java.lang.IllegalStateException

The IllegalComponentStateException is thrown when a component is not in the appropriate state for a requested operation.

Syntax & Usage As of Java 1.1, this exception is thrown only by the getLocale() method from the Component class, indicating that the Locale of this Component cannot be determined:

```
public Locale compLocale(Component comp)
{
  try
  {
    return comp.getLocale();
  }
  catch(IllegalComponentStateException e)
  {
    System.out.println(e.getMessage());
    return null;
  }
}
```

Fields None

Constructors

Modifiers	Constructor
public	IllegalComponentStateException()
public	IllegalComponentStateException(String)

Methods None

See Also java.lang.IllegalStateException • java.util.Locale

Class Image

public abstract synchronized java.awt.Image extends java.lang.Object implements java.io.Serializable

The Image class is used to represent an image that you can use and display in your Java programs.

Syntax & Usage The Image class is an **abstract** class and is implemented differently for each environment supported by Java. That's because each environment loads and handles images in different ways.

Tip

The MediaTracker class can be used to track a number of images in your Java programs.

Because it is **abstract**, the Image class cannot be instantiated directly. However, if you use the getImage() method (from the java.applet.Applet class) or the createImage() method (from the java.awt.Component class) you can have an instance of its platform-specific subclass returned.

The following example demonstrates the usage of the Image class to load an arbitrary image and consistently display it in the center of the applet's panel (no matter what size the panel is specified to be):

```
public class MyApplet extends java.applet.Applet {
  Image m_Image = null;
  int m_w, m_h;

  public void init()
  {
    MediaTracker mtracker = new
      MediaTracker(this);
    m_Image = getImage(getDocumentBase(),
      "myImage.gif");
    mtracker.addImage(m_Image, 0);

    try
    {
      mtracker.waitForAll();
    }
    catch (InterruptedException e)
    {
      m_Image = null;
      System.out.println(e.getMessage());
    }

    m_w = m_Image.getWidth(this);
    m_h = m_Image.getHeight(this);
    repaint();
  }

  public void paint(Graphics g)
  {
    if (m_Image != null)
    {
      int x = (getSize().width - m_w)/2;
      int y = (getSize().height - m_h)/2;
      g.drawImage(m_Image, x, y, this);
    }
  }
}
```

The applet starts by declaring the Image object m_Image, with **int** m_w used to hold the image's width and **int** m_h used to hold the image's height.

In the init() method, you start by constructing a MediaTracker object specifying a **this** reference. Then you load an image using the getImage() method from the java.applet.Applet class specifying the image's location (as retrieved by the getDocumentBase() method) and the filename for the image ('myImage.gif' in this case) that will be displayed later in the applet's panel when the paint() method is called. However, since Java does not wait for the getImage() method to complete before it decides to paint the applet (by calling the paint() method), the applet uses a MediaTracker object to make sure the image has been completely downloaded before being displayed (the actual code that does this is explained a little later on). You do this by adding the loading image to the MediaTracker object using the addImage() method.

Tip

You can gather all loading images into one place and add all loading images to one MediaTracker object that will take care of them.

Then in a **try/catch** block, the applet calls the waitForAll() method that will wait for the m_Image to finish loading. If, in the process of waiting, something gets interrupted, the method will throw an InterruptedException, and m_Image will be set to **null**.

Following that, you have the applet's paint() method, which starts by verifying that the image actually has been loaded. If this is **true**, then paint() draws the image in the center of the applet's panel using the getSize() method to calculate the appropriate coordinates. Note that if you resize the applet's panel, it will reinvoke the paint() method, which will in turn recalculate the image's position, thereby redrawing it in the center of the panel.

Fields

Modifiers	Type	Field
public static final	int	SCALE_AVERAGE
public static final	int	SCALE_DEFAULT
public static final	int	SCALE_FAST
public static final	int	SCALE_REPLICATE
public static final	int	SCALE_SMOOTH
public static final	Object	UndefinedProperty

Constructors

Modifiers	Constructor
public	Image()

Methods

Modifiers	Return Type	Method
public abstract	void	flush()
public abstract	Graphics	getGraphics()
public abstract	int	getHeight(ImageObserver)

Modifiers	Return Type	Method
public abstract	Object	getProperty(String, ImageObserver)
public	Image	getScaledInstance(int, int, int)
public abstract	ImageProducer	getSource()
public abstract	int	getWidth(ImageObserver)

See Also java.applet.Applet • java.awt.Component • java.awt.Graphics • java.awt.MediaTracker • java.awt.image.ImageObserver • java.io.Serializable • java.lang.Object

Class Insets

public synchronized java.awt.Insets extends java.lang.Object implements java.lang.Cloneable, java.io.Serializable

The Insets class is used to represent four margins (top, bottom, left, and right) for a variety of things in Java; the Container, Component, and GridBagConstraints classes all make use of Insets objects.

Tip

Margins are specified as a measurement of pixels.

Syntax & Usage The following example uses the Insets class to resize the working area of a sample frame to the given size (width 200, height 150):

```
int w = 200, h = 150;
Frame frame = new Frame("Sample Frame");
frame.setVisible(true);
Insets ins = frame.getInsets();
frame.setSize(w+ins.left+ins.right,
   h+ins.top+ins.bottom);
```

Note that the Container object must be visible before the Insets object can give you the size of the Container's unusable margins.

Tip

All windows created by untrusted applets display the following message at the bottom: "Untrusted applet window." The height of that message line is not included in an Insets object fields.

Fields

Modifiers	Type	Field
public	int	bottom
public	int	left
public	int	right
public	int	top

Constructors

Modifiers	Constructor
public	Insets(int, int, int, int)

Methods

Modifiers	Return Type	Method
public	Object	clone()
public	boolean	equals(Object)
public	String	toString()

See Also java.awt.Component • java.awt.Container • java.awt.GridBagConstraints • java.awt.GridBagLayout • java.io.Serializable • java.lang.Cloneable • java.lang.Object

Interface ItemSelectable

public abstract synchronized interface java.awt.ItemSelectable

The ItemSelectable class is an interface that is used for objects that contain a list of items that can be selected.

Note

The List component is an excellent example of an object that implements ItemSelectable's functionality.

Syntax & Usage Please see the examples under the Checkbox, CheckboxMenuItem, Choice, and List classes, all of which implement this interface.

Fields None

Constructors None

Methods

Modifiers	Return Type	Method
public abstract	void	addItemListener(ItemListener)
public abstract	Object[]	getSelectedObjects()
public abstract	void	removeItemListener(ItemListener)

See Also java.awt.Checkbox • java.awt.CheckboxMenuItem • java.awt.Choice • java.awt.List • java.awt.event.ItemListener

Class Label

public synchronized java.awt.Label extends java.awt.Component

The Label class is a GUI component that is a string of text displayed as a component in a container of your Java program. In essence, this is the same as using the drawString() method you worked with to print text on the applet pane. However, the advantage of using Label objects over the drawString() method is that Label objects are components and can be housed with other UI components, thus allowing it to be handled by a layout making it much more versatile.

Syntax & Usage The following example creates three labels with different alignments (left, center, and right) specified in their constructors, as shown in Figure 2-18:

```
setLayout(new GridLayout(3, 1, 20, 10));
add(new Label("Left Alignment", Label.LEFT));
add(new Label("Center Alignment",
  Label.CENTER));
add(new Label("Right Alignment",
  Label.RIGHT));
```

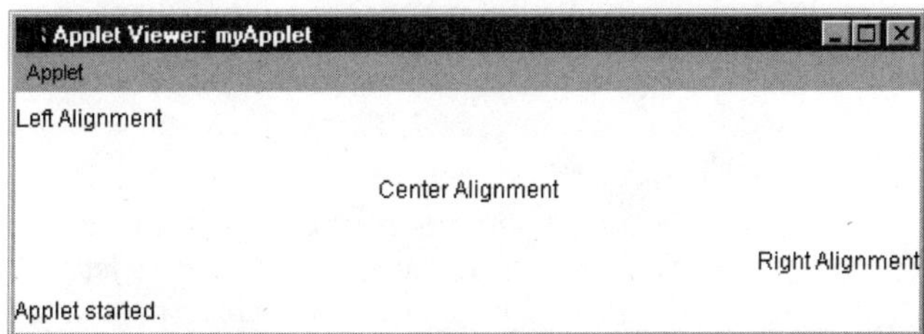

Figure 2-18: Label.

Fields

Modifiers	Type	Field
public static final	int	CENTER
public static final	int	LEFT
public static final	int	RIGHT

Constructors

Modifiers	Constructor
public	Label()
public	Label(String)
public	Label(String, int)

Methods

Modifiers	Return Type	Method
public	void	addNotify()
public	int	getAlignment()
public	String	getText()
protected	String	paramString()
public synchronized	void	setAlignment(int)
public synchronized	void	setText(String)

See Also java.awt.Button • java.awt.Canvas • java.awt.Checkbox • java.awt.CheckboxGroup • java.awt.Choice • java.awt.Component • java.awt.List • java.awt.Scrollbar • java.awt.TextArea • java.awt.TextComponent • java.awt.TextField

Interface LayoutManager

public abstract synchronized interface java.awt.LayoutManager

The LayoutManager class is an interface that is used to define the standard functionality for how all layout managers are to behave. BorderLayout, CardLayout, FlowLayout, and GridLayout all implement this interface.

Tip

GridBagLayout now implements the LayoutManager2 interface—as opposed to the LayoutManager as defined in Java 1.0. LayoutManager2 extends LayoutManager's functionality, providing additional support for any constraint-based layouts.

Syntax & Usage You can create your own layout managers to do just about anything you want them to. All you need to do is create a class that implements the LayoutManager interface and override the five methods defined in that interface, listed as follows:

- **addLayoutComponent(String, Component).** This method is used to add a specified component and give it the name specified in the String parameter.
- **removeLayoutComponent(Component).** This method is used to remove the specified component.
- **component.preferredLayoutSize(Container).** This method returns a Dimension object giving the recommended dimensions for the specified panel based on the components present in the specified parent container.
- **minimumLayoutSize(Container).** This method returns a Dimension object giving the minimum dimensions for the specified panel based on the components present in the specified parent container.
- **layoutContainer(Container).** This method lays out the container.

Please see the examples under the BorderLayout, CardLayout, and GridBagLayout classes for more information.

> **Tip**
>
> *The good thing about all layouts is that they take care of placing and sizing your components. The bad thing is that they may not always give you the freedom that you need. Usually, you can achieve desirable results by combining several layouts (see the example under "Class Panel," later in this chapter).*
>
> *Nevertheless, Java does provide an alternative: Don't use a layout manager to begin with. Instead, set the layout manager to **null** and explicitly resize your components using the setBounds() method.*

Fields None

Constructors None

Methods

Modifiers	Return Type	Method
public abstract	void	addLayoutComponent(String, Component)
public abstract	void	layoutContainer(Container)
public abstract	Dimension	minimumLayoutSize(Container)
public abstract	Dimension	preferredLayoutSize(Container)
public abstract	void	removeLayoutComponent(Component)

See Also java.awt.BorderLayout • java.awt.CardLayout • java.awt.Component • java.awt.FlowLayout • java.awt.GridBagLayout • java.awt.GridLayout • java.awt.LayoutManager2

Interface LayoutManager2

public abstract synchronized interface java.awt.LayoutManager2 implements java.awt.LayoutManager

The LayoutManager2 class is an interface that implements the LayoutManager interface, thus extending LayoutManager's functionality. This interface is used specifically for layouts that use constraint-based objects to specify the layout of components and containers—based on the terms defined in the corresponding constraint object(s).

Syntax & Usage Please see the examples for the FlowLayout and GridLayout classes, earlier in this chapter.

Tip

LayoutManager2 also is useful for programmers wishing to create their own custom constraint-based layouts.

Fields None

Constructors None

Methods

Modifiers	Return Type	Method
public abstract	void	addLayoutComponent(Component, Object)
public abstract	float	getLayoutAlignmentX(Container)
public abstract	float	getLayoutAlignmentY(Container)
public abstract	void	invalidateLayout(Container)
public abstract	Dimension	maximumLayoutSize(Container)

See Also java.awt.FlowLayout • java.awt.GridBagLayout • java.awt.GridLayout • java.awt.LayoutManager

Class List

public synchronized java.awt.List extends java.awt.Component implements java.awt.ItemSelectable

The List class is a GUI component that displays a list of items in a scrolling format. The functionality of List is very similar to that of Choice. However, a list is always in a drop-down state. List is also unique in that it can be configured to have more than one selection in one box at one time (i.e., it facilitates support for multiple selections).

Syntax & Usage The following example demonstrates usage of a list with multiple selections including notification via an ItemListener object:

```
public class myApplet extends Applet
{
  List m_List;

  public void init()
  {
    m_List = new List(4, true);
    m_List.addItem("Ann");
    m_List.addItem("John");
    m_List.addItem("Bill");
    m_List.addItem("George");
    m_List.addItem("Susan");
    for (int k=0; k<m_List.getItemCount();
      k++)
      m_List.select(k);
    m_List.addItemListener(new
      ItemAdapter());
    add(m_List);
  }

  class ItemAdapter implements ItemListener
  {
    public void itemStateChanged(
      ItemEvent ev)
    {
      int index;
      try
      {
        index = Integer.parseInt(
        ev.getItem().toString());
      }
```

```
            catch(NumberFormatException e)
            {
              return;
            }
            String str = m_List.getItem(index)+
              " has been "+
              (ev.getStateChange()
              ==ItemEvent.SELECTED ?
              "selected" : "deselected");
            System.out.println(str);
          }
      }
}
```

You first create a new List object, specifying four rows and setting the multiple selections flag to **true**. Then you add several items to the list and select all of them using the select() method in the **for** loop that follows. An ItemAdapter object is set as ItemListener for this list.

The ItemAdapter class defines the itemStateChanged() method, which will be invoked every time the user selects or deselects an item in the list. The ItemEvent object contains information about the event. The getItem() method retrieves the item's index as an Object, and getStateChange() retrieves the current item's state (i.e., whether it is selected or not). Figure 2-19 shows the previous code in action.

Tip

Unfortunately, to convert the Object object containing the selected item to an integer value is not an easy process in the JDK 1.1: First, you need to convert the value contained in the Object object to a String. Then, you need to invoke the parseInt() method from the java.lang.Integer class and catch any possible NumberFormatExceptions.

You also can use the ActionListener interface to handle ActionEvents that occur when a user double-clicks on an item contained in a List object.

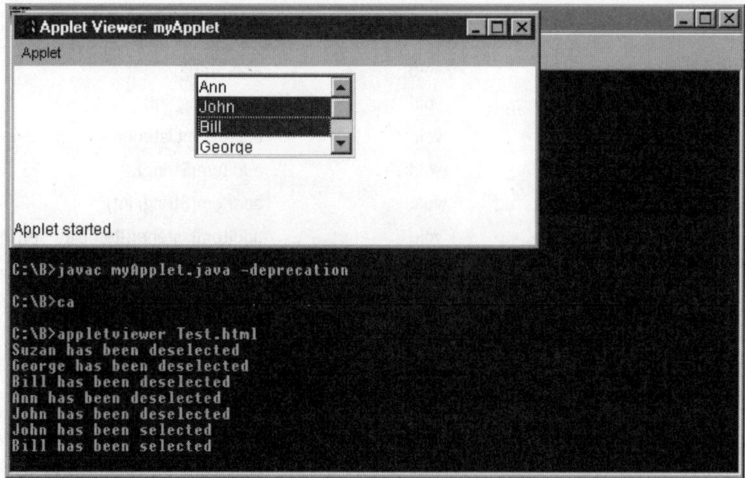

Figure 2-19: List.

Some methods in the List class have been deprecated in the JDK 1.1.

Deprecated Method	Replaced By
Boolean allowsMultipleSelections()	boolean isMultipleMode()
void clear()	void removeAll()
int countItems()	int getItemCount()
void delItems(int, int)	Not for public use in the JDK 1.1
boolean isSelected(int)	boolean isIndexSelected(int)
Dimension minimumSize()	Dimension getMinimumSize()
Dimension minimumSize(int)	Dimension getMinimumSize(int)
Dimension preferredSize()	Dimension getPreferredSize()
Dimension preferredSize(int)	Dimension getPreferredSize(int)
void setMultipleSelections(boolean)	void setMultipleMode(boolean)

Fields None

Constructors

Modifiers	Constructor
public	List()
public	List(int)
public	List(int, boolean)

Methods

Modifiers	Return Type	Method
public	void	add(String)
public synchronized	void	add(String, int)
public	void	addActionListener(ActionListener)
public	void	addItem(String)
public synchronized	void	addItem(String, int)
public	void	addItemListener(ItemListener)
public	void	addNotify()
public	boolean	allowsMultipleSelections()
public synchronized	void	clear()
public	int	countItems()
public synchronized	void	delItem(int)
public synchronized	void	delItems(int, int)
public synchronized	void	deselect(int)
public	String	getItem(int)
public	int	getItemCount()
public synchronized	String[]	getItems()
public	Dimension	getMinimumSize()
public	Dimension	getMinimumSize(int)
public	Dimension	getPreferredSize()
public	Dimension	getPreferredSize(int)
public	int	getRows()
public synchronized	int	getSelectedIndex()
public synchronized	int[]	getSelectedIndexes()
public synchronized	String	getSelectedItem()
public synchronized	String[]	getSelectedItems()
public	Object[]	getSelectedObjects()
public	int	getVisibleIndex()
public	boolean	isIndexSelected(int)
public	boolean	isMultipleMode()
public	boolean	isSelected(int)
public synchronized	void	makeVisible(int)
public	Dimension	minimumSize()
public	Dimension	minimumSize(int)
protected	String	paramString()
public	Dimension	preferredSize()
public	Dimension	preferredSize(int)
protected	void	processActionEvent(ActionEvent)
protected	void	processEvent(AWTEvent)

Modifiers	Return Type	Method
protected	void	processItemEvent(ItemEvent)
public synchronized	void	remove(int)
public synchronized	void	remove(String)
public	void	removeActionListener(ActionListener)
public synchronized	void	removeAll()
public	void	removeItemListener(ItemListener)
public	void	removeNotify()
public synchronized	void	replaceItem(String, int)
public synchronized	void	select(int)
public synchronized	void	setMultipleMode(boolean)
public synchronized	void	setMultipleSelections(boolean)

See Also java.awt.Button • java.awt.Canvas • java.awt.Checkbox • java.awt.CheckboxGroup • java.awt.Choice • java.awt.Component • java.awt.ItemSelectable • java.awt.Label • java.awt.Scrollbar • java.awt.TextArea • java.awt.TextComponent • java.awt.TextField • java.awt.event.ActionListener • java.awt.event.ItemListener

Class MediaTracker

public synchronized java.awt.MediaTracker extends java.lang.Object implements java.io.Serializable

The MediaTracker class is used to track a variety of media-based objects including audio files and images.

Syntax & Usage Please see the example under "Class Image," earlier in this chapter.

Fields

Modifiers	Type	Field
public static final	int	ABORTED
public static final	int	COMPLETE
public static final	int	ERRORED
public static final	int	LOADING

Constructors

Modifiers	Constructor
public	MediaTracker(Component)

Methods

Modifiers	Return Type	Method
public	void	addImage(Image, int)
public synchronized	void	addImage(Image, int, int, int)
public	boolean	checkAll()
public synchronized	boolean	checkAll(boolean)
public	boolean	checkID(int)
public synchronized	boolean	checkID(int, boolean)
public synchronized	Object[]	getErrorsAny()
public synchronized	Object[]	getErrorsID(int)
public synchronized	boolean	isErrorAny()
public synchronized	boolean	isErrorID(int)
public synchronized	void	removeImage(Image)
public synchronized	void	removeImage(Image, int)
public synchronized	void	removeImage(Image, int, int, int)
public synchronized	int	statusAll(boolean)
public synchronized	int	statusID(int, boolean)
public	void	waitForAll()
public synchronized	boolean	waitForAll(long)
public	void	waitForID(int)
public synchronized	boolean	waitForID(int, long)

See Also java.awt.Image • java.io.Serializable • java.lang.Object

Class Menu

public synchronized java.awt.Menu extends java.awt.MenuItem implements java.awt.MenuContainer

The Menu class is a menu-based GUI component that represents the actual menus for your menu bar.

Note

The Menu class contains the setHelpMenu() method which is used to specify a menu object as the program's standard help menu.

Syntax & Usage To use menus, you first need to create a Frame object that will hold the menu. The following example demonstrates this, as well as Menu, MenuItem, MenuBar, and MenuShortcut:

> **Tip**
>
> *You need at least one text object to be added to Frame, otherwise the menu shortcuts mechanism will not work.*

```
public class myFrame extends Frame
{

   TextArea m_txtEdit;

   public myFrame()
   {
      super("Sample Menu");
      setSize(200, 200);

      Menu mFile = new Menu("File");
      MenuItem mNew = new MenuItem("New",
         new MenuShortcut('n'));
      mNew.setActionCommand("New");
      mNew.addActionListener(new
         ActionAdapter(1));
      mFile.add(mNew);

      MenuItem mOpen = new MenuItem("Open",
         new MenuShortcut('o'));
      mOpen.setActionCommand("Open");
      mOpen.addActionListener(new
         ActionAdapter(2));
      mFile.add(mOpen);

      MenuItem mClose = new MenuItem("Close");
      mClose.addActionListener(new
         ActionAdapter(3));
      mFile.add(mClose);

      mFile.addSeparator();
      MenuItem mExit = new MenuItem("Exit",
         new MenuShortcut('x'));
      mExit.setActionCommand("Exit");
      mExit.addActionListener(new
         ActionAdapter(4));
      mFile.add(mExit);
```

```
        Menu mHelp = new Menu("Help");
        MenuItem mAbout = new MenuItem("About");
        mAbout.addActionListener(new
          ActionAdapter(5));
        mHelp.add(mAbout);

        MenuItem mIndex = new MenuItem(
          "Help Index",
          new MenuShortcut(KeyEvent.VK_F1));
        mIndex.setActionCommand("Help Index");
        mIndex.addActionListener(new
          ActionAdapter(6));
        mHelp.add(mIndex);

        MenuBar mBar = new MenuBar();
        mBar.add(mFile);
        mBar.add(mHelp);
        mBar.setHelpMenu(mHelp);

        setMenuBar(mBar);
        m_txtEdit = new TextArea(15, 40);
        add(m_txtEdit);
        pack();
        m_txtEdit.requestFocus();
        setVisible(true);
      }

      class ActionAdapter implements
        ActionListener
      {
        private int m_commandID;

        ActionAdapter(int commandID)
        {
          m_commandID = commandID;
        }

        public void actionPerformed(
          ActionEvent e)
        {
          m_txtEdit.append("Get command \""+
          e.getActionCommand()+
          "\" (ID: "+m_commandID+")\n");
        }

      }
    }
```

Looking at the constructor for the myFrame class, the first two lines construct a Frame object labeled 'Sample Menu' and resize it.

Then you create two menu objects labeled File and Help. Menu File holds menu items labeled New, Open, Close, Exit, and also holds a menu separator. The menu item New has the keyboard shortcut Ctrl+N, which is assigned by creating a new MenuShortcut object with the key n. Menu Help holds menu items labeled About and Help Index.

Tip

All menu shortcuts in the JDK 1.1 work on a combination of the Control key and a specified key. Additionally, you can specify the Shift key by adding a second parameter true to the constructor. For alphabetical symbols, just specify the corresponding character in single quotes. For other keys, use virtual codes constants defined in java.awt.event.KeyEvent class (as in Help Index in this example).

JDK 1.1 automatically adds shortcut names to menu labels, like Open Ctrl+O, so you don't need to do it twice.

For menu items with shortcuts, you use the setActionCommand() method to specify the command text that will be assigned to generated action events (mouse-activated action events automatically will receive MenuItem's label as a name).

Each menu item receives its own ActionAdapter object as an ActionListener with a unique ID for each. In a real application, you would specify Menu's IDs as **static final int** fields (see the example for "Class Button," earlier in this chapter).

As soon as all menu items are created and added to their menus, you create a MenuBar object and add these menus to it. Menu mHelp is specified as the help menu for this frame using the setHelpMenu() method. Finally, you create and add a TextArea object and pack() the Frame.

Class ActionAdapter implements ActionListener and uses it to receive notification from the menus you just created. It's defined as an inner class and holds the ID values specified at construction. As soon as an action event occurs, it displays the event's name and ID in the text area.

Running this example, you can see that ActionListener is the response to both mouse menu selections and keyboard shortcuts.

Note

JDK 1.1 displays the F1 shortcut as Ctrl+P, and it works equally for Ctrl+F1 and Ctrl+P (see Figure 2-20).

Figure 2-20: Menu.

One method in the Menu class has been deprecated in the JDK 1.1.

Deprecated Method	Replaced By
int countItems()	int getItemCount()

Fields None

Constructors

Modifiers	Constructor
public	Menu()
public	Menu(String)
public	Menu(String, boolean)

Methods

Modifiers	Return Type	Method
public synchronized	MenuItem	add(MenuItem)
public	void	add(String)
public	void	addNotify()
public	void	addSeparator()
public	int	countItems()
public	MenuItem	getItem(int)
public	int	getItemCount()
public synchronized	void	insert(MenuItem, int)
public	void	insert(String, int)
public	void	insertSeparator(int)
public	boolean	isTearOff()

Modifiers	Return Type	Method
public	String	paramString()
public synchronized	void	remove(int)
public synchronized	void	remove(MenuComponent)
public synchronized	void	removeAll()
public	void	removeNotify()

See Also java.awt.CheckboxMenuItem • java.awt.MenuBar • java.awt.MenuContainer • java.awt.MenuItem • java.awt.PopupMenu

Class MenuBar

public synchronized java.awt.MenuBar extends java.awt.MenuComponent implements java.awt.MenuContainer

The MenuBar class is a menu-based GUI component that represents the actual menu bar for your Java program.

Syntax & Usage MenuBar is the first class that you need to work with to create a menu in Java. Let's take a look at a typical scenario for adding a complete menu system to a frame in your Java program:

1. Declare a MenuBar object and add it to your frame using the setMenubar() method from the Frame class.
2. Construct the menu objects you wish to use, passing a string for the name of each.
3. Construct all the menu-based components (MenuItem object, CheckboxMenuItem objects, separators, etc.) you need and add them to their respective menus.
4. Add the menus to the MenuBar object you created in step 1.

Please see the example under "Class Menu," the previous subsection, for a real example.

One method in the MenuBar class has been deprecated in the JDK 1.1.

Deprecated Method	Replaced By
int countMenus()	int getMenuCount()

Fields None

Constructors

Modifiers	Constructor
public	MenuBar()

Methods

Modifiers	Return Type	Method
public synchronized	Menu	add(Menu)
public	void	addNotify()
public	int	countMenus()
public	void	deleteShortcut(MenuShortcut)
public	Menu	getHelpMenu()
public	Menu	getMenu(int)
public	int	getMenuCount()
public	MenuItem	getShortcutMenuItem(MenuShortcut)
public synchronized	void	remove(int)
public synchronized	void	remove(MenuComponent)
public	void	removeNotify()
public synchronized	void	setHelpMenu(Menu)
public synchronized	Enumeration	shortcuts()

See Also java.awt.CheckboxMenuItem • java.awt.Menu • java.awt.MenuComponent • java.awt.MenuContainer • java.awt.MenuItem • java.awt.PopupMenu

Class MenuComponent

public abstract synchronized java.awt.MenuComponent extends java.lang.Object implements java.io.Serializable

The MenuComponent **abstract** class is the root of all menu-based classes components used in Java.

Syntax & Usage

MenuComponent is itself an **abstract** class. Thus, you cannot instantiate it directly. However, you can benefit from its functionality by instantiating its subclasses, which are as follows:

- CheckboxMenuItem
- Menu
- MenuBar
- MenuItem
- PopupMenu

Tip

You can specify the font to be used for your menu-based component using the setFont() method contained in this class and passing it an instance of a Font object.

Please see the example under "Class Menu," earlier in this chapter for more information.

One method in the MenuComponent class has been deprecated in the JDK 1.1.

Deprecated Method	Replaced By
MenuComponentPeer getPeer()	In the JDK 1.1, programs should not directly manipulate peers

Fields None

Constructors

Modifiers	Constructor
public	MenuComponent()

Methods

Modifiers	Return Type	Method
public final	void	dispatchEvent(AWTEvent)
public	Font	getFont()
public	String	getName()
public	MenuContainer	getParent()
public	MenuComponentPeer	getPeer()
protected	String	paramString()
public	boolean	postEvent(Event)
protected	void	processEvent(AWTEvent)
public	void	removeNotify()
public	void	setFont(Font)
public	void	setName(String)
public	String	toString()

See Also java.awt.CheckboxMenuItem • java.awt.Font • java.awt.Menu • java.awt.MenuBar • java.awt.MenuContainer • java.awt.MenuItem • java.awt.PopupMenu • java.io.Serializable • java.lang.Object

Interface MenuContainer

public abstract synchronized interface java.awt.MenuContainer

The MenuContainer class is an **abstract** interface that defines the methods necessary to add and use menus in various containers. Classes that implement MenuContainer include java.awt.Frame, java.awt.Menu, and java.awt.MenuBar.

Syntax & Usage In most cases you will not need to implement this interface directly.

> **Note**
>
> *If you are creating your own container and need to add menu-based functionality to it, you need to implement this interface.*

Fields None

Constructors None

Methods

Modifiers	Return Type	Method
public abstract	Font	getFont()
public abstract	boolean	postEvent(Event)
public abstract	void	remove(MenuComponent)

See Also java.awt.CheckboxMenuItem • java.awt.Frame • java.awt.Menu • java.awt.MenuBar • java.awt.MenuComponent • java.awt.MenuContainer • java.awt.MenuItem • java.awt.PopupMenu

Class MenuItem

public synchronized java.awt.MenuItem extends java.awt.MenuComponent

The MenuItem class is a menu-based GUI component that is used for creating menu items that you specify and add to your menus you wish to add to your Java programs.

Syntax & Usage Please see the example under "Class Menu," earlier in this chapter for an example of this class in action.

Several methods in MenuItem class have been deprecated in the JDK 1.1.

Deprecated Method	Replaced By
void disable()	void setEnabled(false)
void enable()	void setEnabled(true)
void enable(boolean)	void setEnabled(boolean)

Fields None

Constructors

Modifiers	Constructor
public	MenuItem()
public	MenuItem(String)
public	MenuItem(String, MenuShortcut)

Methods

Modifiers	Return Type	Method
public	void	addActionListener(ActionListener)
public	void	addNotify()
public	void	deleteShortcut()
public synchronized	void	disable()
protected final	void	disableEvents(long)
public synchronized	void	enable()
public	void	enable(boolean)
protected final	void	enableEvents(long)
public	String	getActionCommand()
public	String	getLabel()
public	MenuShortcut	getShortcut()
public	boolean	isEnabled()
public	String	paramString()
protected	void	processActionEvent(ActionEvent)
protected	void	processEvent(AWTEvent)
public	void	removeActionListener(ActionListener)
public	void	setActionCommand(String)
public synchronized	void	setEnabled(boolean)
public synchronized	void	setLabel(String)
public	void	setShortcut(MenuShortcut)

See Also java.awt.CheckboxMenuItem • java.awt.Menu • java.awt.MenuBar • java.awt.MenuComponent • java.awt.MenuContainer • java.awt.PopupMenu

Class MenuShortcut

public synchronized java.awt.MenuShortcut extends java.awt.Event

The MenuShortcut class is an event that gets generated when a menu shortcut for a menu item is invoked.

Syntax & Usage Please see the example under "Class Menu," earlier in this chapter.

Fields None

Constructors

Modifiers	Constructor
public	MenuShortcut(int)
public	MenuShortcut(int, boolean)

Methods

Modifiers	Return Type	Method
public	boolean	equals(MenuShortcut)
public	int	getKey()
protected	String	paramString()
public	String	toString()
public	boolean	usesShiftModifier()

See Also java.awt.CheckboxMenuItem • java.awt.Event • java.awt.Menu • java.awt.MenuBar • java.awt.MenuComponent • java.awt.MenuContainer • java.awt.MenuItem • java.awt.PopupMenu

Class Panel

public synchronized java.awt.Panel extends java.awt.Container

The Panel class is a Container subclass that is used to hold components (and potentially other panels).

Syntax & Usage Unlike its siblings (e.g., Frame), a Panel object does not create a separate window for itself. Instead, the Panel object is added to a Frame or another Panel object, which makes Panel objects very useful for designing a piece of your GUI at one time and grouping it into one "subcontainer."

Note

The java.applet.Applet class actually extends from this class. That is how Java applets are able to hold UI components and use layouts without having to explicitly construct a Container-based object.

Unless otherwise specified, the default layout manager for a Panel object is FlowLayout.

The following example uses a Panel object to localize the area of different layout managers and achieve a more desirable placement for components:

```
Panel pn1 = new Panel();
pn1.setLayout(new GridLayout(3, 2, 20, 10));

pn1.add(new Label("First name:"));
pn1.add(new TextField(15));
pn1.add(new Label("Last name:"));
pn1.add(new TextField(15));
pn1.add(new Label("Telephone:"));
pn1.add(new TextField(15));

pn1.setSize(200, 100);
add(pn1);

Panel pn2 = new Panel();
pn2.setLayout(new FlowLayout());

pn2.add(new Button("Add new record"));
pn2.add(new Button("Edit record"));
pn2.add(new Button("Delete record"));

pn2.setSize(200, 30);
add(pn2);
```

Panel pn1 uses GridLayout, whereas Panel pn2 uses FlowLayout. When both are added to the applet's panel, they produce the result shown in Figure 2-21.

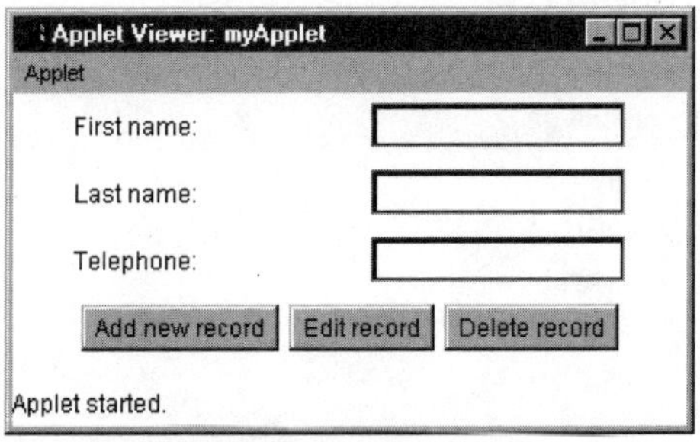

Figure 2-21: Panel.

Fields None

Constructors

Modifiers	Constructor
public	Panel()
public	Panel(LayoutManager)

Methods

Modifiers	Return Type	Method
public	void	addNotify()

See Also java.awt.Container • java.awt.FlowLayout • java.awt.Frame
java.awt.ScrollPanel

Class Point

public synchronized java.awt.Point extends java.lang.Object implements java.io.Serializable

The Point class encapsulates an ordered pair (X, Y) for a two-dimensional plane.

Syntax & Usage Please see the example under "Class Rectangle," later in this chapter.

Note

The Point class comes in handy for drawing various two-dimensional graphics.

Fields

Modifiers	Type	Field
public	int	x
public	int	y

Constructors

Modifiers	Constructor
public	Point()
public	Point(int, int)
public	Point(Point)

Methods

Modifiers	Return Type	Method
public	boolean	equals(Object)
public	Point	getLocation()
public	int	hashCode()
public	void	move(int, int)
public	void	setLocation(int, int)
public	void	setLocation(Point)
public	String	toString()
public	void	translate(int, int)

See Also java.awt.Graphics • java.awt.Rectangle • java.io.Serializable java.lang.Object

Class Polygon

public synchronized java.awt.Polygon extends java.lang.Object implements java.awt.Shape, java.io.Serializable

The Polygon class is used to define an array of X points and an array of Y points that can vary in size.

Syntax & Usage A Polygon object is used to draw custom polygons using the drawPolygon() or fillPolygon() methods from the java.awt.Graphics class.

Note

The methods getBoundingBox() and inside() have both been replaced in Java 1.1:

The getBoundingBox() method returns a Rectangle object that is the smallest representation of a Polygon object. The new method that should be used in its place is getBounds().

*The inside() method takes two integers that represent an X- and a Y-coordinate. This method returns **true** if the coordinate point is located inside of a given Polygon object. The new method that should be used in its place is contains().*

The following example uses the Polygon class to draw a star:

```
public class myApplet extends Applet
{
   Polygon m_Poly;
   public void init()
   {
      m_Poly = new Polygon();
      double teta = 2.0*Math.PI/5.0;
      double R1 = 50.0, R2 = 25.0;
      int x0 = getSize().width/2;
      int y0 = getSize().height/2;
      for (int k=0; k<5; k++)
      {
         int x = x0+
         (int)(R1*Math.sin(teta*k));
         int y = y0-
         (int)(R1*Math.cos(teta*k));
         m_Poly.addPoint(x, y);
         x = x0+
         (int)(R2*Math.sin(teta*(k+0.5)));
         y = y0-
         (int)(R2*Math.cos(teta*(k+0.5)));
         m_Poly.addPoint(x, y);
      }
   }

   public void paint(Graphics g)
   {
      g.setColor(Color.blue);
      g.fillPolygon(m_Poly);
      g.setColor(Color.black);
      g.drawPolygon(m_Poly);
   }
}
```

Starting with the init() method of this sample applet, it constructs a Polygon object and adds the star's vertices to that Polygon. The method paint() uses this Polygon to draw the star, using the fillPolygon() and drawPolygon() methods from the Graphics class (see Figure 2-22).

Figure 2-22: Polygon.

As explained earlier, two methods in the Polygon class have been deprecated in the JDK 1.1.

Deprecated Method	Replaced By
Rectangle getBoundingBox()	Rectangle getBounds()
boolean inside(int, int)	boolean contains(int, int)

Fields

Modifiers	Type	Field
protected	Rectangle	bounds
public	int	npoints
public	int[]	xpoints
public	int[]	ypoints

Constructors

Modifiers	Constructor
public	Polygon()
public	Polygon(int[], int[], int)

Methods

Modifiers	Return Type	Method
public	void	addPoint(int, int)
public	boolean	contains(int, int)
public	boolean	contains(Point)
public	Rectangle	getBoundingBox()
public	Rectangle	getBounds()
public	boolean	inside(int, int)
public	void	translate(int, int)

See Also java.awt.Graphics • java.awt.Point • java.awt.Rectangle • java.awt.Shape • java.io.Serializable • java.lang.Object

Class PopupMenu

public synchronized java.awt.PopupMenu extends java.awt.Menu

The PopupMenu class, which is a java.awt.Menu subclass, is a new class added to the AWT 1.1. PopupMenu gives you the ability to add a pop-up menu functionality to your Java programs. A pop-up menu is a temporary menu that appears next to your mouse arrow after right-clicking (mouse button two for Windows or three for Motif) your mouse.

Syntax & Usage

The PopupMenu class uses the three methods: add(), remove(), and show(). The first two come from the Menu class and the third is defined in this one. The add() and remove() methods let you add and remove menu items to and from a pop-up menu. The show() method displays the given PopupMenu object based on three parameters: The first is the component/container in which you wish to have the pop-up menu display; the second and third represent the exact X- and Y-coordinates of where it is to be displayed.

Looking at the following example, the construction of a PopupMenu object is very similar to the construction of a Menu object. The difference is that you add a PopupMenu object direct to your component. Then you need to enable the mouse events for this component by invoking the enableEvents() method:

```
public class myApplet extends Applet
{
   PopupMenu popup;

   public void init()
   {
      popup = new PopupMenu("Colors");
      popup.add(new MenuItem("Cut"));
      popup.add(new MenuItem("Copy"));
      popup.add(new MenuItem("Paste"));
      popup.addSeparator();
      popup.add(new MenuItem("Properties"));
      add(popup);

      enableEvents(AWTEvent.MOUSE_EVENT_MASK);
   }
```

```
  public void processMouseEvent(MouseEvent e)
  {
    if (e.isPopupTrigger())
      popup.show(e.getComponent(),
        e.getX(), e.getY());
    super.processMouseEvent(e);
  }
}
```

The processMouseEvent() method verifies that this mouse event is the pop-up menu trigger event by invoking the isPopupTrigger() method from the MouseEvent class. If so, it activates the pop-up menu, using the show() method from the PopupMenu class specifying the current mouse position. Finally, this method invokes super.processMouseEvent(), which is used to process all mouse-based events that contain a call to the show() method to display the PopupMenu object at the specified location (see Figure 2-23). This provides event-handling support so when a user right-clicks their mouse in the Java program, the pop-up menu is displays.

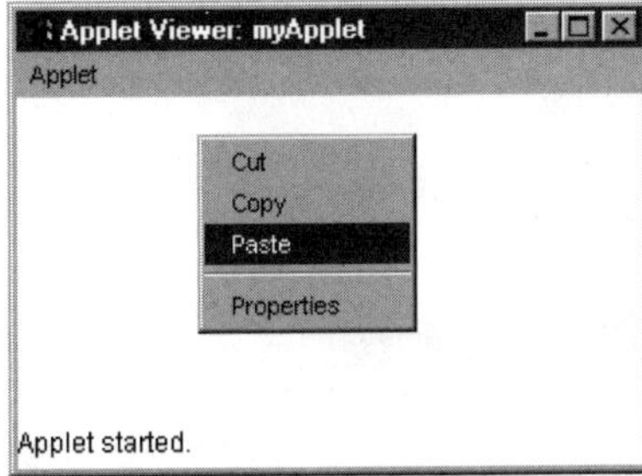

Figure 2-23: PopupMenu.

Fields None

Constructors

Modifiers	Constructor
public	PopupMenu()
public	PopupMenu(String)

Methods

Modifiers	Return Type	Method
public synchronized	void	addNotify()
public	void	show(Component, int, int)

See Also java.awt.CheckboxMenuItem • java.awt.Menu • java.awt.MenuBar java.awt.MenuItem

Interface PrintGraphics

public abstract synchronized interface java.awt.PrintGraphics

PrintGraphics is an **abstract** interface that defines the graphics context to be used for printing in Java.

Syntax & Usage You can use the **instanceof** operator on this interface to check whether your Graphics object in the paint() method refers to printing:

```
public void paint(Graphics g)
{
   if (g instanceof PrintGraphics)
     // now printing
     ;
}
```

Fields None

Constructors None

Methods

Modifiers	Return Type	Method
public abstract	PrintJob	getPrintJob()

See Also java.awt.Graphics • java.awt.PrintJob • java.awt.Toolkit

Class PrintJob

public abstract synchronized java.awt.PrintJob extends java.lang.Object

The PrintJob class is an **abstract** class used to initiate and execute a print job in Java. It provides the functionality to render graphics to be printed to the user's printing device.

Syntax & Usage PrintJob is itself an **abstract** class. Thus, you cannot instantiate it directly. However, you can benefit from its functionality by calling the getPrintJob() method from the java.awt.Toolkit class.

Note

The Toolkit class provides a natively-based subclass for the ***abstract*** *AWT-based classes.*

The following example demonstrates the PrintJob class. It takes the frame to be printed and returns **true** if the printing is successful or **false** if an error occurs.

Note

Any attempt to use the PrintJob class from an untrusted applet will cause a security exception.

```
public boolean printFrame(Frame frame)
{
  PrintJob prnJob;
  try
  {
  prnJob = frame.getToolkit().getPrintJob(frame,
    "Print", null);
  }
  catch(Exception e)
  {
  return false;
  }

  if (prnJob == null)
    return false;

  Graphics pg;
  try
  {
    pg = prnJob.getGraphics();
  }
  catch(InternalError e)
  {
  return false;
  }

  if (pg != null)
  {
    frame.paintAll(pg);
    pg.dispose();
  }
  prnJob.end();
  return true;
}
```

First you obtain the reference to the Toolkit object for the frame to be printed. Then you invoke the getPrintJob() method, which displays the user's platform-dependent Print dialog. If the user successfully follows through to print this job, it returns a reference to the PrintJob object; otherwise, **null** is returned. For this reason, several exceptions and/or errors need to be caught if some error occurs.

If prnJob is not **null**, you can obtain a Graphics object to be used for printing purposes by calling the getGraphics() method.

If everything runs smoothly, then you will have a Graphics object that is used for printing purposes. At this point, you invoke the paintAll() method for the given frame. That will print (by invoking the frame's corresponding paint() method) the component and any subcomponents contained in the frame. The dispose() method from the Graphics class is used to clean up by flashing the page to the printer and performing all necessary cleanup. Finally, you call the end() method for this PrintJob object and return **true** to indicate that printing was successful.

Tip

You can use the ***instanceof*** *operator on the PrintGraphics interface to check whether your Graphics object in the paint() method refers to printing. This is very useful to avoid having a NullPointerException thrown.*

Fields None

Constructors

Modifiers	Constructor
public	PrintJob()

Methods

Modifiers	Return Type	Method
public abstract	void	end()
public	void	finalize()
public abstract	Graphics	getGraphics()
public abstract	Dimension	getPageDimension()
public abstract	int	getPageResolution()
public abstract	boolean	lastPageFirst()

See Also java.awt.Graphics • java.awt.PrintGraphics • java.lang.Object

Class Rectangle

public synchronized java.awt.Rectangle extends java.lang.Object implements java.awt.Shape, java.io.Serializable

The Rectangle class encapsulates a rectangle specified by x, y, width, and height values through which the rectangle is defined.

Syntax & Usage Rectangle is frequently used with the java.awt.Graphics class, using drawRect() or fillRect() to draw rectangles.

The following example demonstrates the usage of Rectangle, creating an object of it based on the specified Point objects and using the MouseAdapter classes so it can handle mouse events. Specifically, if a user clicks inside the rectangle, it toggles between the colors red and blue. Otherwise, if the user clicks outside the drawn rectangle (but still inside the applet pane), the rectangle grows in the corresponding direction:

```
public class myApplet extends Applet
{

   Rectangle m_Rect;
   boolean   m_bRed = false;

   public void init()
   {
      Point center = new Point(
         getSize().width/2,
         getSize().height/2);
      m_Rect = new Rectangle(center);
      m_Rect.grow(30, 30);
      addMouseListener(new MsAdapter());
      repaint();
   }

   public void paint(Graphics g)
   {
      g.setColor(m_bRed ? Color.red :
         Color.blue);
      g.fillRect(m_Rect.x, m_Rect.y,
         m_Rect.width, m_Rect.height);
   }
```

```
    class MsAdapter extends MouseAdapter
    {
      public void mouseClicked(MouseEvent e)
      {
        Point mousePt = e.getPoint();
        if (m_Rect.contains(mousePt))
          m_bRed = !m_bRed;
        else
          m_Rect.add(mousePt);
        repaint();
      }
    }
}
```

This sample applet holds two fields: Rectangle m_Rect is drawn on the screen, and **boolean** m_bRed holds information about the current color.

The init() method calculates the central point of the applet's panel and constructs m_Rect based on that point (using zero width and height). Then the grow() method expands the rectangle by 30 pixels in both directions. Then a new MsAdapter object is set as a mouse listener for the applet using the addMouseListener() method. Following that is the paint() method that draws a red rectangle (when m_bRed is **true**) or a blue one (when m_bRed is **false**).

Class MsAdapter is defined as an inner class. It extends the MouseAdapter class and overrides only one method from that class: mouseClicked(MouseEvent e). This method gets a Point object corresponding to the location of the mouse click. If this point is inside the applet's rectangle, this method triggers the color flag. Otherwise, it increases the rectangle using the add() method from this class. Finally, it repaints the applet's panel to display changes made (see Figure 2-24).

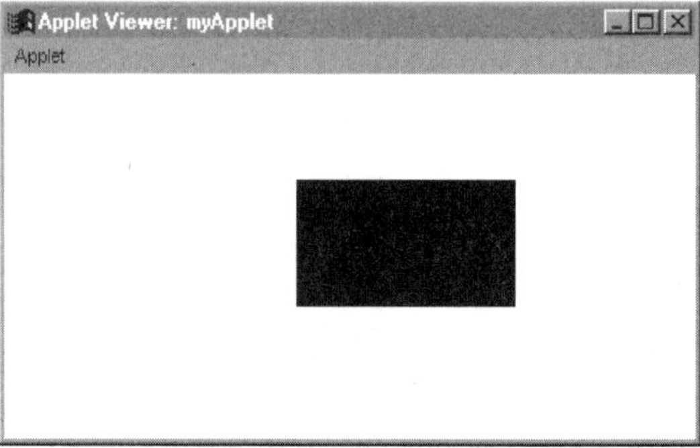

Figure 2-24: Rectangle.

Some methods in the Rectangle class have been deprecated in the JDK 1.1.

Deprecated Method	Replaced By
boolean inside(int, int)	Boolean contains(int, int)
void move(int, int)	Void setLocation(int, int)
void reshape(int, int, int, int)	Void setBounds(int, int, int, int)
void resize(int, int)	void setSize(int, int)

Fields

Modifiers	Type	Field
public	int	height
public	int	width
public	int	x
public	int	y

Constructors

Modifiers	Constructor
public	Rectangle()
public	Rectangle(Dimension)
public	Rectangle(int, int)
public	Rectangle(int, int, int, int)
public	Rectangle(Point)
public	Rectangle(Point, Dimension)
public	Rectangle(Rectangle)

Methods

Modifiers	Return Type	Method
public	void	add(int, int)
public	void	add(Point)
public	void	add(Rectangle)
public	boolean	contains(int, int)
public	boolean	contains(Point)
public	boolean	equals(Object)
public	Rectangle	getBounds()
public	Point	getLocation()
public	Dimension	getSize()
public	void	grow(int, int)
public	int	hashCode()
public	boolean	inside(int, int)
public	Rectangle	intersection(Rectangle)

Modifiers	Return Type	Method
public	boolean	intersects(Rectangle)
public	boolean	isEmpty()
public	void	move(int, int)
public	void	reshape(int, int, int, int)
public	void	resize(int, int)
public	void	setBounds(int, int, int, int)
public	void	setBounds(Rectangle)
public	void	setLocation(int, int)
public	void	setLocation(Point)
public	void	setSize(Dimension)
public	void	setSize(int, int)
public	String	toString()
public	void	translate(int, int)
public	Rectangle	union(Rectangle)

See Also java.awt.Graphics • java.awt.Point • java.awt.Shape • java.io.Serializable • java.lang.Object

Class Scrollbar

public synchronized java.awt.Scrollbar extends java.awt.Component implements java.awt.Adjustable

The Scrollbar class is a GUI component that lets a user scroll through a continuous range of predetermined integer values.

Syntax & Usage You can create stand-alone scrollbars. You also can create scrollbars that are dependent on other components in your GUI, just like the scrollbars that appear on the corner of a word processor document when it grows larger than one page.

The following example demonstrates the Scrollbar class and the AdjustmentListener interface:

```
public class myApplet extends Applet
{
   Scrollbar m_scrl;
   TextField m_txt;
   public void init()
   {
```

```
        setLayout(null);

        m_scrl = new Scrollbar(
          Scrollbar.HORIZONTAL);
        m_scrl.setBounds(20, 20, 300, 18);
        m_scrl.setValues(50, 10, 0, 100);
        m_scrl.setUnitIncrement(1);
        m_scrl.setBlockIncrement(10);
        m_scrl.addAdjustmentListener(new
          AdjustmentAdapter());
        add(m_scrl);

        m_txt = new TextField(5);
        m_txt.setBounds(130, 100, 80, 20);
        m_txt.setEditable(false);
        add(m_txt);
    }

    class AdjustmentAdapter implements
        AdjustmentListener
    {
        public void adjustmentValueChanged(
          AdjustmentEvent e)
        {
          int nVal = e.getValue();
          m_txt.setText(String.valueOf(nVal));
        }
    }
}
```

This sample applet starts off by setting the layout to **null**. Then it creates a horizontal scrollbar using the following parameters:

- Initial value to 50
- Visible (the range of values represented by the width of the scrollbar's bubble) to 10
- Minimum value to 0
- Maximum value to 100
- Unit increment (will be added or subtracted when the user hits the unit down/up gadgets) to 1
- Block increment (will be added or subtracted when the user hits the block down/up gadgets) to 10

Then you set an AdjustmentAdapter instance as the AdjustmentListener for this scrollbar for event-handling purposes. Finally, a text field is declared and will be used to display the current value for the scrollbar. The AdjustmentAdapter class is defined as an inner class and implements the AdjustmentListener interface. It contains the adjustmentValueChanged()

method, which will be invoked when the scrollbar's value changes in any way. This method retrieves the new value for the scrollbar using the getValue() method from the AdjustementEvent class and then displays it in the text area (see Figure 2-25).

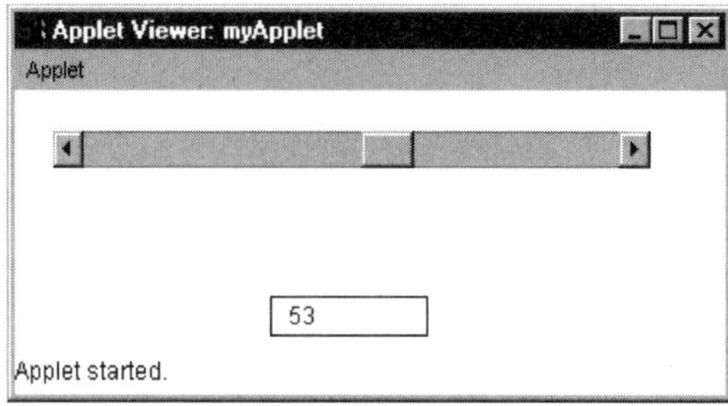

Figure 2-25: Scrollbar.

Several methods in the Scrollbar class have been deprecated in the JDK 1.1.

Deprecated Method	Replaced By
int getLineIncrement()	int getUnitIncrement()
int getPageIncrement()	int getBlockIncrement()
int getVisible()	int getVisibleAmount()
void setLineIncrement(int)	void setUnitIncrement(int)
void setPageIncrement(int)	void setBlockIncrement(int)

Fields

Modifiers	Type	Field
public static final	int	HORIZONTAL
public static final	int	VERTICAL

Constructors

Modifiers	Constructor
public	Scrollbar()
public	Scrollbar(int)
public	Scrollbar(int, int, int, int, int)

Methods

Modifiers	Return Type	Method
public	void	addAdjustmentListener(AdjustmentListener)
public	void	addNotify()
public	int	getBlockIncrement()
public	int	getLineIncrement()
public	int	getMaximum()
public	int	getMinimum()

Modifiers	Return Type	Method
public	int	getOrientation()
public	int	getPageIncrement()
public	int	getUnitIncrement()
public	int	getValue()
public	int	getVisible()
public	int	getVisibleAmount()
protected	String	paramString()
protected	void	processAdjustmentEvent(AdjustmentEvent)
protected	void	processEvent(AWTEvent)
public	void	removeAdjustmentListener(AdjustmentListener)
public synchronized	void	setBlockIncrement(int)
public	void	setLineIncrement(int)
public synchronized	void	setMaximum(int)
public synchronized	void	setMinimum(int)
public synchronized	void	setOrientation(int)
public	void	setPageIncrement(int)
public synchronized	void	setUnitIncrement(int)
public synchronized	void	setValue(int)
public synchronized	void	setValues(int, int, int, int)
public synchronized	void	setVisibleAmount(int)

See Also java.awt.Adjustable • java.awt.Canvas • java.awt.Checkbox • java.awt.CheckboxGroup • java.awt.Choice • java.awt.Component • java.awt.Label • java.awt.List • java.awt.TextArea • java.awt.TextComponent • java.awt.TextField • java.awt.event.AdjustmentListener

Class ScrollPane

public synchronized java.awt.ScrollPane extends java.awt.Container

Java 1.0 supports the use of scrolling with most components and containers in the AWT package by explicitly programming this functionality, using the java.awt.Scrollbar class and specific code that you need to write to catch scrollbar events.

Java 1.1, however, has added functionality that enables automatic, always, or never scrolling features for any component or container. Furthermore, all event handling is handled internally, thus making it very easy to implement scrolling capabilities.

This is facilitated through the addition of the ScrollPane class that provides all the necessary functionality to implement this automated scrolling.

Syntax & Usage In order to set the type of scrolling you want (horizontal or vertical), you need to implement the java.awt.Adjustable Interface. Then, using methods from Adjustable, you can specify various scrolling preferences.

> **Note**
>
> *Only one object can be added to ScrollPane. Probably the best candidate is a Panel object, which can hold any number of your components.*

The following example shows how to use the ScrollPane class:

```
Panel panToScroll = new Panel();
panToScroll.setLayout(null);
panToScroll.setSize(300, 200);
panToScroll.setBackground(Color.blue);

Button btnl = new Button("North-West");
btnl.setBounds(10, 10, 80, 20);
panToScroll.add(btnl);
Button btn2 = new Button("South-East");
btn2.setBounds(210, 170, 80, 20);
panToScroll.add(btn2);

ScrollPane m_ScrollPan = new ScrollPane(
   ScrollPane.SCROLLBARS_AS_NEEDED);
Adjustable vAdjust =
   m_ScrollPan.getVAdjustable();
vAdjust.setUnitIncrement(10);
Adjustable hAdjust =
   m_ScrollPan.getHAdjustable();
hAdjust.setUnitIncrement(10);

m_ScrollPan.setSize(200, 150);
m_ScrollPan.add(panToScroll);
add(m_ScrollPan);
```

This example starts by creating a Panel object (containing two buttons), called panToScroll, to be added to a ScrollPane object. Then you create a ScrollPane object specifying SCROLLBARS_AS_NEEDED. You also set the unit increment for both horizontal and vertical scrollbars to 10 (please see the example under "Class Scrollbar," the previous subsection, for more information on how this is done).

Finally, you add the panToScroll to the ScrollPane object. Since the Panel object has a larger size (300 x 200) than the ScrollPane (200 x 150), it forces ScrollPane to display scrollbars. Notice in Figure 2-26 that only one button is visible at once; to see the other, you need to scroll to it.

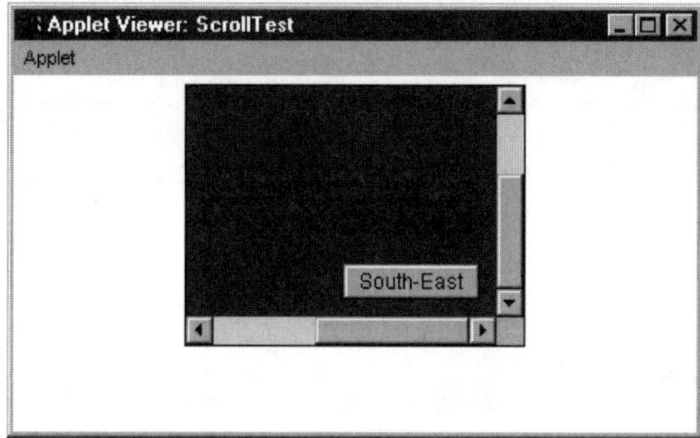

Figure 2-26: ScrollPane.

Fields

Modifiers	Type	Field
public static final	int	SCROLLBARS_ALWAYS
public static final	int	SCROLLBARS_AS_NEEDED
public static final	int	SCROLLBARS_NEVER

Constructors

Modifiers	Constructor
public	ScrollPane()
public	ScrollPane(int)

Methods

Modifiers	Return Type	Method
protected final	void	addImpl(Component, Object, int)
public	void	addNotify()
public	void	doLayout()
public	Adjustable	getHAdjustable()
public	int	getHScrollbarHeight()

Modifiers	Return Type	Method
public	int	getScrollbarDisplayPolicy()
public	Point	getScrollPosition()
public	Adjustable	getVAdjustable()
public	Dimension	getViewportSize()
public	int	getVScrollbarWidth()
public	void	layout()
public	String	paramString()
public	void	printComponents(Graphics)
public final	void	setLayout(LayoutManager)
public	void	setScrollPosition(int, int)
public	void	setScrollPosition(Point)

See Also java.awt.Adjustable • java.awt.Container • java.awt.Graphics • java.awt.Panel • java.awt.Scrollbar

Interface Shape

public abstract synchronized interface java.awt.Shape

The Shape interface is an **abstract** class that describes how to represent geometric shapes in Java.

Syntax & Usage Classes Polygon and Rectangle implement the Shape class. Please see those classes for more information.

Fields None

Constructors None

Methods

Modifiers	Return Type	Method
public abstract	Rectangle	getBounds()

See Also java.awt.Polygon • java.awt.Rectangle

Class SystemColor

public final synchronized java.awt.SystemColor extends java.awt.Color implements java.io.Serializable

Most environments (Windows, Solaris, etc.) supported by Java provide a user-definable color scheme for their desktop environment. This means that any entity (a program, icon, trash can, etc.) belonging to the desktop conforms to this user-definable color scheme. With 1.0 the AWT does not provide any kind of support for Java programs to conform to this functionality. All AWT components and objects are set in a sort of default gray color scheme.

However, the AWT 1.1 now provides Java programs support for different colors other than a default gray. Along with this is the ability to query the current desktop to determine the color scheme used and match it as closely as possible.

Note

Do not confuse this with being able to change the desktop color scheme. Java 1.1 does not let you change system colors during program execution (for example, most Windows programs process the WM_SYSCOLORCHANGE message).

The functionality for this has been facilitated by the addition of the java.awt.SystemColor class.

Syntax & Usage The SystemColor class contains a set of static fields that you use in conjunction with the methods setBackground() and setColor() from the Graphics class to use the user's environmental colors in the program.

Tip

Be sure to use proper colors from the SystemColor class when you implement the paint() method in your application.

The following example shows you how to use the **static** fields to implement a Canvas-based component that resembles a button on the user's screen (see Figure 2-27):

```
class MyButton extends Canvas
{
  public void paint(Graphics g)
  {
    int w = getSize().width-1;
    int h = getSize().height-1;
    g.setColor(SystemColor.control);
    g.fillRect(0, 0, w, h);
    g.setColor(
      SystemColor.controlLtHighlight);
    g.drawLine(0, 0, w, 0);
    g.drawLine(0, 0, 0, h);
    g.setColor(SystemColor.controlDkShadow);
    g.drawLine(w, h, w, 1);
    g.drawLine(w, h, 1, h);
    g.setColor(SystemColor.controlShadow);
    g.drawLine(w-1, h-1, w-1, 2);
    g.drawLine(w-1, h-1, 2, h-1);

    g.setColor(Color.white);
    g.drawOval(10, 10, w-20, h-20);
    g.setColor(Color.red);
    g.drawOval(11, 11, w-20, h-20);
  }
}
```

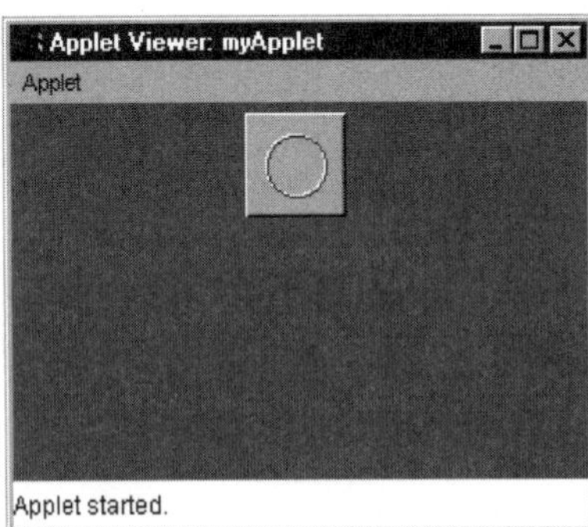

Figure 2-27: SystemColor.

Fields

Modifiers	Type	Field
public static final	SystemColor	activeCaption
public static final	SystemColor	activeCaptionBorder
public static final	SystemColor	activeCaptionText
public static final	int	ACTIVE_CAPTION

Modifiers	Type	Field
public static final	int	ACTIVE_CAPTION_BORDER
public static final	int	ACTIVE_CAPTION_TEXT
public static final	int	CONTROL
public static final	SystemColor	control
public static final	SystemColor	controlDkShadow
public static final	SystemColor	controlHighlight
public static final	SystemColor	controlLtHighlight
public static final	SystemColor	controlShadow
public static final	SystemColor	controlText
public static final	int	CONTROL_DK_SHADOW
public static final	int	CONTROL_HIGHLIGHT
public static final	int	CONTROL_LT_HIGHLIGHT
public static final	int	CONTROL_SHADOW
public static final	int	CONTROL_TEXT
public static final	int	DESKTOP
public static final	SystemColor	desktop
public static final	SystemColor	inactiveCaption
public static final	SystemColor	inactiveCaptionBorder
public static final	SystemColor	inactiveCaptionText
public static final	int	INACTIVE_CAPTION
public static final	int	INACTIVE_CAPTION_BORDER
public static final	int	INACTIVE_CAPTION_TEXT
public static final	int	INFO
public static final	SystemColor	info
public static final	SystemColor	infoText
public static final	int	INFO_TEXT
public static final	int	MENU
public static final	SystemColor	menu
public static final	SystemColor	menuText
public static final	int	MENU_TEXT
public static final	int	NUM_COLORS
public static final	int	SCROLLBAR
public static final	SystemColor	scrollbar
public static final	int	TEXT
public static final	SystemColor	text
public static final	SystemColor	textHighlight
public static final	SystemColor	textHighlightText
public static final	SystemColor	textInactiveText
public static final	SystemColor	textText
public static final	int	TEXT_HIGHLIGHT

Modifiers	Type	Field
public static final	int	TEXT_HIGHLIGHT_TEXT
public static final	int	TEXT_INACTIVE_TEXT
public static final	int	TEXT_TEXT
public static final	int	WINDOW
public static final	SystemColor	window
public static final	SystemColor	windowBorder
public static final	SystemColor	windowText
public static final	int	WINDOW_BORDER
public static final	int	WINDOW_TEXT

Constructors None

Methods

Modifiers	Return Type	Method
public	int	getRGB()
public	String	toString()

See Also java.awt.Color • java.awt.Graphics • java.io.Serializable

Class TextArea

public synchronized java.awt.TextArea extends java.awt.TextComponent

TextArea is nothing more than a text field that can have more than one row for inputting information.

Syntax & Usage This example shows how to process keyboard input in the TextArea and TextField classes so that only digits can be displayed in the text field and upper case characters in the text area:

```
TextField txtDigits = new TextField(8);
txtDigits.addKeyListener(new
  KAdapter(KAdapter.DIGITS));
add(txtDigits);

TextArea txtCapital = new TextArea(5, 30);
txtCapital.addKeyListener(new
  KAdapter(KAdapter.CAPITAL));
add(txtCapital);
```

This snippet of code starts by creating and adding TextField and TextArea objects, respectively. TextField is intended to accept only numerical values, whereas TextArea is intended to covert its characters to upper case. To accomplish this, the KAdapter object with the KAdapter.DIGITS flag raised is set as the KeyListener for the text field, and another KAdapter object is set as the the listener for the text area. However, this time the KAdapter.CAPITAL flag is set.

```
class KAdapter extends KeyAdapter
{
  public static final int CAPITAL = 1;
  public static final int DIGITS = 2;
  static final String OTHER_CHARS =
    "~`!@#$%^&*()_+={[}]|\\:;\"'<,>?/";

  private int m_Type = 0;

  public KAdapter(int type)
  {
    m_Type = type;
  }

  public void keyPressed(KeyEvent ev)
  {
    char c = ev.getKeyChar();
    if (c == KeyEvent.CHAR_UNDEFINED)
      return;

    switch (m_Type)
    {
    case CAPITAL:
      ev.setModifiers(ev.getModifiers() |
        InputEvent.SHIFT_MASK);
      ev.setKeyChar(
        Character.toUpperCase(c));
      break;

    case DIGITS:
      if (Character.isLetter(c) ||
        Character.isWhitespace(c) ||
        OTHER_CHARS.indexOf(c)>=0)
        ev.consume();
      break;
    }
  }
}
```

Class KAdapter extends KeyAdapter and is defined as an outer class (it cannot be an inner class because it holds **static** variables). It holds the **private** variable m_Type which determines the adapter's behavior and two **static int** variables, CAPITAL and DIGITS. String OTHER_CHARS holds all characters that are printable but do not fall into the digit and alphanumeric categories.

The constructor for the KAdapter class simply accepts the adapter's type. All the useful functionality is located in the keyPressed() method, which processes key events. It does this by first extracting the character from the key event. If no character exists, it does nothing.

The rest of the method works in a twofold manner:

- If CAPITAL has been specified, it mandatorily adds the SHIFT_MASK to the event's modifier and sets the character to uppercase, using the Character.toUpperCase() method.
- If DIGITS has been specified, it consumes the event (so it will not be processed by the parent TextComponent object) for nondigital characters (i.e., letters, white spaces, and other characters defined in the OTHER_CHARS string) so that it will not be displayed in the text field. Note that periods (.) and hyphens (-) will be processed in a transparent manner (see Figure 2-28).

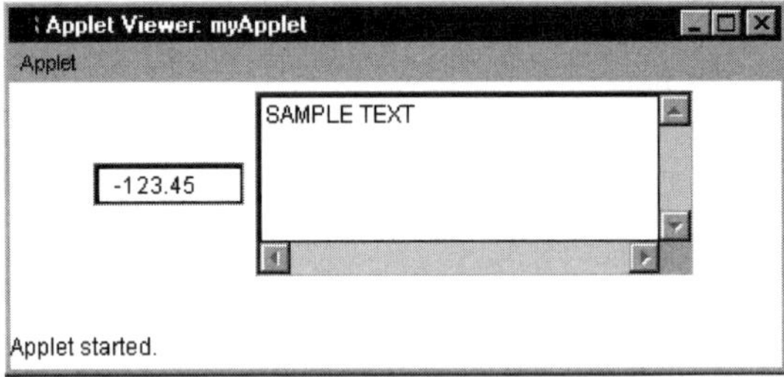

Figure 2-28: TextField and TextArea.

Several methods in the TextArea class have been deprecated in the JDK 1.1.

Deprecated Method	Replaced By
void appendText(String str)	void append(String str)
void insertText(String, int)	void insert(String, int)
Dimension minimumSize()	Dimension getMinimumSize()
Dimension minimumSize(int, int)	Dimension getMinimumSize(int, int)
Dimension preferredSize()	Dimension getPreferredSize()
Dimension preferredSize(int, int)	Dimension getPreferredSize(int, int)
void replaceText(String, int, int)	void replaceRange(String, int, int)

Fields

Modifiers	Type	Field
public static final	int	SCROLLBARS_BOTH
public static final	int	SCROLLBARS_HORIZONTAL_ONLY
public static final	int	SCROLLBARS_NONE
public static final	int	SCROLLBARS_VERTICAL_ONLY

Constructors

Modifiers	Constructor
public	TextArea()
public	TextArea(int, int)
public	TextArea(String)
public	TextArea(String, int, int)
public	TextArea(String, int, int, int)

Methods

Modifiers	Return Type	Method
public	void	addNotify()
public synchronized	void	append(String)
public	void	appendText(String)
public	int	getColumns()
public	Dimension	getMinimumSize()
public	Dimension	getMinimumSize(int, int)
public	Dimension	getPreferredSize()
public	Dimension	getPreferredSize(int, int)
public	int	getRows()
public	int	getScrollbarVisibility()
public synchronized	void	insert(String, int)
public	void	insertText(String, int)
public	Dimension	minimumSize()
public	Dimension	minimumSize(int, int)
protected	String	paramString()
public	Dimension	preferredSize()
public	Dimension	preferredSize(int, int)
public synchronized	void	replaceRange(String, int, int)
public	void	replaceText(String, int, int)
public	void	setColumns(int)
public	void	setRows(int)

See Also java.awt.Button • java.awt.Canvas • java.awt.Checkbox • java.awt.CheckboxGroup • java.awt.Choice • java.awt.Component • java.awt.Label • java.awt.List • java.awt.Scrollbar • java.awt.TextComponent • java.awt.TextField

Class TextComponent

public synchronized java.awt.TextComponent extends java.awt.Component

The TextComponent class is used for any kind of AWT-based component that is used for editing. TextComponent does not in and of itself have any constructors. However, this class is a superclass to TextField and TextArea.

Syntax & Usage Please see the example in the previous section, "Class TextArea."

Fields

Modifiers	Type	Field
protected	TextListener	textListener

Constructors None

Methods

Modifiers	Return Type	Method
public	void	addTextListener(TextListener)
public	int	getCaretPosition()
public synchronized	String	getSelectedText()
public synchronized	int	getSelectionEnd()
public synchronized	int	getSelectionStart()
public synchronized	String	getText()
public	boolean	isEditable()
protected	String	paramString()
protected	void	processEvent(AWTEvent)
protected	void	processTextEvent(TextEvent)
public	void	removeNotify()
public	void	removeTextListener(TextListener)
public synchronized	void	select(int, int)
public synchronized	void	selectAll()
public	void	setCaretPosition(int)
public synchronized	void	setEditable(boolean)
public synchronized	void	setSelectionEnd(int)
public synchronized	void	setSelectionStart(int)
public synchronized	void	setText(String)

See Also java.awt.Button • java.awt.Canvas • java.awt.Checkbox • java.awt.CheckboxGroup • java.awt.Choice • java.awt.Component • java.awt.Label • java.awt.List • java.awt.Scrollbar • java.awt.TextArea • java.awt.TextField

Class TextField

public synchronized java.awt.TextField extends java.awt.TextComponent

TextField is a class that represents an area for a user to enter data. A text field can be considered an editable label designed for input. Note that a text field can be only one row in height. However, the number of columns (i.e., width) of a text field is customizable.

Syntax & Usage Please see the examples under "Class Menu" and "Class TextArea," earlier in the chapter.

Several methods in the TextField class have been deprecated in the JDK 1.1.

Deprecated Method	Replaced By
Dimension minimumSize()	Dimension getMinimumSize()
Dimension minimumSize(int)	Dimension getMinimumSize(int)
Dimension preferredSize()	Dimension getPreferredSize()
Dimension preferredSize(int)	Dimension getPreferredSize(int)
void setEchoCharacter(char)	void setEchoChar(char)

Fields None

Constructors

Modifiers	Constructor
public	TextField()
public	TextField(int)
public	TextField(String)
public	TextField(String, int)

Methods

Modifiers	Return Type	Method
public	void	addActionListener(ActionListener)
public	void	addNotify()
public	boolean	echoCharIsSet()
public	int	getColumns()
public	char	getEchoChar()
public	Dimension	getMinimumSize()
public	Dimension	getMinimumSize(int)
public	Dimension	getPreferredSize()
public	Dimension	getPreferredSize(int)

Modifiers	Return Type	Method
public	Dimension	minimumSize()
public	Dimension	minimumSize(int)
protected	String	paramString()
public	Dimension	preferredSize()
public	Dimension	preferredSize(int)
protected	void	processActionEvent(ActionEvent)
protected	void	processEvent(AWTEvent)
public	void	removeActionListener(ActionListener)
public	void	setColumns(int)
public	void	setEchoChar(char)
public	void	setEchoCharacter(char)

See Also java.awt.Button • java.awt.Canvas • java.awt.Checkbox • java.awt.CheckboxGroup • java.awt.Choice • java.awt.Component • java.awt.Label • java.awt.List • java.awt.Scrollbar • java.awt.TextArea • java.awt.TextComponent

Class Toolkit

public abstract synchronized java.awt.Toolkit extends java.lang.Object

The Toolkit class is used to house all of the native-platform-specific implementations needed by various abstract AWT-based classes.

Syntax & Usage The Toolkit class provides functionality to get the user's screen size and resolution (using getScreenSize() and getScreenResolution(), respectively).

Tip

Toolkit provides printing functionality for Java, using the getPrintJob() method. Also, Toolkit provides the native functionality to get an instance of the user's native operating system clipboard to facilitate clipboard functionality. For more information on implementing clipboard functionality in your Java programs, go to Chapter 3, "The java.awt.datatransfer Package."

The getFontList() method returns a list of supported fonts for this user's environment. Toolkit provides a variety of useful methods that are specific to a user's environment in one way or another.

Tip

Another useful method is beep(), which when invoked causes the user's computer to beep.

The following example demonstrates the usage of the Toolkit class to get and display the list of available fonts:

```
public void paint(Graphics g)
{
   Toolkit toolkit = getToolkit();
   String[] sFonts = toolkit.getFontList();
   int y = 20;
   for (int k=0; k<sFonts.length; k++)
   {
      g.setFont(new Font(sFonts[k], 12,
         Font.PLAIN));
      g.drawString(sFonts[k], 20, y);
      y += 20;
   }
}
```

The getToolkit() method from the Component class is used to get the Toolkit for the current component. Then the getFontList() method from the Toolkit class retrieves the list of names of available fonts in the user's environment. Finally, this example lists each available font in its respective style (see Figure 2-29).

Figure 2-29: Toolkit.

Fields None

Constructors

Modifiers	Constructor
public	Toolkit()

Methods

Modifiers	Return Type	Method
public abstract	void	beep()
public abstract	int	checkImage(Image, int, int, ImageObserver)
protected abstract	ButtonPeer	createButton(Button)
protected abstract	CanvasPeer	createCanvas(Canvas)
protected abstract	CheckboxPeer	createCheckbox(Checkbox)
protected abstract	CheckboxMenuItemPeer	createCheckboxMenuItem(CheckboxMenuItem)
protected abstract	ChoicePeer	createChoice(Choice)
protected	LightweightPeer	createComponent(Component)
protected abstract	DialogPeer	createDialog(Dialog)
protected abstract	FileDialogPeer	createFileDialog(FileDialog)
protected abstract	FramePeer	createFrame(Frame)
public	Image	createImage(byte[])
public	abstract Image	createImage(byte[], int, int)
public	abstract Image	createImage(ImageProducer)
protected abstract	LabelPeer	createLabel(Label)
protected abstract	ListPeer	createList(List)
protected abstract	MenuPeer	createMenu(Menu)
protected abstract	MenuBarPeer	createMenuBar(MenuBar)
protected abstract	MenuItemPeer	createMenuItem(MenuItem)
protected abstract	PanelPeer	createPanel(Panel)
protected abstract	PopupMenuPeer	createPopupMenu(PopupMenu)
protected abstract	ScrollbarPeer	createScrollbar(Scrollbar)
protected abstract	ScrollPanePeer	createScrollPane(ScrollPane)
protected abstract	TextAreaPeer	createTextArea(TextArea)
protected abstract	TextFieldPeer	createTextField(TextField)
protected abstract	WindowPeer	createWindow(Window)
public abstract	ColorModel	getColorModel()
public static synchronized	Toolkit	getDefaultToolkit()
public abstract	String[]	getFontList()
public abstract	FontMetrics	getFontMetrics(Font)
protected abstract	FontPeer	getFontPeer(String, int)
public abstract	Image	getImage(String)
public abstract	Image	getImage(URL)

Modifiers	Return Type	Method
public	int	getMenuShortcutKeyMask()
protected static	Container	getNativeContainer(Component)
public abstract	PrintJob	getPrintJob(Frame, String, Properties)
public static	String	getProperty(String, String)
public abstract	int	getScreenResolution()
public abstract	Dimension	getScreenSize()
public abstract	Clipboard	getSystemClipboard()
public final	EventQueue	getSystemEventQueue()
protected abstract	EventQueue	getSystemEventQueueImpl()
protected	void	loadSystemColors(int[])
public abstract	boolean	prepareImage(Image, int, int, ImageObserver)
public abstract	void	sync()

See Also java.awt.Color • java.awt.PrintGraphics • java.awt.PrintJob • java.awt.SystemColor • java.lang.Object

Class Window

public synchronized java.awt.Window extends java.awt.Container

The Window class encapsulates a basic window that has no borders or menu bar. The Window class is used to implement the Frame and in Java 1.1, to implement pop-up menus.

Syntax & Usage Please see the examples under "Class Dialog" and "Class Frame," earlier in this chapter.

One method in the Window class has been deprecated in the JDK 1.1.

Deprecated Method	Replaced By
boolean postEvent(Event)	dispatchEvent(AWTEvent)

Fields None

Constructors

Modifiers	Constructor
public	Window(Frame)

Methods

Modifiers	Return Type	Method
public	void	addNotify()
public synchronized	void	addWindowListener(WindowListener)
public	void	dispose()
public	Component	getFocusOwner()
public	Locale	getLocale()
public	Toolkit	getToolkit()
public final	String	getWarningString()
public	boolean	isShowing()
public	void	pack()
public	boolean	postEvent(Event)
protected	void	processEvent(AWTEvent)
protected	void	processWindowEvent(WindowEvent)
public synchronized	void	removeWindowListener(WindowListener)
public	void	show()
public	void	toBack()
public	void	toFront()

See Also java.awt.Container • java.awt.Frame • java.awt.PopupMenu

The java.awt.datatransfer Package

3

The java.awt.datatransfer package is a subpackage to the java.awt package. This is a rather small package in the Java Class Library; however, it can (and will) house all the functionality needed to perform a variety of data-transfer-based operations including clipboard operations (which are available in version 1.1 of the JDK) and drag-and-drop applications (which will be functional in the next version of the JDK).

Class Clipboard

public synchronized java.awt.datatransfer.Clipboard extends java.lang.Object

Clipboard operations represent a very useful way for a user to send and retrieve data between programs (regardless of their relation to each other). This is possible because the host operating system acts as an intermediary holding tank for the communication to take place.

Note

The Clipboard class is the class used to implement cut/copy/paste clipboard operations in Java.

In order to instantiate the Clipboard class you need to get a link to the native clipboard on the host's operating system. This is done by calling the getToolkit().getSystemClipboard() methods from the java.awt.Toolkit class.

Syntax & Usage

This example shows how to use Clipboard and StringSelection classes:

```
class ClipboardTextArea extends TextArea
   implements ClipboardOwner
{
   Clipboard m_clBoard = getToolkit().
      getSystemClipboard();

   public void copy()
   {
      String sCopy = getSelectedText();
      if (sCopy != null)
      {
         StringSelection sSelection = new
            StringSelection(sCopy);
         m_clBoard.setContents(sSelection,
            this);
      }
   }
```

```
public void cut()
{
   String sCopy = getSelectedText();
   if (sCopy != null)
   {
      StringSelection sSelection = new
         StringSelection(sCopy);
      m_clBoard.setContents(sSelection,
         this);
      replaceRange("",
         getSelectionStart(),
         getSelectionEnd());
   }
}

public void paste()
{
   Transferable sTransf = m_clBoard.
      getContents(this);
   if (sTransf != null)
   {
      try
      {
         String sPaste =
            (String)sTransf.
            getTransferData(
            DataFlavor.stringFlavor);
         replaceRange(sPaste,
            getSelectionStart(),
            getSelectionEnd());
      }
      catch (UnsupportedFlavorException e)
      {
         System.out.println(
         "Unsupported Flavor Exception:"
         +e.getMessage());
      }
      catch (IOException e)
      {
         System.out.println(
         "IO Exception:"
         +e.getMessage());
      }
   }
}
```

```
    public void lostOwnership(
        Clipboard clipboard,
        Transferable contents)
    {
    }
}
```

To use Clipboard, your Component first needs to obtain a reference to the instance of Clipboard class by using Toolkit.getSystemClipboard() method. Normally, when a component supports clipboard operations it should support the copy, cut, and paste operations. The above example exemplifies each of the three operations in three respective methods.

Tip

You can use menu items, keyboard accelerators, or pop-up menu items to invoke these methods. Please see examples to java.awt.Menu and java.awt.PopupMenu classes.

The copy() method first takes selected text as String from this TextArea. If some text is selected it creates the instance of StringSelection class based on selected text. Then it sets that text as a contents of clipboard by Clipboard.setContents() method. To do this, our class must implement ClipboardOwner interface and define lostOwnership() method (which does nothing in our example). The cut() method is identical to copy() except that this methods removes selected text.

The paste() method gets the contents of the system clipboard by using the getContents() method, which is used as a reference to Transferable object. If this operation is successful, the method extracts a String object from the Transferable object using the getTransferData() method. The DataFlavor.stringFlavor is specified as the required flavor. Then extracted String is actually pasted to this TextArea replacing selected text (if no text is selected it's inserted at the cursor location). All of the operation is included into **try/catch** block to catch possible exceptions.

Fields

Modifiers	Type	Field
protected	Transferable	contents
protected	ClipboardOwner	owner

Constructors

Modifiers	Constructor
public	Clipboard(String)

Methods

Modifiers	Return Type	Method
public synchronized	Transferable	getContents(Object)
public	String	getName()
public synchronized	void	setContents(Transferable, ClipboardOwner)

See Also java.awt.datatransfer.ClipboardOwner • java.awt.datatransfer.StringSelection • java.awt.Toolkit • java.lang.Object

Interface ClipboardOwner

public abstract interface java.awt.datatransfer.ClipboardOwner

The ClipboardOwner interface provides the necessary data formats for transferring (either through cut/copy/paste clipboard or drag-and-drop operations) to take place in a Java program.

This interface needs to be implemented by any Java program that needs to use clipboard operations.

Syntax & Usage Please see the example in the "Class Clipboard" section earlier in this chapter.

Fields None

Constructors None

Methods

Modifiers	Return Type	Method
public abstract	void	lostOwnership(Clipboard, Transferable)

See Also java.awt.datatransfer.Clipboard • java.awt.datatransfer.DataFlavor • java.awt.datatransfer.StringSelection

Class DataFlavor

public synchronized java.awt.datatransfer.DataFlavor extends java.lang.Object

The DataFlavor class represents the actual data format for any kind of data transfer to take place within a Java program, between two Java programs, or between a Java program and another program.

Note

For clipboard operations, you usually do not need to concern yourself with DataFlavor.

Syntax & Usage

DataFlavor class provides two static fields:

- plainTextFlavor for plain text with Unicode encoding
- stringFlavor representing a Java Unicode String class

However, you're free to create your own DataFlavor using two constructors defined in this class:

```
DataFlavor imageFlavor = new DataFlavor(
    Class.forName("java.awt.Image",
    "Image Flavor");
```

Your implementation of Transferable interface should accept this kind of DataFlavor and retrieve it.

Fields

Modifiers	Type	Field
public static	DataFlavor	plainTextFlavor
public static	DataFlavor	stringFlavor

Constructors

Modifiers	Constructor
public	DataFlavor(Class, String)
public	DataFlavor(String, String)

Methods

Modifiers	Return Type	Method
public	boolean	equals(DataFlavor)
public	String	getHumanPresentableName()
public	String	getMimeType()
public	Class	getRepresentationClass()
public final	boolean	isMimeTypeEqual(DataFlavor)
public	boolean	isMimeTypeEqual(String)
protected	String	normalizeMimeType(String)
protected	String	normalizeMimeTypeParameter(String, String)
public	void	setHumanPresentableName(String)

See Also java.awt.datatransfer.Clipboard • java.awt.datatransfer.ClipboardOwner • java.lang.Object

Class StringSelection

public synchronized java.awt.datatransfer.StringSelection extends java.lang.Object implements java.awt.datatransfer.Transferable, ClipboardOwner

The StringSelection class facilitates the ability to transfer a Java String in a plain text format. It also implements the Transferable interface, thus making it a vital key in the implementation of clipboard operations.

Syntax & Usage Please see the example in the "Class Clipboard" section earlier in this chapter.

Fields None

Constructors

Modifiers	Constructor
public	StringSelection(String)

Methods

Modifiers	Return Type	Method
public synchronized	Object	getTransferData(DataFlavor)
public synchronized	DataFlavor[]	getTransferDataFlavors()
public	boolean	isDataFlavorSupported(DataFlavor)
public	void	lostOwnership(Clipboard, Transferable)

See Also java.awt.datatransfer.Clipboard • java.awt.datatransfer.ClipboardOwner • java.awt.datatransfer.Transferable • java.lang.Object

Interface Transferable

public abstract interface java.awt.datatransfer.Transferable

The Transferable abstract interface is the key component for any type of data transferring taking place in Java. Only objects that have implemented this interface can be transferred by any of the current (and future) means provided in the java.awt.datatransfer package.

Tip

For basic cut/copy/paste clipboard operations you do not need to implement this interface directly. Instead, use the class java.awt.datatransfer.StringSelection that has already implemented this interface, thus simplifying the entire task of adding cut/copy/paste clipboard functionality.

Syntax & Usage Using this interface you can implement your own type of data transfer (images, Rich Text Format, etc.). For that, you need to implement these methods:

- **Object getTransferData(DataFlavor).** This method retrieves the current contents of Transferable as an Object.
- **DataFlavor[] getTransferDataFlavors().** This method retrieves an array of supported getTransferDataFlavors.
- **boolean isDataFlavorSupported(DataFlavor).** This method returns **true** if the specified DataFlavor is supported.

Fields None

Constructors None

Methods

Modifiers	Return Type	Method
public abstract	Object	getTransferData(DataFlavor)
public abstract	DataFlavor[]	getTransferDataFlavors()
public abstract	boolean	isDataFlavorSupported(DataFlavor)

See Also java.awt.datatransfer.Clipboard • java.awt.datatransfer.ClipboardOwner • java.awt.datatransfer.DataFlavor • java.awt.datatransfer.StringSelection

Class UnsupportedFlavorException

public synchronized java.awt.datatransfer.UnsupportedFlavorException extends java.lang.Exception

This exception class is thrown when data are in an unsupported format (or flavor) for data transfer to/from Java.

Syntax & Usage Please see the example in the "Class Clipboard" section earlier in this chapter.

Fields None

Constructors

Modifiers	Constructor
public	UnsupportedFlavorException(DataFlavor)

Methods None

See Also java.awt.datatransfer.DataFlavor • java.lang.Exception

The java.awt.event Package

4

Java 1.1 has replaced the java.awt.Event class with the java.awt.event package. Its sole purpose is focused on event handling using the 1.1 delegation model. Essentially, classes in this package can be categorized in two groups:

- **Low-level or detail-oriented types of events.** These include subclasses of java.awt.event.ComponentEvent: ContainerEvent, FocusEvent, InputEvent, KeyEvent, MouseEvent, and WindowEvent.
- **A higher-level group called semantic events.** These include java.awt.event.ActionEvent, AdjustmentEvent, ItemEvent, and TextEvent.

In order to catch an event you need to "listen" to a part (or component) in your Java program. This is done by implementing one of the following listener interfaces and using an appropriate add*XXX*Listener() method:

- **Low-level listeners.** These include ComponentListener, ContainerListener, FocusListener, KeyListener, MouseListener, MouseMotionListener, and WindowListener.
- **High-level listeners.** These include ActionListener, AdjustmentListener, ItemListener, and TextListener.

The methods defined in these interfaces are the ones that you implement to perform an action based on the event. However, the low-level listeners define a number of methods to catch a variety of related events and for most practical solutions you would extend its corresponding adapter class (which is abstract and does nothing), which has already implemented the listener. This way you can create a subclass to the adapter class (using an inner class of your program) and override only those methods that you need.

This package is connected closely to the java.awt package, covered in Chapter 2. Many of the examples for that package are related to this package. So, you will see many cross-references indicated between the two in this chapter.

Note

JDK 1.1 also provides java.beans.PropertyChangeEvent, which is used in Java Beans. For more information, see Chapter 7.

Class ActionEvent

public synchronized java.awt.event.ActionEvent extends java.awt.AWTEvent

The ActionEvent class is part of the higher-level (semantic) group of event-handling classes used to handle action events (e.g., button clicks).

Syntax & Usage

Action events occur when a user clicks on a button or selects a menu item. You can implement the ActionListener interface to process these kinds of events.

For details, please see the examples for the java.awt.AWTEventMulticaster, java.awt.Button, and java.awt.Menu classes in Chapter 2.

Fields

Modifiers	Type	Field
public static final	int	ACTION_FIRST
public static final	int	ACTION_LAST
public static final	int	ACTION_PERFORMED
public static final	int	ALT_MASK
public static final	int	CTRL_MASK
public static final	int	META_MASK
public static final	int	SHIFT_MASK

Constructors

Modifiers	Constructor
public	ActionEvent(Object, int, String)
public	ActionEvent(Object, int, String, int)

Methods

Modifiers	Return Type	Method
public	String	getActionCommand()
public	int	getModifiers()
public	String	paramString()

See Also java.awt.AWTEvent • java.awt.event.ActionListener

Interface ActionListener

public abstract interface java.awt.event.ActionListener implements java.util.EventListener

The ActionListener interface is used for listening to action events (e.g., button clicks).

Syntax & Usage You implement the ActionListener interface to process action events that occur when a user clicks on a button or selects a menu item.

For details, please see the examples for the java.awt.AWTEventMulticaster, java.awt.Button, and java.awt.Menu classes in Chapter 2.

Fields None

Constructors None

Methods

Modifiers	Return Type	Method
public abstract	void	actionPerformed(ActionEvent)

See Also java.awt.event.ActionEvent • java.util.EventListener

Class AdjustmentEvent

public synchronized java.awt.event.AdjustmentEvent extends java.awt.AWTEvent

The AdjustmentEvent class is part of the higher-level (semantic) group of event-handling classes used for adjustment events (e.g., changing the value of a scrollbar).

Syntax & Usage

Adjustment events occur when the user changes the value of a Scrollbar component. You implement AdjustmentListener to process these events.

For details, please see the example for the java.awt.Scrollbar class in Chapter 2.

Fields

Modifiers	Type	Field
public static final	int	ADJUSTMENT_FIRST
public static final	int	ADJUSTMENT_LAST
public static final	int	ADJUSTMENT_VALUE_CHANGED
public static final	int	BLOCK_DECREMENT
public static final	int	BLOCK_INCREMENT
public static final	int	TRACK
public static final	int	UNIT_DECREMENT
public static final	int	UNIT_INCREMENT

Constructors

Modifiers	Constructor
public	AdjustmentEvent(Adjustable, int, int, int)

Methods

Modifiers	Return Type	Method
public	Adjustable	getAdjustable()
public	int	getAdjustmentType()
public	int	getValue()
public	String	paramString()

See Also

java.awt.AWTEvent • java.awt.Adjustable • java.awt.List • java.awt.ScrollPane • java.awt.event.AdjustmentListener

Interface AdjustmentListener

public abstract interface java.awt.event.AdjustmentListener implements java.util.EventListener

The AdjustmentListener interface is used for listening to adjustment events (e.g., changing the value of a scrollbar).

Syntax & Usage You implement this interface to process adjustment events, which occur when the user changes the value of a Scrollbar component.

For details, please see the example for the java.awt.Scrollbar class in Chapter 2.

Fields None

Constructors None

Methods

Modifiers	Return Type	Method
public abstract	void	adjustmentValueChanged(AdjustmentEvent)

See Also java.awt.event.AdjustmentEvent • java.util.EventListener

Class ComponentAdapter

public abstract synchronized java.awt.event.ComponentAdapter extends java.lang.Object implements java.awt.event.ComponentListener

ComponentAdapter is an **abstract** class used for receiving component events.

Syntax & Usage You can use ComponentAdapter as an alternative to implementing ComponentListener in your Java programs, and override only the methods that you need.

The following example uses the ComponentAdapter class to show the current size of a frame:

```
class myFrame extends Frame
{
   public myFrame()
   {
      super("Frame");
      addComponentListener(new CompAdapter());
   }

   class CompAdapter extends ComponentAdapter
   {
      public void componentResized(
         ComponentEvent ev)
      {
         setTitle("Frame ("+
            getSize().width+"x"+
            getSize().height+")");
      }
   }
}
```

The class myFrame instantiates CompAdapter and sets it as a ComponentListener for myFrame.

Underneath that, you have the class CompAdapter which extends ComponentAdapter and overrides one method: componentResized(). This method is invoked when the parent is resized. When this happens, the method displays the current frame size in myFrame's title (see Figure 4-1).

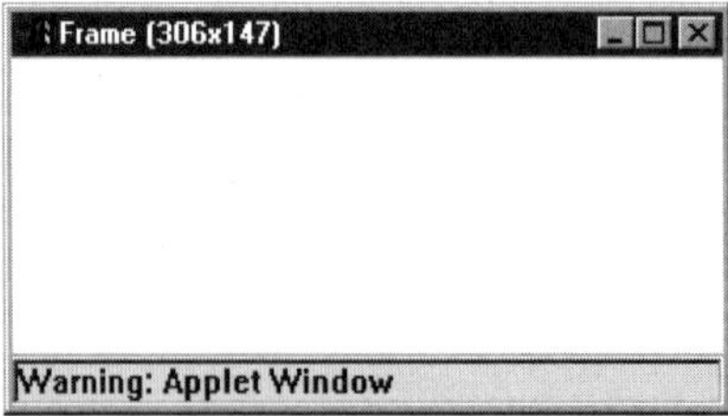

Figure 4-1: ComponentAdapter.

Fields None

Constructors

Modifiers	Constructor
public	ComponentAdapter()

Methods

Modifiers	Return Type	Method
public	void	componentHidden(ComponentEvent)
public	void	componentMoved(ComponentEvent)
public	void	componentResized(ComponentEvent)
public	void	componentShown(ComponentEvent)

See Also java.awt.event.ComponentEvent • java.awt.event.ComponentListener • java.lang.Object

Class ComponentEvent

public synchronized java.awt.event.ComponentEvent extends java.awt.AWTEvent

The ComponentEvent class is part of the lower-level group of event-handling classes used for component events (e.g., resizing a Java component).

Syntax & Usage All component events are handled internally by the Abstract Window Toolkit (AWT). You do not need to program event-handling functionality explicitly for your Java programs to work.

Please see the example in the previous section, "Class ComponentAdapter."

Fields

Modifiers	Type	Field
public static final	int	COMPONENT_FIRST
public static final	int	COMPONENT_HIDDEN
public static final	int	COMPONENT_LAST
public static final	int	COMPONENT_MOVED
public static final	int	COMPONENT_RESIZED
public static final	int	COMPONENT_SHOWN

Constructors

Modifiers	Constructor
public	ComponentEvent(Component, int)

Methods

Modifiers	Return Type	Method
public	Component	getComponent()
public	String	paramString()

See Also java.awt.AWTEvent • java.awt.event.ComponentAdapter • java.awt.event.ComponentListener

Interface ComponentListener

public abstract interface java.awt.event.ComponentListener implements java.util.EventListener

The ComponentListener interface is used for listening to component events (e.g., resizing a Java component).

Syntax & Usage Instead of implementing the ComponentListener interface, you can extend the ComponentAdapter class and override only those methods that you need.

All component events are handled internally by the AWT. You do not need to program event-handling functionality explicitly for your Java programs to work.

Please see the example under "Class ComponentAdapter," earlier in this chapter.

Fields None

Constructors None

Methods

Modifiers	Return Type	Method
public abstract	void	componentHidden(ComponentEvent)
public abstract	void	componentMoved(ComponentEvent)
public abstract	void	componentResized(ComponentEvent)
public abstract	void	componentShown(ComponentEvent)

See Also java.awt.event.ComponentAdapter • java.awt.event.ComponentEvent • java.util.EventListener

Class ContainerAdapter

public abstract synchronized java.awt.event.ContainerAdapter extends java.lang.Object implements java.awt.event.ContainerListener

ContainerAdapter is an **abstract** class that can be extended for receiving container events, which can occur when a Java program adds or removes components from a Container.

Syntax & Usage

You can use this class as an alternative to ContainerListener and not have to override every method in the ContainerListener interface. To use this adapter, you need to extend it and override only those methods that you need.

In the following example, ContainerAdapter subclass is used to perform various actions when a component is added to the panel container:

```
public void init()
{
   Panel pn = new Panel();
   pn.setSize(200, 200);
   pn.addContainerListener(new CntAdapter());
   add(pn);

   pn.add(new Button("OK"));
   pn.add(new Button("Cancel"));
   pn.add(new Button("Help"));
}

class CntAdapter extends ContainerAdapter
{
   int counter = 0;
   public void componentAdded(
      ContainerEvent ev)
   {
      Component cmp = ev.getChild();
      if (cmp instanceof Button)
      {
         Button btn = (Button)cmp;
         counter++;
         btn.setLabel(btn.getLabel()+
         " (#"+counter+")");
      }
   }
}
```

You can see the ContainerAdapter subclass (CntAdapter) object is added as a listener to the Panel object (pn) using the addContainerListener. As a listener, it receives notification about the buttons added to pn. The CntAdapter object then counts all the buttons added to pn and changes their titles to display the number based on their order in being added to pn (see Figure 4-2).

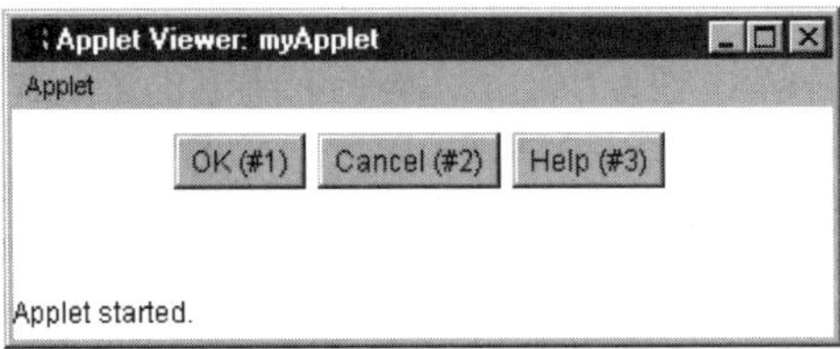

Figure 4-2: ContainerAdapter.

Fields None

Constructors

Modifiers	Constructor
public	ContainerAdapter()

Methods

Modifiers	Return Type	Method
public	void	componentAdded(ContainerEvent)
public	void	componentRemoved(ContainerEvent)

See Also java.awt.event.ContainerEvent • java.awt.event.ContainerListener • java.lang.Object

Class ContainerEvent

public synchronized java.awt.event.ContainerEvent extends java.awt.event.ComponentEvent

The ContainerEvent class is part of the lower-level group of event-handling classes used for container events (e.g., removing a Java component from a container).

Syntax & Usage You can use container events to do special processing during the addition or removal of a component (or components) to and from your Container object (e.g., for dragging and dropping purposes).

All container events are handled internally by the AWT. You do not need to program event-handling functionality explicitly for your Java programs to work.

Please see the example in the previous section, "Class ContainerAdapter."

Fields

Modifiers	Type	Field
public static final	int	COMPONENT_ADDED
public static final	int	COMPONENT_REMOVED
public static final	int	CONTAINER_FIRST
public static final	int	CONTAINER_LAST

Constructors

Modifiers	Constructor
public	ContainerEvent(Component, int, Component)

Methods

Modifiers	Return Type	Method
public	Component	getChild()
public	Container	getContainer()
public	String	paramString()

See Also java.awt.event.ComponentEvent • java.awt.event.ContainerListener

Interface ContainerListener

public abstract interface java.awt.event.ContainerListener implements java.util.EventListener

The ContainerListener interface is used for listening to container events (e.g., adding or removing a Java component from a container).

Syntax & Usage You can implement this interface to process container events, which occur when a Java program adds or removes a component from a container. Alternatively, you can extend the ContainerAdapter class that provides the default (empty) implementation, letting you override only those methods that you need.

All container events are handled internally by the AWT. You do not need to program event-handling functionality explicitly for your Java programs to work.

Please see the example under "Class ContainerAdapter," earlier in this chapter.

Fields None

Constructors None

Methods

Modifiers	Return Type	Method
public abstract	void	componentAdded(ContainerEvent)
public abstract	void	componentRemoved(ContainerEvent)

See Also java.awt.event.ContainerAdapter • java.awt.event.ContainerEvent • java.util.EventListener

Class FocusAdapter

public abstract synchronized java.awt.event.FocusAdapter extends java.lang.Object implements java.awt.event.FocusListener

FocusAdapter is an **abstract** class used for processing focus events, which occur when a component gains or loses the input focus.

Syntax & Usage You can use this class as opposed to implementing FocusListener in your Java programs. To use this adapter you need to extend it and override only those methods that you need.

In the following code snippet, FocusAdapter receives notification about moving focus between text fields and automatically changes the background color of the field that gained focus:

```
public void init()
{
   setLayout(new GridLayout(4, 2, 20, 10));
   add(new Label("First name:"));
   TextField txtFirst = new TextField(15);
   txtFirst.addFocusListener(new
     FocAdapter());
   add(txtFirst);
   add(new Label("Last name:"));
   TextField txtLast = new TextField(15);
   txtLast.addFocusListener(new FocAdapter());
   add(txtLast);
```

```
    add(new Label("Telephone:"));
    TextField txtTel = new TextField(15);
    txtTel.addFocusListener(new FocAdapter());
    add(txtTel);
    txtFirst.requestFocus();
}

class FocAdapter extends FocusAdapter
{
    public void focusGained(FocusEvent ev)
    {
        Component cmp = ev.getComponent();
        if (cmp instanceof TextField)
        {
            cmp.setBackground(Color.green);
        }
    }

    public void focusLost(FocusEvent ev)
    {
        Component cmp = ev.getComponent();
        if (cmp instanceof TextField)
        {
            cmp.setBackground(Color.white);
        }
    }
}
```

In this example, an extended FocusAdapter class is used to process a focus event generated by three TextFields that also are declared. The method focusGained() verifies that the component that gains focus is a TextField object and changes the background color of that TextField to green. When the TextField loses the focus and the focusLost() method is invoked, the background color is changed back to white (which is assumed to be the default background). In this way, a user can easily keep track of which field currently has focus (see Figure 4-3).

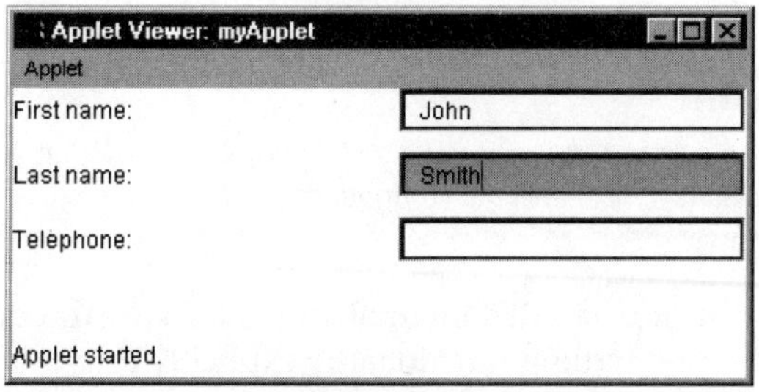

Figure 4-3: FocusAdapter.

Fields None

Constructors

Modifiers	Constructor
public	FocusAdapter()

Methods

Modifiers	Return Type	Method
public	void	focusGained(FocusEvent)
public	void	focusLost(FocusEvent)

See Also java.awt.event.FocusEvent • java.awt.event.FocusListener • java.lang.Object

Class FocusEvent

public synchronized java.awt.event.FocusEvent extends java.awt.event.ComponentEvent

The FocusEvent class is part of the lower-level group of event-handling classes used for focus events.

Syntax & Usage There are two types of focus events:

- **Permanent focus change events.** These focus events occur when focus is directly gained or lost in a component. Permanent focus change events can be initiated direct by the user, as the result of a click on a tab, or by specific focus method calls in your Java program.
- **Temporary focus change events.** These occur when focus is gained or lost in a component as the result of an operation. Once the operation finishes, permanent focus returns to the original component.

Tip

You can use the requestFocus() method from the java.awt.Component class to give a specific component focus.

All focus events are handled internally by the AWT. You do not need to program this event-handling functionality explicitly for your Java programs to work.

Please see the example in the previous section, "Class FocusAdapter."

Fields

Modifiers	Type	Field
public static final	int	FOCUS_FIRST
public static final	int	FOCUS_GAINED
public static final	int	FOCUS_LAST
public static final	int	FOCUS_LOST

Constructors

Modifiers	Constructor
public	FocusEvent(Component, int)
public	FocusEvent(Component, int, boolean)

Methods

Modifiers	Return Type	Method
public	boolean	isTemporary()
public	String	paramString()

See Also java.awt.Component • java.awt.event.ComponentEvent • java.awt.event.FocusAdapter • java.awt.event.FocusListener

Interface FocusListener

public abstract interface java.awt.event.FocusListener implements java.util.EventListener

The FocusListener interface is used for listening to focus events (e.g., a Java component loses focus).

Syntax & Usage The FocusListener interface can be implemented to process focus events, which occur when a component gains or loses the input focus.

Instead of implementing the FocusListener interface, you can extend the FocusAdapter class and override only those methods that you need.

For details, please see the example under "Class FocusAdapter," earlier in this chapter.

Fields None

Constructors None

Methods

Modifiers	Return Type	Method
public abstract	void	focusGained(FocusEvent)
public abstract	void	focusLost(FocusEvent)

See Also java.awt.event.FocusAdapter • java.awt.event.FocusEvent • java.util.EventListener

Class InputEvent

public abstract synchronized java.awt.event.InputEvent extends java.awt.event.ComponentEvent

The InputEvent class is part of the lower-level group of event-handling classes used as the radix for handling component events.

Syntax & Usage

Because events are passed to a listener (or listeners) before they are sent to their originator, a component subclass can intercept the event and "consume" it.

Please see the example for the java.awt.TextField class in Chapter 2.

Fields

Modifiers	Type	Field
public static final	int	ALT_MASK
public static final	int	BUTTON1_MASK
public static final	int	BUTTON2_MASK
public static final	int	BUTTON3_MASK
public static final	int	CTRL_MASK
public static final	int	META_MASK
public static final	int	SHIFT_MASK

Constructors None

Methods

Modifiers	Return Type	Method
public	void	consume()
public	int	getModifiers()
public	long	getWhen()

Modifiers	Return Type	Method
public	boolean	isAltDown()
public	boolean	isConsumed()
public	boolean	isControlDown()
public	boolean	isMetaDown()
public	boolean	isShiftDown()

See Also java.awt.event.ComponentEvent

Class ItemEvent

public synchronized java.awt.event.ItemEvent extends java.awt.AWTEvent

The ItemEvent class is part of the higher-level (semantic) group of event-handling classes used to handle item events for components that implement the ItemSelectable interface.

> **Note**
>
> *Checkbox, CheckboxMenuItem, Choice, and List are all components in the AWT that implement the ItemSelectable interface.*

Syntax & Usage The ItemEvent class encapsulates events for checking and unchecking checkboxes (and checkbox groups), checkbox menu items, and selecting an item contained in a Choice or List component. You implement the ItemListener interface to process these events.

> **Tip**
>
> *A double mouse click on a List component generates an ActionEvent, not an ItemEvent.*

For details, please see the example for the java.awt.Checkbox class in Chapter 2.

Fields

Modifiers	Type	Field
public static final	int	DESELECTED
public static final	int	ITEM_FIRST
public static final	int	ITEM_LAST
public static final	int	ITEM_STATE_CHANGED
public static final	int	SELECTED

Constructors

Modifiers	Constructor
public	ItemEvent(ItemSelectable, int, Object, int)

Methods

Modifiers	Return Type	Method
public	Object	getItem()
public	ItemSelectable	getItemSelectable()
public	int	getStateChange()
public	String	paramString()

See Also java.awt.AWTEvent • java.awt.Checkbox • java.awt.CheckboxMenuItem • java.awt.Choice • java.awt.ItemSelectable • java.awt.List • java.awt.event.ItemListener

Interface ItemListener

public abstract interface java.awt.event.ItemListener implements java.util.EventListener

The ItemListener interface is used for listening to item events for components that implement the ItemSelectable interface (e.g., checking or unchecking a Checkbox object).

Syntax & Usage Please see the example for the java.awt.Checkbox class in Chapter 2.

Fields None

Constructors None

Methods

Modifiers	Return Type	Method
public abstract	void	itemStateChanged(ItemEvent)

See Also java.awt.Checkbox • java.awt.CheckboxMenuItem • java.awt.Choice • java.awt.ItemSelectable • java.awt.List • java.awt.event.ItemEvent • java.util.EventListener

Class KeyAdapter

public abstract synchronized java.awt.event.KeyAdapter extends java.lang.Object implements java.awt.event.KeyListener

KeyAdapter is an **abstract** class used for receiving keyboard events.

Syntax & Usage This adapter provides default implementation (which does nothing) of the KeyListener interface to process all events connected to keyboard input. To use this adapter, you need to extend it and override only those methods that you need.

Please see the example for the java.awt.TextField class in Chapter 2.

Fields None

Constructors

Modifiers	Constructor
public	KeyAdapter()

Methods

Modifiers	Return Type	Method
public	void	keyPressed(KeyEvent)
public	void	keyReleased(KeyEvent)
public	void	keyTyped(KeyEvent)

See Also java.awt.event.KeyEvent • java.awt.event.KeyListener • java.lang.Object

Class KeyEvent

public synchronized java.awt.event.KeyEvent extends java.awt.event.InputEvent

The KeyEvent class is part of the lower-level group of event-handling classes used for keyboard events (e.g., keys pressed on a user's keyboard).

Syntax & Usage This class encapsulates all events relating to keyboard input. It also provides a complete set of int identifiers for all keys present on a user's keyboard. You normally extend KeyAdapter if you want to directly process keyboard input in your Java program.

For details, please see the example for the java.awt.TextField class in Chapter 2.

Fields

Modifiers	Type	Field
public static final	char	CHAR_UNDEFINED
public static final	int	KEY_FIRST
public static final	int	KEY_LAST
public static final	int	KEY_PRESSED
public static final	int	KEY_RELEASED
public static final	int	KEY_TYPED
public static final	int	VK_0
public static final	int	VK_1
public static final	int	VK_2
public static final	int	VK_3
public static final	int	VK_4
public static final	int	VK_5
public static final	int	VK_6
public static final	int	VK_7
public static final	int	VK_8
public static final	int	VK_9
public static final	int	VK_A
public static final	int	VK_ACCEPT
public static final	int	VK_ADD
public static final	int	VK_ALT
public static final	int	VK_B
public static final	int	VK_BACK_QUOTE
public static final	int	VK_BACK_SLASH
public static final	int	VK_BACK_SPACE
public static final	int	VK_C
public static final	int	VK_CANCEL
public static final	int	VK_CAPS_LOCK
public static final	int	VK_CLEAR
public static final	int	VK_CLOSE_BRACKET
public static final	int	VK_COMMA
public static final	int	VK_CONTROL
public static final	int	VK_CONVERT

Modifiers	Type	Field
public static final	int	VK_D
public static final	int	VK_DECIMAL
public static final	int	VK_DELETE
public static final	int	VK_DIVIDE
public static final	int	VK_DOWN
public static final	int	VK_E
public static final	int	VK_END
public static final	int	VK_ENTER
public static final	int	VK_EQUALS
public static final	int	VK_ESCAPE
public static final	int	VK_F
public static final	int	VK_F1
public static final	int	VK_F10
public static final	int	VK_F11
public static final	int	VK_F12
public static final	int	VK_F2
public static final	int	VK_F3
public static final	int	VK_F4
public static final	int	VK_F5
public static final	int	VK_F6
public static final	int	VK_F7
public static final	int	VK_F8
public static final	int	VK_F9
public static final	int	VK_FINAL
public static final	int	VK_G
public static final	int	VK_H
public static final	int	VK_HELP
public static final	int	VK_HOME
public static final	int	VK_I
public static final	int	VK_INSERT
public static final	int	VK_J
public static final	int	VK_K
public static final	int	VK_KANA
public static final	int	VK_KANJI
public static final	int	VK_L
public static final	int	VK_LEFT
public static final	int	VK_M
public static final	int	VK_META
public static final	int	VK_MODECHANGE

Modifiers	Type	Field
public static final	int	VK_MULTIPLY
public static final	int	VK_N
public static final	int	VK_NONCONVERT
public static final	int	VK_NUMPAD0
public static final	int	VK_NUMPAD1
public static final	int	VK_NUMPAD2
public static final	int	VK_NUMPAD3
public static final	int	VK_NUMPAD4
public static final	int	VK_NUMPAD5
public static final	int	VK_NUMPAD6
public static final	int	VK_NUMPAD7
public static final	int	VK_NUMPAD8
public static final	int	VK_NUMPAD9
public static final	int	VK_NUM_LOCK
public static final	int	VK_O
public static final	int	VK_OPEN_BRACKET
public static final	int	VK_P
public static final	int	VK_PAGE_DOWN
public static final	int	VK_PAGE_UP
public static final	int	VK_PAUSE
public static final	int	VK_PERIOD
public static final	int	VK_PRINTSCREEN
public static final	int	VK_Q
public static final	int	VK_QUOTE
public static final	int	VK_R
public static final	int	VK_RIGHT
public static final	int	VK_S
public static final	int	VK_SCROLL_LOCK
public static final	int	VK_SEMICOLON
public static final	int	VK_SEPARATOR
public static final	int	VK_SHIFT
public static final	int	VK_SLASH
public static final	int	VK_SPACE
public static final	int	VK_SUBTRACT
public static final	int	VK_T
public static final	int	VK_TAB
public static final	int	VK_U
public static final	int	VK_UNDEFINED
public static final	int	VK_UP
public static final	int	VK_V

Modifiers	Type	Field
public static final	int	VK_W
public static final	int	VK_X
public static final	int	VK_Y
public static final	int	VK_Z

Constructors

Modifiers	Constructor
public	KeyEvent(Component, int, long, int, int)
public	KeyEvent(Component, int, long, int, int, char)

Methods

Modifiers	Return Type	Method
public	char	getKeyChar()
public	int	getKeyCode()
public static	String	getKeyModifiersText(int)
public static	String	getKeyText(int)
public	boolean	isActionKey()
public	String	paramString()
public	void	setKeyChar(char)
public	void	setKeyCode(int)
public	void	setModifiers(int)

See Also java.awt.event.InputEvent • java.awt.event.KeyAdapter • java.awt.event.KeyListener

Interface KeyListener

public abstract interface java.awt.event.KeyListener implements java.util.EventListener

The KeyListener interface is used for listening to KeyEvents (e.g., keys that users press on their keyboards).

Syntax & Usage This listener declares methods to process all events connected to keyboard input. Instead of implementing the KeyListener interface, you can extend the KeyAdapter class and override only those methods that you need.

For more information, please see the example for the java.awt.TextField class in Chapter 2.

Fields None

Constructors None

Methods

Modifiers	Return Type	Method
public abstract	void	keyPressed(KeyEvent)
public abstract	void	keyReleased(KeyEvent)
public abstract	void	keyTyped(KeyEvent)

See Also java.awt.event.KeyAdapter • java.awt.event.KeyEvent • java.util.EventListener

Class MouseAdapter

public abstract synchronized java.awt.event.MouseAdapter extends java.lang.Object implements java.awt.event.MouseListener

MouseAdapter is an **abstract** class used for receiving mouse events.

Syntax & Usage To use this adapter, you need to extend it and override only those methods that you need. Here's the outline for subclassing this adapter:

```
class MsAdapter extends MouseAdapter
{
   public void mousePressed(MouseEvent ev)
   {
      // Get point where the mouse click occurs
      int x = ev.getX();
      int y = ev.getY();
      // Process mouse click
   }
}
```

For an example of this class in action, please see the examples for the java.awt.Rectangle class in Chapter 2 and the MouseMotionAdapter class, later in this chapter.

Fields None

Constructors

Modifiers	Constructor
public	MouseAdapter()

Methods

Modifiers	Return Type	Method
public	void	mouseClicked(MouseEvent)
public	void	mouseEntered(MouseEvent)
public	void	mouseExited(MouseEvent)
public	void	mousePressed(MouseEvent)
public	void	mouseReleased(MouseEvent)

See Also Java.awt.event.MouseEvent • java.awt.event.MouseListener • java.lang.Object

Class MouseEvent

public synchronized java.awt.event.MouseEvent extends java.awt.event.InputEvent

The MouseEvent class is part of the lower-level group of event-handling classes used for mouse-clicking and mouse-movement events.

Syntax & Usage

Mouse events actually have two listeners and their corresponding adapter classes: MouseListener, MouseAdapter and MouseMotionListener, MouseMotionAdapter. The former is used for listening to mouse clicks and location, while the latter is used for listening to mouse movement and dragging.

Note

Not all applications need to process mouse-motion events (which is an important factor because mouse movements usually generate a large number of consecutive events). That's why Java 1.1 separates MouseEvents from MouseMotionEvents.

Please see the examples for the java.awt.Rectangle class in Chapter 2 and the MouseAdapter and MouseMotionAdapter classes, elsewhere in this chapter.

Fields

Modifiers	Type	Field
public static final	int	MOUSE_CLICKED
public static final	int	MOUSE_DRAGGED
public static final	int	MOUSE_ENTERED
public static final	int	MOUSE_EXITED
public static final	int	MOUSE_FIRST
public static final	int	MOUSE_LAST
public static final	int	MOUSE_MOVED
public static final	int	MOUSE_PRESSED
public static final	int	MOUSE_RELEASED

Constructors

Modifiers	Constructor
public	MouseEvent(Component, int, long, int, int, int, int, boolean)

Methods

Modifiers	Return Type	Method
public	int	getClickCount()
public	Point	getPoint()
public	int	getX()
public	int	getY()
public	boolean	isPopupTrigger()
public	String	paramString()
public synchronized	void	translatePoint(int, int)

See Also java.awt.event.InputEvent • java.awt.event.MouseAdapter • java.awt.event.MouseListener • java.awt.event.MouseMotionAdapter • java.awt.event.MouseMotionListener

Interface MouseListener

public abstract interface java.awt.event.MouseListener implements java.util.EventListener

The MouseListener interface is used for listening to mouse events (e.g., mouse clicks).

Syntax & Usage This listener declares methods to process all events connected to mouse clicks. Instead of implementing the MouseListener interface, you can extend the MouseAdapter class and override only those methods that you need.

For an example of this class in action, please see the examples for the java.awt.Rectangle class, in Chapter 2, and the MouseMotionAdapter class, which is the next section.

Fields None

Constructors None

Methods

Modifiers	Return Type	Method
public abstract	void	mouseClicked(MouseEvent)
public abstract	void	mouseEntered(MouseEvent)
public abstract	void	mouseExited(MouseEvent)
public abstract	void	mousePressed(MouseEvent)
public abstract	void	mouseReleased(MouseEvent)

See Also java.awt.event.MouseAdapter • java.awt.event.MouseEvent • java.awt.event.MouseMotionAdapter • java.awt.event.MouseMotionListener • java.util.EventListener

Class MouseMotionAdapter

public abstract synchronized java.awt.event.MouseMotionAdapter extends java.lang.Object implements java.awt.event.MouseMotionListener

MouseMotionAdapter is an **abstract** class used for receiving mouse-movement events.

Syntax & Usage To use this adapter, you need to extend it and override only the methods you need.

The following example applet uses MouseMotionAdapter and MouseAdapter to drag a simple image (circle) over an applet's panel:

```
public class myApplet extends Applet
{

  int m_x, m_y;
  boolean m_dragging = false;

  public void init()
  {
    m_x = getSize().width/2;
    m_y = getSize().height/2;
    addMouseListener(new MsAdapter());
    addMouseMotionListener(new
      MsMotionAdapter());
  }

  public void paint(Graphics g)
  {
    drawObject(g);
  }

  public void drawObject(Graphics g)
  {
    g.setColor(m_dragging ? Color.red :
      Color.blue);
    g.fillOval(m_x-5, m_y-5, 10, 10);
    g.setColor(Color.black);
    g.drawOval(m_x-5, m_y-5, 10, 10);
  }

  protected void eraseObject(Graphics g)
  {
    g.clearRect(m_x-6, m_y-6, 12, 12);
  }

  class MsAdapter extends MouseAdapter
  {
    public void mousePressed(MouseEvent ev)
    {
      if (Math.abs(ev.getX()-m_x)<=5 &&
        Math.abs(ev.getY()-m_y)<=5)
      {
        m_dragging = true;
        drawObject(getGraphics());
      }
    }
```

```
        public void mouseReleased(MouseEvent ev)
        {
            if (m_dragging)
            {
                m_dragging = false;
                drawObject(getGraphics());
            }
        }
    }

    class MsMotionAdapter extends
        MouseMotionAdapter
    {
        public void mouseDragged(MouseEvent ev)
        {
            if (m_dragging)
            {
                Graphics g = getGraphics();
                eraseObject(g);
                m_x = Math.min(
                Math.max(ev.getX(), 0),
                    getSize().width);
                m_y = Math.min(
                Math.max(ev.getY(), 0),
                    getSize().height);
                drawObject(g);
            }
        }
    }
}
```

This applet holds the current coordinates of the image (m_x and m_y) and contains a flag for the dragging state (m_dragging). The method drawObject() draws a circle (in red during the dragging state, in blue otherwise) at the current position, and the method eraseObject() erases the circle at the current position.

Following that is an implementation of the MouseAdapter method mousePressed(). This mousePressed() method verifies that the mouse has been pressed close enough to the circle so it can turn on the dragging flag. Following that is the mouseReleased() method that turns the dragging flag off.

Finally, you come to the implementation of the MouseMotionAdapter class, which uses the mouseDragged() method to verify that the dragging flag is turned on. Then it erases the circle at the current position, takes new coordinates from the mouse's newer position, verifies them to be inside the applet's panel, and draws the circle at the new position.

Fields None

Constructors

Modifiers	Constructor
public	MouseMotionAdapter()

Methods

Modifiers	Return Type	Method
public	void	mouseDragged(MouseEvent)
public	void	mouseMoved(MouseEvent)

See Also java.awt.event.MouseAdapter • java.awt.event.MouseEvent • java.awt.event.MouseListener • java.awt.event.MouseMotionListener • java.lang.Object

Interface MouseMotionListener

public abstract interface java.awt.event.MouseMotionListener implements java.util.EventListener

The MouseMotionListener interface is used for listening to mouse-movement events (e.g., dragging something across a component).

Syntax & Usage Instead of implementing the MouseMotionListener interface, you can extend the MouseMotionAdapter class and override only those methods that you need.

Please see the example in the previous section, "Class MouseMotionAdapter."

Fields None

Constructors None

Methods

Modifiers	Return Type	Method
public abstract	void	mouseDragged(MouseEvent)
public abstract	void	mouseMoved(MouseEvent)

See Also java.awt.event.MouseAdapter • java.awt.event.MouseEvent • java.awt.event.MouseListener • java.awt.event.MouseMotionAdapter • java.util.EventListener

Class PaintEvent

public synchronized java.awt.event.PaintEvent extends java.awt.event.ComponentEvent

The PaintEvent class is used for paint events (i.e., when a component/ container gets painted or repainted).

Syntax & Usage PaintEvent does not have a corresponding event-listener interface. Instead, you should subclass your components and containers and override the paint() methods for your Java programs to be drawn properly. Nevertheless, this event class has been designed for complete encapsulation of all possible events in Java applications.

Fields

Modifiers	Type	Field
public static final	int	PAINT
public static final	int	PAINT_FIRST
public static final	int	PAINT_LAST
public static final	int	UPDATE

Constructors

Modifiers	Constructor
public	PaintEvent(Component, int, Rectangle)

Methods

Modifiers	Return Type	Method
public	Rectangle	getUpdateRect()
public	String	paramString()
public	void	setUpdateRect(Rectangle)

See Also java.awt.event.ComponentEvent

Class TextEvent

public synchronized java.awt.event.TextEvent extends java.awt.AWTEvent

The TextEvent class is part of the higher-level (semantic) group of event-handling classes used for text events that can originate from java.awt.TextComponent. This includes java.awt.TextArea, java.awt.TextField, or any custom components that extend TextComponent.

Syntax & Usage

The TextEvent class is very similar to keyboard events. Although keyboard input generates most of the text changes for TextComponents, the text also can be changed programmatically or through pasting from a clipboard. To make the programmer's life easier, Java encapsulates any text changes into special text events. You can process these events if you need to keep track of text changes without regard to the origins of the changes.

For an example of this class in action, please see "Interface TextListener" in the next section.

Fields

Modifiers	Type	Field
public static final	int	TEXT_FIRST
public static final	int	TEXT_LAST
public static final	int	TEXT_VALUE_CHANGED

Constructors

Modifiers	Constructor
public	TextEvent(Object, int)

Methods

Modifiers	Return Type	Method
public	String	paramString()

See Also

java.awt.AWTEvent • java.awt.TextArea • java.awt.TextComponent • java.awt.TextField • java.awt.event.TextListener

Interface TextListener

public abstract interface java.awt.event.TextListener implements java.util.EventListener

The TextListener interface is used for listening to TextEvents from TextComponent components.

Syntax & Usage The TextListener class processes changes in text for several reasons, not necessarily just for keyboard input. For example, a clipboard paste or programmatically invoked text change can invoke TextListener to process changes.

The following example uses a TextListener implementation to process any text changes in the TextField m_Search to search through a List:

```
public class myApplet extends Applet
{
  List      m_List;
  TextField m_Search;

  public void init()
  {
    m_Search = new TextField(10);
    m_Search.addTextListener(new
      TxtAdapter());
    add(m_Search);

    m_List = new List(5);
    m_List.addItem("Andrea");
    m_List.addItem("Ann");
    m_List.addItem("Antony");
    m_List.addItem("Jack");
    m_List.addItem("Jeff");
    m_List.addItem("John");
    add(m_List);

    m_Search.requestFocus();
  }

  class TxtAdapter implements TextListener
  {
    public void  textValueChanged(
      TextEvent ev)
    {
```

```
            String target = m_Search.
              getText().toUpperCase();
            int n = target.length();
            for (int k=0; k<m_List.
              getItemCount(); k++)
            {
              String str = m_List.
                getItem(k).toUpperCase();
              if (str.length()>=n &&
                str.substring(0, n).
                equals(target))
              {
                m_List.select(k);
                break;
              }
            }
          }
        }
      }
```

The init() method creates a TextField search pattern, and a List object is filled by an ordered list of names. Following that, you have the TextAdapter class containing the textValueChanged() method that takes the current contents of m_Search and performs a non-case-sensitive search through the list using the first letters entered (see Figure 4-4).

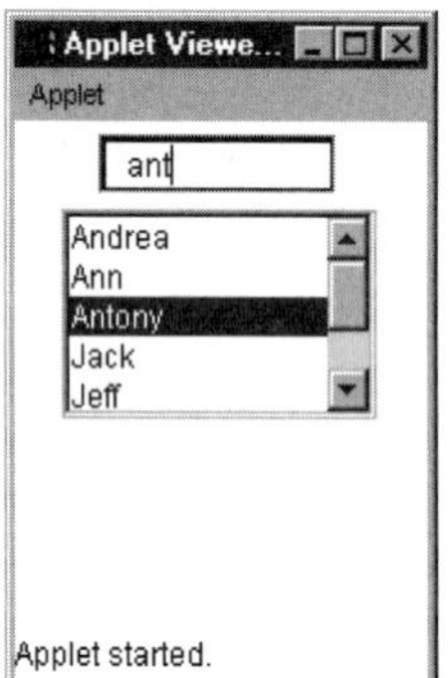

Figure 4-4: TextListener.

Fields None

Constructors None

Methods

Modifiers	Return Type	Method
public abstract	void	textValueChanged(TextEvent)

See Also java.awt.TextComponent • java.util.EventListener

Class WindowAdapter

public abstract synchronized java.awt.event.WindowAdapter extends java.lang.Object implements java.awt.event.WindowListener

WindowAdapter is an **abstract** class used for receiving window events.

Syntax & Usage

To use this adapter, you need to extend it and override any methods that you need for event-handling purposes. This can be more efficient than implementing WindowListener, which forces you to implement all methods contained in that interface.

The following example uses a WindowAdapter subclass (WndAdapter) object to dispose of the frame when the system's Close button is clicked on:

```
Frame frame = new Frame("Sample Frame");
frame.addWindowListener(new WndAdapter());

class WndAdapter extends WindowAdapter
{
   public void windowClosing(WindowEvent e)
   {
      e.getWindow().dispose();
   }
}
```

Fields None

Constructors

Modifiers	Constructor
public	WindowAdapter()

Methods

Modifiers	Return Type	Method
public	void	windowActivated(WindowEvent)
public	void	windowClosed(WindowEvent)
public	void	windowClosing(WindowEvent)
public	void	windowDeactivated(WindowEvent)
public	void	windowDeiconified(WindowEvent)
public	void	windowIconified(WindowEvent)
public	void	windowOpened(WindowEvent)

See Also java.awt.Frame • java.awt.event.WindowEvent • java.awt.event.WindowListener • java.lang.Object

Class WindowEvent

public synchronized java.awt.event.WindowEvent extends java.awt.event.ComponentEvent

The WindowEvent class is part of the lower-level group of event-handling classes used for window events (e.g., closing a window).

Syntax & Usage Java encapsulates events for window closing, minimizing, resizing, and so on into WindowEvents. Usually, you will need to at least process the WINDOW_CLOSED event; otherwise, your frames and dialogs in Java will not be closed by the native-system menu.

Please see the example in the previous section, "Class WindowAdapter."

Fields

Modifiers	Type	Field
public static final	int	WINDOW_ACTIVATED
public static final	int	WINDOW_CLOSED
public static final	int	WINDOW_CLOSING
public static final	int	WINDOW_DEACTIVATED
public static final	int	WINDOW_DEICONIFIED
public static final	int	WINDOW_FIRST
public static final	int	WINDOW_ICONIFIED
public static final	int	WINDOW_LAST
public static final	int	WINDOW_OPENED

Constructors

Modifiers	Constructor
public	WindowEvent(Window, int)

Methods

Modifiers	Return Type	Method
public	Window	getWindow()
public	String	paramString()

See Also java.awt.Frame • java.awt.event.ComponentEvent • java.awt.event.WindowAdapter • java.awt.event.WindowListener

Interface WindowListener

public abstract interface java.awt.event.WindowListener implements java.util.EventListener

The WindowListener interface is used for listening to window events (e.g., closing a window).

Syntax & Usage Instead of implementing the WindowListener interface, you can extend the WindowAdapter class and override only those methods that you need.

Please see the example under "Class WindowAdapter," earlier in this chapter.

Fields None

Constructors None

Methods

Modifiers	Return Type	Method
public abstract	void	windowActivated(WindowEvent)
public abstract	void	windowClosed(WindowEvent)
public abstract	void	windowClosing(WindowEvent)
public abstract	void	windowDeactivated(WindowEvent)
public abstract	void	windowDeiconified(WindowEvent)
public abstract	void	windowIconified(WindowEvent)
public abstract	void	windowOpened(WindowEvent)

See Also java.awt.Frame • java.awt.event.WindowAdapter • java.awt.event.WindowEvent • java.util.EventListener

The java.awt.image Package

5

The java.awt.image package contains the classes that are necessary for image processing in Java. Using this package you can perform a variety of operations including cropping, scaling, and other forms of image filtering. You can also convert image data between various color models. This package also contains the framework necessary for you to add your own custom image processing functionality if the need should arise.

Class AreaAveragingScaleFilter

public synchronized java.awt.image.AreaAveragingScaleFilter extends java.awt.image.ReplicateScaleFilter

The AreaAveragingScaleFilter class is used for scaling images using the area-averaging algorithm.

Syntax & Usage Use this class primarily when you intend to enlarge or contract the overall size of an image. Please see the example under "Class ImageFilter," later in the chapter.

Fields None

Constructors

Modifiers	Constructor
public	AreaAveragingScaleFilter(int, int)

Methods

Modifiers	Return Type	Method
public	void	setHints(int)
public	void	setPixels(int, int, int, int, ColorModel, byte[], int, int)
public	void	setPixels(int, int, int, int, ColorModel, int[], int, int)

See Also java.awt.image.ReplicateScaleFilter

Class ColorModel

public abstract synchronized java.awt.image.ColorModel extends java.lang.Object

ColorModel is an abstract class used to represent pixel values as standard RGB values (Red-Green-Blue) or an alpha transparency value, color model.

Syntax & Usage Please see the examples under "Class DirectColorModel" and "Class IndexColorModel" later in this chapter.

Fields

Modifiers	Type	Field
protected	int	pixel_bits

Constructors

Modifiers	Constructor
public	ColorModel(int)

Methods

Modifiers	Return Type	Method
public	void	finalize()
public abstract	int	getAlpha(int)
public abstract	int	getBlue(int)
public abstract	int	getGreen(int)
public	int	getPixelSize()
public abstract	int	getRed(int)
public	int	getRGB(int)
public static	ColorModel	getRGBdefault()

See Also java.awt.image.DirectColorModel • java.awt.image.IndexColorModel • java.lang.Object

Class CropImageFilter

public synchronized java.awt.image.CropImageFilter extends java.awt.image.ImageFilter

The CropImageFilter class is used for cropping images.

Syntax & Usage You use this class to extract a specified rectangle in an image, thereby, making a new image out of a designated part of the original image. This class facilitates the functionality to extract the specified rectangle for the original image and provide a destination for the new resulting image.

CropImageFilter is meant to be used in conjunction with FilteredImageSource and should not be called directly.

Please see the example under "Class ImageFilter" later in this chapter.

Fields None

Constructors

Modifiers	Constructor
public	CropImageFilter(int, int, int, int)

Methods

Modifiers	Return Type	Method
public	void	setDimensions(int, int)
public	void	setPixels(int, int, int, int, ColorModel, byte[], int, int)
public	void	setPixels(int, int, int, int, ColorModel, int[], int, int)
public	void	setProperties(Hashtable)

See Also java.awt.image.FilteredImageSource • java.awt.image.ImageFilter

Class DirectColorModel

public synchronized java.awt.image.DirectColorModel extends java.awt.image.ColorModel

The DirectColorModel class extends ColorModel's functionality; it is used to convert pixel values into a standard RGB (Red-Green-Blue) or alpha transparency value, color model. Specifically, DirectColorModel is used for images that have RGB colors directly embedded in their pixel bits.

Syntax & Usage This example shows how to create a DirectColorModel instance by specifying three color masks (color masks for DirectColorModel must have a contiguous set of bytes):

```
new DirectColorModel(24, 0x000000ff,
   0x0000ff00, 0x00ff0000);
```

Fields None

Constructors

Modifiers	Constructor
public	DirectColorModel(int, int, int, int)
public	DirectColorModel(int, int, int, int, int)

Methods

Modifiers	Return Type	Method
public final	int	getAlpha(int)
public final	int	getAlphaMask()
public final	int	getBlue(int)
public final	int	getBlueMask()
public final	int	getGreen(int)
public final	int	getGreenMask()
public final	int	getRed(int)
public final	int	getRedMask()
public final	int	getRGB(int)

See Also java.awt.image.ColorModel • java.awt.image.IndexColorModel

Class FilteredImageSource

public synchronized java.awt.image.FilteredImageSource extends java.lang.Object implements java.awt.image.ImageProducer

The FilteredImageSource class takes an image and a filter object that you use to produce a new image, which has had its image data filtered in some way based on the image filter specified. For instance, cropping an image using FilteredImageSource as the filter is an example of filtering an image.

Syntax & Usage Please see the example under "Class ImageFilter" later in this chapter.

Fields None

Constructors

Modifiers	Constructor
public	FilteredImageSource(ImageProducer, ImageFilter)

Methods

Modifiers	Return Type	Method
public synchronized	void	addConsumer(ImageConsumer)
public synchronized	boolean	isConsumer(ImageConsumer)
public synchronized	void	removeConsumer(ImageConsumer)
public	void	requestTopDownLeftRightResend(ImageConsumer)
public	void	startProduction(ImageConsumer)

See Also java.awt.image.ImageProducer • java.lang.Object

Interface ImageConsumer

public abstract interface java.awt.image.ImageConsumer

ImageConsumer is an interface that facilitates methods to process image data and communicate with other classes that produce image data (i.e., ImageProducer interfaces). ImageFilter is an example of a class that implements the ImageProducer interface.

Syntax & Usage PixelGrabber represents a class in the java.awt.image package that implements the ImageConsumer interface.

For most solutions, Java programs usually do not need to implement this interface, but instead use ImageProducer or PixelGrabber, which already implement this interface.

Please see the example under "Class PixelGrabber" later in this chapter.

Fields

Modifiers	Type	Field
public static final	int	COMPLETESCANLINES
public static final	int	IMAGEABORTED
public static final	int	IMAGEERROR
public static final	int	RANDOMPIXELORDER
public static final	int	SINGLEFRAME
public static final	int	SINGLEFRAMEDONE
public static final	int	SINGLEPASS
public static final	int	STATICIMAGEDONE
public static final	int	TOPDOWNLEFTRIGHT

Constructors None

Methods

Modifiers	Return Type	Method
public abstract	void	imageComplete(int)
public abstract	void	setColorModel(ColorModel)
public abstract	void	setDimensions(int, int)
public abstract	void	setHints(int)
public abstract	void	setPixels(int, int, int, int, ColorModel, byte[], int, int)
public abstract	void	setPixels(int, int, int, int, ColorModel, int[], int, int)
public abstract	void	setProperties(Hashtable)

See Also java.awt.image.ImageProducer • java.awt.image.PixelGrabber

Class ImageFilter

public synchronized java.awt.image.ImageFilter extends java.lang.Object implements java.awt.image.ImageConsumer, java.lang.Cloneable

The ImageFilter class is the root class for all image filters used in Java. It is used in conjunction with a FilteredImageSource object.

Syntax & Usage Effectively, the ImageFilter class sends image data from an ImageProducer to an ImageConsumer as specified in the regulating FilteredImageSource, thus filtering the image data in the transition process.

While ImageFilter is a filter in and of itself, it does not contain any inherent filtering functionality. Instead, you need to subclass it. Three such classes that already reside in the java.awt.image package are CropImageFilter (used for cropping images), RGBImageFilter (used to modify the RGB values of the image), and AreaAveragingFilter (used to enlarge or shrink images).

This example uses different implementations of ImageFilter (CropImageFilter, RGBImageFilter, AreaAveragingScaleFilter, and ReplicateScaleFilter) to rescale and modify an original image. An instance of java.awt.MediaTracker synchronizes the process. Finally, method paint() draws all produced images along with their numbers.

```
public class myApplet extends Applet
{

   Image   m_Image[] = new Image[5];
   boolean m_bLoaded = false;

   public void init()
   {
      MediaTracker mtracker = new
         MediaTracker(this);

      m_Image[0] = getImage(getDocumentBase(),
         "myImage.gif");
      mtracker.addImage(m_Image[0], 0);
      m_Image[1] = createImage(new
         FilteredImageSource(
         m_Image[0].getSource(),
         new CropImageFilter(5, 5, 30, 30)));
      mtracker.addImage(m_Image[1], 0);
      m_Image[2] = createImage(new
         FilteredImageSource(
         m_Image[0].getSource(),
         new RedBlueSwapFilter()));
      mtracker.addImage(m_Image[2], 0);
      m_Image[3] = createImage(new
         FilteredImageSource(
         m_Image[0].getSource(),
         new AreaAveragingScaleFilter(
         50, 50)));
      mtracker.addImage(m_Image[3], 0);
      m_Image[4] = createImage(new
         FilteredImageSource(
         m_Image[0].getSource(),
         new ReplicateScaleFilter(60, 60)));
      mtracker.addImage(m_Image[4], 0);

      try
      {
         mtracker.waitForAll();
         m_bLoaded = true;
      }
```

```
        catch (InterruptedException e)
        {
            m_bLoaded = false;
            System.out.println(e.getMessage());
        }

        repaint();
    }

    public void paint(Graphics g)
    {
        if (m_bLoaded)
        {
            for (int k=0; k<m_Image.length; k++)
            {
                int x = k*60+20;
                g.drawString(
                    String.valueOf(k+1)+".",
                     x, 15);
                g.drawImage(m_Image[k],
                    x, 20, this);
            }
        }
    }

    class RedBlueSwapFilter extends
        RGBImageFilter
    {
        public RedBlueSwapFilter()
        {
            canFilterIndexColorModel = true;
        }

        public int filterRGB(int x, int y,
            int rgb)
        {
            return ((rgb & 0xff00ff00)
                | ((rgb & 0xff0000) >> 16)
            | ((rgb & 0xff) << 16));
        }
    }
}
```

Class RedBlueSwapFilter extends RGBImageFilter to swap red and blue components of each pixel.

Figure 5-1 shows generated images: 1. CropImageFilter, 2. RGBImageFilter, 3. AreaAveragingScaleFilter, 4. ReplicateScaleFilter.

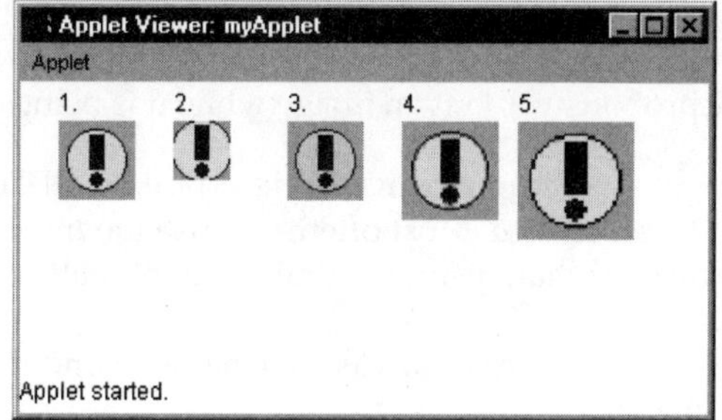

Figure 5-1: Subclasses of ImageFilter.

Fields

Modifiers	Type	Field
protected	ImageConsumer	consumer

Constructors

Modifiers	Constructor
public	ImageFilter()

Methods

Modifiers	Return Type	Method
public	Object	clone()
public	ImageFilter	getFilterInstance(ImageConsumer)
public	void	imageComplete(int)
public	void	resendTopDownLeftRight(ImageProducer)
public	void	setColorModel(ColorModel)
public	void	setDimensions(int, int)
public	void	setHints(int)
public	void	setPixels(int, int, int, int, ColorModel, byte[], int, int)
public	void	setPixels(int, int, int, int, ColorModel, int[], int, int)
public	void	setProperties(Hashtable)

See Also java.awt.image.AreaAveragingScaleFilter • java.awt.image.CropImageFilter • java.awt.image.FilteredImageSource • java.awt.image.ImageConsumer • java.awt.image.ImageProducer • java.awt.image.ReplicateScaleFilter • java.awt.image.RGBImageFilter

Interface ImageObserver

public abstract interface java.awt.image.ImageObserver

The ImageObserver interface is used for classes that need to receive status information asynchronously about an image while it is being constructed.

Syntax & Usage

Class java.awt.Component implements this interface, so all Component subclasses inherit this interface. Most often, you use the ImageObserver interface as a parameter when using the drawImage() method from the java.awt.Graphics class.

See the example under "Class Canvas" in Chapter 2 and the examples elsewhere in this chapter.

Fields

Modifiers	Type	Field
public static final	int	ABORT
public static final	int	ALLBITS
public static final	int	ERROR
public static final	int	FRAMEBITS
public static final	int	HEIGHT
public static final	int	PROPERTIES
public static final	int	SOMEBITS
public static final	int	WIDTH

Constructors

None

Methods

Modifiers	Return Type	Method
public abstract	boolean	imageUpdate(Image, int, int, int, int, int)

See Also

java.awt.Graphics • java.awt.image.ImageConsumer • java.awt.image.ImageProducer

Interface ImageProducer

public abstract interface java.awt.image.ImageProducer

The ImageProducer interface is used for classes that produce image data for an image (or images). By implementing this class, they must define communication with an ImageConsumer.

Syntax & Usage Any class that implements ImageProducer and needs to communicate with an ImageConsumer object must be registered (via the addConsumer() method) with that ImageProducer. FilteredImageSource and MemoryImageSource represent classes in the java.awt.image package that implement the ImageProducer interface.

> **Note**
>
> *Every Image in Java contains an ImageProducer object used to redraw the image when needed.*

For most solutions, you do not need to implement this interface, but should instead use the FilteredImageSource or MemoryImageSource classes.

Please see the example under "Class MemoryImageSource" later in this chapter.

Fields None

Constructors None

Methods

Modifiers	Return Type	Method Name
public abstract	void	addConsumer(ImageConsumer)
public abstract	boolean	isConsumer(ImageConsumer)
public abstract	void	removeConsumer(ImageConsumer)
public abstract	void	requestTopDownLeftRightResend(ImageConsumer)
public abstract	void	startProduction(ImageConsumer)

See Also java.awt.image.FilteredImageSource • java.awt.image.ImageConsumer • java.awt.image.ImageObserver • java.awt.image.MemoryImageSource

Class IndexColorModel

public synchronized java.awt.image.IndexColorModel extends java.awt.image.ColorModel

The IndexColorModel class extends the ColorModel class. It is used to convert pixel values into a standard RGB (Red-Green-Blue) or an alpha transparency value, color model. Specifically, IndexColorModel is used for pixel indices that belong to a fixed color map.

Syntax & Usage This example shows how to create an IndexColorModel object using three arrays of bytes:

```
byte r[] = new byte[] {(byte)0x00, (byte)0x40,
  (byte)0x80, (byte)0xC0, (byte)0xFF};
byte g[] = new byte[] {(byte)0x00, (byte)0x40,
  (byte)0x80, (byte)0xC0, (byte)0xFF};
byte b[] = new byte[] {(byte)0x00, (byte)0x40,
  (byte)0x80, (byte)0xC0, (byte)0xFF};
IndexColorModel indexModel = new
  IndexColorModel(24, 5, r, g, b);
```

Note

You also can specify an optional transparent pixel value representing a completely transparent pixel regardless of the alpha value (if any) recorded for that pixel.

Fields None

Constructors

Modifiers	Constructor
public	IndexColorModel(int, int, byte[], byte[], byte[])
public	IndexColorModel(int, int, byte[], byte[], byte[], byte[])
public	IndexColorModel(int, int, byte[], byte[], byte[], int)
public	IndexColorModel(int, int, byte[], int, boolean)
public	IndexColorModel(int, int, byte[], int, boolean, int)

Methods

Modifiers	Return Type	Method
public final	int	getAlpha(int)
public final	void	getAlphas(byte[])
public final	int	getBlue(int)
public final	void	getBlues(byte[])
public final	int	getGreen(int)
public final	void	getGreens(byte[])
public final	int	getMapSize()
public final	int	getRed(int)
public final	void	getReds(byte[])
public final	int	getRGB(int)
public final	int	getTransparentPixel()

See Also java.awt.image.ColorModel • java.awt.image.DirectColorModel

Class MemoryImageSource

public synchronized java.awt.image.MemoryImageSource extends java.lang.Object implements java.awt.image.ImageProducer

The MemoryImageSource class is an ImageProducer that can produce an image through an array of data stored in memory.

Syntax & Usage This example uses MemoryImageSource to create and modify an image modeling Brownian motion. Array m_Pixels[] holds color values of the image's pixels (see Figure 5-2):

```
public class myApplet extends Applet
   implements Runnable
{
   Thread   m_Anim;
   MemoryImageSource m_ImgSrc;
   Image m_MemImg;
   int[] m_Pixels;
   int x0 = 50, y0 = 50;

   public void init()
   {
      m_Pixels = new int[100 * 100];
      for (int k=0; k<m_Pixels.length; k++)
         m_Pixels[k] = 0;
      m_ImgSrc = new MemoryImageSource(100,
         100, m_Pixels, 0, 100);
      m_MemImg = createImage(m_ImgSrc);
      m_MemImg.flush();
      repaint();
   }

   public void start()
   {
      m_Anim = new Thread(this);
      m_Anim.start();
   }

   public synchronized void stop()
   {
      m_Anim = null;
      notify();
   }
```

```
    public synchronized void run()
    {
        while (Thread.currentThread() == m_Anim)
        {
            int x = x0 + (int)Math.round(
                Math.random()*4)-2;
            x = Math.min(Math.max(x, 0), 99);
            x0 = x;
            int y = y0 + (int)Math.round(
                Math.random()*4)-2;
            y = Math.min(Math.max(y, 0), 99);
            y0 = y;
            int nBlue = m_Pixels[y * 100 + x]
                & 0x000000ff;
            nBlue = Math.min(nBlue+64, 255);
            m_Pixels[y * 100 + x] = nBlue |
                (0xff<<24);
            m_MemImg.flush();
            repaint(x, y, 1, 1);
            try
            {
                wait(50);
            }
            catch (InterruptedException e)
            {
                return;
            }
        }
    }

    public void paint(Graphics g)
    {
        g.drawImage(m_MemImg, 0, 0, this);
    }
}
```

Figure 5-2: MemoryImageSource.

This applet uses threads to model Brownian motion. 0, 0 are current coordinates of the point. Every time the moving point hits some pixel, the blue component of that pixel increases by 64 to give impression about the density of motion.

Fields None

Constructors

Modifiers	Constructor
public	MemoryImageSource(int, int, ColorModel, byte[], int, int)
public	MemoryImageSource(int, int, ColorModel, byte[], int, int, Hashtable)
public	MemoryImageSource(int, int, ColorModel, int[], int, int)
public	MemoryImageSource(int, int, ColorModel, int[], int, int, Hashtable)
public	MemoryImageSource(int, int, int[], int, int)
public	MemoryImageSource(int, int, int[], int, int, Hashtable)

Methods

Modifiers	Return Type	Method
public synchronized	void	addConsumer(ImageConsumer)
public synchronized	boolean	isConsumer(ImageConsumer)
public	void	newPixels()
public synchronized	void	newPixels(byte[], ColorModel, int, int)
public synchronized	void	newPixels(int, int, int, int)
public synchronized	void	newPixels(int, int, int, int, boolean)
public synchronized	void	newPixels(int[], ColorModel, int, int)
public synchronized	void	removeConsumer(ImageConsumer)
public	void	requestTopDownLeftRightResend(ImageConsumer)
public synchronized	void	setAnimated(boolean)
public synchronized	void	setFullBufferUpdates(boolean)
public	void	startProduction(ImageConsumer)

See Also java.awt.image.ImageProducer • java.lang.Object

Class PixelGrabber

public synchronized java.awt.image.PixelGrabber extends java.lang.Object implements java.awt.image.ImageConsumer

The PixelGrabber class is an ImageConsumer class that can be attached to an Image or ImageProducer object to return a rectangular array of pixels based on the image.

Syntax & Usage This example uses a PixelGrabber instance to calculate average red, green, and blue components of the specified part for a given image:

```
public void calcAverColors(Image img, int x,
   int y, int w, int h)
{
   int[] pixels = new int[w * h];
   PixelGrabber pg = new PixelGrabber(img, x,
      y, w, h, pixels, 0, w);
   try
   {
      pg.grabPixels();
   }
   catch (InterruptedException e)
   {
      System.err.println(e.getMessage());
      return;
   }
   if ((pg.getStatus() & ImageObserver.ABORT) != 0)
   {
      System.err.println(
         "PixelGrabber aborted");
      return;
   }

   long lRed = 0;
   long lGreen = 0;
   long lBlue = 0;
   long lCount = 0;

   for (int j = 0; j < h; j++)
   for (int i = 0; i < w; i++)
   {
      int pixel = pixels[j * w + i];
      lRed   += (pixel >> 16) & 0xff;
      lGreen += (pixel >>  8) & 0xff;
      lBlue  += (pixel      ) & 0xff;
      lCount ++;
   }

   System.out.println(
      "Total pixels processed:\t"+lCount);
   System.out.println(
      "Average red component:\t"+lRed/lCount);
```

```
  System.out.println(
     "Average green component:\t"+
     lGreen/lCount);
  System.out.println(
     "Average blue component:\t"+
     lBlue/lCount);
}
```

This output corresponds to the image used in the example under "Class ImageFilter" earlier in this chapter:

```
Total pixels processed:  1600
Average red component:   195
Average green component: 179
Average blue component:  101
```

Fields None

Constructors

Modifiers	Constructor
public	PixelGrabber(Image, int, int, int, int, boolean)
public	PixelGrabber(Image, int, int, int, int, int[], int, int)
public	PixelGrabber(ImageProducer, int, int, int, int, int[], int, int)

Methods

Modifiers	Return Type	Method
public synchronized	void	abortGrabbing()
public synchronized	ColorModel	getColorModel()
public synchronized	int	getHeight()
public synchronized	Object	getPixels()
public synchronized	int	getStatus()
public synchronized	int	getWidth()
public	boolean	grabPixels()
public synchronized	boolean	grabPixels(long)
public synchronized	void	imageComplete(int)
public	void	setColorModel(ColorModel)
public	void	setDimensions(int, int)
public	void	setHints(int)
public	void	setPixels(int, int, int, int, ColorModel, byte[], int, int)
public	void	setPixels(int, int, int, int, ColorModel, int[], int, int)
public	void	setProperties(Hashtable)
public synchronized	void	startGrabbing()
public synchronized	int	status()

See Also java.awt.image.ImageConsumer • java.awt.image.ImageProducer

Class RGBImageFilter

public abstract synchronized java.awt.image.RGBImageFilter extends java.awt.image.ImageFilter

The RGBImageFilter class is used for modifying the colors in an image on a pixel-by-pixel basis.

Syntax & Usage

To use RGBImageFilter, you need to subclass it to add the needed functionality. RGBImageFilter is meant to be used in conjunction with FilteredImageSource and should not be called directly.

Please see the example under "Class ImageFilter" earlier in this chapter.

Fields

Modifiers	Type	Field
protected	boolean	canFilterIndexColorModel
protected	ColorModel	newmodel
protected	ColorModel	origmodel

Constructors

Modifiers	Constructor
public	RGBImageFilter()

Methods

Modifiers	Return Type	Method
public	IndexColorModel	filterIndexColorModel(IndexColorModel)
public abstract	int	filterRGB(int, int, int)
public	void	filterRGBPixels(int, int, int, int, int[], int, int)
public	void	setColorModel(ColorModel)
public	void	setPixels(int, int, int, int, ColorModel, byte[], int, int)
public	void	setPixels(int, int, int, int, ColorModel, int[], int, int)
public	void	substituteColorModel(ColorModel, ColorModel)

See Also

java.awt.image.CropImageFilter • java.awt.image.ImageFilter • java.awt.image.ReplicateScaleFilter

Class ReplicateScaleFilter

public synchronized java.awt.image.ReplicateScaleFilter extends java.awt.image.ImageFilter

The ReplicateScaleFilter class is used for scaling images.

Syntax & Usage

This class uses a very simple algorithm in which the pixels in the original image are sampled for the destination image. If you are scaling up, the ReplicateScaleFilter replicates the rows and columns of pixels to scale up. When scaling down, it omits rows and columns of pixels.

ReplicateImageFilter is meant to be used in conjunction with FilteredImageSource and should not be called directly.

Please see the example under "Class ImageFilter" earlier in this chapter.

Fields

Modifiers	Type	Field
protected	int	destHeight
protected	int	destWidth
protected	Object	outpixbuf
protected	int[]	srccols
protected	int	srcHeight
protected	int[]	srcrows
protected	int	srcWidth

Constructors

Modifiers	Constructor
public	ReplicateScaleFilter(int, int)

Methods

Modifiers	Return Type	Method
public	void	setDimensions(int, int)
public	void	setPixels(int, int, int, int, ColorModel, byte[], int, int)
public	void	setPixels(int, int, int, int, ColorModel, int[], int, int)
public	void	setProperties(Hashtable)

See Also

java.awt.image.CropImageFilter • java.awt.image.ImageFilter • java.awt.image.RGBImageFilter

The java.awt.peer Package

6

The java.awt.peer package is merely a collection of interfaces that define an abstract model, which is implemented by its respective components housed in the java.awt package. Currently, each Java environment implements the AWT components natively and uses these peers to tie in each native implementation to a common (i.e., abstract) foundation. This rather cumbersome native/peer implementation is due to be replaced with a better solution in the version that follows the AWT 1.1.

These peer interfaces are practically never used directly by a programmer but are instead part of the internal implementation Java uses for components defined in the java.awt package.

Note

Since these interfaces have effectively been covered in the java.awt package, and are almost never used directly by the programmer, there are no definitions or examples of usage in this chapter.

Tip

Normally, you should not use these peer interfaces directly in your Java programs; instead, you should use the corresponding java.awt component, which can create peer objects internally on an as-needed basis.

Interface ButtonPeer

public abstract interface java.awt.peer.ButtonPeer implements java.awt.peer.ComponentPeer

Fields None

Constructors None

Methods

Modifiers	Return Type	Method
public abstract	void	setLabel(String)

See Also java.awt.Button • java.awt.peer.ComponentPeer

Interface CanvasPeer

public interface java.awt.peer.CanvasPeer implements java.awt.peer.ComponentPeer

Fields None

Constructors None

Methods None

See Also java.awt.Canvas • java.awt.peer.ComponentPeer

Interface CheckboxMenuItemPeer

public abstract interface java.awt.peer.CheckboxMenuItemPeer implements java.awt.peer.MenuItemPeer

Fields None

Constructors None

Methods

Modifiers	Return Type	Method
public abstract	void	setState(boolean)

See Also java.awt.CheckboxMenuItem • java.awt.peer.MenuItemPeer

Interface CheckboxPeer

public abstract interface java.awt.peer.CheckboxPeer implements java.awt.peer.ComponentPeer

Fields None

Constructors None

Methods

Modifiers	Return Type	Method
public abstract	void	setCheckboxGroup(CheckboxGroup)
public abstract	void	setLabel(String)
public abstract	void	setState(boolean)

See Also java.awt.Checkbox • java.awt.peer.ComponentPeer

Interface ChoicePeer

public abstract interface java.awt.peer.ChoicePeer implements java.awt.peer.ComponentPeer

Fields None

Constructors None

Methods

Modifiers	Return Type	Method
public abstract	void	add(String, int)
public abstract	void	addItem(String, int)
public abstract	void	remove(int)
public abstract	void	select(int)

See Also java.awt.Choice • java.awt.peer.ComponentPeer

Interface ComponentPeer

public abstract interface java.awt.peer.ComponentPeer

Fields None

Constructors None

Methods

Modifiers	Return Type	Method
public abstract	int	checkImage(Image, int, int, ImageObserver)
public abstract	Image	createImage(ImageProducer)
public abstract	Image	createImage(int, int)
public abstract	void	disable()
public abstract	void	dispose()
public abstract	void	enable()
public abstract	ColorModel	getColorModel()
public abstract	FontMetrics	getFontMetrics(Font)
public abstract	Graphics	getGraphics()
public abstract	Point	getLocationOnScreen()
public abstract	Dimension	getMinimumSize()
public abstract	Dimension	getPreferredSize()
public abstract	Toolkit	getToolkit()
public abstract	void	handleEvent(AWTEvent)
public abstract	void	hide()
public abstract	boolean	isFocusTraversable()
public abstract	Dimension	minimumSize()

Modifiers	Return Type	Method
public abstract	void	paint(Graphics)
public abstract	Dimension	preferredSize()
public abstract	boolean	prepareImage(Image, int, int, ImageObserver)
public abstract	void	print(Graphics)
public abstract	void	repaint(long, int, int, int, int)
public abstract	void	requestFocus()
public abstract	void	reshape(int, int, int, int)
public abstract	void	setBackground(Color)
public abstract	void	setBounds(int, int, int, int)
public abstract	void	setCursor(Cursor)
public abstract	void	setEnabled(boolean)
public abstract	void	setFont(Font)
public abstract	void	setForeground(Color)
public abstract	void	setVisible(boolean)
public abstract	void	show()

See Also java.awt.Component

Interface ContainerPeer

public abstract interface java.awt.peer.ContainerPeer implements java.awt.peer.ComponentPeer

Fields None

Constructors None

Methods

Modifiers	Return Type	Method
public abstract	void	beginValidate()
public abstract	void	endValidate()
public abstract	Insets	getInsets()
public abstract	Insets	insets()

See Also java.awt.Container • java.awt.peer.ComponentPeer

Interface DialogPeer

public abstract interface java.awt.peer.DialogPeer implements java.awt.peer.WindowPeer

Fields None

Constructors None

Methods

Modifiers	Return Type	Method
public abstract	void	setResizable(boolean)
public abstract	void	setTitle(String)

See Also java.awt.Dialog • java.awt.peer.WindowPeer

Interface FileDialogPeer

public abstract interface java.awt.peer.FileDialogPeer implements java.awt.peer.DialogPeer

Fields None

Constructors None

Methods

Modifiers	Return Type	Method
public abstract	void	setDirectory(String)
public abstract	void	setFile(String)
public abstract	void	setFilenameFilter(FilenameFilter)

See Also java.awt.FileDialog • java.awt.peer.DialogPeer

Interface FontPeer

public interface java.awt.peer.FontPeer

Fields None

Constructors None

Methods None

See Also java.awt.Font

Interface FramePeer

public abstract interface java.awt.peer.FramePeer implements java.awt.peer.WindowPeer

Fields None

Constructors None

Methods

Modifiers	Return Type	Method
public abstract	void	setIconImage(Image)
public abstract	void	setMenuBar(MenuBar)
public abstract	void	setResizable(boolean)
public abstract	void	setTitle(String)

See Also java.awt.Frame • java.awt.peer.WindowPeer

Interface LabelPeer

public abstract interface java.awt.peer.LabelPeer implements java.awt.peer.ComponentPeer

Fields None

Constructors None

Methods

Modifiers	Return Type	Method
public abstract	void	setAlignment(int)
public abstract	void	setText(String)

See Also java.awt.Label • java.awt.peer.ComponentPeer

Interface LightweightPeer

public interface java.awt.peer.LightweightPeer implements java.awt.peer.ComponentPeer

Fields None

Constructors None

Methods None

See Also java.awt.peer.ComponentPeer

Interface ListPeer

public abstract interface java.awt.peer.ListPeer implements java.awt.peer.ComponentPeer

Fields None

Constructors None

Methods

Modifiers	Return Type	Method
public abstract	void	add(String, int)
public abstract	void	addItem(String, int)
public abstract	void	clear()
public abstract	void	delItems(int, int)
public abstract	void	deselect(int)
public abstract	Dimension	getMinimumSize(int)
public abstract	Dimension	getPreferredSize(int)
public abstract	int[]	getSelectedIndexes()
public abstract	void	makeVisible(int)
public abstract	Dimension	minimumSize(int)
public abstract	Dimension	preferredSize(int)
public abstract	void	removeAll()
public abstract	void	select(int)
public abstract	void	setMultipleMode(boolean)
public abstract	void	setMultipleSelections(boolean)

See Also java.awt.List • java.awt.peer.ListPeer

Interface MenuBarPeer

public abstract interface java.awt.peer.MenuBarPeer implements java.awt.peer.MenuComponentPeer

Fields None

Constructors None

Methods

Modifiers	Return Type	Method
public abstract	void	addHelpMenu(Menu)
public abstract	void	addMenu(Menu)
public abstract	void	delMenu(int)

See Also java.awt.MenuBar • java.awt.peer.MenuBarPeer

Interface MenuComponentPeer

public abstract interface java.awt.peer.MenuComponentPeer

Fields None

Constructors None

Methods

Modifiers	Return Type	Method
public abstract	void	dispose()

See Also java.awt.MenuComponent

Interface MenuItemPeer

public abstract interface java.awt.peer.MenuItemPeer implements java.awt.peer.MenuComponentPeer

Fields None

Constructors None

Methods

Modifiers	Return Type	Method
public abstract	void	disable()
public abstract	void	enable()
public abstract	void	setEnabled(boolean)
public abstract	void	setLabel(String)

See Also java.awt.MenuItem • java.awt.peer.MenuComponentPeer

Interface MenuPeer

public abstract interface java.awt.peer.MenuPeer implements java.awt.peer.MenuItemPeer

Fields None

Constructors None

Methods

Modifiers	Return Type	Method
public abstract	void	addItem(MenuItem)
public abstract	void	addSeparator()
public abstract	void	delItem(int)

See Also java.awt.Menu • java.awt.MenuItemPeer

Interface PanelPeer

public interface java.awt.peer.PanelPeer implements java.awt.peer.ContainerPeer

Fields None

Constructors None

Methods None

See Also java.awt.Panel • java.awt.ContainerPeer

Interface PopupMenuPeer

public abstract interface java.awt.peer.PopupMenuPeer implements java.awt.peer.MenuPeer

Fields None

Constructors None

Methods

Modifiers	Return Type	Method
public abstract	void	show(Event)

See Also java.awt.PopupMenu • java.awt.peer.MenuPeer

Interface ScrollbarPeer

public abstract interface java.awt.peer.ScrollbarPeer implements java.awt.peer.ComponentPeer

Fields None

Constructors None

Methods

Modifiers	Return Type	Method
public abstract	void	setLineIncrement(int)
public abstract	void	setPageIncrement(int)
public abstract	void	setValues(int, int, int, int)

See Also java.awt.Scrollbar • java.awt.ComponentPeer

Interface ScrollPanePeer

public abstract interface java.awt.peer.ScrollPanePeer implements java.awt.peer.ContainerPeer

Fields None

Constructors None

Methods

Modifiers	Return Type	Method
public abstract	void	childResized(int, int)
public abstract	int	getHScrollbarHeight()
public abstract	int	getVScrollbarWidth()
public abstract	void	setScrollPosition(int, int)
public abstract	void	setUnitIncrement(Adjustable, int)
public abstract	void	setValue(Adjustable, int)

See Also java.awt.ScrollPane • java.awt.peer.ContainerPeer

Interface TextAreaPeer

public abstract interface java.awt.peer.TextAreaPeer implements java.awt.peer.TextComponentPeer

Fields None

Constructors None

Methods

Modifiers	Return Type	Method
public abstract	Dimension	getMinimumSize(int, int)
public abstract	Dimension	getPreferredSize(int, int)
public abstract	void	insert(String, int)
public abstract	void	insertText(String, int)

Modifiers	Return Type	Method
public abstract	Dimension	minimumSize(int, int)
public abstract	Dimension	preferredSize(int, int)
public abstract	void	replaceRange(String, int, int)
public abstract	void	replaceText(String, int, int)

See Also java.awt.TextArea • java.awt.TextComponentPeer

Interface TextComponentPeer

public abstract interface java.awt.peer.TextComponentPeer implements java.awt.peer.ComponentPeer

Fields None

Constructors None

Methods

Modifiers	Return Type	Method
public abstract	int	getCaretPosition()
public abstract	int	getSelectionEnd()
public abstract	int	getSelectionStart()
public abstract	String	getText()
public abstract	void	select(int, int)
public abstract	void	setCaretPosition(int)
public abstract	void	setEditable(boolean)
public abstract	void	setText(String)

See Also java.awt.TextComponent • java.awt.ComponentPeer

Interface TextFieldPeer

public abstract interface java.awt.peer.TextFieldPeer implements java.awt.peer.TextComponentPeer

Fields None

Constructors None

Methods

Modifiers	Return Type	Method
public abstract	Dimension	getMinimumSize(int)
public abstract	Dimension	getPreferredSize(int)
public abstract	Dimension	minimumSize(int)
public abstract	Dimension	preferredSize(int)
public abstract	void	setEchoChar(char)
public abstract	void	setEchoCharacter(char)

See Also java.awt.TextField • java.awt.peer.ComponentPeer

Interface WindowPeer

public abstract interface java.awt.peer.WindowPeer implements java.awt.peer.ContainerPeer

Fields None

Constructors None

Methods

Modifiers	Return Type	Method
public abstract	void	toBack()
public abstract	void	toFront()

See Also java.awt.Window • java.awt.peer.ContainerPeer

The java.beans Package

7

The java.beans package comprises the JavaBeans API, giving you the ability to create and use reusable software components. Furthermore, the JavaBeans design is neutral from a component architecture standpoint. This means that when you create a bean it can be bridged with other component technologies including:

- ActiveX using Microsoft's Component Object Model (COM)
- Live Object using OpenDoc
- LiveConnect using Netscape Navigator

Class BeanDescriptor

public synchronized java.beans.BeanDescriptor extends java.beans.FeatureDescriptor

The BeanDescriptor class returns global information about a specified bean.

Note

BeanDescriptor is one of the objects that can be returned by a BeanInfo object.

Syntax & Usage The following example uses a BeanDescriptor object to retrieve the actual class for a bean. Then it retrieves the bean's Customizer class (if one is specified):

```
try
{
   Class source = Class.forName("myBean");
   BeanInfo beanInfo = Introspector.
      getBeanInfo(source);
   BeanDescriptor beanDescr = beanInfo.
      getBeanDescriptor();

   Class beanClass = beanDescr.getBeanClass();
   System.out.println("Bean class: "+
      beanClass.getName());
   Class custClass = beanDescr.
      getCustomizerClass();
   if (custClass != null)
      System.out.println("Customizer: "+
         custClass.getName());
}
catch(IntrospectionException e)
{
   System.err.println(
      "IntrospectionException:"+
      e.getMessage());
}
catch(ClassNotFoundException e)
{
   System.err.println(
      "ClassNotFoundException: "+
      e.getMessage());
}
```

This example uses the BeanDescriptor class to retrieve the bean's Java class using the getBeanClass() method from this class. It also uses the getCustomizerClass() method from this class to retrieve information on the customizer for this bean (or **null** if one isn't specified). Notice that Exceptions IntrospectionException and ClassNotFoundException must be caught.

Fields None

Constructors

Modifiers	Constructor
public	BeanDescriptor(Class)
public	BeanDescriptor(Class, Class)

Methods

Modifiers	Return Type	Method
public	Class	getBeanClass()
public	Class	getCustomizerClass()

See Also java.beans.BeanInfo • java.beans.EventSetDescriptor • java.beans.FeatureDescriptor • java.beans.IndexedPropertyDescriptor • java.beans.MethodDescriptor • java.beans.ParameterDescriptor • java.beans.PropertyDescriptor

Interface BeanInfo

public abstract interface java.beans.BeanInfo

The BeanInfo interface is implemented to provide explicit information about a specified bean (i.e. properties, events, and so on).

Syntax & Usage Effectively, when calling this implemented object it returns a descriptor object containing information about the specified bean. This allows you to gather information about a bean explicitly, and it allows the bean to be selective about what behavior it wishes to expose through this interface. Note that this selectiveness is not designed for hiding bean behavior.

> **Tip**
>
> *If you must obtain a complete picture for a given bean, you should use the Introspector interface.*

Please see examples for the BeanDescriptor, MethodDescriptor, and PropertyDescriptor classes, elsewhere in this chapter.

Fields

Modifiers	Type	Field
public static final	int	ICON_COLOR_16x16
public static final	int	ICON_COLOR_32x32
public static final	int	ICON_MONO_16x16
public static final	int	ICON_MONO_32x32

Constructors None

Methods

Modifiers	Return Type	Method
public abstract	BeanInfo[]	getAdditionalBeanInfo()
public abstract	BeanDescriptor	getBeanDescriptor()
public abstract	int	getDefaultEventIndex()
public abstract	int	getDefaultPropertyIndex()
public abstract	EventSetDescriptor[]	getEventSetDescriptors()
public abstract	Image	getIcon(int)
public abstract	MethodDescriptor[]	getMethodDescriptors()
public abstract	PropertyDescriptor[]	getPropertyDescriptors()

See Also java.beans.BeanDescriptor • java.beans.EventSetDescriptor • java.beans.FeatureDescriptor • java.beans.IndexedPropertyDescriptor • java.beans.MethodDescriptor • java.beans.ParameterDescriptor • java.beans.PropertyDescriptor

Class Beans

public synchronized java.beans.Beans extends java.lang.Object

The Beans class is used to facilitate seven basic utility methods used for beans-related purposes. The premise of these methods is to help tailor your bean to its given environment. For example, consider the methods isDesignTime() and setDesignTime(). The former lets you check and the latter lets you set whether a given bean is in an application building environment.

Syntax & Usage The following example uses several **static** methods in this class to verify that the given instance can be represented as the java.awt.Button class. If so, this example adds the given bean as a button:

```
try
{
   myBean btnBean = new myBean();
   Button btn = null;
   Class target = Class.forName("myBean");
   if (Beans.isInstanceOf(btnBean, target))
   {
      btn = (Button)Beans.
         getInstanceOf(btnBean, target);
      add(btn);
   }
}
catch (Exception e) {}
```

Fields None

Constructors

Modifiers	Constructor
public	Beans()

Methods

Modifiers	Return Type	Method
public static	Object	getInstanceOf(Object, Class)
public static	Object	instantiate(ClassLoader, String)
public static	boolean	isDesignTime()
public static	boolean	isGuiAvailable()
public static	boolean	isInstanceOf(Object, Class)
public static	void	setDesignTime(boolean)
public static	void	setGuiAvailable(boolean)

See Also java.lang.Object

Interface Customizer

public abstract interface java.beans.Customizer

The Customizer interface is used to provide a customizer for a Java bean. A customizer is a wizard-like tool used for editing properties in more sophisticated bean components. Any class wishing to be a customizer must implement this interface, and should extend the java.awt.Component class so that it can have a visual presence in a frame or panel in Java.

Note

Customizers also can include property editors for the bean.

Syntax & Usage The following example demonstrates how to implement a Customizer interface in a typical Beans class. It extends a TextField object (thereby indirectly extending the java.awt.Component class) to enter integer values for a bean property. Implementation of the Customizer interface allows myBean class to add and remove PropertyChangeListener objects, while the PropertyChangeSupport instance manages them.

The myBean class holds one property: Integer X. This property can be modified using the setX() method defined in the myBean class, which notifies all registered PropertyChangeListeners by firing a PropertyChangeEvent event. Correspondingly, the X property can be retrieved using the getX() method defined in the Beans class.

You should never modify a bean property directly. Instead, use the appropriate setXXX() (where *XXX* is the name of the property type) methods. This is because the setXXX() method normally notifies all the PropertyChangeListeners and lets any assigned listeners know that a bean property has been changed.

```
class myBean extends TextField
   implements Customizer, TextListener
{
   private Integer X;
   private PropertyChangeSupport m_ChSupp;

   public myBean()
   {
      m_ChSupp = new
         PropertyChangeSupport(this);
      addTextListener(this);
      X = new Integer(0);
   }

   public void setX(Integer value)
   {
      m_ChSupp.firePropertyChange("X",
         X, value);
      X = value;
      setText(String.valueOf(X));
   }

   public Integer getX()
   {
      return X;
   }
```

```
    public void textValueChanged(TextEvent evt)
    {
       try
       {
          int newX = Integer.parseInt(
             getText());
          if (newX != X.intValue())
             setX(new Integer(newX));
       }
       catch(NumberFormatException e)
       {
          setText(String.valueOf(X));
       }
    }

    public void addPropertyChangeListener(
       PropertyChangeListener Listener)
    {
       m_ChSupp.addPropertyChangeListener(
          Listener);
    }

    public void removePropertyChangeListener(
       PropertyChangeListener Listener)
    {
       m_ChSupp.removePropertyChangeListener(
          Listener);
    }

    public void setObject(Object bean) {}

}
```

In this simple example, you use a TextField object to edit an integer value and implement the textValueChanged() method from the TextListener interface. This method verifies that the content of the field represents an integer number. If this number differs from the current property's value, it invokes the setX() method.

Note

If it is not set up in this way (i.e., that setX() only gets called if the new value differs from the old one), an endless loop crops up. Without doing this, the textValueChanged() method would invoke the setX() method, which in turn would display the new property value using the setText() method. This would result in the generation of another TextEvent and result in the calling of the textValueChanged() method again, causing an indefinite loop. That is why to avoid this problem, invoke the setX() method only if the old and new values differ.

The following applet creates and adds a new instance of the myBean class. It then registers itself as a PropertyChangeListener for that bean's object. Finally, the method propertyChange() displays the new value for that property in the Label (see Figure 7-1):

```
public class myApplet extends Applet
   implements PropertyChangeListener
{
   myBean m;
   Label l;

   public void init()
   {
      setLayout(null);
      l = new Label();
      l.setBounds(10, 50, 80, 25);
      add(l);

      m = new myBean();
      m.addPropertyChangeListener(this);
      m.setX(new Integer(50));
      m.setBounds(10, 10, 80, 25);
      add(m);
   }

   public void propertyChange(
      PropertyChangeEvent evt)
   {
      l.setText(evt.getNewValue().toString());
   }
}
```

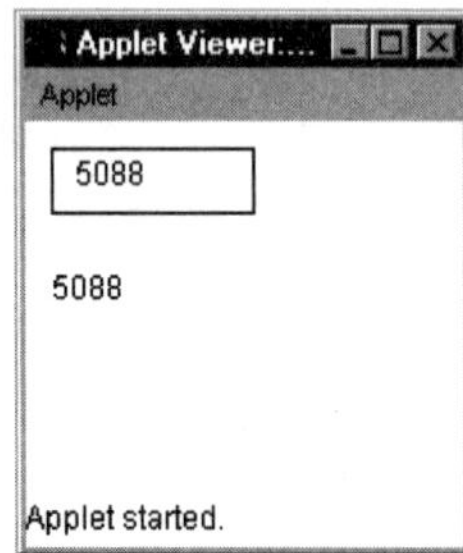

Figure 7-1: Customizer.

Note

Notice how Label gets its initial value. When the setX() method is called, the myApplet instance is already registered as PropertyChangeListener. So, it receives notification back and the propertyChange() method sets the value 50 to the Label.

Fields None

Constructors None

Methods

Modifiers	Return Type	Method
public abstract	void	addPropertyChangeListener(PropertyChangeListener)
public abstract	void	removePropertyChangeListener(PropertyChangeListener)
public abstract	void	setObject(Object)

See Also java.beans.PropertyChangeEvent • java.beans.PropertyChangeListener • java.beans.PropertyChangeSupport • java.beans.PropertyEditor • java.beans.PropertyEditorManager • java.beans.PropertyEditorSupport

Class EventSetDescriptor

public synchronized java.beans.EventSetDescriptor extends java.beans.FeatureDescriptor

The EventSetDescriptor class is used to describe the events, listeners, and any add*XXX*Listener() or remove*XXX*Listener() methods for a specified bean.

Syntax & Usage The following example uses the EventSetDescriptor class to retrieve information about registered events and their listeners and the add*XXX*Listener() and remove*XXX*Listener() methods for a specified bean:

```
try
{
  Class source = Class.forName("myBean");
  BeanInfo beanInfo = Introspector.
    getBeanInfo(source);
  BeanDescriptor beanDescr = beanInfo.
    getBeanDescriptor();
```

```
    EventSetDescriptor[] events =
      beanInfo.getEventSetDescriptors();
    if (events != null)
      for (int k=0; k<events.length; k++)
      {
        Class listener = events[k].
          getListenerType();
        if (listener!=null)
          System.out.println(
          "Listener:\t"+listener.
          getName());
        Method add = events[k].
          getAddListenerMethod();
        if (add!=null)
          System.out.println(
            "Add method:\t"+add.
            toString());
        Method remove = events[k].
          getRemoveListenerMethod();
        if (remove!=null)
          System.out.println(
            "Remove method:\t"+
            remove.toString());
      }
  }
  catch(IntrospectionException e)
  {
    System.err.println(
      "IntrospectionException:"+
      e.getMessage());
  }
  catch(ClassNotFoundException e)
  {
    System.err.println(
      "ClassNotFoundException: "+
      e.getMessage());
  }
```

Fields None

Constructors

Modifiers	Constructor
public	EventSetDescriptor(Class, String, Class, String)
public	EventSetDescriptor(Class, String, Class, String[], String, String)
public	EventSetDescriptor(String, Class, MethodDescriptor[], Method, Method)
public	EventSetDescriptor(String, Class, Method[], Method, Method)

Methods

Modifiers	Return Type	Method
public	Method	getAddListenerMethod()
public	MethodDescriptor[]	getListenerMethodDescriptors()
public	Method[]	getListenerMethods()
public	Class	getListenerType()
public	Method	getRemoveListenerMethod()
public	boolean	isInDefaultEventSet()
public	boolean	isUnicast()
public	void	setInDefaultEventSet(boolean)
public	void	setUnicast(boolean)

See Also java.beans.BeanDescriptor • java.beans.BeanInfo • java.beans.FeatureDescriptor • java.beans.IndexedPropertyDescriptor • java.beans.MethodDescriptor • java.beans.ParameterDescriptor • java.beans.PropertyDescriptor

Class FeatureDescriptor

public synchronized java.beans.FeatureDescriptor extends java.lang.Object

The FeatureDescriptor class is the root class for descriptor classes that are used by beans to facilitate information about themselves.

Syntax & Usage This class is the superclass for the following descriptor classes:

- java.beans.BeanDescriptor
- java.beans.EventSetDescriptor
- java.beans.IndexedPropertyDescriptor
- java.beans.MethodDescriptor
- java.beans.ParameterDescriptor
- java.beans.PropertyDescriptor

This class defines the commonalties that are used by all introspection-based descriptor classes. The FeatureDescriptor class also provides the ability to associate various attribute/value pairs with a design pattern.

For more information, please see the previous classes in this chapter. For examples of usage, please see the the BeanDescriptor, MethodDescriptor, and PropertyDescriptor classes, specifically.

Fields None

Constructors

Modifiers	Constructor
public	FeatureDescriptor()

Methods

Modifiers	Return Type	Method
public	Enumeration	attributeNames()
public	String	getDisplayName()
public	String	getName()
public	String	getShortDescription()
public	Object	getValue(String)
public	boolean	isExpert()
public	boolean	isHidden()
public	void	setDisplayName(String)
public	void	setExpert(boolean)
public	void	setHidden(boolean)
public	void	setName(String)
public	void	setShortDescription(String)
public	void	setValue(String, Object)

See Also java.beans.BeanDescriptor • java.beans.BeanInfo • java.beans.EventSetDescriptor • java.beans.IndexedPropertyDescriptor • java.beans.MethodDescriptor • java.beans.ParameterDescriptor • java.beans.PropertyDescriptor • java.lang.Object

Class IndexedPropertyDescriptor

public synchronized java.beans.IndexedPropertyDescriptor extends java.beans.PropertyDescriptor

The IndexedPropertyDescriptor is used to describe any indexed (i.e., array-like) properties for a given bean. Usually, this class also describes the necessary methods that give you the ability to read or write to a specific element in the indexed property.

This class may also return information about generic read*XXX*()/write*XXX*() methods (if available) that address the array-like property in its entirety.

Syntax & Usage The following code snippet uses this class to retrieve information about the read*XXX*() and write*XXX*() methods of the indexed properties contained in a given PropertyDescriptor object.

Please also see the example under "Class PropertyDescriptor," later in this chapter.

```
PropertyDescriptor prop;
if (prop instanceof IndexedPropertyDescriptor)
{
  IndexedPropertyDescriptor indProp =
    (IndexedPropertyDescriptor)prop;
  Method mRead = indProp.
    getIndexedReadMethod();
  if (mRead != null)
    System.out.println(
      "Read method:\t"+mRead.toString());
  Method mWrite = indProp.
    getIndexedWriteMethod();
  if (mWrite != null)
    System.out.println(
      "Write method:\t"+
      mWrite.toString());
}
```

Fields None

Constructors

Modifiers	Constructor
public	IndexedPropertyDescriptor(String, Class)
public	IndexedPropertyDescriptor(String, Class, String, String, String, String)
public	IndexedPropertyDescriptor(String, Method, Method, Method, Method)

Methods

Modifiers	Return Type	Method
public	Class	getIndexedPropertyType()
public	Method	getIndexedReadMethod()
public	Method	getIndexedWriteMethod()

See Also java.beans.BeanDescriptor • java.beans.BeanInfo • java.beans.EventSetDescriptor • java.beans.FeatureDescriptor • java.beans.MethodDescriptor • java.beans.ParameterDescriptor • java.beans.PropertyDescriptor

Class IntrospectionException

public synchronized java.beans.IntrospectionException extends java.lang.Exception

The IntrospectionException class is thrown anytime an introspection-related exception occurs.

Syntax & Usage For examples of where this exception is potentially caught, please see the BeanDescriptor, MethodDescriptor, and PropertyDescriptor classes.

Fields None

Constructors

Modifiers	Constructor
public	IntrospectionException(String)

Methods None

See Also java.lang.Exception

Class Introspector

public synchronized java.beans.Introspector extends java.lang.Object

The Introspector class facilitates a uniform and comprehensive way to gather information on the methods, properties, and events of a specified bean.

Syntax & Usage This class works by "walking" through the bean and its superclasses, looking for explicit and implicit information, and returning all of its results as a new BeanInfo instance. The explicit process involves using a design pattern to look for any implemented instances of the BeanInfo class and gathering any information about the bean contained therein. The implicit process involves using the low-level reflection to introspect the bean class and its superclasses.

Please see the examples for the BeanDescriptor, MethodDescriptor, and PropertyDescriptor classes, elsewhere in this chapter.

Fields None

Constructors None

Methods

Modifiers	Return Type	Constructor
public static	String	decapitalize(String)
public static	BeanInfo	getBeanInfo(Class)
public static	BeanInfo	getBeanInfo(Class, Class)
public static	String[]	getBeanInfoSearchPath()
public static	void	setBeanInfoSearchPath(String[])

See Also java.beans.BeanDescriptor • java.beans.BeanInfo • java.beans.MethodDescriptor • java.beans.PropertyDescriptor • java.lang.Object

Class MethodDescriptor

public synchronized java.beans.MethodDescriptor extends java.beans.FeatureDescriptor

The MethodDescriptor class is used to facilitate information about a method supported by the specified bean's class.

Syntax & Usage The following example uses this class to retrieve the methods in a specified bean by using the getMethodDescriptors() method from the BeanInfo class and returning only the methods defined in the bean's class and none of the inherited ones. Note that exceptions IntrospectionException and ClassNotFoundException must be caught:

```
try
{
  Class source = Class.forName("myBean");
  BeanInfo beanInfo = Introspector.
    getBeanInfo(source);

  MethodDescriptor[] beanMethods = beanInfo.
    getMethodDescriptors();
```

```
    if (beanMethods != null)
      for (int k=0; k<beanMethods.length; k++)
      {
        Method mthd =
          beanMethods[k].getMethod();
        if (mthd.getDeclaringClass()==
          beanClass)
        {
        System.out.println(
          "\t"+mthd.toString());
        ParameterDescriptor[] params =
          beanMethods[k].
          getParameterDescriptors();
        if (params != null)
          for (int i=0; i<params.length;
            i++)
          {
            String str = params[i].
              getDisplayName();
            if (str != null)
              System.out.println(
                "\t\t"+str);
          }
        }
      }
  }
  catch(IntrospectionException e)
  {
    System.err.println(
      "IntrospectionException:"+
      e.getMessage());
  }
  catch(ClassNotFoundException e)
  {
    System.err.println(
      "ClassNotFoundException: "+
      e.getMessage());
  }
```

Fields None

Constructors

Modifiers	Constructor
public	MethodDescriptor(Method)
public	MethodDescriptor(Method, ParameterDescriptor[])

Methods

Modifiers	Return Type	Method
public	Method	getMethod()
public	ParameterDescriptor[]	getParameterDescriptors()

See Also java.beans.BeanDescriptor • java.beans.BeanInfo • java.beans.EventSetDescriptor • java.beans.FeatureDescriptor • java.beans.IndexedPropertyDescriptor • java.beans.ParameterDescriptor • java.beans.PropertyDescriptor

Class ParameterDescriptor

public synchronized java.beans.ParameterDescriptor extends java.beans.FeatureDescriptor

The ParameterDescriptor class is used to facilitate extra information (beyond what normally is attained using reflection and the java.lang.reflect.Method class) on a parameter for a specified bean.

Syntax & Usage Aside from one **public** constructor, this class looks empty. That's because the methods and other functionality you need to use this class are inherited from the FeatureDescriptor class. Please see that class for more information.

Also, please see the example in the previous section, "Class MethodDescriptor."

Fields None

Constructors

Modifiers	Constructor
public	ParameterDescriptor()

Methods None

See Also java.beans.BeanDescriptor • java.beans.BeanInfo • java.beans.EventSetDescriptor • java.beans.FeatureDescriptor • java.beans.IndexedPropertyDescriptor • java.beans.MethodDescriptor • java.beans.PropertyDescriptor

Class PropertyChangeEvent

public synchronized java.beans.PropertyChangeEvent extends java.util.EventObject

The PropertyChangeEvent class represents an event that gets delivered when a constrained or bound property changes in value. Usually, PropertyChangeEvent objects contain a reference to the source bean, the property name, and the old and new values for the property.

A **null** value can be substituted for the old and/or the new property value if they are unavailable. Also, **null** can be used for notification that more than one property has been changed. In that case, **null** would also be specified for the property name and the old and new property values. If the old or new value happens to be a primitive type, it must be wrapped in a corresponding object type.

Syntax & Usage Depending on the type of property, there are two listeners that you use to receive notification for this event:

- If the property is a bound one, you use a PropertyChangeListener object to receive the property change event notification. (A bound property is one that provides change notification to its container or another bean component.) This is done through event handling—a PropertyChangeEvent object is passed to a PropertyChangeListener listener interface if the value of the source property has changed.

  The JavaBeans API also facilitates the PropertyChangeSupport class, which is used to keep track of all the property change listeners that are currently available and to fire the actual property change events.
- If the property is a constrained one, you use a VetoableChangeListener object to receive property change events. Constrained properties facilitate transaction-like functionality wherein a property for a bean component needs to either (1) validate the updated value or (2) reject it, throw the PropertyVetoException, and revert back to the original value.

  Basically, you use a VetoableChangeListener object to report when a constrained property has been updated, and you use the VetoableChangeSupport class to keep track of veto change listeners and to fire property change events.

For an example of this class in action, please see "Interface Customizer," earlier in this chapter.

Fields None

Constructors

Modifiers	Constructor
public	PropertyChangeEvent(Object, String, Object, Object)

Methods

Modifiers	Return Type	Method
public	Object	getNewValue()
public	Object	getOldValue()
public	Object	getPropagationId()
public	String	getPropertyName()
public	void	setPropagationId(Object)

See Also java.beans.PropertyChangeListener • java.beans.PropertyChangeSupport • java.beans.PropertyVetoException • java.beans.VetoableChangeListener • java.beans.VetoableChangeSupport • java.util.EventObject

Interface PropertyChangeListener

public abstract interface java.beans.PropertyChangeListener implements java.util.EventListener

The PropertyChangeListener interface is used for listening to bounded bean properties to see when a PropertyChangeEvent object will be delivered. This happens when the designated property changes in value.

Syntax & Usage You can specify this object to listen to an entire bean so you can receive notification if any bound property in the designated bean changes in value.

Please see the example under "Interface Customizer," earlier in this chapter.

Fields None

Constructors None

Methods

Modifiers	Return Type	Method
public abstract	void	propertyChange(PropertyChangeEvent)

See Also java.beans.Customizer • java.beans.PropertyChangeEvent • java.util.EventListener

Class PropertyChangeSupport

public synchronized java.beans.PropertyChangeSupport extends java.lang.Object implements java.io.Serializable

The PropertyChangeSupport class is used to keep track of all the property change listeners that are currently available for bounded bean properties and to fire the actual property change events.

Syntax & Usage

This class is used in conjunction with beans containing bounded properties. Usually, you extend this class's functionality by subclassing it or instantiating an object in this class as a field in your bean.

Please see "Interface Customizer," earlier in this chapter, for an example of usage.

Fields

None

Constructors

Modifiers	Constructor
public	PropertyChangeSupport(Object)

Methods

Modifiers	Return Type	Method
public synchronized	void	addPropertyChangeListener(PropertyChangeListener)
public	void	firePropertyChange(String, Object, Object)
public synchronized	void	removePropertyChangeListener(PropertyChangeListener)

See Also

java.beans.Customizer • java.beans.PropertyChangeEvent • java.beans.PropertyChangeListener • java.io.Serializable • java.lang.Object

Class PropertyDescriptor

public synchronized java.beans.PropertyDescriptor extends java.beans.FeatureDescriptor

The PropertyDescriptor class is used to facilitate information about an exported (via accessor method, e.g., get*XXX*() and set*XXX*()) property for a specified bean.

Syntax & Usage The following example uses the PropertyDescriptor class to retrieve the property *Ben*, including the read*XXX*() and write*XXX*() methods for the property:

```
try
{
   Class source = Class.forName("myBean");
   BeanInfo beanInfo = Introspector.
      getBeanInfo(source);

   PropertyDescriptor[] beanPropr =
      beanInfo.getPropertyDescriptors();
   if (beanPropr != null)
      for (int k=0; k<beanPropr.length; k++)
      {
         System.out.println("Property: "+
            beanPropr[k].getName());
         Method mthdGet = beanPropr[k].
            getReadMethod();
         if (mthdGet!=null)
            System.out.println(
            "\t"+mthdGet.toString());
         Method mthdSet = beanPropr[k].
            getWriteMethod();
         if (mthdSet!=null)
            System.out.println(
            "\t"+mthdSet.toString());
      }
}
```

```
catch(IntrospectionException e)
{
   System.err.println(
      "IntrospectionException:"+
      e.getMessage());
}
catch(ClassNotFoundException e)
{
   System.err.println(
      "ClassNotFoundException: "+
      e.getMessage());
}
```

Fields None

Constructors

Modifiers	Constructor
public	PropertyDescriptor(String, Class)
public	PropertyDescriptor(String, Class, String, String)
public	PropertyDescriptor(String, Method, Method)

Methods

Modifiers	Return Type	Method
public	Class	getPropertyEditorClass()
public	Class	getPropertyType()
public	Method	getReadMethod()
public	Method	getWriteMethod()
public	boolean	isBound()
public	boolean	isConstrained()
public	void	setBound(boolean)
public	void	setConstrained(boolean)
public	void	setPropertyEditorClass(Class)

See Also java.beans.BeanDescriptor • java.beans.BeanInfo • java.beans.EventSetDescriptor • java.beans.FeatureDescriptor • java.beans.IndexedPropertyDescriptor • java.beans.MethodDescriptor • java.beans.ParameterDescriptor

Interface PropertyEditor

public abstract interface java.beans.PropertyEditor

The PropertyEditor interface defines the semantics of a property editor. A property editor lets the user graphically change a given bean property for a specified data type. Property editors facilitate a variety of ways to edit a property and a bean's implementation does not have to support them all.

Note

For customization in your Java bean, you usually use one or more property editors. However, in a professional component editor or graphical user interface (GUI) builder, editors can be scattered coming from a variety of places. Therefore, most of these professional environments should put all the properties for a given bean into one property sheet.

Syntax & Usage Please see the example under "Class PropertyEditorSupport," later in this chapter.

Fields None

Constructors None

Methods

Modifiers	Return Type	Method
public abstract	void	addPropertyChangeListener(PropertyChangeListener)
public abstract	String	getAsText()
public abstract	Component	getCustomEditor()
public abstract	String	getJavaInitializationString()
public abstract	String[]	getTags()
public abstract	Object	getValue()
public abstract	boolean	isPaintable()
public abstract	void	paintValue(Graphics, Rectangle)
public abstract	void	removePropertyChangeListener(PropertyChangeListener)
public abstract	void	setAsText(String)
public abstract	void	setValue(Object)
public abstract	boolean	supportsCustomEditor()

See Also java.beans.PropertyChangeEvent • java.beans.PropertyChangeListener • java.beans.PropertyChangeSupport • java.beans.PropertyEditorManager • java.beans.PropertyEditorSupport

Class PropertyEditorManager

public synchronized java.beans.PropertyEditorManager extends java.lang.Object

The PropertyEditorManager class is used to locate the appropriate property editors that have been facilitated by the bean developer and by an application builder environment. This class also is responsible for maintaining a registry of available property editors for each type.

Syntax & Usage

This class lets you explicitly register a Java class as a property editor for a given type, using the registerEditor() method. Alternatively, if an appropriate type was not explicitly registered, this class will search for a property editor by property type name, or if that fails it will append "Editor" to the property type and look for the editor in the specified package. Finally, if that doesn't work, it appends "Editor" to the property type and looks for it in a property editor package based on a search path.

Note

The Beans Development Kit comes with preloaded property editors registered for the following types: byte, short, int, long, boolean, float, double, java.lang.String, java.awt.Color, java.awt.Font.

The following code snippet uses the **static** method findEditor() from the PropertyEditorManager class to retrieve a PropertyEditor for the specified bean:

```
try
{
   Class target = Class.forName("myBean");
   PropertyEditor editor = PropertyEditorManager.findEditor(target);
   // Use PropertyEditor
}
catch(ClassNotFoundException e)
{
   System.err.println(
      "ClassNotFoundException: "+
      e.getMessage());
}
```

Fields None

Constructors

Modifiers	Constructor
public	PropertyEditorManager()

Methods

Modifiers	Return Type	Method
public static	PropertyEditor	findEditor(Class)
public static	String[]	getEditorSearchPath()
public static	void	registerEditor(Class, Class)
public static	void	setEditorSearchPath(String[])

See Also java.awt.Color • java.awt.Font • java.beans.PropertyChangeEvent • java.beans.PropertyChangeListener • java.beans.PropertyChangeSupport • java.beans.PropertyEditor • java.beans.PropertyEditorSupport • java.lang.Object • java.lang.String

Class PropertyEditorSupport

public synchronized java.beans.PropertyEditorSupport extends java.lang.Object implements java.beans.PropertyEditor

The PropertyEditorSupport class implements the PropertyEditor interface, allowing you to extend it and use it to edit a property in your own bean without having to implement all the methods in the PropertyEditor interface.

Syntax & Usage This implementation of the PropertyEditor interface uses this class to avoid overriding all methods of that interface. The editor allows editing of the property Integer X in the following three ways:

- Using the pair of setValue() and getValue() methods specifying Integer arguments.
- Using the pair of setAsText() and getAsText() methods specifying String arguments.
- Using a graphical interface approach in which the paintValue() method draws the current value in the specifier Rectangle. Also, the isPaintable() method must return true in this case.

The method getJavaInitializationString() returns the current property as a String suitable for initialization of Java object in the program's text:

```
class MyEditor extends PropertyEditorSupport
{
  private Integer X = new Integer(0);

  public void setValue(Object value)
  {
    if (value instanceof Integer)
      X = (Integer)value;
  }

  public Object getValue()
  {
    return (Object)X;
  }

  public void setAsText(String text)
    throws IllegalArgumentException
  {
    try
    {
      int newX = Integer.parseInt(text);
      X = new Integer(newX);
    }
    catch(NumberFormatException e)
    {
      throw new IllegalArgumentException(
        "Illegal value for X");
    }
  }

  public String getAsText()
  {
    return X.toString();
  }

  public String getJavaInitializationString()
  {
    return X.toString();
  }
```

```
   public boolean isPaintable()
   {
      return true;
   }

   public void paintValue(Graphics g,
      Rectangle rc)
   {
      g.drawString(X.toString(), rc.x,
         rc.y+rc.height-2);
   }
}
```

Fields None

Constructors

Modifiers	Constructor
protected	PropertyEditorSupport()
protected	PropertyEditorSupport(Object)

Methods

Modifiers	Return Type	Method
public synchronized	void	addPropertyChangeListener(PropertyChangeListener)
public	void	firePropertyChange()
public	String	getAsText()
public	Component	getCustomEditor()
public	String	getJavaInitializationString()
public	String[]	getTags()
public	Object	getValue()
public	boolean	isPaintable()
public	void	paintValue(Graphics, Rectangle)
public synchronized	void	removePropertyChangeListener(PropertyChangeListener)
public	void	setAsText(String)
public	void	setValue(Object)
public	boolean	supportsCustomEditor()

See Also java.beans.PropertyChangeEvent • java.beans.PropertyChangeListener • java.beans.PropertyChangeSupport • java.beans.PropertyEditor • java.beans.PropertyEditorManager • java.lang.Object

Class PropertyVetoException

public synchronized java.beans.PropertyVetoException extends java.lang.Exception

This exception class is thrown when the intended new value of a constrained bean property is outside the specified range.

Syntax & Usage Please see the example under "Class VetoableChangeSupport," later in this chapter.

Fields None

Constructors

Modifiers	Constructor
public	PropertyVetoException(String, PropertyChangeEvent)

Methods

Modifiers	Return Type	Method
public	PropertyChangeEvent	getPropertyChangeEvent()

See Also java.beans.VetoableChangeListener • java.beans.VetoableChangeSupport • java.lang.Exception

Class SimpleBeanInfo

public synchronized java.beans.SimpleBeanInfo extends java.lang.Object implements java.beans.BeanInfo

The SimpleBeanInfo class is a supporting class of the BeanInfo class. It facilities an easier way to allow BeanInfo classes to give explicit information on a bean.

This class always defaults with denying that it has explicit information on a requested item for the specified bean. The Introspector class uses this as a cue to invoke low-level reflective introspection and design patterns on the bean.

Syntax & Usage Please see the examples for the BeanDescriptor, MethodDescriptor, and PropertyDescriptor classes earlier in this chapter.

Fields None

Constructors

Modifiers	Constructor
public	SimpleBeanInfo()

Methods

Modifiers	Return Type	Method
public	BeanInfo[]	getAdditionalBeanInfo()
public	BeanDescriptor	getBeanDescriptor()
public	int	getDefaultEventIndex()
public	int	getDefaultPropertyIndex()
public	EventSetDescriptor[]	getEventSetDescriptors()
public	Image	getIcon(int)
public	MethodDescriptor[]	getMethodDescriptors()
public	PropertyDescriptor[]	getPropertyDescriptors()
public	Image	loadImage(String)

See Also java.beans.BeanDescriptor • java.beans.BeanInfo • java.beans.MethodDescriptor • java.beans.PropertyDescriptor • java.lang.Object

Interface VetoableChangeListener

public abstract interface java.beans.VetoableChangeListener implements java.util.EventListener

The VetoableChangeListener interface is used for listening to constrained bean properties to see when a PropertyChangeEvent object will be delivered, which happens when the designated property changes in value.

Syntax & Usage You can specify this object to listen to an entire bean so that you receive notification if any constrained property in the designated bean changes in value.

Please see the example in the next section, "Class VetoableChangeSupport."

Fields None

Constructors None

Methods

Modifiers	Return Type	Method
public abstract	void	vetoableChange(PropertyChangeEvent)

See Also java.beans.PropertyVetoException • java.beans.VetoableChangeSupport • java.util.EventListener

Class VetoableChangeSupport

public synchronized java.beans.VetoableChangeSupport extends java.lang.Object implements java.io.Serializable

The VetoableChangeSupport class is used to keep track of all the property change listeners available to constrained bean properties and to fire the actual property change events.

Syntax & Usage This class is used in conjunction with bounded bean properties. You extend this class's functionality by subclassing it or by instantiating an object of this class as a field in your bean.

This example modifies the program shown under "Interface Customizer," earlier in the chapter, to support vetoable changes to the bean's property (i.e., make it a constrained property). It holds a VetoableChangeSupport object, which adds and removes VetoableChangeListeners. The method setX() in this example throws PropertyVetoException if the value passed lies outside the permitted interval (1-100):

> **Note**
>
> *You have to catch PropertyVetoException every time you modify a constrained property.*

```
class myBean extends TextField
  implements TextListener
{
  private Integer X;
  private VetoableChangeSupport m_ChSupp;
```

```
public myBean()
{
   m_ChSupp = new
      VetoableChangeSupport(this);
   addTextListener(this);
   X = new Integer(0);
}

public void setX(Integer value)
   throws PropertyVetoException
{
   int newX = value.intValue();
   if (newX<0 || newX>100)
      throw new PropertyVetoException(
      "Allowed values: 0 - 100",
      new PropertyChangeEvent(
      this, "X", X, X) );

   m_ChSupp.fireVetoableChange("X",
      X, value);
   X = value;
   setText(String.valueOf(X));
}

public Integer getX()
{
   return X;
}

public void textValueChanged(TextEvent evt)
{
   try
   {
      int newX = Integer.parseInt(
         getText());
      if (newX != X.intValue())
         setX(new Integer(newX));
   }
   catch(Exception e)
   {
      setText(String.valueOf(X));
   }
}

public void addVetoableChangeListener(
   VetoableChangeListener Listener)
{
```

```
        m_ChSupp.addVetoableChangeListener(
            Listener);
    }

    public void removeVetoableChangeListener(
        VetoableChangeListener Listener)
    {
        m_ChSupp.removeVetoableChangeListener(
            Listener);
    }
}
```

The following creates the applet myApplet to exemplify how you would use the Customizer interface. It also implements the VetoableChangeListener interface to support vetoable changes to the constrained bean property. You can control the value for this bean so that it cannot be moved outside the defined interval 1-100.

```
public class myApplet extends Applet
    implements VetoableChangeListener
{
    myBean m;
    Label l;

    public void init()
    {
        setLayout(null);
        l = new Label();
        l.setBounds(10, 50, 80, 25);
        add(l);

        m = new myBean();
        m.addVetoableChangeListener(this);
        try
        {
            m.setX(new Integer(50));
        }
        catch(PropertyVetoException e) {}
        m.setBounds(10, 10, 80, 25);
        add(m);
    }

    public void vetoableChange(
        PropertyChangeEvent evt)
    {
        l.setText(evt.getNewValue().toString());
    }
}
```

Fields None

Constructors

Modifiers	Constructor
public	VetoableChangeSupport(Object)

Methods

Modifiers	Return Type	Method
public synchronized	void	addVetoableChangeListener(VetoableChangeListener)
public	void	fireVetoableChange(String, Object, Object)
public synchronized	void	removeVetoableChangeListener(VetoableChangeListener)

See Also java.beans.PropertyVetoException • java.beans.VetoableChangeListener • java.io.Serializable • java.lang.Object

Interface Visibility

public abstract interface java.beans.Visibility

This class is used only for high-end bean components that are designed to run in different states. Some states may allow for a GUI of the bean to be present while others may not (i.e., if the bean is executed on a server).

Syntax & Usage This interface defines a set of methods that beans can use to determine the GUI relationship for the bean.

> **Note**
>
> *These methods do not follow the standard design pattern get/set method name format used in other parts of the JavaBeans API.*

The following example shows the class myBean, which can run with the GUI interface and without GUI (automatically) to indicate that it implements the Visibility interface:

```
class myBean implements Visibility
{
  boolean m_bUseGUI = true;
```

```
    public boolean needsGui()
    {
      return false;
    }

    public void dontUseGui()
    {
      m_bUseGUI = false;
    }

    public void okToUseGui()
    {
      m_bUseGUI = true;
    }

    public boolean avoidingGui()
    {
      return !m_bUseGUI;
    }
}
```

The variable m_bUseGUI is a flag showing whether to use GUI. It can be modified by dontUseGui() and okToUseGui() methods. The method needsGui() returns false since this class can run without GUI. The method avoidingGui() returns **false** if this class is currently avoiding GUI.

Fields None

Constructors None

Methods

Modifiers	Return Type	Method
public abstract	boolean	avoidingGui()
public abstract	void	dontUseGui()
public abstract	boolean	needsGui()
public abstract	void	okToUseGui()

See Also java.beans.Customizer • java.beans.PropertyEditor

The java.io Package

8

The java.io package ranks as one of the larger packages in the Java Class Library. It contains the functionality for any kind of input/output that you would use in Java, including the ability to send and retrieve data from streams—streams you can use to communicate with files, network connections, pipes, and so on.

Java 1.1 has introduced two new bodies of classes to this package. The first body is a collection of reader- and writer-based classes that have been added to support Java in its internationalization efforts by supporting full 16-bit Unicode character-encoding sets. The second body of classes added to this package deals with object serialization and the ability to send and receive objects over a stream.

Note

The internationalization and object serialization classes have been flagged with icons noting the category to which they belong.

Class BufferedInputStream

public synchronized java.io.BufferedInputStream extends java.io.FilterInputStream

The BufferedInputStream is a FilterInputStream subclass that lets you use internal buffers to store data coming in from an input stream.

Syntax & Usage

Buffered input streams come in handy for improving the efficiency of your incoming data by storing them in a buffer. So, when your Java program requests data from the stream, they can be retrieved more quickly from the buffer.

The following example shows how to use the BufferedInputStream class by creating a BufferedInputStream object based on a FileInputStream object and a buffer size of 512 bytes:

```
try
{
   FileInputStream fi = new FileInputStream(
      "myFile.txt");
   BufferedInputStream bi = new
      BufferedInputStream(fi, 512);
   byte[] buffer = new byte[512];
   while (bi.available() > 0)
   {
      int n = bi.read(buffer, 0,
         buffer.length);
      String str = new String(buffer, 0, n);
      System.out.print(str);
   }
   fi.close();
}
catch (FileNotFoundException e)
{
   System.err.println("File not found");
}
catch (IOException e)
{
   System.err.println("IO error");
}
```

This snippet of code starts by instantiating a FileInputStream object (fi) and a BufferedInputStream object (bi) specifying the FileInputStream object in bi's constructor. Then, using the read() method, bi reads up to 512 bytes from the BufferedInputStream instance, which then is converted into a String object.

Note

Reading data into a buffer does not necessarily mean that you have retrieved a complete line of text. The buffer will fill up to its limit, possibly stopping in the middle of text.

Finally, this String is displayed using the System.out.print() method. Notice that the exceptions FileNotFoundException and IOException must be handled.

Fields

Modifiers	Type	Field
protected	byte[]	buf
protected	int	count
protected	int	marklimit
protected	int	markpos
protected	int	pos

Constructors

Modifiers	Constructor
public	BufferedInputStream(InputStream)
public	BufferedInputStream(InputStream, int)

Methods

Modifiers	Return Type	Method
public synchronized	int	available()
public synchronized	void	mark(int)
public	boolean	markSupported()
public synchronized	int	read()
public synchronized	int	read(byte[], int, int)
public synchronized	void	reset()
public synchronized	long	skip(long)

See Also java.io.BufferedOutputStream • java.io.FileInputStream • java.io.FilterInputStream

Class BufferedOutputStream

public synchronized java.io.BufferedOutputStream extends java.io.FilterOutputStream

The BufferedOutputStream is a FilterOutputStream subclass that lets you use internal buffers to store the data that you intend to send out. It is not until the buffer fills up or you explicitly call the flush() method that the data are emptied from the buffer and sent to the output stream.

Syntax & Usage

Buffered output streams can come in handy for improving the efficiency of your outgoing data by storing them in a buffer. Therefore, when the buffer fills up (or it is explicitly emptied via the flush() method), the data will be sent in one call to the output stream (rather than having to hit the output stream every time a byte is to be sent).

The following example shows how to use the BufferedOutputStream class by creating a buffered output stream to the specified file and sending the specified array of text. Using a 512-byte buffer, the method calls the output stream only after the buffer has been filled:

```
static boolean writeText(String fName,
  String[] text)
{
  try
  {
    FileOutputStream fo = new
      FileOutputStream(fName);
    BufferedOutputStream bo = new
      BufferedOutputStream(fo, 512);
    for (int k=0; k<text.length; k++)
    {
      String str = text[k] + "\n";
      byte[] buffer = str.getBytes();
      bo.write(buffer, 0, buffer.length);
    }
    bo.flush();
    fo.close();
    return true;
  }
  catch (IOException e)
  {
    System.err.println("IO error");
    return false;
  }
}
```

This snippet of code starts by instantiating a FileOutputStream object (fo) and a BufferedOutputStream object (bo) specifying the FileOutputStream object in bo's constructor. Then, the code uses the getBytes() method to retrieve the individual bytes contained in the string array and send them to the output buffer using the write() method. Once 512 bytes have been filled in the buffer, it will empty the buffer to the actual output stream.

Finally, the code calls the flush() method to make sure any data remaining in the buffer are sent to the output stream and a call to the close() method to close the output stream. Notice that the IOException exception must be handled.

Fields

Modifiers	Type	Field
protected	byte[]	buf
protected	int	count

Constructors

Modifiers	Constructor
public	BufferedOutputStream(OutputStream)
public	BufferedOutputStream(OutputStream, int)

Methods

Modifiers	Return Type	Method
public synchronized	void	flush()
public synchronized	void	write(byte[], int, int)
public synchronized	void	write(int)

See Also java.io.BufferedInputStream • java.io.FileOutputStream • java.io.FilterOutputStream

Class BufferedReader

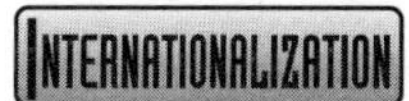

public synchronized java.io.BufferedReader extends java.io.Reader

The BufferedReader class is a Reader subclass that lets you use internal buffers to store data (which can be characters, arrays, or lines) coming in from a character input stream.

Syntax & Usage Buffered readers can come in handy for improving the efficiency of your incoming data by storing them in a buffer. So, when your Java program requests data from the stream using read() or readLine(), they can be retrieved more quickly from the buffer. Please see the example under "Class LineNumberReader," later in this chapter.

Fields None

Constructors

Modifiers	Constructor
public	BufferedReader(Reader)
public	BufferedReader(Reader, int)

Methods

Modifiers	Return Type	Method
public	void	close()
public	void	mark(int)
public	boolean	markSupported()
public	int	read()
public	int	read(char[], int, int)
public	String	readLine()
public	boolean	ready()
public	void	reset()
public	long	skip(long)

See Also java.io.BufferedWriter • java.io.Reader

Class BufferedWriter

public synchronized java.io.BufferedWriter extends java.io.Writer

The BufferedWriter class is a Writer subclass that lets you use internal buffers to store the data (characters, arrays, and strings) that you intend to send out to a character stream. It is not until the buffer fills up or you explicitly call the flush() method that the data are emptied from the buffer and sent to the character output stream.

Syntax & Usage Buffered writers come in handy for improving the efficiency of your outgoing data by storing them in a buffer. Therefore, when the buffer fills up (or it is explicitly emptied via the flush() method), the data is sent in one call to the output stream (rather than having to call the output stream for each byte to be sent).

The following example shows how to use the BufferedWriter class by creating a buffered output stream to the FileWriter object and sending the specified array of text. Using a 512-byte buffer, the method calls the output stream only after the buffer has been filled:

```
static boolean writeText(String fName,
   String[] text)
{
   try
   {
      FileWriter fw = new
         FileWriter(fName);
      BufferedWriter bw = new
         BufferedWriter(fw, 512);
      for (int k=0; k<text.length; k++)
      {
         bw.write(text[k], 0,
            text[k].length());
         if (k<text.length-1)
            bw.newLine();
      }
      bw.flush();
      fw.close();
      return true;
   }
   catch (IOException e)
   {
      System.err.println("IO error");
      return false;
   }
}
```

This snippet of code starts by instantiating a FileWriter object (fw) and a BufferedWriter object (bw) specifying fw in bw's constructor. Then, the code uses the write() method to send a line of text to the output buffer and uses the newLine() method to move to the next line in the string (except when it has moved to the last line in the string array). Once 512 bytes have been filled in the buffer, it will empty the data to the actual output stream.

Finally, the code calls the flush() method to make sure any data remaining in the buffer are sent to the output stream and the close() method to close the output stream. Notice that the IOException exception must be caught.

Fields None

Constructors

Modifiers	Constructor
public	BufferedWriter(Writer)
public	BufferedWriter(Writer, int)

Methods

Modifiers	Return Type	Method
public	void	close()
public	void	flush()
public	void	newLine()
public	void	write(char[], int, int)
public	void	write(int)
public	void	write(String, int, int)

See Also java.io.BufferedReader • java.io.FileWriter • java.io.Writer

Class ByteArrayInputStream

public synchronized java.io.ByteArrayInputStream extends java.io.InputStream

The ByteArrayInputStream is an InputStream subclass that lets you use byte arrays to store the data coming from an input stream.

Syntax & Usage For an example of usage please see the next section, "Class ByteArrayOutputStream."

Fields

Modifiers	Type	Field
protected	byte[]	buf
protected	int	count
protected	int	mark
protected	int	pos

Constructors

Modifiers	Constructor
public	ByteArrayInputStream(byte[])
public	ByteArrayInputStream(byte[], int, int)

Methods

Modifiers	Return Type	Method
public synchronized	int	available()
public	void	mark(int)
public	boolean	markSupported()
public synchronized	int	read()
public synchronized	int	read(byte[], int, int)
public synchronized	void	reset()
public synchronized	long	skip(long)

See Also java.io.ByteArrayOutputStream • java.io.InputStream

Class ByteArrayOutputStream

public synchronized java.io.ByteArrayOutputStream extends java.io.OutputStream

The ByteArrayOutputStream is an OutputStream subclass that lets you use byte arrays for the data you intend to send to the output stream.

Syntax & Usage When using the ByteArrayOutputStream, there are several key methods of which you should be aware:

- **toByteArray().** This method is used to create a byte array based on data contained in the buffer and corresponding output stream.
- **toString().** This method is very useful in converting the contents contained in the buffer of a ByteArrayOutputStream object. Note that it converts the bytes to characters using the host's native character-encoding set.
- **writeTo().** This method is used to write the entire contents of a buffer for a given ByteArrayOutputStream object to a specified output stream.
- **reset().** This method empties the buffer of a ByteArrayOutputStream object by discarding any data contained in the buffer.

The following example uses the ByteArrayOutputStream class, specifying 1024 bytes in the buffer, to create a byte array and send it to an output stream and the ByteArrayInputStream class, wherein it reads 256 bytes of the byte array that was just created.

```
ByteArrayOutputStream bo = new
  ByteArrayOutputStream(1024);
for (int k=0; k<256; k++)
  bo.write(k);
byte[] buffer = bo.toByteArray();
```

```
ByteArrayInputStream bi = new
  ByteArrayInputStream(buffer);
while (bi.available()>0)
{
  char c = (char)bi.read();
  System.out.print(c);
}
```

This snippet of code starts by instantiating a ByteArrayOutputStream object (bo) specifying a 1024-byte buffer size. Then the code prints 256 bytes into the buffer for bo creating a byte array, using the toByteArray() method. Following that is a ByteArrayInputStream instance (bi) used to read and display the byte array that was just created.

Fields

Modifiers	Type	Field
protected	byte[]	buf
protected	int	count

Constructors

Modifiers	Constructor
public	ByteArrayOutputStream()
public	ByteArrayOutputStream(int)

Methods

Modifiers	Return Type	Method
public synchronized	void	reset()
public	int	size()
public synchronized	byte[]	toByteArray()
public	String	toString()
public	String	toString(int)
public	String	toString(String)
public synchronized	void	write(byte[], int, int)
public synchronized	void	write(int)
public synchronized	void	writeTo(OutputStream)

See Also java.io.ByteArrayInputStream • java.io.OutputStream

Class CharArrayReader

public synchronized java.io.CharArrayReader extends java.io.Reader

The CharArrayReader class is a Reader subclass that can be used for reading in character arrays from a character input stream. Note that this class utilizes a dynamic buffer that grows and shrinks based on the size of the character array.

Syntax & Usage

Please see the example in the next section, "Class CharArrayWriter."

Fields

Modifiers	Type	Field
protected	char[]	buf
protected	int	count
protected	int	markedPos
protected	int	pos

Constructors

Modifiers	Constructor
public	CharArrayReader(char[])
public	CharArrayReader(char[], int, int)

Methods

Modifiers	Return Type	Method
public	void	close()
public	void	mark(int)
public	boolean	markSupported()
public	int	read()
public	int	read(char[], int, int)
public	boolean	ready()
public	void	reset()
public	long	skip(long)

See Also

java.io.CharArrayWriter • java.io.Reader

Class CharArrayWriter

public synchronized java.io.CharArrayWriter extends java.io.Writer

The CharArrayWriter class is a Writer subclass that lets you use character arrays to send a character array to a character output stream. Note that this class uses a dynamic buffer that grows and shrinks based on the size of the character array.

Syntax & Usage

When using the CharArrayWriter, there are several key methods you should be aware of:

- **toCharArray().** This method is used to create a char array based on data contained in the buffer and its corresponding output stream.
- **toString().** This method is very useful in converting the contents contained in the buffer for a given CharArrayWriter object. Note that it returns a String object using the host's native character set.
- **writeTo().** This method is used to write the entire contents of a buffer for a CharArrayWriter object to a specified character output stream.
- **reset().** This method empties the buffer of a CharArrayWriter object by discarding any data contained in the buffer, giving you a chance to start over.

The following example uses the CharArrayWriter class to create a char array and send it to an output stream. Then a CharArrayReader instance is used to read and display the contents of the stream.

```
CharArrayWriter cw = new
  CharArrayWriter(1024);
for (int k=0; k<256; k++)
  cw.write(k);
char[] buffer = cw.toCharArray();
cw.close();

CharArrayReader cr = new
  CharArrayReader(buffer);

for (int k=0; k<256; k++)
```

```
{
   try
   {
      char c = (char)cr.read();
      System.out.print(c);
   }
   catch(IOException e)
   {
      break;
   }
}
cr.close();
```

This snippet of code starts by instantiating a CharArrayWriter object (cw) specifying a 1024-byte buffer size. Then the code prints 256 bytes into the buffer for cw creating a char array, using the toCharArray() method. Following that is a CharArrayReader instance (cr) used to read and display the char array that was just created.

Fields

Modifiers	Type	Field
protected	char[]	buf
protected	int	count

Constructors

Modifiers	Constructor
public	CharArrayWriter()
public	CharArrayWriter(int)

Methods

Modifiers	Return Type	Method
public	void	close()
public	void	flush()
public	void	reset()
public	int	size()
public	char[]	toCharArray()
public	String	toString()
public	void	write(char[], int, int)
public	void	write(int)
public	void	write(String, int, int)
public	void	writeTo(Writer)

See Also java.io.CharArrayReader • java.io.Writer

Class CharConversionException

public synchronized java.io.CharConversionException extends java.io.IOException

The CharConversionException represents the base class for any character-conversion-based exceptions.

Syntax & Usage This exception does not get thrown by methods in the JDK 1.1. Instead, you can subclass it and add your own specific functionality.

Fields None

Constructors

Modifiers	Constructor
public	CharConversionException()
public	CharConversionException(String)

Methods None

See Also java.io.IOException

Interface DataInput

public abstract interface java.io.DataInput

The DataInput interface is implemented by classes that need to read primitive data types from a stream.

> **Note**
>
> *This reading takes place in a machine-independent manner.*

Syntax & Usage There are two key classes that implement this interface in the java.io package: DataInputStream and RandomAccessFile. For more information, please see the sections on those classes, later in this chapter.

Fields None

Constructors None

Methods

Modifiers	Return Type	Method
public abstract	boolean	readBoolean()
public abstract	byte	readByte()
public abstract	char	readChar()
public abstract	double	readDouble()
public abstract	float	readFloat()
public abstract	void	readFully(byte[])
public abstract	void	readFully(byte[], int, int)
public abstract	int	readInt()
public abstract	String	readLine()
public abstract	long	readLong()
public abstract	short	readShort()
public abstract	int	readUnsignedByte()
public abstract	int	readUnsignedShort()
public abstract	String	readUTF()
public abstract	int	skipBytes(int)

See Also java.io.DataInputStream • java.io.DataOutput • java.io.RandomAccessFile

Class DataInputStream

public synchronized java.io.DataInputStream extends java.io.FilterInputStream implements java.io.DataInput

The DataInputStream class is a FilterInputStream subclass used to read primitive data types from a data input stream.

Syntax & Usage This class is used primarily for reading in data from a binary source. The class also contains a variety of read*XXX*() methods (where *XXX* represents various data types among other things, see the "Methods" section below for details) that let you read in various types of data from the input stream in a variety of ways.

The following example uses the DataInputStream class to read and display **double**, **float**, **int**, and **long** values from a file called myFile.data:

```
try
{
   FileInputStream fi = new FileInputStream(
      "myFile.data");
   DataInputStream ds = new
      DataInputStream(fi);
   double d = ds.readDouble();
   System.out.println("double value\t"+d);
   float f = ds.readFloat();
   System.out.println("float value\t"+f);
   int i = ds.readInt();
   System.out.println("int value\t"+i);
   long l = ds.readLong();
   System.out.println("long value\t"+l);
   fi.close();
}
catch (IOException e)
{
   System.err.println("IO error");
}
```

This snippet of code starts by creating a FileInputStream object (fi) and a DataInputStream object (ds) specifying fi in ds's constructor. It then uses the readDouble(), readFloat(), readInt(), and readLong() methods to retrieve the appropriate values from ds and display them for the user to see.

Fields None

Constructors

Modifiers	Constructor
public	DataInputStream(InputStream)

Methods

Modifiers	Return Type	Method
public final	int	read(byte[])
public final	int	read(byte[], int, int)
public final	boolean	readBoolean()
public final	byte	readByte()
public final	char	readChar()
public final	double	readDouble()
public final	float	readFloat()
public final	void	readFully(byte[])
public final	void	readFully(byte[], int, int)
public final	int	readInt()

Modifiers	Return Type	Method
public final	String	readLine()
public final	long	readLong()
public final	short	readShort()
public final	int	readUnsignedByte()
public final	int	readUnsignedShort()
public final	String	readUTF()
public static final	String	readUTF(DataInput)
public final	int	skipBytes(int)

See Also java.io.DataInput • java.io.DataOutputStream • java.io.FileInputStream • java.io.FilterInputStream

Interface DataOutput

public abstract interface java.io.DataOutput

The DataOutput interface is implemented by classes that need to write primitive data types to a stream.

Note

This writing takes place in a machine-independent manner.

Syntax & Usage There are two key classes that implement this interface in the java.io package: DataOutputStream and RandomAccessFile. For more information, please go to the sections for those classes, elsewhere in this chapter.

Fields None

Constructors None

Methods

Modifiers	Return Type	Method
public abstract	void	write(byte[])
public abstract	void	write(byte[], int, int)
public abstract	void	write(int)
public abstract	void	writeBoolean(boolean)
public abstract	void	writeByte(int)

Modifiers	Return Type	Method
public abstract	void	writeBytes(String)
public abstract	void	writeChar(int)
public abstract	void	writeChars(String)
public abstract	void	writeDouble(double)
public abstract	void	writeFloat(float)
public abstract	void	writeInt(int)
public abstract	void	writeLong(long)
public abstract	void	writeShort(int)
public abstract	void	writeUTF(String)

See Also java.io.DataInput • java.io.DataOutputStream • java.io.RandomAccessFile

Class DataOutputStream

public synchronized java.io.DataOutputStream extends java.io.FilterOutputStream implements java.io.DataOutput

The DataOutputStream class is a FilterOutputStream subclass used to write primitive data types to a data output stream.

Syntax & Usage This class is used primarily to write in data to a binary source. The class also contains a variety of write*XXX*() methods that let you write various types of data to an output stream in a variety of ways.

The following example uses the DataOutputStream class to write to the file myFile.data, sending it arbitrary **double**, **float**, **int**, and **long** values.

```
try
{
   FileOutputStream fo = new FileOutputStream(
      "myFile.data");
   DataOutputStream ds = new
      DataOutputStream(fo);
   ds.writeDouble(1.234e-5);
   ds.writeFloat((float)8.9e6);
   ds.writeInt(-5);
   ds.writeLong(32000);
   ds.flush();
   fo.close();
   System.out.println(ds.size()+
      " bytes have been written");
}
```

```
catch (EOFException e)
{
   System.err.println("EOF has been reached");
}
catch (IOException e)
{
   System.err.println("IO error");
}
```

This snippet of code starts by creating a FileOutputStream object (fo) and a DataOutputStream object (ds) specifying fo in ds's constructor. It then uses the writeDouble(), writeFloat(), writeInt(), and writeLong() methods to write the appropriate values to ds. Finally, the code uses the size() method to display the number of bytes used. Note that the code handles the EOFException and IOException exceptions.

Fields

Modifiers	Type	Field
protected	int	written

Constructors

Modifiers	Constructor
public	DataOutputStream(OutputStream)

Methods

Modifiers	Return Type	Method
public	void	flush()
public final	int	size()
public synchronized	void	write(byte[], int, int)
public synchronized	void	write(int)
public final	void	writeBoolean(boolean)
public final	void	writeByte(int)
public final	void	writeBytes(String)
public final	void	writeChar(int)
public final	void	writeChars(String)
public final	void	writeDouble(double)
public final	void	writeFloat(float)
public final	void	writeInt(int)
public final	void	writeLong(long)
public final	void	writeShort(int)
public final	void	writeUTF(String)

See Also java.io.DataInputStream • java.io.DataOutput • java.io.FileOutputStream

Class EOFException

public synchronized java.io.EOFException extends java.io.IOException

The EOFException is thrown during an input operation when the end of the file or end of the stream is reached unexpectedly (i.e., either prematurely or after the file/stream should have ended).

Syntax & Usage This exception is used primarily for data streams. For an example of the EOFException being handled, see the previous section, "Class DataOutputStream."

Fields None

Constructors

Modifiers	Constructor
public	EOFException()
public	EOFException(String)

Methods None

See Also java.io.DataInputStream • java.io.DataOutputStream • java.io.IOException

Interface Externalizable

public abstract interface java.io.Externalizable implements java.io.Serializable

The Externalizable interface contains two method definitions: readExternal() and writeExternal(). An object of a class implementing this interface uses these to write its contents to a stream or to read its contents back from a stream.

Syntax & Usage Using the two methods in this interface, a class can have complete control over the format and content of the stream it reads itself from or writes itself to.

This interface also can be useful for object persistence, in which any object that needs to be stored is checked to see if it implements the Externalizable interface. If it does, the writeExternal() method for this object is called. Later, when the object needs to be retrieved, its constructor (with no parameters specified) is called along with the method readExternal().

In the following example, the myString class implements the Externalizable interface and overrides the methods readExternal() and writeExternal() to store the value m_Str that would be contained in an instantiated myString class:

```
class myString implements Externalizable
{
  String m_Str;

  public void readExternal(ObjectInput in)
    throws ClassNotFoundException,
    InvalidClassException, IOException
  {
    Object obj = in.readObject();
    if (obj instanceof String)
      m_Str = (String)obj;
    else
      throw new ClassNotFoundException();
  }

  public void writeExternal(ObjectOutput out)
    throws NotSerializableException,
    IOException
  {
    out.writeObject(m_Str);
  }
}
```

Fields None

Constructors None

Methods

Modifiers	Return Type	Method
public abstract	void	readExternal(ObjectInput)
public abstract	void	writeExternal(ObjectOutput)

See Also java.io.Serializable

Class File

public synchronized java.io.File extends java.lang.Object implements java.io.Serializable

The File class is used to encapsulate all the functionality necessary to read, write, and find the attributes of a specified directory and/or file on the user's file system.

Specifically, you instantiate the File class specifying a file or directory in Java you want to access.

Syntax & Usage

The core concept of this class is to encapsulate a given file or directory on the user's file system. This class also provides a variety of methods to perform standard file operations including checking access to, deleting, creating, and renaming the specified file or directory. (See the following Methods table for the list of self-explanatory methods corresponding to available operations.)

Note

While the actual operations used in this class are platform independent, the conventions (i.e., whether the directory will be specified with a slash, /, or a backslash, \) are based on the hosting file system.

The following example uses the File class to print the list of files (and several of their attributes) contained in the current directory of the user's system:

```
File curDir = new File(".");
String[] files = curDir.list();
for (int k=0; k<files.length; k++)
{
   File f = new File(files[k]);
   String str = files[k]+"\t"+
      (f.isDirectory() ? "DIR" : "")+"\t"+
      (f.canRead() ? "R " : "  ")+
      (f.canWrite() ? "W " : "  ");
   System.out.println(str);
}
```

This snippet of code starts by creating a File object (curDir) specifying the current directory in the hosting system. Then, using the list() method, it gets the name of each file in that directory and puts it in the file's String array.

Finally, there is a **for** loop that goes through each element in the file's array making a File object (f) and using the methods isDirectory(), canRead(), and canWrite() to find out if the current file/directory in f is a directory, and if f has read and write access; flagging each property in the following manner:

- **DIR.** If this is present, it indicates the File object is a directory.
- **R.** If this is present, it indicates that the application can read from this File object.
- **W.** If this is present, it indicates that the application can write to this File object.

The last thing the **for** loop does before it continues with the next k value is display the constructed string for the user to see.

Fields

Modifiers	Type	Field
public static final	String	pathSeparator
public static final	char	pathSeparatorChar
public static final	String	separator
public static final	char	separatorChar

Constructors

Modifiers	Constructor
public	File(File, String)
public	File(String)
public	File(String, String)

Methods

Modifiers	Return Type	Method
public	boolean	canRead()
public	boolean	canWrite()
public	boolean	delete()
public	boolean	equals(Object)
public	boolean	exists()
public	String	getAbsolutePath()
public	String	getCanonicalPath()
public	String	getName()
public	String	getParent()
public	String	getPath()
public	int	hashCode()
public native	boolean	isAbsolute()
public	boolean	isDirectory()
public	boolean	isFile()
public	long	lastModified()
public	long	length()
public	String[]	list()
public	String[]	list(FilenameFilter)

Modifiers	Return Type	Method
public	boolean	mkdir()
public	boolean	mkdirs()
public	boolean	renameTo(File)
public	String	toString()

See Also java.io.FileInputStream • java.io.FileOutputStream • java.io.Serializable • java.lang.Object

Class FileDescriptor

public final synchronized java.io.FileDescriptor extends java.lang.Object

The FileDescriptor class is used to represent a handle to a given file or socket.

Syntax & Usage The FileDescriptor class does not contain any public constructors. However, you can instantiate it using the getFD() method from the following classes:

- FileInputStream
- FileOutputStream
- RandomAccessFile

Once you have a handle to a given file or socket (i.e., an instance of this class), you can use the appropriate **static** fields in, out, and err to represent a standard input stream, output stream, and error stream for the handle.

The following example uses the valid() method to verify that the FileDescriptor corresponding to the given FileInputStream is valid:

```
static public boolean isStreamValid(
  FileInputStream stream)
{
  try
  {
    FileDescriptor fd = stream.getFD();
    if (fd==null)
      return false;
    else
      return fd.valid();
  }
  catch (IOException e)
  {
    return false;
  }
}
```

Fields

Modifiers	Type	Field
public static final	FileDescriptor	err
public static final	FileDescriptor	in
public static final	FileDescriptor	out

Constructors

Modifiers	Constructor
public	FileDescriptor()

Methods

Modifiers	Return Type	Method
public native	void	sync()
public native	boolean	valid()

See Also java.io.FileInputStream • java.io.FileOutputStream • java.lang.Object • java.io.RandomAccessFile

Class FileInputStream

public synchronized java.io.FileInputStream extends java.io.InputStream

The FileInputStream class is an InputStream subclass that is used to read data in from a physical file.

Syntax & Usage You can create a FileInputStream object that specifies a filename (and location), a File object, or a FileDescriptor object. Usually, you do not use FileInputStream but instead use BufferedInputStream (for improved efficiency) or DataInputStream (to retrieve primitive data types and strings).

Tip

To read character files, you need to use character streams, which is done with the FileReader class instead of the FileInputStream class. Please see the FileReader class for more information.

For examples that use the FileInputStream class, please see the BufferedInputStream and FileDescriptor classes, elsewhere in this chapter.

Fields None

Constructors

Modifiers	Constructor
public	FileInputStream(File)
public	FileInputStream(FileDescriptor)
public	FileInputStream(String)

Methods

Modifiers	Return Type	Method
public native	int	available()
public native	void	close()
protected	void	finalize()
public final	FileDescriptor	getFD()
public native	int	read()
public	int	read(byte[])
public	int	read(byte[], int, int)
public native	long	skip(long)

See Also java.io.BufferedInputStream • java.io.DataInputStream • java.io.File • java.io.FileDescriptor • java.io.FileOutputStream • java.io.InputStream

Interface FilenameFilter

public abstract interface java.io.FilenameFilter

The FilenameFilter interface defines methods that are used to filter filenames. For example, imagine you had the following directory listing:

```
one.htm
Test.java
Test.class
two.htm
TestTwo.java
TestTwo.class
```

Table 8-1 shows the several example filters with their results.

Filter	Results
*.class	Test.class; Test2.class
*.htm	one.htm; two.htm
*.java	Test.java; TestTwo.java

Table 8-1: Example filters and their results.

Syntax & Usage The java.awt.FileDialog class and the list() method in the File class implement this interface, giving you the ability to filter filenames.

The following shows the class myFilter, which implements the FilenameFilter interface:

```
class myFilter implements FilenameFilter
{
   String m_Extension;
   public myFilter(String Extension)
   {
      m_Extension = Extension;
   }

   public boolean accept(File dir,
      String name)
   {
      return name.endsWith(m_Extension);
   }
}
```

In this class's constructor is the specification for the filename extension you wish to use. Then it overrides the method accept() from this class.

The following snippet of code instantiates the FileNameFilter class (myFilter) to list only files containing a *.java extension for the current directory:

```
myFilter mf = new myFilter(".java");
File curDir = new File(".");
String[] files = curDir.list(mf);
for (int k=0; k<files.length; k++)
   System.out.println(files[k]);
```

Fields None

Constructors None

Methods

Modifiers	Return Type	Method
public abstract	boolean	accept(File, String)

See Also java.awt.FileDialog • java.io.File

Class FileNotFoundException

public synchronized java.io.FileNotFoundException extends java.io.IOException

The FileNotFoundException exception is raised any time a physical file could not be found.

Syntax & Usage When this exception is raised, it lets you know that a file that has been specified in your program could not be located. Examples of how to handle this exception are shown under the BufferedInputStream and LineNumberReader classes, elsewhere in this chapter.

Fields None

Constructors

Modifiers	Constructor
public	FileNotFoundException()
public	FileNotFoundException(String)

Methods None

See Also java.io.BufferedInputStream • java.io.IOException • java.io.LineNumberReader

Class FileOutputStream

public synchronized java.io.FileOutputStream extends java.io.OutputStream

The FileOutputStream class is an OutputStream subclass that is used to write data to a physical file.

Syntax & Usage You can create a FileOutputStream object specifying a filename (and location), a File object, or a FileDescriptor object. Usually, you do not use FileOutputStream, but instead use BufferedOutputStream (for improved efficiency) or DataOutputStream (to use primitive data types and strings).

For examples that use the FileOutputStream class, please see the BufferedOutputStream and FileDescriptor classes, earlier in this chapter.

Tip

To write to a character file, you need to use character stream which is done with the FileWriter class instead of the FileOutputStream class. Please see the FileWriter class for more informaiton.

Fields None

Constructors

Modifiers	Constructor
public	FileOutputStream(File)
public	FileOutputStream(FileDescriptor)
public	FileOutputStream(String)
public	FileOutputStream(String, boolean)

Methods

Modifiers	Return Type	Method
public native	void	close()
protected	void	finalize()
public final	FileDescriptor	getFD()
public	void	write(byte[])
public	void	write(byte[], int, int)
public native	void	write(int)

See Also java.io.BufferedOutputStream • java.io.DataOutputStream • java.io.File • java.io.FileDescriptor • java.io.FileInputStream • java.io.OutputStream

Class FileReader

public synchronized java.io.FileReader extends java.io.InputStreamReader

The FileReader class is used to read in data from a file using a default character-encoding set and buffer size.

Tip

If you wish to use a specific character-encoding set and/or buffer size, you should use the InputStreamReader class instead.

Syntax & Usage You can create a FileReader object specifying a filename (and location) and a File object or a FileDescriptor object. For an example that uses this class, please see "Class LineNumberReader," later in this chapter.

Fields None

Constructors

Modifiers	Constructor
public	FileReader(File)
public	FileReader(FileDescriptor)
public	FileReader(String)

Methods None

See Also java.io.FileWriter • java.io.InputStreamReader • java.io.LineNumberReader

Class FileWriter

public synchronized java.io.FileWriter extends java.io.OutputStreamWriter

The FileWriter class is used to read in data from a file using a default character-encoding set and buffer size.

> **Tip**
>
> *To use a specific character-encoding set and/or buffer size, you should use the OutputStreamWriter class instead.*

Syntax & Usage You can create a FileWriter object specifying a filename (and location), a File object, or a FileDescriptor object. For an example of this class in action, please see "Class BufferedWriter," earlier in this chapter.

Fields None

Constructors

Modifiers	Constructor
public	FileWriter(File)
public	FileWriter(FileDescriptor)
public	FileWriter(String)
public	FileWriter(String, boolean)

Methods None

See Also java.io.BufferedWriter • java.io.FileReader • java.io.OutputStreamWriter

Class FilterInputStream

public synchronized java.io.FilterInputStream extends java.io.InputStream

The FilterInputStream class is an InputStream subclass that provides the method definitions necessary to filter data coming from an input stream in some way.

Syntax & Usage The FilterInputStream does nothing more than override the methods in the InputStream class to facilitate filtering. However, it is not meant to be used directly (that is why it does not have any public constructors); instead, it should be subclassed. The following is a list of FilterInputStream subclasses currently available:

- BufferedInputStream
- java.util.zip.CheckedInputStream
- DataInputStream
- java.security.DigestInputStream
- java.util.zip.GZIPInputStream
- java.util.zip.InflaterInputStream
- LineNumberInputStream
- PushbackInputStream
- java.util.zip.ZIPInputStream

For examples that relate to FilterInputStream, go to the sections for the classes in the preceding list.

Fields

Modifiers	Type	Field
protected	InputStream	in

Constructors

Modifiers	Constructor
protected	FilterInputStream(InputStream)

Methods

Modifiers	Return Type	Method
public	int	available()
public	void	close()
public synchronized	void	mark(int)
public	boolean	markSupported()
public	int	read()
public	int	read(byte[])
public	int	read(byte[], int, int)
public synchronized	void	reset()
public	long	skip(long)

See Also java.io.BufferedInputStream • java.io.DataInputStream • java.io.FilterOutputStream • java.io.InputStream • java.io.LineNumberInputStream • java.io.PushbackInputStream • java.security.DigestInputStream • java.util.zip.CheckedInputStream • java.util.zip.GZIPInputStream • java.util.zip.InflaterInputStream • java.util.zip.ZipInputStream

Class FilterOutputStream

public synchronized java.io.FilterOutputStream extends java.io.OutputStream

The FilterOutputStream class is an OutputStream subclass that provides the method definitions necessary to filter data going to an output stream in some way.

Syntax & Usage

The FilterOutputStream does nothing more than override the methods in the OutputStream class that facilitate filtering. However, it is not meant to be used directly (that is why it does not have any public constructors); instead, it should be subclassed. The following is a list of FilterOutputStream subclasses currently available:

- BufferedOutputStream
- java.util.zip.CheckOutputStream
- DataOutputStream
- java.rmi.server.LogStream
- java.util.zip.DeflaterOutputStream
- java.security.DigestOutputStream
- java.util.zip.GZIPOutputStream
- PrintStream
- java.util.zip.ZipOutputStream

For examples that relate to FilterOutputStream, see the sections for the classes in this list, elsewhere in this chapter.

Fields

Modifiers	Type	Field
protected	OutputStream	out

Constructors

Modifiers	Constructor
public	FilterOutputStream(OutputStream)

Methods

Modifiers	Return Type	Method
public	void	close()
public	void	flush()
public	void	write(byte[])
public	void	write(byte[], int, int)
public	void	write(int)

See Also

java.io.BufferedOutputStream • java.io.DataOutputStream • java.io.FilterInputStream • java.io.OutputStream • java.io.PrintStream • java.rmi.server.LogStream • java.security.DigestOutputStream • java.util.zip.CheckedOutputStream • java.util.zip.DeflaterOutputStream • java.util.zip.GZIPOutputStream • java.util.zip.ZipOutputStream

Class FilterReader

public abstract synchronized java.io.FilterReader extends java.io.Reader

The FilterReader class is an **abstract** class that subclasses Reader. It provides the framework for implementing reading filters in character-based input streams.

Syntax & Usage

To use this class, you need to subclass it or use the one class in this package that extends FilterReader, which is PushbackReader. PushbackReader enables you to push characters read back to the input stream. For more information and an example, please see "Class PushbackReader," later in this chapter.

Fields

Modifiers	Type	Field
protected	Reader	in

Constructors

Modifiers	Constructor
protected	FilterReader(Reader)

Methods

Modifiers	Return Type	Method
public	void	close()
public	void	mark(int)
public	boolean	markSupported()
public	int	read()
public	int	read(char[], int, int)
public	boolean	ready()
public	void	reset()
public	long	skip(long)

See Also java.io.FilterWriter • java.io.PushbackReader • java.io.Reader

Class FilterWriter

public abstract synchronized java.io.FilterWriter extends java.io.Writer

The FilterWriter class is an **abstract** class that subclasses Writer. It provides the framework for implementing writing filters in character-based output streams.

Syntax & Usage

To use this class, you need to subclass it as there are not classes currently present in this package that have subclassed it.

The following example TabFilter class is a Writer subclass that converts the tabulation symbol (\t) character to a specific number of spaces (based on what is specified in FilterWriter's constructor):

```
class TabFilter extends FilterWriter
{
   int m_Tab;
   int m_Cnt;

   public TabFilter(Writer wr, int tab)
   {
      super(wr);
      m_Tab = Math.max(tab, 1);
      m_Cnt = 0;
   }

   public void write(char cbuf[],
      int offset, int len) throws IOException
   {
      for (int k=0; k<len; k++)
         write((int)cbuf[offset+k]);
   }

   public void write(String str,
      int offset, int len) throws IOException
   {
      for (int k=0; k<len; k++)
         write((int)str.charAt(offset+k));
   }

   public void write(int c) throws IOException
   {
```

```
            switch ((char)c)
            {
            case '\n':
            case '\r':
               m_Cnt = 0;
               super.write(c);
               break;
            case '\t':
               int n = m_Tab - m_Cnt%m_Tab;
               for (int k=0; k<n; k++)
                  super.write(' ');
               break;
            default:
               super.write(c);
               m_Cnt++;
               break;
            }
      }
}
```

The constructor for TabFilter takes an instance of the Writer class (i.e., for instance FileWriter) and the size of tabulation. Two overloaded methods, write(char[], int, int) and write(char[], int, int), use the method write(int) (that actually performs the writing). This method counts the number of characters written after the last end-of-line symbol. Then, when a tabulation symbol comes along, this method calculates the corresponding number of spaces, using the following logic:

```
m_Tab - m_Cnt % m_Tab,
```

Finally, it replaces the tabulation symbol (i.e., \t) with the calculated number of spaces.

Fields

Modifiers	Type	Field
protected	Writer	out

Constructors

Modifiers	Constructor
protected	FilterWriter(Writer)

Methods

Modifiers	Return Type	Method
public	void	close()
public	void	flush()

Modifiers	Return Type	Method
public	void	write(char[], int, int)
public	void	write(int)
public	void	write(String, int, int)

See Also java.io.FilterReader • java.io.Writer

Class InputStream

public abstract synchronized java.io.InputStream extends java.lang.Object

The InputStream class is an **abstract** class that is subclassed by any class needing to represent a byte-based input stream.

Syntax & Usage The following lists InputStream subclasses:

- BufferedInputStream
- ByteArrayInputStream
- DataInputStream
- FileInputStream
- FilterInputStream
- LineNumberInputStream
- ObjectInputStream
- PipedInputStream
- PushbackInputStream
- SequenceInputStream
- StringBufferInputStream
- java.security.DigestInputStream
- java.util.zip.CheckedInputStream
- java.util.zip.GZIPInputStream
- java.util.zip.InflaterInputStream
- java.util.zip.ZipInputStream

For more information on how InputStream is implemented, please see the appropriate sections for each of these classes. For examples of usage, go to the BufferedInputStream, ByteArrayOutputStream, and DataInputStream classes.

Fields None

Constructors

Modifiers	Constructor
public	InputStream()

Methods

Modifiers	Return Type	Method
public	int	available()
public	void	close()
public synchronized	void	mark(int)
public	boolean	markSupported()
public abstract	int	read()
public	int	read(byte[])
public	int	read(byte[], int, int)
public synchronized	void	reset()
public	long	skip(long)

See Also java.io.BufferedInputStream • java.io.BufferedOutputStream • java.io.ByteArrayInputStream • java.io.DataInputStream • java.io.FileInputStream • java.io.FilterInputStream • java.io.LineNumberInputStream • java.io.ObjectInputStream • java.io.OutputStream • java.io.PipedInputStream • java.io.PushbackInputStream • java.io.SequenceInputStream • java.io.StringBufferInputStream • java.lang.Object • java.security.DigestInputStream • java.util.zip.CheckedInputStream • java.util.zip.GZIPInputStream • java.util.zip.InflaterInputStream • java.util.zip.ZipInputStream

Class InputStreamReader

public synchronized java.io.InputStreamReader extends java.io.Reader

The InputStreamReader class is used to link a byte-based input stream to a character-based one. The character-encoding set to which it converts can be specified by name in the constructor; otherwise, the hosting environment's default will be applied.

Syntax & Usage You can use this class to take read operations from a character-based stream to a byte-based one. Instances of this class can be used to create instances of other readers. For an example of InputStreamReader, please see the example under "Class LineNumberReader," later in this chapter.

Fields None

Constructors

Modifiers	Constructor
public	InputStreamReader(InputStream)
public	InputStreamReader(InputStream, String)

Methods

Modifiers	Return Type	Method
public	void	close()
public	String	getEncoding()
public	int	read()
public	int	read(char[], int, int)
public	boolean	ready()

See Also java.io.BufferedReader • java.io.LineNumberReader • java.io.OutputStreamWriter • java.io.Reader

Class InterruptedIOException

public synchronized java.io.InterruptedIOException extends java.io.IOException

The InterruptedIOException exception is raised any time there is an input/output (I/O) operation that has faltered or been interrupted in any way.

Syntax & Usage Usually, you handle this exception when doing various operations with streams, which can be interrupted.

> **Note**
>
> *If you are in the middle of an I/O operation on its own thread and you call the interrupt() method from the java.lang.Thread class, an InterruptedIOException exception will be thrown.*

Fields

Modifiers	Type	Field
public	int	bytesTransferred

Constructors

Modifiers	Constructor
public	InterruptedIOException()
public	InterruptedIOException(String)

Methods None

See Also java.io.InputStream • java.io.IOException • java.io.OutputStream

Class InvalidClassException

public synchronized java.io.InvalidClassException extends java.io.ObjectStreamException

The InvalidClassException exception is used during object serialization operations if the serial version of the class does not match the actual class, unknown data types were detected in the class, the class is not **public** or does not have a constructor (with no parameters), or the class does not override both the writeObject() and readObject() methods.

Syntax & Usage For an example of this exception being handled, please see "Interface Externalizable," earlier in this chapter.

Fields

Modifiers	Type	Field
public	String	classname

Constructors

Modifiers	Constructor
public	InvalidClassException(String)
public	InvalidClassException(String, String)

Methods

Modifiers	Return Type	Method
public	String	getMessage()

See Also java.io.Externalizable • java.io.ObjectStreamException

Class InvalidObjectException

public synchronized java.io.InvalidObjectException extends java.io.ObjectStreamException

The InvalidClassException class is used during object serialization operations and can be raised if the object is invalid.

Syntax & Usage For an example of this exception being caught, please see "Interface ObjectInputValidation," later in this chapter.

Fields None

Constructors

Modifiers	Constructor
public	InvalidObjectException(String)

Methods None

See Also java.io.ObjectInputValidation • java.io.ObjectStreamException

Class IOException

public synchronized java.io.IOException extends java.lang.Exception

The IOException class can be raised when any I/O-related exception occurs. All exceptions declared in this package are subclasses to this one.

Syntax & Usage

If you don't need to reconcile specific exceptions in this package, you can catch them all by catching IOException.

You will find examples of this exception being caught in the sections for almost every class in this chapter.

Fields

None

Constructors

Modifiers	Constructor
public	IOException()
public	IOException(String)

Methods

None

See Also

java.lang.Exception

Class LineNumberInputStream

public synchronized java.io.LineNumberInputStream extends java.io.FilterInputStream

The LineNumberInputStream is a FilterInputStream subclass that represents the number of lines read in from a given input stream. Unfortunately, with the introduction of character streams in Java 1.1, this class has been deprecated.

Syntax & Usage

Since this class is deprecated in JDK 1.1, the preferred class to use is LineNumberReader. Please go to the next section for more information.

Fields

None

Constructors

Modifiers	Constructor
public	LineNumberInputStream(InputStream)

Methods

Modifiers	Return Type	Method
public	int	available()
public	int	getLineNumber()
public	void	mark(int)
public	int	read()
public	int	read(byte[], int, int)
public	void	reset()
public	void	setLineNumber(int)
public	long	skip(long)

See Also java.io.FilterInputStream • java.io.LineNumberReader

Class LineNumberReader

public synchronized java.io.LineNumberReader extends java.io.BufferedReader

The LineNumberReader class is used to keep track of the number of lines read from a character-based input stream.

Syntax & Usage This class is best used for situations in which you wish to read in data from a text file on a line-by-line basis. The following snippet of code shows how to read in data from an arbitrary text file using the LineNumberReader class:

```
try
{
   FileReader fr = new FileReader(
      "myFile.txt");
   LineNumberReader lr = new
      LineNumberReader(fr, 512);
   while (true)
   {
      String str = lr.readLine();
      if (str==null)
         break;
      int n = lr.getLineNumber();
      System.out.println(n+"\t"+str);
   }
   lr.close();
```

```
}
catch (FileNotFoundException e)
{
   System.err.println("File not found");
}
catch (IOException e)
{
   System.err.println("IO error");
}
```

This code instantiates a FileReader object (fr) specifying the file myFile.txt to be read. Then it instantiates a LineNumberReader object (lr) specifying fr as the file you wish to read. Following that, in a **while** loop, you use the readLine() method inherited from the BufferedReader class to read each line of text in myFile.txt as a string without carriage return (CR) and line feed (LF) characters. Following that, if the String returned equals **null**, this indicates that the end of the file has been reached and the loop is broken. If there is data (i.e., the String object doesn't equal **null**) in the String object then the getLineNumber() method used to retrieve the number of the current line and both the line number and its contents are displayed to the user.

Fields None

Constructors

Modifiers	Constructor
public	LineNumberReader(Reader)
public	LineNumberReader(Reader, int)

Methods

Modifiers	Return Type	Method
public	int	getLineNumber()
public	void	mark(int)
public	int	read()
public	int	read(char[], int, int)
public	String	readLine()
public	void	reset()
public	void	setLineNumber(int)
public	long	skip(long)

See Also java.io.BufferedReader • java.io.FileReader

Class NotActiveException

public synchronized java.io.NotActiveException extends java.io.ObjectStreamException

The NotActiveException class can be raised when a serialization (or deserialization) process is not active.

Syntax & Usage For a look at this exception being handled, please see the example under "Interface ObjectInputValidation," later in this chapter.

Fields None

Constructors

Modifiers	Constructor
public	NotActiveException()
public	NotActiveException(String)

Methods None

See Also java.io.ObjectInputValidation • java.io.ObjectStreamException

Class NotSerializableException

public synchronized java.io.NotSerializableException extends java.io.ObjectStreamException

The NotSerializableException class can be raised any time a class cannot be serialized.

Syntax & Usage This exception contains two constructs, one of which takes a parameter specifying the name of the class. For an example of this exception being handled, please see "Interface Externalizable," earlier in this chapter.

Fields None

Constructors

Modifiers	Constructor
public	NotSerializableException()
public	NotSerializableException(String)

Methods None

See Also java.io.Externalizable • java.io.ObjectStreamException

Interface ObjectInput

public abstract interface java.io.ObjectInput implements java.io.DataInput

The ObjectInput interface extends the DataInput interface, facilitating methods specifically for sending objects, arrays, and strings to an input stream.

Syntax & Usage Usually, unless you intend to implement your own object-based input stream class, you do not need to implement this interface directly. Instead, you use the ObjectInputStream class contained in this package that implements this interface for you. For an example of ObjectInputStream in action, please see "Interface ObjectInputValidation," later in this chapter.

Fields None

Constructors None

Methods

Modifiers	Return Type	Method
public abstract	int	available()
public abstract	void	close()
public abstract	int	read()
public abstract	int	read(byte[])
public abstract	int	read(byte[], int, int)
public abstract	Object	readObject()
public abstract	long	skip(long)

See Also java.io.DataInput • java.io.ObjectInputStream • java.io.ObjectInputValidation • java.io.ObjectOutput

Class ObjectInputStream

public synchronized java.io.ObjectInputStream extends java.io.InputStream implements java.io.ObjectInput, java.io.ObjectStreamConstants

The ObjectInputStream class is an InputStream subclass that facilitates the ability to read in primitive data types and, more importantly, objects from an input stream.

> **Note**
>
> *This class implements the non-**public** ObjectStreamConstants interface; it is not documented because it is not **public**.*

Syntax & Usage This class is one of the key classes in object serialization and is used to deserialize data that were formerly were serialized using the ObjectOutputStream class.

> **Note**
>
> *Only objects implementing the Serializable or Externalizable interface can be used in object serialization.*

This class can be used with any type of InputStream including FileInputStream to deserialize objects that have been saved to a particular file. Reading in an object from an input stream is very similar to calling that object's constructor (passing no arguments) and restoring values for fields and so on that were saved. Note that this does not include fields declared **transient** or **static**. Objects that were referenced by this class that also have been saved in the graph will be restored as well.

> **Note**
>
> *Allocating new memory and putting the serialized data in that new object guarantee that data will not be overwritten accidentally.*

For an example of ObjectInputStream in action, please see the next section, "Interface ObjectInputValidation."

Fields None

Constructors

Modifiers	Constructor
public	ObjectInputStream(InputStream)

Methods

Modifiers	Return Type	Method
public	int	available()
public	void	close()
public final	void	defaultReadObject()
protected final	boolean	enableResolveObject(boolean)
public	int	read()
public	int	read(byte[], int, int)
public	boolean	readBoolean()
public	byte	readByte()
public	char	readChar()
public	double	readDouble()
public	float	readFloat()
public	void	readFully(byte[])
public	void	readFully(byte[], int, int)
public	int	readInt()
public	String	readLine()
public	long	readLong()
public final	Object	readObject()
public	short	readShort()
protected	void	readStreamHeader()
public	int	readUnsignedByte()
public	int	readUnsignedShort()
public	String	readUTF()
public synchronized	void	registerValidation(ObjectInputValidation, int)
protected	Class	resolveClass(ObjectStreamClass)
protected	Object	resolveObject(Object)
public	int	skipBytes(int)

See Also java.io.Externalizable • java.io.InputStream • java.io.ObjectInput • java.io.ObjectInputValidation • java.io.Serializable

Interface ObjectInputValidation

public abstract interface java.io.ObjectInputValidation

The ObjectInputValidation interface allows you to validate objects within its graph of supporting objects (e.g., superclass and subclass objects).

Syntax & Usage This is extremely useful when you wish to verify an object and its graph. The following class, myString, shows an example of this by facilitating the ability to serialize and validate itself:

```
class myString implements Serializable,
   ObjectInputValidation
{
   public String str;
   private int   hash;

   private void readObject(
      ObjectInputStream stream)
      throws IOException,
         ClassNotFoundException,
         NotActiveException,
         InvalidObjectException
   {
      str = (String)stream.readObject();
      hash  = stream.readInt();
      stream.registerValidation(this, 0);
   }

   private void writeObject(
      ObjectOutputStream stream)
      throws IOException
   {
      hash  = str.hashCode();
      stream.writeObject(str);
      stream.writeInt(hash);
   }
```

```
    public void validateObject()
        throws InvalidObjectException
    {
        if (hash != str.hashCode())
            throw new InvalidObjectException(
            "Invalid hash code");
    }
}
```

Notice that this class implements the Serializable and ObjectInputValidation interfaces. It also holds two fields: String str and **int** hash used for the hash code of the String.

Following that is the readObject() method, which reads the object for this class from an ObjectInputStream instance. It also invokes the registerValidation() method from the ObjectInputStream class to allow this object to be validated after being read.

The writeObject() method saves the hash code for the str String into the hash field and writes the object for this class to an ObjectOutputStream instance.

Note

Notice that the readObject() and writeObject() methods in this class are declared ***private****, so you cannot access them directly from outside the class. Instead, they will be called internally by the system during the reading/writing of objects for this class.*

Finally, the validateObject() method verifies that the hash field (read from input) equals the string's hash code and throws an InvalidObjectException exception if they differ.

The following snippet of code shows the previously explained class in action. Here you have a main() method that instantiates the previous class, serializes it, and desexualizes it:

```
myString s = new myString();
s.str = "This is a test string";
try
{
    FileOutputStream fOut =
        new FileOutputStream("Test.data");
    ObjectOutput oOut =
        new ObjectOutputStream(fOut);
    oOut.writeObject(s);
    oOut.close();
    fOut.close();
```

```
    FileInputStream fIn =
      new FileInputStream("Test.data");
    ObjectInput  oIn  =
      new  ObjectInputStream(fIn);
    s = (myString)oIn.readObject();
    oIn.close();
    fIn.close();
}
catch (Exception e)
{
    e.printStackTrace();
    System.out.println(
      "Error: "+e.getMessage());
}
System.out.println(s.str);
```

This snippet starts by creating one instance of the myString class. Than the code writes that instance to file Test.data and immediately restores the objects that were just saved in that file. If no exceptions are thrown, it prints the contents of str in the newly restored myString instance.

Fields None

Constructors None

Methods

Modifiers	Return Type	Method
public abstract	void	validateObject()

See Also java.io.Externalizable • java.io.FileOutputStream • java.io.ObjectInputStream • java.io.ObjectOutputStream • java.io.Serializable

Interface ObjectOutput

public abstract interface java.io.ObjectOutput implements java.io.DataOutput

The ObjectOutput interface extends the DataOutput interface, facilitating methods specifically for sending objects, arrays, and strings to an output stream.

Syntax & Usage Usually, unless you intend to implement your own object-based output stream class, you do not need to implement this interface directly. Instead, you use the ObjectOutputStream class contained in this package that implements this interface for you. For an example of ObjectOutputStream in action, please see the previous section, "Interface ObjectInputValidation."

Fields None

Methods

Modifiers	Return Type	Method
public abstract	void	close()
public abstract	void	flush()
public abstract	void	write(byte[])
public abstract	void	write(byte[], int, int)
public abstract	void	write(int)
public abstract	void	writeObject(Object)

See Also java.io.DataOutput • java.io.ObjectInput • java.io.ObjectInputValidation • java.io.ObjectOutputStream

Class ObjectOutputStream

public synchronized java.io.ObjectOutputStream extends java.io.OutputStream implements java.io.ObjectOutput, java.io.ObjectStreamConstants

The ObjectOutputStream class is an OutputStream subclass that facilitates the ability to write primitive data types and, more importantly, objects to an output stream.

Note

*This class implements the non-**public** ObjectStreamConstants interface; it is not documented because it is not **public**.*

Syntax & Usage This class is one of the key classes in object serialization and is used to serialize data so that they can be sent to a stream and be deserialized later on using the ObjectInputStream class.

Note

Only objects implementing the Serializable or Externalizable interface can be used with streams via object serialization.

This class can be used with any type of OutputStream instance, including FileOutputStream, to serialize objects and send them to a particular file. When writing an object to an output stream, it also saves any instantiated objects that were referenced by the original object into a graph. Note that this does not include fields declared **transient** or **static**.

For an example of ObjectOutputStream in action, please see "Interface ObjectInputValidation," earlier in this chapter.

Fields None

Constructors

Modifiers	Constructor
public	ObjectOutputStream(OutputStream)

Methods

Modifiers	Return Type	Method
protected	void	annotateClass(Class)
public	void	close()
public final	void	defaultWriteObject()
protected	void	drain()
protected final	boolean	enableReplaceObject(boolean)
public	void	flush()
protected	Object	replaceObject(Object)
public	void	reset()
public	void	write(byte[])
public	void	write(byte[], int, int)
public	void	write(int)
public	void	writeBoolean(boolean)
public	void	writeByte(int)
public	void	writeBytes(String)
public	void	writeChar(int)
public	void	writeChars(String)
public	void	writeDouble(double)
public	void	writeFloat(float)
public	void	writeInt(int)
public	void	writeLong(long)

Modifiers	Return Type	Method
public final	void	writeObject(Object)
public	void	writeShort(int)
protected	void	writeStreamHeader()
public	void	writeUTF(String)

See Also java.io.Externalizable • java.io.ObjectInputValidation • java.io.ObjectOutput • java.io.OutputStream • java.io.Serializable

Class ObjectStreamClass

public synchronized java.io.ObjectStreamClass extends java.lang.Object implements java.io.Serializable

The ObjectStreamClass is used to describe a class that is to be used for object serialization and/or deserialization purposes.

Syntax & Usage The ObjectStreamClass can be used to find information about a given class for a local Java virtual machine (VM). This includes the ability to get a reference to the class (using the forClass() method), to find the name of the class (using the getName() method), to get its serial version user identifier (UID) (using the getSerialVersionUID() method), to find the location of the class, and to determine if it can be used in object serialization (using the lookup() method).

The following snippet of code uses the ObjectStreamClass class to find an arbitrary class (myClass) in the local Java VM and, if found, display the name and serial version UID for it:

```
try
{
Class cl = Class.forName("myClass");
ObjectStreamClass osc =
   ObjectStreamClass.lookup(cl);
if (osc != null)
   System.out.println(
      "Serialized class: "+osc.getName()+
      " VersionUID: "+
      osc.getSerialVersionUID());
}
catch (ClassNotFoundException e) {}
```

Fields None

Constructors None

Methods

Modifiers	Return Type	Method
public	Class	forClass()
public	String	getName()
public	long	getSerialVersionUID()
public static	ObjectStreamClass	lookup(Class)
public	String	toString()

See Also java.io.Externalizable • java.io.Serializable • java.lang.Object

Class ObjectStreamException

public abstract synchronized java.io.ObjectStreamException extends java.io.IOException

The ObjectStreamException class represents the superclass for all object-stream-based exceptions in object serialization.

Syntax & Usage The following lists subclass exceptions that extend ObjectStreamException:

- InvalidClassException
- InvalidObjectException
- NotActiveException
- NotSerializableException
- OptionalDataException
- StreamCorruptedException
- WriteAbortedException

For more information, please go to the sections for each of the classes in this list, elsewhere in this chapter.

Fields None

Constructors

Modifiers	Constructor
protected	ObjectStreamException()
protected	ObjectStreamException(String)

Methods None

See Also java.io.InvalidClassException • java.io.InvalidObjectException • java.io.IOException • java.io.NotActiveException • java.io.NotSerializableException • java.io.OptionalDataException • java.io.StreamCorruptedException • java.io.WriteAbortedException

Class OptionalDataException

public synchronized java.io.OptionalDataException extends java.io.ObjectStreamException

The OptionalDataException exception is thrown during object deserialization if a readObject() method has optional data.

Syntax & Usage This exception can be raised any time raw bytes are found in a stream instead of an object. The following method reads a String object from an ObjectInputStream instance, catching the OptionalDataException exception (if necessary):

```
static public String readString(ObjectInputStream stream)
{
   try
   {
      Object obj = stream.readObject();
      if (obj instanceof String)
         return (String)obj;
      else
         return null;
   }
```

```
    catch (OptionalDataException e)
    {
        if (!e.eof)
        {
            byte[] data = new byte[e.length];
            try
            {
                stream.read(data, 0, e.length);
                return new String(data);
            }
            catch (IOException e1)
            {
                return null;
            }
        }
    }
    catch (StreamCorruptedException e)
    {
        System.err.println(
        "Stream is corrupted: "+e.getMessage());
    }
    catch (Exception e)
    {
        System.err.println(
        "Error: "+e.getMessage());
    }
    return null;
}
```

If such an exception occurs, the method takes optional data in the stream and attempts to read it and return it as a String object.

Note

*This example uses nested **try/catch** blocks, which is legal in Java.*

Fields

Modifiers	Type	Field
public	boolean	eof
public	int	length

Constructors None

Methods None

See Also java.io.IOException • java.io.ObjectInputStream • java.io.ObjectStreamException • java.io.StreamCorruptedException

Class OutputStream

public abstract synchronized java.io.OutputStream extends java.lang.Object

The OutputStream class is an **abstract** class that is subclassed by any class needing to represent a byte-based output stream.

Syntax & Usage The following lists OutputStream subclasses:

- java.io.BufferedOutputStream
- java.io.ByteArrayOutputStream
- java.io.DataOutputStream
- java.io.FileOutputStream
- java.io.FilterOutputStream
- java.io.PrintStream
- java.security.DigestOutputStream
- java.util.zip.CheckedOutputStream
- java.util.zip.DeflaterOutputStream
- java.util.zip.GZIPOutputStream
- java.util.zip.ZipOutputStream

For more information on how OutputStream is implemented, see the sections throughout this book for each of the classes in this list. For examples of usage, go to the BufferedOutputStream, ByteArrayOutputStream, and DataOutputStream classes, earlier in this chapter.

Fields None

Constructors

Modifiers	Constructor
public	OutputStream()

Methods

Modifiers	Return Type	Method
public	void	close()
public	void	flush()
public	void	write(byte[])
public	void	write(byte[], int, int)
public abstract	void	write(int)

See Also java.io.BufferedOutputStream • java.io.ByteArrayOutputStream • java.io.DataOutputStream • java.io.FileOutputStream • java.io.FilterOutputStream • java.io.InputStream • java.io.PrintStream • java.lang.Object • java.security.DigestOutputStream • java.util.zip.CheckedOutputStream • java.util.zip.DeflaterOutputStream • java.util.zip.GZIPOutputStream • java.util.zip.ZipOutputStream

Class OutputStreamWriter

public synchronized java.io.OutputStreamWriter extends java.io.Writer

The OutputStreamWriter class is used to link a character-based output stream to a byte-based one. The character-encoding set it uses for conversion can be specified by name in its constructor; otherwise, the hosting environment's default character-encoding set will be applied.

Syntax & Usage You can use this class to send write operations to any output stream. Instances of this class can be used to create instances of other writers. For example, the following uses BufferedWriter to convert characters so they can be sent to a byte-based output stream:

```
OutputStream stream;
OutputStreamWriter outWr = new
  OutputStreamWriter(stream);
BufferedWriter buffWr = new
  BufferedWriter(outWr, 1024);
```

Fields None

Constructors

Modifiers	Constructor
public	OutputStreamWriter(OutputStream)
public	OutputStreamWriter(OutputStream, String)

Methods

Modifiers	Return Type	Method
public	void	close()
public	void	flush()
public	String	getEncoding()
public	void	write(char[], int, int)
public	void	write(int)
public	void	write(String, int, int)

See Also java.io.BufferedWriter • java.io.InputStreamReader • java.io.Writer

Class PipedInputStream

public synchronized java.io.PipedInputStream extends java.io.InputStream

The PipedInputStream class is an InputStream subclass used to receive data from a communications pipe. This class represents the receiving end of the pipe, with the PipedOutputStream class used for the sending end.

Syntax & Usage

You can use a piped input stream in conjunction with a piped output stream to exchange data between two processes. For instance, two threads can communicate using pipes: one thread sends data through a PipedOutputStream instance, and the other thread reads the data through a PipedInputStream instance.

The following snippet of code shows an example of constructing a PipedOutputStream and a PipedInputStream:

```
PipedOutputStream m_out = new
   PipedOutputStream();
PipedInputStream m_in = new
   PipedInputStream();
```

The class ThreadOut obtains data (in the form of bytes) and writes them to a piped output stream:

```
class ThreadOut extends Thread
{
```

```
   public synchronized void run()
   {
      byte b;
      while(true)
      {
         try
         {
            // Obtain byte value
            m_out.write(b);
         }
         catch (IOException e) {}
         sleep(10);
      }
   }
}
```

The class ThreadIn connects to a piped input stream corresponding to the piped output stream created by ThreadOut. Its primary function is to read and process bytes written from an instance of the ThreadOut class (described previously):

```
class ThreadIn extends Thread
{
   public synchronized void run()
   {
      try
      {
         m_in.connect(m_out);
      }
      catch (IOException e) { return; }

      byte b;
      while(true)
      {
         try
         {
            if (m_in.available() > 0)
               b = (byte)m_in.read();
            // Process received byte
         }
         catch (IOException e) {}
         sleep(10);
      }
   }
}
```

Fields

Modifiers	Type	Field
protected	byte[]	buffer
protected	int	in
protected	int	out
protected static final	int	PIPE_SIZE

Constructors

Modifiers	Constructor
public	PipedInputStream()
public	PipedInputStream(PipedOutputStream)

Methods

Modifiers	Return Type	Method
public synchronized	int	available()
public	void	close()
public	void	connect(PipedOutputStream)
public synchronized	int	read()
public synchronized	int	read(byte[], int, int)
protected synchronized	void	receive(int)

See Also java.io.InputStream • java.io.PipedOutputStream • java.lang.Thread

Class PipedOutputStream

public synchronized java.io.PipedOutputStream extends java.io.OutputStream

The PipedOutputStream class is an OutputStream subclass used to send data to a communications pipe. This class represents the sending end of a pipe, with the PipedInputStream class used as the receiving end.

Syntax & Usage

You can use a piped output stream in conjunction with a piped input stream to exchange data between two processes. For instance, two threads can communicate using pipes: one thread sends data through a PipedOutputStream instance, and the other thread reads the data through a PipedInputStream instance. For an example of the PipedOutputStream in action, please see the previous section, "Class PipedInputStream."

Fields None

Constructors

Modifiers	Constructor
public	PipedOutputStream()
public	PipedOutputStream(PipedInputStream)

Methods

Modifiers	Return Type	Method
public	void	close()
public	void	connect(PipedInputStream)
public synchronized	void	flush()
public	void	write(byte[], int, int)
public	void	write(int)

See Also java.io.OutputStream • java.io.PipedInputStream

Class PipedReader

public synchronized java.io.PipedReader extends java.io.Reader

The PipedReader class is a Reader subclass used to receive data on a character-based communications pipe. This class represents the receiving end of a given character pipe, with the PipedWriter class used for the sending end.

Syntax & Usage

You use the PipedReader class in conjunction with the PipedWriter class for piped communication between two processes. The following example creates instances of these two classes and connects them:

```
PipedWriter wr = new
  PipedWriter();
PipedReader rd = new
  PipedReader();
rd.connect(wr);
```

Then you can use these two instances similar to the example in the PipedInputStream class using a communications pipe between two threads.

Fields None

Constructors

Modifiers	Constructor
public	PipedReader()
public	PipedReader(PipedWriter)

Methods

Modifiers	Return Type	Method
public	void	close()
public	void	connect(PipedWriter)
public	int	read(char[], int, int)

See Also java.io.PipedInputStream • java.io.PipedWriter • java.io.Reader

Class PipedWriter

public synchronized java.io.PipedWriter extends java.io.Writer

The PipedWriter class is a Writer subclass used to send data on a character-based communications pipe. This class represents the sending end of a given character pipe, with the PipedReader class used as the sending end.

Syntax & Usage You can use the PipedWriter class in conjunction with the PipedReader class for piped communication between two processes. Please see the example in the previous section, "Class PipedReader."

Fields None

Constructors

Modifiers	Constructor
public	PipedWriter()
public	PipedWriter(PipedReader)

Methods

Modifiers	Return Type	Method
public	void	close()
public	void	connect(PipedReader)
public	void	flush()
public	void	write(char[], int, int)

See Also java.io.PipedReader • java.io.Writer

Class PrintStream

public synchronized java.io.PrintStream extends java.io.FilterOutputStream

The PrintStream class is a FilterOutputStream subclass used for sending textual data to an output stream. This class also is used for displaying textual material to the user.

Syntax & Usage This class automatically uses the given platform's native character-encoding set. Because this class cannot handle Unicode (it can only support the standard 8-bit Latin-1 characters), its constructors have been deprecated so no example is supplied here. The preferred way to print textual data in Java 1.1 is to use the PrintWriter class, which supports 16-bit character encoding.

Fields None

Constructors

Modifiers	Constructor
public	PrintStream(OutputStream)
public	PrintStream(OutputStream, boolean)

Methods

Modifiers	Return Type	Method
public	boolean	checkError()
public	void	close()
public	void	flush()
public	void	print(boolean)
public	void	print(char)
public	void	print(char[])
public	void	print(double)
public	void	print(float)
public	void	print(int)
public	void	print(long)
public	void	print(Object)
public	void	print(String)
public	void	println()
public	void	println(boolean)
public	void	println(char)
public	void	println(char[])
public	void	println(double)
public	void	println(float)

Modifiers	Return Type	Method
public	void	println(int)
public	void	println(long)
public	void	println(Object)
public	void	println(String)
protected	void	setError()
public	void	write(byte[], int, int)
public	void	write(int)

See Also java.io.FilterOutputStream • java.io.PrintWriter

Class PrintWriter

public synchronized java.io.PrintWriter extends java.io.Writer

The PrintWriter class is a Writer subclass that is used for sending textual data to a character output stream. This class also is used for displaying textual material to the user.

Syntax & Usage This class behaves just like the PrintStream class except that it supports character-encoding sets other than 8-bit Latin-1. The PrintWriter class also supports the use of automatic buffers, which get flushed every time a println() method is invoked.

The following snippet of code opens device LPT1: as a FileOutputStream, creates a PrintWriter instance based on that stream, and prints sample text:

```
try
{
   FileOutputStream stream = new
      FileOutputStream("LPT1:");
   PrintWriter wr = new PrintWriter(stream,
      true);
   wr.println("This is a test");
   wr.close();
   stream.flush();
   stream.close();
}
catch (Exception e)
{
   e.printStackTrace();
}
```

Tip

The more sophisticated way of printing in Java 1.1 is to use the standard print dialogs and open a print job. Please see the example under "Class java.awt.PrintJob" in Chapter 2.

Fields None

Constructors

Modifiers	Constructor
public	PrintWriter(OutputStream)
public	PrintWriter(OutputStream, boolean)
public	PrintWriter(Writer)
public	PrintWriter(Writer, boolean)

Methods

Modifiers	Return Type	Method
public	boolean	checkError()
public	void	close()
public	void	flush()
public	void	print(boolean)
public	void	print(char)
public	void	print(char[])
public	void	print(double)
public	void	print(float)
public	void	print(int)
public	void	print(long)
public	void	print(Object)
public	void	print(String)
public	void	println()
public	void	println(boolean)
public	void	println(char)
public	void	println(char[])
public	void	println(double)
public	void	println(float)
public	void	println(int)
public	void	println(long)
public	void	println(Object)
public	void	println(String)
protected	void	setError()
public	void	write(char[])

Modifiers	Return Type	Method
public	void	write(char[], int, int)
public	void	write(int)
public	void	write(String)
public	void	write(String, int, int)

See Also java.awt.PrintJob • java.io.PrintStream • java.io.Writer

Class PushbackInputStream

public synchronized java.io.PushbackInputStream extends java.io.FilterInputStream

The PushbackInputStream class is a FilterInputStream subclass that enables a 1-byte pushback buffer. This gives you the ability to push the last byte read back to the input stream.

Syntax & Usage

Usually, the advantage of using 1-byte pushback is for detecting the end-of-stream character and using the unread() method to push back that byte, as well as other bytes read from the stream, so that another operation can reread that same segment of bytes. This is particularly useful in parsing operations.

Usage of the PushbackInputStream class is similar to usage of the PushbackReader class. For an example of 1-byte pushback in action, please see the example in the next section, "Class PushbackReader."

Fields

Modifiers	Type	Field
protected	byte[]	buf
protected	int	pos

Constructors

Modifiers	Constructor
public	PushbackInputStream(InputStream)
public	PushbackInputStream(InputStream, int)

Methods

Modifiers	Return Type	Method
public	int	available()
public	boolean	markSupported()
public	int	read()

Modifiers	Return Type	Method
public	int	read(byte[], int, int)
public	void	unread(byte[])
public	void	unread(byte[], int, int)
public	void	unread(int)

See Also java.io.FilterInputStream • java.io.PushbackReader

Class PushbackReader

public synchronized java.io.PushbackReader extends java.io.FilterReader

The PushbackReader class is a FilterReader subclass that enables a one-character pushback buffer.

Syntax & Usage Usually, the advantage of using one-character pushback is for detecting the end-of-stream character and using the unread() method to push back that byte, as well as other bytes read from the stream, so that another operation can reread this segment of characters. This is particularly useful in parsing operations.

This method uses an instance of the PushbackReader class to extract keywords denoted by << and >> symbols from a given character stream, thus giving you the ability to extract and parse keywords from that stream:

```
static public void findKeys(char[] buffer)
{
  CharArrayReader cr = new
    CharArrayReader(buffer);
  PushbackReader pr = new PushbackReader(cr);
  boolean bKey = false;
  String sKey = "";
  int c, c1;
  while (true)
  {
    try
    {
      c = pr.read();
      if (c < 0)
        break;
      switch (c)
```

```
            {
            case (int)'<':
               c1 = pr.read();
               if (c1 == (int)'<')
               {
                  bKey = true;
                  sKey = "";
               }
               else
                  pr.unread(c1);
               break;

            case (int)'>':
               c1 = pr.read();
               if (c1 == (int)'>')
               {
                  bKey = false;
                  System.out.println(
                     "Key: "+sKey);
               }
               else
                  pr.unread(c1);
               break;

            default:
               if (bKey)
                  sKey += (char)c;
               break;
            }
         }
         catch (IOException e)
         {
            break;
         }
      }
      try { pr.close(); }
      catch (IOException e) {}
   }
```

This example analyses the next character (c) read from the Reader instance. If c<0, then the end of stream has been reached. If c equals < it reads and analyzes the next character (c1). If c1 also equals <, it raises the bKey flag, which will signal that we've reached a keyword. Otherwise, it pushes back that character using the unread() method.

Analogously, if c equals >, then it reads and analyzes the next character c1. If c1 also equals >, it prints the value of the key obtained and lowers the bKey flag. Otherwise, it pushes back that character using the unread() method.

Fields None

Constructors

Modifiers	Constructor
public	PushbackReader(Reader)
public	PushbackReader(Reader, int)

Methods

Modifiers	Return Type	Method
public	void	close()
public	boolean	markSupported()
public	int	read()
public	int	read(char[], int, int)
public	boolean	ready()
public	void	unread(char[])
public	void	unread(char[], int, int)
public	void	unread(int)

See Also java.io.FilterReader • java.io.PushbackInputStream • java.io.Reader

Class RandomAccessFile

public synchronized java.io.RandomAccessFile extends java.lang.Object implements java.io.DataOutput, java.io.DataInput

The RandomAccessFile class facilitates the ability to read and/or write bytes to an arbitrary file at a specified location.

Syntax & Usage The following snippet of code shows how to use the RandomAccessFile class by reading and writing data to various locations of the file myFile.txt:

```
RandomAccessFile file = null;
try
{
   file = new RandomAccessFile("myFile.txt",
     "rw");
   byte[] b = new byte[10];
   file.read(b, 0, 10);
   file.seek(file.length()-10);
   file.write(b, 0, 10);
}
catch (Exception e) {}
```

```
try
{
   if (file != null)
      file.close();
}
catch (Exception e) {}
```

The code starts by opening the file for reading and writing, reading 10 bytes from the beginning, seeking to the 10th position prior to the end of the file, and writing the 10 bytes there.

Note

Since the method close() throws the IOException exception, you must put it in a try/catch block.

Fields None

Constructors

Modifiers	Constructor
public	RandomAccessFile(File, String)
public	RandomAccessFile(String, String)

Methods

Modifiers	Return Type	Method
public native	void	close()
public final	FileDescriptor	getFD()
public native	long	getFilePointer()
public native	long	length()
public native	int	read()
public final	boolean	readBoolean()
public	int	read(byte[])
public	int	read(byte[], int, int)
public final	byte	readByte()
public final	char	readChar()
public final	double	readDouble()
public final	float	readFloat()
public final	void	readFully(byte[])
public final	void	readFully(byte[], int, int)

Modifiers	Return Type	Method
public final	int	readInt()
public final	String	readLine()
public final	long	readLong()
public final	short	readShort()
public final	int	readUnsignedByte()
public final	int	readUnsignedShort()
public final	String	readUTF()
public native	void	seek(long)
public	int	skipBytes(int)
public	void	write(byte[])
public	void	write(byte[], int, int)
public native	void	write(int)
public final	void	writeBoolean(boolean)
public final	void	writeByte(int)
public final	void	writeBytes(String)
public final	void	writeChar(int)
public final	void	writeChars(String)
public final	void	writeDouble(double)
public final	void	writeFloat(float)
public final	void	writeInt(int)
public final	void	writeLong(long)
public final	void	writeShort(int)
public final	void	writeUTF(String)

See Also java.io.DataInput • java.io.DataOutput • java.lang.Object

Class Reader

public abstract synchronized java.io.Reader extends java.lang.Object

The Reader class is the **abstract** class that defines all reader classes that are used for reading data from character-based streams.

Syntax & Usage

Normally, you do not subclass this class, but instead you use its subclasses, which also are defined in this package:

- BufferedReader
- CharArrayReader
- FileReader
- FilterReader
- InputStreamReader
- LineNumberReader
- PipedReader
- PushbackReader
- StringReader

For more information, please see the sections for each of the classes in the preceding list, elsewhere in this chapter. For examples of usage, please see the CharArrayReader, LineNumberReader, PipedReader, and PushbackReader classes.

Fields

Modifiers	Type	Field
protected	Object	lock

Constructors

Modifiers	Constructor
protected	Reader()
protected	Reader(Object)

Methods

Modifiers	Return Type	Method
public abstract	void	close()
public	void	mark(int)
public	boolean	markSupported()
public	int	read()
public	int	read(char[])
public abstract	int	read(char[], int, int)
public	boolean	ready()
public	void	reset()
public	long	skip(long)

See Also

java.io.BufferedReader • java.io.CharArrayReader • java.io.FileReader • java.io.FilterReader • java.io.InputStreamReader • java.io.LineNumberReader • java.io.PipedReader • java.io.PushbackReader • java.io.StringReader • java.lang.Object

Class SequenceInputStream

public synchronized java.io.SequenceInputStream extends java.io.InputStream

The SequenceInputStream class is an InputStream subclass that lets you read and concatenate several input streams into one combined input stream.

Syntax & Usage

The SequenceInputStream operates by reading in each of the specified input streams based on the order given. Once it finishes reading one stream, it moves to the next stream and adds the data contained in that stream to the first one. It continues to do this until all specified input streams have been read and combined into one large input stream.

The following snippet of code uses the SequenceInputStream class to read two files as one stream:

```
try
{
   FileInputStream stream1 = new
     FileInputStream("myFile1.txt");
   FileInputStream stream2 = new
     FileInputStream("myFile2.txt");
   SequenceInputStream seqStream = new
     SequenceInputStream(stream1, stream2);

   while (seqStream.available() > 0)
   {
     byte b = (byte)seqStream.read();
     // process bytes...
   }

   seqStream.close();
   stream1.close();
   stream2.close();
}
catch (Exception e)
{
   e.printStackTrace();
}
```

Fields

None

Constructors

Modifiers	Constructor
public	SequenceInputStream(Enumeration)
public	SequenceInputStream(InputStream, InputStream)

Methods

Modifiers	Return Type	Method
public	int	available()
public	void	close()
public	int	read()
public	int	read(byte[], int, int)

See Also java.io.InputStream

Interface Serializable

public interface java.io.Serializable

The Serializable interface is used for object serialization purposes. Any class (or deriving subclass) that implements this interface can be serialized/deserialized.

Syntax & Usage

While this interface does not contain any fields or methods, it serves to facilitate the semantics for any class needing to have part of its state serialized or deserialized. Classes needing special treatment during either the serialization or deserialization process need to implement these methods:

- **private void readObject(java.io.ObjectInputStream in) throws IOException, ClassNotFoundException.** This method is responsible for deserialization of its object.
- **private void writeObject(java.io.ObjectOutputStream out) throws IOException.** This method is responsible for the serialization of its object.

The following snippet of code can be used to verify that the given object can be serialized and, if this is true, the object is written to the ObjectOutputStream instance (obj):

```
ObjectOutputStream stream;
Object obj;
if (obj instanceof Serializable)
   stream.writeObject(obj);
```

Fields None

Constructors None

Methods None

See Also java.io.Externalizable

Class StreamCorruptedException

public synchronized java.io.StreamCorruptedException extends java.io.ObjectStreamException

The StreamCorruptedException is raised any time control information from an object stream differs from the internal consistency-checking patterns.

Syntax & Usage For an example using this exception, see "Class OptionalDataException," earlier in this chapter.

Fields None

Constructors

Modifiers	Constructor
public	StreamCorruptedException()
public	StreamCorruptedException(String)

Methods None

See Also java.io.ObjectStreamException

Class StreamTokenizer

public synchronized java.io.StreamTokenizer extends java.lang.Object

The StreamTokenizer class is used for parsing operations in which you want to read in an input stream and break it up into various tokens. Once you have tokenized the stream (or a segment of it), you then can analyze it on a token-by-token basis.

Syntax & Usage The StreamTokenizer class can be used to positively identify numbers, text, quoted strings, identifiers, and a wide variety of comment styles (including C/C++).

> **Note**
>
> *The constructor for StreamTokenizer takes an InputStream object for a parameter that has been deprecated. So, you should use the constructor that lets you pass a Reader object to it.*

The following snippet of code uses the StreamTokenizer class to parse sample text string into tokens:

```
String sample = "int x = -123;\nx = x*2;";
StringReader reader = new
   StringReader(sample);
StreamTokenizer token = new
   StreamTokenizer(reader);

try
{
   while (token.nextToken() !=
      StreamTokenizer.TT_EOF)
   {
      switch (token.ttype)
      {
      case StreamTokenizer.TT_WORD:
         System.out.println(
            "Word: "+token.sval);
         break;
      case StreamTokenizer.TT_NUMBER:
         System.out.println(
            "Number: "+token.nval);
         break;
      }
   }
}
catch (IOException e)
{
   e.printStackTrace();
}

reader.close();
```

The code starts by declaring a basic String object (sample). Then in a **while** loop that will end when the end of the stream is met, the nextToken()

method fetches the next token. Field ttype contains information about the next token: value TT_WORD means that field sval contains a String token; value TT_NUMBER means that field nval contains a number token.

If the previous code were executed, this would be its corresponding output:

```
Word: int
Word: x
Number: -123.0
Word: x
Word: x
Number: 2.0
```

Fields

Modifiers	Type	Field
public	double	nval
public	String	sval
public	int	ttype
public static final	int	TT_EOF
public static final	int	TT_EOL
public static final	int	TT_NUMBER
public static final	int	TT_WORD

Constructors

Modifiers	Constructor
public	StreamTokenizer(InputStream)
public	StreamTokenizer(Reader)

Methods

Modifiers	Return Type	Method
public	void	commentChar(int)
public	void	eolIsSignificant(boolean)
public	int	lineno()
public	void	lowerCaseMode(boolean)
public	int	nextToken()
public	void	ordinaryChar(int)
public	void	ordinaryChars(int, int)
public	void	parseNumbers()
public	void	pushBack()
public	void	quoteChar(int)
public	void	resetSyntax()
public	void	slashSlashComments(boolean)

Modifiers	Return Type	Method
public	void	slashStarComments(boolean)
public	String	toString()
public	void	whitespaceChars(int, int)
public	void	wordChars(int, int)

See Also java.io.InputStream • java.io.Reader • java.lang.Object

Class StringBufferInputStream

public synchronized java.io.StringBufferInputStream extends java.io.InputStream

The StringBufferInputStream is an InputStream subclass used for reading in bytes from a specified String object. These bytes then are put into a buffer for improved efficiency.

Syntax & Usage This class has been deprecated, so no example is supplied. Instead, it is recommended you use the StringReader class. For more information, please see the next section.

Fields

Modifiers	Type	Field
protected	String	buffer
protected	int	count
protected	int	pos

Constructors

Modifiers	Constructor
public	StringBufferInputStream(String)

Methods

Modifiers	Return Type	Method
public synchronized	int	available()
public synchronized	int	read()
public synchronized	int	read(byte[], int, int)
public synchronized	void	reset()
public synchronized	long	skip(long)

See Also java.io.InputStream • java.io.StringReader

Class StringReader

public synchronized java.io.StringReader extends java.io.Reader

The StringReader class is a Reader subclass that lets you read in character-based streams that contain strings.

Syntax & Usage You can use instances of this class as a source for creating more advanced readers. For instance, the following snippet of code uses a StringReader object to instance a StreamTokenizer class:

```
StringReader reader = new
   StringReader(sample);
StreamTokenizer token = new
   StreamTokenizer(reader);
```

Fields None

Constructors

Modifiers	Constructor
public	StringReader(String)

Methods

Modifiers	Return Type	Method
public	void	close()
public	void	mark(int)
public	boolean	markSupported()
public	int	read()
public	int	read(char[], int, int)
public	boolean	ready()
public	void	reset()
public	long	skip(long)

See Also java.io.Reader • java.io.StreamTokenizer • java.io.StringWriter

Class StringWriter

public synchronized java.io.StringWriter extends java.io.Writer

The StringWriter class is a Writer subclass that lets you create strings by collecting from the contents of its outgoing buffer.

Syntax & Usage

You can use instances of this class as a source for creating more advanced writers. In the following snippet of code, you create a PrintWriter instance (wr) based on the specified StringWriter (writer) object:

```
StringWriter writer = new
  StringWriter (sample);
PrintWriter wr = new
  PrintWriter (writer);
```

With this setup, you now can use various print() and println() methods to format your strings.

Fields

None

Constructors

Modifiers	Constructor
public	StringWriter()
protected	StringWriter(int)

Methods

Modifiers	Return Type	Method
public	void	close()
public	void	flush()
public	StringBuffer	getBuffer()
public	String	toString()
public	void	write(char[], int, int)
public	void	write(int)
public	void	write(String)
public	void	write(String, int, int)

See Also

java.io.PrintWriter • java.io.StringReader • java.io.Writer

Class SyncFailedException

public synchronized java.io.SyncFailedException extends java.io.IOException

The SyncFailedException exception can be raised if all the buffers for a given stream (or streams) are unable to synchronize.

Syntax & Usage This exception may be thrown by the sync() method from the FileDescriptor class to indicate that during an attempt to force all system buffers to synchronize the underlying device fails.

Fields None

Constructors

Modifiers	Constructor
public	SyncFailedException(String)

Methods None

See Also java.io.IOException

Class UnsupportedEncodingException

public synchronized java.io.UnsupportedEncodingException extends java.io.IOException

The UnsupportedEncodingException exception can be thrown by any class implementing the DataInput interface and by those classes that read from a data input stream in which a malformed UTF-8 String has been found.

Syntax & Usage This exception may be thrown by some of the constructors of the java.lang.String class indicating that the specified encoding format is not supported:

```
public String(byte bytes[],int offset,
     int length, String enc) throws
     UnsupportedEncodingException
```

Fields None

Constructors

Modifiers	Constructor
public	UnsupportedEncodingException()
public	UnsupportedEncodingException(String)

Methods None

See Also java.io.DataInput • java.io.DataInputStream • java.io.IOException • java.lang.String

Class UTFDataFormatException

public synchronized java.io.UTFDataFormatException extends java.io.IOException

The UTFDataFormatException exception is thrown any time an operation with a UTF-8-formatted string has failed.

Syntax & Usage The following snippet of code shows where this exception might be caught:

```
DataInputStream stream;
try
{
   String str = stream.readUTF();
}
catch (UTFDataFormatException e) {}
```

Fields None

Constructors

Modifiers	Constructor
public	UTFDataFormatException()
public	UTFDataFormatException(String)

Methods None

See Also java.io.DataInputStream • java.io.IOException • java.lang.String

Class WriteAbortedException

public synchronized java.io.WriteAbortedException extends java.io.ObjectStreamException

The WriteAbortedException exception can be thrown when an ObjectStreamException is raised during object serialization in a read operation that has been aborted.

Syntax & Usage When this exception is thrown, the stream involved during this write operation is reset, and any data deserialized is discarded.

Fields

Modifiers	Type	Field
public	Exception	detail

Constructors

Modifiers	Constructor
public	WriteAbortedException(String, Exception)

Methods

Modifiers	Return Type	Method
public	String	getMessage()

See Also java.io.ObjectStreamException

Class Writer

public abstract synchronized java.io.Writer extends java.lang.Object

The Writer class is the **abstract** class that defines all writer classes that are used for writing to character-based output streams.

Syntax & Usage

Normally, you do not subclass this class, but instead you use its subclasses, which also are defined in this package:

- BufferedWriter
- CharArrayWriter
- FileWriter
- FilterWriter
- OutputStreamWriter
- PipedWriter
- PrintWriter
- StringWriter

For more information, please see the sections for each of the classes in this list, elsewhere in this chapter. For examples of usage, please see the BufferedWriter, CharArrayWriter, FilterWriter, OutputStreamWriter, PipedWriter, and PrintWriter classes.

Fields

Modifiers	Type	Field
protected	Object	lock

Constructors

Modifiers	Constructor
protected	Writer()
protected	Writer(Object)

Methods

Modifiers	Return Type	Method
public abstract	void	close()
public abstract	void	flush()
public	void	write(char[])
public abstract	void	write(char[], int, int)
public	void	write(int)
public	void	write(String)
public	void	write(String, int, int)

See Also java.io.BufferedWriter • java.io.CharArrayWriter • java.io.FileWriter • java.io.FilterWriter • java.io.OutputStreamWriter • java.io.PipedWriter • java.io.PrintWriter • java.io.StringWriter • java.lang.Object

9 The java.lang Package

The java.lang package is the only package automatically imported to every Java program. It contains the key root classes that are the backbone of the Java and the Java Class Library, including Object, Exception, and Error.

This package also contains the bulk of the basic classes used in the Java language. For instance, all the object-wrapped versions of the Java primitive types are part of this package, as are classes that directly relate to the Java virtual machine (VM) and the system in general. Also contained in this package is a variety of exceptions and errors (some hardly ever seen).

Tip

Optionally, you can explicitly import this package in your Java program. However, that is necessary only for illustration purposes.

Class AbstractMethodError

public synchronized java.lang.AbstractMethodError extends java.lang.IncompatibleClassChangeError

The AbstractMethodError error is thrown any time a Java program attempts to invoke an **abstract** method.

Syntax & Usage Usually this type of error is caught at compile time when the compiler checks for the instantiation of **abstract** classes—including classes derived from **abstract** ones that have not implemented all the superclass's abstract methods—as well as the instantiation of **abstract** methods. However, this error is reserved for those odd situations (perhaps relating to having compiled class files that have been updated but were not recompiled and were mixed with other updated and recompiled class files) during run time when the program attempts to invoke an **abstract** method.

Fields None

Constructors

Modifiers	Constructor
public	AbstractMethodError()
public	AbstractMethodError(String)

Methods None

See Also java.lang.IncompatibleClassChangeError

Class ArithmeticException

public synchronized java.lang.ArithmeticException extends java.lang.RuntimeException

The ArithmeticException exception is thrown any time an illegal mathematical operation is performed (e.g., attempting to divide by zero).

Syntax & Usage The following example catches the ArithmeticException exception to prevent the division-by-zero operation:

```
int x = 0;
try
{
   int y = 123/x;
}
catch (ArithmeticException e)
{
   System.out.println("Divide by zero");
}
```

Note

Floating-point operations in Java 1.1 do not throw exceptions in situations that involve illegal parameters. Instead, the operation sets its result to the Double.NaN value, indicating an invalid floating-point value.

Fields None

Constructors

Modifiers	Constructor
public	ArithmeticException()
public	ArithmeticException(String)

Methods None

See Also java.lang.RuntimeException

Class ArrayIndexOutOfBoundsException

public synchronized java.lang.ArrayIndexOutOfBoundsException extends java.lang.IndexOutOfBoundsException

The ArrayIndexOutOfBoundsException exception is thrown any time an index that does not exist in the array has been referenced.

Syntax & Usage The following example catches the ArrayIndexOutOfBoundsException exception to prevent accessing an illegal index of the y array:

```
int x = 5;
try
```

```
{
   int[] y = {1, 2, 3, 4};
   int k = y[x];
}
catch (ArrayIndexOutOfBoundsException e)
{
   System.out.println(
      "Array Index Out Of Bounds: ");
}
```

Fields None

Constructors

Modifiers	Constructor
public	ArrayIndexOutOfBoundsException()
public	ArrayIndexOutOfBoundsException(int)
public	ArrayIndexOutOfBoundsException(String)

Methods None

See Also java.lang.IndexOutOfBoundsException

Class ArrayStoreException

public synchronized java.lang.ArrayStoreException extends java.lang.RuntimeException

The ArrayStoreException exception is thrown any time a program attempts to store the wrong type (primitive or otherwise) in an array.

Syntax & Usage The following example catches the ArrayStoreException exception to prevent storing illegal arguments into an array of objects:

```
try
{
   Object obj[] = new Integer[5];
   obj[0] = new String("Sample");
}
catch (ArrayStoreException e)
{
   System.out.println("Trying store wrong type of object into an array
   of objects");
}
```

Notice that in the preceding example, if you change Object obj[] to Integer obj[], it will cause a compile-time error with the following message: "Incompatible type for =. Can't convert java.lang.String to java.lang.Integer." However since all classes in Java are derived from the Object class, this code does not cause a compile-time error, but throws a run-time exception since it is still an illegal operation.

Fields None

Constructors

Modifiers	Constructor
public	ArrayStoreException()
public	ArrayStoreException(String)

Methods None

See Also java.lang.RuntimeException

Class Boolean

public final synchronized java.lang.Boolean extends java.lang.Object implements java.io.Serializable

The Boolean class represents an object wrapper for the **boolean** primitive type. The **boolean** primitive type is very simple to understand in that it can contain only two values: either **true** or **false**.

Syntax & Usage This class uses two fields (TRUE and FALSE) to represent its values, and it contains a number of methods to convert between primitive **boolean** and object Boolean values and vice versa.

The following example uses the Boolean class to parse a String to a **boolean** value:

```
String s = "True";
Boolean bool = Boolean.valueOf(s);
boolean b = bool.booleanValue();
```

Notice that the Boolean.valueOf() method does not throw any exception if an illegal parameter is passed to it. Instead, it simply sets the result to **false**. The following is the output for the preceding example:

```
b=true
```

Fields

Modifiers	Type	Field
public static final	Boolean	FALSE
public static final	Boolean	TRUE
public static final	Class	TYPE

Constructors

Modifiers	Constructor
public	Boolean(boolean)
public	Boolean(String)

Methods

Modifiers	Return Type	Method
public	boolean	booleanValue()
public	boolean	equals(Object)
public static	boolean	getBoolean(String)
public	int	hashCode()
public	String	toString()
public static	Boolean	valueOf(String)

See Also java.io.Serializable • java.lang.Object

Class Byte

public final synchronized java.lang.Byte extends java.lang.Number

The Byte class represents an object wrapper for the **byte** primitive type. The **byte** primitive type is the smallest primitive integer data type in Java, being only 8 bits wide. Since **byte** is the smallest size of integer in Java, it is the most efficient to use. However, as a result, **byte** also has the smallest range. You can assign a **byte** to have a value of -128 to +127.

Syntax & Usage

This class contains methods that let you convert to other primitive Java types. The following snippet of code uses the Byte class to parse a String to a byte value. Notice that a NumberFormatException exception will be thrown if the String passed is illegal:

```
String s = "123";
try
{
```

```
   Byte bt = Byte.valueOf(s);
   byte b = bt.byteValue();
   System.out.println("b="+b);
}
catch (NumberFormatException e)
{
   System.out.println(
      "Can't parse string to byte");
}
```

The following shows the output for the preceding example:

```
b=123
```

Fields

Modifiers	Type	Field
public static final	byte	MAX_VALUE
public static final	byte	MIN_VALUE
public static final	Class	TYPE

Constructors

Modifiers	Constructor
public	Byte(byte)
public	Byte(String)

Methods

Modifiers	Return Type	Method
public	byte	byteValue()
public static	Byte	decode(String)
public	double	doubleValue()
public	boolean	equals(Object)
public	float	floatValue()
public	int	hashCode()
public	int	intValue()
public	long	longValue()
public static	byte	parseByte(String)
public static	byte	parseByte(String, int)
public	short	shortValue()
public	String	toString()
public static	String	toString(byte)
public static	Byte	valueOf(String)
public static	Byte	valueOf(String, int)

See Also java.lang.Integer • java.lang.Long • java.lang.Number • java.lang.Short • java.lang.String

Class Character

public final synchronized java.lang.Character extends java.lang.Object implements java.io.Serializable

The Character class represents an object wrapper for the **char** primitive type. The **char** primitive type is like **char** in C/C++, with only one major difference: The **char** type in Java stores its values using the 16-bit Unicode character set as opposed to the 8-bit ASCII set used in most C/C++ language environments.

Syntax & Usage

This class provides a set of useful **static** methods to determine the character type and other methods to convert to another character or character type. These methods are especially useful in conjunction with methods contained in the String class. Consider the following:

```
static public String toTitleCase(String str)
{
   char[] chars = str.toCharArray();
   for (int k=0; k< str.length(); k++)
      chars[k] = k==0 ?
         Character.toTitleCase(chars[k]) :
         Character.toLowerCase(chars[k]);
   return new String(chars);
}
```

This example method converts the specified String (str) into an array of characters using the toCharArray() method from the String class. Then it processes all the characters (capitalizing the first using the toTitleCase() method from the Character class and lowercasing the rest using the toLowerCase() method also from the Character class). Finally, it creates and returns a new String based on the formatted array.

Fields

Modifiers	Type	Field
public static final	byte	COMBINING_SPACING_MARK
public static final	byte	CONNECTOR_PUNCTUATION
public static final	byte	CONTROL
public static final	byte	CURRENCY_SYMBOL
public static final	byte	DASH_PUNCTUATION
public static final	byte	DECIMAL_DIGIT_NUMBER
public static final	byte	ENCLOSING_MARK
public static final	byte	END_PUNCTUATION
public static final	byte	FORMAT
public static final	byte	LETTER_NUMBER

Modifiers	Type	Field
public static final	byte	LINE_SEPARATOR
public static final	byte	LOWERCASE_LETTER
public static final	byte	MATH_SYMBOL
public static final	int	MAX_RADIX
public static final	char	MAX_VALUE
public static final	int	MIN_RADIX
public static final	char	MIN_VALUE
public static final	byte	MODIFIER_LETTER
public static final	byte	MODIFIER_SYMBOL
public static final	byte	NON_SPACING_MARK
public static final	byte	OTHER_LETTER
public static final	byte	OTHER_NUMBER
public static final	byte	OTHER_PUNCTUATION
public static final	byte	OTHER_SYMBOL
public static final	byte	PARAGRAPH_SEPARATOR
public static final	byte	PRIVATE_USE
public static final	byte	SPACE_SEPARATOR
public static final	byte	START_PUNCTUATION
public static final	byte	SURROGATE
public static final	byte	TITLECASE_LETTER
public static final	Class	TYPE
public static final	byte	UNASSIGNED
public static final	byte	UPPERCASE_LETTER

Constructors

Modifiers	Constructor
public	Character(char)

Methods

Modifiers	Return Type	Method
public	char	charValue()
public static	int	digit(char, int)
public	boolean	equals(Object)
public static	char	forDigit(int, int)
public static	int	getNumericValue(char)
public static	int	getType(char)
public	int	hashCode()
public static	boolean	isDefined(char)
public static	boolean	isDigit(char)
public static	boolean	isIdentifierIgnorable(char)
public static	boolean	isISOControl(char)

Modifiers	Return Type	Method
public static	boolean	isJavaIdentifierPart(char)
public static	boolean	isJavaIdentifierStart(char)
public static	boolean	isJavaLetter(char)
public static	boolean	isJavaLetterOrDigit(char)
public static	boolean	isLetter(char)
public static	boolean	isLetterOrDigit(char)
public static	boolean	isLowerCase(char)
public static	boolean	isSpace(char)
public static	boolean	isSpaceChar(char)
public static	boolean	isTitleCase(char)
public static	boolean	isUnicodeIdentifierPart(char)
public static	boolean	isUnicodeIdentifierStart(char)
public static	boolean	isUpperCase(char)
public static	boolean	isWhitespace(char)
public static	char	toLowerCase(char)
public	String	toString()
public static	char	toTitleCase(char)
public static	char	toUpperCase(char)

See Also java.io.Serializable • java.lang.Object • java.lang.String

Class Class

public final synchronized java.lang.Class extends java.lang.Object implements java.io.Serializable

The Class class is used to reference the class for a Java object. Because this class does not have any constructors, it is instantiated automatically by the Java VM. However, you can return an instance of it by calling several of the methods from either the Object class or the Class class.

Note

The Class class has been considerably extended in 1.1. Specifically, Class has the added functionality to indirectly access all fields, constructors, and methods of a Java class.

As of Java 1.1, from a functionality standpoint, this class should be part of the java.lang.reflect package. However, for the purpose of backward compatibility with 1.0, it remains in this package.

Syntax & Usage You can obtain a reference to a Java class as an instance of this class in one of two ways:

1. From the fully qualified class name using the static method Class.forName():

```
Class clsRef = Class.forName("MyPackage.MyClass");
```

2. From an existing instance of the Object class using the Object.getClass() method:

```
MyClass obj;
Class clsRef = obj.getClass();
```

Once you have a reference to a class, you can get a reference to any field, constructor, or method declared in the class or inherited by it. Following are several examples:

```
Field Xref = clsRef.getField("X");
```

The preceding gets a reference to field X.

```
Method setRef = clsRef.getMethod("setX",
   new Class[] { int.class } );
```

This gets a reference to method setX(int).

```
Method constrRef = clsRef.getConstructor(
   new Class[] { int.class });
```

This third example gets a reference to the constructor MyClass(int).

Note

Please see the examples in Chapter 10, "The java.lang.reflect Package," which explain how to use these references to access the fields, constructors, and methods of a Java class indirectly.

Those Java classes in this package that encapsulate primitive Java types often are used as arguments for Remote Method Invocation (RMI) method calls. To make a programmer's life simpler, Java 1.1 provides class literals to use as a Class instance of the classes, as shown in Table 9-1. See Chapters 13 through 16 for more information on RMI.

Expression	Meaning
boolean.class	Represents Boolean class
char.class	Represents Character class
byte.class	Represents Byte class

Expression	Meaning
short.class	Represents Short class
int.class	Represents Integer class
long.class	Represents Long class
float.class	Represents Float class
double.class	Represents Double class
void.class	Represents Void class

Table 9-1: Class literals.

Fields None

Constructors None

Methods

Modifiers	Return Type	Method
public static native	Class	forName(String)
public	Class[]	getClasses()
public native	ClassLoader	getClassLoader()
public native	Class	getComponentType()
public	Constructor	getConstructor(Class[])
public	Constructor[]	getConstructors()
public	Class[]	getDeclaredClasses()
public	Constructor	getDeclaredConstructor(Class[])
public	Constructor[]	getDeclaredConstructors()
public	Field	getDeclaredField(String)
public	Field[]	getDeclaredFields()
public	Method	getDeclaredMethod(String, Class[])
public	Method[]	getDeclaredMethods()
public	Class	getDeclaringClass()
public	Field	getField(String)
public	Field[]	getFields()
public native	Class[]	getInterfaces()
public	Method	getMethod(String, Class[])
public	Method[]	getMethods()
public	int	getModifiers()
public native	String	getName()
public	URL	getResource(String)
public	InputStream	getResourceAsStream(String)
public native	Object[]	getSigners()
public native	Class	getSuperclass()
public native	boolean	isArray()

Modifiers	Return Type	Method
public native	boolean	isAssignableFrom(Class)
public native	boolean	isInstance(Object)
public native	boolean	isInterface()
public native	boolean	isPrimitive()
public native	Object	newInstance()
public	String	toString()

See Also java.io.Serializable • java.lang.Object • java.lang.reflect.*

Class ClassCastException

public synchronized java.lang.ClassCastException extends java.lang.RuntimeException

ClassCastException is thrown any time an incorrect cast has been attempted (i.e., a cast from an object to a subclass that it is not an instance of).

Syntax & Usage The following code generates a ClassCastException:

```
Object num = new Long(0);
System.out.println((BigDecimal)num);
```

Tip

To avoid casting issues, it is always a good idea to use the ***instanceof*** *operator to check the relationship between the object and the class to which it is being cast before attempting to perform the actual cast.*

Fields None

Constructors

Modifiers	Constructor
public	ClassCastException()
public	ClassCastException(String)

Methods None

See Also java.lang.RuntimeException

Class ClassCircularityError

public synchronized java.lang.ClassCircularityError extends java.lang.LinkageError

ClassCircularityError is thrown any time a class or interface names itself as its own superclass or superinterface.

Syntax & Usage Primarily, this error is thrown during the initialization of a class that specifies itself for its superclass or superinterface.

Fields None

Constructors

Modifiers	Constructor
public	ClassCircularityError()
public	ClassCircularityError(String)

Methods None

See Also java.lang.LinkageError

Class ClassFormatError

public synchronized java.lang.ClassFormatError extends java.lang.LinkageError

ClassFormatError is thrown when the physical class file for a class is corrupted or is in an otherwise unreadable format.

Syntax & Usage This error occurs when the Java VM attempts to read a corrupted class file. Please see the example in the next section, "Class ClassLoader," for more information.

Fields None

Constructors

Modifiers	Constructor
public	ClassFormatError()
public	ClassFormatError(String)

Methods None

See Also java.lang.LinkageError

Class ClassLoader

public abstract synchronized java.lang.ClassLoader extends java.lang.Object

The ClassLoader class is responsible for facilitating the added functionality to enhance the Java VM's processes for loading a class. Primarily, this is useful if you wish to load a class from an untraditional source (i.e., sources outside the normal places the Java VM would look).

Syntax & Usage To use this class in your application you need to subclass it. In the subclass, you need to implement at least one method: loadClass(String name, boolean resolve), in which the name parameter is the name of the class to be loaded and the resolve equals **true**, indicating that the class must be resolved. The following example shows a way to extend the ClassLoader class:

```
class MyClassLoader extends ClassLoader
{
  private Hashtable classes = new
    Hashtable();

  public synchronized Class loadClass(
    String name, boolean  resolve)
    throws ClassNotFoundException
  {
    Class cl = (Class)classes.get(name);
    if (cl != null)
      return cl;

    byte data[];
    // Get class's data bytes...
```

```
            try
            {
                cl = defineClass(name, data,
                    0, data.length);
            }
            catch (ClassFormatError e)
            {
                System.err.println(
                    "ClassFormatError");
                return null;
            }

            classes.put(name, cl);
            if (resolve)
                resolveClass(cl);
            return cl;
        }
}
```

The Hashtable objects are used to keep track of classes already loaded. If the requested class has not been loaded yet, the example assumes that the bytes will be read from some external source and uses the defineClass() method to define a new class from that byte array.

Fields None

Constructors

Modifiers	Constructor
protected	ClassLoader()

Methods

Modifiers	Return Type	Method
protected final	Class	defineClass(byte[], int, int)
protected final	Class	defineClass(String, byte[], int, int)
protected final	Class	findLoadedClass(String)
protected final	Class	findSystemClass(String)
public	URL	getResource(String)
public	InputStream	getResourceAsStream(String)
public static final	URL	getSystemResource(String)
public static final	InputStream	getSystemResourceAsStream(String)
public	Class	loadClass(String)
protected abstract	Class	loadClass(String, boolean)
protected final	void	resolveClass(Class)
protected final	void	setSigners(Class, Object[])

See Also java.lang.Class • java.lang.Object • java.util.Hashtable

Class ClassNotFoundException

public synchronized java.lang.ClassNotFoundException extends java.lang.Exception

The ClassNotFoundException exception is thrown whenever a specified class definition can't be found.

Syntax & Usage This exception is thrown by the forName() method in the Class class, and by the findSystemClass() and the loadClass() methods both from the ClassLoader class in the event that a specified class to be loaded could not be found. For an example, please see the preceding section "Class ClassLoader."

Fields None

Constructors

Modifiers	Constructor
public	ClassNotFoundException()
public	ClassNotFoundException(String)

Methods None

See Also java.lang.Class • java.lang.ClassLoader • java.lang.Exception

Interface Cloneable

public interface java.lang.Cloneable

The Cloneable interface contains no methods or fields but must be implemented by any class that needs to facilitate the ability to be cloned in Java.

Syntax & Usage This interface is used by any class that needs to have the ability to be cloned, which is done using the clone() method in the Object class. If a program attempts to clone a class that does not implement this interface, a CloneNotSupportedException exception will be thrown. However, you can use the **instanceof** operator to verify that a given object can be cloned before actually attempting to clone it. The following shows an example of this test being performed:

```
Object obj;
if (obj instanceof Cloneable)
   System.out.println(
      "This object can be cloned");
```

Fields None

Constructors None

Methods None

See Also java.lang.CloneNotSupportedException • java.lang.Object

Class CloneNotSupportedException

public synchronized java.lang.CloneNotSupportedException extends java.lang.Exception

The CloneNotSupportedException is thrown any time there is an attempt to clone an object that does not implement the Cloneable interface.

Syntax & Usage Specifically, this exception is thrown by the clone() method from the Object class. The following method creates a clone of a specified java.security.Signature instance and returns a new object:

```
static public Object cloneSignature(
   Signature sgn)
{
   try
   {
      return sgn.clone();
   }
   catch (CloneNotSupportedException e)
   {
      return null;
   }
}
```

If the operation should fail for some reason, **null** is returned; otherwise this code returns the cloned Signature instance as an Object object.

Fields None

Constructors

Modifiers	Constructor
public	CloneNotSupportedException()
public	CloneNotSupportedException(String)

Methods None

See Also java.lang.Cloneable • java.lang.Exception • java.lang.Object

Class Compiler

public final synchronized java.lang.Compiler extends java.lang.Object

The Compiler class is used to define several **native static** methods used in native compilers for Java.

Syntax & Usage This class is used for Just In Time (JIT) compiler implementations.

Basically, when the Java VM starts up, it looks for the system property *java.compiler*. If found, this property will point out the native compiler's library, and the Java VM will use the loadLibrary() method from the System class to load that library. At that point, you can use the **static** methods defined in the Compiler class to compile Java classes natively. For instance, the following shows the code you would use to compile the MyClass class:

```
Class cl = Class.forName("MyClass");
if (Compiler.compileClass(cl))
   System.out.println(
      "MyClass has been compiled");
```

Fields None

Constructors None

Methods

Modifiers	Return Type	Method
public static native	Object	command(Object)
public static native	boolean	compileClass(Class)
public static native	boolean	compileClasses(String)
public static native	void	disable()
public static native	void	enable()

See Also java.lang.Object • java.lang.System

Class Double

public final synchronized java.lang.Double extends java.lang.Number

The Double class represents an object wrapper for the **double** primitive type. The **double** primitive type is used for handling large floating-point values in Java. It is 64 bits in length, giving it a range of +/-1.79769313486231570E+308 to +/- 4.94065645841246544e-324, and can hold 15 significant digits.

Note

*Both the **double** and **float** primitive types conform to the IEEE 754 specifications. (IEEE stands for the Institute of Electrical and Electronic Engineers, an organization noted for setting standards in the industry.)*

Syntax & Usage

This class contains methods that let you convert to other primitive Java types. It also contains a few handy constants. The following snippet of code uses the Double class to parse a String to a **double**. Note that a NumberFormatException exception will be thrown if the operation is unsuccessful (i.e., the String is not able to be parsed):

```
String s = "123.98e5";
try
{
   Double dbl = Double.valueOf(s);
   double d = dbl.doubleValue();
   System.out.println("d="+d);
}
catch (NumberFormatException e)
{
   System.out.println(
      "Can't parse string to double");
}
```

The output for the preceding example would be as follows:

```
d=1.2398E7
```

Fields

Modifiers	Type	Field
public static final	double	MAX_VALUE
public static final	double	MIN_VALUE
public static final	double	NaN

Modifiers	Type	Field
public static final	double	NEGATIVE_INFINITY
public static final	double	POSITIVE_INFINITY
public static final	Class	TYPE

Constructors

Modifiers	Constructor
public	Double(double)
public	Double(String)

Methods

Modifiers	Return Type	Method
public	byte	byteValue()
public static native	long	doubleToLongBits(double)
public	double	doubleValue()
public	boolean	equals(Object)
public	float	floatValue()
public	int	hashCode()
public	int	intValue()
public	boolean	isInfinite()
public static	boolean	isInfinite(double)
public	boolean	isNaN()
public static	boolean	isNaN(double)
public static native	double	longBitsToDouble(long)
public	long	longValue()
public	short	shortValue()
public	String	toString()
public static	String	toString(double)
public static	Double	valueOf(String)

See Also java.lang.Float • java.lang.Number • java.lang.NumberFormatException

Class Error

public synchronized java.lang.Error extends java.lang.Throwable

The Error class represents the root for all errors in Java, and since it extends Throwable, errors can be thrown just like exceptions. Technically, an Error subclass represents a problem in the program (and/or underlying Java VM) and, unlike exceptions, would not need to be caught if the program were behaving normally.

Syntax & Usage Exceptions represent potential feasible issues that need to be caught in certain situations; errors are abnormal by nature. Errors are thrown only in the event that there is a serious problem with the program; that is why methods do not have errors in their **throws** clauses. However, since this class extends the Throwable class, it can be caught. Consider the following:

```
try
{
  // do something
}
catch (Error e)
{
  // React to the error
}
```

Usually, you don't catch an instance of this class or one of its subclasses in your Java programs, as errors represent abnormal behavior on the part of the Java program (or Java VM).

> **Note**
>
> *ThreadDeath is a unique error in Java: it is always thrown to kill a given thread. For more information, please see "Class ThreadDeath," later in this chapter.*

Fields None

Constructors

Modifiers	Constructor
public	Error()
public	Error(String)

Methods None

See Also java.lang.Exception • java.lang.ThreadDeath • java.lang.Throwable

Class Exception

public synchronized java.lang.Exception extends java.lang.Throwable

The Exception class is the root class for all exceptions in Java. Since it extends from the Throwable class, it can be thrown in Java.

Syntax & Usage Any exception subclasses (or the Exception class itself) declared in the **throws** clause of a method or class must be caught when the method or class is used.

If you are not interested in catching all the exceptions or errors in a given operation, you need to catch only the Exception class. This is useful in situations where you are only interested in the fact that an exception was thrown—and not necessarily what particular exception was thrown. The following code snippet outlines how to do this:

```
try
{
   // do something
}
catch (Exception e)
{
   // Process all exceptions in the code here
}
```

Fields None

Constructors

Modifiers	Constructor
public	Exception()
public	Exception(String)

Methods None

See Also java.lang.Error • java.lang.Throwable

Class ExceptionInInitializerError

public synchronized java.lang.ExceptionInInitializerError extends java.lang.LinkageError

The ExceptionInInitializerError signals that some sort of unexpected exception occurred during initialization of a **static** block.

Syntax & Usage You can use the getException() method from this class to determine exactly what exception occurred to raise this error.

Note

A ***static*** *initialization block starts from the* ***static*** *keyword and can be used for initialization of static variables. It executes before any other code in the class. For example, the following uses a* ***static*** *block to initialize the* ***static*** *factors array:*

```
class B {
   static long[] factors = new long[10];
   static {
     factors = 1;
     for (int k=1; k < factors.length; k++)
     factors[k] = factors[k-1]*k;
   }
```

Fields None

Constructors

Modifiers	Constructor
public	ExceptionInInitializerError()
public	ExceptionInInitializerError(String)
public	ExceptionInInitializerError(Throwable)

Methods

Modifiers	Return Type	Method
public	Throwable	getException()

See Also java.lang.LinkageError

Class Float

public final synchronized java.lang.Float extends java.lang.Number

The Float class represents an object wrapper for the float primitive type. The float primitive type is used for handling floating-point values in Java. It is 32 bits in length, giving it a range of +/-3.40282347E+38 to +/-1.40239846e-45, and holds seven significant digits.

Note

Like the ***double*** *primitive type, the* ***float*** *primitive type conforms to the IEEE 754 specifications.*

Syntax & Usage

This class contains methods that let you convert to other primitive Java types. It also contains a few handy constants. The following snippet of code uses the Float class to parse a String to a **float** value. Note that a NumberFormatException exception is thrown if the operation is unsuccessful (i.e., the String is not able to be parsed):

```
String s = "123.98e5";
try
{
   Float fl = Float.valueOf(s);
   float f = fl.floatValue();
   System.out.println("f="+f);
}
catch (NumberFormatException e)
{
   System.out.println(
      "Can't parse string to float");
}
```

The output for the preceding example is as follows:

```
f=1.2398E7
```

Fields

Modifiers	Type	Field
public static final	float	MAX_VALUE
public static final	float	MIN_VALUE
public static final	float	NaN
public static final	float	NEGATIVE_INFINITY
public static final	float	POSITIVE_INFINITY
public static final	Class	TYPE

Constructors

Modifiers	Constructor
public	Float(double)
public	Float(float)
public	Float(String)

Methods

Modifiers	Return Type	Method
public	byte	byteValue()
public	double	doubleValue()
public	boolean	equals(Object)
public static native	int	floatToIntBits(float)
public	float	floatValue()
public	int	hashCode()

Modifiers	Return Type	Method
public static native	float	intBitsToFloat(int)
public	int	intValue()
public	boolean	isInfinite()
public static	boolean	isInfinite(float)
public	boolean	isNaN()
public static	boolean	isNaN(float)
public	long	longValue()
public	short	shortValue()
public	String	toString()
public static	String	toString(float)
public static	Float	valueOf(String)

See Also java.lang.Double • java.lang.Number • java.lang.String

Class IllegalAccessError

public synchronized java.lang.IllegalAccessError extends java.lang.IncompatibleClassChangeError

IllegalAccessError can be thrown if a Java program attempts to access or modify the member of a class to which it should not have access.

Syntax & Usage This error is typically caught during compile time by the Java compiler. Nonetheless, you can still see this error at run time if the definition of a class has changed abnormally.

Fields None

Constructors

Modifiers	Constructor
public	IllegalAccessError()
public	IllegalAccessError(String)

Methods None

See Also java.lang.IncompatibleClassChangeError

Class IllegalAccessException

public synchronized java.lang.IllegalAccessException extends java.lang.Exception

IllegalAccessException is thrown any time the Java program (or environment) attempts to access a member of a class to which it does not have access.

Syntax & Usage This exception is thrown by the forName() method in the Class class and by the findSystemClass() and the loadClass() methods from the ClassLoader class in the event that code calls a member of a nonpublic class residing in another package.

The following example method constructs a new instance of the class specified in className, catching this exception among others:

```
static Object createInstance(String className)
{
   try
   {
      Class cl = Class.forName(className);
      return cl.newInstance();
   }
   catch (ClassNotFoundException e1)
   {
      System.err.println("Class not found: "
         +e1.getMessage());
   }
   catch (InstantiationException e2)
   {
      System.err.println(
         "Instantiation Exception: "
         +e2.getMessage());
   }
   catch (IllegalAccessException e3)
   {
      System.err.println(
         "Illegal Access Exception: "
         +e3.getMessage());
   }
   return null;

}
```

The method starts by taking a reference to a Class object and invokes the zero-parameter (default) constructor of that class, using the newInstance() method from the Class class. If this succeeds, the method returns a new object. Otherwise, the method catches the following three exceptions:

- **ClassNotFoundException.** The class cannot be found by the given name.
- **InstantiationException.** An object cannot be instantiated because it is an interface or is an abstract class.
- **IllegalAccessException.** The current method does not have access to the appropriate zero-parameter constructor.

If any of the preceding exceptions occur, this method prints out an error message and returns **null**.

Fields None

Constructors

Modifiers	Constructor
public	IllegalAccessException()
public	IllegalAccessException(String)

Methods None

See Also java.lang.Class • java.lang.ClassLoader • java.lang.Exception • java.lang.Object

Class IllegalArgumentException

public synchronized java.lang.IllegalArgumentException extends java.lang.RuntimeException

IllegalArgumentException can be thrown any time an illegal parameter is passed to a given method, constructor, and so on.

Syntax & Usage This exception can be thrown by many Java methods in the event that an illegal parameter is passed. The following example method sets the alignment of the specified Label (lbl) instance and catches the IllegalArgumentException if an invalid alignment were passed:

```
static public void setAlignment(Label lbl,
  int alignment)
{
  try
  {
    lbl.setAlignment(alignment);
  }
```

```
    catch (IllegalArgumentException e)
    {
        System.err.println(
        "Illegal argument for setAlignment(): "
        +alignment);
    }
}
```

Tip

If you are writing a method that can accept only a limited range of parameter values, you can throw this exception in the event that an invalid parameter is passed to your method.

Fields None

Constructors

Modifiers	Constructor
public	IllegalArgumentException()
public	IllegalArgumentException(String)

Methods None

See Also java.lang.RuntimeException

Class IllegalMonitorStateException

public synchronized java.lang.IllegalMonitorStateException extends java.lang.RuntimeException

IllegalMonitorStateException is thrown any time a thread, that has not been specified to listen to an object, attempts to wait or notify that object's monitor.

Syntax & Usage The following example uses the notify() method from the Object class to notify the object's monitor for a given Thread instance and catches an IllegalMonitorStateException if the current thread is not the owner of this object's monitor:

```
static public void notify(Thread thread)
{
    try
    {
        thread.notify();
    }
```

```
    catch (IllegalMonitorStateException e)
    {
      System.err.println(
      "IllegalMonitorStateException: "
      +e.getMessage());
    }
}
```

Fields None

Constructors

Modifiers	Constructor
public	IllegalMonitorStateException()
public	IllegalMonitorStateException(String)

Methods None

See Also java.lang.Object • java.lang.RuntimeException • java.lang.Thread

Class IllegalStateException

public synchronized java.lang.IllegalStateException extends java.lang.RuntimeException

IllegalStateException is thrown any time a Java program invokes a method at the wrong time.

Syntax & Usage Basically, this exception is thrown when a Java program is not in the correct state to have a given method be invoked to do its job. For an example of this exception, please see the section in Chapter 2, "ClassIllegalComponentStateException," which subclasses this one.

Fields None

Constructors

Modifiers	Constructor
public	IllegalStateException()
public	IllegalStateException(String)

Methods None

See Also java.awt.IllegalComponentStateException • java.lang.RuntimeException

Class IllegalThreadStateException

public synchronized java.lang.IllegalThreadStateException extends java.lang.IllegalArgumentException

IllegalThreadStateException is thrown any time a thread program is not in the correct state (or time) to have its request operation completed.

Syntax & Usage This exception is thrown when invoking a method (i.e., sleep(), suspend() and resume(), and so on from the Thread class) when the thread is not in the proper state. The following example method returns the number of stack frames in the given thread and catches an IllegalThreadStateException exception if the thread is not in a suspended state:

```
static public int countStackFrames(
  Thread thread)
{
  try
  {
    return thread.countStackFrames();
  }
  catch (IllegalThreadStateException e)
  {
    System.err.println(
    "IllegalThreadStateException: "
    +e.getMessage());
    return 0;
  }
}
```

Fields None

Constructors

Modifiers	Constructor
public	IllegalThreadStateException()
public	IllegalThreadStateException(String)

Methods None

See Also java.lang.IllegalArgumentException • java.lang.Thread

Class IncompatibleClassChangeError

public synchronized java.lang.IncompatibleClassChangeError extends java.lang.LinkageError

IncompatibleClassChangeError can be thrown if the definition of some class has been changed and the currently executing method cannot complete execution because of those changes.

Syntax & Usage

This class contains a number of subclasses that derive more precise errors relating to abnormal changes in various definitions of classes (and their members). The following is a list of its subclasses:

- AbstractMethodError
- IllegalAccessError
- InstantiationError
- NoSuchFieldError
- NoSuchMethodError

For more information, please see the sections, elsewhere in this chapter, for each of the subclasses in the preceding list.

Fields

None

Constructors

Modifiers	Constructor
public	IncompatibleClassChangeError()
public	IncompatibleClassChangeError(String)

Methods

None

See Also

java.lang.AbstractMethodError • java.lang.IllegalAccessError • java.lang.InstantiationError • java.lang.LinkageError • java.lang.NoSuchFieldError • java.lang.NoSuchMethodError

Class IndexOutOfBoundsException

public synchronized java.lang.IndexOutOfBoundsException extends java.lang.RuntimeException

IndexOutOfBoundsException is thrown any time an array has been referenced to a value outside of its range.

Syntax & Usage Usually this exception occurs with arrays, strings, or vectors. However, you also can subclass this exception to create your own custom exception of this type.

The following example method returns an array element for the specified array called index and catches the IndexOutOfBoundsException exception in the event that an illegal index value has been specified:

```
static public int getInt(int[] array,
  int index)
{
  try
  {
    return array[index];
  }
  catch (IndexOutOfBoundsException e)
  {
    System.err.println(
    "IndexOutOfBoundsException: "+index);
    return 0;
  }
}
```

Fields None

Constructors

Modifiers	Constructor
public	IndexOutOfBoundsException()
public	IndexOutOfBoundsException(String)

Methods None

See Also java.lang.RuntimeException • java.lang.String • java.util.Vector

Class InstantiationError

public synchronized java.lang.InstantiationError extends java.lang.IncompatibleClassChangeError

InstantiationError is thrown any time a Java program tries to instantiate a class that has been declared **abstract**.

Syntax & Usage Normally, you will not see this error because it is almost always caught at compile time. The rare event that might cause this error at run time is if the class declaration has been changed in an incompatible manner.

Fields None

Constructors

Modifiers	Constructor
public	InstantiationError()
public	InstantiationError(String)

Methods None

See Also java.lang.IncompatibleClassChangeError

Class InstantiationException

public synchronized java.lang.InstantiationException extends java.lang.Exception

InstantiationException is thrown any time a program attempts to invoke the constructor of an **abstract** class.

Syntax & Usage In particular, this exception is thrown by the newInstance() method from the Class class if the specified class to be instantiated is defined as **abstract**. Please see "Class IllegalAccessException," earlier in this chapter, for an example of its usage.

Fields None

Constructors

Modifiers	Constructor
public	InstantiationException()
public	InstantiationException(String)

Methods None

See Also java.lang.Class • java.lang.Exception

Class Integer

public final synchronized java.lang.Integer extends java.lang.Number

The Integer class represents an object wrapper for the int primitive type. The int primitive type is a 32-bit integer value with a range of -2,147,483,648 to +2,147,483,647.

Syntax & Usage This class contains methods that let you convert to other primitive Java types and to other number systems. The following snippet of code uses the Integer class to parse a String value to an int value. Note that a NumberFormatException exception will be thrown if the String passed is illegal:

```
String s = "123";
try
{
   Integer I = Integer.valueOf(s);
   int i = I.intValue();System.out.println("i="+i);
}
catch (NumberFormatException e)
{
   System.out.println(
      "Can't parse string to int");
}
```

The output for the preceding example would be:

```
i=123
```

Fields

Modifiers	Type	Field
public static final	int	MAX_VALUE
public static final	int	MIN_VALUE
public static final	Class	TYPE

Constructors

Modifiers	Constructor
public	Integer(int)
public	Integer(String)

Methods

Modifiers	Return Type	Method
public	byte	byteValue()
public static	Integer	decode(String)
public	double	doubleValue()
public	boolean	equals(Object)
public	float	floatValue()
public static	Integer	getInteger(String)
public static	Integer	getInteger(String, int)
public static	Integer	getInteger(String, Integer)
public	int	hashCode()
public	int	intValue()
public	long	longValue()
public static	int	parseInt(String)
public static	int	parseInt(String, int)
public	short	shortValue()
public static	String	toBinaryString(int)
public static	String	toHexString(int)
public static	String	toOctalString(int)
public	String	toString()
public static	String	toString(int)
public static	String	toString(int, int)
public static	Integer	valueOf(String)
public static	Integer	valueOf(String, int)

See Also java.lang.Byte • java.lang.Long. • java.lang.Number • java.lang.Short • java.lang.String

Class InternalError

public synchronized java.lang.InternalError extends java.lang.VirtualMachineError

InternalError is thrown any time an unexpected internal error occurs in the Java VM.

Syntax & Usage Since this rare error relates directly to the Java VM, a typical programmer does not have any direct use for it.

Fields None

Constructors

Modifiers	Constructor
public	InternalError()
public	InternalError(String)

Methods None

See Also java.lang.VirtualMachineError

Class InterruptedException

public synchronized java.lang.InterruptedException extends java.lang.Exception

InterruptedException can be thrown any time a thread that is not in a running state is interrupted.

Syntax & Usage This exception can be thrown when another thread calls interrupt() to interrupt an executing thread that has already paused (e.g., waiting or sleeping) in some fashion. For an example of this, please see "Class Thread," later in this chapter.

Fields None

Constructors

Modifiers	Constructor
public	InterruptedException()
public	InterruptedException(String)

Methods None

See Also java.lang.Exception • java.lang.Thread

Class LinkageError

public synchronized java.lang.LinkageError extends java.lang.Error

LinkageError can be thrown if a class on which another class depends has changed in an incompatible manner after compilation.

Syntax & Usage This class actually contains a number of subclasses that derive more precise errors relating to interclass dependency anomalies. The following is a list of its subclasses:

- AbstractMethodError
- ClassFormatError
- ExceptionInInitializerError
- IllegalAccessError
- IncompatibleClassChangeError
- InstantiationError
- NoClassDefFoundError
- NoSuchFieldError
- NoSuchMethodError
- UnsatisfiedLinkError
- VerifyError

For more information on these error classes, please see the appropriate sections elsewhere in this chapter.

Fields None

Constructors

Modifiers	Constructor
public	LinkageError()
public	LinkageError(String)

Methods None

See Also java.lang.AbstractMethodError • java.lang.ClassFormatError • java.lang.Error • java.lang.ExceptionInInitializerError • java.lang.IllegalAccessError • java.lang.IncompatibleClassChangeError • java.lang.InstantiationError • java.lang.NoClassDefFoundError • java.lang.NoSuchFieldError • java.lang.NoSuchMethodError • java.lang.UnsatisfiedLinkError • java.lang.VerifyError

Class Long

public final synchronized java.lang.Long extends java.lang.Number

The Long class represents an object wrapper for the long primitive type. The long primitive type is a 64-bit integer value with a range of –9,223,372,036,854,775,808 to +9,223,372,036,854,775,807.

Syntax & Usage This class contains methods that let you convert to other primitive Java types and other number systems. The following snippet of code uses the Integer class to parse a String value to a **long** value. Note that a NumberFormatException exception is thrown if the String passed is illegal:

```
String s = "123";
try
{
   Long L = Long.valueOf(s);
   long l = L.longValue();
   System.out.println("l="+l);
}
catch (NumberFormatException e)
{
   System.out.println(
      "Can't parse string to long");
}
```

The output for the preceding example would be:

```
i=123
```

Fields

Modifiers	Type	Field
public static final	long	MAX_VALUE
public static final	long	MIN_VALUE
public static final	Class	TYPE

Constructors

Modifiers	Constructor
public	Long(long)
public	Long(String)

Methods

Modifiers	Return Type	Method
public	byte	byteValue()
public	double	doubleValue()
public	boolean	equals(Object)
public	float	floatValue()
public static	Long	getLong(String)
public static	Long	getLong(String, long)
public static	Long	getLong(String, Long)
public	int	hashCode()
public	int	intValue()
public	long	longValue()
public static	long	parseLong(String)
public static	long	parseLong(String, int)
public	short	shortValue()
public static	String	toBinaryString(long)
public static	String	toHexString(long)
public static	String	toOctalString(long)
public	String	toString()
public static	String	toString(long)
public static	String	toString(long, int)
public static	Long	valueOf(String)
public static	Long	valueOf(String, int)

See Also java.lang.Byte • java.lang.Integer • java.lang.Number • java.lang.Short • java.lang.String

Class Math

public final synchronized java.lang.Math extends java.lang.Object

The Math class contains the necessary methods and fields for performing a variety of mathematical operations.

Note

This class uses algorithms present from fdlibm. Therefore, the functionality present in this class is similar to that of the <math.h> header file used in C—which also is based on the algorithms present in fdlibm.

Syntax & Usage

This class contains a useful collection of static methods that are necessary in a variety of mathematical calculations including those that relate to trigonometry and exponentiation. This class also defines two common mathematical constants: *e* (represented as Math.E) and p (represented as Math.PI).

The following snippet uses methods from the Math class to convert Cartesian coordinates *(x, y)* to polar *(r, f)* coordinates:

```
double x, y, r, f;

r = Math.sqrt(x*x + y*y);
f = Math.atan2(x, y);
```

Notice that the Math.atan2(x, y) method computes an arctangent from the y/x ratio in the range -p to p, not from x/y as the function of the same name does it in C.

The following snippet uses methods from the Math class to convert polar coordinates *(r, f)* back to Cartesian *(x, y)*:

```
x = r*Math.cos(f);
y = r*Math.sin(f);
```

Fields

Modifiers	Type	Field
public static final	double	E
public static final	double	PI

Constructors None

Methods

Modifiers	Return Type	Method
public static	double	abs(double)
public static	float	abs(float)
public static	int	abs(int)
public static	long	abs(long)
public static native	double	acos(double)
public static native	double	asin(double)
public static native	double	atan(double)
public static native	double	atan2(double, double)
public static native	double	ceil(double)

Modifiers	Return Type	Method
public static native	double	cos(double)
public static native	double	exp(double)
public static native	double	floor(double)
public static native	double	IEEEremainder(double, double)
public static native	double	log(double)
public static	double	max(double, double)
public static	float	max(float, float)
public static	int	max(int, int)
public static	long	max(long, long)
public static	double	min(double, double)
public static	float	min(float, float)
public static	int	min(int, int)
public static	long	min(long, long)
public static	double	pow(double, double)
public static synchronized	double	random()
public static native	double	rint(double)
public static	long	round(double)
public static	int	round(float)
public static native	double	sin(double)
public static native	double	sqrt(double)
public static native	double	tan(double)

See Also java.lang.Object

Class NegativeArraySizeException

public synchronized java.lang.NegativeArraySizeException extends java.lang.RuntimeException

The NegativeArraySizeException exception is thrown any time a Java program attempts to create an array with a negative size.

Syntax & Usage This exception can crop up when you are performing calculations and use the results of those calculations to initialize an array. For an example of this exception being used, please see the java.lang.reflect.Array class in Chapter 10.

Fields None

Constructors

Modifiers	Constructor
public	NegativeArraySizeException()
public	NegativeArraySizeException(String)

Methods None

See Also java.lang.Object • java.lang.reflect.Array • java.lang.RuntimeException

Class NoClassDefFoundError

public synchronized java.lang.NoClassDefFoundError extends java.lang.LinkageError

NoClassDefFoundError can be thrown any time the definition for a class cannot be found.

Syntax & Usage Specifically, this error deals with a class that existed at compile time, thereby letting the program compile successfully but for some reason is no longer present during run time when the program attempts to load it.

Fields None

Constructors

Modifiers	Constructor
public	NoClassDefFoundError()
public	NoClassDefFoundError(String)

Methods None

See Also java.lang.LinkageError

Class NoSuchFieldError

public synchronized java.lang.NoSuchFieldError extends java.lang.IncompatibleClassChangeError

The NoSuchFieldError error is thrown any time a Java program tries to access a field of an instantiated class that has disappeared in an anomalous fashion.

Syntax & Usage Normally, this error is caught by the compiler at compile time. The only time you might see this error is when the definition of that class has abnormally changed during run time.

Fields None

Constructors

Modifiers	Constructor
public	NoSuchFieldError()
public	NoSuchFieldError(String)

Methods None

See Also java.lang.IncompatibleClassChangeError • java.lang.NoSuchMethodError

Class NoSuchFieldException

public synchronized java.lang.NoSuchFieldException extends java.lang.Exception

NoSuchFieldException is thrown any time a Java program attempts to access a nonexistent field of an object.

Syntax & Usage Usually, you do not see this exception thrown in your Java programs because the compiler catches such issues.

Fields None

Constructors

Modifiers	Constructor
public	NoSuchFieldException()
public	NoSuchFieldException(String)

Methods None

See Also java.lang.Exception • java.lang.NoSuchMethodException

Class NoSuchMethodError

public synchronized java.lang.NoSuchMethodError extends java.lang.IncompatibleClassChangeError

NoSuchMethodError can be thrown any time a Java program tries to access a method (static or otherwise) of an instantiated class that has "disappeared" in an anomalous fashion.

Syntax & Usage Normally this error is caught by the compiler at compile time. The only time you might see this error is when the definition of a class has abnormally changed during run time.

Fields None

Constructors

Modifiers	Constructor
public	NoSuchMethodError()
public	NoSuchMethodError(String)

Methods None

See Also java.lang.IncompatibleClassChangeError • java.lang.NoSuchFieldError

Class NoSuchMethodException

public synchronized java.lang.NoSuchMethodException extends java.lang.Exception

NoSuchMethodException is thrown any time a Java program attempts to access a nonexistent field of an object.

Syntax & Usage Usually, you do not see this exception raised in your Java programs because the compiler catches such issues. For more information, please see the example for the java.lang.reflect.Field class in Chapter 10.

Fields None

Constructors

Modifiers	Constructor
public	NoSuchMethodException()
public	NoSuchMethodException(String)

Methods None

See Also java.lang.Exception • java.lang.NoSuchFieldException

Class NullPointerException

public synchronized java.lang.NullPointerException extends java.lang.RuntimeException

NullPointerException is thrown by a number of methods in Java in the event that a null reference is passed. More often, this exception can occur when you receive an object reference from a Java method and attempt to use it to invoke methods from that object.

Syntax & Usage This exception crops up particularly with arrays in the event that you try to take the length of an array that is currently **null** or access its elements. It also shows up when you attempt to access members of an instantiated object that is currently set to **null**.

Note

*Throwing **null** as if it were a Throwable object also results in this exception being raised.*

Consider the following code snippet, which obtains a PrintJob instance by invoking the getPrintJob() method from the java.awt.Toolkit class, returning a Graphics instance. Then the snippet performs printing by invoking the paintAll() method and flashes the page using the dispose() method:

```
Frame myFrame;

PrintJob prnJob = getToolkit().getPrintJob(
   myFrame, "Printing Test", null);
Graphics pg = prnJob.getGraphics();
myFrame.paintAll(pg); // print myFrame
pg.dispose();         // flush page
```

So, what's wrong with that example? The method getPrintJob() will return **null** if the user has canceled the print dialog or if some other error occurs. In cases like this, a NullPointerException exception will be thrown when the program tries to call getGraphics() on a **null** object reference. For another example of this exception being used, please see the java.lang.reflect.Array class in Chapter 10.

> **Note**
>
> *Although Java does not use pointers, this exception has the word* pointer *as a part of its name. It obviously is carried over from C/C++ errors relating to NULL pointers.*

Fields None

Constructors

Modifiers	Constructor
public	NullPointerException()
public	NullPointerException(String)

Methods None

See Also java.awt.Toolkit • java.lang.RuntimeException • java.lang.reflect.Array

Class Number

public abstract synchronized java.lang.Number extends java.lang.Object implements java.io.Serializable

The Number class is an **abstract** class that is the superclass for any integer-based classes in Java. It defines the methods necessary for any of its subclasses to convert between various primitive numerical types in Java.

Syntax & Usage To use this class, you need to subclass it. In most cases, you can use one of its subclasses that represent the object wrappers for the integer-based primitive types available in Java. The following is a list of java.lang.Number subclasses:

- Byte
- Double
- Float
- Integer
- Long
- Short

For more information on each of these classes, please see the appropriate sections elsewhere in this chapter.

Fields None

Constructors

Modifiers	Constructor
public	Number()

Methods

Modifiers	Return Type	Method
public	byte	byteValue()
public abstract	double	doubleValue()
public abstract	float	floatValue()
public abstract	int	intValue()
public abstract	long	longValue()
public	short	shortValue()

See Also java.io.Serializable • java.lang.Byte • java.lang.Double • java.lang.Float • java.lang.Integer • java.lang.Long • java.lang.Object • java.lang.Short

Class NumberFormatException

public synchronized java.lang.NumberFormatException extends java.lang.IllegalArgumentException

NumberFormatException is thrown any time a conversion operation from a String to a numerical type has failed. Specifically, this failure relates to the fact that the given String did not contain appropriate values to be converted to the specified primitive type.

Syntax & Usage When performing various conversions from String to various primitive numerical types, it is extremely important that they are formatted properly: otherwise, this exception will be thrown. For examples of this exception, please see the sections, elsewhere in this chapter, for the Byte, Double, Float, Integer, Long, and Short classes.

Fields None

Constructors

Modifiers	Constructor
public	NumberFormatException()
public	NumberFormatException(String)

Methods None

See Also java.lang.Byte • java.lang.Double • java.lang.Float • java.lang.IllegalArgumentException • java.lang.Integer • java.lang.Long • java.lang.Short

Class Object

public synchronized java.lang.Object

The Object class is the root class to every class present in Java.

Note

Arrays also implement methods from this class.

Syntax & Usage You may find it useful to override methods in the Object class when creating your own Java classes. The following lists three important methods inherited from this class that may be useful when creating your own Java classes:

- **public boolean equals(Object obj)**. This method returns true if the specified object can be considered as equaling the given object. However, when implementing this method, you must obey the following algebraic rules:
  - Reflexive: X == X
  - Symmetric: if X == Y, when Y == X
  - Transitive: if X == Y and Y == Z when X == Z
  - Consistent: The relation (equals or not) between X and Y will be the same for any references on X and Y.
  - Not null: X != null

- **protected Object clone()**. This method returns an identical copy of this object. Note that this works only on objects that implement the Cloneable interface.
- **protected void finalize()**. This method is invoked when this instance is destroyed by the garbage collector. Note that, because the garbage collector runs on a background thread, you may not always know exactly when it is called.

> **Note**
>
> *You can invoke the runFinalization() method from the System (or Runtime) class to force any unreferenced objects that have not been cleaned up yet to call their respective finalize() methods.*

The following shows an example class called MyClass that extends Object and overrides the three methods listed earlier:

```
class MyClass extends Object
{
   protected int X;

   public MyClass(int x)
   {
      X = x;
   }

   public boolean equals(Object obj)
   {
      if (obj instanceof MyClass)
         return (((MyClass)obj).X == X);
      else
         return false;
   }

   protected Object clone()
   {
      return new MyClass(X);
   }

   protected void finalize()
   {
      System.out.println(
         "I have been finalized");
   }
}
```

Note

If a Java class does not extend another class explicitly, it is assumed to have extended the Object class. However, you can extend the Object class explicitly.

In the preceding example, we've shown the 'extends Object' clause for clarity only. If you are new to Java (or are working with junior programmers), for simplicity's sake, you may want to extend Object explicitly for classes that normally would appear not to extend any class.

Fields None

Constructors

Modifiers	Constructor
public	Object()

Methods

Modifiers	Return Type	Method
protected native	Object	clone()
public	boolean	equals(Object)
protected	void	finalize()
public final native	Class	getClass()
public native	int	hashCode()
public final native	void	notify()
public final native	void	notifyAll()
public	String	toString()
public final	void	wait()
public final native	void	wait(long)
public final	void	wait(long, int)

See Also java.lang.Cloneable

Class OutOfMemoryError

public synchronized java.lang.OutOfMemoryError extends java.lang.VirtualMachineError

OutOfMemoryError can be thrown any time the program runs out of memory.

Syntax & Usage Specifically, this error gets thrown if an object is allocated more memory than the garbage collector has available. The following snippet of code initializes a very large array of integers (i.e., 1024 by 1024 bytes)—thus needing about 1 megabyte (MB) of memory. If there is not enough available memory on the user's system to complete this operation, the OutOfMemoryError error will be thrown:

```
try
{
   int[][] array = new int[1024][1024];
}
catch (OutOfMemoryError e)
{
   System.err.println(
      "Can't allocate memory for array");
}
```

Fields None

Constructors

Modifiers	Constructor
public	OutOfMemoryError()
public	OutOfMemoryError(String)

Methods None

See Also java.lang.VirtualMachineError

Class Process

public abstract synchronized java.lang.Process extends java.lang.Object

The Process class is an **abstract** class that lets applications (or digitally signed applets) execute system commands on the user's system.

Syntax & Usage Since this class is **abstract**, you cannot use it directly. However, you can gain an instance of a subclass of this class using the exec() method from the Runtime class. Once you have a subclass instance, you can execute commands (e.g., invoke non-Java applications) on the user's system. The following snippet of code shows how to execute a batch file from your Java program:

```
Runtime runtime = Runtime.getRuntime();
try
{
   Process child = runtime.exec("dr.bat");
   InputStream in = child.getInputStream();
   int k;
   while ((k = in.read()) != -1)
   {
      System.out.print((char)k);
   }
   child.waitFor();
}
catch (IOException e)
{
   e.printStackTrace();
   System.err.println("IOException: "+
      e.getMessage());
}
catch (InterruptedException e)
{
   System.err.println("InterruptedException"+
      e.getMessage());
}
```

Using the exec() method from the Runtime class, this code starts execution of the batch file dr.bat, obtains an input stream for that, subclasses Process, and redirects all output characters to the System.out stream. Then, the method waitFor() from this class waits until this process finishes execution.

Fields None

Constructors

Modifiers	Constructor
public	Process()

Methods

Modifiers	Return Type	Method
public abstract	void	destroy()
public abstract	int	exitValue()
public abstract	InputStream	getErrorStream()
public abstract	InputStream	getInputStream()
public abstract	OutputStream	getOutputStream()
public abstract	int	waitFor()

See Also java.io.InputStream • java.io.OutputStream • java.lang.Object

Interface Runnable

public abstract interface java.lang.Runnable

The Runnable interface should be implemented by any class needing to use threads.

Tip

This provides an alternative to facilitate support of threads without having to subclass the Thread class. This is quite useful for Java applets, which by definition must subclass the Applet class.

Syntax & Usage This interface provides a way of using threads without subclassing java.lang.Thread (please see the example for "Class Thread," later in this chapter, for more information). If your class implements this interface, it must override the run() method, which can use a Thread instance assigned to it. The following example outlines how to do this:

```
class MyRunnable implements Runnable
{
   // Constructor
   public MyRunnable()
   {
      // Place initialization code here
   }

   public void run()
   {
      while (true)
      {
         // do something...
         System.out.println("I'm alive");
         try
         {
            Thread.sleep(1000);
         }
         catch (InterruptedException e)
         {
            System.out.println(
               "I'm interrupted");
            return;
         }
      }
   }
}
```

To start this, you need to create a new instance of the MyRunnable class, create a Thread instance for it, and implement the run() method for the Thread object:

```
Runnable toRun = new MyRunnable();
new Thread(toRun).start();
```

Fields None

Constructors None

Methods

Modifiers	Return Type	Method
public abstract	void	run()

See Also java.lang.Thread

Class Runtime

public synchronized java.lang.Runtime extends java.lang.Object

The Runtime class is used for performing various platform-specific operations (e.g., starting a new external process).

Syntax & Usage Since this class does not contain any constructors, you can gain an instance of it using the **static** getRuntime() method. Once you have an instance of it, you can perform a variety of platform-dependent operations, including the ability to start a new process (using an exec() method), query information about the memory, and other related operations.

This class also defines methods that are useful for interpreters including the traceInstructions() and the traceMethodCalls() methods that let you enable (or disable) tracing. For an example of this class in action, please see "Class Process," earlier in this chapter.

Fields None

Constructors None

Methods

Modifiers	Return Type	Method
public	Process	exec(String)
public	Process	exec(String, String[])
public	Process	exec(String[])
public	Process	exec(String[], String[])

Modifiers	Return Type	Method
public	void	exit(int)
public native	long	freeMemory()
public native	void	gc()
public	InputStream	getLocalizedInputStream(InputStream)
public	OutputStream	getLocalizedOutputStream(OutputStream)
public static	Runtime	getRuntime()
public synchronized	void	load(String)
public synchronized	void	loadLibrary(String)
public native	void	runFinalization()
public static	void	runFinalizersOnExit(boolean)
public native	long	totalMemory()
public native	void	traceInstructions(boolean)
public native	void	traceMethodCalls(boolean)

See Also java.lang.Object • java.lang.Process

Class RuntimeException

public synchronized java.lang.RuntimeException extends java.lang.Exception

RuntimeException is thrown when there is a problem during the normal execution of the Java VM.

Syntax & Usage This exception serves as the superclass for numerous exceptions in Java. For instance, ArithmeticException, ArrayStoreException, ClassCastException, and IllegalArgumentException to name a few. For more information, see the examples in the sections, elsewhere in this chapter, for the previous classes.

Fields None

Constructors

Modifiers	Constructor
public	RuntimeException()
public	RuntimeException(String)

Methods None

See Also java.lang.ArithmeticException • java.lang.ArrayStoreException • java.lang.ClassCastException • java.lang.Exception • java.lang.IllegalArgumentException

Class SecurityException

public synchronized java.lang.SecurityException extends java.lang.RuntimeException

SecurityException is thrown any time there is a violation in the security model for your Java program.

Syntax & Usage

This exception can be thrown if the Java program is considered "untrusted" by the Java VM (i.e., an unsigned Java applet) and the program attempts to access the user's file system, make an arbitrary network connection, send data to the user's printer, or perform other activities that give it direct access to the user's resources. For an example where this exception needs to be caught, please see the next section, "Class SecurityManager."

Fields

None

Constructors

Modifiers	Constructor
public	SecurityException()
public	SecurityException(String)

Methods

None

See Also

java.lang.RuntimeException • java.lang.SecurityManager

Class SecurityManager

public abstract synchronized java.lang.SecurityManager extends java.lang.Object

The SecurityManager class is an **abstract** class that is used to regulate the restrictions and privileges of a Java program.

Syntax & Usage

Any Java applet downloaded off the Net that is not digitally signed is considered untrusted by the Java VM. Thus, it will not be allowed access to various resources on the user's system. It is this class's job to actually implement the security restrictions for an untrusted applet. This class also contains methods to check whether your Java applet is allowed to perform certain actions.

The following snippet of code uses this class to check to see if read, write, and delete operations are permitted for the arbitrarily specified file myFile.txt:

```
SecurityManager security =
   System.getSecurityManager();
if (security != null)
{
   String sFile = "myFile.txt";

   boolean bCanRead = true;
   try { security.checkRead(sFile); }
   catch (SecurityException er)
   { bCanRead = false; }

   boolean bCanWrite = true;
   try { security.checkWrite(sFile); }
   catch (SecurityException ew)
   { bCanWrite = false; }

   boolean bCanDelete = true;
   try { security.checkDelete(sFile); }
   catch (SecurityException ed)
   { bCanDelete = false; }

   System.out.println(
   "Can read:\t"+(bCanRead ? "YES" : "NO")+
   "\nCan write:\t"+(bCanWrite ?
   "YES" : "NO")+
   "\nCan delete:\t"+(bCanDelete ?
   "YES" : "NO"));
}
```

This code snippet starts by obtaining an instance of this class using the getSecurityManager() method from the System class and then calls the checkRead(), checkWrite(), and checkDelete() methods for the given file name. If the operation (i.e., reading, writing, or deleting) is not permitted, the corresponding method will throw a SecurityException exception. Catching the exception (or exceptions) lets you verify whether your applet is not permitted to do that action.

Following is the corresponding output if a nonsigned Java applet were to perform the preceding checks:

```
Can read:      YES
Can write:     NO
Can delete:    NO
```

Note

For Java applications, the getSecurityManager() method from the System class returns ***null****; the preceding example can be used only for Java applets. However, you can use this method to check to see whether your Java appletcation is executing as a Java applet or application.*

Fields

Modifiers	Type	Field
protected	boolean	inCheck

Constructors

Modifiers	Constructor
protected	SecurityManager()

Methods

Modifiers	Return Type	Method
public	void	checkAccept(String, int)
public	void	checkAccess(Thread)
public	void	checkAccess(ThreadGroup)
public	void	checkAwtEventQueueAccess()
public	void	checkConnect(String, int)
public	void	checkConnect(String, int, Object)
public	void	checkCreateClassLoader()
public	void	checkDelete(String)
public	void	checkExec(String)
public	void	checkExit(int)
public	void	checkLink(String)
public	void	checkListen(int)
public	void	checkMemberAccess(Class, int)
public	void	checkMulticast(InetAddress)
public	void	checkMulticast(InetAddress, byte)
public	void	checkPackageAccess(String)
public	void	checkPackageDefinition(String)
public	void	checkPrintJobAccess()
public	void	checkPropertiesAccess()
public	void	checkPropertyAccess(String)
public	void	checkRead(FileDescriptor)
public	void	checkRead(String)
public	void	checkRead(String, Object)

Modifiers	Return Type	Method
public	void	checkSecurityAccess(String)
public	void	checkSetFactory()
public	void	checkSystemClipboardAccess()
public	boolean	checkTopLevelWindow(Object)
public	void	checkWrite(FileDescriptor)
public	void	checkWrite(String)
protected native	int	classDepth(String)
protected native	int	classLoaderDepth()
protected native	ClassLoader	currentClassLoader()
protected	Class	currentLoadedClass()
protected native	Class[]	getClassContext()
public	boolean	getInCheck()
public	Object	getSecurityContext()
public	ThreadGroup	getThreadGroup()
protected	boolean	inClass(String)
protected	boolean	inClassLoader()

See Also java.lang.Object • java.lang.SecurityException • java.lang.System

Class Short

public final synchronized java.lang.Short extends java.lang.Number

The Short class represents an object wrapper for the **short** primitive type. The **short** primitive type is an integer data type in Java. Since byte is 16 bits in length, it has a range of -32,768 to 32,767.

Syntax & Usage

This class contains methods that let you convert to other primitive Java types. The following snippet of code uses the Short class to parse a String to a short value. Notice that a NumberFormatException exception will be thrown if the String passed is illegal:

```
String s = "123";
try
{
```

```
   Short sh = Short.valueOf(s);
   short s = bt.shortValue();
   System.out.println("s="+s);
}
catch (NumberFormatException e)
{
   System.out.println(
      "Can't parse string to short");
}
```

The output for the preceding example would be as follows:

```
b=123
```

Fields

Modifiers	Type	Field
public static final	short	MAX_VALUE
public static final	short	MIN_VALUE
public static final	Class	TYPE

Constructors

Modifiers	Constructor
public	Short(short)
public	Short(String)

Methods

Modifiers	Return Type	Method
public	byte	byteValue()
public static	Short	decode(String)
public	double	doubleValue()
public	boolean	equals(Object)
public	float	floatValue()
public	int	hashCode()
public	int	intValue()
public	long	longValue()
public static	short	parseShort(String)
public static	short	parseShort(String, int)
public	short	shortValue()
public	String	toString()
public static	String	toString(short)
public static	Short	valueOf(String)
public static	Short	valueOf(String, int)

See Also java.lang.Byte • java.lang.Integer • java.lang.Long • java.lang.Number • java.lang.String

Class StackOverflowError

public synchronized java.lang.StackOverflowError extends java.lang.VirtualMachineError

StackOverFlowError is thrown any time a Java program overflows its stack.

Syntax & Usage This error can be thrown if a stack overflow occurs, which often happens when a Java program creates too many local variables—most likely in some sort of a recursive fashion—for the current stack to hold.

Fields None

Constructors

Modifiers	Constructor
public	StackOverflowError()
public	StackOverflowError(String)

Methods None

See Also java.lang.VirtualMachineError

Class String

public final synchronized java.lang.String extends java.lang.Object implements java.io.Serializable

The String class is a key class used in Java to represent a string of characters.

Note

In C/C++, a string is an array of characters. Unfortunately, without the direct use of pointers (and pointer arithmetic) in Java, you lose the functionality of arrays (and ultimately the character array). That is why Java has the String class for you to use instead. However, this class does have special privileges that are not available to a typical class in Java.

Syntax & Usage One of the extra hooks that Java provides this class is that a String object will automatically initialize any time the compiler runs into double quotes (").This means that you can declare a String as if it were a primitive data type:

```
String s = "My test string.";
```

Note

This also applies to string literals, which means that they are represented as String objects as well.

The String class provides a variety of methods used to perform various string-based operations.

Note

This class uses functionality that is similar to that defined in the <string.h> header file used in C.

When performing operations, it is important to note that the contents of the String instance cannot be changed after its creation (i.e., Strings are immutable). Instead, you must create new String objects that will contain the results of the String operations that will result from using the methods defined in this class. Notwithstanding, you can concatenate strings using the + operator.

Note

It is possible to perform in-place modifications of a string using the StringBuffer class.

The following example method shows how to extract the middle part of the specified string safely and return it as a new String object:

```
static public String mid(String str,
   int index, int len)
{
   int n = str.length();
   if (index>n || len<=0)
      return ""; // nothing to return
   // 0-based 1-st char
   int index1 = Math.max(index, 0);
   // 0-based last char
   int index2 = Math.min(index+len, n);
   try
```

```
    {
       return str.substring(index1, index2);
    }
    catch (StringIndexOutOfBoundsException e)
    {
       return "";
    }
}
```

Notice that this **static** method takes a String object (str) parameter for the original string, an int (index) for the starting index in the middle of the string, and another int (len) representing the length of the portion to be returned. The method then calculates the position of the zero-based first and last characters from the requested portion and uses the substring() method from the String class to extract that portion as a new String object. A StringIndexOutOfBoundsException exception may be thrown during this operation if the starting index and length parameters (in relation to the specified String str) were not set to valid values.

Once you have extracted the middle portion of the string successfully, you can then easily extract its remaining left and right portions, as follows:

```
// Returns left portion of given string
static public String left(String str, int len)
{
   return mid(str, 0, len);
}

// Returns right portion of given string
static public String right(String str,
   int len)
{
   return mid(str, str.length()-len, len);
}
```

Tip

*Class String is **final** and therefore cannot be extended. If you need to add some functionality to String objects, you can create **static** methods like the examples shown above.*

Fields None

Constructors

Modifiers	Constructor
public	String()
public	String(byte[])
public	String(byte[], int)

Modifiers	Constructor
public	String(byte[], int, int)
public	String(byte[], int, int, int)
public	String(byte[], int, int, String)
public	String(byte[], String)
public	String(char[])
public	String(char[], int, int)
public	String(String)
public	String(StringBuffer)

Methods

Modifiers	Return Type	Method
public	char	charAt(int)
public	int	compareTo(String)
public	String	concat(String)
public static	String	copyValueOf(char[])
public static	String	copyValueOf(char[], int, int)
public	boolean	endsWith(String)
public	boolean	equals(Object)
public	boolean	equalsIgnoreCase(String)
public	byte[]	getBytes()
public	void	getBytes(int, int, byte[], int)
public	byte[]	getBytes(String)
public	void	getChars(int, int, char[], int)
public	int	hashCode()
public	int	indexOf(int)
public	int	indexOf(int, int)
public	int	indexOf(String)
public	int	indexOf(String, int)
public native	String	intern()
public	int	lastIndexOf(int)
public	int	lastIndexOf(int, int)
public	int	lastIndexOf(String)
public	int	lastIndexOf(String, int)
public	int	length()
public	boolean	regionMatches(boolean, int, String, int, int)
public	boolean	regionMatches(int, String, int, int)
public	String	replace(char, char)
public	boolean	startsWith(String)
public	boolean	startsWith(String, int)
public	String	substring(int)

Modifiers	Return Type	Method
public	String	substring(int, int)
public	char[]	toCharArray()
public	String	toLowerCase()
public	String	toLowerCase(Locale)
public	String	toString()
public	String	toUpperCase()
public	String	toUpperCase(Locale)
public	String	trim()
public static	String	valueOf(boolean)
public static	String	valueOf(char)
public static	String	valueOf(char[])
public static	String	valueOf(char[], int, int)
public static	String	valueOf(double)
public static	String	valueOf(float)
public static	String	valueOf(int)
public static	String	valueOf(long)
public static	String	valueOf(Object)

See Also java.io.Serializable • java.lang.Object • java.lang.StringBuffer • java.lang.StringIndexOutOfBoundsException

Class StringBuffer

public final synchronized java.lang.StringBuffer extends java.lang.Object implements java.io.Serializable

The StringBuffer class facilities the ability to create and work with mutable strings in Java.

Syntax & Usage This class gives you the ability to create strings that can have various in-place modifications performed on them. The following example **static** method takes a String object and returns it as an inverted string using this class to perform the operation:

```
// Returns inverted string
static public String invert(String str)
{
   StringBuffer buffer = new
      StringBuffer(str);
   // "pointer" to the beginning
   int p = 0;
   // "pointer" to the end
   int q = str.length()-1;
   while (p < q)
   {
      // Swap the contents of the pointers
      char c = buffer.charAt(p);
      buffer.setCharAt(p, buffer.charAt(q));
      buffer.setCharAt(q, c);
      // Move pointers
      p++;
      q--;
   }
   return new String(buffer);
}
```

This creates a StringBuffer instance from the specified String (str) and uses two references (p and q) to point to the beginning and end of the noninverted area of str. While that area is not empty, the program swaps the contents of the pointers and moves these pointers closer to each other.

Implementation of + Operators for Strings

A Java compiler uses this class to implement operation buffers that are used by the compiler to perform String concatenation with the + and += operators. For example, consider the following code:

```
str += "abc";
```

which is compiled to the equivalent of:

```
str = new StringBuffer().
   append("abc").toString()
```

Fields None

Constructors

Modifiers	Constructor
public	StringBuffer()
public	StringBuffer(int)
public	StringBuffer(String)

Methods

Modifiers	Return Type	Method
public	StringBuffer	append(boolean)
public synchronized	StringBuffer	append(char)
public synchronized	StringBuffer	append(char[])
public synchronized	StringBuffer	append(char[], int, int)
public	StringBuffer	append(double)
public	StringBuffer	append(float)
public	StringBuffer	append(int)
public	StringBuffer	append(long)
public synchronized	StringBuffer	append(Object)
public synchronized	StringBuffer	append(String)
public	int	capacity()
public synchronized	char	charAt(int)
public synchronized	void	ensureCapacity(int)
public synchronized	void	getChars(int, int, char[], int)
public	StringBuffer	insert(int, boolean)
public synchronized	StringBuffer	insert(int, char)
public synchronized	StringBuffer	insert(int, char[])
public	StringBuffer	insert(int, double)
public	StringBuffer	insert(int, float)
public	StringBuffer	insert(int, int)
public	StringBuffer	insert(int, long)
public synchronized	StringBuffer	insert(int, Object)
public synchronized	StringBuffer	insert(int, String)
public	int	length()
public synchronized	StringBuffer	reverse()
public synchronized	void	setCharAt(int, char)
public synchronized	void	setLength(int)
public	String	toString()

See Also java.io.Serializable • java.lang.Object • java.lang.String

Class StringIndexOutOfBoundsException

public synchronized java.lang.StringIndexOutOfBoundsException extends java.lang.IndexOutOfBoundsException

StringIndexOutOfBoundsException is thrown any time the index for a given String object is out of the bounds of that object or is negative in value.

Syntax & Usage Several methods in the String and StringBuffer classes throw this exception; they include the subString() and charAt() methods in the String class and the charAt(), insert(), and setCharAt() methods in the StringBuffer class. For an example, please see "Class String," earlier in this chapter.

Fields None

Constructors

Modifiers	Constructor
public	StringIndexOutOfBoundsException()
public	StringIndexOutOfBoundsException(int)
public	StringIndexOutOfBoundsException(String)

Methods None

See Also java.lang.IndexOutOfBoundsException • java.lang.String • java.lang.StringBuffer

Class System

public final synchronized java.lang.System extends java.lang.Object

The System class provides a collection of **static** methods that encapsulate various system properties and functions that you can call from your Java program.

Syntax & Usage The usefulness of this class primarily rests in its methods, which let you perform various system functions in a platform-independent manner. Let's take a closer look at several of the methods in this class:

- The fields *out* and *err* are used in conjunction with the print() and println() methods. Consider the following:

```
int x = 10;
System.out.print("x= "+x);

Exception e;
System.err.println("Exception: "
   +e.getMessage());
```

- The currentTimeMillis() method returns the current system time in milliseconds since January 1, 1970 GMT. You can use this method to measure time required for calculations in Java:

```
long t1 = System.currentTimeMillis();
myMethod();
long t2 = System.currentTimeMillis();
double dSec = (double)(t2 - t1)/1000.0;
System.out.println("myMethod takes "+
   dSec + " sec.");
```

- The gc() method invokes the garbage collector. You can use this method as a manual override for invoking the garbage collector and freeing up memory:

```
System.gc();
```

- The exit() method terminates the Java application and sets return code. It is usually a good idea in your Java program to call the exit() method (passing it zero to state that the program has exited normally), as follows:

```
System.exit(0);
```

Note

System.exit() cannot be used to terminate a Java applet that is running in a browser.

- The loadLibrary() method is used to load a native (platform-dependent) library. For example, the following loads the library myLibrary:

```
System.loadLibrary("myLibrary");
```

For other uses of the methods in this class, please see "Class SecurityManager," earlier in this chapter.

Fields

Modifiers	Type	Field
public static final	PrintStream	err
public static final	InputStream	in
public static final	PrintStream	out

Constructors None

Methods

Modifiers	Return Type	Method
public static native	void	arraycopy(Object, int, Object, int, int)
public static native	long	currentTimeMillis()
public static	void	exit(int)
public static	void	gc()
public static	String	getenv(String)
public static	Properties	getProperties()
public static	String	getProperty(String)
public static	String	getProperty(String, String)
public static	SecurityManager	getSecurityManager()
public static native	int	identityHashCode(Object)
public static	void	load(String)
public static	void	loadLibrary(String)
public static	void	runFinalization()
public static	void	runFinalizersOnExit(boolean)
public static	void	setErr(PrintStream)
public static	void	setIn(InputStream)
public static	void	setOut(PrintStream)
public static	void	setProperties(Properties)
public static	void	setSecurityManager(SecurityManager)

See Also java.lang.Object • java.lang.SecurityManager

Class Thread

public synchronized java.lang.Thread extends java.lang.Object implements java.lang.Runnable

The Thread class represents a single thread of execution in Java. Since Java is a multithreaded environment, you can explicitly program more than one thread to execute a body of code at the same time.

Note

A program is considered to be finished when all of the nondaemon threads have completed execution or are explicitly killed (by calling the exit() method from the System class).

Syntax & Usage To explicitly use threads in a Java program, you can choose one of two ways: Either subclass this class or implement the Runnable interface. The subclassing technique will be outlined here. Please see "Interface Runnable," earlier in this chapter, for more information about using the Runnable interface technique.

To subclass Thread, you typically need to override the following methods:

- **A constructor to create your thread instance.** You can pass parameters to be used in this thread through its constructor. For instance, you might want to reference the parent Java program.
- **The run() method.** It contains the code to actually perform the primary actions for the thread. Typically this method contains an endless **while(true)** loop that contains useful code, followed by a call to the sleep() method. If the thread has been interrupted (for instance, the program has been closed), the InterruptedException exception is thrown and the loop terminates.

> **Note**
>
> *The endless loop discussed here is a common programming practice often used in animations.*

- **The destroy() method.** It contains all necessary cleanup code.

The following example outlines a sample class that extends the thread called MyThread:

```
class MyThread extends Thread
{

   // Constructor
   public MyThread()
   {
      // Place initialization code here
   }

   // run() thread
   public void run()
   {
      while (true)
      {
         // do something...
         try
         {
            sleep(1000); // sleep 1 sec.
         }
```

```
            catch (InterruptedException e)
            {
               stop();
               break;
            }
         }
      }

      // destroy() thread
      public void destroy()
      {
         // Place cleanup code here
      }
   }
```

Note

The reason you don't need to implement the Runnable interface when subclassing Thread is that the Thread class has already implemented it for you.

To start MyThread, you need to create a new instance of the MyThread class and call start(), as follows:

```
MyThread thread = new MyThread();
thread.start();
```

The start() method then automatically calls the run() method and, once that method has finished, the thread is destroyed by having its destroy() method called.

Fields

Modifiers	Type	Field
public static final	int	MAX_PRIORITY
public static final	int	MIN_PRIORITY
public static final	int	NORM_PRIORITY

Constructors

Modifiers	Constructor
public	Thread()
public	Thread(Runnable)
public	Thread(Runnable, String)
public	Thread(String)
public	Thread(ThreadGroup, Runnable)
public	Thread(ThreadGroup, Runnable, String)
public	Thread(ThreadGroup, String)

Methods

Modifiers	Return Type	Method
public static	int	activeCount()
public	void	checkAccess()
public native	int	countStackFrames()
public static native	Thread	currentThread()
public	void	destroy()
public static	void	dumpStack()
public static	int	enumerate(Thread[])
public final	String	getName()
public final	int	getPriority()
public final	ThreadGroup	getThreadGroup()
public	void	interrupt()
public static	boolean	interrupted()
public final native	boolean	isAlive()
public final	boolean	isDaemon()
public	boolean	isInterrupted()
public final	void	join()
public final synchronized	void	join(long)
public final synchronized	void	join(long, int)
public final	void	resume()
public	void	run()
public final	void	setDaemon(boolean)
public final	void	setName(String)
public final	void	setPriority(int)
public static native	void	sleep(long)
public static	void	sleep(long, int)
public native synchronized	void	start()
public final	void	stop()
public final synchronized	void	stop(Throwable)
public final	void	suspend()
public	String	toString()
public static native	void	yield()

See Also java.lang.Object • java.lang.Runnable • java.lang.ThreadDeath • java.lang.ThreadGroup

Class ThreadDeath

public synchronized java.lang.ThreadDeath extends java.lang.Error

The ThreadDeath error, unlike other errors, gets thrown every time the stop() method of a thread has been called.

The Uniqueness of ThreadDeath

The reason this error behaves like an exception (in the sense that it is a regular occurrence every time a thread dies) but is not an exception is that it has to reconcile itself from being caught in a **try/catch** block that catches the Exception class. If ThreadDeath were declared as an exception, it would prove troublesome, as this class must be rethrown so that the thread can actually die.

Syntax & Usage Java programs need to concern themselves with this error only if they must clean up after being terminated in an asynchronous fashion. To do this, you add the following code to the try/catch block in the run() method of your Thread subclass (or class that implements the Runnable interface):

```
catch (ThreadDeath e)
{
   // Place cleanup code here...
   throw new ThreadDeath();
}
```

Note

If ThreadDeath is caught by a method, it is important that it be rethrown; otherwise, the thread will not die.

Fields None

Constructors

Modifiers	Constructor
public	ThreadDeath()

Methods None

See Also java.lang.Error • java.lang.Runnable • java.lang.Thread

Class ThreadGroup

public synchronized java.lang.ThreadGroup extends java.lang.Object

The ThreadGroup class is used in connection with the threads in your Java program. It gives you the ability to collect otherwise-unrelated threads (and even other thread groups) to have them belong to one thread group.

Syntax & Usage

You use the thread group as a sort of management class for a collection of threads and thread groups. The advantage of managing threads via thread groups is that you can specify one change in the thread group and it automatically affects all the threads (or other thread groups) that belong to it.

> **Tip**
>
> *Thread groups are useful in situations dealing with a minimum of three or four threads executing concurrently.*

The following example method lists the active threads belonging to the specified ThreadGroup object (group):

```
static void printThreadGroup(
   ThreadGroup group)
{
   Thread list = new Thread(
      group.activeCount());
   group.enumerate(list);
   for (int k=0; k<list.length; k++)
      System.out.println(list[k].toString());
}
```

This starts by creating an array of Thread references and then fills this array using the enumerate() method. Finally, it invokes the toString() method on each Thread in the list, printing out for the user to see.

Fields

None

Constructors

Modifiers	Constructor
public	ThreadGroup(String)
public	ThreadGroup(ThreadGroup, String)

Methods

Modifiers	Return Type	Method
public	int	activeCount()
public	int	activeGroupCount()
public	boolean	allowThreadSuspension(boolean)
public final	void	checkAccess()
public final	void	destroy()
public	int	enumerate(ThreadGroup[])
public	int	enumerate(ThreadGroup[], boolean)
public	int	enumerate(Thread[])
public	int	enumerate(Thread[], boolean)
public final	int	getMaxPriority()
public final	String	getName()
public final	ThreadGroup	getParent()
public final	boolean	isDaemon()
public synchronized	boolean	isDestroyed()
public	void	list()
public final	boolean	parentOf(ThreadGroup)
public final	void	resume()
public final	void	setDaemon(boolean)
public final	void	setMaxPriority(int)
public final	void	stop()
public final	void	suspend()
public	String	toString()
public	void	uncaughtException(Thread, Throwable)

See Also java.lang.Object • java.lang.Runnable • java.lang.Thread • java.lang.ThreadDeath

Class Throwable

public synchronized java.lang.Throwable extends java.lang.Object implements java.io.Serializable

The Throwable class is the root class for all errors and exceptions in Java. Any class that needs to be thrown by the Java VM and/or that needs to be caught in a **try/catch** block, must be a subclass of Throwable.

Syntax & Usage

This class provides useful functionality to retrieve information about the error or exception thrown. The following example uses the printStackTrace() method to print the stack trace of the specified error or exception:

```
catch (Exception e)
{
  e.printStackTrace();
  System.out.println("Exception: "
    +e.getMessage());
}
```

Fields

None

Constructors

Modifiers	Constructor
public	Throwable()
public	Throwable(String)

Methods

Modifiers	Return Type	Method
public native	Throwable	fillInStackTrace()
public	String	getLocalizedMessage()
public	String	getMessage()
public	void	printStackTrace()
public	void	printStackTrace(PrintStream)
public	void	printStackTrace(PrintWriter)
public	String	toString()

See Also

java.io.Serializable • java.lang.Object • java.lang.Error • java.lang.Exception

Class UnknownError

public synchronized java.lang.UnknownError extends java.lang.VirtualMachineError

UnknownError is thrown any time there is a serious error that does not relate to any of the defined errors in Java.

Syntax & Usage This error is thrown by the Java VM and is rarely seen.

Fields None

Constructors

Modifiers	Constructor
public	UnknownError()
public	UnknownError(String)

Methods None

See Also java.lang.VirtualMachineError

Class UnsatisfiedLinkError

public synchronized java.lang.UnsatisfiedLinkError extends java.lang.LinkageError

UnsatisfiedLinkError is thrown any time the method definition cannot be found for a method declared **native** in a Java program.

Syntax & Usage This error is thrown by the Java VM if it cannot find an appropriate native-language definition of a native method.

Fields None

Constructors

Modifiers	Constructor
public	UnsatisfiedLinkError()
public	UnsatisfiedLinkError(String)

Methods None

See Also java.lang.LinkageError

Class VerifyError

public synchronized java.lang.VerifyError extends java.lang.LinkageError

VerifyError is thrown any time a class file is found but contains an internal issue.

Syntax & Usage This error is thrown if a class file exists and is properly formed but contains an internal inconsistency or security issue.

Fields None

Constructors

Modifiers	Constructor
public	VerifyError()
public	VerifyError(String)

Methods None

See Also java.lang.LinkageError

Class VirtualMachineError

public abstract synchronized java.lang.VirtualMachineError extends java.lang.Error

VirtualMachineError is thrown any time the Java VM is not operating properly or has run out of available resources (usually memory related) to continue operation.

Syntax & Usage This class actually contains a number of subclasses that derive more precise errors relating to Java VM anomalies. The following is a list of its subclasses:

- InternalError
- OutOfMemoryError
- StackOverflowError
- UnknownError

For more information on each of these classes, please see the appropriate sections, elsewhere in this chapter.

Fields None

Constructors

Modifiers	Constructor
public	VirtualMachineError()
public	VirtualMachineError(String)

Methods None

See Also java.lang.Error • java.lang.InternalError • java.lang.OutOfMemoryError • java.lang.StackOverflowError • java.lang.UnknownError

Class Void

public final synchronized java.lang.Void extends java.lang.Object

The Void class represents an object wrapper for the void primitive type used in Java.

Syntax & Usage This class does not provide any functionality. Basically, it is useful only when working with the Reflection application programming interface (API) methods as a parameter for a method's return type (please see examples in Chapter 10 for more information).

> **Note**
>
> *If the method's parameters list is empty, do not use the Void class as a method's parameter; just leave it empty.*

Fields

Modifiers	Type	Field
public static final	Class	TYPE

Constructors None

Methods None

See Also java.lang.Object • java.lang.reflect.*

The java.lang.reflect Package

10

This package (new to the JDK) introduces the Reflection API. The Reflection API is a set of tools that you can use to look at (i.e., reflect) information about your Java program during run time. Further, you can use the Reflection API to make calls back to the original (or underlying) class to access and/or modify its fields or invoke its methods and constructors.

In a typical Java program, all references to classes and methods are established by the compiler during compilation and thus hard coded in Java byte codes. However, using reflection, you can obtain references dynamically at run time—something that is not possible in Java 1.0. Furthermore, you can use the Reflection API to indirectly access fields, constructors, and methods in the classes that make up your Java program.

Note that Java checks all reflected objects for access modifiers imposed on the original object (or member). So, when a reflected object accesses or changes the value of a field, invokes a method, or constructs a new object, it must still adhere to the restrictions defined in the original object. In the future, unrestricted access may be granted if certain conditions are met. Effectively, reflection mirrors the same information hiding that a typical Java program uses.

Tip

Using the Reflection API can be extremely advantageous in situations in which you need to retrieve and manipulate information precisely at run time. For example, reflection is very useful if you are writing a Java interpreter or debugger for your Java programs.

Security & Java Applets

An unsigned Java applet can access only **public** members of a **public** class, assuming that it is using the same class loader that belongs to the applet. Also, a reflected object (or member) in an unsigned Java applet may use only the original constructors (or members) based on the standard access control model.

Class Array

public final synchronized java.lang.reflect.Array extends java.lang.Object

This class provides a collection of **static** methods that allow you to create an Object object that represents an array of objects or primitive types.

Syntax & Usage You can use this class for the dynamic creation and access of Java arrays. The class provides two newInstance() methods to dynamically create arrays:

- **Object newInstance(Class componentType, int length).** This method is used for creating a new one-dimensional array.
- **Object newInstance(Class componentType, int dimensions).** This method is used for creating a new multidimensional array.

The following example creates an array of int elements and sets and retrieves elements in that array. Note that several exceptions must be caught:

```
int length = 10;
int index = 5;
try
{
   Object array = Array.newInstance(int.class,
      length);
   Array.setInt(array, index, 123);
   int k = Array.getInt(array, index);
   System.out.println("array["+index+"]="+k);
}
catch (NullPointerException e1)
{
   System.err.println(
      "Class type object is null");
}
catch (NegativeArraySizeException e2)
```

```
{
   System.err.println(
      "Array size is negative");
}
catch (ArrayIndexOutOfBoundsException e3)
{
   System.err.println(
      "Array index out of bounds");
}
catch (IllegalArgumentException e4)
{
   System.err.println(
      "Illegal argument exception");
}
```

The preceding code produces the following corresponding output:

```
array[5]=123
```

Fields None

Constructors None

Methods

Modifiers	Return Type	Method
public static native	Object	get(Object, int)
public static native	boolean	getBoolean(Object, int)
public static native	byte	getByte(Object, int)
public static native	char	getChar(Object, int)
public static native	double	getDouble(Object, int)
public static native	float	getFloat(Object, int)
public static native	int	getInt(Object, int)
public static native	int	getLength(Object)
public static native	long	getLong(Object, int)
public static native	short	getShort(Object, int)
public static	Object	newInstance(Class, int)
public static	Object	newInstance(Class, int[])
public static native	void	set(Object, int, Object)
public static native	void	setBoolean(Object, int, boolean)
public static native	void	setByte(Object, int, byte)
public static native	void	setChar(Object, int, char)
public static native	void	setDouble(Object, int, double)
public static native	void	setFloat(Object, int, float)
public static native	void	setInt(Object, int, int)
public static native	void	setLong(Object, int, long)
public static native	void	setShort(Object, int, short)

See Also java.lang.Object

Class Constructor

public final synchronized java.lang.reflect.Constructor extends java.lang.Object implements java.lang.reflect.Member

The Constructor class provides reflection access to constructors of Java classes.

Syntax & Usage

This class does not have any constructors you can use direct. However, you can instantiate this class and get a reference to one or more constructors of a specified class using the following methods from the java.lang.Class class:

- **Constructor getConstructor(Class[]).** This method returns a reference to a public constructor of a given class, corresponding to a specified array of argument types (i.e., an array of Class objects).
- **Constructor[] getConstructors().** This method returns an array of references to public constructors of a given class.
- **Constructor getDeclaredConstructors().** Returns an array of references to *any* constructors of a given class.

The following example shows how to create a new instance of the sample class MyClass using the Reflection API and this class. Here is the definition of MyClass:

```
class MyClass
{
   private int X;
   public MyClass(int xx)
      { X = xx; }
}
```

This example method takes a reference using reflection (and this class) to invoke a new instance of MyClass:

```
static Object createX(int value)
{
   try
   {
      // Get Class reference
      Class clsRef = Class.forName("MyClass");

      // Get reference to constructor
      Constructor constrRef =
         clsRef.getConstructor(
         new Class[] { int.class });

      // Invoke constructor
      Object newObj = constrRef.newInstance(
```

```
        new Object[] { new Integer(
        value) });

      // Return newly created object
      return newObj;
    }
    catch (InvocationTargetException e1)
    {
      System.err.println(
        "Invocation Target Exception: "
        +e1.getMessage());
    }
    catch (Exception e2)
    {
      System.err.println("Exception: "
        +e2.getMessage());
    }
    // If any exception occurs, return null
    return null;
}
```

The code starts by invoking the forName() method from the java.lang.Class class to get a reference to MyClass. Then it obtains the reference to that class's constructor instance using the getConstructor() method from the java.lang.Class class and creates a new instance of MyClass using the newInstance() method from this class. Note the usage of the anonymous array of the constructor's arguments. Also note that InvocationTargetException as well as other exceptions must be caught.

Fields None

Constructors None

Methods

Modifiers	Return Type	Method
public	boolean	equals(Object)
public	Class	getDeclaringClass()
public	Class[]	getExceptionTypes()
public native	int	getModifiers()
public	String	getName()
public	Class[]	getParameterTypes()
public	int	hashCode()
public native	Object	newInstance(Object[])
public	String	toString()

See Also java.lang.Class • java.lang.Object

Class Field

public final synchronized java.lang.reflect.Field extends java.lang.Object implements java.lang.reflect.Member

The Field class provides reflection access to fields (both **static** and instance) of Java classes.

Syntax & Usage

This class does not provide any constructor. However, you can instantiate this class and get a reference to fields in an underlying class using several methods in java.lang.Class, outlined as follows:

- **Field getField(String fieldName).** This method returns a reference to a public field for a given class.
- **Field[] getDeclaredField(String fieldName).** This method returns a reference to any field of a given class.
- **Field[] getFields().** This method returns an array of public fields of a given class.
- **Field[] getDeclaredFields().** This method returns an array of all fields of a given class.

Consider the following:

```
class MyClass
{
   private int X;
   public MyClass(int xx)
      { X = xx; }
}
```

The following snippet of code shows how to access and modify the public field X in the class MyClass (declared previously):

```
MyClass obj = new MyClass();
try
{
   // Get Class reference
   Class clsRef = obj.getClass();

   // Get Field reference
   Field Xref = clsRef.getField("X");

   // Access Field value
   int valueX = Xref.getInt(obj);
```

```
    // Modify value
    valueX++;

    // Set modified value
    Xref.setInt(obj, valueX);
}
catch (NoSuchFieldException e1)
{
    System.err.println("No Such Field: X");
}
catch (SecurityException e2)
{
    System.err.println("Security Exception: "
        +e2.getMessage());
}
catch (Exception e3)
{
    System.err.println("Exception: "
        +e3.getMessage());
}
```

This code takes a reference to a Class instance by invoking the getClass() method from the java.lang.Class class specifying the MyClass instance. Then it obtains a reference to field X using the getField() method from the java.lang.Class class. Next, it gets that field's value using the getInt() method, modifies the value, and sets the new value to field X using the setInt() method. Notice that exceptions NoSuchFieldException and SecurityException as well as a few others have to be caught.

Fields None

Constructors None

Methods

Modifiers	Return Type	Method
public	boolean	equals(Object)
public native	Object	get(Object)
public native	boolean	getBoolean(Object)
public native	byte	getByte(Object)
public native	char	getChar(Object)
public	Class	getDeclaringClass()
public native	double	getDouble(Object)
public native	float	getFloat(Object)
public native	int	getInt(Object)
public native	long	getLong(Object)

Modifiers	Return Type	Method
public native	int	getModifiers()
public	String	getName()
public native	short	getShort(Object)
public	Class	getType()
public	int	hashCode()
public native	void	set(Object, Object)
public native	void	setBoolean(Object, boolean)
public native	void	setByte(Object, byte)
public native	void	setChar(Object, char)
public native	void	setDouble(Object, double)
public native	void	setFloat(Object, float)
public native	void	setInt(Object, int)
public native	void	setLong(Object, long)
public native	void	setShort(Object, short)
public	String	toString()

See Also java.lang.Class • java.lang.Object

Class InvocationTargetException

public synchronized java.lang.reflect.InvocationTargetException extends java.lang.Exception

InvocationTargetException is thrown any time there is an exception during the innovation of a method or constructor using reflection.

Syntax & Usage Specifically, this exception is thrown during any reflection operation that is attempting to invoke something (i.e., a method or constructor), and that something throws an exception. You can use the getTargetException() method to get the actual exception thrown by that something. For examples of where this exception may be thrown, please see the sections for the Constructor and Method classes, elsewhere in this chapter.

Fields None

Constructors

Modifiers	Constructor
protected	InvocationTargetException()
public	InvocationTargetException(Throwable)
public	InvocationTargetException(Throwable, String)

Methods

Modifiers	Return Type	Method
public	Throwable	getTargetException()

See Also java.lang.Exception • java.lang.reflect.Constructor • java.lang.reflect.Method

Interface Member

public abstract interface java.lang.reflect.Member

The Member interface is the only interface defined in this package and the only one used in the Reflection API. Any class that reflects information about a member (i.e., a field, method, or constructor) of an underlying class implements this interface.

Syntax & Usage This interface is implemented by the following classes:

- Constructor
- Field
- Method

For more information on the classes in the preceding list, please see the appropriate sections elsewhere in this chapter.

Fields

Modifiers	Type	Field
public static final	int	DECLARED
public static final	int	PUBLIC

Methods

Modifiers	Return Type	Method
public abstract	Class	getDeclaringClass()
public abstract	int	getModifiers()
public abstract	String	getName()

See Also java.lang.reflect.Constructor • java.lang.reflect.Field • java.lang.reflect.Method

Class Method

public final synchronized java.lang.reflect.Method extends java.lang.Object implements java.lang.reflect.Member

The Method class provides reflection access to methods in Java classes.

Syntax & Usage

This class does not have a constructor. However, you can instantiate Method and get a reference to methods in an underlying class using the following methods from the java.lang.Class class:

- **Method getMethod(String, Class[]).** This method returns a reference to a public method for a given class corresponding to the specified name and given array of argument types (array of Class objects).
- **Method[] getDeclaredMethod(String, Class[]).** This method returns a reference to any method for a given class corresponding to the specified name and given array of argument types (array of Class objects).
- **Method[] getMethods().** This method returns an array of public methods for a given class.
- **Method[] getDeclaredMethods().** This method returns an array of all methods of a given class.

Consider the following:

```
class MyClass
{
  private int X;
  public MyClass(int xx)
    { X = xx; }
```

```
    public void setX(int xx)
      { X = xx; }
    public int getX()
      { return X; }
}
```

The following example method shows how to access public methods of the sample class MyClass (shown previously), using the Reflection API:

```
void incrementX(MyClass obj)
{
    try
    {
        // Get Class reference
        Class clsRef = obj.getClass();

        // Get reference to getX()
        Method GetRef = clsRef.getMethod("getX",
            new Class[] {});

        // Invoke getX() method
        Integer IntX = (Integer)GetRef.invoke(
            obj, new Object[] {});
        int valueX = IntX.intValue();

        // Modify value
        valueX++;

        // Get reference to setX()
        Method SetRef = clsRef.getMethod(
            "setX", new Class[] { int.class });

        // Invoke setX() method
        SetRef.invoke(obj, new Object[] {
            new Integer(valueX) });
    }
    catch (InvocationTargetException e1)
    {
        System.err.println(
            "Invocation Target Exception: "
            +e1.getMessage());
    }
    catch (Exception e2)
    {
        System.err.println("Exception: "
            +e2.getMessage());
    }
}
```

This example gets a reference of a Class instance by invoking the getClass() method from the java.lang.Object class. Then the code obtains a reference to the getX() method using the getMethod() method from the java.lang.Class class. That method is then invoked from the MyClass instance using the invoke() method from the Method class, which returns the value of the private field X (see MyClass, previously).

At this point, you can modify the value of X interlay and send it back to X in MyClass using the setX() method. Note the usage of anonymous arrays of methods arguments in the preceding code. Also, notice that InvocationTargetException as well as other exceptions have to be caught.

Fields None

Constructors None

Methods

Modifiers	Return Type	Method
public	boolean	equals(Object)
public	Class	getDeclaringClass()
public	Class[]	getExceptionTypes()
public native	int	getModifiers()
public	String	getName()
public	Class[]	getParameterTypes()
public	Class	getReturnType()
public	int	hashCode()
public native	Object	invoke(Object, Object[])
public	String	toString()

See Also java.lang.Class • java.lang.Object

Class Modifier

public synchronized java.lang.reflect.Modifier extends java.lang.Object

The Modifier class contains a group of **static** methods and fields that you can use to determine the modifiers present for a given underlying class or the modifiers for a given field or method.

Syntax & Usage This class is used in conjunction with the getModifiers() method that is available from several classes in this package, including Constructor, Field, and Method, as well as java.lang.Class and others. This method retrieves all the modifier flags (**abstract**, **final**, **interface**, etc.) encoded into a single integer value. The example method that follows takes an instance of Member and prints its modifiers using the isAbstract(), isFinal(), and isInterface() methods, all from the Modifier class:

```
void displayModifiers(Member m)
{
   int flags = m.getModifiers();
   if (Modifier.isAbstract(flags))
      System.out.print("abstract");
   if (Modifier.isFinal(flags))
      System.out.print("final");
   if (Modifier.isInterface(flags))
      System.out.print("interface");
   // Repeat the above steps for the native,
   // private, protected, public, static,
   // synchronized, transient, volatile
   // modifiers
}
```

Fields

Modifiers	Type	Field
public static final	int	ABSTRACT
public static final	int	FINAL
public static final	int	INTERFACE
public static final	int	NATIVE
public static final	int	PRIVATE
public static final	int	PROTECTED
public static final	int	PUBLIC
public static final	int	STATIC
public static final	int	SYNCHRONIZED
public static final	int	TRANSIENT
public static final	int	VOLATILE

Constructors

Modifiers	Constructor
public	Modifier()

Methods

Modifiers	Return Type	Method
public static	boolean	isAbstract(int)
public static	boolean	isFinal(int)
public static	boolean	isInterface(int)

Modifiers	Return Type	Method
public static	boolean	isNative(int)
public static	boolean	isPrivate(int)
public static	boolean	isProtected(int)
public static	boolean	isPublic(int)
public static	boolean	isStatic(int)
public static	boolean	isSynchronized(int)
public static	boolean	isTransient(int)
public static	boolean	isVolatile(int)
public static	String	toString(int)

See Also java.lang.Class • java.lang.Object • java.lang.reflect.Constructor • java.lang.reflect.Field • java.lang.reflect.Member • java.lang.reflect.Method

The java.math Package

11

This small package, which is new to the JDK, contains only two classes. Both of these classes facilitate support for extremely precise or extremely large numerical values. Instances of the first class (BigDecimal) can be used for values that need an absolute amount of precision and/or a customizable rounding format, and instances of the second class (BigInteger) are used for values that need an arbitrarily definable (and potentially unlimited) length. Both classes do more than just encapsulate extreme values; they also contain a variety of methods that you can use to perform various arithmetical and other related operations.

Class BigDecimal

public synchronized java.math.BigDecimal extends java.lang.Number

The BigDecimal class gives you the ability to specify a virtually unlimited degree of precision (decimal places) based on a specified precision scale or rounding. Each BigDecimal instance encapsulates an immutable value. This class also contains the ability to round numbers based on scientific, business, or customizable formats, which you can specify for each instance of the BigDecimal object.

Tip

When working with Java Database Connectivity (JDBC), this class is used to receive NUMERIC and DECIMAL—two Structured Query Language (SQL) types that are fixed-point numbers needing absolute precision. It is now possible to use this class to receive any other numerically based SQL types as well.

Syntax & Usage

BigDecimal contains a variety of options that let you customize the rounding format you wish to use. It also contains several math-based methods that enable you to mathematically handle BigDecimal values. Let's take a closer look.

This class provides eight types of rounding, which can be selected by invoking the setScale(int scale, int roundingMode) method on a BigDecimal instance. You can pass any one of the eight constants listed in Table 11-1 as the second parameter to this method, thereby specifying its rounding behavior for the given BigDecimal object.

Constant	Definition
ROUND_DOWN	Never increment the last remaining digit.
ROUND_HALF_DOWN	Never increment the last remaining digit if the discarded fraction is less than or equal to one-half.
ROUND_HALF_UP	Increase the last remaining digit if the discarded fraction is greater than or equal to one-half.
ROUND_UP	Always increase the remaining digit (assuming the discarded fraction is not zero).

Constant	Definition
ROUND_CEILING	If the BigDecimal number is positive, increment the remaining digit.
ROUND_FLOOR	If the BigDecimal number is negative, increment the remaining digit.
ROUND_UNNECESSARY	No rounding is necessary.
ROUND_HALF_EVEN	If the remaining digit is odd, increment it if the discarded fraction is greater than or equal to one-half. If the remaining digit is even, decrement it if the discarded fraction is less than or equal to one-half.

Table 11-1: Rounding constants in the BigDecimal class.

This class also comes with a host of arithmetical operations that you can use on your BigDecimal values. Table 11-2 shows examples.

Java	BigDecimal
a = x + y;	a = x.add(y);
a = x – y;	a = x.subtract(y);
a = x * y;	a = x.multiply(y);
a = x / y;	a = x.divide(y);
a += x;	a = a.add(x);
a *= 10;	a = a.movePointRight(1);
a /= 10;	a = a.movePointLeft(1);

Table 11-2: Examples of BigDecimal operations corresponding to usual arithmetic operations.

Let's take a look at an example of where BigDecimal is useful. The following shows the equation used to compound interest on an initial principal value:

$$Pr * (1 + R/100)^P$$

In this equation, Pr is the initial balance, R is the rate of interest, and P is the period or number of iterations of compounding. The following shows an example method that performs the calculations for the preceding formula by using several BigDecimal instances to hold various values for the method. In this case, Pr is represented as the parameter dAmount, R is represented as the parameter dRate, and P is represented as the parameter nPeriod. Finally, the last parameter (nRoundMode) is used to specify the rounding mode that will be used:

```
static BigDecimal bgnDeposit(
  double dAmount, double dRate,
  int nPeriod, int nRoundMode)
{
```

```
    BigDecimal bRate = (new
      BigDecimal(dRate/100.0)).
      setScale(5, nRoundMode);
    BigDecimal bResult = (new
      BigDecimal(dAmount)).
      setScale(2, nRoundMode);
    BigDecimal bInterest = (new
      BigDecimal(0)).
      setScale(2, nRoundMode);
    for (int k=0; k<nPeriod; k++)
    {
      bInterest = bResult.multiply(bRate).
        setScale(2, nRoundMode);
      bResult = bResult.add(bInterest).
        setScale(2, nRoundMode);
    }
    return bResult;
}
```

The first three lines of code construct three BigDecimal objects. The first (bRate) represents the rate specified in dRate, set to a scale of 5. The second and third—bResult (used for holding the result) and bInterest (the actual interest that will be calculated from bRate)—are both set to a scale of 2. All three are specified with the rounding mode nRoundMode.

Following that is a **for** loop that lasts for the duration of nPeriod. With each pass, it calculates the interest using the multiply() method, from this class, and adds the resulting interest (bInterest) to the result (bResult) using the add() method, also from this class.

The following code snippet shows three examples of invoking the bgnDeposit() method. The interesting thing to note is that calculations for each are the same, but the rounding is different:

```
  BigDecimal b1 = bgnDeposit(1000, 5.25, 20, BigDecimal.ROUND_DOWN);
  BigDecimal b2 = bgnDeposit(1000, 5.25, 20,
  BigDecimal.ROUND_HALF_UP);
  BigDecimal b3 = bgnDeposit(1000, 5.25, 20, BigDecimal.ROUND_UP);

System.out.println("b1 = "+ b1);
System.out.println("b2 = "+ b2);
System.out.println("b3 = "+ b3);
```

The following shows what the output would be for the preceding code snippet. Notice that the calculation is exactly the same, but the rounding used causes each to yield a slightly different result:

```
b1 = 2781.84
b2 = 2782.59
b3 = 2782.68
```

Fields

Modifiers	Type	Field
public static final	int	ROUND_CEILING
public static final	int	ROUND_DOWN
public static final	int	ROUND_FLOOR
public static final	int	ROUND_HALF_DOWN
public static final	int	ROUND_HALF_EVEN
public static final	int	ROUND_HALF_UP
public static final	int	ROUND_UNNECESSARY
public static final	int	ROUND_UP

Constructors

Modifiers	Constructor
public	BigDecimal(BigInteger)
public	BigDecimal(BigInteger, int)
public	BigDecimal(double)
public	BigDecimal(String)

Methods

Modifiers	Return Type	Method
public	BigDecimal	abs()
public	BigDecimal	add(BigDecimal)
public	int	compareTo(BigDecimal)
public	BigDecimal	divide(BigDecimal, int)
public	BigDecimal	divide(BigDecimal, int, int)
public	double	doubleValue()
public	boolean	equals(Object)
public	float	floatValue()
public	int	hashCode()
public	int	intValue()
public	long	longValue()
public	BigDecimal	max(BigDecimal)
public	BigDecimal	min(BigDecimal)
public	BigDecimal	movePointLeft(int)
public	BigDecimal	movePointRight(int)
public	BigDecimal	multiply(BigDecimal)
public	BigDecimal	negate()
public	int	scale()
public	BigDecimal	setScale(int)
public	BigDecimal	setScale(int, int)
public	int	signum()

Modifiers	Return Type	Method
public	BigDecimal	subtract(BigDecimal)
public	BigInteger	toBigInteger()
public	String	toString()
public static	BigDecimal	valueOf(long)
public static	BigDecimal	valueOf(long, int)

See Also java.lang.Number • java.math.BigInteger

Class BigInteger

public synchronized java.math.BigInteger extends java.lang.Number

The BigInteger class is used for calculations requiring extremely large (virtually unlimited) integer values.

Syntax & Usage Java 1.1 actually uses this class to perform its security calculations in several methods contained in the following classes:

- java.security.interfaces.DSAParams
- java.security.interfaces.DSAPrivateKey
- java.security.interfaces.DSAPublicKey

Please refer to Chapter 19 for more information.

Just like the BigDecimal class, the BigInteger class comes with a host of arithmetical operations that you can use on your BigInteger values. Table 11-3 details some of them.

Java	BigInteger
a = x & mask;	a = x.and(mask);
a = ! a;	a = a.not();
a = x | y;	a = x.or(y);
a = - x;	a = x.negate();
a = x % y;	a = x.mod(y);
a = Math.max(x,y);	a = x.max(y);

Java	BigInteger
a = Math.min(x,y);	a = x.min(y);
a = x + y;	a = x.add(y);
a = x – y;	a = x.subtract(y);
a = x * y;	a = x.multiply(y);
a = x / y;	a = x.divide(y);
a += x;	a = a.add(x);
a *= 10;	a = a.movePointRight(1);
a /= 10;	a = a.movePointLeft(1);

Table 11-3: Examples of BigInteger operations corresponding to usual arithmetic operations.

Fields None

Constructors

Modifiers	Constructor
public	BigInteger(byte[])
public	BigInteger(int, byte[])
public	BigInteger(int, int, Random)
public	BigInteger(int, Random)
public	BigInteger(String)
public	BigInteger(String, int)

Methods

Modifiers	Return Type	Method
public	BigInteger	abs()
public	BigInteger	add(BigInteger)
public	BigInteger	and(BigInteger)
public	BigInteger	andNot(BigInteger)
public	int	bitCount()
public	int	bitLength()
public	BigInteger	clearBit(int)
public	int	compareTo(BigInteger)
public	BigInteger	divide(BigInteger)
public	BigInteger[]	divideAndRemainder(BigInteger)
public	double	doubleValue()
public	boolean	equals(Object)
public	BigInteger	flipBit(int)
public	float	floatValue()
public	BigInteger	gcd(BigInteger)
public	int	getLowestSetBit()

Modifiers	Return Type	Method
public	int	hashCode()
public	int	intValue()
public	boolean	isProbablePrime(int)
public	long	longValue()
public	BigInteger	max(BigInteger)
public	BigInteger	min(BigInteger)
public	BigInteger	mod(BigInteger)
public	BigInteger	modInverse(BigInteger)
public	BigInteger	modPow(BigInteger, BigInteger)
public	BigInteger	multiply(BigInteger)
public	BigInteger	negate()
public	BigInteger	not()
public	BigInteger	or(BigInteger)
public	BigInteger	pow(int)
public	BigInteger	remainder(BigInteger)
public	BigInteger	setBit(int)
public	BigInteger	shiftLeft(int)
public	BigInteger	shiftRight(int)
public	int	signum()
public	BigInteger	subtract(BigInteger)
public	boolean	testBit(int)
public	byte[]	toByteArray()
public	String	toString()
public	String	toString(int)
public static	BigInteger	valueOf(long)
public	BigInteger	xor(BigInteger)

See Also java.lang.Number • java.math.BigDecimal • java.security.interfaces.DSAParams • java.security.interfaces.DSAPrivateKey • java.security.interfaces.DSAPublicKey

The java.net Package

12

The java.net package houses the networking functionality available in Java. It facilitates a wide range of lower-level communication possibilities between your Java program and another Java program or entity over a network (via TCP/IP). The given network can be local, global, or the actual Net.

Note

For security reasons, unsigned applets are allowed to make connections only back to their host.

Java 1.1 has tweaked this package with several new errors that catch more precise network-based exceptions. Functionality has been added to support extendable sockets, which you can use to upgrade existing socket implementations and add your own custom functionality like encryption, peer authentication, and even compression. Also, the ability to send broadcast messages (via multicast sockets) has been added.

Class BindException

public synchronized java.net.BindException extends java.net.SocketException

The BindException exception is thrown any time an attempt to bind a socket to a port (and/or an address) fails.

Syntax & Usage Usually, this exception is thrown when the specified port is in use.

> **Tip**
>
> *To avoid this exception being thrown, you might want to specify zero for the port number when instantiating ServerSocket. This tells Java to use any available port.*

You can use this exception to signal the user that the socket can't be bound to the specified InetAddress:

```
ServerSocket getSocket(int port, int backlog,
   InetAddress iAddr)
{
   try
   {
      return new ServerSocket(port, backlog,
         iAddr);
   }
   catch (BindException e)
   {
      System.out.println("port "+port+
      " in use, or can't bind to "
      +iAddr.getHostAddress()+
      "as a local address: "
      +e.getMessage());
      return null;
   }
   catch (IOException e)
   {
      System.out.println("IOException: "
         +e.getMessage());
      return null;
   }
}
```

This creates an instance of ServerSocket using the specified port and InetAddress. If BindException is caught, it prints a warning message and returns **null**.

Fields None

Constructors

Modifiers	Constructor
public	BindException()
public	BindException(String)

Methods None

See Also java.net.InetAddress • java.net.ServerSocket • java.net.SocketException

Class ConnectException

public synchronized java.net.ConnectException extends java.net.SocketException

ConnectException is thrown any time an attempt to connect to a specified port and address has failed.

Syntax & Usage This exception usually gets thrown when the remote side refuses a connection. This exception can also be thrown if the given port is not being listened to for a connection on the remote side. In such situations, it is a good idea to find out the correct port to request a connection from and try that port. Alternatively, you can systematically (or randomly) try another port till you locate the port to which the host is listening. You can use this exception to signal the user that the Socket object can't be created to connect to the specified host:

```
Socket getSocket(String  host, int port)
{
   try
   {
      return new Socket(host, port);
   }
   catch (ConnectException e)
```

```
    {
      System.out.println("Connection to "
        +host+"refused: "+e.getMessage());
      return null;
    }
    catch (IOException e)
    {
      System.out.println("IOException: "+e.getMessage());
      return null;
    }
}
```

This creates an instance of Socket using a specified port and host. If the ConnectException exception is caught, it prints a warning message and returns **null**.

Fields None

Constructors

Modifiers	Constructor
public	ConnectException()
public	ConnectException(String)

Methods None

See Also java.net.Socket • java.net.SocketException

Class ContentHandler

public abstract synchronized java.net.ContentHandler extends java.lang.Object

The ContentHandler class is an **abstract** class that facilitates the ability for any subclass to be able to read in Object objects from a given URLConnection.

Syntax & Usage In most solutions, you do not work with this class directly; instead, you let it be created on an as-needed basis by the registered ContentHandlerFactory object, with each subclass of this class representing a specific Multipurpose Internet Mail Extensions (MIME) type. For most solutions, you simply use the getContent() method from the URL and/or URLConnection classes and everything else is taken care of automatically.

Tip

You can register a ContentHandlerFactory object via a call to the setContentHandlerFactory() method from the URLConnection class.

However, if you wish to add your own custom parsing functionality, you can extend this **abstract** class to read an Object object from a given URLConnection. The only method you implement is the getContent() method, which reads data from a given URLConnection instance and returns them as an Object object. The following example class reads text from a specified URLConnection and returns that text as a String object:

```
class StringHandler extends ContentHandler
{
  public  Object getContent(
    URLConnection urlc)
    throws IOException
  {
    InputStream stream =
      urlc.getInputStream();
    InputStreamReader r = new
      InputStreamReader(stream);
    LineNumberReader lr = new
      LineNumberReader(r);

    String str = "";
    while (true)
    {
      try
      {
        String sLine = lr.readLine();
        if (sLine == null)
          break;
        str += sLine + "\n";
      }
      catch (Exception e)
      { break; }
    }
    try
    { lr.close(); }
    catch (Exception e) {}

    return (Object)str;
  }
}
```

This example takes an InputStream from a given URLConnection using the getInputStream() method. Then it sequentially creates java.io.InputStreamReader and java.io.LineNumberReader instances to read text from that stream using the using readLine() method. The resulting String then is converted into an Object reference and returned to the program that called it.

Tip

*It's a good idea to use the **instanceof** operator to verify that the object returned from the getContent() method belongs to the right class.*

Fields None

Constructors

Modifiers	Constructor
public	ContentHandler()

Methods

Modifiers	Return Type	Method
public abstract	Object	getContent(URLConnection)

See Also java.io.InputStreamReader • java.io.LineNumberReader • java.lang.Object • java.net.ContentHandlerFactory • java.net.URL • java.net.URLConnection

Interface ContentHandlerFactory

public abstract interface java.net.ContentHandlerFactory

The ContentHandlerFactory interface defines the method that is used to map specified MIME types to an appropriate ContentHandler object.

Syntax & Usage You can implement this interface to process various MIME types and return the proper instances of subclasses of the ContentHandler class to retrieve data from a given URLConnection (please refer to the previous section, "Class ContentHandler," for details). Here's an example:

```
class MyContentHandlerFactory implements
  ContentHandlerFactory
{
  public ContentHandler createContentHandler(
    String mimetype)
```

```
    {
        if (mimetype.equals(
            "application/x-string"))
            return new StringHandler();

        // Process other MIME types here.

        // Return null for unknown type
        return null;
    }
}
```

This implementation of ContentHandlerFactory returns a new instance of the StringHandler class (defined under "Syntax & Usage" in the previous section) if the MIME type is equal to "application/x-string." Otherwise, the createContentHandler() method returns **null**, resulting in an UnknownServiceException exception being thrown.

In your program, use the setContentHandlerFactory() method from the URLConnection class to register an instance of the MyContentHandlerFactory class as the content handler factory for the given URLConnection, shown as follows:

```
URLConnection myConnection;
// Open connection here.
myConnection .setContentHandlerFactory(
    new MyContentHandlerFactory());
```

Fields None

Constructors None

Methods

Modifiers	Return Type	Method
public abstract	ContentHandler	createContentHandler(String)

See Also java.net.ContentHandler • java.net.URLConnection

Class DatagramPacket

public final synchronized java.net.DatagramPacket extends java.lang.Object

The DatagramPacket class is used to represent an individual packet (commonly referred to as a datagram) used in the User Datagram Protocol/Internet Protocol (UDP/IP) part of the TCP/IP suite. Each DatagramPacket object contains a binary array used to hold the actual data being transmitted.

Syntax & Usage This class encapsulates UDP packets that are used to implement a connectionless UDP transmission. UDP protocol, while more efficient than TCP, is more prone to failure as each datagram is sent on its own and without verification that it has been properly received.

Note

Java also provides support for TCP connections. Please refer to the sections for the ServerSocket and Socket classes, later in this chapter, for more information.

This class is used by the DatagramSocket class to represent the actual datagrams to be sent or received. Please refer to the next section for details.

Fields None

Constructors

Modifiers	Constructor
public	DatagramPacket(byte[], int)
public	DatagramPacket(byte[], int, InetAddress, int)

Methods

Modifiers	Return Type	Method
public synchronized	InetAddress	getAddress()
public synchronized	byte[]	getData()
public synchronized	int	getLength()
public synchronized	int	getPort()
public synchronized	void	setAddress(InetAddress)
public synchronized	void	setData(byte[])
public synchronized	void	setLength(int)
public synchronized	void	setPort(int)

See Also java.lang.Object • java.net.DatagramSocket • java.net.ServerSocket • java.net.Socket

Class DatagramSocket

public synchronized java.net.DatagramSocket extends java.lang.Object

The DatagramSocket class represents the socket end points in a UDP transmission.

Syntax & Usage You can use the DatagramSocket class as a sending or receiving point for a connectionless delivery service of packets encapsulated into DatagramPacket objects. The following example class shows how to use the DatagramSocket and DatagramPacket classes to retrieve incoming packets, display their contents, and send notification back to the sender:

```
class DatagramMail implements Runnable
{
  DatagramSocket socket;

  public DatagramMail(int port,
    InetAddress iaddr)
    throws SocketException
  {
    socket = new DatagramSocket(port, iaddr);
    socket.setSoTimeout(10000);
  }

  public void run()
  {
    byte[]  data = new byte[1024];
    DateFormat dFormat =
      DateFormat.getDateInstance();

    while (true)
    {
      DatagramPacket packet = new
        DatagramPacket(data,
        data.length);
      try
      {
        socket.receive(packet);
      }
      catch (InterruptedIOException e) {}
      catch (IOException e)
      {
        System.err.println(
        "Error receiving package: "
        +e.getMessage());
        return;
      }

      int lenData = packet.getLength();
      if (lenData > 0)
      {
        String sData = new
          String(data);
        System.out.println(
          "Got message: "+sData);
```

```
                String sResponce = "Received "
                  +lenData+" bytes at "+
                  dFormat.format(new Date())
                  +" Thanks.";
                byte[] bResponce =
                  sResponce.getBytes();
                InetAddress address =
                  packet.getAddress();
                int port = packet.getPort();
                packet = new DatagramPacket(
                  bResponce,
                  bResponce.length,
                  address, port);

                try
                {
                  socket.send(packet);
                }
                catch (IOException e)
                {
                  System.err.println(
                  "Error sending package: "
                  +e.getMessage());
                  return;
                }
              }

              try
              {
                Thread.sleep(10000);
              }
              catch (InterruptedException e)
              {
                return;
              }
            }
          }
        }
```

Notice that the instance of the class DatagramMail implements the java.lang.Runnable interface so it can be executed on a thread.

The first thing to look at in DatagramMail is its constructor, which takes a port number and an InetAddress instance to construct a DatagramSocket object used for the connection. Timeout is set to 10 seconds using the setSoTimeout() method. Also, note that SocketException can be thrown and must be caught by the program calling this constructor.

Following that is the run() method, which implements the active part of this class. First, it creates an array of bytes to be used as data storage. Then an instance of java.text.DateFormat is created to get the current date and time. Following is an endless **while** loop that creates a new instance of DatagramPacket for the **byte** array and invokes the receive() method to receive the packet from the network. If the operation times out, InterruptedIOException is thrown and the method simply continues execution outside of the loop. If IOException is thrown, an error message is printed and the method halts. If data were received (i.e., length greater than zero), run() does the following:

1. Displays the data retrieved to the user.
2. Creates a notification String that includes the number of bytes received and the current date and time (as formatted by the DateFormat instance) to be sent back to the sender.
3. Obtains the port and InetAddress of the received packet.
4. Creates and sends a new DatagramPacket object with the notification String back to the sender using the sender's port and InetAddress.

If IOException is thrown, the method prints an error message and halts. Finally, the run() method sleeps for 10 seconds and continues to cycle, waiting for a new package to be received.

Fields None

Constructors

Modifiers	Constructor
public	DatagramSocket()
public	DatagramSocket(int)
public	DatagramSocket(int, InetAddress)

Methods

Modifiers	Return Type	Method
public	void	close()
public	InetAddress	getLocalAddress()
public	int	getLocalPort()
public synchronized	int	getSoTimeout()
public synchronized	void	receive(DatagramPacket)
public	void	send(DatagramPacket)
public synchronized	void	setSoTimeout(int)

See Also java.lang.Object • java.lang.Runnable • java.lang.Thread • java.net.DatagramPacket • java.net.MulticastSocket • java.text.DateFormat

Class DatagramSocketImpl

public abstract synchronized java.net.DatagramSocketImpl extends java.lang.Object implements java.net.SocketOptions

The DatagramSocketImpl class is an **abstract** class that defines the default declaration used for all datagram sockets in Java.

Note

*The SocketOptions that is implemented by DatagramSocketImpl is a non-**public** interface (which is why it is not documented), containing various constants and methods used by this class and potentially used in your own subclasses of DatagramSocketImpl.*

Syntax & Usage

This **abstract** class provides default declaration, used for all UDP sockets in Java. Unless you wish to add your own functionality for environmentally specific situations in which you need to do something natively for a UDP communication to take place (e.g., go through a firewall), you do not need to worry about this class.

The PlainDatagramSocketImpl class

Java 1.1 provides the PlainDatagramSocketImpl class, which was derived from the DatagramSocketImpl class. PlainDatagramSocketImpl is not **public** and therefore has not been described in Java 1.1 documentation, nor in this book. Native methods from the net library are used to implement this class. Refer to the PlainDatagramSocketImpl.java file, in the JDK1.1 source code files, for details on this class.

Fields

Modifiers	Type	Field
protected	FileDescriptor	fd
protected	int	localPort

Constructors

Modifiers	Constructor
public	DatagramSocketImpl()

Methods

Modifiers	Return Type	Method
protected abstract	void	bind(int, InetAddress)
protected abstract	void	close()
protected abstract	void	create()
protected	FileDescriptor	getFileDescriptor()
protected	int	getLocalPort()
public abstract	Object	getOption(int)
protected abstract	byte	getTTL()
protected abstract	void	join(InetAddress)
protected abstract	void	leave(InetAddress)
protected abstract	int	peek(InetAddress)
protected abstract	void	receive(DatagramPacket)
protected abstract	void	send(DatagramPacket)
public abstract	void	setOption(int, Object)
protected abstract	void	setTTL(byte)

See Also java.lang.Object • java.net.DatagramPacket • java.net.DatagramSocket

Interface FileNameMap

public abstract interface java.net.FileNameMap

The FileNameMap interface is used to determine MIME types from various filenames and their extensions.

Syntax & Usage This interface contains only one method: getContentTypeFor(), which takes a String parameter specifying the filename and extension. Implementations of this method will return the appropriate MIME type for the specified filename. The following class shows an example:

```
class MyFileNameMap implements FileNameMap
{
  public String getContentTypeFor(
    String fileName)
  {
    if (fileName.endsWith(".txt"))
      return "application/x-string";
```

```
        // Process other file extensions here.

        // Return null for unknown extension
        return null;
    }
}
```

FileNameMap returns the "application/x-string" MIME type if the specified filename has a .txt extension. Otherwise, the getContentTypeFor() method returns **null**, which indicates that the given file cannot be classified for a known MIME type.

To instantiate an implementation of FileNameMap, you can use the **static** field fileNameMap from URLConnection:

```
URLConnection.fileNameMap = new
  MyFileNameMap();
```

Fields None

Constructors None

Methods

Modifiers	Return Type	Method
public abstract	String	getContentTypeFor(String)

See Also java.net.URLConnection

Class HttpURLConnection

public abstract synchronized java.net.HttpURLConnection extends java.net.URLConnection

The HttpURLConnection class is an **abstract** class that extends the URLConnection class, providing additional support for various HTTP/1.1 features.

Syntax & Usage You can extend this class to support HTTP-specific features including HTTP request methods (i.e., GET, POST, PUT, and so on) and HTTP redirects.

The minimum set of methods to be overridden includes:

- **public void connect().** This method opens a communications link to the resource referenced by this URL. Note that this method is inherited from URLConnection.
- **public void disconnect().** This method closes the connection to the given server.

- **public boolean usingProxy().** This method returns **true** if the connection is going through a proxy.

The following outlines how you would extend this class:

```
class MyHttpConnection extends
  HttpURLConnection
{
  protected MyHttpConnection(URL u)
  {
    // Constructor
    super(u);
  }

  public void connect() throws IOException
  {
    // Opens a communications link to the
    // resource referenced by this URL.
  }

  public void disconnect()
  {
    // Close the connection to the server.
  }

  public boolean usingProxy()
  {
    // Indicates if the connection is going
    // through a proxy.
    return false;
  }
}
```

Fields

Modifiers	Type	Field
public static final	int	HTTP_ACCEPTED
public static final	int	HTTP_BAD_GATEWAY
public static final	int	HTTP_BAD_METHOD
public static final	int	HTTP_BAD_REQUEST
public static final	int	HTTP_CLIENT_TIMEOUT
public static final	int	HTTP_CONFLICT
public static final	int	HTTP_CREATED
public static final	int	HTTP_ENTITY_TOO_LARGE
public static final	int	HTTP_FORBIDDEN
public static final	int	HTTP_GATEWAY_TIMEOUT

Modifiers	Type	Field
public static final	int	HTTP_GONE
public static final	int	HTTP_INTERNAL_ERROR
public static final	int	HTTP_LENGTH_REQUIRED
public static final	int	HTTP_MOVED_PERM
public static final	int	HTTP_MOVED_TEMP
public static final	int	HTTP_MULT_CHOICE
public static final	int	HTTP_NOT_ACCEPTABLE
public static final	int	HTTP_NOT_AUTHORITATIVE
public static final	int	HTTP_NOT_FOUND
public static final	int	HTTP_NOT_MODIFIED
public static final	int	HTTP_NO_CONTENT
public static final	int	HTTP_OK
public static final	int	HTTP_PARTIAL
public static final	int	HTTP_PAYMENT_REQUIRED
public static final	int	HTTP_PRECON_FAILED
public static final	int	HTTP_PROXY_AUTH
public static final	int	HTTP_REQ_TOO_LONG
public static final	int	HTTP_RESET
public static final	int	HTTP_SEE_OTHER
public static final	int	HTTP_SERVER_ERROR
public static final	int	HTTP_UNAUTHORIZED
public static final	int	HTTP_UNAVAILABLE
public static final	int	HTTP_UNSUPPORTED_TYPE
public static final	int	HTTP_USE_PROXY
public static final	int	HTTP_VERSION
protected	String	method
protected	int	responseCode
protected	String	responseMessage

Constructors

Modifiers	Constructor
protected	HttpURLConnection(URL)

Methods

Modifiers	Return Type	Method
public abstract	void	disconnect()
public static	boolean	getFollowRedirects()
public	String	getRequestMethod()
public	int	getResponseCode()
public	String	getResponseMessage()
public static	void	setFollowRedirects(boolean)

Modifiers	Return Type	Method
public	void	setRequestMethod(String)
public abstract	boolean	usingProxy()

See Also java.net.URL • java.net.URLConnection

Class InetAddress

public final synchronized java.net.InetAddress extends java.lang.Object implements java.io.Serializable

The InetAddress class is used to encapsulate an IP address.

Syntax & Usage This class does not provide a **public** constructor. So, to obtain an instance of InetAddress, you can use one of the three **static** methods from the InetAddress class, shown as follows:

- **getByName().** This method retrieves an InetAddress for the specified host—a String that is either its hexadecimal address or its text name.
- **getAllByName().** This method retrieves an array of all the InetAddresses for the specified host—a String that is either its hexadecimal address or its text name.
- **getLocalHost().** This method retrieves the IP address of the specified local host.

The following example uses these three methods to obtain three distinct instances of InetAddress:

```
try
{
   InetAddress iHost  = InetAddress.
      getByName("www.microsoft.com");
   InetAddress[] iAll = InetAddress.
      getAllByName("208.226.1.800");
   InetAddress iLocal = InetAddress.
      getLocalHost();
}
catch (UnknownHostException e) {}
```

Instances of the InetAddress class are used to create Socket instances used in TCP connections (either explicitly or internally wherein an InetAddress is created from the specified host name) and DatagramSocket instances used in UDP transmissions. Please see the example under "Class DatagramSocket," earlier in this chapter, for details.

Fields None

Constructors None

Methods

Modifiers	Return Type	Method
public	boolean	equals(Object)
public	byte[]	getAddress()
public static	InetAddress[]	getAllByName(String)
public static	InetAddress	getByName(String)
public	String	getHostAddress()
public	String	getHostName()
public static	InetAddress	getLocalHost()
public	int	hashCode()
public	boolean	isMulticastAddress()
public	String	toString()

See Also java.io.Serializable • java.lang.Object • java.net.DatagramSocket • java.net.Socket

Class MalformedURLException

public synchronized java.net.MalformedURLException extends java.io.IOException

MalformedURLException is thrown any time there is a problem with a specified URL.

Syntax & Usage This exception can be thrown, for instance, by the constructor for the URL class to indicate that the specified URL is malformed. Please see the example under "Class URL," later in this chapter, for details.

Fields None

Constructors

Modifiers	Constructor
public	MalformedURLException()
public	MalformedURLException(String)

Methods None

See Also java.io.IOException • java.net.URL

Class MulticastSocket

public synchronized java.net.MulticastSocket extends java.net.DatagramSocket

The MulticastSocket class is used to send and receive IP multicast packets (via UDP/IP).

Syntax & Usage This class is the same as the DatagramSocket class, with additional capabilities for specifying multicast groups on the Internet. Without having to necessarily be a member of the given group, anyone can send messages to the group, causing all members of the group to receive the message.

> **Note**
>
> *Untrusted applets are not allowed to use multicast sockets.*

Consider the following example method:

```
void sendHiToGroup(InetAddress group,
   int port)
{
   // Join the group
   MulticastSocket s = new
      MulticastSocket(port);
   s.joinGroup(group);

   String hi = "Hi there";
   byte[] b = str.getBytes();
   DatagramPacket p = new DatagramPacket(
      b, b.length, group, port);
   s.send(p);

// Read responses here (see the DatagramPacket
// class).

   // Leave the group
   s.leaveGroup(group);
}
```

This creates an instance of the MulticastSocket class based on the specified port and joins the group at the specified InetAddress using the joinGroup() method. The DatagramPacket is created and sent to all the members of the group using the send() method. You also can read responses from group members using the receive() method (inherited from the DatagramSocket class). Finally, the example leaves the group, using the leaveGroup() method.

Fields None

Constructors

Modifiers	Constructor
public	MulticastSocket()
public	MulticastSocket(int)

Methods

Modifiers	Return Type	Method
public	InetAddress	getInterface()
public	byte	getTTL()
public	void	joinGroup(InetAddress)
public	void	leaveGroup(InetAddress)
public synchronized	void	send(DatagramPacket, byte)
public	void	setInterface(InetAddress)
public	void	setTTL(byte)

See Also java.net.DatagramSocket • java.net.InetAddress

Class NoRouteToHostException

public synchronized java.net.NoRouteToHostException extends java.net.SocketException

NoRouteToHostException is thrown any time an attempt to connect a socket to a specified address and port has timed out (i.e., the remote host is unreachable for some reason).

Syntax & Usage You can use this exception to signal the user that a timeout occurred when trying to connect to a remote host. Typically, this indicates some kind of network failure (i.e., a down router). The following shows an example method that returns a TCP connection using the specified host and port. If for some reason it cannot contact the host, NoRouteToHostException is thrown:

```
Socket getSocket(String  host, int port)
{
  try
  {
    return new Socket(host, port);
  }
  catch (NoRouteToHostException e)
  {
    System.out.println(
    "The connect attempt to "+host+
    " has failed: "+e.getMessage());
    return null;
  }
  catch (IOException e)
  {
    System.out.println("IOException: "
    +e.getMessage());
    return null;
  }
}
```

This example creates an instance of Socket for the specified port and host. If NoRouteToHostException is caught, it prints an error message and returns **null**.

> **Note**
>
> *If there is a firewall between the sender and receiver, this exception is thrown. In such cases, you should try connecting through a proxy when the exception is caught.*

Fields None

Constructors

Modifiers	Constructor
public	NoRouteToHostException()
public	NoRouteToHostException(String)

Methods None

See Also java.net.Socket • java.net.SocketException

Class ProtocolException

public synchronized java.net.ProtocolException extends java.io.IOException

The ProtocolException exception is thrown any time there is an error relating to the underlying TCP/IP protocol being used.

Syntax & Usage This exception is thrown by a native method in the PlainSocketImpl class (see the sidebar under "Class SocketImpl," later in this chapter, for more information on this class), indicating that there was a protocol error. Consider the following:

```
HttpURLConnection u;
Try
{
   u.setRequestMethod("TRACE");
}
catch(ProtocolException e)
{
   System.err.println(
      "Protocol exception: "+e.getMessage());
}
```

This snippet of code catches ProtocolException, which can be thrown by the setRequestMethod() method from the HttpURLConnection class when trying to set the method for the URL request.

Fields None

Constructors

Modifiers	Constructor
public	ProtocolException()
public	ProtocolException(String)

Methods None

See Also java.io.IOException • java.net.HttpURLConnection • java.net.SocketImpl

Class ServerSocket

public synchronized java.net.ServerSocket extends java.lang.Object

The ServerSocket class is a key class used in the server implementation of a TCP connection. ServerSocket is responsible for retrieving a port when an instance of the ServerSocket class is created and listening to that port to respond to client connection requests.

Note

The actual functionality for the socket used in this class is housed in a natively implemented SocketImpl subclass. Alternatively, you can specify your own SocketImpl subclass using the setSocketFactory() method from this class, which can be useful if you have to do something environmentally specific (i.e., go through a firewall).

Syntax & Usage

When programming sockets, you design the server to listen to connection requests from a client (or clients). Then, if this request is granted, a network connection between the client and the server is opened. The following list shows the protocol needed to implement the server side of the TCP connection:

1. Designate a port and listen for activity.
2. Respond to requests from clients at the designated port.
3. Use streams to read the incoming data and respond accordingly.
4. Continue to communicate back and forth as needed.

You designate a port and listen for activity by instantiating ServerSocket and calling the accept() method. This method cycles continually, listening to the designated port until a client contacts this port with a request for communication. If a request comes through and is successful, the method accept() returns an instance of the Socket class that encapsulates a connection between the server and the client.

When a socket is created from the method accept(), a connection has been opened successfully between the client and the server. To establish a connection, a Socket object can use an IP address or host name, a port, or both at the same time. Following is a discussion and example of the three constructors available in the ServerSocket class.

This constructor specifies a port for a socket connection:

```
ServerSocket(int port)
```

Here's an example:

```
ServerSocket srvSocket = new
  ServerSocket(0);
```

Note

A port designated 0 creates a socket connection on any free port.

This constructor specifies a port and sets the maximum queue length for the number of incoming connection requests:

```
ServerSocket(int port, int backlog)
```

The following shows an example:

```
ServerSocket srvSocket = new
  ServerSocket(0, 1024);
Socket s = srvSocket.accept();
```

This constructor specifies a port, sets the maximum queue length for the number of incoming connection requests, and allows you to specify an InetAddress object:

```
ServerSocket(int port, int backlog,
  InetAddress bindAddr)
```

The following shows an example:

```
InetAddress iAddr =
  InetAddress.getLocalHost();
ServerSocket srvSocket = new
  ServerSocket(0, 1024, iAddr);
Socket s = srvSocket.accept();
```

Note

Remember to catch any potential IOException exceptions when you create a new instance of ServerSocket. (This is not done in the previous examples.)

Java 1.1 has added the functionality that allows you to extend the ServerSocket class to create your own implementation of the server sockets.

Note

*Since the ServerSocket class is now extendable, the methods responsible for interacting with the security manager in Java are now declared **final**. This is to prevent anyone from extending these methods and programming them to bypass the security manager.*

The following shows an example of extending the ServerSocket class:

```
public class MyServerSocket extends
  ServerSocket
{
  public MyServerSocket(int port)
  {
    super(port);
    // Set options for server socket
    try
    {
      // Set I/O timeout to 10 sec.
      setSoTimeout(10000);
    }
    catch (SocketException e)
    {
      System.err.println(
      "Error creating socket: "
      +e.getMessage());
    }
    //Provide your implementation here.
  }
}
```

Notice that inside the constructor for MyServerSocket you call the constructor for ServerSocket through a **super** reference. After that, you specify the setSoTimeout() option for MySocket. This method is used to set IO timeout to 10 sec (10000 ms). As you can see, it is easy to add to the basic functionality of the ServerSocket class.

Fields None

Constructors

Modifiers	Constructor
public	ServerSocket(int)
public	ServerSocket(int, int)
public	ServerSocket(int, int, InetAddress)

Methods

Modifiers	Return Type	Method
public	Socket	accept()
public	void	close()
public	InetAddress	getInetAddress()
public	int	getLocalPort()
public synchronized	int	getSoTimeout()
protected final	void	implAccept(Socket)
public static synchronized	void	setSocketFactory(SocketImplFactory)
public synchronized	void	setSoTimeout(int)
public	String	toString()

See Also java.io.IOException • java.lang.Object • java.net.Socket

Class Socket

public synchronized java.net.Socket extends java.lang.Object

The Socket class represents the client implementation of a TCP connection.

Note

The actual functionality for this class is housed in a natively implemented SocketImpl subclass.

Syntax & Usage In Java, a client uses the Socket class to connect to a server through a specified port. Creating a client is a fairly simple process:

1. The client requests a connection with the server.
2. The client uses streams to send data and wait for a response from the server.
3. The client and server continue to communicate back and forth as needed.

The following code snippet shows an example of creating an instance of the Socket class, which requests a socket connection to the remote host (i.e., the server); the first parameter specifies the IP address (alternatively, you can use a host name), and the second parameter specifies the port to which the server is listening:

```
try
{
  Socket s = new Socket(
    "205.12.1.123", 2345);
}
catch(IOException e) {}
```

When a connection has been successfully established, you can use the getOutputStream() and the getInputStream() methods from the Socket class to send and retrieve data from the connection.

The following shows an example of using these methods to communicate with a server. The first method, readSocket(), shows you how to read in data from the network connection, and the second method, writeSocket(), shows you how to send information back to the connection. Starting with readSocket():

```
public boolean readSocket(Socket socket,
  byte[] b)
{
  try
  {
    InputStream stream =
      socket.getInputStream();
    stream.read(b);
  }
  catch (IOException e)
  {
    System.err.println(
      "Error reading from socket: "
      +e.getMessage());
    return false;
  }
  return true;
}
```

Method readSocket() takes a reference to the existing Socket instance and obtains an InputStream instance using the getInputStream() method from the Socket class. Then it reads in an array of bytes using the read() method from the InputStream class and returns **true** if the operation is successful. On the other hand, if an IOException exception occurs, this method prints an error message and returns **false**.

Method writeSocket() takes a reference to the existing Socket instance and obtains an OutputStream instance using the getOutputStream() method from the Socket class. Then it writes an array of bytes using a write() method from the OutputStream class and returns **true** if the operation is successful. If an IOException exception occurs, this method prints an error message and returns **false**.

Tip

You can create a new input stream (or reader instance for a character stream) or output stream (or writer instance for a character stream) based on the input or output stream reference you have from the Socket object. You then can use any methods from various classes in the java.io package to read from the input stream or write to the output stream over the TCP connection.

Java 1.1 allows you to extend the Socket class to create your own implementation of the sockets.

Note

*Since the Socket class is now extendable, the methods responsible for interacting with the security manager in Java are now declared **final**. This is to prevent anyone from extending these methods and programming them to bypass the security manager.*

The following shows an example of extending the Socket class:

```
public class MySocket extends Socket
{
   public MySocket(String sHost, int nPort)
      throws UnknownHostException,
      IOException
   {
      super(sHost, nPort);

      // Set options for socket.
      try
      {
         // Set I/O timeout to 10 sec.
         setSoTimeout(10000);
         // Set SO_LINGER on.
         // (linger time 5 sec.)
         setSoLinger(true, 5000);
         // Enable Nagle's algorithm.
         setTcpNoDelay(true);
      }
      catch (SocketException e)
      {
         System.err.println(
         "Error creating socket: "
         +e.getMessage());
      }
      //Provide your implementation here.
   }
}
```

Notice that inside the constructor for MySocket you call the constructor for Socket through a **super** reference. After that, you specify any of your options for MySocket:

- **setSoTimeout().** This method is used to set IO timeout to 10 sec (10000 ms).
- **setSoLinger().** This method is used to set linger time to 5 sec.
- **setTcpNoDelay().** This method is used to enable Nagle's algorithm for this socket.

As you can see, it is easy to add functionality to the Socket class.

Fields None

Constructors

Modifiers	Constructor
protected	Socket()
public	Socket(InetAddress, int)
public	Socket(InetAddress, int, boolean)
public	Socket(InetAddress, int, InetAddress, int)
protected	Socket(SocketImpl)
public	Socket(String, int)
public	Socket(String, int, boolean)
public	Socket(String, int, InetAddress, int)

Methods

Modifiers	Return Type	Method
public synchronized	void	close()
public	InetAddress	getInetAddress()
public	InputStream	getInputStream()
public	InetAddress	getLocalAddress()
public	int	getLocalPort()
public	OutputStream	getOutputStream()
public	int	getPort()
public	int	getSoLinger()
public synchronized	int	getSoTimeout()
public	boolean	getTcpNoDelay()
public static synchronized	void	setSocketImplFactory(SocketImplFactory)
public	void	setSoLinger(boolean, int)
public synchronized	void	setSoTimeout(int)
public	void	setTcpNoDelay(boolean)
public	String	toString()

See Also java.io.* • java.lang.Object • java.net.ServerSocket • java.net.SocketImpl

Class SocketException

public synchronized java.net.SocketException extends java.io.IOException

SocketException is thrown any time there is a problem during a socket connection.

Syntax & Usage This exception can be thrown to indicate that there is an error in the underlying protocol, such as a TCP error. Please see the two previous sections, the ServerSocket and Socket classes, for examples of where this exception is handled.

Fields None

Constructors

Modifiers	Constructor
public	SocketException()
public	SocketException(String)

Methods None

See Also java.io.IOException • java.net.ServerSocket • java.net.Socket

Class SocketImpl

public abstract synchronized java.net.SocketImpl extends java.lang.Object implements java.net.SocketOptions

The SocketImpl class is an **abstract** class that defines the default declaration used for all sockets in a TCP connection in Java.

Note

*The SocketOptions that is implemented by DatagramSocketImpl is a non-**public** interface (which is why it is not documented), containing various constants and methods used by this class and potentially used in your own subclasses of DatagramSocketImpl.*

Syntax & Usage Unless you wish to add your own functionality for environmentally specific situations in which you need to do something natively for a TCP communication to take place (e.g., go through a firewall), you do not need to worry about this class.

The PlainSocketImpl class

Java 1.1 provides the PlainSocketImpl class, which was derived from the SocketImpl class. The PlainSocketImpl class is not **public**; therefore, it is not described in Java 1.1 documentation, nor in this book. This class is implemented by native methods from the net library. Refer to the PlainSocketImpl.java file, in the JDK 1.1 source code files, for more information.

Fields

Modifiers	Type	Field
protected	InetAddress	address
protected	FileDescriptor	fd
protected	int	localport
protected	int	port

Constructors

Modifiers	Constructor
public	SocketImpl()

Methods

Modifiers	Return Type	Method
protected abstract	void	accept(SocketImpl)
protected abstract	int	available()
protected abstract	void	bind(InetAddress, int)
protected abstract	void	close()
protected abstract	void	connect(InetAddress, int)
protected abstract	void	connect(String, int)
protected abstract	void	create(boolean)
protected	FileDescriptor	getFileDescriptor()
protected	InetAddress	getInetAddress()
protected abstract	InputStream	getInputStream()
protected	int	getLocalPort()
public abstract	Object	getOption(int)
protected abstract	OutputStream	getOutputStream()
protected	int	getPort()
protected abstract	void	listen(int)
public abstract	void	setOption(int, Object)
public	String	toString()

See Also java.lang.Object • java.net.ServerSocket • java.net.Socket • java.net.SocketImplFactory

Interface SocketImplFactory

public abstract interface java.net.SocketImplFactory

The SocketImplFactory interface defines the method used to create SocketImpl objects that implement the actual Socket socket and ServerSocket sockets of a TCP connection.

Syntax & Usage The implementations of this **abstract** interface are used to generate the sockets that serve both the client and the server in a TCP connection. The following methods can be used to set an instance of SocketImplFactory as the Sockets generator:

- setSocketImplFactory(SocketImplFactory) from the Socket class
- setSocketImplFactory(SocketImplFactory) from the ServerSocket class

Fields None

Constructors None

Methods

Modifiers	Return Type	Method
public abstract	SocketImpl	createSocketImpl()

See Also java.net.ServerSocket • java.net.Socket • java.net.SocketImpl

Class UnknownHostException

public synchronized java.net.UnknownHostException extends java.io.IOException

UnknownHostException is thrown any time a specified IP address cannot be resolved.

Syntax & Usage You can use this exception to signal a spelling-related error (among other things) in the specified host name:

```
Socket getSocket(String  host, int port)
{
  try
  {
    return new Socket(host, port);
  }
```

```
        catch (UnknownHostException e)
        {
            System.out.println(
            "Check spelling of hostname "+host+
            ": "+e.getMessage());
            return null;
        }
        catch (IOException e)
        {
            System.out.println("IOException: "
            +e.getMessage());
            return null;
        }
    }
```

This example method creates an instance of the Socket class based on the specified port and host. If the UnknownHostException exception is caught, it prints a warning message and returns **null**.

Fields None

Constructors

Modifiers	Constructor
public	UnknownHostException()
public	UnknownHostException(String)

Methods None

See Also java.io.IOException • java.net.InetAddress • java.net.Socket

Class UnknownServiceException

public synchronized java.net.UnknownServiceException extends java.io.IOException

UnknownServiceException is thrown any time an unknown service is encountered (i.e., an unknown MIME type) or a URL connection is not writable.

Syntax & Usage This exception may be thrown to indicate that an unknown service exception has occurred. Consider the following:

```
URLConnection uc;
// Open URL connection here
try
{
   Object obj = uc.getContent();
}
catch (UnknownServiceException e)
{
   System.err.println(
   "UnknownServiceException: "
   +e.getMessage());
}
catch (IOException e)
{
   System.err.println("IOException: "
   +e.getMessage());
}
```

This example tries to retrieve the contents of the specified URLConnection and catches UnknownServiceException, if necessary.

Fields None

Constructors

Modifiers	Constructor
public	UnknownServiceException()
public	UnknownServiceException(String)

Methods None

See Also java.io.IOException • java.net.URL • java.net.URLConnection

Class URL

public final synchronized java.net.URL extends java.lang.Object implements java.io.Serializable

The URL class represents a URL that you use to send and retrieve data from a particular source on the Internet. A URL can use the HTTP protocol for hypertext documents, FTP for transferring files, or several other Internet-supported protocols (Gopher, for example). In your Java programs, you can use URL objects to connect to a specific resource on the Net, which allows you to send and retrieve data from the Net.

Syntax & Usage This class encapsulates a URL, a pointer to a resource on the World Wide Web. You can use it to create a URL instance for a specified protocol and host and to open a connection to that URL. The following shows a simple example pointing to the Web site http://www.microsoft.com:

```
try {
    URL myMsURL= new URL("http://www.microsoft.com ");
  URL myMsURL2 = new URL("http", "www.microsoft.com", 80,
  "index.html")
} catch(MalformedURLException e) {}
```

Notice that there are two URL objects created, both connecting to the same site (http://www.microsoft.com). The first takes the String http://www.microsoft.com. The second has four input parameters specifying the following: the protocol, the site, the port, and the file to load. Notice MalformedURLException must be handled.

> **Note**
>
> *You can use both relative and absolute URLs with the URL class.*

However, constructing a URL object and communicating with the actual URL are two different things. To actually use the URL, you need to implement a way to retrieve data from the site. That can be done in one of several ways:

- One way is to use the URLConnection class (that you instantiate using the openConnection() method in the URL class). This is the most versatile way to connect, because it allows you to retrieve and send data. For more information, please see the next section, "Class URLConnection."
- It also is possible to retrieve data directly from the URL class by using the getContent() method from the URL class. You also can open an input stream from the specified URL using the openStream() method from the URL class. Note that these methods only let you retrieve data from a given URL; if you wish to send data, your best bet is to use URLConnection (or HttpURLConnection).

The following shows an example of using a URL object to connect to a Web site and using URLConnection and streams to retrieve data from a specified URL:

```
try
{
  URL myURL = new URL("ftp",
    "ftp.myHost.com", -1, "myFile.html");
  URLConnection connection =
    myURL.openConnection();
  InputStream stream =
    connection.getInputStream();
```

```
    // Read data from input stream

    stream.close();
}
catch (MalformedURLException e)
{
    System.err.println(
        "Malformed URL: "+e.getMessage());
}
catch (IOException e)
{
    System.err.println(
        "IO exception: "+e.getMessage());
}
```

This example creates a URL instance using the specified protocol, host, port (-1 means the default port), and the specified filename. Then a URLConnection instance is returned from a call to the openConnection() method from the URL class. Following that is a newly created input stream to the specified URL obtained using the getInputStream() method. At this point you can read data from that URL. Note that IOException and MalformedURLException have to be handled.

Fields None

Constructors

Modifiers	Constructor
public	URL(String)
public	URL(String, String, int, String)
public	URL(String, String, String)
public	URL(URL, String)

Methods

Modifiers	Return Type	Method
public	boolean	equals(Object)
public final	Object	getContent()
public	String	getFile()
public	String	getHost()
public	int	getPort()
public	String	getProtocol()
public	String	getRef()
public	int	hashCode()
public	URLConnection	openConnection()
public final	InputStream	openStream()
public	boolean	sameFile(URL)
protected	void	set(String, String, int, String, String)

Modifiers	Return Type	Method
public static synchronized	void	setURLStreamHandlerFactory(URLStreamHandlerFactory)
public	String	toExternalForm()
public	String	toString()

See Also java.io.InputStream • java.io.OutputStream • java.io.Serializable • java.lang.Object • java.net.HttpURLConnection • java.net.URLConnection

Class URLConnection

public abstract synchronized java.net.URLConnection extends java.lang.Object

The URLConnection class represents the actual network connection to a specified URL on the Net. Using URLConnection in conjunction with URL gives you the ability to retrieve and send data to and from a particular site on the Net.

Syntax & Usage The **abstract** class URLConnection represents a communications link between a Java program and a specified URL. You can gain an instance of it using the openConnection() method from the URL class (wherein Java will return an appropriate subclass object). The following example creates a URLConnection:

```
try {
    URL myMsURL = new URL("http://www.microsoft.com ");

    URLConnection myMsConnection = myMsURL.openConnection();
} catch(MalformedURLException e)
```

This example instantiates myMsURL to point to http://www.microsoft.com. Then it retrieves a URLConnection object for myMsURL using the openConnection() method from the URL class. Once this is done, you can retrieve data from the specified location using methods contained in this class. Please see the examples in the sections for the ContentHandler, ContentHandlerFactory, FileNameMap, HttpURLConnection, and URL classes, elsewhere in this chapter, for more examples.

Note

There are other methods in this class, but not discussed here, that let you communicate with a URL on the Net. Please see the following "Methods" subsection for more information.

Fields

Modifiers	Type	Field
protected	boolean	allowUserInteraction
protected	boolean	connected
protected	boolean	doInput
protected	boolean	doOutput
public static	FileNameMap	fileNameMap
protected	long	ifModifiedSince
protected	URL	url
protected	boolean	useCaches

Constructors

Modifiers	Constructor
protected	URLConnection(URL)

Methods

Modifiers	Return Type	Method
public abstract	void	connect()
public	boolean	getAllowUserInteraction()
public	Object	getContent()
public	String	getContentEncoding()
public	int	getContentLength()
public	String	getContentType()
public	long	getDate()
public static	boolean	getDefaultAllowUserInteraction()
public static	String	getDefaultRequestProperty(String)
public	boolean	getDefaultUseCaches()
public	boolean	getDoInput()
public	boolean	getDoOutput()
public	long	getExpiration()
public	String	getHeaderField(int)
public	String	getHeaderField(String)
public	long	getHeaderFieldDate(String, long)
public	int	getHeaderFieldInt(String, int)
public	String	getHeaderFieldKey(int)
public	long	getIfModifiedSince()
public	InputStream	getInputStream()
public	long	getLastModified()
public	OutputStream	getOutputStream()
public	String	getRequestProperty(String)
public	URL	getURL()
public	boolean	getUseCaches()
protected static	String	guessContentTypeFromName(String)

Modifiers	Return Type	Method
public static	String	guessContentTypeFromStream(InputStream)
public	void	setAllowUserInteraction(boolean)
public static synchronized	void	setContentHandlerFactory(ContentHandlerFactory)
public static	void	setDefaultAllowUserInteraction(boolean)
public static	void	setDefaultRequestProperty(String, String)
public	void	setDefaultUseCaches(boolean)
public	void	setDoInput(boolean)
public	void	setDoOutput(boolean)
public	void	setIfModifiedSince(long)
public	void	setRequestProperty(String, String)
public	void	setUseCaches(boolean)
public	String	toString()

See Also java.lang.Object • java.net.ContentHandler • java.net.ContentHandlerFactory • java.net.FileNameMap • java.net.HttpURLConnection • java.net.URL

Class URLEncoder

public synchronized java.net.URLEncoder extends java.lang.Object

The URLEncoder class is used to convert strings to the URL-encoded format, commonly used in CGI scripts.

Syntax & Usage The class contains one **static** method—encode()—used for converting a string into a MIME format called "x-www-form-urlencoded" format. This format basically leaves all alphanumeric and numeric values unchanged, but converts all spaces to the plus sign (+), and converts any other 8-bit characters into two-digit hexadecimal addresses, each preceded by a percentage symbol (%). Consider the following:

```
String mime = URLEncoder.encode("http://www.test.com/ help");
System.out.println(mime);
```

This snippet of code uses the encode() method to convert the specified string. Here's the corresponding output:

```
http%3a%2f%2fwww.test.com%2f+help
```

Fields None

Constructors None

Methods

Modifiers	Return Type	Method
public static	String	encode(String)

See Also java.lang.Object • java.net.HttpURLConnection • java.net.URL • java.net.URLConnection

Class URLStreamHandler

public abstract synchronized java.net.URLStreamHandler extends java.lang.Object

The URLStreamHandler class is an **abstract** class with each subclass defining a particular protocol (e.g., HTTP, FTP, or Gopher).

Syntax & Usage In most cases, you do not create URLStreamHandler subclasses directly. All necessary stream protocol handlers are included with Java and are loaded automatically on an as-needed basis whenever you construct a URL object.

If you ever need to override your Java program's handling of a particular protocol, you can do so by subclassing this class. Then you need to implement the URLStreamHandlerFactory interface in another object and set that object as the stream-handling factory using the **static** method setURLStreamHandlerFactory(URLStreamHandlerFactory) from the URL factory. Please see the URLStreamHandlerFactory interface for more information.

Fields None

Constructors

Modifiers	Constructor
public	URLStreamHandler()

Methods

Modifiers	Return Type	Method
protected abstract	URLConnection	openConnection(URL)
protected	void	parseURL(URL, String, int, int)
protected	void	setURL(URL, String, String, int, String, String)
protected	String	toExternalForm(URL)

See Also java.lang.Object • java.net.URL • java.net.URLConnection • java.net.URLStreamHandlerFactory

Interface URLStreamHandlerFactory

public abstract interface java.net.URLStreamHandlerFactory

The URLStreamHandlerFactory interface is used to define one method necessary to create URLStreamHandler subclass objects to handle a particular protocol (e.g., HTTP, FTP, or Gopher).

Syntax & Usage

This class is used internally by the URL class to create an appropriate StreamHandler for the given protocol.

The only time you need to implement this interface is when you want to use your own URLStreamHandler classes. In such cases, you need to implement the createURLStreamHandler() method, which returns a new instance of URLStreamHandler for each applicable protocol name or **null** otherwise (please refer to the example under "Interface ContentHandlerFactory," earlier in this chapter, which performs a similar task). Then, you set this instance of URLStreamHandlerFactory as a stream-handler factory using the **static** method setURLStreamHandlerFactory(URLStreamHandlerFactory) from the URL class.

Fields

None

Constructors

None

Methods

Modifiers	Return Type	Method
public abstract	URLStreamHandler	createURLStreamHandler(String)

See Also

java.net.ContentHandlerFactory • java.net.URL • java.net.URLStreamHandler

The java.rmi Package

13

The java.rmi package is not terribly large. Basically, this is a "utility" package for the Remote Method Invocation (RMI) system. It contains two very useful miscellaneous classes (java.rmi.Naming and java.rmi.RMISecurityManager) and one interface (java.rmi.Remote), plus a number of RMI-related exceptions.

Class AccessException

public synchronized java.rmi.AccessException extends java.rmi.RemoteException

The AccessException exception is thrown any time there is an access violation.

Syntax & Usage This exception is thrown by methods in the java.rmi, java.rmi.registry, and java.rmi.server packages to indicate an access violation. Please see "Interface java.rmi.registry.Registry" in Chapter 15 for more information.

Fields None

Constructors

Modifiers	Constructor
public	AccessException(String)
public	AccessException(String, Exception)

Methods None

See Also java.rmi.RemoteException • java.rmi.registry.Registry

Class AlreadyBoundException

public synchronized java.rmi.AlreadyBoundException extends java.lang.Exception

The AlreadyBoundException exception can be thrown any time there is an attempt to bind a registry to a name that is already being used to represent another registry entry.

Syntax & Usage This exception is thrown by the bind() method in the java.rmi.registry.Registry interface, indicating that a specified name is already bound into the RMI database (names cannot be bound twice). Please see "Interface java.rmi.registry.Registry" in Chapter 15 for more information.

Fields None

Constructors

Modifiers	Constructor
public	AlreadyBoundException()
public	AlreadyBoundException(String)

Methods None

See Also java.lang.Exception • java.lang.RemoteException • java.rmi.registry.Registry

Class ConnectException

public synchronized java.rmi.ConnectException extends java.rmi.RemoteException

The ConnectException exception is thrown any time a connection to a host is refused.

Syntax & Usage The following code snippet invokes the getX() remote method from the MyServer remote object (assumed to have already been located in the Naming database) and catches a ConnectException exception if the connection to the host is refused:

```
MyServer remote;
// Look it up in the Naming database
try
{
   int x = remote.getX();
}
catch (ConnectException e)
{
   System.err.println(
   "Remote host refused connection: "
   +e.getMessage());
}
catch (Exception e)
{
   // Process other exceptions here
}
```

Fields None

Constructors

Modifiers	Constructor
public	ConnectException(String)
public	ConnectException(String, Exception)

Methods None

See Also java.rmi.RemoteException

Class ConnectIOException

public synchronized java.rmi.ConnectIOException extends java.rmi.RemoteException

The ConnectIOException exception is thrown any time there is an error related to input/output (I/O) during an attempt to create a connection to invoke a remote method.

Syntax & Usage The following code snippet calls the remote method getX() from the MyServer remote object (which is assumed to have already been found in the Naming database) and catches a ConnectIOException exception if an I/O error occurs when trying to create the actual connection:

```
MyServer remote;
// Look it up in the Naming database
try
{
   int x = remote.getX();
}
catch (ConnectIOException e)
{
   System.err.println(
   "IO exception when connecting to host: "
   +e.getMessage());
}
catch (Exception e)
{
   // Process other exceptions here
}
```

Fields None

Constructors

Modifiers	Constructor
public	ConnectIOException(String)
public	ConnectIOException(String, Exception)

Methods None

See Also java.rmi.RemoteException

Class MarshalException

public synchronized java.rmi.MarshalException extends java.rmi.RemoteException

The MarshalException exception is thrown any time there is an I/O or protocol error while marshaling the transport header, call header, or parameters. *Marshaling* is a process of sending various data (in this case parameters) to a buffer prior to transmission, usually converting all data to one uniform format (using object serialization).

Syntax & Usage The following code snippet invokes the remote method getX() from the MyServer remote object (assumed to already be found in the Naming database) and catches a MarshalException exception if an I/O marshaling-related error occurs:

```
MyServer remote;
// Look it up in the Naming database
try
{
   int x = remote.getX();
}
catch (MarshalException e)
{
   System.err.println(
"Marshal exception when connecting to host:"
   +e.getMessage());
}
catch (Exception e)
{
   // Process other exceptions here
}
```

Fields None

Constructors

Modifiers	Constructor
public	MarshalException(String)
public	MarshalException(String, Exception)

Methods None

See Also java.rmi.RemoteException • java.rmi.UnmarshalException

Class Naming

public final synchronized java.rmi.Naming extends java.lang.Object

The Naming class represents the mechanism for obtaining references to remote objects using a specified URL pointing to the location of a remote object.

Syntax & Usage On the server side, you need to register your server class by entering the following:

```
Naming.rebind(m_ServerName, appl);
```

In this rebind() method call, *m_ServerName* represents a URL reference to a remote object and *appl* represents the remote object (implementing the Remote interface).

On the client side, you need to find the server by constructing its location and name using URL syntax in the form rmi://*host*:*port*/*name* (if *host* and *port* are not specified, the current host and port will be used):

```
MyServer server = (MyServer)
   Naming.lookup("rmi://" + getCodeBase().
   getHost() + "/"+ ServerName);
```

This example constructs the name of the remote server, wherein the lookup() method searches for it in the naming database and returns it as an instance of the MyServer class.

Fields None

Constructors None

Methods

Modifiers	Return Type	Method
public static	void	bind(String, Remote)
public static	String[]	list(String)
public static	Remote	lookup(String)
public static	void	rebind(String, Remote)
public static	void	unbind(String)

See Also java.lang.Object • java.rmi.Remote

Class NoSuchObjectException

public synchronized java.rmi.NoSuchObjectException extends java.rmi.RemoteException

The NoSuchObjectException exception is thrown any time there is an attempt to invoke a remote method for an object that is no longer accessible.

Syntax & Usage This code snippet invokes the remote method getX() on the MyServer remote object (assumed to be found in the Naming database) and catches a NoSuchObjectException exception for the remote object that is no longer accessible for some reason:

```
MyServer remote;
// Look it up in the Naming database
try
{
  int x = remote.getX();
}
catch (NoSuchObjectException  e)
{
  System.err.println("Attempt to invoke a method on an object that is
  no longer available: "+e.getMessage());
}
catch (Exception e)
{
  // Process other exceptions here
}
```

Fields None

Constructors

Modifiers	Constructor
public	NoSuchObjectException(String)

Methods None

See Also java.rmi.RemoteException

Class NotBoundException

public synchronized java.rmi.NotBoundException extends java.lang.Exception

The NotBoundException exception is thrown any time a specified name is not bound into the RMI registry database.

Syntax & Usage This exception is thrown by methods in the java.rmi.registry.Registry interface and the java.rmi.Naming class to indicate that the specified name does not exist in the RMI registry. Please see the example under "Interface java.rmi.registry.Registry" in Chapter 15 for more information.

Fields None

Constructors

Modifiers	Constructor
public	NotBoundException()
public	NotBoundException(String)

Methods None

See Also java.lang.Exception • java.rmi.Naming • java.rmi.registry.Registry

Interface Remote

public interface java.rmi.Remote

The Remote interface is used to identify remote objects.

Syntax & Usage This interface does not contain any fields or methods, but any object needing to be a remote object must implement or inherit it; otherwise, it will not be considered a remote object by the RMI system.

> **Tip**
>
> *You can use the **instanceof** operator to determine whether an object implements this interface. Consider the following example that performs this check on myObj:*
>
> ```
> if (myObj instanceof java.rmi.Remote)
>    { }
> ```

Fields None

Constructors None

Methods None

See Also java.lang.Object

Class RemoteException

public synchronized java.rmi.RemoteException extends java.io.IOException

The RemoteException class is the root class for RMI-related exceptions.

Syntax & Usage

The RemoteException exception is the superclass for a number of exceptions contained in this package and the java.rmi.server package. The following is a list of subclasses to this exception:

- AccessException
- ConnectException
- ConnectIOException
- MarshalException
- NoSuchObjectException
- ServerError
- ServerException
- ServerRuntimeException
- StubNotFoundException
- UnexpectedException
- UnknownHostException
- UnmarshalException
- java.rmi.server.ExportException
- java.rmi.server.SkeletonMismatchException
- java.rmi.server.SkeletonNotFoundException
- java.rmi.server.SocketSecurityException

For more information on the classes in the preceding list, please see the appropriate sections elsewhere in this chapter and also see Chapter 16.

Note

You can catch RemoteException if you don't want to reconcile various subclasses of this exception.

This class also contains the **public** Throwable detail field, which can hold one of the more specific exception subclasses wrapped by this exception. That way, you can extract a more precise exception.

Fields

Modifiers	Type	Field
public	Throwable	detail

Constructors

Modifiers	Constructor
public	RemoteException()
public	RemoteException(String)
public	RemoteException(String, Throwable)

Methods

Modifiers	Return Type	Method
public	String	getMessage()

See Also java.io.IOException • java.rmi.AccessException • java.rmi.ConnectException • java.rmi.ConnectIOException • java.rmi.MarshalException • java.rmi.NoSuchObjectException • java.rmi.ServerError • java.rmi.ServerException • java.rmi.ServerRuntimeException • java.rmi.StubNotFoundException • java.rmi.UnexpectedException • java.rmi.UnknownHostException • java.rmi.UnmarshalException • java.rmi.server.ExportException • java.rmi.server.SkeletonMismatchException • java.rmi.server.SkeletonNotFoundException • java.rmi.server.SocketSecurityException

Class RMISecurityException

public synchronized java.rmi.RMISecurityException extends java.lang.SecurityException

The RMISecurityException exception is thrown any time access to a specified remote object and/or method is denied.

Syntax & Usage This example invokes the remote method getX() on the MyServer remote object (assumed to already be found in the Naming database) and catches an RMISecurityException exception if access to that method is denied by the currently installed RMI security manager. The following code snippet shows a simple example:

```
MyServer remote;
// Look it up in the Naming database
try
{
   int x = remote.getX();
}
catch (RMISecurityException e)
{
   System.err.println("Security exception:"
   "+e.getMessage());
}
catch (Exception e)
```

```
{
   // Process other exceptions here
}
```

Fields None

Constructors

Modifiers	Constructor
public	RMISecurityException(String)
public	RMISecurityException(String, String)

Methods None

See Also java.lang.SecurityException • java.rmi.RMISecurityManager

Class RMISecurityManager

public synchronized java.rmi.RMISecurityManager extends java.lang.SecurityManager

This class overrides java.lang.SecurityManager and manages RMI security for Java applications (specifically). Not specifying an RMI security manager will result in the Java application being able to call only local methods (which is the default).

Syntax & Usage In the main() method of your Java application, you can specify an RMI security manager using the setSecurityManager() method from the java.lang.System class. You can specify either an RMISecurityManager instance or a security manager you have defined yourself. Consider the following code snippet example:

```
RMISecurityManager rmiSecurity =
   RMISecurityManager();
System.setSecurityManager(rmiSecurity);
rmiSecurity.checkConnect(myHost, myPort);
```

This example creates a new instance of the RMISecurityManager class, sets it as a system's security manager, and then checks that stubs can make connections through the specified host (myHost) and port (myPort).

Fields None

Constructors

Modifiers	Constructor
public	RMISecurityManager()

Methods

Modifiers	Return Type	Method
public synchronized	void	checkAccept(String, int)
public synchronized	void	checkAccess(Thread)
public synchronized	void	checkAccess(ThreadGroup)
public	void	checkAwtEventQueueAccess()
public synchronized	void	checkConnect(String, int)
public	void	checkConnect(String, int, Object)
public synchronized	void	checkCreateClassLoader()
public	void	checkDelete(String)
public synchronized	void	checkExec(String)
public synchronized	void	checkExit(int)
public synchronized	void	checkLink(String)
public synchronized	void	checkListen(int)
public	void	checkMemberAccess(Class, int)
public	void	checkMulticast(InetAddress)
public	void	checkMulticast(InetAddress, byte)
public synchronized	void	checkPackageAccess(String)
public synchronized	void	checkPackageDefinition(String)
public	void	checkPrintJobAccess()
public synchronized	void	checkPropertiesAccess()
public synchronized	void	checkPropertyAccess(String)
public synchronized	void	checkRead(FileDescriptor)
public synchronized	void	checkRead(String)
public	void	checkRead(String, Object)
public	void	checkSecurityAccess(String)
public synchronized	void	checkSetFactory()
public	void	checkSystemClipboardAccess()
public synchronized	boolean	checkTopLevelWindow(Object)
public synchronized	void	checkWrite(FileDescriptor)
public synchronized	void	checkWrite(String)
public	Object	getSecurityContext()

See Also java.lang.SecurityManager • java.lang.System • java.rmi.RMISecurityException

Class ServerError

public synchronized java.rmi.ServerError extends java.rmi.RemoteException

The ServerError error is thrown any time there is a server-side problem during the execution of a remote method.

Syntax & Usage Because this is an error, you do not need to worry about catching it in your Java programs. Please see the java.lang.Error class for more information on errors.

Fields None

Constructors

Modifiers	Constructor
public	ServerError(String, Error)

Methods None

See Also java.lang.Error • java.rmi.RemoteException

Class ServerException

public synchronized java.rmi.ServerException extends java.rmi.RemoteException

The ServerException exception is thrown any time there is an exception during the execution of a remote method.

Syntax & Usage This class wraps any remote exception that occurs while the server is executing a remote method. To retrieve the original exception, you need to use the **public** Throwable detail field, inherited from RemoteException. The following is a list of exceptions wrapped by this one:

- MarshalException
- RemoteException
- UnmarshalException
- java.rmi.server.SkeletonMismatchException

Please see the appropriate sections on the above classes elsewhere in the chapter for more information.

The following code snippet shows an example:

```
try
{
  // Do something remote here
}
catch (ServerException e)
{
  Throwable e1 = e.detail;
  System.err.println("Remote exception:"
  "+e1.getMessage());
}
```

Fields None

Constructors

Modifiers	Constructor
public	ServerException(String)
public	ServerException(String, Exception)

Methods None

See Also java.rmi.MarshalException • java.rmi.RemoteException • java.rmi.UnmarshalException • java.rmi.server.SkeletonMismatchException

Class ServerRuntimeException

public synchronized java.rmi.ServerRuntimeException extends java.rmi.RemoteException

The ServerRuntimeException exception is thrown any time there is a run-time-related exception while the server is executing a remote method.

Syntax & Usage This class wraps any run-time exception—even if the exception is declared in the signature of the method. To retrieve the original exception, use the Throwable detail field, inherited from the RemoteException superclass. The following shows a simple example:

```
try
{
   // Do something remote here
}
catch (ServerRuntimeException e)
{
   Throwable e1 = e.detail;
   System.err.println("Remote exception:"
   "+e1.getMessage());
}
```

Fields None

Constructors

Modifiers	Constructor
public	ServerRuntimeException(String, Exception)

Methods None

See Also java.rmi.RemoteException

Class StubNotFoundException

public synchronized java.rmi.StubNotFoundException extends java.rmi.RemoteException

The StubNotFoundException exception is thrown any time there is a problem exporting (i.e., being called by a foreign Java virtual machine—VM—or being sent as a parameter or result in a remote method call) or if, during the execution of a remote method, its corresponding remote object was not exported properly.

Note

Only instances of classes extending the java.rmi.server.UnicastRemoteObject class can be exported.

Syntax & Usage

This exception can be thrown during the remote object export process if one of the following occurs:

- The class for the stub is not found.
- A name collision has occurred (a class has the same name as a stub, causing the stub to fail to be instantiated).
- There is bad URL due to an incorrect code base reference.
- The stub simply represents an incorrect class (usually resulting from a name collision).

Fields

None

Constructors

Modifiers	Constructor
public	StubNotFoundException(String)
public	StubNotFoundException(String, Exception)

Methods

None

See Also

java.rmi.RemoteException

Class UnexpectedException

public synchronized java.rmi.UnexpectedException extends java.rmi.RemoteException

The UnexpectedException exception is thrown any time an exception that was not defined in the signature of the method occurs.

Syntax & Usage You can retrieve the actual exception using the **public** Throwable detail field, inherited from the RemoteException superclass. The following shows a simple example:

```
try
{
   // get some value from a remote object
}
catch (UnexpectedException e)
{
   Throwable e1 = e.detail;
   System.err.println("Unexpected exception:"
   "+e1.getMessage());
}
```

Fields None

Constructors

Modifiers	Constructor
public	UnexpectedException(String)
public	UnexpectedException(String, Exception)

Methods None

See Also java.rmi.RemoteException

Class UnknownHostException

public synchronized java.rmi.UnknownHostException extends java.rmi.RemoteException

The UnknownHostException exception is thrown any time the host for a given remote object is not known.

Syntax & Usage

The following code snippet invokes the remote method getX() from the MyServer remote object (assumed to already be found in the Naming database) and catches an UnknownHostException exception if the host is not recognized:

```
MyServer remote;
// lookup in the Naming database
try
{
   int x = remote.getX();
}
catch (UnknownHostException e)
{
   System.err.println(
   " Unknown Host Exception: "
   +e.getMessage());
}
catch (Exception e)
{
   // Process other exceptions here
}
```

Fields

None

Constructors

Modifiers	Constructor
public	UnknownHostException(String)
public	UnknownHostException(String, Exception)

Methods

None

See Also

java.rmi.RemoteException

Class UnmarshalException

public synchronized java.rmi.UnmarshalException extends java.rmi.RemoteException

The UnmarshalException exception is thrown any time there is an I/O or protocol-related exception with data coming back from a remote object.

Syntax & Usage

This exception is thrown in the event that there is a corrupted I/O stream or a protocol error during the marshaling of the returning header, the checking of the return code and type, or the unmarshaling of the return. RMI uses object serialization to unmarshal the data. Please see "Class MarshalException," earlier in this chapter, for more information.

Fields

None

Constructors

Modifiers	Constructor
public	UnmarshalException(String)
public	UnmarshalException(String, Exception)

Methods

None

See Also

java.rmi.MarshalException • java.rmi.RemoteException

The java.rmi.dgc Package

14

The java.rmi.dgc package is a tiny package containing only two classes and one interface. The letters *dgc* in the package name stand for *d*istributed *g*arbage *c*ollector. The distributed garbage collector is used by the Remote Method Invocation (RMI) system to perform garbage collection of remote objects among client and server Java virtual machines (VMs). Besides the three classes in this package, two classes in the java.rmi.server package also relate to distributed garbage collection; they are:

- java.rmi.server.ObjID
- java.rmi.server.UID

For more information, please see the appropriate sections for these two classes in Chapter 16.

Interface DGC

public abstract interface java.rmi.dgc.DGC implements java.rmi.Remote

The DGC interface is an **abstract** interface that is part of the distributed garbage collection algorithm used to handle the server-side aspect of garbage collection in RMI.

Syntax & Usage

This interface contains two methods—dirty() and clean(). These two methods are called by a client Java VM, when a particular remote object is referenced, to manage the references it has, and to determine when it is no longer being referenced—all of which is managed by a master reference list (containing client VMIDs with their references) that the distributed garbage collector uses for each remote object. The distributed garbage collector grants a lease period for each reference, and if this lease is not renewed by the client Java VM before the lease expires, the distributed garbage collector assumes that there are no longer any references to the given remote object.

The client must make an initial dirty() method call (as well as subsequent renewal dirty() calls), letting the distributed garbage collector know that a particular remote object is being referenced. Correspondingly, it also must make a clean() method call, letting the distributed garbage collector know when a particular remote object is no longer being referenced. Let's take a closer look at the semantics of each of these methods.

```
public abstract Lease dirty(ObjID ids[],
   long sequenceNum, Lease lease)
   throws RemoteException
```

Let's look at the parameters:

- **ObjID ids[].** This parameter represents an array of the remote object identifiers (see the section on the java.rmi.server.ObjID class in Chapter 16 for details) that represent remote references to various remote objects from this client Java VM.
- **long sequenceNum.** This is a sequence of numbers used to recognize and ignore any late method calls to the distributed garbage collector.
- **Lease lease.** This object contains a unique VMID and a lease period (see the next section, "Class Lease," for more information)—either the period requested by the client or the one specified by the server.

```
public abstract void clean(ObjID ids[],
   long sequenceNum, VMID vmid,
   boolean strong) throws RemoteException
```

Now let's look at these parameters:

- **ObjID ids[].** This represents an array of the object identifiers (see the section for the java.rmi.server.ObjID class in Chapter 16 for details) that represent remote references to various remote objects from the given client Java VM.
- **long sequenceNum.** This value is used to recognize late clean() method calls.
- **VMID vmid.** This is the VMID to be removed from the reference list of each remote object in the ids[] array.
- **boolean strong.** If this is **true**, then this clean() method call is the result of a failed dirty() method call, so the sequence number for this client must be retained to recognize future methods calls that will be out of order.

Fields None

Constructors None

Methods

Modifiers	Return Type	Method
public abstract	void	clean(ObjID[], long, VMID, boolean)
public abstract	Lease	dirty(ObjID[], long, Lease)

See Also java.rmi.Remote • java.rmi.dgc.Lease • java.rmi.dgc.VMID • java.rmi.server.ObjID • java.rmi.server.UID

Class Lease

public final synchronized java.rmi.dgc.Lease extends java.lang.Object implements java.io.Serializable

The Lease class is used by the distributed garbage collector in RMI to request and grant leases for a specified remote reference (or set of remote references). A lease is a license for a remote reference—from the server—containing a unique VMID used to identify the client Java VM responsible for the reference and an expellable duration for the lease.

Syntax & Usage Instances of this class are used to request and grant leases to remote object references:

```
Lease lease = new Lease(new VMID(),
  3600*1000);
```

This example creates a new instance of the Lease class for a new VMID instance (see the next section, "Class VMID," for more information) and a requested lease duration of one hour (3,600 seconds). Note that it is up to the server to decide how long the lease period should be.

Fields None

Constructors

Modifiers	Constructor
public	Lease(VMID, long)

Methods

Modifiers	Return Type	Method
public	long	getValue()
public	VMID	getVMID()

See Also java.io.Serializable • java.lang.Object • java.rmi.dgc.DGC • java.rmi.dgc.VMID • java.rmi.server.ObjID • java.rmi.server.UID

Class VMID

public final synchronized java.rmi.dgc.VMID extends java.lang.Object implements java.io.Serializable

The VMID class is used as part of the distributed garbage collector model to represent a unique way to identify Java VMs in an RMI system.

Syntax & Usage You can use this class to obtain a unique ID based on the UID and hosting address of your Java VM. Sometimes (due to security restorations), it is not possible to obtain a universally unique VMID wherein the distributed garbage collector assigns a VMID for the given client Java VM. You can use the **static** isUnique() method to determine if the VMID you have is universally unique:

```
if (VMID.isUnique())
{
   VMID myVMID = new VMID();
   System.out.println("Unique VM ID: "
      +myVMID.toString());
}
else
   System.out.println("Unique VM ID not available.");
```

This code snippet checks whether there is a universally unique ID for the given Java VM. If so, it creates a VMID instance and displays it; otherwise, it prints a warning message.

Fields None

Constructors

Modifiers	Constructor
public	VMID()

Methods

Modifiers	Return Type	Method
public	boolean	equals(Object)
public	int	hashCode()
public static	boolean	isUnique()
public	String	toString()

See Also java.io.Serializable • java.lang.Object • java.rmi.dgc.DGC • java.rmi.dgc.Lease • java.rmi.server.ObjID • java.rmi.server.UID

The java.rmi.registry Package

15

The registry acts as a naming service for the Remote Method Invocation (RMI) system. The registry keeps a database of available remote objects based on a uniquely bound name used to represent each remote object reference. This registry is used by the RMI client to locate the remote object for a remote method (or methods) it wishes to invoke. However, these remote objects are not added automatically to this registry; instead, the server must register its remote object(s) explicitly. The overall functionality for this registry is defined in the three classes that make up this package.

Class LocateRegistry

public final synchronized java.rmi.registry.LocateRegistry extends java.lang.Object

The LocateRegistry class is used to obtain references to an RMIregistry based on a specified host.

Syntax & Usage On the server side, you can use this class to locate the registry so you can register your server under a certain name using the bind() method from the Registry class:

```
// On server side
Registry registry = LocateRegistry.
   getRegistry();
registry.bind(m_Name, server);
```

On the client side, you can use this class to locate the registry so you can get a reference to your server's host address and registered name, using the lookup() method from the Registry class:

```
// On client side
Registry registry = LocateRegistry.
   getRegistry(myHostAddr);
MyServer server = (MyServer)registry.
   lookup(m_Name);
// Access server
server.requestData();
```

Fields None

Constructors None

Methods

Modifiers	Return Type	Method
public static	Registry	createRegistry(int)
public static	Registry	getRegistry()
public static	Registry	getRegistry(int)
public static	Registry	getRegistry(String)
public static	Registry	getRegistry(String, int)

See Also java.lang.Object • java.rmi.registry.Registry

Interface Registry

public abstract interface java.rmi.registry.Registry implements java.rmi.Remote

The Registry interface describes methods used to perform various registry-related operations.

> **Note**
>
> *The registry does not provide persistent storage.*

Syntax & Usage Usually you do not implement this interface directly; instead, you use the java.rmi.Naming class, which implements this interface to support a registry based on URL names. Nonetheless, the following example outlines how to implement this interface:

```
class MyRegistry implements Registry
{
  String[] names;
  Remote[] remotes;

  public MyRegistry()
  {
  // place initialization code here
  }

  public void bind(String name, Remote obj)
    throws RemoteException,
    AlreadyBoundException, AccessException
  {
  // Check that the given name is not already
  // bound and add it to the registry along
  // with the Remote reference. Otherwise
  // throw an exception.
  }

  public void unbind(String name)
    throws RemoteException,
    NotBoundException, AccessException
  {
```

```
    // Check that the given name is already
    // bound and remove it from the registry
    // along with the Remote reference.
    // Otherwise throw an exception.
    }

    public void rebind(String name, Remote obj)
      throws RemoteException, AccessException
    {
    // Find the given name the registry and
    // replace the Remote reference.
    }

    public Remote lookup(String name) throws
      RemoteException, NotBoundException,
      AccessException
    {
    // Find the given name in the registry and
    //return the corresponding Remote
    //reference.
    }

    public String[] list() throws
      RemoteException, AccessException
    {
    // Return the names currently listed in the
    //registry
      return names;
    }
}
```

This implementation holds an array of names and another array of corresponding remote objects, which together make up the anatomy of a typical registry. Method bind() checks that the specified name is not bound already and, if this is true, adds it to the registry along with its corresponding Remote object reference. Otherwise, the AlreadyBoundException exception is thrown. Note that RemoteException and AccessException also can be thrown and must either be rethrown or caught here.

Method unbind() checks whether a specified name already is bound and, if it is, removes it from the registry along with its corresponding Remote object reference. Otherwise, the NotBoundException exception is thrown. Note that RemoteException and AccessException also can be thrown and must either be rethrown or caught here.

Method rebind() finds the specified name in the registry and replaces the corresponding Remote object reference with the specified one. Note that RemoteException and AccessException can be thrown and must either be rethrown or caught here.

Method lookup() checks to see if the specified name exists in the registry and, if it does, returns the corresponding Remote object reference. Otherwise, the NotBoundException exception is thrown. Note that RemoteException and AccessException also can be thrown and must either be rethrown or caught here.

Method list() returns the whole list of names currently bound in this registry.

Fields

Modifiers	Type	Field
public static final	int	REGISTRY_PORT

Constructors None

Methods

Modifiers	Return Type	Method
public abstract	void	bind(String, Remote)
public abstract	String[]	list()
public abstract	Remote	lookup(String)
public abstract	void	rebind(String, Remote)
public abstract	void	unbind(String)

See Also java.rmi.AccessException • java.rmi.AlreadyBoundException • java.rmi.Naming • java.rmi.NotBoundException • java.rmi.Remote • java.rmi.RemoteException • java.rmi.registry.LocateRegistry • java.rmi.registry.RegistryHandler

Interface RegistryHandler

public abstract interface java.rmi.registry.RegistryHandler

The RegistryHandler interface is used to contact the remote Registry instance.

Syntax & Usage There are two methods that implementations of this interface need to provide for: registryImpl() and registryStub(). The following example outlines how to do this:

```
class MyRegHandler implements RegistryHandler
{
```

```
    public Registry registryStub(String host,
       int port) throws RemoteException,
       UnknownHostException
    {
    // Return a stub to contact the remote
    // registry using the specified host and
    // port here
    }

    public Registry registryImpl(int port)
       throws RemoteException
    {
    // Create and export a Registry instance
    // using the specified port here
    }
}
```

The method registryStub() returns a stub that is used to contact the remote registry on the specified host and port. Method registryImpl() creates and exports a Registry instance on the specified port.

Fields None

Constructors None

Methods

Modifiers	Return Type	Method
public abstract	Registry	registryImpl(int)
public abstract	Registry	registryStub(String, int)

See Also java.rmi.registry.LocateRegistry • java.rmi.registry.Registry

The java.rmi.server Package

16

The java.rmi.server package is much more populated than its siblings, the java.rmi, the java.rmi.dgc, and the java.rmi.registry packages. The java.rmi.server package contains classes that relate to several key Remote Method Invocation (RMI) topics:

- **Server classes.** These are used to implement the server in RMI.
- **Stub and skeleton classes.** This group of classes is used by the RMI compiler rmic.exe when it generates stub and skeleton class files. Usually, you do not need to work with these classes.
- **Distributed garbage collector classes.** This package contains several classes used for distributed garbage collection in the RMI system. The rest of the distributed garbage collection setup is contained in the java.rmi.dgc package, covered in Chapter 14.

Class ExportException

public synchronized java.rmi.server.ExportException extends java.rmi.RemoteException

ExportException is thrown any time there is a problem exporting a given object.

Syntax & Usage Specifically, this exception is thrown when the port specified for object exportation is in use or otherwise unavailable. In situations such as these, upon catching this exception, you should try using another port.

Fields None

Constructors

Modifiers	Constructor
public	ExportException(String)
public	ExportException(String, Exception)

Methods None

See Also java.rmi.RemoteException

Interface LoaderHandler

public abstract interface java.rmi.server.LoaderHandler

The LoaderHandler interface must be implemented by a class called LoaderHandler. The methods implemented from this interface in a LoaderHandler class are used by the RMIClassLoader class to help it load classes.

Syntax & Usage This interface declares the same methods as the RMIClassLoader class. You can implement this interface to develop your own RMI class loader. Consider the following:

```
Class MyLoader implements RMIClassLoader
{
  public static Class loadClass(URL codebase,
    String name) throws
      MalformedURLException,
      ClassNotFoundException
  {
    // Load class specified by name from the
    // given URL.
  }

  public static Class loadClass(
    String name) throws
      MalformedURLException,
      ClassNotFoundException
  {
    // Load class specified by name from the
    //  URL specified in the
    // java.rmi.server.codebase system
    // property.
  }

  Object getSecurityContext(ClassLoader
    loader)
  {
    // Returns the security context for the
    // loader class loader.
  }
}
```

You see two overloaded loadClass() methods that load a class using the name in the specified URL or the URL specified in the java.rmi.server.codebase system property. The method getSecurityContext() returns the security context for the specified class loader.

Fields

Modifiers	Type	Field
public static final	String	packagePrefix

Constructors None

Methods

Modifiers	Return Type	Method
public abstract	Object	getSecurityContext(ClassLoader)
public abstract	Class	loadClass(String)
public abstract	Class	loadClass(URL, String)

See Also java.rmi.server.RMIClassLoader

Class LogStream

public synchronized java.rmi.server.LogStream extends java.io.PrintStream

The LogStream class is used to log messages (including error messages) during an RMI connection session. It automatically appends the date, time, and registered name for each message logged. This class also is used internally by the RMI system for logging server calls.

Syntax & Usage

This class does not contain any **public** constructors. However, you can instantiate it using one of the **static** methods available in this class. From there, you can send data to the specified log stream using one of the available write() methods. The following example method uses the log() method from this class to instantiate LogStream and append several newly created messages to a test.log file:

```
public static void logMessage(String message)
{
  try
  {
    FileOutputStream fStream =
      new FileOutputStream(
      "test.log", true);
    LogStream myLog = LogStream.log(
    "My Log");
    myLog.setOutputStream(fStream);

    String s = message+"\r\n";
    byte b[] = s.getBytes();
    myLog.write(b, 0, b.length);

    myLog.getOutputStream().close();
  }
  catch (IOException e) {}
}
```

This example creates a FileOutputStream object (fStream) for the file test.log and a LogStream instance (myLog) with the "My Log" message setting the log output stream to fStream. The actual logging is made using the write() method from this class. Here's what the output might look like for the messages "This is a log message" and "Test" based on the preceding example method:

```
Fri Mar 14 17:32:37 PST 1997:My Log:main:This is a log message
Fri Mar 14 17:35:52 PST 1997:My Log:main:Test
```

Fields

Modifiers	Type	Field
public static final	int	BRIEF
public static final	int	SILENT
public static final	int	VERBOSE

Constructors None

Modifiers	Return Type	Method
public static synchronized	PrintStream	getDefaultStream()
public synchronized	OutputStream	getOutputStream()
public static	LogStream	log(String)
public static	int	parseLevel(String)
public static synchronized	void	setDefaultStream(PrintStream)
public synchronized	void	setOutputStream(OutputStream)
public	String	toString()
public	void	write(byte[], int, int)
public	void	write(int)

See Also java.io.FileOutputStream • java.io.PrintStream

Class ObjID

public final synchronized java.rmi.server.ObjID extends java.lang.Object implements java.io.Serializable

The ObjID class is used to generate unique identifiers for objects on a particular Java virtual machine (VM) for purposes relating to RMI's distributed garbage collector.

Syntax & Usage

Each ObjID object contains a unique object number (assigned during object exportation) represented as a **long** value and an address space identifier (that is unique to the host) encapsulated in a UID object. Consider the following:

```
ObjID oID = new ObjID(REGISTRY_ID);
objStream.write(oID);
```

This snippet of code creates an ObjID instance specifying REGISTRY_ID and writes the instance to the specified ObjectOutputStream object objStream.

Fields

Modifiers	Type	Field
public static final	int	DGC_ID
public static final	int	REGISTRY_ID

Constructors

Modifiers	Constructor
public	ObjID()
public	ObjID(int)

Methods

Modifiers	Return Type	Method
public	boolean	equals(Object)
public	int	hashCode()
public static	ObjID	read(ObjectInput)
public	String	toString()
public	void	write(ObjectOutput)

See Also

java.io.Serializable • java.lang.Object • java.rmi.dgc.DGC • java.rmi.dgc.Lease • java.rmi.dgc.VMID • java.rmi.server.UID

Class Operation

public synchronized java.rmi.server.Operation extends java.lang.Object

The Operation class is used to hold descriptions for a specified Java method belonging to a given remote object.

Syntax & Usage Operation objects usually are constructed using the method signature of the method the Operation object is to describe. The following code snippet constructs a simple Operation object based on the method signature for myMethod() and retrieves that object's String representation by using the getOperation() method from this class:

```
Operation op = new Operation(
   "void myMethod(String)");
String str = op.getOperation();
```

Fields None

Constructors

Modifiers	Constructor
public	Operation(String)

Methods

Modifiers	Return Type	Method
public	String	getOperation()
public	String	toString()

See Also java.lang.Object

Interface RemoteCall

public interface java.rmi.server.RemoteCall

The RemoteCall interface is implemented by the stubs and skeletons of remote objects to perform the actual method calls to a given remote object.

Syntax & Usage The executeCall() method in this class is used to process the call while the other declared methods retrieve or release communication streams. The following outlines a simple implementation of this interface:

```
class MyCall implements RemoteCall
{
   public MyCall()
   {
   // Construct a MyCall object.
   }
```

```
    void executeCall() throws Exception
    {
    // Implement your call here.
    }

    // Implement other methods of the interface here.
}
```

Fields None

Constructors None

Methods

Modifiers	Return Type	Method
public abstract	void	done()
public abstract	void	executeCall()
public abstract	ObjectInput	getInputStream()
public abstract	ObjectOutput	getOutputStream()
public abstract	ObjectOutput	getResultStream(boolean)
public abstract	void	releaseInputStream()
public abstract	void	releaseOutputStream()

See Also java.rmi.server.Skeleton

Class RemoteObject

public abstract synchronized java.rmi.server.RemoteObject extends java.lang.Object implements java.rmi.Remote, java.io.Serializable

The RemoteObject class is declared as an **abstract** class and used to facilitate the basic functionality for remote objects. Effectively, it extends the java.lang.Object class and overrides three of the Object class's methods (hashCode(), equals(), and toString()) so they can work in a remote setting.

Syntax & Usage

This class represents the java.lang.Object for remote objects. The following is a list of its subclasses:

- RemoteServer
- RemoteStub
- UnicastRemoteObject

Please see the appropriate sections for these classes for more information.

Fields

Modifiers	Type	Field
protected transient	RemoteRef	ref

Constructors

Modifiers	Constructor
protected	RemoteObject()
protected	RemoteObject(RemoteRef)

Methods

Modifiers	Return Type	Method
public	boolean	equals(Object)
public	int	hashCode()
public	String	toString()

See Also

java.io.Serializable • java.lang.Object • java.rmi.Remote • java.rmi.server.RemoteServer • java.rmi.server.RemoteStub • java.rmi.server.UnicastRemoteObject

Interface RemoteRef

public abstract interface java.rmi.server.RemoteRef implements java.io.Externalizable

The RemoteRef interface is declared as an **abstract** interface and represents a reference to a remote object. Each stub implements this interface to provide a distinct handle for a given remote object.

Syntax & Usage This remote reference is used to execute remote method calls on the remote object to which it refers. This example shows a sample implementation of this interface:

```
class MyRef implements RemoteRef
{
   public MyRef (Remote obj)
   {
   // Construct MyRef object for obj.
   }

   public RemoteCall newCall(RemoteObject obj,
      Operation op[],int opnum,
      long hash) throws RemoteException
   {
      return new MyCall();
   }

   // Implement other methods of the interface here.
}
```

This implementation of the newCall() method returns a new instance of the MyCall class (please see the example under "Interface RemoteCall," earlier in this chapter, for more information).

Fields

Modifiers	Type	Field
public static final	String	packagePrefix

Constructors None

Methods

Modifiers	Return Type	Method
public abstract	void	done(RemoteCall)
public abstract	String	getRefClass(ObjectOutput)
public abstract	void	invoke(RemoteCall)
public abstract	RemoteCall	newCall(RemoteObject, Operation[], int, long)
public abstract	boolean	remoteEquals(RemoteRef)
public abstract	int	remoteHashCode()
public abstract	String	remoteToString()

See Also java.io.Externalizable • java.rmi.server.RemoteCall

Class RemoteServer

public abstract synchronized java.rmi.server.RemoteServer extends java.rmi.server.RemoteObject

The RemoteServer class is declared as an **abstract** class that defines a remote server in the RMI system.

Syntax & Usage Currently, the only class that subclasses this one is UnicastRemoteObject, which implements a TCP connection stream.

> **Tip**
>
> *Alternatively, you can subclass this class to implement a User Datagram Protocol (UDP) connection in RMI.*

This class also provides three useful **static** methods:

- **getClientHost().** This method returns a String object containing the hostname for the current client.
- **getLog().** This method returns a PrintStream object used to retrieve the RMI method call logs (please see "Class LogStream," earlier in this chapter, for more information).
- **setLog(OutputStream).** This method is used to set the specified OutputStream object as the stream that you can use to log RMI calls.

Fields None

Constructors

Modifiers	Constructor
protected	RemoteServer()
protected	RemoteServer(RemoteRef)

Methods

Modifiers	Return Type	Method
public static	String	getClientHost()
public static	PrintStream	getLog()
public static	void	setLog(OutputStream)

See Also java.rmi.server.LogStream • java.rmi.server.RemoteObject • java.rmi.server.RemoteStub • java.rmi.server.UnicastRemoteObject

Class RemoteStub

public abstract synchronized java.rmi.server.RemoteStub extends java.rmi.server.RemoteObject

The RemoteStub class is declared as an **abstract** class that defines the foundation for implementations of a remote client stub in the RMI system.

Syntax & Usage

This class provides the framework to support remote references in RMI. The following example shows the MyStub class extending RemoteStub:

```
class MyStub extends RemoteStub
{
   RemoteRef m_ref;
   MyStub(RemoteRef ref)
   {
      m_ref = ref;
   }
}
```

This example holds the RemoteRef m_ref instance variable, which is set by the constructor.

Fields

None

Constructors

Modifiers	Constructor
protected	RemoteStub()
protected	RemoteStub(RemoteRef)

Methods

Modifiers	Return Type	Method
protected static	void	setRef(RemoteStub, RemoteRef)

See Also

java.rmi.server.RemoteObject • java.rmi.server.RemoteServer

Class RMIClassLoader

public synchronized java.rmi.server.RMIClassLoader extends java.lang.Object

The RMIClassLoader class is used as a way for Java programs to load classes remotely of a network using a specified URL.

Syntax & Usage This class has no constructor but provides two overloaded **static** loadClass() methods for loading classes from a specified URL or from the URL specified in the java.rmi.server.codebase system property:

```
try
{
  Class cls = RMIClassLoader.loadClass(
    myURL, myClassName);
}
catch (MalformedURLException e) {}
catch (ClassNotFoundException e) {}
```

This example shows how to load classes by specifying URL and name, using an RMIClassLoader object. Note that MalformedURLException and ClassNotFoundException must be handled here.

Fields None

Constructors None

Methods

Modifiers	Return Type	Method
public static	Object	getSecurityContext(ClassLoader)
public static	Class	loadClass(String)
public static	Class	loadClass(URL, String)

See Also java.lang.Object • java.rmi.server.LoaderHandler

Interface RMIFailureHandler

public abstract interface java.rmi.server.RMIFailureHandler

The RMIFailureHandler interface declares only one method (failure()), which is implemented to respond to a failed TCP connection in RMI.

Syntax & Usage

An RMIFailureHandler implementation must be registered before you can use it. You can register an RMIFailureHandler implementation using the setFailureHandler() method from the RMISocketFactory class.

The only method declared in this interface is failure(), which returns **true** or **false** indicating whether there should be a retry connection attempt. Consider the following:

```
RMISocketFactory.setFailureHandler(new
  MyHandler());

Class MyHandler implements RMIFailureHandler
{
  int failureCounter = 0;

  public boolean failure(Exception ex)
  {
    failureCounter++;
    return (failureCounter < 3);
  }
}
```

This example implements this interface. Class MyHandler holds field failureCounter, which counts the number of unsuccessful attempts to create a socket. The method failure() returns **true** for the first three attempts and then returns **false** on the fourth (and any attempts after the fourth).

Fields

None

Constructors

None

Methods

Modifiers	Return Type	Method
public abstract	boolean	failure(Exception)

See Also

java.rmi.server.RMISocketFactory

Class RMISocketFactory

public abstract synchronized java.rmi.server.RMISocketFactory extends java.lang.Object

The RMISocketFactory is used by the RMI system to obtain both the client- and server-side sockets.

Syntax & Usage This class uses three procedures for attempting a TCP connection to a given remote Java VM: The first and most common procedure uses the default direct approach. The second and third procedures are employed only if the first should fail, due to an intervening firewall.

```
RMISocketFactory sf =
   RMISocketFactory.getSocketFactory();
Socket mySocket = sf.createSocket(
   myHost, myPort);
```

This snippet of code uses an instance of this class to create a socket to the specified host address and port.

Fields None

Constructors

Modifiers	Constructor
public	RMISocketFactory()

Methods

Modifiers	Return Type	Method
public abstract	ServerSocket	createServerSocket(int)
public abstract	Socket	createSocket(String, int)
public static	RMIFailureHandler	getFailureHandler()
public static	RMISocketFactory	getSocketFactory()
public static	void	setFailureHandler(RMIFailureHandler)
public static	void	setSocketFactory(RMISocketFactory)

See Also java.lang.Object • java.net.ServerSocket • java.net.Socket • java.rmi.server.RMIFailureHandler

Class ServerCloneException

public synchronized java.rmi.server.ServerCloneException extends java.lang.CloneNotSupportedException

ServerCloneException is thrown any time an attempt to clone a remote object fails.

Syntax & Usage

This exception may be thrown only by the clone() method from the UnicastRemoteObject class, indicating a clone operation on a given remote object has failed, usually because the object is not replicable. Please see "Class UnicastRemoteObject," later in this chapter, for more information.

Fields

Modifiers	Type	Field
public	Exception	detail

Constructors

Modifiers	Constructor
public	ServerCloneException(String)
public	ServerCloneException(String, Exception)

Methods

Modifiers	Return Type	Method
public	String	getMessage()

See Also

java.lang.CloneNotSupportedException
• java.rmi.server.UnicastRemoteObject

Class ServerNotActiveException

public synchronized java.rmi.server.ServerNotActiveException extends java.lang.Exception

ServerNotActiveException is thrown any time there is a failed attempt to retrieve the host of a given client.

Syntax & Usage This exception may be thrown by the getClientHost() method in the RemoteServer class. Please see the example under "Interface ServerRef," in the next section, for an example of where this exception can be thrown.

Fields None

Constructors

Modifiers	Constructor
public	ServerNotActiveException()
public	ServerNotActiveException(String)

Methods None

See Also java.lang.Exception • java.rmi.server.RemoteServer • java.rmi.server.ServerRef

Interface ServerRef

public abstract interface java.rmi.server.ServerRef implements java.rmi.server.RemoteRef

The ServerRef interface is declared as an **abstract** interface that represents a server-side reference to a remote object.

Syntax & Usage The method exportObject() in this class creates a client stub object for the specified Remote object. The method getClientHost() returns the host name of the current client or throws an exception if the host is not available. Consider the following example:

```
class MyServerRef implements ServerRef
{
  Thread runner;

  RemoteStub exportObject(Remote obj,
    Object data)
    throws RemoteException
  {
    return MyStub(new MyRef(obj));
  }
```

```
    String getClientHost() throws
      ServerNotActiveException
    {
      if (runner.isAlive())
        return runner.getName();
      else
        throw new
        ServerNotActiveException();
    }
}
```

This example holds an instance of a Thread named runner. The exportObject() method returns a new instance of the MyStub class created from the MyRef class (please see the sections for the RemoteRef and RemoteStub classes, elsewhere in this chapter, for more information).

The getClientHost() method returns the name of runner if this thread is alive or throws a ServerNotActiveException exception otherwise.

Fields None

Constructors None

Methods

Modifiers	Type	Method
public abstract	RemoteStub	exportObject(Remote, Object)
public abstract	String	getClientHost()

See Also java.lang.Thread • java.rmi.server.RemoteRef • java.rmi.server.RemoteStub

Interface Skeleton

public abstract interface java.rmi.server.Skeleton

The Skeleton interface is declared as an **abstract** interface that is implemented by server skeleton classes in the RMI system.

Syntax & Usage Skeletons are the objects that actually dispatch calls to the given remote object. You do not need to implement this class directly because all skeleton classes (i.e., classes implementing this interface) are generated using the rmic stub compiler and implement this interface. This example shows a sample implementation of this interface:

```
class MySkeleton implements Skeleton
{
  Operation[] ops;

  public void dispatch(Remote obj,
    RemoteCall call, int opnum,
    long hash) throws Exception
  {
    ObjectInput input = call.
      getInputStream();
    // Take arguments from the input.

    Operation op = ops[opnum];
    // Invoke this operation op on the obj.

    ObjectOutput output = call.
      getOutputStream();
    // Write return value to the output.
  }

  public Operation[] getOperations()
  {
    return ops;
  }
}
```

The method dispatch() takes any parameters from the input stream obtained from the call object, invokes the method (indicated by the operation number opnum), and writes the return value to the output stream obtained from the call object or throws an exception.

Fields None

Constructors None

Methods

Modifiers	Type	Method
public abstract	void	dispatch(Remote, RemoteCall, int, long)
public abstract	Operation[]	getOperations()

See Also java.rmi.server.RemoteStub • java.rmi.server.ServerRef

Class SkeletonMismatchException

public synchronized java.rmi.server.SkeletonMismatchException extends java.rmi.RemoteException

SkeletonMismatchException is thrown any time there is a hash mismatch between a client and server during the execution of a remote method.

Syntax & Usage This exception is wrapped in the java.rmi.ServerException class. Please see "Class ServerException," in Chapter 13, for more information.

Fields None

Constructors

Modifiers	Constructor
public	SkeletonMismatchException(String)

Methods None

See Also java.rmi.RemoteException • java.rmi.server.Skeleton • java.rmi.server.SkeletonNotFoundException

Class SkeletonNotFoundException

public synchronized java.rmi.server.SkeletonNotFoundException extends java.rmi.RemoteException

SkeletonNotFoundException is thrown any time there is a problem exporting or if the corresponding remote object of an executing remote method was not properly exported to begin with.

Syntax & Usage This exception can be thrown during the remote object export process if the class for the skeleton is not found or a name collision has occurred (i.e., another class has the same name as a skeleton, causing the skeleton class to fail to be instantiated). This exception also can occur if there is a bad URL due to an incorrect code base reference, or the skeleton simply represents an incorrect class—usually resulting from the name collision just mentioned.

Fields None

Constructors

Modifiers	Constructor
public	SkeletonNotFoundException(String)
public	SkeletonNotFoundException(String, Exception)

Methods None

See Also java.rmi.RemoteException • java.rmi.StubNotFoundException

Class SocketSecurityException

public synchronized java.rmi.server.SocketSecurityException extends java.rmi.server.ExportException

SocketSecurityException is thrown any time a security issue is raised when there is an attempt to export an object on a specified port.

Syntax & Usage This exception extends the ExportException class. Usually this exception is thrown if an unsigned applet attempts to export an object on an arbitrary port, which violates the applet security model.

Fields None

Constructors

Modifiers	Constructor
public	SocketSecurityException(String)
public	SocketSecurityException(String, Exception)

Methods None

See Also java.rmi.server.ExportException

Class UID

public final synchronized java.rmi.server.UID extends java.lang.Object implements java.io.Serializable

The UID class is used by the distributed garbage collector (dgc) in RMI to uniquely identify a given host.

Syntax & Usage This class is used to create an address space identifier that is unique with respect to the host that generated it. Consider the following:

```
UID uID = new UID();
uID.write(dataOut);
InetAddress iAddr =
   InetAddress.getLocalHost();
DataOut.write(iAddr.getAddress());
```

This example creates an instance of the UID class and writes it to the specified DataOutput stream. To make this ID globally unique, this example also takes the local InetAddress and writes it to the same stream as a byte array.

> **Note**
>
> *Objects of this class are encapsulated in ObjID objects. Please see the section for that class, earlier in this chapter, for more information.*

Fields None

Constructors

Modifiers	Constructor
public	UID()
public	UID(short)

Methods

public	boolean	equals(Object)
public	int	hashCode()
public static	UID	read(DataInput)
public	String	toString()
public	void	write(DataOutput)

See Also java.io.Serializable • java.lang.Object • java.rmi.dgc.DGC • java.rmi.dgc.Lease • java.rmi.dgc.VMID • java.rmi.server.ObjID

Class UnicastRemoteObject

public synchronized java.rmi.server.UnicastRemoteObject extends java.rmi.server.RemoteServer

The UnicastRemoteObject represents a non-cloneable remote object using RMI's default socket-based transport.

Syntax & Usage

This class indirectly extends the RemoteObject class and defines a remote object that cannot be cloned and exists only while a corresponding server process remains alive. Classes needing to be remote objects normally should extend the UnicastRemoteObject class (and thus the RemoteObject class):

```
Class MyRemote extends UnicastRemoteObject
{
  // Use functionality inherited from
  // UnicastRemoteObject.
  Object obj = this.clone()
}
```

Note

Extending a remote object (such as UnicastRemoteObject) is optional. However, if you do create a remote object that extends from a non-remote class, you will need to export the remote object explicitly using the ***static*** *exportObject() method from this class.*

Fields

None

Constructors

Modifiers	Constructor
protected	UnicastRemoteObject()

Methods

Modifiers	Return Type	Method
public	Object	clone()
public static	RemoteStub	exportObject(Remote)

See Also

java.rmi.server.RemoteObject • java.rmi.server.RemoteServer

Interface Unreferenced

public abstract interface java.rmi.server.Unreferenced

The Unreferenced interface defines one method (unreferenced()) that is used to notify remote objects that they are no longer referenced by any client objects.

Syntax & Usage This interface works in conjunction with the distributed garbage collector (dgc). The dgc maintains an active list of client references to a given remote object. As long as there are client references, the dgc keeps a local reference to the remote object. However, any time there are no longer any client references to a given remote object, the unreferenced() method for that remote object is invoked.

The following example suspends a thread when the MyRemote remote object becomes unreferenced:

```
Class MyRemote extends RemoteObject implements Unreferenced
{
   Thread runner;
   public void unreferenced()
   {
      runner.suspend();
   }
}
```

You see that the thread runner for MyRemote class is suspended in the event that the unreferenced() method is called.

Fields None

Constructors None

Methods

Modifiers	Return Type	Method
public abstract	void	unreferenced()

See Also java.rmi.server.RemoteObject

17 The java.security Package

The java.security package is the root package for the classes and subpackages that make up the Java Security API—which is new to the JDK 1.1. This API represents the framework (due for major upgrades and revisions in the version following 1.1).

However, a default provider (i.e., Provider subclass) facilitating concrete implementations for the various engine classes is available in the JDK 1.1 supports the ability to create message digests using MD4 and SHA-1, public/private keys and key management facilities, and operations relating to digital signatures using the DSA algorithm. This provider is named the SUN provider and, unless specified otherwise, is the default provider in the JDK 1.1.

Interface Certificate

public abstract interface java.security.Certificate

The Certificate interface defines an abstract framework of methods to be used by its implementations to facilitate a specific certificate format (e.g., X.509 or Pretty Good Privacy—PGP).

Syntax & Usage This interface provides no functionality of its own; instead, it provides the common framework that all certificates share. In light of this, it is important to note that it is up to the program implementing this interface to verify a given certificate's validity.

Note

The SUN provider facilitates an implementation of this interface, providing support and management for X.509 v1 certificates.

These Certificate implementation objects represent digital certificates in which their public keys are used to verify the validity of the signature of a public key for a given Identity object. You can add or remove a Certificate implementation object in a given Identity object using the addCertificate() or removeCertificate() method from the Identity class. The following example method adds the specified Certificate object (certificate) to the specified Identity object (identity):

```
void addCert(Identity identity,
   Certificate certificate)
{
   try
   {
      identity.addCertificate(certificate);
   }
   catch (KeyManagementException e)
   {
      System.err.println(
         "Key Management Exception: "
         +e.getMessage());
   }
}
```

Notice that KeyManagementException must be caught in the event that the specified certificate is not valid, the public key in the certificate conflicts with the identity's public key, or some other key-related exception occurs.

Fields None

Constructors None

Methods

Modifiers	Return Type	Method
public abstract	void	decode(InputStream)
public abstract	void	encode(OutputStream)
public abstract	String	getFormat()
public abstract	Principal	getGuarantor()
public abstract	Principal	getPrincipal()
public abstract	PublicKey	getPublicKey()
public abstract	String	toString(boolean)

See Also java.security.KeyException • java.security.Identity

Class DigestException

public synchronized java.security.DigestException extends java.lang.Exception

DigestException is thrown any time a message-digest-related exception occurs.

Syntax & Usage This exception is not thrown directly by any methods in Java 1.1. However, you can use it in your own implementations of the Message Digest API. Please see the example under "Class MessageDigest," later in this chapter, for more information.

Fields None

Constructors

Modifiers	Constructor
public	DigestException()
public	DigestException(String)

Methods None

See Also java.lang.Exception • java.security.DigestException

Class DigestInputStream

public synchronized java.security.DigestInputStream extends java.io.FilterInputStream

The DigestInputStream is a FilterInputStream subclass that lets you read in data to be "digested" so a message digest can be created for the data contained in this stream. Note that this class does not make any inherent changes to the data in the specified InputStream object.

Note

This class behaves like the DigestOutputStream class except that this one is used with InputStream objects.

Syntax & Usage

This class works in conjunction with the MessageDigest class and is used to read data from a specified InputStream object and to create a message digest for those data by using a MessageDigest object. Assuming that you have turned on the digesting option (using the on() method from this class), each call to this object's read() method updates its corresponding message digest. Finally, to complete the message digest computations, you call the digest() method from the MessageDigest class.

Tip

If you wish to obtain multiple message digests on various parts of a given InputStream object, you should clone the corresponding MessageDigest object.

The following example method getStreamDigest() takes a specified InputStream object (stream) and a message digest algorithm (name), which it uses to compute the message digest for the specified InputStream object and return the computed message digest as an array of bytes:

```
static public byte[] getStreamDigest(
   String algorithm, InputStream stream)
   throws IOException,
   NoSuchAlgorithmException
```

```
{
  MessageDigest dg = MessageDigest.
    getInstance(algorithm);
  DigestInputStream ds = new
    DigestInputStream(stream, dg);
  ds.on(true);
  while (ds.read() != -1);
  return ds.getMessageDigest().digest();
}
```

This example instantiates the MessageDigest class specifying the algorithm in the **static** getInstance() method from the MessageDigest class. The NoSuchAlgorithmException exception must be handled.

Note

For a list of standard algorithm names used in the Java Security API, please see Appendix A of the Java Cryptography Architecture API Specification and Reference at http://www.javasoft.com/products/jdk/1.1/docs/guide/security/CryptoSpec.html#AppA.

Then this example creates a DigestInputStream object from the newly instantiated MessageDigest class and InputStream parameter specified in the method signature. Following that, you need to turn on the message-digesting option, which is done using the on() method from this class.

At this point you are ready to read in the data and compute the message digest. A **while** loop reads bytes from the input stream until the end of the stream is reached. Notice how all the work is done in the while clause, so the body of the loop is empty. Also note that an IOException exception must be handled here.

Finally, once the loop has finished, the digest() method is called from the MessageDigest class on the associated MessageDigest instance to complete calculations and return the resulting array of bytes, which represents the message digest for the InputStream.

Fields

Modifiers	Type	Field
protected	MessageDigest	digest

Constructors

Modifiers	Constructor
public	DigestInputStream(InputStream, MessageDigest)

Methods

Modifiers	Return Type	Method
public	MessageDigest	getMessageDigest()
public	void	on(boolean)
public	int	read()
public	int	read(byte[], int, int)
public	void	setMessageDigest(MessageDigest)
public	String	toString()

See Also java.io.FilterInputStream • java.io.InputStream • java.security.DigestOutputStream • java.security.MessageDigest

Class DigestOutputStream

public synchronized java.security.DigestOutputStream extends java.io.FilterOutputStream

The DigestOutputStream is a FilterOutputStream subclass that lets you read in data to be "digested" so a message digest can be created for data contained in the given output stream. This class does not make any inherent changes to the specified OutputStream.

Note

This class behaves like the DigestInputStream class except that this one is used with OutputStream objects.

Syntax & Usage This class works in conjunction with the MessageDigest class and is used to read data from a specified OutputStream object and create a message digest for those data, using a MessageDigest object. Assuming that you have turned on the digesting option (using the on() method from this class), each call to this object's read() method updates its corresponding message digest. Finally, to complete the message digest, you can call the digest() method from the MessageDigest class.

Tip

If you wish to obtain multiple message digests on various parts of a given OutputStream object, you should clone its corresponding MessageDigest object.

The following example method getStreamDigest() takes a specified OutputStream object (stream) and a message digest algorithm (name), which it uses to compute the message digest for the specified OutputStream object and return the computed digest as an array of bytes:

```
static public byte[] getStreamDigest(String algorithm, OutputStream
   stream, byte[] data)
   throws IOException,
   NoSuchAlgorithmException
{
   MessageDigest dg = MessageDigest.getInstance(algorithm);
   DigestOutputStream ds = new DigestOutputStream(stream, dg);
   ds.on(true);
   ds.write(data, 0, data.length);
   return ds.getMessageDigest().digest();
}
```

This example instantiates the MessageDigest class, specifying the name in the **static** getInstance() method from the MessageDigest class. The NoSuchAlgorithmException exception may be thrown by this method call and therefore must be caught.

Then this example creates a DigestOutputStream object from the newly instantiated MessageDigest class and OutputStream parameter specified in the method signature. Method on() from this class turns digest calculations on.

The write() method writes the specified array of bytes to the output stream, and that automatically updates the associated MessageDigest object. Note that IOException must be caught.

Finally, the digest() method from the MessageDigest class is called to complete the message digest and return it as an array of bytes.

Fields

Modifiers	Type	Field
protected	MessageDigest	digest

Constructors

Modifiers	Constructor
public	DigestOutputStream(OutputStream, MessageDigest)

Methods

Modifiers	Return Type	Method
public	MessageDigest	getMessageDigest()
public	void	on(boolean)
public	void	setMessageDigest(MessageDigest)
public	String	toString()
public	void	write(byte[], int, int)
public	void	write(int)

See Also java.io.FilterOutputStream • java.io.OutputStream • java.security.DigestInputStream • java.security.MessageDigest

Class Identity

public abstract synchronized java.security.Identity extends java.lang.Object implements java.security.Principal, java.io.Serializable

This class represents an entity (i.e., a person, organization, department, etc.) that has a name, a public key, and a corresponding digital certificate to authenticate that public key.

> **Note**
>
> *Each Identity's name is represented as an immutable String.*

Optionally, you can select an IdentityScope object to specify that any Identity object in that scope has a unique name and public key (see the IdentityScope class for details).

Syntax & Usage

You can use this class directly or subclass it to facilitate your own custom functionality. For instance, say you are using this class to represent employees in your company. You might want to subclass this class and add functionality to support identifying an employee by his/her social security or employee number. The following example subclasses this class to provide support for adding a name and address:

```
class MyIdentity extends Identity
{
   String m_Phone;
   String m_Address;

   public MyIdentity(String name,
      String phone, String address,
      IdentityScope scope) throws
      KeyManagementException
   {
      super(name, scope);
      m_Phone = phone;
      m_Address = address;
   }

   public String toString(boolean detailed)
   {
      if (detailed)
         return getName()+
         "\n"+m_Phone+"\n"+m_Address;
      else
         return toString();
   }
}
```

Class MyIdentity extends Identity to hold additional information including a phone number and address (both represented as String objects) for each entity. The constructor creates a new instance of this class using the specified name, phone number, address, and IdentityScope instance. Note that KeyManagementException must be handled in the constructor. Following that is the overridden toString() method, which returns detailed information (i.e., the address and phone number of the given identity) if the detailed parameter is **true**; if **false,** the toString() method inherited from the parent class is called instead.

More sophisticated solutions might include such things as image capabilities, thereby facilitating a visual ID for each entity.

Fields None

Constructors

Modifiers	Constructor
protected	Identity()
public	Identity(String)
public	Identity(String, IdentityScope)

Methods

Modifiers	Return Type	Method
public	void	addCertificate(Certificate)
public	Certificate[]	certificates()
public final	boolean	equals(Object)
public	String	getInfo()
public final	String	getName()
public	PublicKey	getPublicKey()
public final	IdentityScope	getScope()
public	int	hashCode()
protected	boolean	identityEquals(Identity)
public	void	removeCertificate(Certificate)
public	void	setInfo(String)
public	void	setPublicKey(PublicKey)
public	String	toString()
public	String	toString(boolean)

See Also java.io.Serializable • java.lang.Object • java.lang.String • java.security.IdentityScope • java.security.Principal

Class IdentityScope

public abstract synchronized java.security.IdentityScope extends java.security.Identity

The IdentityScope represents a group of identities. Any Identity (or related) objects belonging to a given IdentityScope object will have a unique name, public key, and a corresponding certificate.

Syntax & Usage Interestingly enough, this class is actually an Identity subclass, meaning that it is in and of itself an identity. Each IdentityScope has a name, public key, and a corresponding certificate (if available). The following example method displays any Identity (if any) objects belonging to the specified IdentityScope object (scope) that contain the specified PublicKey object (key):

```
static public void displayIdentity(
   IdentityScope scope, PublicKey key)
{
   Identity idt = scope.getIdentity(key);
   if (idt==null)
      System.out.println(
      "Identity not found for this key");
   else
      System.out.println("Identity found: "
      +idt.toString(true));
}
```

This example uses the getIdentity() method from this class to retrieve an Identity instance that has the specified public key. If an appropriate Identity instance cannot be located, the method returns **null**, and a warning message is printed. If a matching Identity is found, detailed information about that object is displayed.

Fields None

Constructors

Modifiers	Constructor
protected	IdentityScope()
public	IdentityScope(String)
public	IdentityScope(String, IdentityScope)

Methods

Modifiers	Return Type	Method
public abstract	void	addIdentity(Identity)
public	Identity	getIdentity(Principal)
public abstract	Identity	getIdentity(PublicKey)
public abstract	Identity	getIdentity(String)
public static	IdentityScope	getSystemScope()
public abstract	Enumeration	identities()
public abstract	void	removeIdentity(Identity)
protected static	void	setSystemScope(IdentityScope)
public abstract	int	size()
public	String	toString()

See Also java.security.Identity

Class InvalidKeyException

public synchronized java.security.InvalidKeyException extends java.security.KeyException

InvalidKeyException is a KeyException subclass that is thrown any time there is a problem with a given key.

Syntax & Usage This exception is found in several methods of the Signature class. Please see "Class Signature," later in this chapter, for an example of where this exception may be thrown.

Fields None

Constructors

Modifiers	Constructor
public	InvalidKeyException()
public	InvalidKeyException(String)

Methods None

See Also java.security.KeyException • java.security.PrivateKey • java.security.PublicKey • java.security.Signature

Class InvalidParameterException

public synchronized java.security.InvalidParameterException extends java.lang.IllegalArgumentException

InvalidParameterException is thrown any time an incorrect parameter is passed to a given method.

Syntax & Usage This exception is used by various methods in the Java Security API to indicate an invalid parameter was passed. The following code snippet sets a parameter named size for the given Signature object (which implements an arbitrary custom algorithm) and catches an InvalidParameterException exception if the parameter contains an invalid size:

```
try
{
  mySignature.setParameter("size",
    new Integer(128));
}
catch (InvalidParameterException e)
{
  System.err.println("Invalid size: "
    +e.getMessage());
}
```

Fields None

Constructors

Modifiers	Constructor
public	InvalidParameterException()
public	InvalidParameterException(String)

Methods None

See Also java.lang.IllegalArgumentException • java.security.Signature

Interface Key

public abstract interface java.security.Key implements java.io.Serializable

The Key interface is an **abstract** interface used as the base class to define a key in the Java Security API. Objects implementing this class contain a key (encoded in a given format), the name of this key's encoding format, and the actual cryptographic algorithm (e.g., DSA or RSA).

Syntax & Usage This class represents the base class for implementations of the PrivateKey and PublicKey classes. Please see the sections on those classes, later in this chapter, for more information.

Fields None

Constructors None

Methods

Modifiers	Return Type	Method
public abstract	String	getAlgorithm()
public abstract	byte[]	getEncoded()
public abstract	String	getFormat()

See Also java.io.Serializable • java.security.PrivateKey • java.security.PublicKey

Class KeyException

public synchronized java.security.KeyException extends java.lang.Exception

The KeyException exception (or its subclasses) is thrown to indicate a variety of key-related problems.

Syntax & Usage This class actually is the root class for two more specific key-related exceptions:

- InvalidKeyException
- KeyManagementException

If you don't want to reconcile these two key exceptions, you can catch them all by catching KeyException. Please see the sections for the two exceptions in this list for more information.

Fields None

Constructors

Modifiers	Constructor
public	KeyException()
public	KeyException(String)

Methods None

See Also java.lang.Exception • java.security.InvalidKeyException • java.security.KeyManagementException

Class KeyManagementException

public synchronized java.security.KeyManagementException extends java.security.KeyException

KeyManagementException is a KeyException subclass thrown any time there is a management-related problem with a given key. For instance, this exception is thrown if a specified certificate is not valid—the public key in the certificate conflicts with the corresponding identity's public key.

Syntax & Usage This exception can be thrown if, during the management of a given key (or keys), the key has expired, there are conflicting keys, or a key fails authentication. Please see "Interface Certificate," earlier in this chapter, for an example of where this exception may be thrown.

Fields None

Constructors

Modifiers	Constructor
public	KeyManagementException()
public	KeyManagementException(String)

Methods None

See Also java.security.Certificate • java.security.KeyException

Class KeyPair

public final synchronized java.security.KeyPair extends java.lang.Object

The KeyPair class is used as a holding tank for a given public/private key pair (as specified by a PublicKey object and a PrivateKey object).

Syntax & Usage This class does nothing more than hold a PublicKey and PrivateKey object pair, which are specified in this class's constructor and can be retrieved using the getPublic() and getPrivate() methods. Objects of this class also are returned from the getInstance() method of the KeyPairGenerator class (please see that section for more information). For an example of this class in action, please see the example under "Class Signature," later in this chapter.

Fields None

Constructors

Modifiers	Constructor
public	KeyPair(PublicKey, PrivateKey)

Methods

Modifiers	Return Type	Method
public	PrivateKey	getPrivate()
public	PublicKey	getPublic()

See Also java.lang.Object • java.security.KeyPairGenerator • java.security.PrivateKey • java.security.PublicKey • java.security.Signature

Class KeyPairGenerator

public abstract synchronized java.security.KeyPairGenerator extends java.lang.Object

The KeyPairGenerator class is used to generate public/private key pairs (as a KeyPair object that contains a corresponding PublicKey object and a PrivateKey object, which respectively represent the generated public key and private key).

Syntax & Usage This class is an engine class in the Java Security API; it can be used to generate public/private key pairs. In order to generate a key pair, you need to instantiate this class using the getInstance() method specifying an algorithm. Then you call the initialize() method to initialize the algorithm, specifying a strength and, optionally, a cryptographically based random-number generator.

Finally, you can generate the key pair by calling the generateKeyPair() method.

Note

For a list of standard algorithm names used in the Java Security API, please see Appendix A of the Java Cryptography Architecture API Specification and Reference at http://www.javasoft.com/products/jdk/1.1/docs/guide/security/CryptoSpec.html#AppA.

Specifying Parameters Unique to an Algorithm

Sometimes there may be situations in which you need to specify parameters a specific algorithm. As you can see, the initialize() method does not support such custom functionality. However, in these situations, you would implement an interface that would define the initialize() method with the appropriate algorithm-specific parameters added. One such example of this implementation that is part of the Java Security API used to specify parameters for the DSA algorithm is the java.security.interfaces.DSAKeyPairGenerator interface. For more information, please see the section for that interface in Chapter 19.

The following example method takes a specified algorithm and provider to generate a public/private key pair:

```
static public KeyPair getKeyPair(
   String algorithm, String provider)
{
   try
   {
      KeyPairGenerator generator =
         KeyPairGenerator.getInstance(
         algorithm, provider);
      generator.initialize(1024);
      return generator.generateKeyPair();
   }
   catch (NoSuchAlgorithmException e)
   {
      System.err.println("No Such Algorithm: "
         +algorithm);
   }
   catch (NoSuchProviderException e)
   {
      System.err.println("No Such Provider: "
         +provider);
   }
   return null;
}
```

This example method obtains an instance of the KeyPairGenerator class using the getInstance() method from this class specifying the algorithm and security provider. Following that is a call to the initialize() method that initializes the algorithm using the specified strength. After that, the generateKeyPair() method actually generates and returns the pair of public and private keys, returning from the method as a KeyPair object. Notice that NoSuchAlgorithmException and NoSuchProviderException must be caught. If either of these exceptions should be thrown, the method prints out an error message and returns **null**.

> **Note**
>
> *Multiple calls to the generateKeyPair() method will yield different key pairs.*

Fields None

Constructors

Modifiers	Constructor
protected	KeyPairGenerator(String)

Methods

Modifiers	Return Type	Method
public abstract	KeyPair	generateKeyPair()
public	String	getAlgorithm()
public static	KeyPairGenerator	getInstance(String)
public static	KeyPairGenerator	getInstance(String, String)
public	void	initialize(int)
public abstract	void	initialize(int, SecureRandom)

See Also java.lang.Object • java.security.PrivateKey • java.security.Provider • java.security.PublicKey • java.security.SecureRandom • java.security.interfaces.DSAKeyPairGenerator

Class MessageDigest

public abstract synchronized java.security.MessageDigest extends java.lang.Object

The MessageDigest class is used to represent a message digest in the Java Security API. A message digest is a fixed-length value that is computed using a one-way hash algorithm (e.g., MD5 or SHA) on given data (the actual length of which is irrelevant). Note that the message digest and the data from which it was created are indistinguishable. These message digests are used to uniquely identify the given data.

Note

Some implementations of digital signatures sign the message digest for a given piece of data rather than digitally signing the actual data. This is particularly useful in situations in which the given data is very large in size.

Syntax & Usage This class provides methods for message-digest-related operations (referred to as the Message Digest API) and engine-based methods implemented by a given provider (referred to as the Message Digest Service Provider Interface—SPI). The following example method creates a message digest for the specified input stream:

```
static public byte[] getStreamDigest(
   String algorithm, InputStream stream)
   throws DigestException,
   NoSuchAlgorithmException
{
   MessageDigest dg = MessageDigest.
      getInstance(algorithm);
   while (true)
   {
      try
      {
         int k = stream.read();
         if (k == -1)
            break;
         dg.update((byte)k);
      }
      catch (IOException e)
      {
         throw new DigestException(
         "IO error when reading input");
      }
   }
   return dg.digest();
}
```

This example obtains an instance of the MessageDigest class specifying an algorithm in a call to the getInstance() method from this class. Then this example reads bytes from the input stream and updates the message digest using the update() method from this class. Note that an IOException exception may be caught; if so, it is rethrown as a DigestException exception. Finally, the digest() method is called to complete calculations and return the message digest in the form of an array of bytes.

Fields None

Constructors

Modifiers	Constructor
protected	MessageDigest(String)

Methods

Modifiers	Return Type	Method
public	Object	clone()
public	byte[]	digest()
public	byte[]	digest(byte[])
protected abstract	byte[]	engineDigest()
protected abstract	void	engineReset()
protected abstract	void	engineUpdate(byte)
protected abstract	void	engineUpdate(byte[], int, int)
public final	String	getAlgorithm()
public static	MessageDigest	getInstance(String)
public static	MessageDigest	getInstance(String, String)
public static	boolean	isEqual(byte[], byte[])
public	void	reset()
public	String	toString()
public	void	update(byte)
public	void	update(byte[])
public	void	update(byte[], int, int)

See Also java.lang.Object • java.security.DigestInputStream • java.security.DigestOutputStream

Class NoSuchAlgorithmException

public synchronized java.security.NoSuchAlgorithmException extends java.lang.Exception

The NoSuchAlgorithmException exception is thrown any time a specified algorithm is unavailable.

Syntax & Usage

This exception may be thrown by various methods in the Java Security API if an algorithm specified by its name cannot be found.

Note

For a list of standard algorithm names used in the Java Security API, please see Appendix A of the Java Cryptography Architecture API Specification and Reference at http://www.javasoft.com/products/jdk/1.1/docs/guide/security/CryptoSpec.html#AppA.

For examples of where this exception may be thrown, please see the sections for the DigestInputStream, DigestOutputStream, KeyPairGenerator, and MessageDigest classes, elsewhere in this chapter.

Fields None

Constructors

Modifiers	Constructor
public	NoSuchAlgorithmException()
public	NoSuchAlgorithmException(String)

Methods None

See Also java.lang.Exception • java.security.DigestInputStream • java.security.DigestOutputStream • java.security.KeyPairGenerator • java.security.MessageDigest

Class NoSuchProviderException

public synchronized java.security.NoSuchProviderException extends java.lang.Exception

The NoSuchProviderException exception is thrown any time a specified provider is unavailable.

Syntax & Usage This exception may be thrown by various methods in the Java Security API if the security provider specified by its name cannot be found. For an example of where this exception may be thrown, please see "Class KeyPairGenerator," earlier in this chapter.

Fields None

Constructors

Modifiers	Constructor
public	NoSuchProviderException()
public	NoSuchProviderException(String)

Methods None

See Also java.lang.Exception • java.security.KeyPairGenerator • java.security.Provider

Interface Principal

public abstract interface java.security.Principal

The Principal interface is an **abstract** interface used to encapsulate a principal in the Java Security API. A principal is defined as any entity that has the ability to be referred to by a name.

Syntax & Usage The following example begins to outline the implementation of this interface. It holds the **private** String field m_Name, which can be set by the constructor and retrieved by the getName() method:

```
class MyPrincipal implements Principal
{
  private String m_Name;

  public MyPrincipal(String name)
  {
    m_Name = name;
  }

  public String getName()
  {
    return m_Name;
  }

  // Implement other methods here.
}
```

Note

The Principal interface is used by several methods of classes contained in the java.security.acl package. Please see Chapter 18 for more information.

Fields None

Constructors None

Methods

Modifiers	Return Type	Method
public abstract	boolean	equals(Object)
public abstract	String	getName()
public abstract	int	hashCode()
public abstract	String	toString()

See Also java.security.acl.*

Interface PrivateKey

public interface java.security.PrivateKey implements java.security.Key

The PrivateKey interface extends the Key class and is used to define a private key in the Java Security API.

Syntax & Usage This interface is used for organizational purposes only. It contains no methods or fields; instead, it serves as a way to categorize a specific type of key. Please see "Class Signature," later in this chapter, for an example involving this class.

> **Note**
>
> *The Java Security API also has defined another PrivateKey-related interface that is designed for private keys using the DSA algorithm. It is the java.security.interfaces.DSAPrivateKey. Please see the section for that class in Chapter 19 for more information.*

Fields None

Constructors None

Methods None

See Also java.security.Key • java.security.PublicKey • java.security.Signature • java.security.interfaces.DSAPrivateKey

Class Provider

public abstract synchronized java.security.Provider extends java.util.Properties

The Provider class is an **abstract** class that is subclassed to implement various parts of the Java Security API. Providers are responsible for the implementation and location of the actual cryptographically related algorithms and other key-related technologies. Note that these implementations do not have to be hard coded in the provider subclass but can be retrieved from a file or pulled from some arbitrary source at run time.

Note

The Java Security API comes with a default provider referred to as the SUN provider.

Syntax & Usage

Provider subclasses must override the following methods:

- **String getInfo().** This method returns information about this Provider.
- **String getName().** This method returns the name for this Provider.
- **double getVersion().** This method returns the Provider's version number.

Thus, each provider must have a name, a version number, and, optionally, a way to give additional information about itself.

Fields

None

Installing Your Own Provider

To install your own provider on a given Java virtual machine, you use the text file java.security located in the java\lib\security directory and modify the following line:

```
security.provider.n=providerClassName
```

where *n* is the provider's number and providerClassName is the name of your Java class that implements the Provider interface. By default, this is set to the sun.security.provider.Sun class.

Constructors

Modifiers	Constructor
protected	Provider(String, double, String)

Methods

Modifiers	Return Type	Method
public	String	getInfo()
public	String	getName()
public	double	getVersion()
public	String	toString()

See Also java.security.ProviderException • java.util.Properties

Class ProviderException

public synchronized java.security.ProviderException extends java.lang.RuntimeException

The ProviderException exception is thrown any time there is a provider-related exception. This exception can crop if there is a problem directly related to the current provider (please see the Provider class for more information).

Syntax & Usage This exception is used during run time by Provider subclasses. Optionally, you can subclass this class to throw specific provider-related exceptions for a given provider.

Fields None

Constructors

Modifiers	Constructor
public	ProviderException()
public	ProviderException(String)

Methods None

See Also java.lang.RuntimeException • java.security.Provider

Interface PublicKey

public interface java.security.PublicKey implements java.security.Key

The PublicKey interface extends the Key class and is used to define a public key in the Java Security API.

Syntax & Usage This interface is used for organizational purposes only. It contains no methods or fields; instead, it serves as a way to categorize a specific type of key. Please see "Class Signature," later in this chapter, for an example using this class.

> **Note**
>
> *The Java Security API also has defined another PublicKey-related interface that is designed for private keys using the DSA algorithm. It is the java.security.interfaces.DSAPublicKey. Please see the section for that class in Chapter 19 for more information.*

Fields None

Constructors None

Methods None

See Also java.security.Key • java.security.PrivateKey • java.security.Signature • java.security.interfaces.DSAPublicKey

Class SecureRandom

public synchronized java.security.SecureRandom extends java.util.Random

The SecureRandom class is used as a pseudo random-number generator in various cryptographic solutions.

Syntax & Usage

This class is used by the KeyPairGenerator class to help it generate key pairs in the Java Security API. This class also can be used for any solution needing cryptographically "strong" random numbers (i.e., results whose logic can in no way be deciphered). The following example demonstrates the usage of the SecureRandom class by generating five sets of random values using this class:

```
SecureRandom sRandom = new SecureRandom();
Date d = new Date();
sRandom.setSeed(d.getTime());
byte[] b = new byte[10];
for (int k=0; k<5; k++)
{
  sRandom.nextBytes(b);
  for (int i=0; i<b.length; i++)
    System.out.print(b[i]+" ");
  System.out.println("");
}
```

This example creates a new instance of the SecureRandom class and sets the seed (using the setSeed() method from this class) to the current date and time to ensure that all values will be unique each time the example is executed. Then it obtains five random values represented as an array of bytes. Here's what the output could look like:

```
103 -47 37 123 88 -45 47 -49 4 -56
-89 31 88 42 -83 104 -1 -18 -116 74
90 -39 -117 120 -2 110 81 -17 -42 -110
51 6 43 -20 -68 25 -118 -1 39 -126
-87 47 58 -57 -114 75 -112 0 -87 43
```

Fields None

Constructors

Modifiers	Constructor
public	SecureRandom()
public	SecureRandom(byte[])

Methods

Modifiers	Return Type	Method
public static	byte[]	getSeed(int)
protected final	int	next(int)
public synchronized	void	nextBytes(byte[])
public synchronized	void	setSeed(byte[])
public	void	setSeed(long)

See Also java.security.KeyPairGenerator • java.util.Random

Class Security

public final synchronized java.security.Security extends java.lang.Object

The Security class is used to manage all security properties (including providers) and common security methods in the Java Security API.

Syntax & Usage This class holds and manages all security properties. It also provides a set of **static** methods that you can use in your Java programs (note that you cannot instantiate this class directly as it does not have any constructors). The following is a selected list of **static** methods from this class that let you work with providers:

- **addProvider(Provider provider).** This method adds the new specified provider to a list of available providers.
- **removeProvider(String name).** This method removes the provider specified by its name from a list of available providers.
- **getProvider(String name).** This method retrieves the provider specified by its name.

The following code snippet uses the getProviders() method from this class to retrieve a list of all providers currently available:

```
Provider[] prList = Security.getProviders();
for (int k=0; k< prList.length; k++)
   System.out.println(prList[k].toString());
```

By default, the only provider available in the Java Security API is the SUN security provider (referred to as SUN). So, unless you've added other providers, the output for the preceding code will be as follows:

```
SUN version 1.0
```

Fields None

Constructors None

Methods

Modifiers	Return Type	Method
public static	int	addProvider(Provider)
public static	String	getAlgorithmProperty(String, String)
public static	String	getProperty(String)
public static	Provider	getProvider(String)
public static	Provider[]	getProviders()
public static	int	insertProviderAt(Provider, int)
public static	void	removeProvider(String)
public static	void	setProperty(String, String)

See Also java.lang.Object • java.security.Provider

Class Signature

public abstract synchronized java.security.Signature extends java.lang.Object

The Signature class is an **abstract** class that is subclassed by a provider to implement a particular digital signature algorithm (for example, DSA) to be used by the Java Security API for creating digital signatures.

Digital signatures work in the following way: Using a digital signature algorithm and a given public/private key pair on some data, a randomly based code for the message is generated. This code—or more accurately, this signature—belongs to the specified data and is passed, along with the data's public key, to the recipient. When retrieved, the user uses the public key on the signature to verify the identity of the sender and the integrity of the data.

Note

A digital signature, a public key, and their corresponding data are unreconcilable.

Syntax & Usage This class provides methods for digital-signature-related operations (referred to as the Digital Signature API) and engine-based methods implemented by a given provider (referred to as the Digital Signature SPI).

> **Note**
>
> *The SUN provider facilitates an implementation of this interface providing support and management for DSA algorithm.*

This class is an engine class in the Java Security API that can be used to generate digital signatures on some data. In order to generate a digital signature, you need to instantiate this class using the getInstance() method specifying an algorithm. Then you call the initialize() method to initialize the algorithm specifying a strength and, optionally, a random-number generator.

> **Note**
>
> *For a list of standard algorithm names used in the Java Security API, please see Appendix A of the Java Cryptography Architecture API Specification and Reference at http://www.javasoft.com/products/jdk/1.1/docs/guide/security/CryptoSpec.html#AppA.*

The following example uses this class, along with the KeyPair, PrivateKey, and PublicKey classes, to generate a public/private key pair on a given file, read in and sign that file, and finally to look at and verify this file via the newly created digital signature and public key:

```
class SignFile
{
   private Signature m_Signature;
   private KeyPair   m_KPair;
   byte[] realSignature;

   // Initialization
   public void initSignature()
      throws NoSuchAlgorithmException,
      KeyException
   {
      m_Signature =
         Signature.getSignature("DSA");
      m_Signature.initGenerateKeyPair(1024);

      // Generate key pair
      KeyPairGenerator keyGen =
         KeyPairGenerator.getInstance("DSA");
      keyGen.initialize(1024, new
         SecureRandom());
```

```
      m_KPair = keyGen.generateKeyPair();
      System.out.println(
         "Key pair has been generated");
}

   // Calculate signature for a given file
   public void signFile(String sName)
      throws FileNotFoundException,
      IOException, InvalidKeyException,
      SignatureException
   {
      System.out.println(
         "Signing file "+sName);
      m_Signature.initSign(
         m_KPair.getPrivate());

      FileInputStream stream = new
         FileInputStream(sName);
      while (stream.available() != 0)
      {
         int next = stream.read();
         m_Signature.update((byte)next);
      }
      realSignature = m_Signature.sign();
      stream.close();
      System.out.println("File "+sName+
         " has been signed");
   }

   // Verify signature for a given file
   public void verifyFile(String sName)
      throws FileNotFoundException,
      IOException, InvalidKeyException,
      SignatureException
   {
   System.out.println(
      "Verifying file "+sName);
   m_Signature.initVerify(
      m_KPair.getPublic());

      FileInputStream stream = new
         FileInputStream(sName);
      while (stream.available() != 0)
      {
         int next = stream.read();
         m_Signature.update((byte)next);
      }
      stream.close();
```

```
        if (m_Signature.verify(realSignature))
           System.out.println(
              "Signature check OK");
        else
           System.out.println(
              "Signature check fails");
     }
  }
```

The declaration of the SignFile class includes three class variables: m_Signature, which is an instance variable for the Signature object; m_KeyPair, which is an instance variable for the KeyPair class; and realSignature, which is used to hold the binary data for the actual signature.

Following the declaration, the first method in the SignFile class is initSignature(), which is used for the initialization of the signing process used to generate a public/private key pair. Notice that this method rethrows the NoSuchAlgorithm and KeyException exceptions. The first thing the method does is construct the m_Signature Signature object using the **static** method getSignature(), which specifies you wish to use the DSA algorithm. Then you initialize key pair generation using the initGenerateKeyPair() method and specifying 1,024 strength. Now you are ready to actually generate a key pair by instantiating the KeyPairGenerator class. Following the initialization, you call the generateKeyPair() method to generate the key pair and put it in the m_KPair variable. Finally, you send a message via System.out, letting the user know that the key pair has been generated.

The second method in the SignFile class, signFile(), performs the actual calculations necessary to generate the signature for the file specified in sName. Notice that this method rethrows the FileNotFoundException, IOException, InvalidKeyException, and SignatureException exceptions. The first thing the method does is initialize a Signature object by invoking the initSign() method and specifying the private key generated earlier in the initSignature() method. Then the method opens an input stream and reads in the file specified in sName. As soon as there are no more bytes to read in from the file, this method performs signature calculations, closes the input stream, and displays a message via System.out to the terminal, letting the user know that the file specified in sName has been signed.

Finally, the third method of the SignFile class, verifyFile(), provides the necessary functionality to verify the file specified in the sName String. Notice that this method rethrows the FileNotFoundException, IOException, InvalidKeyException, and SignatureException exceptions. The first thing the method does is initialize the Signature object's verification functionality by invoking the initVerify() method and specifying the public key generated earlier in the initSignature() method. Then the method opens an input stream and reads in the file specified in sName. As soon as there are no more bytes to read, this method closes the input stream, performs the signature-verification process, and displays the results (pass or fail) via System.out to the user.

Fields

Modifiers	Type	Field
protected static final	int	SIGN
protected	int	state
protected static final	int	UNINITIALIZED
protected static final	int	VERIFY

Constructors

Modifiers	Constructor
protected	Signature(String)

Methods

Modifiers	Return Type	Method
public	Object	clone()
protected abstract	Object	engineGetParameter(String)
protected abstract	void	engineInitSign(PrivateKey)
protected abstract	void	engineInitVerify(PublicKey)
protected abstract	void	engineSetParameter(String, Object)
protected abstract	byte[]	engineSign()
protected abstract	void	engineUpdate(byte)
protected abstract	void	engineUpdate(byte[], int, int)
protected abstract	boolean	engineVerify(byte[])
public final	String	getAlgorithm()
public static	Signature	getInstance(String)
public static	Signature	getInstance(String, String)
public final	Object	getParameter(String)
public final	void	initSign(PrivateKey)
public final	void	initVerify(PublicKey)
public final	void	setParameter(String, Object)
public final	byte[]	sign()
public	String	toString()
public final	void	update(byte)
public final	void	update(byte[])
public final	void	update(byte[], int, int)
public final	boolean	verify(byte[])

See Also java.lang.Object • java.security.KeyPair • java.security.PrivateKey • java.security.PublicKey • java.security.SignatureException

Class SignatureException

public synchronized java.security.SignatureException extends java.lang.Exception

SignatureException is thrown any time a digital-signature-related exception occurs.

Syntax & Usage This can be thrown during various digital-signature operations involving the Signature class. For instance, it may be thrown by the sign(), update(), and verify() methods in the Signature class if the given Signature object is not initialized properly. Please see the previous section, "Class Signature," for an example of where this exception may be thrown.

Fields None

Constructors

Modifiers	Constructor
public	SignatureException()
public	SignatureException(String)

Methods None

See Also java.lang.Exception • java.security.Signature

Class Signer

public abstract synchronized java.security.Signer extends java.security.Identity

The Signer class is an Identity subclass customized to support identities that can have the ability to digitally sign something.

Syntax & Usage

This class has the added capabilities of holding public/private key pair objects for the given Signer (which is needed for the Signer to digitally sign anything). This class also can hold a KeyPair instance and can retrieve its PublicKey. The two important **public** methods from this class are:

- **setKeyPair(KeyPair).** This method lets you set the KeyPair for this Signer object.
- **getPrivateKey().** This method retrieves the PublicKey of this Signer's object.

Please see the sections for the KeyPair, PrivateKey, and PublicKey classes earlier in this chapter for more information.

Fields

None

Constructors

Modifiers	Constructor
protected	Signer()
public	Signer(String)
public	Signer(String, IdentityScope)

Methods

Modifiers	Return Type	Method
public	PrivateKey	getPrivateKey()
public final	void	setKeyPair(KeyPair)
public	String	toString()

See Also

java.security.Identity • java.security.KeyPair • java.security.KeyPairGenerator • java.security.PrivateKey • java.security.PublicKey

The java.security.acl Package

18

The java.security.acl package is part of the Java Security API used for designing Access Control Lists (ACLs) in Java. This class has no internal use in Java, but is here to provide Java programs a way to grant and deny permissions for a principal (or set of principals), to have access to a given resource based on that principal's own permissions and the permissions of the group of principals to which it belongs.

Interface Acl

public abstract interface java.security.acl.Acl implements java.security.acl.Owner

The ACL interface is used to describe an Access Control List (ACL). This class holds a list of entries and calculates a set of granted permissions.

Syntax & Usage

The idea behind an ACL is to limit access of principals to various resources on the given system *after* they've logged in (so to speak). It's based on the concept of permissions, which may be one of the following two forms:

- **Positive permission** grants access to the specified system resource.
- **Negative permission** denies access to the specified system resource.

Note

The ACL assumes that each principal may belong to one or more groups and can have either a positive or a negative permission from an individual and group perspective. It also assumes that individual permissions always dominate group permissions. For instance, person X belongs to the group A. This group A has a positive permission to use some resource, but X has a personal negative permission for that resource. In this case, access of this resource from person X will be denied by the ACL.

An ACL uses set algebra to calculate the final permission for a given resource. The final formula to calculate the set of granted permission is as follows:

$$(P_+ \cup (G_+ - P_-)) - (P_- \cup (G_- - P_+))$$

where » means the union of two sets and the minus sign (-) is their difference. Here, P_+ is the set of individual positive permissions, P_- is the set of individual negative permissions, G_+ is the set of group positive permissions, and G_- is the set of group negative permissions. To implement this interface, you need to provide all its methods, including:

- **addEntry(Principal, AclEntry).** This method adds a new AclEntry for the specified Principal object, with the specified AclEntry object being an owner initiating the call.

- **checkPermission(Principal, Permission).** This method returns **true** if the specified Principal object has the specified Permission.
- **entries().** This method returns an Enumeration object containing all the AclEntry objects in this ACL.
- **getPermissions(Principal).** This method returns an Enumeration object containing all the Permission objects for the specified Principal object.
- **removeEntry (Principal, AclEntry).** This method removes the specified AclEntry from this ACL, with the specified Principal object being an owner initiating the call.

Fields None

Constructors None

Methods

Modifiers	Return Type	Method
public abstract	boolean	addEntry(Principal, AclEntry)
public abstract	boolean	checkPermission(Principal, Permission)
public abstract	Enumeration	entries()
public abstract	String	getName()
public abstract	Enumeration	getPermissions(Principal)
public abstract	boolean	removeEntry(Principal, AclEntry)
public abstract	void	setName(Principal, String)
public abstract	String	toString()

See Also java.security.Principal • java.security.acl.AclEntry • java.security.acl.Group • java.security.acl.Owner

Interface AclEntry

public abstract interface java.security.acl.AclEntry implements java.lang.Cloneable

The AclEntry class is used to describe an entry in an Access Control List (ACL) for a particular principal. A typical ACL contains a set of AclEntry entities.

Syntax & Usage Each AclEntry instance represents a set of various permissions for a given principal (or group of principals) and also contains a designated permission (either positive or negative) for the entry as a whole.

> **Note**
>
> *By default, all permissions are positive. They can be set to negative by the setNegativePermissions() method in this interface.*

To implement this interface, you need to provide all its methods, including:

- **setPrincipal(Principal).** This method sets the specified Principal object to this AclEntry.
- **getPrincipal().** This method returns the Principal object for this AclEntry.
- **addPermission(Permission).** This method adds the specified Permission object to this AclEntry.
- **checkPermission(Permission).** This method returns **true** if this AclEntry has the specified Permission (regardless of whether that permission is positive or negative).
- **removePermission(Permission).** This method removes the specified Permission object from this AclEntry.
- **isNegative().** This method returns **true** if this AclEntry describes a set of negative permissions.

Fields None

Constructors None

Methods

Modifiers	Return Type	Method
public abstract	boolean	addPermission(Permission)
public abstract	boolean	checkPermission(Permission)
public abstract	Object	clone()
public abstract	Principal	getPrincipal()
public abstract	boolean	isNegative()
public abstract	Enumeration	permissions()
public abstract	boolean	removePermission(Permission)
public abstract	void	setNegativePermissions()
public abstract	boolean	setPrincipal(Principal)
public abstract	String	toString()

See Also java.lang.Cloneable • java.security.Principal • java.security.acl.Acl • java.security.acl.Group

Class AclNotFoundException

public synchronized java.security.acl.AclNotFoundException extends java.lang.Exception

The AclNotFoundException exception is thrown any time a specified ACL could not be located.

Syntax & Usage You can use this exception in your ACL implementations to be thrown when a given ACL cannot be located.

Fields None

Constructors

Modifiers	Constructor
public	AclNotFoundException()

Methods None

See Also java.lang.Exception • java.security.acl.Acl

Interface Group

public abstract interface java.security.acl.Group extends java.security.Principal

The Group interface is used to describe an assemblage of principals.

Syntax & Usage This interface extends the Principal class, making it possible to seamlessly use a Group wherever you can use a Principal.

Note

When creating an ACL implementation, you must be able to process both groups and principals that are passed to your methods that take a Principal instance as a parameter.

To implement this interface, you need to provide for all its methods, including:

- **addMember(Principal).** This method adds the specified Principal object to this Group instance.
- **isMember(Principal).** This method returns **true** if the specified Principal object is a member of this Group instance.
- **members().** This method returns an Enumeration object containing all of the Principal objects that are members of this Group instance.
- **removeMember(Principal).** This method removes the specified Principal object from this Group instance.

Fields None

Constructors None

Methods

Modifiers	Return Type	Method
public abstract	boolean	addMember(Principal)
public abstract	boolean	isMember(Principal)
public abstract	Enumeration	members()
public abstract	boolean	removeMember(Principal)

See Also java.security.Principal • java.security.acl.Acl • java.security.acl.AclEntry

Class LastOwnerException

public synchronized java.security.acl.LastOwnerException extends java.lang.Exception

The LastOwnerException exception is thrown any time there is an attempt to remove the last owner in a ACL system.

Syntax & Usage This exception must be thrown in your ACL implementation in case there is an attempt to delete its last owner:

```
static public void delOwner(Owner aclOwner,
  Principal caller, Principal owner)
{
  try
  {
    aclOwner.deleteOwner(caller, owner);
  }
  catch(NotOwnerException e)
  {
    System.err.println(caller.toString() +
    " is not owner of this ACL");
  }
  catch(LastOwnerException e)
  {
    System.err.println(owner.toString() +
    " is the last owner of this ACL");
  }
}
```

This example invokes the deleteOwner() method from the Owner class to delete the specified owner with caller being the owner initiating this deletion. Note that the following two exceptions must be caught:

- **NotOwnerException.** This must be caught in case the caller is not an owner of aclOwner.
- **LastOwnerException.** This must be caught in case this is the last owner of aclOwner.

Fields None

Constructors

Modifiers	Constructor
public	LastOwnerException()

Methods None

See Also java.lang.Exception • java.security.acl.Acl • java.security.acl.NotOwnerException • java.security.acl.Owner

Class NotOwnerException

public synchronized java.security.acl.NotOwnerException extends java.lang.Exception

The NotOwnerException exception is thrown any time a specified principal is attempting to perform modification to a given ACL of which it is not an owner.

Syntax & Usage This exception can be thrown by several methods in the java.security.acl package. Please see the example in the previous section, "Class LastOwnerException," for details.

Fields None

Constructors

Modifiers	Constructor
public	NotOwnerException()

Methods None

See Also java.lang.Exception • java.security.Principal • java.security.acl.Acl • java.security.acl.LastOwnerException

Interface Owner

public abstract interface java.security.acl.Owner

The Owner interface is used to describe the owner of a given ACL (or set of ACLs). Only specified owners are allowed to modify an ACL. For example, only an owner can call the ACL's removeEntry() method to remove an actual ACL entry from the ACL.

Syntax & Usage To implement this interface, you need to provide all its methods, including:

- **addOwner(Principal caller, Principal owner).** This method takes the specified Principal object (caller) and adds the new Principal object (owner).

- **deleteOwner(Principal caller, Principal owner).** This method uses the specified Principal object (caller) and removes the specified Principal (owner).
- **isOwner(Principal).** This method returns **true** if the specified principal is an owner of this ACL.

Fields None

Constructors None

Methods

Modifiers	Return Type	Method
public abstract	boolean	addOwner(Principal, Principal)
public abstract	boolean	deleteOwner(Principal, Principal)
public abstract	boolean	isOwner(Principal)

See Also java.security.Principal • java.security.acl.Acl • java.security.acl.owner

Interface Permission

public abstract interface java.security.acl.Permission

The Permission interface is used to represent a permission (either positive or negative) to a specified resource.

Syntax & Usage To implement this interface, you need to provide all its methods, including:

- **equals(Object).** This method returns **true** if this Permission instance is equal to the specified Object object.
- **toString().** This method returns a String object for this permission.

Fields None

Constructors None

Methods

Modifiers	Return Type	Method
public abstract	boolean	equals(Object)
public abstract	String	toString()

See Also java.security.acl.Acl

The java.security.interfaces Package

19

The java.security.interfaces package mirrors the key-related classes and interfaces in the java.security package providing specific support for the Digital Signature Algorithm (DSA).

The classes in the java.security package have been designed from a cryptographic algorithm-independent standpoint. However, there are certain options that are not shared by every algorithm. In such cases, the Java Security API has the built in framework to allow you to create a set of interfaces that handle algorithm-specific options for a given algorithm, which is exactly what the interfaces in this package represent for DSA.

Note

Currently, DSA is the only digital signature algorithm that comes with the Java Security API. However, JavaSoft also is completing a set of interfaces for the RSA algorithm. Go to http://www.javasoft.com/security/ for more information.

To use the algorithm-specific approach, you need to instantiate the corresponding algorithm-independent class from the java.security package and cast it to your algorithm-specific interface, which will have implemented methods that let you set various algorithm-specific parameters to perform the operation.

Interface DSAKey

public abstract interface java.security.interfaces.DSAKey

The DSAKey interface is an **abstract** interface used to describe a DSA key in the Java Security API.

Syntax & Usage

To implement this interface, you need to provide for the getParams() method, which returns DSA-specific key parameters for a given DSA key.

Fields

None

Constructors

None

Methods

Modifiers	Return Type	Method
public abstract	DSAParams	getParams()

See Also

java.security.Key • java.security.interfaces.DSAKeyPairGenerator • java.security.interfaces.DSAPrivateKey • java.security.interfaces.DSAPublicKey

Interface DSAKeyPairGenerator

public abstract interface java.security.interfaces.DSAKeyPairGenerator

The KeyPairGenerator interface is used to generate public/private DSA key pairs.

Syntax & Usage

To implement this interface, you need to provide for all its methods, including:

- **initialize(DSAParams, SecureRandom).** This method initializes the key pair generator using the specified DSA parameters and a SecureRandom instance.
- **initialize(int, boolean, SecureRandom).** This method initializes the key pair generator using the specified modulus length and a SecureRandom instance.

Fields None

Constructors None

Methods

Modifiers	Return Type	Method
public abstract	void	initialize(DSAParams, SecureRandom)
public abstract	void	initialize(int, boolean, SecureRandom)

See Also java.security.KeyPairGenerator
• java.security.interfaces.DSAKeyPairGenerator
• java.security.interfaces.DSAParams

Interface DSAParams

public abstract interface java.security.interfaces.DSAParams

The DSAParams interface is used to describe DSA-specific parameters when using DSA for various operations.

Syntax & Usage To implement this interface, you need to provide for all its methods, including:

- **getG().** This method returns a BigInteger object representing the DSA parameter: base, g.
- **getP().** This method returns a BigInteger object representing the DSA parameter prime, p.
- **getQ().** This method returns a BigInteger object representing the DSA parameter subprime, q.

Fields None

Constructors None

Methods

Modifiers	Return Type	Method
public abstract	BigInteger	getG()
public abstract	BigInteger	getP()
public abstract	BigInteger	getQ()

See Also java.security.interfaces.DSAKeyPairGenerator

Interface DSAPrivateKey

public abstract interface java.security.interfaces.DSAPrivateKey implements java.security.interfaces.DSAKey, java.security.PrivateKey

The DSAPrivateKey interface implements the java.security.interfaces.DSAKey and java.security.PrivateKey interfaces and is used to define a DSA private key in the Java Security API.

Syntax & Usage To implement this interface, you need to provide for the getX() method. This method returns a BigInteger object, which represents the value of the private key.

Fields None

Constructors None

Methods

Modifiers	Return Type	Method
public abstract	BigInteger	getX()

See Also java.security.PrivateKey • java.security.interfaces.DSAKey • java.security.interfaces.DSAKeyPairGenerator • java.security.interfaces.DSAPublicKey

Interface DSAPublicKey

public abstract interface java.security.interfaces.DSAPublicKey implements java.security.interfaces.DSAKey, java.security.PublicKey

The PublicKey interface implements the java.security.interfaces.DSAKey and java.security.PublicKey interfaces. It is used to define a DSA public key in the Java Security API.

Syntax & Usage To implement this interface, you need to provide for the getY() method. This method returns a BigInteger object, which represents the y value of the public key.

Fields None

Constructors None

Methods

Modifiers	Return Type	Method
public abstract	BigInteger	getY()

See Also java.security.PublicKey • java.security.interfaces.DSAKey • java.security.interfaces.DSAPrivateKey

20 The java.sql Package

Java Database Connectivity (JDBC) is encapsulated in the java.sql package and is a very important addition to the JDK 1.1. JDBC is a set of application programming interfaces (APIs) that lays the framework for allowing Java programs to connect to a database. JDBC is designed to be somewhat of an Open Database Connectivity (ODBC) look-alike. Specifically, ODBC could not be implemented directly in Java because ODBC was designed in C (using pointers). However, Java 1.1 does contain a JDBC-ODBC bridge you can use to connect your JDBC applications to an ODBC data source. Further, a variety of third-party JDBC drivers are also available, or, if you desire, you can even write your own.

Specifically, JDBC is designed around the X/Open Call Level Interface (CLI). A CLI allows you to query a database direct using Structured Query Language (SQL) and receive "raw" results. It is a somewhat crude format, but it gets the job done.

Interface CallableStatement

public abstract interface java.sql.CallableStatement implements java.sql.PreparedStatement

The CallableStatement class extends PreparedStatement (which in turn extends Statement). This class is used in conjunction with SQL stored procedures and has the ability to specify IN, OUT, and INOUT parameters. IN parameters let you pass values to a given stored procedure. OUT parameters let you retrieve values direct from the stored procedure—note that this does not involve using a ResultSet object. INOUT parameters give you the functionality of both for the same parameter of a given stored procedure.

Syntax & Usage

Obviously, when working with stored procedures, you need to know what procedures are available for the given database, but you do not need to worry about the proprietary syntax of calling the procedure. Fortunately, JDBC has devised a standard way to call all stored procedures from Java, so you won't need to worry about the semantics of the actual call.

To start, you use the prepareCall() method from Connection to instantiate CallableStatement. Then you can specify the stored procedure using Java's SQL escape syntax (i.e., placing the procedure inside curly brackets and adding a keyword; in the case of stored procedures, that keyword would be **call**) and using a question mark (?) to represent a parameter.

> **Tip**
>
> *You can use SQL escape syntax to call more than stored procedures. You also can call scalar functions (using the* ***fn*** *keyword and the name of the function), dates and times (using* **d** *and* **ts**, *respectively), and even outer joins.*

Then, if you want to add an IN parameter to a given stored procedure, use one of the setXXX() methods inherited from the PreparedStatement class and specify the location of this parameter and the value you wish to use. Please see the example under "Interface PreparedStatement," later in this chapter, for more information.

To add an OUT parameter to a given stored procedure, use one of the two available registerOutParameter() methods. The first one takes two parameters, specifying the index and the location and the SQL data type (using a constant from the Types field) for this parameter. Then, after the query has executed, you retrieve the results of this parameter using an appropriate get*XXX*() method from this class. The following code snippet specifies the stored procedure getTheData() specifying one OUT parameter:

```
Connection myCon;

// Create the connection here.

CallableStatement myCallStmt =
  myCon.prepareCall("{call getTheData(?)}");
myCallStmt.registerOutParameter(1,
  java.sql.Types.INTEGER);
myCallStmt.executeUpdate();
int theParam = myCallStmt.getInt(1);
```

Note

The following shows syntax if the stored procedure were to also return a value:

```
String myQuery = "{? = getTheData(?)}");
```

This snippet of code uses the Connection instance myCon and creates an instance of CallableStatement by calling the prepareCall() method from this class, assuming that you have the stored procedure getTheData(), which you access via the CallableStatement myCallStmt. Notice that right under the prepareCall() method call, you register the OUT parameters before actually executing the query. Finally, you can retrieve the parameter by using the appropriate get*XXX*() method, which in this case is getInt().

Adding an INOUT parameter is merely a mixing of the two processes described previously. First, use a set*XXX*() method call on the parameter specifying a value for it, then use the registerOutParameter() method specifying the same parameter with a SQL data type. Once it has executed, you use an appropriate get*XXX*(), retrieving the results from this same parameter. The following code snippet specifies the stored procedure changeTheData() specifying one INOUT parameter:

```
Connection myCon;

// Create the connection here.
CallableStatement myCallStmt =
  myCon.prepareCall("{ call changeTheData(?)}");

setInt(1, 5);

myCallStmt.registerOutParameter(1,
  java.sql.Types.INTEGER);

myCallStmt.executeUpdate();

int theParam = myCallStmt.getInt(1);
```

This snippet of code uses the Connection instance myCon to create an instance of CallableStatement. Using the assumed stored procedure changeTheData(), you specify one INOUT parameter. Notice that right under the prepareCall() method (which creates the statement) you use the setInt() method specifying 5 as the IN value for this parameter. Then you register the same parameter as an OUT parameter, using the registerOutParameter() method. Finally, you actually execute the query and retrieve the returned value for the INOUT parameter, using getInt().

Note

In some situations, you may return parameters and a ResultSet from a SQL query. In these cases, you need to retrieve both the parameter and ResultSet. However, it is preferable that the results are pulled out of the ResultSet first and OUT parameters second.

Fields None

Constructors None

Methods

Modifiers	Return Type	Method
public abstract	BigDecimal	getBigDecimal(int, int)
public abstract	boolean	getBoolean(int)
public abstract	byte	getByte(int)
public abstract	byte[]	getBytes(int)
public abstract	Date	getDate(int)
public abstract	double	getDouble(int)
public abstract	float	getFloat(int)
public abstract	int	getInt(int)
public abstract	long	getLong(int)
public abstract	Object	getObject(int)
public abstract	short	getShort(int)
public abstract	String	getString(int)
public abstract	Time	getTime(int)
public abstract	Timestamp	getTimestamp(int)
public abstract	void	registerOutParameter(int, int)
public abstract	void	registerOutParameter(int, int, int)
public abstract	boolean	wasNull()

See Also java.sql.PreparedStatement • java.sql.ResultSet • java.sql.Statement • java.sql.Types

Interface Connection

public abstract interface java.sql.Connection

The Connection class describes a given connection with the SQL database. This class is the backbone for being able to send a Statement object to a database or to get a ResultSet object containing the results of a specified SQL query. Furthermore, Connection supports the use of transaction processing with a SQL database.

Syntax & Usage By using Connection, SQL queries can be executed and results can be returned from a given database. A variety of programming techniques also can be employed in using Connection with SQL queries or stored procedures.

The following shows a simple but very effective process for constructing an instance of Connection using one of the overloaded **static** getConnection() methods from DriverManager:

```
Connection myCon = DriverManager.getConnection ("jdbc:odbc:data",
   "joshid", "password");
```

Let's take a look at the three parameters: The first represents a URL specifying the driver and location of your database. In this case, it represents a connection to an ODBC data source using the JDBC-ODBC driver that comes with Java 1.1. The second and third (both optional) parameters are my user ID and password for logging into that data source.

At the end of your JDBC session, don't forget to use the close() method from this class to ensure that you are properly disconnected from the database:

```
myCon.close();
```

The URL Syntax

The URL syntax is based on the premise of URLs used on the Internet. The format is as follows:

```
jdbc:<subprotocol>:<subname>
```

The *subprotocol* is where you put the particular type of database mechanism. And the *subname* is used to actually connect to a database.

Subprotocols are being defined continually. For example, the JDBC-ODBC bridge driver, used in the previous example, is defined as odbc. Other major protocols such as Oracle have also been introduced.

Fields

Modifiers	Type	Field
public static final	int	TRANSACTION_NONE
public static final	int	TRANSACTION_READ_COMMITTED
public static final	int	TRANSACTION_READ_UNCOMMITTED
public static final	int	TRANSACTION_REPEATABLE_READ
public static final	int	TRANSACTION_SERIALIZABLE

Constructors None

Methods

Modifiers	Return Type	Method
public abstract	void	clearWarnings()
public abstract	void	close()
public abstract	void	commit()
public abstract	Statement	createStatement()
public abstract	boolean	getAutoCommit()
public abstract	String	getCatalog()
public abstract	DatabaseMetaData	getMetaData()
public abstract	int	getTransactionIsolation()
public abstract	SQLWarning	getWarnings()
public abstract	boolean	isClosed()
public abstract	boolean	isReadOnly()
public abstract	String	nativeSQL(String)
public abstract	CallableStatement	prepareCall(String)
public abstract	PreparedStatement	prepareStatement(String)
public abstract	void	rollback()
public abstract	void	setAutoCommit(boolean)
public abstract	void	setCatalog(String)
public abstract	void	setReadOnly(boolean)
public abstract	void	setTransactionIsolation(int)

See Also java.sql.Driver • java.sql.DriverManager • java.sql.ResultSet • java.sql.Statement

Interface DatabaseMetaData

public abstract interface java.sql.DatabaseMetaData

The DatabaseMetaData interface describes information about the database to which your JDBC program is connected. This includes information on what is supported and how in this database.

Syntax & Usage This interface provides information about a given database as a whole. In order to use DatabaseMetaData, you need to already have a connection (i.e., a Connection instance) to that database. Then you can return a DatabaseMetaData object using the getMetaData() method from the Connection class. In the following example, the myCon object represents a database connection that will use DatabaseMetaData to retrieve information about the database and database driver:

```
DatabaseMetaData myDBMetaData = myCon.getMetaData();

System.out.println("Connected to " +
  myDBMetaData.getURL());
System.out.println("\n Using the Driver " +
  myDBMetaData.getDriverName());
```

In this snippet of code, you create the myDBMetaData through the getMetaData() method from the Connection class. Then, using the getURL() method from the DatabaseMetaData class, you retrieve the URL for the database to which myCon is connected. Then, in the following line, you retrieve the name of the database driver you are using to connect to the specified database by calling getDriverName() from the DatabaseMetaData class.

Note

This interface defines more than 150 members (listed under "Methods," later in this section) corresponding to numerous options in the SQL92 standard.

Fields

Modifiers	Type	Field
public static final	int	bestRowNotPseudo
public static final	int	bestRowPseudo
public static final	int	bestRowSession
public static final	int	bestRowTemporary
public static final	int	bestRowTransaction
public static final	int	bestRowUnknown
public static final	int	columnNoNulls
public static final	int	columnNullable
public static final	int	columnNullableUnknown
public static final	int	importedKeyCascade
public static final	int	importedKeyInitiallyDeferred
public static final	int	importedKeyInitiallyImmediate
public static final	int	importedKeyNoAction
public static final	int	importedKeyNotDeferrable
public static final	int	importedKeyRestrict
public static final	int	importedKeySetDefault
public static final	int	importedKeySetNull
public static final	int	procedureColumnIn
public static final	int	procedureColumnInOut
public static final	int	procedureColumnOut
public static final	int	procedureColumnResult
public static final	int	procedureColumnReturn
public static final	int	procedureColumnUnknown
public static final	int	procedureNoNulls
public static final	int	procedureNoResult
public static final	int	procedureNullable
public static final	int	procedureNullableUnknown
public static final	int	procedureResultUnknown
public static final	int	procedureReturnsResult
public static final	short	tableIndexClustered
public static final	short	tableIndexHashed
public static final	short	tableIndexOther
public static final	short	tableIndexStatistic
public static final	int	typeNoNulls
public static final	int	typeNullable
public static final	int	typeNullableUnknown
public static final	int	typePredBasic
public static final	int	typePredChar
public static final	int	typePredNone
public static final	int	typeSearchable

Modifiers	Type	Field
public static final	int	versionColumnNotPseudo
public static final	int	versionColumnPseudo
public static final	int	versionColumnUnknown

Constructors None

Methods

Modifiers	Return Type	Method
public abstract	boolean	allProceduresAreCallable()
public abstract	boolean	allTablesAreSelectable()
public abstract	boolean	dataDefinitionCausesTransactionCommit()
public abstract	boolean	dataDefinitionIgnoredInTransactions()
public abstract	boolean	doesMaxRowSizeIncludeBlobs()
public abstract	ResultSet	getBestRowIdentifier(String, String, String, int, boolean)
public abstract	ResultSet	getCatalogs()
public abstract	String	getCatalogSeparator()
public abstract	String	getCatalogTerm()
public abstract	ResultSet	getColumnPrivileges(String, String, String, String)
public abstract	ResultSet	getColumns(String, String, String, String)
public abstract	ResultSet	getCrossReference(String, String, String, String, String, String)
public abstract	String	getDatabaseProductName()
public abstract	String	getDatabaseProductVersion()
public abstract	int	getDefaultTransactionIsolation()
public abstract	int	getDriverMajorVersion()
public abstract	int	getDriverMinorVersion()
public abstract	String	getDriverName()
public abstract	String	getDriverVersion()
public abstract	ResultSet	getExportedKeys(String, String, String)
public abstract	String	getExtraNameCharacters()
public abstract	String	getIdentifierQuoteString()
public abstract	ResultSet	getImportedKeys(String, String, String)
public abstract	ResultSet	getIndexInfo(String, String, String, boolean, boolean)
public abstract	int	getMaxBinaryLiteralLength()
public abstract	int	getMaxCatalogNameLength()
public abstract	int	getMaxCharLiteralLength()
public abstract	int	getMaxColumnNameLength()
public abstract	int	getMaxColumnsInGroupBy()
public abstract	int	getMaxColumnsInIndex()
public abstract	int	getMaxColumnsInOrderBy()
public abstract	int	getMaxColumnsInSelect()
public abstract	int	getMaxColumnsInTable()

Modifiers	Return Type	Method
public abstract	int	getMaxConnections()
public abstract	int	getMaxCursorNameLength()
public abstract	int	getMaxIndexLength()
public abstract	int	getMaxProcedureNameLength()
public abstract	int	getMaxRowSize()
public abstract	int	getMaxSchemaNameLength()
public abstract	int	getMaxStatementLength()
public abstract	int	getMaxStatements()
public abstract	int	getMaxTableNameLength()
public abstract	int	getMaxTablesInSelect()
public abstract	int	getMaxUserNameLength()
public abstract	String	getNumericFunctions()
public abstract	ResultSet	getPrimaryKeys(String, String, String)
public abstract	ResultSet	getProcedureColumns(String, String, String, String)
public abstract	ResultSet	getProcedures(String, String, String)
public abstract	String	getProcedureTerm()
public abstract	ResultSet	getSchemas()
public abstract	String	getSchemaTerm()
public abstract	String	getSearchStringEscape()
public abstract	String	getSQLKeywords()
public abstract	String	getStringFunctions()
public abstract	String	getSystemFunctions()
public abstract	ResultSet	getTablePrivileges(String, String, String)
public abstract	ResultSet	getTables(String, String, String, String[])
public abstract	ResultSet	getTableTypes()
public abstract	String	getTimeDateFunctions()
public abstract	ResultSet	getTypeInfo()
public abstract	String	getURL()
public abstract	String	getUserName()
public abstract	ResultSet	getVersionColumns(String, String, String)
public abstract	boolean	isCatalogAtStart()
public abstract	boolean	isReadOnly()
public abstract	boolean	nullPlusNonNullIsNull()
public abstract	boolean	nullsAreSortedAtEnd()
public abstract	boolean	nullsAreSortedAtStart()
public abstract	boolean	nullsAreSortedHigh()
public abstract	boolean	nullsAreSortedLow()
public abstract	boolean	storesLowerCaseIdentifiers()
public abstract	boolean	storesLowerCaseQuotedIdentifiers()
public abstract	boolean	storesMixedCaseIdentifiers()
public abstract	boolean	storesMixedCaseQuotedIdentifiers()

Modifiers	Return Type	Method
public abstract	boolean	storesUpperCaseIdentifiers()
public abstract	boolean	storesUpperCaseQuotedIdentifiers()
public abstract	boolean	supportsAlterTableWithAddColumn()
public abstract	boolean	supportsAlterTableWithDropColumn()
public abstract	boolean	supportsANSI92EntryLevelSQL()
public abstract	boolean	supportsANSI92FullSQL()
public abstract	boolean	supportsANSI92IntermediateSQL()
public abstract	boolean	supportsCatalogsInDataManipulation()
public abstract	boolean	supportsCatalogsInIndexDefinitions()
public abstract	boolean	supportsCatalogsInPrivilegeDefinitions()
public abstract	boolean	supportsCatalogsInProcedureCalls()
public abstract	boolean	supportsCatalogsInTableDefinitions()
public abstract	boolean	supportsColumnAliasing()
public abstract	boolean	supportsConvert()
public abstract	boolean	supportsConvert(int, int)
public abstract	boolean	supportsCoreSQLGrammar()
public abstract	boolean	supportsCorrelatedSubqueries()
public abstract	boolean	supportsDataDefinitionAndDataManipulationTransactions()
public abstract	boolean	supportsDataManipulationTransactionsOnly()
public abstract	boolean	supportsDifferentTableCorrelationNames()
public abstract	boolean	supportsExpressionsInOrderBy()
public abstract	boolean	supportsExtendedSQLGrammar()
public abstract	boolean	supportsFullOuterJoins()
public abstract	boolean	supportsGroupBy()
public abstract	boolean	supportsGroupByBeyondSelect()
public abstract	boolean	supportsGroupByUnrelated()
public abstract	boolean	supportsIntegrityEnhancementFacility()
public abstract	boolean	supportsLikeEscapeClause()
public abstract	boolean	supportsLimitedOuterJoins()
public abstract	boolean	supportsMinimumSQLGrammar()
public abstract	boolean	supportsMixedCaseIdentifiers()
public abstract	boolean	supportsMixedCaseQuotedIdentifiers()
public abstract	boolean	supportsMultipleResultSets()
public abstract	boolean	supportsMultipleTransactions()
public abstract	boolean	supportsNonNullableColumns()
public abstract	boolean	supportsOpenCursorsAcrossCommit()
public abstract	boolean	supportsOpenCursorsAcrossRollback()
public abstract	boolean	supportsOpenStatementsAcrossCommit()
public abstract	boolean	supportsOpenStatementsAcrossRollback()
public abstract	boolean	supportsOrderByUnrelated()
public abstract	boolean	supportsOuterJoins()

Modifiers	Return Type	Method
public abstract	boolean	supportsPositionedDelete()
public abstract	boolean	supportsPositionedUpdate()
public abstract	boolean	supportsSchemasInDataManipulation()
public abstract	boolean	supportsSchemasInIndexDefinitions()
public abstract	boolean	supportsSchemasInPrivilegeDefinitions()
public abstract	boolean	supportsSchemasInProcedureCalls()
public abstract	boolean	supportsSchemasInTableDefinitions()
public abstract	boolean	supportsSelectForUpdate()
public abstract	boolean	supportsStoredProcedures()
public abstract	boolean	supportsSubqueriesInComparisons()
public abstract	boolean	supportsSubqueriesInExists()
public abstract	boolean	supportsSubqueriesInIns()
public abstract	boolean	supportsSubqueriesInQuantifieds()
public abstract	boolean	supportsTableCorrelationNames()
public abstract	boolean	supportsTransactionIsolationLevel(int)
public abstract	boolean	supportsTransactions()
public abstract	boolean	supportsUnion()
public abstract	boolean	supportsUnionAll()
public abstract	boolean	usesLocalFilePerTable()
public abstract	boolean	usesLocalFiles()

See Also java.sql.Connection • java.sql.ResultSetMetaData

Class DataTruncation

public synchronized java.sql.DataTruncation extends java.sql.SQLWarning

The DataTruncation class represents a warning or exception when there is an unexpected truncation of data during a JDBC read/write operation.

Syntax & Usage This class is used as a SQLWarning when unexpected data truncation takes place. Data truncation takes place if a given read or write operation hits an internal limitation in the database that is being accessed and/or in the JDBC driver. A DataTruncation instance contains complete information about a truncation-related error. Consider the following:

```
static public void displayTruncation(
  DataTruncation dt)
{
  System.err.println("Data Truncation in "
    +dt.getIndex()+" column:\n"+
    "Expected\t"+dt.getDataSize()+" bytes\n"+
    "Transferred\t"+dt. getTransferSize()+
    " bytes\n"+
    "Operation\t"+(dt.getRead() ? "READ" :
    "WRITE"));
}
```

This code prints detailed information about the specified DataTruncation instance to the standard error output stream.

Fields None

Constructors

Modifiers	Constructor
public	DataTruncation(int, boolean, boolean, int, int)

Methods

Modifiers	Return Type	Method
public	int	getDataSize()
public	int	getIndex()
public	boolean	getParameter()
public	boolean	getRead()
public	int	getTransferSize()

See Also java.sql.SQLWarning

Class Date

public synchronized java.sql.Date extends java.util.Date

The Date class wraps the java.util.Date class, providing support for the SQL DATE data type.

Syntax & Usage The following example method retrieves and displays a Date instance from the specified column and result set:

```
static public void displayDate(Recordset rs,
  int columnIndex)
{
  try
  {
    Date date = rs.getDate(columnIndex);
    if (date != null)
      System.out.println(
      "Date: "+date.toString());
    else
      System.out.println("Date is null");
  }
  catch (SQLException e)
  {
    System.err.println("SQLException: "
      +e.getMessage());
  }
}
```

Notice that SQLException has to be caught.

Note

*You always should check whether the results of a given getXXX() method call from the ResultSet class is **null** before attempting to use those results.*

Tip

Since this class inherits from the java.util.Date class, you can use various methods available from that class to format your dates retrieved from this class, including locale-sensitive methods. Please see Chapters 21 and 22 for more information on the java.text and java.util packages.

Fields None

Constructors

Modifiers	Constructor
public	Date(int, int, int)
public	Date(long)

Methods

Modifiers	Return Type	Method
public	int	getHours()
public	int	getMinutes()
public	int	getSeconds()

Modifiers	Return Type	Method
public	void	setHours(int)
public	void	setMinutes(int)
public	void	setSeconds(int)
public	void	setTime(long)
public	String	toString()
public static	Date	valueOf(String)

See Also java.sql.ResultSet • java.sql.Time • java.sql.Timestamp • java.util.Date

Interface Driver

public abstract interface java.sql.Driver

The Driver is an interface that you implement when creating an actual JDBC driver. This interface usually is not used directly in your JDBC programs except when loading its class or calling some of the methods defined in this interface to facilitate information about the driver.

Syntax & Usage This interface describes common methods that all JDBC drivers must implement.

In theory, the DriverManager will go through, look for, and load all available drivers when your JDBC program starts up. However, it is always a good idea to explicitly load the JDBC Driver class, using the forName() method from java.lang.Class:

```
Class.forName("companyName.databaseName.DriverName");
```

In this code snippet, notice the naming convention is to have the company name, database name, and the actual driver name all printed in the forName() method. Java takes this and looks for the file DriverName.class in \companyName\databaseName\ located in your CLASSPATH directory.

Note

JavaSoft has developed a JDBC driver that acts as a bridge to the ODBC. You can use this JDBC-ODBC driver to connect to an ODBC database. Also, other major vendors have implemented various types of JDBC drivers. For more information on both of these topics, please go to http://splash.javasoft.com.

As soon as you've loaded your Driver class and created its instance using an appropriately supplied constructor, you can use the connect() method to obtain a connection to the specified database and manage that driver and connection yourself. Or you can call the getConnection() **static** method from the DriverManager class and let the JDBC's DriverManager manage these details for you. Please see the sections for the Connection and DriverManager classes, elsewhere in this chapter, for more information.

Fields None

Constructors None

Methods

Modifiers	Return Type	Method
public abstract	boolean	acceptsURL(String)
public abstract	Connection	connect(String, Properties)
public abstract	int	getMajorVersion()
public abstract	int	getMinorVersion()
public abstract	DriverPropertyInfo[]	getPropertyInfo(String, Properties)
public abstract	boolean	jdbcCompliant()

See Also java.sql.Connection • java.sql.DriverManager • java.sql.DriverPropertyInfo

Class DriverManager

public synchronized java.sql.DriverManager extends java.lang.Object

The DriverManager class is responsible for keeping track of and loading appropriate JDBC drivers (which can originate from various sources) and for creating new database connections. This class also manages the log and error message streams during a JDBC session.

Syntax & Usage This class provides a number of **static** methods (note that it does not contain any constructors) to manage a set of JDBC drivers. The following two are used often:

- **register().** This method should be called to register the JDBC driver with this DriverManager instance.

- **getConnection().** This set of overloaded methods creates a connection to a particular data source using a JDBC driver that has already been registered. Please see "Interface Connection," earlier in this chapter, for an example.

Fields None

Constructors None

Methods

Modifiers	Return Type	Method
public static	void	deregisterDriver(Driver)
public static synchronized	Connection	getConnection(String)
public static synchronized	Connection	getConnection(String, Properties)
public static synchronized	Connection	getConnection(String, String, String)
public static	Driver	getDriver(String)
public static	Enumeration	getDrivers()
public static	int	getLoginTimeout()
public static	PrintStream	getLogStream()
public static	void	println(String)
public static synchronized	void	registerDriver(Driver)
public static	void	setLoginTimeout(int)
public static	void	setLogStream(PrintStream)

See Also java.lang.Object • java.sql.Connection • java.sql.Driver

Class DriverPropertyInfo

public synchronized java.sql.DriverPropertyInfo extends java.lang.Object

The DriverPropertyInfo class is used to access properties on a connection for a particular driver.

Syntax & Usage To get properties for a particular Driver, use the getPropertyInfo() method from the Driver class, which returns an array of DriverPropertyInfo objects based on the specified URL and java.util.Properties instance specifying the property (or properties) about which you wish to receive information. In this class there is a set of **public** fields that describes the various attributes for a given property in the JDBC driver. They are listed in Table 20-1.

Field	Description
String[] choices	Describes a set of possible values (if any) that can be selected for the given driver property
String description	Facilitates additional information for the given driver property; if none is available, **null** is returned
String name	Specifies the name of the given driver property
Boolean required	If **true,** then this driver property must be specified in the connect() method call from the Driver class
String value	Specifies the current value for the given driver property

Table 20-1: Fields of DriverPropertyInfo class.

Fields

Modifiers	Type	Field
public	String[]	choices
public	String	description
public	String	name
public	boolean	required
public	String	value

Constructors

Modifiers	Constructor
public	DriverPropertyInfo(String, String)

Methods None

See Also java.lang.Object • java.sql.Driver • java.sql.DriverManager • java.util.Properties

Interface PreparedStatement

public abstract interface java.sql.PreparedStatement implements java.sql.Statement

The PreparedStatement class extends the Statement class. This class's primary use is for queries that may execute more than once. Thus, using PreparedStatement, you can create precompiled queries that can optionally contain IN parameters. This optimizes the query for improved performance each time it is executed.

Syntax & Usage This object then can be used to efficiently execute a SQL query. The following shows an example of using a PreparedStatement specifying one IN parameter:

```
PreparedStatement myPrepStmt =
  myCon.prepareStatement(
  "SELECT * FROM Test WHERE State = ?")
```

In this code, you can see that you use the prepareStatement() method from the Connection class to create the PreparedStatement myPrepStmt instance using a SQL query containing one parameter (as denoted by the question mark character). Now you can execute this query multiple times, passing different values for State:

```
myPrepStmt.setString(1, "CA");
ResultSet myCAResults =
  myPrepStmt.executeQuery();
```

In this code, you use the setString() method to specify the location (in this case, 1) as the first parameter in the SQL query. The second parameter in setString() is to fill in the ? parameter for State to equal CA.

> **Tip**
>
> *You can use the setObject() method to set an IN parameter that contains a data format that does not have a corresponding setXXX() method in this class.*

The results of this query will be the same as if you executed the following SQL query:

```
SELECT * FROM Test WHERE State = "CA"
```

Now imagine that later in your JDBC program you want to run this same query, but this time find results where State equals OH. You do the following:

```
myPrepStmt.setString(1, "OH");
ResultSet myOHResults = myPrepStmt.executeQuery();
```

Here you are effectively taking the same prepared SQL statement but changing State from CA to OH so that the actual query in SQL would look like the following:

```
SELECT * FROM Test WHERE State = "OH"
```

You then can retrieve the results from myOHResults.

Fields None

Constructors None

Methods

Modifiers	Return Type	Method
public abstract	void	clearParameters()
public abstract	boolean	execute()
public abstract	ResultSet	executeQuery()
public abstract	int	executeUpdate()
public abstract	void	setAsciiStream(int, InputStream, int)
public abstract	void	setBigDecimal(int, BigDecimal)
public abstract	void	setBinaryStream(int, InputStream, int)
public abstract	void	setBoolean(int, boolean)
public abstract	void	setByte(int, byte)
public abstract	void	setBytes(int, byte[])
public abstract	void	setDate(int, Date)
public abstract	void	setDouble(int, double)
public abstract	void	setFloat(int, float)
public abstract	void	setInt(int, int)
public abstract	void	setLong(int, long)
public abstract	void	setNull(int, int)
public abstract	void	setObject(int, Object)
public abstract	void	setObject(int, Object, int)
public abstract	void	setObject(int, Object, int, int)
public abstract	void	setShort(int, short)
public abstract	void	setString(int, String)
public abstract	void	setTime(int, Time)
public abstract	void	setTimestamp(int, Timestamp)
public abstract	void	setUnicodeStream(int, InputStream, int)

See Also java.sql.CallableStatement • java.sql.Connection • java.sql.Statement

Interface ResultSet

public abstract interface java.sql.ResultSet

The ResultSet interface is used by JDBC to house the results of a SQL query from a given Statement object. Once you have executed a Statement object, it returns one or more ResultSet objects. You then can use various get*XXX*() methods to retrieve the data contained therein.

Syntax & Usage The result of a query execution is a ResultSet instance. ResultSet stores its results in sequential rows and columns and has a current position that you can move using the next() method from this class. You also can use varying forms of the get*XXX*() methods from this class to retrieve data from a specified row and/or column by using that column's name (if any) or positional index. Consider the following:

```
ResultSet myResults = myStmt.executeQuery("SELECT * FROM Test");
while (myResults.next ())
{
   for (i=1; i<=numofCols; i++)
   {
      System.out.print(myResults.getString(i));
   }
   System.out.println("");
}
myResults.close();
```

> **Note**
>
> *In the previous code example, you have the variable* numofCols *that represents the number of columns contained in the ResultSet. Unless you know ahead of time how many rows the SQL query will return, you need to use the ResultSetMetaData interface. Please see the next section, "Interface ResultSetMetaData," for more information.*

This snippet of code is generated using the executeQuery() method. Then the **while** loop cycles through, using the next() method to go through each row of the result until the end of the file is reached. Then the **for** loop inside goes through each column in the row and displays information from it using the print() and the getString() methods. In this way, the results of the query are displayed onto the screen. Finally, the last line closes the ResultSet object.

> **Tip**
>
> *Usually, the ResultSet object closes automatically when the Statement object that generated it is closed. However, it is a good idea to close it explicitly anyway.*

Fields None

Constructors None

Methods

Modifiers	Return Type	Method
public abstract	void	clearWarnings()
public abstract	void	close()
public abstract	int	findColumn(String)
public abstract	InputStream	getAsciiStream(int)
public abstract	InputStream	getAsciiStream(String)
public abstract	BigDecimal	getBigDecimal(int, int)
public abstract	BigDecimal	getBigDecimal(String, int)
public abstract	InputStream	getBinaryStream(int)
public abstract	InputStream	getBinaryStream(String)
public abstract	boolean	getBoolean(int)
public abstract	boolean	getBoolean(String)
public abstract	byte	getByte(int)
public abstract	byte	getByte(String)
public abstract	byte[]	getBytes(int)
public abstract	byte[]	getBytes(String)
public abstract	String	getCursorName()
public abstract	Date	getDate(int)
public abstract	Date	getDate(String)
public abstract	double	getDouble(int)
public abstract	double	getDouble(String)
public abstract	float	getFloat(int)
public abstract	float	getFloat(String)
public abstract	int	getInt(int)
public abstract	int	getInt(String)
public abstract	long	getLong(int)
public abstract	long	getLong(String)
public abstract	ResultSetMetaData	getMetaData()
public abstract	Object	getObject(int)
public abstract	Object	getObject(String)
public abstract	short	getShort(int)
public abstract	short	getShort(String)
public abstract	String	getString(int)
public abstract	String	getString(String)
public abstract	Time	getTime(int)
public abstract	Time	getTime(String)
public abstract	Timestamp	getTimestamp(int)
public abstract	Timestamp	getTimestamp(String)
public abstract	InputStream	getUnicodeStream(int)

Modifiers	Return Type	Method
public abstract	InputStream	getUnicodeStream(String)
public abstract	SQLWarning	getWarnings()
public abstract	boolean	next()
public abstract	boolean	wasNull()

See Also java.sql.Connection • java.sql.ResultSetMetaData

Interface ResultSetMetaData

public abstract interface java.sql.ResultSetMetaData

The ResultSetMetaData interface is used to gather information and properties about the columns and rows in a given ResultSet object.

Syntax & Usage Consider the following example:

```
//Get the label of each column in myResults.
ResultSetMetaData myMetaData =
  myResults.getMetaData();

int numOfCols= myMetaData.getColumnCount ();

for (i=1; i<=numOfCols; i++)
{
  if (i > 1)
    System.out.print("\t");
  System.out.print(myMetaData.
    getColumnLabel(i));
}
```

Notice that the first thing you do is construct the myMetaData object from the myResults object using the getMetaData() method from the ResultSet class. Then, in the following line, you retrieve the number of columns in myResults using the getColumnCount() from this class. Finally, you have a **for** loop that goes through and uses the getColumnLabel() method from this class to retrieve the names of all columns in myResults and display them, separated by tabs.

Fields

Modifiers	Type	Field
public static final	int	columnNoNulls
public static final	int	columnNullable
public static final	int	columnNullableUnknown

Constructors None

Methods

Modifiers	Return Type	Method
public abstract	String	getCatalogName(int)
public abstract	int	getColumnCount()
public abstract	int	getColumnDisplaySize(int)
public abstract	String	getColumnLabel(int)
public abstract	String	getColumnName(int)
public abstract	int	getColumnType(int)
public abstract	String	getColumnTypeName(int)
public abstract	int	getPrecision(int)
public abstract	int	getScale(int)
public abstract	String	getSchemaName(int)
public abstract	String	getTableName(int)
public abstract	boolean	isAutoIncrement(int)
public abstract	boolean	isCaseSensitive(int)
public abstract	boolean	isCurrency(int)
public abstract	boolean	isDefinitelyWritable(int)
public abstract	int	isNullable(int)
public abstract	boolean	isReadOnly(int)
public abstract	boolean	isSearchable(int)
public abstract	boolean	isSigned(int)
public abstract	boolean	isWritable(int)

See Also java.sql.ResultSet

Class SQLException

public synchronized java.sql.SQLException extends java.lang.Exception

SQLException is thrown any time there is a database-related exception.

Syntax & Usage This exception is thrown by most methods in this package, indicating a SQL-, JDBC-, or database-related exception. This class contains several methods for retrieving specific information (either Java or vendor related) about the given exception. This class also has the ability to chain several exceptions together to facilitate more information about the exception.

The following example method shows how to extract and display various information from a specified SQLException instance:

```
static public void displaySQLException(
   SQLException e)
{
   System.err.println("SQLException: "
      +e.getMessage());
   System.err.println(
      "\tSQL state:\t"+e.getSQLState());
   System.err.println(
      "\tError Code:\t"+e.getErrorCode());
   SQLException eNext = e.getNextException();
   if (eNext != null)
      displaySQLException(eNext);
}
```

This code uses the getSQLState() method from this class to retrieve the current SQL state and the getErrorCode() method from this class to get the vendor-specific error code(s). Finally, if the specified SQLException has a chain of exceptions, this method will recursively call itself to display each chained exception.

Fields None

Constructors

Modifiers	Constructor
public	SQLException()
public	SQLException(String)
public	SQLException(String, String)
public	SQLException(String, String, int)

Methods

Modifiers	Return Type	Method
public	int	getErrorCode()
public	SQLException	getNextException()
public	String	getSQLState()
public synchronized	void	setNextException(SQLException)

See Also java.lang.Exception • java.sql.DataTruncation • java.sql.SQLWarning

Class SQLWarning

public synchronized java.sql.SQLWarning extends java.sql.SQLException

The SQLWarning class facilitates warnings to Java that originate from the database that the given JDBC program is accessing.

Syntax & Usage Although this class is derived from the SQLException class, it is not thrown as an exception and therefore does not interrupt program execution. Rather, a SQLWarning is appended to the given object whose method caused it. You can use the getWarnings() method from the Connection, Statement, and ResultSet classes to retrieve the actual warnings for those objects. The following example method shows how to extract and display various information from the specified SQLWarning instance:

```
static public void displaySQLWarning(
   SQLWarning e)
{
   System.err.println("SQLWarning: "
      +e.getMessage());
   System.err.println(
      "\tSQL state:\t"+e.getSQLState());
   System.err.println(
      "\tError Code:\t"+e.getErrorCode());
   SQLWarning eNext = e.getNextWarning();
   if (eNext != null)
      displaySQLWarning(eNext);
}
```

This example uses the getSQLState() method (inherited from SQLException) to retrieve the current SQL state and the getErrorCode() method to get the database vendor's error messages. Since one SQLWarning has the potential to hold a reference to another, this method recursively calls itself to display all of the chained warnings.

Fields None

Constructors

Modifiers	Constructor
public	SQLWarning()
public	SQLWarning(String)
public	SQLWarning(String, String)
public	SQLWarning(String, String, int)

Methods

Modifiers	Return Type	Method
public	SQLWarning	getNextWarning()
public	void	setNextWarning(SQLWarning)

See Also java.sql.Connection • java.sql.DataTruncation • java.sql.ResultSet • java.sql.SQLException • java.sql.Statement

Interface Statement

public abstract interface java.sql.Statement

The Statement class is used to house and execute static SQL queries. Once a Statement executes, it returns a ResultSet object. Sometimes (although it's rather rare), more than one ResultSet object can be returned.

Note

This interface is also the base class for the PreparedStatement and CallableStatement classes. The former is used for executing precompiled SQL statements (and optionally specifying IN parameters), and the latter is used for executing stored procedures (and optionally specifying IN, OUT, and/or INOUT parameters).

Syntax & Usage This class is effective only after you have made a connection to a SQL database. Then the Statement class should be executed using one of the following methods from this class:

- **execute(String query).** This method is used to execute the specified SQL statement in situations in which more than a ResultSet object and/or an update count may be returned. The method returns a **boolean,** letting you know if the next result is a ResultSet (**true**), update count (**false**), or no other results (**false**).
- **executeQuery(String query).** This method is used to execute the specified SQL statement returning a single ResultSet object, which contains the results for the query.
- **executeUpdate(String query).** This method is used to execute the specified DELETE, INSERT, or UPDATE SQL statement. It also is used for executing Data Definition Language (DDL) statements. The method returns an **int** specifying the number of rows affected or zero otherwise.

The following code snippet executes a simple SQL query using the executeQuery() method:

```
Statement myStmt = myCon.createStatement();
ResultSet myResults = myStmt.executeQuery("SELECT * FROM Test");
```

In this example, you have a connection to a database, called myCon, in which you create myStmt by using the createStatement() method. Then, in the next line, you use the executeQuery() method to execute the query and receive the results in a ResultSet instance.

Fields None

Constructors None

Methods

Modifiers	Return Type	Method
public abstract	void	cancel()
public abstract	void	clearWarnings()
public abstract	void	close()
public abstract	boolean	execute(String)
public abstract	ResultSet	executeQuery(String)
public abstract	int	executeUpdate(String)
public abstract	int	getMaxFieldSize()
public abstract	int	getMaxRows()
public abstract	boolean	getMoreResults()
public abstract	int	getQueryTimeout()
public abstract	ResultSet	getResultSet()
public abstract	int	getUpdateCount()
public abstract	SQLWarning	getWarnings()
public abstract	void	setCursorName(String)
public abstract	void	setEscapeProcessing(boolean)
public abstract	void	setMaxFieldSize(int)
public abstract	void	setMaxRows(int)
public abstract	void	setQueryTimeout(int)

See Also java.sql.CallableStatement • java.sql.Connection • java.sql.PreparedStatement • java.sql.ResultSet

Class Time

public synchronized java.sql.Time extends java.util.Date

The Time class extends the java.util.Date class, providing support for the SQL TIME data type.

Syntax & Usage This class adds various methods that you can use to format and parse instances of this class.

Note

Since this class inherits from the java.util.Date class, you can use various methods available from that class to format dates retrieved from this class. Please see Chapters 21 and 22 for more information on the java.text and java.util packages.

Fields None

Constructors

Modifiers	Constructor
public	Time(int, int, int)
public	Time(long)

Methods

Modifiers	Return Type	Method
public	int	getDate()
public	int	getDay()
public	int	getMonth()
public	int	getYear()
public	void	setDate(int)
public	void	setMonth(int)
public	void	setTime(long)
public	void	setYear(int)
public	String	toString()
public static	Time	valueOf(String)

See Also java.sql.Date • java.sql.Timestamp • java.text.* • java.util.*

Class Timestamp

public synchronized java.sql.Timestamp extends java.util.Date

The Timestamp class extends the java.util.Date class, providing support for the SQL TIMESTAMP data type.

Syntax & Usage This class adds various methods that you can use to format and parse instances of this class.

Fields None

Constructors

Modifiers	Constructor
public	Timestamp(int, int, int, int, int, int, int)
public	Timestamp(long)

Methods

Modifiers	Return Type	Method
public	boolean	after(Timestamp)
public	boolean	before(Timestamp)
public	boolean	equals(Timestamp)
public	int	getNanos()
public	void	setNanos(int)
public	String	toString()
public static	Timestamp	valueOf(String)

See Also java.sql.Date • java.sql.Time • java.util.Date

Class Types

public synchronized java.sql.Types extends java.lang.Object

The Types class is nothing more than a collection of **final static** fields (a.k.a. Java constants) that you can use to identify various SQL data types.

Syntax & Usage

This class simply defines **final int** constants you can use to identify various SQL types. These constants are used to specify the SQL type for OUT parameters in a CallableStatement object (please see the section for that class, earlier in this chapter, for an example). They also are returned from the getColumnType() method from the ResultSetMetaData class specifying the SQL type of the specified column.

The following **static** method outlines how you would use a **switch** statement to map to a SQL type being used in the specified column:

```
static public String displayType(ResultSetMetaData myMetaData, int
  colIndex) {
  int x = myMetaData.getColumnType(colIndex);

  switch(x) {
  case Types.BIGINT:
    return "Column " + colIndex + "is of type BIGINT";

  case Types.BINARY:
    return "Column " + colIndex + "is of type BINARY";

//Put other implementations here.

  }
}
```

Fields

Modifiers	Type	Field
public static final	int	BIGINT
public static final	int	BINARY
public static final	int	BIT
public static final	int	CHAR
public static final	int	DATE

Modifiers	Return Type	Method
public static final	int	DECIMAL
public static final	int	DOUBLE
public static final	int	FLOAT
public static final	int	INTEGER
public static final	int	LONGVARBINARY
public static final	int	LONGVARCHAR
public static final	int	NULL
public static final	int	NUMERIC
public static final	int	OTHER
public static final	int	REAL
public static final	int	SMALLINT
public static final	int	TIME
public static final	int	TIMESTAMP
public static final	int	TINYINT
public static final	int	VARBINARY
public static final	int	VARCHAR

Constructors None

Methods None

See Also java.lang.Object • java.sql.CallableStatement • java.sql.ResultSetMetaData

21 The java.text Package

The java.text package is new to the JDK 1.1 and is used in various locale-sensitive text operations and procedures. Classes in this package that work directly with Locale objects are usually instantiated from what is known as **static** "factory" methods (e.g., getInstance()), while the others can be instantiated using their constructor.

The java.text.resources package

Note that the JDK 1.1 comes with a java.text.resources package, which contains a set of public classes. These are indirect java.util.ResourceBundle subclasses that are used to hold the properties for the standard locales supported in Java. Note that the classes in this package are never used directly by a Java program and they have been declared public only as a temporary workaround, which is why they have not been documented online at JavaSoft or in this book.

Class BreakIterator

public abstract synchronized java.text.BreakIterator extends java.lang.Object implements java.lang.Cloneable, java.io.Serializable

The BreakIterator class is used to isolate words, sentences, or lines in a given locale-sensitive text. This class is useful for implementing word searches, word wrapping (i.e., deciding when and where to break a line), and tasks that involve extracting sentences.

Note

This class is not designed for tokenizing. Instead, use the java.util.StringTokenizer class (see that class for more information).

Syntax & Usage

This class uses a CharacterIterator instance to scan each character in a given text looking for a specified boundary. This class facilitates several **static** methods that return an instance of this class, which you can use to help you perform a specific task involving boundary analysis. The following list contains some of the more traveled methods:

- **getCharacterInstance().** This method is used for analyzing groups of characters and their boundaries.
- **getLineInstance().** This method is used for analyzing where line breaks are possible.
- **getWordInstance().** This method is used for analyzing words and their boundaries.

Note

Each of the methods in the bulleted list is defined as a pair of overloaded methods respectively. The default (specifying no parameters) method performs its functionality based on the current locale, while the second method lets you specify a request to use a certain Locale object.

You can retrieve an array of currently installed locales that support boundaries by using the getAvailableLocale() method from this class.

Once you have an instance of this class, you need to use one of the setText() methods from this class, specifying the text which you wish to have some type of boundary analysis performed upon. After that, you can then use the various methods available in this class (first(), following(), next(), last(), etc.) to complete your task.

Note

Each instance of this class can perform its analysis on only one given text string. Therefore, you must have an instance for every segment of text you wish to analyze.

The following example shows a sample method getSentences(), which uses this class to return an Enumeration object containing a set of sentences that belongs to the specified text string (using the US Locale):

```
public Enumeration getSentences(final String
   stringToExamine)
{
   return new Enumeration()
   {
      BreakIterator boundary;
      int start, end;
      {
      boundary = BreakIterator.
         getSentenceInstance(Locale.US);
      boundary.setText(stringToExamine);
      start = boundary.first();
      end = boundary.next();
      }

      public boolean hasMoreElements()
      {
         return end != BreakIterator.DONE;
      }

      public Object nextElement()
      {
         String str = stringToExamine.
            substring(start,end);
         start = end;
         end = boundary.next();
         return str;
      }
   }
}
```

This returns an instance of an anonymous class, which implements the Enumeration interface. It holds a BreakIterator instance called boundary, which is created by calling the getSentenceInstance() method from this class, specifying Locale.US. The nextElement() method from the Enumeration interface iterates through the string using the next() method, also from this class.

Here's a code snippet calling the getSentences() method (defined above), passing it the string "Hello, world! It's me." The getSentences() method causes the string to be broken into two separate statements:

```
Enumeration en = getSentences(
   "Hello, world! It's me.");
while (en.hasMoreElements())
   System.out.println(en.nextElement());
```

This snippet produces the following output:

```
Hello, world!
It's me.
```

Fields

Modifiers	Type	Field
public static final	int	DONE

Constructors

Modifiers	Constructor
protected	BreakIterator()

Methods

Modifiers	Return Type	Method
public	Object	clone()
public abstract	int	current()
public abstract	int	first()
public abstract	int	following(int)
public static synchronized	Locale[]	getAvailableLocales()
public static	BreakIterator	getCharacterInstance()
public static	BreakIterator	getCharacterInstance(Locale)
public static	BreakIterator	getLineInstance()
public static	BreakIterator	getLineInstance(Locale)
public static	BreakIterator	getSentenceInstance()
public static	BreakIterator	getSentenceInstance(Locale)
public abstract	CharacterIterator	getText()
public static	BreakIterator	getWordInstance()
public static	BreakIterator	getWordInstance(Locale)
public abstract	int	last()
public abstract	int	next()

Modifiers	Return Type	Method
public abstract	int	next(int)
public abstract	int	previous()
public abstract	void	setText(CharacterIterator)
public	void	setText(String)

See Also java.io.Serializable • java.lang.Cloneable • java.lang.Object • java.text.CharacterIterator • java.text.StringCharacterIterator • java.util.Enumeration • java.util.StringTokenizer

Interface CharacterIterator

public abstract interface java.text.CharacterIterator implements java.lang.Cloneable

The CharacterIterator interface defines methods used to scan characters of a given text string.

Syntax & Usage Implementations of this interface can be used to iterate forwards or backwards through a bounded group of characters (as determined by the implementation). Assuming that you have the instance variable iterate for this class, you can iterate forward using a **for** loop in the following manner:

```
for (char c = iterate.first();
   c != CharacterIterator.DONE;
   c = iter.next())
{
   // Process character c here
}
```

The following example shows backward iteration:

```
for (char c = iterate.last();
   c != CharacterIterator.DONE;
   c = iter.prev())
{
   // Process character c here
}
```

Please see the example under "Class StringCharacterIterator," later in this chapter, for more information.

Fields

Modifiers	Type	Field
public static final	char	DONE

Constructors None

Methods

Modifiers	Return Type	Method
public abstract	Object	clone()
public abstract	char	current()
public abstract	char	first()
public abstract	int	getBeginIndex()
public abstract	int	getEndIndex()
public abstract	int	getIndex()
public abstract	char	last()
public abstract	char	next()
public abstract	char	previous()
public abstract	char	setIndex(int)

See Also java.lang.Cloneable • java.text.BreakIterator • java.text.StringCharacterIterator

Class ChoiceFormat

public synchronized java.text.ChoiceFormat extends java.text.NumberFormat

The ChoiceFormat class is a NumberFormat subclass that allows you to choose among text strings using a numerically based index.

Syntax & Usage Basically, you have a given string of text in a given language wherein you can insert pieces of text based on a specified value. For instance, you can have an index listing the days of the week (represented as 1 through 7). You can then use this class to map those values to a corresponding word (or phrase). Table 21-1 shows an example.

Index	Choice Format #1	Choice Format #2
1	Monday	Beginning of the week
2	Tuesday	(Same as above)
3	Wednesday	Middle of the week
4	Thursday	(Same as above)
5	Friday	End of the week
6	Saturday	Beginning of the weekend
7	Sunday	End of the weekend

Table 21-1: Days of the week formatted for use with the ChoiceFormat class.

The table shows an example of mapping one set of values to either one format (Monday, Tuesday, etc.) or the other (Beginning of the week, Middle of the week, etc.). You also can design formats based on various other forms of logic (i.e., a, b, c, and everything else). This class often is used in conjunction with the MessageFormat class for specifying how plurals of something are to be represented. The following code snippet uses this class to specify a fiscal quarter based to a given month (as denoted by a numerical value):

```
double[] quarters = {1, 4, 7, 10};
String[] quartNames = {"1-st quarter",
   "2-nd quarter","3-rd quarter",
   "4-th quarter"};
ChoiceFormat qForm = new ChoiceFormat(
   quarters, quartNames);
for (int i = 1; i <= 12; i++)
   System.out.println(i + " month is in "
     + qForm.format(i));
```

This example creates an instance of this class and uses the format() method from this class to generate quarter names for numbers from 1 to 12. Here's what the corresponding output looks like:

```
1 month is in 1-st quarter
2 month is in 1-st quarter
3 month is in 1-st quarter
4 month is in 2-nd quarter
5 month is in 2-nd quarter
6 month is in 2-nd quarter
7 month is in 3-rd quarter
8 month is in 3-rd quarter
9 month is in 3-rd quarter
10 month is in 4-th quarter
11 month is in 4-th quarter
12 month is in 4-th quarter
```

Fields None

Constructors

Modifiers	Constructor
public	ChoiceFormat(double[], String[])
public	ChoiceFormat(String)

Methods

Modifiers	Return Type	Method
public	void	applyPattern(String)
public	Object	clone()
public	boolean	equals(Object)
public	StringBuffer	format(double, StringBuffer, FieldPosition)
public	StringBuffer	format(long, StringBuffer, FieldPosition)
public	Object[]	getFormats()
public	double[]	getLimits()
public	int	hashCode()
public static final	double	nextDouble(double)
public static	double	nextDouble(double, boolean)
public	Number	parse(String, ParsePosition)
public static final	double	previousDouble(double)
public	void	setChoices(double[], String[])
public	String	toPattern()

See Also java.text.MessageFormat • java.text.NumberFormat

Class CollationElementIterator

public final synchronized java.text.CollationElementIterator extends java.lang.Object

The CollationElementIterator class is used to iterate through each character of some locale-sensitive text string wherein it determines the primary, secondary, and tertiary (i.e., third) order for each character in that text.

Syntax & Usage This class does not provide any constructor. To get an instance of this class, use the getCollationElementIterator() method from the RuleBasedCollator class specifying a String. Then you can use the primaryOrder(), secondaryOrder(), and tertiaryOrder() methods from this class to determine the primary, secondary, and tertiary key (a.k.a. order) based on the specified collation order in the given RuleBasedCollator object. Consider the following:

```
RuleBasedCollator itCollator =
   (RuleBasedCollator)Collator.getInstance(
   Locale.ITALY);
CollationElementIterator c = itCollator.
   getCollationElementIterator("Oggi è il");

while (true)
{
   int n = c.next();
   if (n == CollationElementIterator.
      NULLORDER)
      break;
   int primOrder = CollationElementIterator.
      primaryOrder(n);
   int secnOrder = CollationElementIterator.
      secondaryOrder(n);
   int tetrOrder = CollationElementIterator.
      tertiaryOrder(n);
   System.out.println("Order: Primary:"+
      primOrder+"\tSecondary:"+secnOrder+
      "\tTertiary:"+tetrOrder);
}
```

This creates an instance of CollationElementIterator by calling the getCollationElementIterator() method from the RuleBasedCollator class. It then iterates through the given text "Oggi è il" using Locale.ITALY, displaying the primary, secondary, and tertiary indices for each character. Here's the corresponding output:

```
Order: Primary:84    Secondary:0   Tertiary:2
Order: Primary:76    Secondary:0   Tertiary:0
Order: Primary:76    Secondary:0   Tertiary:0
Order: Primary:78    Secondary:0   Tertiary:0
Order: Primary:0     Secondary:1   Tertiary:0
Order: Primary:74    Secondary:0   Tertiary:0
Order: Primary:0     Secondary:22  Tertiary:0
Order: Primary:0     Secondary:1   Tertiary:0
Order: Primary:78    Secondary:0   Tertiary:0
Order: Primary:81    Secondary:0   Tertiary:0
```

Fields

Modifiers	Type	Field
public static final	int	NULLORDER

Constructors None

Methods

Modifiers	Return Type	Method
public	int	next()
public static final	int	primaryOrder(int)
public	void	reset()
public static final	short	secondaryOrder(int)
public static final	short	tertiaryOrder(int)

See Also java.lang.Object • java.text.CollationKey • java.text.Collator

Class CollationKey

public final synchronized java.text.CollationKey extends java.lang.Object

The CollationKey class is used for comparing and ordering locale-sensitive strings.

Syntax & Usage This class converts a given string into a binary interpretation, thereby enabling the string-comparison process to use bitwise operations, which are notably faster. However, because the initial conversion process is comprehensive, it can be quite slow. Therefore, this operation is reserved primarily for situations in which some string comparisons take place several times—a common occurrence in various sorting algorithms. This class is used primarily when you wish to sort a given number of strings.

Tip

Alternatively, if you intend to perform a comparison only once on some given strings, your best bet would be to use the compare() method from the Collator class, which examines only parts of the strings (on an as-needed basis) necessary to perform the comparison. Please see the section for that class, which follows, for more information.

To instantiate this class, you need to call the getCollationKey() method from the Collator class specifying the String you wish to be interpreted. Note that you must use the same Collator object to instantiate all the given strings you wish to compare. The following example method implements a procedure to sort an array of Strings using several instances of the CollationKey class:

```
public void sort(String str[])
{
   Collator defCollator = Collator.
      getInstance();
   int n = str.length;
   CollationKey keys[] = new CollationKey[n];
   CollationKey tmp;
   int i, j;
   for (i=0; i<n; i++)
      keys[i] = defCollator.
         getCollationKey(str[i]);

   for (i=0; i<n; i++)
   for (j=i+1; j<n; j++)
      if (keys[i].compareTo(keys[j]) > 0)
      {
         tmp = keys[i];
         keys[i] = keys[j];
         keys[j] = tmp;
      }

   for (i=0; i<n; i++)
      str[i] = keys[i].getSourceString();
}
```

The sort() method takes a String array to be sorted. Then it creates a Collator object based on the default Locale and constructs an array of CollationKey objects from the String array using the newly created Collator object. After that, this method implements a standard sorting algorithm using the compareTo() method from this class. Finally, it converts the now-sorted array of CollationKey objects back to a String.

Note

All primitive parameters in Java are passed by value, so any changes on parameters inside the called method cannot be seen from the calling procedure. However, an array is passed by reference, so changes in an array are accessible from the calling procedure.

The following code snippet uses the previous sorting method to alphabetically sort four names:

```
String str[] = {"John", "Bill", "Ann", "Sam"};
sort(str);
for (int i=0; i<str.length; i++)
   System.out.println(str[i]);
```

Here's the corresponding output:

```
Ann
Bill
John
Sam
```

As you can see, the example alphabetically sorted the list of names based on their first letter (using the default locale of US).

Fields None

Constructors None

Methods

Modifiers	Return Type	Method
public	int	compareTo(CollationKey)
public	boolean	equals(Object)
public	String	getSourceString()
public	int	hashCode()
public	byte[]	toByteArray()

See Also java.lang.Object • java.text.Collator

Class Collator

public abstract synchronized java.text.Collator extends java.lang.Object implements java.lang.Cloneable, java.io.Serializable

The Collator class is an **abstract** class that is used as the base class to define various collation operations with locale-sensitive strings. Primarily, implementations of this class would add the ability to compare, sort, and search through a given number of text strings.

Syntax & Usage

To instantiate this class, you need to call the **static** method getInstance() of this class, either using the default locale or specifying the Locale object you wish to use. From there, you can use the compare() method from this class to perform a one-time comparison of some strings, or you can call the getCollationKey() method from this class for sorting operations that involve multiple comparisons. Please see the previous section, "Class CollationKey," for more information.

Java 1.1 has defined one subclass—RuleBasedCollator—which extends this class. RuleBasedCollator is used to define the collation rules. Please see "Class RuleBasedCollator," later in this chapter, for more information.

Tip

Alternatively, you can extend this class to implement your own collation-based solutions.

Please see the two previous sections, on the CollationElementIterator and CollationKey classes, for examples of how to use this class.

Fields

Modifiers	Type	Field
public static final	int	CANONICAL_DECOMPOSITION
public static final	int	FULL_DECOMPOSITION
public static final	int	IDENTICAL
public static final	int	NO_DECOMPOSITION
public static final	int	PRIMARY
public static final	int	SECONDARY
public static final	int	TERTIARY

Constructors

Modifiers	Constructor
protected	Collator()

Methods

Modifiers	Return Type	Method
public	Object	clone()
public abstract	int	compare(String, String)
public	boolean	equals(Object)
public	boolean	equals(String, String)
public static synchronized	Locale[]	getAvailableLocales()
public abstract	CollationKey	getCollationKey(String)
public synchronized	int	getDecomposition()
public static synchronized	Collator	getInstance()

Modifiers	Return Type	Method
public static synchronized	Collator	getInstance(Locale)
public synchronized	int	getStrength()
public abstract synchronized	int	hashCode()
public synchronized	void	setDecomposition(int)
public synchronized	void	setStrength(int)

See Also java.io.Serializable • java.lang.Cloneable • java.lang.Object • java.text.CollationElementIterator • java.text.CollationKey • java.text.RuleBasedCollator

Class DateFormat

public abstract synchronized java.text.DateFormat extends java.text.Format implements java.lang.Cloneable

A DateFormat class is an **abstract** Format subclass that provides a wide range of methods and various settings for date/time formatting using the default or a specified locale.

Syntax & Usage

This class facilitates four sizes for a date, represented by the fields SHORT, MEDIUM, FULL, and LONG. To use this class, you can call one of the overloaded **static** getDateInstance(), getDateTimeInstance(), or getTimeInstance() methods from this class, using the default locale or specifying the Locale object you wish to use.

The following code snippet demonstrates an example of using the DateFormat class to format the SHORT and FULL date using a specified locale:

```
DateFormat dFull =
  DateFormat.getDateInstance(
  DateFormat.FULL, Locale.UK);
System.out.println("Full date : "+
  dFull.format(new Date()));
DateFormat dShort =
  DateFormat.getDateInstance(
  DateFormat.SHORT, Locale.UK);
System.out.println("Short date: "+
  dShort.format(new Date()));
```

This example creates two instances of the DateFormat class by using the **static** method getDateInstance() from this class: The first DateFormat object (dFull) has been specified with DateFormat.FULL and Locale.UK. The second DateFormat object (dShort) has been specified with DateFormat.SHORT and Locale.UK. Then the code uses the format() method from this class to print a text representation of the current date for both objects. Here's the corresponding output:

```
Full date : 03 March 1997
Short date: 03/03/97
```

Fields

Modifiers	Type	Field
public static final	int	AM_PM_FIELD
protected	Calendar	calendar
public static final	int	DATE_FIELD
public static final	int	DAY_OF_WEEK_FIELD
public static final	int	DAY_OF_WEEK_IN_MONTH_FIELD
public static final	int	DAY_OF_YEAR_FIELD
public static final	int	DEFAULT
public static final	int	ERA_FIELD
public static final	int	FULL
public static final	int	HOUR0_FIELD
public static final	int	HOUR1_FIELD
public static final	int	HOUR_OF_DAY0_FIELD
public static final	int	HOUR_OF_DAY1_FIELD
public static final	int	LONG
public static final	int	MEDIUM
public static final	int	MILLISECOND_FIELD
public static final	int	MINUTE_FIELD
public static final	int	MONTH_FIELD
protected	NumberFormat	numberFormat
public static final	int	SECOND_FIELD
public static final	int	SHORT
public static final	int	TIMEZONE_FIELD
public static final	int	WEEK_OF_MONTH_FIELD
public static final	int	WEEK_OF_YEAR_FIELD
public static final	int	YEAR_FIELD

Constructors

Modifiers	Constructor
protected	DateFormat()

Methods

Modifiers	Return Type	Method
public	Object	clone()
public	boolean	equals(Object)
public final	String	format(Date)
public abstract	StringBuffer	format(Date, StringBuffer, FieldPosition)
public final	StringBuffer	format(Object, StringBuffer, FieldPosition)
public static	Locale[]	getAvailableLocales()
public	Calendar	getCalendar()
public static final	DateFormat	getDateInstance()
public static final	DateFormat	getDateInstance(int)
public static final	DateFormat	getDateInstance(int, Locale)
public static final	DateFormat	getDateTimeInstance()
public static final	DateFormat	getDateTimeInstance(int, int)
public static final	DateFormat	getDateTimeInstance(int, int, Locale)
public static final	DateFormat	getInstance()
public	NumberFormat	getNumberFormat()
public static final	DateFormat	getTimeInstance()
public static final	DateFormat	getTimeInstance(int)
public static final	DateFormat	getTimeInstance(int, Locale)
public	TimeZone	getTimeZone()
public	int	hashCode()
public	boolean	isLenient()
public	Date	parse(String)
public abstract	Date	parse(String, ParsePosition)
public	Object	parseObject(String, ParsePosition)
public	void	setCalendar(Calendar)
public	void	setLenient(boolean)
public	void	setNumberFormat(NumberFormat)
public	void	setTimeZone(TimeZone)

See Also java.lang.Cloneable • java.text.DateFormatSymbols • java.text.Format • java.text.SimpleDateFormat • java.util.Date • java.util.Locale

Class DateFormatSymbols

public synchronized java.text.DateFormatSymbols extends java.lang.Object implements java.io.Serializable, java.lang.Cloneable

The DateFormatSymbols class is used to hold all the date, time, time zone, and related words and symbols for a given locale.

Syntax & Usage

In most situations, you do not use this class directly, but instead use the DateFormat (or its concrete subclass SimpleDateFormat) class to format dates and times for a given locale. However, it is possible for you to create your own format for a specified locale using this class. Consider the following:

```
DateFormatSymbols dfSymbols = new
  DateFormatSymbols(myLocale);
SimpleDateFormat sdf =
  new SimpleDateFormat(myPattern, dfSymbols);
```

Here you use a SimpleDateFormat object to format your times and dates (please see "Class SimpleDateFormat," later in this chapter, for details) based on the specified pattern myPattern and the DateFormatSymbols object dfSymbols.

Fields

None

Constructors

Modifiers	Constructor
public	DateFormatSymbols()
public	DateFormatSymbols(Locale)

Methods

Modifiers	Return Type	Method
public	Object	clone()
public	boolean	equals(Object)
public	String[]	getAmPmStrings()
public	String[]	getEras()
public	String	getLocalPatternChars()
public	String[]	getMonths()

Modifiers	Return Type	Method
public	String[]	getShortMonths()
public	String[]	getShortWeekdays()
public	String[]	getWeekdays()
public	String[]	getZoneStrings()
public	int	hashCode()
public	void	setAmPmStrings(String[])
public	void	setEras(String[])
public	void	setLocalPatternChars(String)
public	void	setMonths(String[])
public	void	setShortMonths(String[])
public	void	setShortWeekdays(String[])
public	void	setWeekdays(String[])
public	void	setZoneStrings(String[])

See Also java.io.Serializable • java.lang.Cloneable • java.lang.Object • java.text.DateFormat • java.text.SimpleDateFormat • java.util.Locale

Class DecimalFormat

public synchronized java.text.DecimalFormat extends java.text.NumberFormat

The DecimalFormat class is a NumberFormat subclass that is used for working with locale-sensitive numerical values.

Syntax & Usage You can use getInstance(), getCurrencyInstance(), or getPercentInstance() **static** methods from the NumberFormat class to get an instance of this class. Here's an example of using this class:

```
Locale locales[] = new Locale[] { Locale.US,
   Locale.UK, Locale.CANADA, Locale.GERMANY,
   Locale.ITALY };
double myNumber = 7985.41, myPercent = 86.93;
for (int i = 0; i < locales.length; i++)
{
   DecimalFormat dfNumber = (DecimalFormat)
      NumberFormat.getInstance(locales[i]);
```

```
    DecimalFormat dfMoney  = (DecimalFormat)
      NumberFormat.getCurrencyInstance(
      locales[i]);

    DecimalFormat dfPercent= (DecimalFormat)
      NumberFormat.getPercentInstance(
      locales[i]);
    try
    {
      System.out.println(
        locales[i].getDisplayCountry()+"\t"
        +dfNumber.format(myNumber)+"\t"
        +dfMoney.format(myNumber)+"\t"
        +dfPercent.format(myPercent));
    }
    catch (IllegalArgumentException e) { }
}
```

This example creates three instances of the DecimalFormat class and displays a number, money amount, and percent for each using a locale in the specified array. The above produces the following output:

```
United States  7,985.41  $7,985.41    8,693%
United Kingdom 7,985.41  £7,985.41    8,693%
Canada         7,985.41  $7,985.41    8,693%
Germany        7.985,41  7.985,41 DM  8.693%
Italy          7.985,41  L 7.985,41   8.693%
```

Fields None

Constructors

Modifiers	Constructor
public	DecimalFormat()
public	DecimalFormat(String)
public	DecimalFormat(String, DecimalFormatSymbols)

Methods

Modifiers	Return Type	Method
public	void	applyLocalizedPattern(String)
public	void	applyPattern(String)
public	Object	clone()
public	boolean	equals(Object)
public	StringBuffer	format(double, StringBuffer, FieldPosition)
public	StringBuffer	format(long, StringBuffer, FieldPosition)
public	DecimalFormatSymbols	getDecimalFormatSymbols()
public	int	getGroupingSize()

Modifiers	Return Type	Method
public	int	getMultiplier()
public	String	getNegativePrefix()
public	String	getNegativeSuffix()
public	String	getPositivePrefix()
public	String	getPositiveSuffix()
public	int	hashCode()
public	boolean	isDecimalSeparatorAlwaysShown()
public	Number	parse(String, ParsePosition)
public	void	setDecimalFormatSymbols(DecimalFormatSymbols)
public	void	setDecimalSeparatorAlwaysShown(boolean)
public	void	setGroupingSize(int)
public	void	setMultiplier(int)
public	void	setNegativePrefix(String)
public	void	setNegativeSuffix(String)
public	void	setPositivePrefix(String)
public	void	setPositiveSuffix(String)
public	String	toLocalizedPattern()
public	String	toPattern()

See Also java.text.DecimalFormatSymbols • java.text.NumberFormat • java.util.Locale

Class DecimalFormatSymbols

public final synchronized java.text.DecimalFormatSymbols extends java.lang.Object implements java.lang.Cloneable, java.io.Serializable

The DecimalFormatSymbols class is used to hold all the numerically related symbols (i.e., characters used to represent a decimal, grouping, positive or negative infinity, etc.) for a given locale.

Syntax & Usage A DecimalFormat instance creates an instance of DecimalFormatSymbols for itself using its locale data and is therefore usually not used directly.

Note

This class contains a variety of getXXX() and setXXX() methods that you can use to retrieve or set a numerically related symbol for a specific operation.

Nonetheless, you can create and set up your own DecimalFormatSymbols. Here's an example of changing the format of the US Locale so that a decimal point is represented as a colon (:) instead of a period (.):

```
DecimalFormatSymbols dfs = new
   DecimalFormatSymbols(Locale.US);
dfs.setDecimalSeparator(':');
DecimalFormat dfNumber = new
   DecimalFormat("###,###.000", dfs);
System.out.println(dfNumber.format(7985.41));
```

This example creates an instance of this class specifying Locale.US and setting the colon character as the new decimal separator. It produces the following output:

```
7,985:410
```

Fields None

Constructors

Modifiers	Constructor
public	DecimalFormatSymbols()
public	DecimalFormatSymbols(Locale)

Methods

Modifiers	Return Type	Method
public	Object	clone()
public	boolean	equals(Object)
public	char	getDecimalSeparator()
public	char	getDigit()
public	char	getGroupingSeparator()
public	String	getInfinity()
public	char	getMinusSign()
public	String	getNaN()
public	char	getPatternSeparator()
public	char	getPercent()
public	char	getPerMill()
public	char	getZeroDigit()

Modifiers	Return Type	Method
public	int	hashCode()
public	void	setDecimalSeparator(char)
public	void	setDigit(char)
public	void	setGroupingSeparator(char)
public	void	setInfinity(String)
public	void	setMinusSign(char)
public	void	setNaN(String)
public	void	setPatternSeparator(char)
public	void	setPercent(char)
public	void	setPerMill(char)
public	void	setZeroDigit(char)

See Also java.io.Serializable • java.lang.Cloneable • java.lang.Object • java.util.Locale

Class FieldPosition

public synchronized java.text.FieldPosition extends java.lang.Object

The FieldPosition class keeps track of the position of a field within some formatted text string.

Syntax & Usage This class is used by Format and its subclasses (particularly NumberFormat and DateFormat) to identify a given location (i.e., a field) in a text string. Text parts, including formatted numbers, dates, and times can have varying lengths in different locales. Using this class, you can format these things properly, despite potential differences in length. The following code snippet uses this class to format numerical output without regard to its size:

```
NumberFormat nf = NumberFormat.getInstance();
StringBuffer sb = new StringBuffer();
FieldPosition fp = new FieldPosition(NumberFormat.INTEGER_FIELD);
double numbers[] = { 7985.41, 34.456, 12000345.5 };
for (int k=0; k<numbers.length; k++)
{
```

```
        StringBuffer s = nf.format(numbers[k],  new StringBuffer(), fp);
        for (int i=0; i < (12 - fp.getEndIndex()); i++) {
            System.out.print(" ");
        }
        System.out.print(s.toString() + "\n");
    }
```

By specifying the NumberFormat.INTEGER_FIELD constant in this FieldPosition object, you can retrieve the size of your output relative to the decimal point and align it by adding the appropriate number of spaces (the inner **for** loop does this by simply printing k spaces) for each number. This produces the following output:

```
     7,985.41
        34.456
  12,000,345.5
```

Fields None

Constructors

Modifiers	Constructor
public	FieldPosition(int)

Methods

Modifiers	Return Type	Method
public	int	getBeginIndex()
public	int	getEndIndex()
public	int	getField()

See Also java.lang.Object • java.text.DateFormat • java.text.Format • java.text.NumberFormat

Class Format

public abstract synchronized java.text.Format extends java.lang.Object implements java.io.Serializable, java.lang.Cloneable

The Format class is an **abstract** class that defines how various locale-sensitive data (e.g., dates, text strings, and numerical values) should be formatted.

Syntax & Usage This class defines the functionality to convert a given locale-sensitive piece of data to a String and vice versa. To go from locale to String, you use the format() method; to go from String to locale, you use the parseObject() method. The following is a list of the Format class's subclasses:

- ChoiceFormat
- DateFormat
- DecimalFormat
- MessageFormat
- NumberFormat
- SimpleDateFormat

For more information, please see the sections for these subclasses elsewhere in this chapter.

Fields None

Constructors

Modifiers	Constructor
public	Format()

Methods

Modifiers	Return Type	Method
public	Object	clone()
public final	String	format(Object)
public abstract	StringBuffer	format(Object, StringBuffer, FieldPosition)
public	Object	parseObject(String)
public abstract	Object	parseObject(String, ParsePosition)

See Also java.io.Serializable • java.lang.Cloneable • java.lang.Object • java.text.ChoiceFormat • java.text.DateFormat • java.text.DecimalFormat • java.text.MessageFormat • java.text.NumberFormat • java.text.ParsePosition • java.text.SimpleDateFormat

Class MessageFormat

public synchronized java.text.MessageFormat extends java.text.Format

The MessageFormat class is a Format subclass that is used for working with locale-sensitive text strings.

Syntax & Usage This class formats a set of specified objects (i.e., converts them to strings) and inserts the newly formatted strings to the appropriate places in some given line of text.

The MessageFormat class uses a special syntax for string patterns in the form {*NumberOfArgument*, *ElementFormat*}, where *NumberOfArgument* is a zero-based index in the array of arguments, and *ElementFormat* may have one of the forms shown in Table 21-2.

Message Type	Example	Description
None	{1}	Simple texts (i.e., Strings)
time	{2, time, full}	The time part of a DateFormat object; has an additional option to specify short, medium, long, and full (please see "Class DateFormat," earlier in this chapter, for more information)
date	{3, date, long}	The date part of a DateFormat object; has an additional option to specify short, medium, long, and full (please see "Class DateFormat," earlier in this chapter, for more information)
number	{4, number, percent}	Numerical values; has an additional option to specify currency, percent, and integer
choice	{5, choice, 0# are no disks|1#is one disk|1# are {5, number, integer} disks}	Allows you to select a string based on a specific pattern (please see "Class ChoiceFormat," earlier in this chapter, for more information)

Table 21-2: Index of ElementFormat forms in the MessageFormat class's special syntax for string patterns.

Let's take a look at a simple example:

```
System.out.println(appointment("Mr. Smith",
   new Date()));

public String appointment(String name,
   Date date) {
   return MessageFormat.format("{0} has an appointment at {1,time} on
   {1,date}", new Object[] {name, date});
   }
```

This produces the following output:

```
Mr. Smith has an appointment at 5:09:02 PM on 03-Mar-97
```

> **Note**
>
> *This example uses an anonymous array to pass arguments to the format() method.*

Fields None

Constructors

Modifiers	Constructor
public	MessageFormat(String)

Methods

Modifiers	Return Type	Method
public	void	applyPattern(String)
public	Object	clone()
public	boolean	equals(Object)
public final	StringBuffer	format(Object, StringBuffer, FieldPosition)
public final	StringBuffer	format(Object[], StringBuffer, FieldPosition)
public static	String	format(String, Object[])
public	Format[]	getFormats()
public	Locale	getLocale()
public	int	hashCode()
public	Object[]	parse(String)
public	Object[]	parse(String, ParsePosition)
public	Object	parseObject(String, ParsePosition)
public	void	setFormat(int, Format)
public	void	setFormats(Format[])
public	void	setLocale(Locale)
public	String	toPattern()

See Also java.text.ChoiceFormat • java.text.Format • java.text.NumberFormat

Class NumberFormat

public abstract synchronized java.text.NumberFormat extends java.text.Format implements java.lang.Cloneable

The NumberFormat class is an **abstract** Format subclass that is used for defining with locale-sensitive numerically base values.

Syntax & Usage This class formats (i.e., converts to strings) a set of specified numerical values and inserts the newly formatted strings in the appropriate places in some given line of text. To use this class you need to call one of its **static** getInstance() (or get*XXX*Instance()) methods.

This class has two subclasses:

- ChoiceFormat
- DecimalFormat

For more information, please see the sections for these two subclasses, earlier in this chapter.

Fields

Modifiers	Type	Field
public static final	int	FRACTION_FIELD
public static final	int	INTEGER_FIELD

Constructors

Modifiers	Constructor
public	NumberFormat()

Methods

Modifiers	Return Type	Method
public	Object	clone()
public	boolean	equals(Object)
public final	String	format(double)
public abstract	StringBuffer	format(double, StringBuffer, FieldPosition)
public final	String	format(long)
public abstract	StringBuffer	format(long, StringBuffer, FieldPosition)
public final	StringBuffer	format(Object, StringBuffer, FieldPosition)
public static	Locale[]	getAvailableLocales()
public static final	NumberFormat	getCurrencyInstance()
public static	NumberFormat	getCurrencyInstance(Locale)
public static final	NumberFormat	getInstance()
public static	NumberFormat	getInstance(Locale)
public	int	getMaximumFractionDigits()
public	int	getMaximumIntegerDigits()
public	int	getMinimumFractionDigits()
public	int	getMinimumIntegerDigits()
public static final	NumberFormat	getNumberInstance()
public static	NumberFormat	getNumberInstance(Locale)
public static final	NumberFormat	getPercentInstance()
public static	NumberFormat	getPercentInstance(Locale)
public	int	hashCode()
public	boolean	isGroupingUsed()

Modifiers	Return Type	Method
public	boolean	isParseIntegerOnly()
public	Number	parse(String)
public abstract	Number	parse(String, ParsePosition)
public final	Object	parseObject(String, ParsePosition)
public	void	setGroupingUsed(boolean)
public	void	setMaximumFractionDigits(int)
public	void	setMaximumIntegerDigits(int)
public	void	setMinimumFractionDigits(int)
public	void	setMinimumIntegerDigits(int)
public	void	setParseIntegerOnly(boolean)

See Also java.lang.Cloneable • java.text.ChoiceFormat • java.text.DecimalFormat • java.text.FieldPosition • java.text.Format • java.text.MessageFormat

Class ParseException

public synchronized java.text.ParseException extends java.lang.Exception

ParseException is thrown any time there is a problem parsing some given data.

Syntax & Usage This exception can be thrown by any implementation of the parse() method of the Format class, signaling a problem or an unexpected error during the parse operation:

```
static public Date parseDate(
  DateFormat df, String text)
{
  try
  {
    return df.parse(text);
  }
  catch (ParseException e)
  {
    System.err.println(
      "Can't parse "+text+" to Date");
    return null;
  }
}
```

This uses the parse() method from the DateFormat class to parse the specific text string to a DateFormat instance. If the ParseException is thrown, this sample method prints an error message and returns **null**.

Fields None

Constructors

Modifiers	Constructor
public	ParseException(String, int)

Methods

Modifiers	Return Type	Method
public	int	getErrorOffset()

See Also java.lang.Exception • java.text.DateFormat • java.text.Format

Class ParsePosition

public synchronized java.text.ParsePosition extends java.lang.Object

The ParsePosition class is used by the Format and subclasses to keep track of the current position during a parse operation. This position is known as the index.

Syntax & Usage Here's a code snippet using this class and DecimalFormat to parse an arbitrary text string:

```
ParsePosition pp = new ParsePosition(0);
String source = "120 boxes";
DecimalFormat format = new DecimalFormat();
String str = format.parse(source, pp).
  toString();
System.out.println(str+"\t"+pp.getIndex());
```

This example uses an instance of the ParsePosition class to retrieve the current index position in the given string using the getIndex() method from this class. This produces the following output:

```
120     3
```

Fields None

Constructors

Modifiers	Constructor
public	ParsePosition(int)

Methods

Modifiers	Return Type	Method
public	int	getIndex()
public	void	setIndex(int)

See Also java.lang.Object • java.text.DecimalFormat • java.text.Format

Class RuleBasedCollator

public synchronized java.text.RuleBasedCollator extends java.text.Collator

The RuleBasedCollator class is used to define a table of collation rules that will be used to determine the various relations and map characters according to a given ordering priority value.

Syntax & Usage Please see the example under "Class CollationElementIterator," earlier in this chapter, for details of using this class.

Fields None

Constructors

Modifiers	Constructor
public	RuleBasedCollator(String)

Methods

Modifiers	Return Type	Method
public	Object	clone()
public	int	compare(String, String)
public	boolean	equals(Object)
public	CollationElementIterator	getCollationElementIterator(String)
public	CollationKey	getCollationKey(String)
public	String	getRules()
public	int	hashCode()

See Also java.text.CollationElementIterator • java.text.Collator

Class SimpleDateFormat

public synchronized java.text.SimpleDateFormat extends java.text.DateFormat

The SimpleDateFormat class is a DateFormat subclass used for working with locale-sensitive dates and times.

Syntax & Usage

This class is a subclass of DateFormat and provides an implementation for DateFormat's format() and parse() methods. This class formats (i.e., converts to String objects) a set of specified numerical values and inserts the newly formatted strings in the appropriate places in some given line of text. The following code snippet uses this class to format dates based on a defined pattern:

```
SimpleDateFormat sFormat =
   new SimpleDateFormat ("yyyy-MMM-dd");
String str = sFormat.format(new Date());
System.out.println(str);
```

For current locale set to Locale.US, this produces the following output:

```
1997-Mar-03
```

> **Tip**
>
> *You also can use the format() method from the DateFormat class for locale-based date formatting.*

Fields

None

Constructors

Modifiers	Constructor
public	SimpleDateFormat()
public	SimpleDateFormat(String)
public	SimpleDateFormat(String, DateFormatSymbols)
public	SimpleDateFormat(String, Locale)

Methods

Modifiers	Return Type	Method
public	void	applyLocalizedPattern(String)
public	void	applyPattern(String)
public	Object	clone()
public	boolean	equals(Object)
public	StringBuffer	format(Date, StringBuffer, FieldPosition)
public	DateFormatSymbols	getDateFormatSymbols()
public	int	hashCode()
public	Date	parse(String, ParsePosition)
public	void	setDateFormatSymbols(DateFormatSymbols)
public	String	toLocalizedPattern()
public	String	toPattern()

See Also java.text.DateFormat • java.util.Locale

Class StringCharacterIterator

public final synchronized java.text.StringCharacterIterator extends java.lang.Object implements java.text.CharacterIterator

The StringCharacterIterator class implements the CharacterIterator interface and is used to iterate through the individual characters (in a forward or reverse manner) of a String object.

Syntax & Usage

The following example demonstrates how to reverse the specified String object (source) using this class:

```
static public String revert(String source)
{
  StringCharacterIterator iter = new
    StringCharacterIterator(source);
  String result = "";
  for (char c = iter.last();
    c != CharacterIterator.DONE;
    c = iter.previous())
    result += c;
  return result;
}
```

This example iterates backwards through the specified String using the previous() method to form a reversed string. So, if you call the revert() method, passing "This is a test," based on the following snippet of code:

```
String t = revert('This is a test');
System.out.println(t);
```

it produces the following output:

```
tset a si sihT
```

Fields None

Constructors

Modifiers	Constructor
public	StringCharacterIterator(String)
public	StringCharacterIterator(String, int)
public	StringCharacterIterator(String, int, int, int)

Methods

Modifiers	Return Type	Method
public	Object	clone()
public	char	current()
public	boolean	equals(Object)
public	char	first()
public	int	getBeginIndex()
public	int	getEndIndex()
public	int	getIndex()
public	int	hashCode()
public	char	last()
public	char	next()
public	char	previous()
public	char	setIndex(int)

See Also java.lang.Object • java.text.CharacterIterator

The java.util Package

22

The java.util package is considered the miscellaneous package containing odds and ends in the Java Class Library. This package contains various classes representing a variety of data structures (among other things) that you can use in your Java programs.

Java 1.1 has added several root classes, including the EventListener and EventObject classes, by which all listener and event type classes must extend. Also, new in 1.1 are several classes belonging to the International application programming interface (API) used to handle locale-sensitive date/time operations.

Class BitSet

public final synchronized java.util.BitSet extends java.lang.Object implements java.lang.Cloneable, java.io.Serializable

The BitSet class represents a vector of bits. Like all vectors, BitSet objects can grow dynamically on an as-needed basis. This class is used for performing various bitwise operations including and, or, and exclusive or.

Syntax & Usage

Each bit in a BitSet object is represented as a **boolean**. If a bit is "set" (via the set() method) it is **true**. If a bit is "clear" (via the clear() method), then it is **false** (which is the default). This example shows usage of the BitSet class:

```
BitSet src = new BitSet(4);
src.set(0);
src.set(3);
BitSet mask = new BitSet(4);
mask.set(2);
mask.set(3);

BitSet bAnd = (BitSet)src.clone();
bAnd.and(mask);
BitSet bOr  = (BitSet)src.clone();
bOr.or(mask);
BitSet bXor = (BitSet)src.clone();
bXor.xor(mask);

for (int k=0; k<4; k++)
   System.out.println(k+" "+bAnd.get(k)+
   " "+bOr.get(k)+" "+bXor.get(k));
```

This example creates two BitSet instances: src and mask. Then it performs the and(), or(), and xor() bitwise operations on these two bit sets, printing their results:

```
0 false true  true
1 false false false
2 false true  true
3 true  true  false
```

Fields

None

Constructors

Modifiers	Constructor
public	BitSet()
public	BitSet(int)

Methods

Modifiers	Return Type	Method
public	void	and(BitSet)
public	void	clear(int)
public	Object	clone()
public	boolean	equals(Object)
public	boolean	get(int)
public	int	hashCode()
public	void	or(BitSet)
public	void	set(int)
public	int	size()
public	String	toString()
public	void	xor(BitSet)

See Also java.io.Serializable • java.lang.Cloneable • java.lang.Object • java.util.Vector

Class Calendar

public abstract synchronized java.util.Calendar extends java.lang.Object implements java.io.Serializable, java.lang.Cloneable

The Calendar class is an **abstract** class used to interpret various locale-sensitive data from a given Date object to either a string or integer format.

Syntax & Usage Subclasses of this class determine how to interpret a Date object according to a specified calendar system. Currently, Java 1.1 has one concrete subclass available: GregorianCalendar. Please see the section for that class, later in this chapter, for more information.

Note

Other subclasses could represent the various types of calendars in use in many parts of the world.

Fields

Modifiers	Type	Field
public static final	int	AM
public static final	int	AM_PM
public static final	int	APRIL
protected	boolean	areFieldsSet
public static final	int	AUGUST
public static final	int	DATE
public static final	int	DAY_OF_MONTH
public static final	int	DAY_OF_WEEK
public static final	int	DAY_OF_WEEK_IN_MONTH
public static final	int	DAY_OF_YEAR
public static final	int	DECEMBER
public static final	int	DST_OFFSET
public static final	int	ERA
public static final	int	FEBRUARY
protected	int[]	fields
public static final	int	FIELD_COUNT
public static final	int	FRIDAY
public static final	int	HOUR
public static final	int	HOUR_OF_DAY
protected	Z[]	isSet
protected	boolean	isTimeSet
public static final	int	JANUARY
public static final	int	JULY
public static final	int	JUNE
public static final	int	MARCH
public static final	int	MAY
public static final	int	MILLISECOND
public static final	int	MINUTE
public static final	int	MONDAY
public static final	int	MONTH
public static final	int	NOVEMBER
public static final	int	OCTOBER
public static final	int	PM
public static final	int	SATURDAY
public static final	int	SECOND
public static final	int	SEPTEMBER
public static final	int	SUNDAY
public static final	int	THURSDAY
protected	long	time

Modifiers	Type	Field
public static final	int	TUESDAY
public static final	int	UNDECIMBER
public static final	int	WEDNESDAY
public static final	int	WEEK_OF_MONTH
public static final	int	WEEK_OF_YEAR
public static final	int	YEAR
public static final	int	ZONE_OFFSET

Constructors

Modifiers	Constructor
protected	Calendar()
protected	Calendar(TimeZone, Locale)

Methods

Modifiers	Return Type	Method
public abstract	void	add(int, int)
public abstract	boolean	after(Object)
public abstract	boolean	before(Object)
public final	void	clear()
public final	void	clear(int)
public	Object	clone()
protected	void	complete()
protected abstract	void	computeFields()
protected abstract	void	computeTime()
public abstract	boolean	equals(Object)
public final	int	get(int)
public static synchronized	Locale[]	getAvailableLocales()
public	int	getFirstDayOfWeek()
public abstract	int	getGreatestMinimum(int)
public static synchronized	Calendar	getInstance()
public static synchronized	Calendar	getInstance(Locale)
public static synchronized	Calendar	getInstance(TimeZone)
public static synchronized	Calendar	getInstance(TimeZone, Locale)
public abstract	int	getLeastMaximum(int)
public abstract	int	getMaximum(int)
public	int	getMinimalDaysInFirstWeek()
public abstract	int	getMinimum(int)
public final	Date	getTime()
protected	long	getTimeInMillis()
public	TimeZone	getTimeZone()

Modifiers	Return Type	Method
protected final	int	internalGet(int)
public	boolean	isLenient()
public final	boolean	isSet(int)
public abstract	void	roll(int, boolean)
public final	void	set(int, int)
public final	void	set(int, int, int)
public final	void	set(int, int, int, int, int)
public final	void	set(int, int, int, int, int, int)
public	void	setFirstDayOfWeek(int)
public	void	setLenient(boolean)
public	void	setMinimalDaysInFirstWeek(int)
public final	void	setTime(Date)
protected	void	setTimeInMillis(long)
public	void	setTimeZone(TimeZone)

See Also java.io.Serializable • java.lang.Cloneable • java.lang.Object • java.text.DateFormat • java.util.Date • java.util.TimeZone

Class Date

public synchronized java.util.Date extends java.lang.Object implements java.io.Serializable, java.lang.Cloneable

The Date class is used to encapsulate a date and time using millisecond precision.

Changes in Java 1.1

In Java 1.0 this class is the basic utility class for anything date related including parsing a given string to a Date object and vice versa. However, with Java 1.1 and its inclusion of the International API, most of the functionality for this class has been turned over to the java.util.Calendar and java.text.DateFormat classes to support locale-sensitive dates. Please see the previous section, "Class Calendar," and "Class DateFormat" in Chapter 21 for more information.

Syntax & Usage This class can retrieve today's date (as determined by your computer's internal clock) or any date that you specify. The time also can be a part of the date retrieved from the Date class.

The following is a list of constructors you can use to create instances of the Date class:

Note

One of the Date constructors (the one that takes a String parameter) has been deprecated for Java 1.1 and therefore is not documented here.

- Date(long milliseconds)
- Date(int year, int month, int date)
- Date(int year, int month, int date, int hours, int minutes)
- Date(int year, int month, int date, int hours, int minutes, int seconds)

Tip

To create an instance of the current date, use the Date constructor without parameters:

```
Date today = new Date();
```

Table 22-1 describes the parameters (with examples) that are passed (in varying combinations) to the four Date constructors.

Type	Format	Example	Value Passed
year	Year - 1900	1956	56
month	0-11	June	5
date	1-31	15	15
day	0-6	Sunday	0
hour	0-23	9:00 PM	21
minute	0-59	25 min. past the hr.	25
second	0-59	30 sec. past the min.	30
milliseconds	May 14 13:18:47 EDT 1997	Number of milliseconds since midnight Jan. 1, 1970	863630327441

Table 22-1: Parameters and examples for Date constructors.

Several methods in this class have been deprecated in the JDK 1.1. To access and modify parts of a Date object, you now need to use implementations of the Calendar class and set the Date object using the setTime() method:

```
Calendar calendar = Calendar.getInstance();
setTime(date);
```

Then you can use get() and set() methods from the Calendar class.

Several methods in the Date class have been deprecated.

Deprecated Method	Replaced by
int getDate()	int Calendar.get(Calendar.DAY_OF_MONTH)
int getDay()	int Calendar.get(Calendar.DAY_OF_WEEK)
int getHours()	int Calendar.get(Calendar.HOUR)
int getMinutes()	int Calendar.get(Calendar.MINUTE)
int getMonth()	int Calendar.get(Calendar.MONTH)
int getSeconds()	int Calendar.get(Calendar.SECOND)
int getYear()	int Calendar.get(Calendar.YEAR)
setDate(int value)	Calendar.set(Calendar.DAY_OF_MONTH, int value)
setDay(int value)	Calendar.set(Calendar.DAY_OF_WEEK, int value)
setHours(int value)	Calendar.set(Calendar.HOUR, int value)
setMinutes(int value)	Calendar.set(Calendar.MINUTE, int value)
setMonth(int value)	Calendar.set(Calendar.MONTH, int value)
setSeconds(int value)	Calendar.set(Calendar.SECOND, int value)
SetYear(int value)	Calendar.set(Calendar.YEAR, int value)

Fields None

Constructors

Modifiers	Constructor
public	Date()
public	Date(int, int, int)
public	Date(int, int, int, int, int)
public	Date(int, int, int, int, int, int)
public	Date(long)
public	Date(String)

Methods

Modifiers	Return Type	Method
public	boolean	after(Date)
public	boolean	before(Date)
public	boolean	equals(Object)
public	int	getDate()
public	int	getDay()
public	int	getHours()
public	int	getMinutes()
public	int	getMonth()
public	int	getSeconds()
public	long	getTime()
public	int	getTimezoneOffset()

Modifiers	Return Type	Method
public	int	getYear()
public	int	hashCode()
public static	long	parse(String)
public	void	setDate(int)
public	void	setHours(int)
public	void	setMinutes(int)
public	void	setMonth(int)
public	void	setSeconds(int)
public	void	setTime(long)
public	void	setYear(int)
public	String	toGMTString()
public	String	toLocaleString()
public	String	toString()
public static	long	UTC(int, int, int, int, int, int)

See Also java.io.Serializable • java.lang.Cloneable • java.lang.Object • java.text.DateFormat • java.util.Calendar • java.util.TimeZone

Class Dictionary

public abstract synchronized java.util.Dictionary extends java.lang.Object

The Dictionary class is an **abstract** class that defines the methods necessary for mapping a name object (referred to as a key) to another object (i.e., referred to as a value). By referencing the key object, you can gain access to the value object. Note that while each key can have only one value, a value can contain several keys.

> **Note**
>
> *No key or value object can be **null**.*

Syntax & Usage The following lists this class's subclasses:

- java.security.Provider
- java.util.Hashtable
- java.util.Properties

For more information on these two packages, please see the appropriate sections, later in this chapter, and also see "Class Provider," in Chapter 17.

Fields None

Constructors

Modifiers	Constructor
public	Dictionary()

Methods

Modifiers	Return Type	Method
public abstract	Enumeration	elements()
public abstract	Object	get(Object)
public abstract	boolean	isEmpty()
public abstract	Enumeration	keys()
public abstract	Object	put(Object, Object)
public abstract	Object	remove(Object)
public abstract	int	size()

See Also java.lang.Object • java.security.Provider • java.util.Hashtable • java.util.Properties

Class EmptyStackException

public synchronized java.util.EmptyStackException extends java.lang.RuntimeException

The EmptyStackException exception is thrown any time an operation is performed on a given stack that is currently empty.

Syntax & Usage This exception can be thrown by the pop() and peek() methods in the Stack class when the corresponding stack is empty.

Tip

*To avoid this exception being thrown, you should call the empty() method from the Stack class, which returns a **true** if this Stack object is empty.*

Please see "Class Stack," later in this chapter, for more information.

Fields None

Constructors

Modifiers	Constructor
public	EmptyStackException()

Methods None

See Also java.lang.RuntimeException • java.util.Stack

Interface Enumeration

public abstract interface java.util.Enumeration

The Enumeration interface provides the functionality to systematically access a data structure (e.g., a hashtable) that does not have an array like index format.

Syntax & Usage In implementing this interface, you must provide two methods: boolean hasMoreElements() and Object nextElement(). Then you can access all elements in a given data structure using these methods in a simple loop, for example:

```
for (Enumeration e = getEnumeration(); e.hasMoreElements(); )
   {
   Object obj = e.nextElement();
   // do something with obj
   }
```

Please see "Class Vector," the last section in this chapter, for more information.

Fields None

Constructors None

Methods

Modifiers	Return Type	Method
public abstract	boolean	hasMoreElements()
public abstract	Object	nextElement()

See Also java.util.Hashtable • java.util.Vector

Interface EventListener

public interface java.util.EventListener

The EventListener interface is the root interface that all interfaces must extend in order to be considered a listener interface.

Syntax & Usage A listener interface is part of the new delegation-event-handling model in which events (i.e., event objects—please see the next section, "Class EventObject," for more information) are originated from a source object (usually a widget or container) and passed to the registered listening objects (i.e., listeners).

For an object to be a listener, it must implement a corresponding listener interface in which that interface will extend (either directly or indirectly) EventListener. For more information, please see the sections for the ActionListener, AdjustmentListener, ComponentListener, and the numerous other listener classes in Chapter 4, "The java.awt.event Package."

Note

The delegation-event-handling model also is used by Java Beans. Please see Chapter 7, "The java.beans Package," for more information.

Fields None

Constructors None

Methods None

See Also java.awt.event.* • java.beans.* • java.util.EventObject

Class EventObject

public synchronized java.util.EventObject extends java.lang.Object implements java.io.Serializable

The EventObject class is the root class that all events must extend in order to be considered an event type.

Syntax & Usage A hierarchy of events that extend this class (either directly or indirectly) is part of the new delegation-event-handling model. In this model, events are no longer represented as a single java.awt.Event object with an ID used to identify the type of event. Instead, there are specific classes to represent specific event types. Please see the sections for the ActionListener, AdjustmentListener, ComponentListener, and the numerous other listener classes in Chapter 4 for details.

Fields

Modifiers	Type	Field
protected transient	Object	source

Constructors

Modifiers	Constructor
public	EventObject(Object)

Methods

Modifiers	Return Type	Method
public	Object	getSource()
public	String	toString()

See Also java.awt.event.* • java.io.Serializable • java.lang.Object • java.util.EventListener

Class GregorianCalendar

public synchronized java.util.GregorianCalendar extends java.util.Calendar

The GregorianCalendar class is a Calendar subclass that implements a Gregorian calendar (a calendar system implemented by Pope Gregory XIII in 1582 changing New Year's Day from March 25 to January 1), using a BC/AD era format.

Syntax & Usage You can get an instance of this class using one of its constructors, which let you specify various combinations of dates and times. There are also constructors that let you specify Locale objects or TimeZone objects as well. The following example extends this class and implements the method diffTime(), computing the time difference between two time moments as specified by a year, month, day, hour, and minute:

```
class myCalendar extends GregorianCalendar
{
   public myCalendar(TimeZone tz)
   {
      super(tz);
   }

   public double diffTime(int y1, int m1,
      int d1, int h1, int n1, int y2, int m2,
      int d2, int h2, int n2)
   {
      try
      {
         set(y1, m1, d1, h1, n1);
         computeTime();
         long l1 = getTimeInMillis();
         set(y2, m2, d2, h2, n2);
         computeTime();
         long l2 = getTimeInMillis();
         return (l2-l1)/(60.0*60.0*1000.0);
      }
      catch(IllegalArgumentException e)
      {
         System.out.println(
            "Error: "+e.getMessage());
         return 0.0;
      }
   }
}
```

The constructor merely takes the specified TimeZone object and passes it to its parent.

The diffTime() method uses the set() method from this class to set the specified values for the year, month, day, and minute so the computTime() method can compute the time that these values specify. The getTimeInMillis() method returns this newly computed time as a **long** value (i.e., the number of milliseconds from epoch (i.e., January 1, 1970)). Notice that the preceding example performs this operation twice: once for the *X1* parameters and again for the *X2* parameters. Then, the method diffTime() returns the difference (in hours) between these two times.

The following example uses an instance of the myCalendar class (shown previously) and creates a SimpleTimeZone object corresponding to Eastern Standard Time (i.e., with a minus 5-hour offset) and sets the rules to start daylight savings on the first Sunday in April and to end daylight savings on the last Sunday in October. Then it uses the myCalendar object to calculate the length of the day for April 6, 1997, and for October 26, 1997:

```
SimpleTimeZone est = new SimpleTimeZone(
   -5 * 60 * 60 * 1000, "EST");
est.setStartRule(Calendar.APRIL, 1,
   Calendar.SUNDAY, 2 * 60 * 60 * 1000);
est.setEndRule(Calendar.OCTOBER, -1,
   Calendar.SUNDAY, 2 * 60 * 60 * 1000);
myCalendar calendar = new myCalendar(est);

double d1 = calendar.diffTime(
   1997, Calendar.APRIL, 6, 0, 0,
   1997, Calendar.APRIL, 7, 0, 0);
System.out.println(
   "Daylight savings begin: "+d1+" hrs.");
double d2 = calendar.diffTime(
   1997, Calendar.OCTOBER, 26, 0, 0,
   1997, Calendar.OCTOBER, 27, 0, 0);
System.out.println(
   "Daylight savings end  : "+d2+" hrs.");
```

This produces the following output:

```
Daylight savings begin: 23.0 hrs.

Daylight savings end  : 25.0 hrs.
```

Note

As you can see, it is not always correct to assume that each and every day in a year has 24 hours. It can be 23 or 25 hours because of daylight savings changes.

Fields

Modifiers	Type	Field
public static final	int	AD
public static final	int	BC

Constructors

Modifiers	Constructor
public	GregorianCalendar()
public	GregorianCalendar(int, int, int)
public	GregorianCalendar(int, int, int, int, int)
public	GregorianCalendar(int, int, int, int, int, int)
public	GregorianCalendar(Locale)
public	GregorianCalendar(TimeZone)
public	GregorianCalendar(TimeZone, Locale)

Methods

Modifiers	Return Type	Method
public	void	add(int, int)
public	boolean	after(Object)
public	boolean	before(Object)
public	Object	clone()
protected	void	computeFields()
protected	void	computeTime()
public	boolean	equals(Object)
public	int	getGreatestMinimum(int)
public final	Date	getGregorianChange()
public	int	getLeastMaximum(int)
public	int	getMaximum(int)
public	int	getMinimum(int)
public synchronized	int	hashCode()
public	boolean	isLeapYear(int)
public	void	roll(int, boolean)
public	void	setGregorianChange(Date)

See Also java.util.Calendar • java.util.TimeZone

Class Hashtable

public synchronized java.util.Hashtable extends java.util.Dictionary implements java.lang.Cloneable, java.io.Serializable

The Hashtable class is a Dictionary subclass that represents a hashtable in Java. A hashtable takes an association between a key name and a given value (see "Class Dictionary," earlier in this chapter, for definitions of these terms) and uses a hash function on the key to create a hash code to index the key to a slot—commonly referred to as a *hash bucket* (which can contain more than one key). These hash buckets are in turn organized using a sorting algorithm.

The advantage of a hashtable is that, if properly tweaked, it can provide an efficient method for storing and retrieving values (i.e., objects) because you do not need to search through the entire table to locate the given key that refers to the desired value.

For example, when you go to look up a topic (i.e., a value) in a set of encyclopedias, you first mentally choose a word or phrase that summarizes the desired topic (i.e., a key). Then you start by pulling the volume (i.e., the hash bucket), based on the first letter of that word or phrase (i.e., the hash for that key), and begin your linear search from there.

Syntax & Usage

Hashtables have two attributes: a capacity and a load factor. Specifying a capacity lets the Hashtable know how many hash buckets it is allowed to use. A load factor represents its entry/bucket ratio. Along these lines in this class's constructor, you optionally can specify a load factor threshold value. This value must be between 0 and 1 (which is used to specify a percentile), representing a cutoff for how full the table is allowed to get before it should be expanded.

Note

If you do not specify a capacity and/or a load factor threshold, the default capacity of 101 and a load factor threshold of 75 percent is implemented.

So, for example, if you specify .5 for the threshold, it means that if the entries have collectively filled 50 percent of the available buckets, the Hashtable object will be rehashed to twice its current capacity. The compromise is that lowering the load factor decreases the access time, but it also increases the amount of space needed. On the other hand, raising the load saves space but increases the opportunity for name collisions (i.e., two or more keys being hashed to the same value, which must in turn be reconciled inside the given bucket), thus resulting in a hit on performance.

Note

Typically, if you are more interested in performance, a load factor of 50 percent is a good figure without being too wasteful of the space needed. On the other hand, if you're more interested in saving space, a load factor of 75 percent is fairly efficient (space-wise) without costing too much in performance. Note that hashtable performance is very dependent on the type of data, so use these figures as starting points only.

The following code snippet creates a Hashtable object (meals) using the put() method from this class to populate the table. It assumes that corresponding classes exist and uses the names of the meals as its keys (i.e., String objects):

```
Hashtable meals = new Hashtable();
meals.put("steak", new Steak());
meals.put("pizza", new Pizza());
meals.put("salad", new Salad());
```

Note

For an object to be used as a key, it must implement the hashCode() and the equals() methods.

To retrieve objects stored in the meals hashtable, the following code snippet uses the get() method from this class to retrieve the stored Pizza object:

```
Object obj = meals.get("pizza");
if (obj != null)
   System.out.println("pizza: " +
   obj.toString());
```

Tip

*To be safe, always verify that an object reference retrieved from Hashtable is not **null**.*

Fields None

Constructors

Modifiers	Constructor
public	Hashtable()
public	Hashtable(int)
public	Hashtable(int, float)

Methods

Modifiers	Return Type	Method
public synchronized	void	clear()
public synchronized	Object	clone()
public synchronized	boolean	contains(Object)
public synchronized	boolean	containsKey(Object)
public synchronized	Enumeration	elements()
public synchronized	Object	get(Object)
public	boolean	isEmpty()
public synchronized	Enumeration	keys()
public synchronized	Object	put(Object, Object)
protected	void	rehash()
public synchronized	Object	remove(Object)
public	int	size()
public synchronized	String	toString()

See Also java.io.Serializable • java.lang.Cloneable • java.lang.String • java.util.Dictionary • java.util.Vector

Class ListResourceBundle

public abstract synchronized java.util.ListResourceBundle extends java.util.ResourceBundle

The ListResourceBundle class is an **abstract** ResourceBundle subclass designed to house various resources for a locale in a list.

Syntax & Usage

To use this class, you need to subclass it, and when doing that, you must override the getContents() method that returns a two-dimensional array of objects. The first object is the key (i.e., a String object), and the second corresponds to the actual resource. The following shows two subclasses of this class, which hold string resources for the English and French languages, respectively:

```
// English language resources (default)
class TextResource extends ListResourceBundle
{
   public Object[][] getContents()
   {
      return contents;
   }

   static final Object[][] contents =
   {
      {"welcome", "Welcome to my international Java application"},
      {"today", "Today is :"},
      {"money", "You have got :"}
   };
}

// French language resources
class TextResource_fr extends
   ListResourceBundle
{
   public Object[][] getContents()
   {
      return contents;
   }

   static final Object[][] contents =
   {
      {"welcome", "Bienvenue dans mon application internationale"},
      {"today", "Date :"},
      {"money", "Vous avez obtenu :"}
   };
}
```

Fields None

Constructors

Modifiers	Constructor
public	ListResourceBundle()

Methods

Modifiers	Return Type	Method
protected abstract	Object[]	getContents()
public	Enumeration	getKeys()
public final	Object	handleGetObject(String)

See Also java.util.Locale • java.util.MissingResourceException • java.util.PropertyResourceBundle • java.util.ResourceBundle

Class Locale

public final synchronized java.util.Locale extends java.lang.Object implements java.lang.Cloneable, java.io.Serializable

The Locale class is used to represent a locale in Java. A locale specifies a geographic location that affects how a program should behave in that surrounding. Locales affect dates, times, numbers, currency, and text and how all of these things are to be displayed. Java 1.1's addition of the International API has provided the functionality to allow your programs to be flexible in all these areas.

Syntax & Usage The Locale class is a collection of rules governing how text, dates, numbers, and so forth are to be formatted based on country- and language-sensitive rules. Other classes in the International API use the Locale class to retrieve and implement these rules. You create a Locale object using one of the two constructors available in this class:

- Locale(String language, String country)
- Locale(String language, String country, String variant)

You also can use the predefined locales represented in this class as **final** fields, for example:

```
Locale default = Locale.US;
```

This class is a key part of the International API and is used by numerous other Java classes. Please see the sections for the BreakIterator, CollationElementIterator, DateFormat, DecimalFormat, and DecimalFormatSymbols classes in Chapter 21 for more information.

Fields

Modifiers	Type	Field
public static final	Locale	CANADA
public static final	Locale	CANADA_FRENCH
public static final	Locale	CHINA
public static final	Locale	CHINESE
public static final	Locale	ENGLISH
public static final	Locale	FRANCE
public static final	Locale	FRENCH
public static final	Locale	GERMAN
public static final	Locale	GERMANY
public static final	Locale	ITALIAN
public static final	Locale	ITALY
public static final	Locale	JAPAN
public static final	Locale	JAPANESE
public static final	Locale	KOREA
public static final	Locale	KOREAN
public static final	Locale	PRC
public static final	Locale	SIMPLIFIED_CHINESE
public static final	Locale	TAIWAN
public static final	Locale	TRADITIONAL_CHINESE
public static final	Locale	UK
public static final	Locale	US

Constructors

Modifiers	Constructor
public	Locale(String, String)
public	Locale(String, String, String)

Methods

Modifiers	Return Type	Method
public	Object	clone()
public	boolean	equals(Object)
public	String	getCountry()
public static synchronized	Locale	getDefault()
public final	String	getDisplayCountry()
public	String	getDisplayCountry(Locale)

Modifiers	Return Type	Method
public final	String	getDisplayLanguage()
public	String	getDisplayLanguage(Locale)
public final	String	getDisplayName()
public	String	getDisplayName(Locale)
public final	String	getDisplayVariant()
public	String	getDisplayVariant(Locale)
public	String	getISO3Country()
public	String	getISO3Language()
public	String	getLanguage()
public	String	getVariant()
public synchronized	int	hashCode()
public static synchronized	void	setDefault(Locale)
public final	String	toString()

See Also java.io.Serializable • java.lang.Cloneable • java.lang.Object • java.text.BreakIterator • java.text.CollationElementIterator • java.text.DateFormat • java.text.DecimalFormat • java.text.DecimalFormatSymbols • java.util.GregorianCalendar • java.util.ResourceBundle

Class MissingResourceException

public synchronized java.util.MissingResourceException extends java.lang.RuntimeException

The MissingResourceException exception is thrown any time a resource could not be located.

Syntax & Usage This exception can be thrown by the get*XXX*() methods in the ResourceBundle class signaling that the resource for the specified key is currently unavailable. Consider the following:

```
static public String getResourceString(
   ResourceBundle bundle, String key)
{
   try
   {
      return bundle.getString(key);
   }
```

```
   catch (MissingResourceException e)
   {
      System.err.println(
         "Can't find resource for "+key);
      return null;
   }
}
```

This example retrieves the specified String resource from the specified ResourceBundle instance and catches MissingResourceException if it is missing.

Note

This exception also may be the result of an improperly named ResourceBundle. Please see "Class ResourceBundle," later in this chapter, for more information.

Fields None

Constructors

Modifiers	Constructor
public	MissingResourceException(String, String, String)

Methods

Modifiers	Return Type	Method
public	String	getClassName()
public	String	getKey()

See Also java.lang.RuntimeException • java.util.ListResourceBundle • java.util.PropertyResourceBundle • java.util.ResourceBundle

Class NoSuchElementException

public synchronized java.util.NoSuchElementException extends java.lang.RuntimeException

NoSuchElementException is thrown any time there is a reference to the next element in some given object implementing the Enumeration interface that has no more elements.

Syntax & Usage This exception may be thrown by the nextElement() method of an Enumeration implementation when you have reached the end of the enumeration. Please see "Interface Enumeration," earlier in this chapter, for details.

> **Note**
>
> *If you use the hasMoreElements() method from the Enumeration interface, you do not need to worry about catching this exception.*

Fields None

Constructors

Modifiers	Constructor
public	NoSuchElementException()
public	NoSuchElementException(String)

Methods None

See Also java.lang.RuntimeException • java.util.Enumeration

Class Observable

public synchronized java.util.Observable extends java.lang.Object

The Observable class is used to encapsulate the class to be "observed" in an Observable/Observer setup. This model view controller concept, borrowed from Smalltalk, lets a registered list of observing objects (i.e., observers) receive notification about various changes in another object (i.e., an observable). This class represents the base class (which must be subclassed) to be an observable.

Syntax & Usage Subclasses of this class have the ability to assign or remove observers (i.e., objects that implement the Observer interface; please see the next section for more information) using the addObserver() and deleteObserver() methods from this class. When a change occurs in the given Observable subclass, it can notify registered observers using the notifyObservers() method, which will call the Observer object's update() methods.

Fields None

Constructors

Modifiers	Constructor
public	Observable()

Methods

Modifiers	Return Type	Method
public synchronized	void	addObserver(Observer)
protected synchronized	void	clearChanged()
public synchronized	int	countObservers()
public synchronized	void	deleteObserver(Observer)
public synchronized	void	deleteObservers()
public synchronized	boolean	hasChanged()
public	void	notifyObservers()
public	void	notifyObservers(Object)
protected synchronized	void	setChanged()

See Also java.lang.Object • java.util.Observer

Interface Observer

public abstract interface java.util.Observer

The Observer interface is an **abstract** interface that is implemented by any class needing to be an "observer" in an Observable/Observer setup. This model view controller concept, borrowed from Smalltalk, lets a list of observing objects (i.e., observers) receive notification about various changes in another object (i.e., an observable). This class represents the base interface (which must be implemented) to be an observer.

Syntax & Usage Implementations of this interface must implement the update(Observable, Object) method, which is called whenever the observed object (i.e., the Observable) is changed and sends notification to its Observers via a notifyObservers() method call from that class.

Fields None

Constructors None

Methods

Modifiers	Return Type	Method
public abstract	void	update(Observable, Object)

See Also java.util.Observable

Class Properties

public synchronized java.util.Properties extends java.util.Hashtable

The Properties class is used in Java to provide a way to generically store and manage properties in a key/value format (please see "Class Dictionary," earlier in this chapter, for more information on those terms) in what is known as a property list.

Syntax & Usage

This class uses streams to store and retrieve various properties and also gives you the (optional) ability to specify a second property list, which can act as a default if the first property list does not contain the requested key.

This class is used throughout Java when there is a need to persistently store properties. For instance, it is used by the java.lang.System class to store various system properties. It also is used in the Java Database Connectivity (JDBC) API to specify various database/driver properties. The following code snippet retrieves and prints a list of system properties using the getProperties() method from the System class:

```
Properties sysProp = System.getProperties();
Enumeration en = sysProp.propertyNames();
while (en.hasMoreElements())
{
   String key  = (String)en.nextElement();
   String text = (String)sysProp.get(key);
   System.out.println(key+"\t"+text);
}
```

You can see that this uses the propertyNames() method from this class to obtain an Enumeration of all keys present in the System property list. Then it prints all keys and corresponding values. Here's what the output might look like:

```
user.language   en
java.home       C:\JAVA\BIN\..
awt.toolkit     sun.awt.windows.WToolkit
file.encoding.pkg       sun.io
java.version    1.1_Final
file.separator  \
line.separator
```

```
user.region     US
file.encoding   8859_1
java.vendor     Sun Microsystems Inc.
user.timezone   EST
user.name       unknown
os.arch x86
os.name Windows 95
java.vendor.url http://www.sun.com/
user.dir        C:\B
java.class.path .;C:\JAVA\BIN\..\classes;
  C:\JAVA\BIN\..\lib\classes.zip
java.class.version      45.3
os.version      4.0
path.separator  ;
user.home       C:\JAVA\BIN\..
```

Tip

To retrieve a single system property, you can use the get(Object key) method inherited from the Dictionary class.

Fields

Modifiers	Type	Field
protected	Properties	defaults

Constructors

Modifiers	Constructor
public	Properties()
public	Properties(Properties)

Methods

Modifiers	Return Type	Method
public	String	getProperty(String)
public	String	getProperty(String, String)
public	void	list(PrintStream)
public	void	list(PrintWriter)
public synchronized	void	load(InputStream)
public	Enumeration	propertyNames()
public synchronized	void	save(OutputStream, String)

See Also java.lang.System • java.util.Dictionary • java.util.Enumeration • java.util.Hashtable

Class PropertyResourceBundle

public synchronized java.util.PropertyResourceBundle extends java.util.ResourceBundle

The PropertyResourceBundle class is a ResourceBundle subclass that lets you manage various resources for a given locale using a set of properties from a given file.

Syntax & Usage This subclass was created so that rather than having to create a variety of ResourceBundle subclasses to provide resources for a given Locale object, you can simply create a PropertyResourceBundle subclass and a properties file that stores the actual key/value pair resources.

> **Note**
>
> *The naming convention for the actual properties file is the same as the one used for ResourceBundles (please see "Class ResourceBundle," later in this chapter, for more information), with the actual properties file having the same name but ending with the .properties extension.*

The following example shows a subclass of this class that retrieves the value for three keys:

```
class myBundle extends PropertyResourceBundle
{
  String m_sTitle;
  Double m_dRate;
  Image  m_Map;

  public myBundle(ObjectInputStream stream)
    throws IOException,ClassNotFoundException
  {
    super(stream);
    m_sTitle = (String)stream.readObject();
    m_dRate  = (Double)stream.readObject();
    m_Map    = (Image)stream.readObject();
  }

  public Object handleGetObject(String key)
  {
    if (key.equals("Title"))
      return m_sTitle;
```

```
        if (key.equals("Rate"))
            return m_dRate;
        if (key.equals("Map"))
            return m_Map;
        return null;
    }
}
```

The handleGetObject() method in this example analyzes the parameter key and returns the correspondingly stored String, Double, or Image object. Otherwise, **null** is returned (alternatively, you could throw a MissingResourceException object here instead).

Fields None

Constructors

Modifiers	Constructor
public	PropertyResourceBundle(InputStream)

Methods

Modifiers	Return Type	Method
public	Enumeration	getKeys()
public	Object	handleGetObject(String)

See Also java.util.ListResourceBundle • java.util.Locale • java.util.MissingResourceException • java.util.ResourceBundle

Class Random

public synchronized java.util.Random extends java.lang.Object implements java.io.Serializable

The Random class is used to generate a stream of pseudorandom numbers. The randomness for these values is based on a 48-bit seed.

Syntax & Usage To use this class, you need to instantiate it wherein you can explicitly set the seed (using a **long**) or use a default seed that is determined internally by retrieving a **long** from a call to the currentTimeMillis() method from the System class representing the current time in milliseconds since January 1, 1970. Needless to say, every time you instantiate this class without explicitly specifying a seed value, it will yield a different set of pseudorandom values. To actually retrieve pseudorandom values, you need to call one of the nextXXX() methods.

The following code snippet uses this class to draw an imitation of a quasirandom signal (from some radio or electrical device):

```
Random m_Random = new Random(1997);
double dispersion = 20.0;

public void paint(Graphics g)
{
   int x, y, x1=0, y1=0;
   g.setColor(Color.yellow);
   for (x = 0; x<100; x++)
   {
      int Signal = -72 + (int)(m_Random.
         nextGaussian()*dispersion);
      y = getY(Signal);
      if (x > 0)
         g.drawLine(x1, y1, x, y);
      x1 = x;
      y1 = y;
   }
}
```

This example uses the nextGaussian() method to generate a sequence of pseudorandom numbers. The method getY() transforms the signal into screen coordinates and was not included in the text of this example for the sake of simplicity. Figure 22-1 shows the example in action (with visual enhancements added).

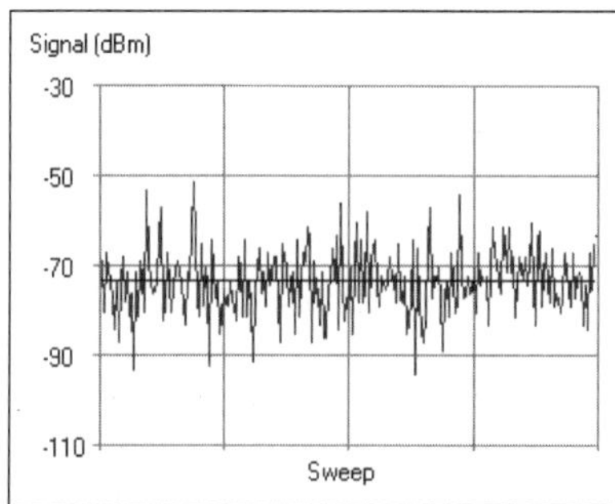

Figure 22-1: A quasirandom signal using the Random class.

Tip

If you are just looking to retrieve a basic pseudorandom value, you can use the ***static*** *random() method from the java.lang.Math class, which returns the value as a* ***double*** *inside the [0, 1] interval. This method does not have the flexibility to set the seed or determine the type of random value to be returned, but it is perfect for simple solutions that just require an arbitrary value.*

Fields None

Constructors

Modifiers	Constructor
public	Random()
public	Random(long)

Methods

Modifiers	Return Type	Method
protected synchronized	int	next(int)
public	void	nextBytes(byte[])
public	double	nextDouble()
public	float	nextFloat()
public synchronized	double	nextGaussian()
public	int	nextInt()
public	long	nextLong()
public synchronized	void	setSeed(long)

See Also java.io.Serializable • java.lang.Math • java.lang.Object

Class ResourceBundle

public abstract synchronized java.util.ResourceBundle extends java.lang.Object

The ResourceBundle class is an **abstract** class that defines a container for specific resources relating to a given locale. Each resource is based on a key/value pair (please see "Class Dictionary," earlier in this chapter, for more information on those terms) wherein the key is a String that can be used to identify the corresponding resource object (i.e., the value). Using resource bundles helps Java programs to reconcile locale-specific parts of a program with regular parts and keeps multiple locales segregated.

Syntax & Usage To use this class, you need to subclass it and override the handleGetKey() method. Usually, you will have to create several subclasses for any given locale.

When creating a subclass, it is important that it is declared as **public** and that you use a specific naming procedure wherein you can append the ISO-639 lowercase language code and also (optionally) the ISO-3166 uppercase country code. You can even (optionally) append a variant value. This way, the **static** getBundle() method (which is used to load a given ResourceBundle object) will be able to locate it automatically.

Java 1.1 defines two subclasses—ListResourceBundle and PropertyResourceBundle—which add specific enhancements to this class. Please see the sections for those two classes, elsewhere in this chapter, for more information.

Fields

Modifiers	Type	Field
protected	ResourceBundle	parent

Constructors

Modifiers	Constructor
public	ResourceBundle()

Methods

Modifiers	Return Type	Method
public static final	ResourceBundle	getBundle(String)
public static final	ResourceBundle	getBundle(String, Locale)
public abstract	Enumeration	getKeys()
public final	Menu	getMenu(String)
public final	MenuBar	getMenuBar(String)
public final	Object	getObject(String)
public final	String	getString(String)
public final	String[]	getStringArray(String)
protected abstract	Object	handleGetObject(String)
protected	void	setParent(ResourceBundle)

See Also java.lang.Object • java.util.ListResourceBundle • java.util.MissingResourceException • java.util.PropertyResourceBundle

Class SimpleTimeZone

public synchronized java.util.SimpleTimeZone extends java.util.TimeZone

The SimpleTimeZone class is a TimeZone subclass and is used in conjunction with the GregorianCalendar class to encapsulate a time zone for a given calendar.

Syntax & Usage This class provides a simple implementation for supporting time zones and daylight savings time. This is done using offsets from UCT (Universal Coordinated Time). This class, however, does not have the sophistication to support the various deviations and historical anomalies associated with time zones.

This class (and its parent TimeZone) closely relate to Calendar and its subclasses. In most cases, you need to work with only the Calendar classes and do not need to use this class directly. Please see "Class GregorianCalendar," earlier in this chapter, for an example of this class in action.

Fields None

Constructors

Modifiers	Constructor
public	SimpleTimeZone(int, String)
public	SimpleTimeZone(int, String, int, int, int, int, int, int, int, int)

Methods

Modifiers	Return Type	Method
public	Object	clone()
public	boolean	equals(Object)
public	int	getOffset(int, int, int, int, int, int)
public	int	getRawOffset()
public synchronized	int	hashCode()
public	boolean	inDaylightTime(Date)
public	void	setEndRule(int, int, int, int)
public	void	setRawOffset(int)
public	void	setStartRule(int, int, int, int)
public	void	setStartYear(int)
public	boolean	useDaylightTime()

See Also java.util.Calendar • java.util.GregorianCalendar • java.util.TimeZone

Class Stack

public synchronized java.util.Stack extends java.util.Vector

The Stack class is used to represent a LIFO (Last In First Out) stack that you can use as a temporary way to store given objects.

Syntax & Usage The stack is a common data structure used for temporarily storing some given set of items using LIFO logic. LIFO is simple to understand: Think of it as a stack of dishes. The last dish to be added to the top of the stack is the first dish to come off.

> **Note**
>
> *This class is a Vector subclass, meaning that it inherits the methods from that class and can grow and shrink dynamically on an as-needed basis.*

The following code snippet demonstrates the usage of this class:

```
Stack stack = new Stack();
for (int k=0; k<5; k++)
  stack.push(new Integer(k));

  stack.push("Five");

while(!stack.empty())
{
  System.out.println(stack.pop().toString());}
```

This example creates an instance of the Stack class and pushes five Integer objects and one String to that stack. Then it pops and prints the value of every object stored in the stack. Here's the output:

```
Five
4
3
2
1
0
```

> **Note**
>
> *The members of a given Stack object do not have to be the same object type.*

Fields None

Constructors

Modifiers	Constructor
public	Stack()

Methods

Modifiers	Return Type	Method
public	boolean	empty()
public synchronized	Object	peek()
public synchronized	Object	pop()
public	Object	push(Object)
public synchronized	int	search(Object)

See Also java.util.EmptyStackException • java.util.Vector

Class StringTokenizer

public synchronized java.util.StringTokenizer extends java.lang.Object implements java.util.Enumeration

The StringTokenizer class is used to tokenize a given String object using either a default delimiter (i.e., a white space), a specified delimiter, or a set of several delimiters. This class is quite useful in various parsing operations.

Syntax & Usage

This class allows an application to break a String into tokens using some sort of delimiter(s). The class implements the Enumeration interface, so you can access the resulting String tokens via the nextElement() method defined in this class (or synonymously the nextToken() method). You specify the String object you wish to be tokenized in this class's constructor. You also (optionally) can set other delimiters and specify a **boolean,** which, if **true,** will return the delimiters as tokens.

The following example method word wraps a given String by converting that String into tokens, using the following conditions:

- Any single text line occupies no more than wMax pixels.
- Only words separated by spaces can be wrapped to the new line (no words breaks).
- New-line characters (\n) included in the original text always make a new line.

Here's the code:

```
public void drawMessage(Graphics g,
  String text, int wMax)
{
  FontMetrics fm = g.getFontMetrics();
  int hLine = fm.getHeight();
  int y = hLine, x = 0;
```

```
    StringTokenizer Token = new
      StringTokenizer(text, " \n", true);
    while (Token.hasMoreTokens())
    {
      String sNext = Token.nextToken();

      if (sNext.equals("\n"))
      {
        y += hLine;
        x = 0;
        continue;
      }

      if (sNext.equals(" "))
      {
        if (!Token.hasMoreTokens())
          break;
        sNext = Token.nextToken();
        if (x+fm.stringWidth(sNext)<wMax)
        { // Add to the same line
          sNext = " " + sNext;
        }
        else
        { // Add to the next line
          y += hLine;
          x = 0;
        }
      }

      g.drawString(sNext, x, y);
      x += fm.stringWidth(sNext);
    }
}
```

This obtains a FontMetrics instance for the specified Graphics object (g). Then it creates a StringTokenizer object (Token), passing the specified String object (text), specifying that breaks (a.k.a. delimiters) will be caused by white spaces and new-line characters (\n) and that these breaks are to be considered tokens in and of themselves. Following that is the initialization of two **int** variables, x and y, used for the current point where the next portion of the text is to be drawn.

Then in a **while** loop, which cycles until the tokenizer is out of tokens (using the hasMoreTokens() method), the code gets the next token and processes it in the following manner:

- The first **if** condition checks to see if the token is a new-line character (\n), and if this is **true,** the code moves to the next line and continues.
- The second **if** conditional checks to see if the token is a white space. If this is **true,** then the program gets the next token (presumably a word) and checks whether we have enough room to place it in the current line. If so, it adds the space before the text. Otherwise, it does not add the space and moves to the next line.
- The code draws the line of text using the current position and adjusts the x-position after drawing.

Figure 22-2 shows a sample dialog box using this method to word wrap the text contained therein.

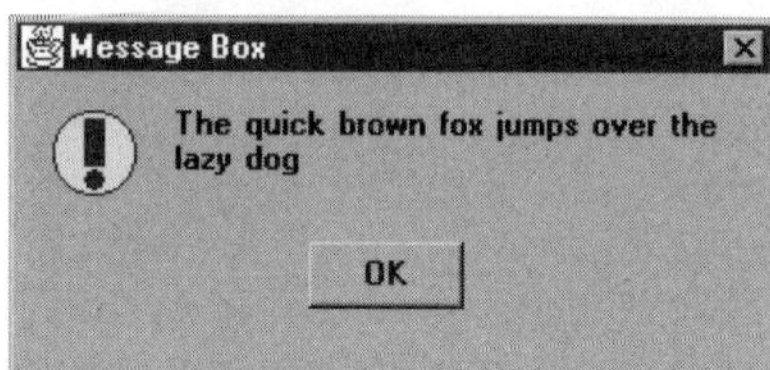

Figure 22-2: Using StringTokenizer to word wrap text.

Fields None

Constructors

Modifiers	Constructor
public	StringTokenizer(String)
public	StringTokenizer(String, String)
public	StringTokenizer(String, String, boolean)

Methods

Modifiers	Return Type	Method
public	int	countTokens()
public	boolean	hasMoreElements()
public	boolean	hasMoreTokens()
public	Object	nextElement()
public	String	nextToken()
public	String	nextToken(String)

See Also java.lang.Object • java.lang.String • java.text.BreakIterator • java.util.Enumeration

Class TimeZone

public abstract synchronized java.util.TimeZone extends java.lang.Object implements java.io.Serializable, java.lang.Cloneable

The TimeZone class is an **abstract** class used to represent various locale-sensitive time zones and daylight savings offsets from UCT.

Syntax & Usage

The TimeZone class represents a time zone offset. It is an **abstract** class, so you need to subclass it to use it. However, it does contain several **static** methods that you can use; they include getDefault() and setDefault(), which let you retrieve and specify the current time zone for a given program. The getAvailableIDs() method also is useful in returning an array of String objects representing all available time zones. Consider the following:

```
int hour = 60 * 60 * 1000;
String[] tzIDs = TimeZone.getAvailableIDs(
   -5 * hour);
TimeZone est = new SimpleTimeZone(
   -5 * hour, tzIDs[0]);
int offset = est.getRawOffset()/hour;
System.out.println("EST offset: "+offset+
" hrs.");
```

This code snippet creates an instance of the SimpleTimeZone class and uses the getRawOffset() method (inherited from this class) to determine the zone's offset in hours.

Fields None

Constructors

Modifiers	Constructor
public	TimeZone()

Methods

Modifiers	Return Type	Method
public	Object	clone()
public static synchronized	String[]	getAvailableIDs()
public static synchronized	String[]	getAvailableIDs(int)
public static synchronized	TimeZone	getDefault()
public	String	getID()

Modifiers	Return Type	Method
public abstract	int	getOffset(int, int, int, int, int, int)
public abstract	int	getRawOffset()
public static synchronized	TimeZone	getTimeZone(String)
public abstract	boolean	inDaylightTime(Date)
public static synchronized	void	setDefault(TimeZone)
public	void	setID(String)
public abstract	void	setRawOffset(int)
public abstract	boolean	useDaylightTime()

See Also java.io.Serializable • java.lang.Cloneable • java.lang.Object • java.util.Calendar • java.util.GregorianCalendar • java.util.SimpleTimeZone

Class TooManyListenersException

public synchronized java.util.TooManyListenersException extends java.lang.Exception

The TooManyListenersException exception is thrown any time there are too many listeners registered to a given object source.

Syntax & Usage The delegation-event-handling model can use this exception in situations in which an implementation of a Java object can have only a limited number of listeners.

Along these lines you can use this exception in your Java Beans implementations wherein you wish to specify a bean event to only tolerate one listener at a time. In such situations this exception is declared in the **throws** clause of the corresponding bean's addXXXListener() method. Not only does this let any users of this bean know that the given event can only tolerate a single listener at a time, but if more than one listener attempts to be registered (using the addXXXListener()), this exception is thrown.

Note

Currently none of the classes in the Java 1.1 Class Library throw this exception. However, you can throw this exception in your implementation of the addXXXListener() method if you need to limit the number of listeners.

Fields None

Constructors

Modifiers	Constructor
public	TooManyListenersException()
public	TooManyListenersException(String)

Methods None

See Also java.lang.Exception • java.util.EventListener • java.util.EventObject

Class Vector

public synchronized java.util.Vector extends java.lang.Object implements java.lang.Cloneable, java.io.Serializable

The Vector class is used to implement an array of objects that can grow and shrink dynamically on an as-needed basis.

Syntax & Usage A vector is just like an array of objects wherein each object can be accessed by an index value. However, vectors have the ability to grow and shrink dynamically and with this added functionality comes the ability to add a value to a given vector specifying a location in between two existing ones.

Tip

It is usually a good idea to specify an initial size for a vector for efficiency reasons even if it is only a hazarded guess.

When constructing a vector, you can specify (optionally) an initial size as well as specify (also optional) its incremental size (i.e., the minimum number of values that should be added when a given vector is full). The following code snippet shows the usage of the Vector class:

```
Vector vector = new Vector(10);
// Fill vector
for (int k=0; k<10; k++)
  vector.addElement(new Integer(k));
```

```
// Access stored elements
for (int j=0; j<10; j+=2)
{
   Integer i = (Integer)vector.elementAt(j);
   System.out.println(i);
}
```

This example creates a Vector object and adds 10 Integer objects to it using the addElement() method from this class. Then these elements are retrieved and printed in order with step 2. Here's the output:

```
0
2
4
6
8
```

Fields

Modifiers	Type	Field
protected	int	capacityIncrement
protected	int	elementCount
protected	Object[]	elementData

Constructors

Modifiers	Constructor
public	Vector()
public	Vector(int)
public	Vector(int, int)

Methods

Modifiers	Return Type	Method
public final synchronized	void	addElement(Object)
public final	int	capacity()
public synchronized	Object	clone()
public final	boolean	contains(Object)
public final synchronized	void	copyInto(Object[])
public final synchronized	Object	elementAt(int)
public final synchronized	Enumeration	elements()
public final synchronized	void	ensureCapacity(int)
public final synchronized	Object	firstElement()
public final	int	indexOf(Object)
public final synchronized	int	indexOf(Object, int)
public final synchronized	void	insertElementAt(Object, int)

Modifiers	Return Type	Method
public final	boolean	isEmpty()
public final synchronized	Object	lastElement()
public final	int	lastIndexOf(Object)
public final synchronized	int	lastIndexOf(Object, int)
public final synchronized	void	removeAllElements()
public final synchronized	boolean	removeElement(Object)
public final synchronized	void	removeElementAt(int)
public final synchronized	void	setElementAt(Object, int)
public final synchronized	void	setSize(int)
public final	int	size()
public final synchronized	String	toString()
public final synchronized	void	trimToSize()

See Also java.io.Serializable • java.lang.Cloneable • java.lang.Object • java.util.Stack

The java.util.zip Package

23

The java.util.zip package is a new face in Java 1.1. This package has been added to provide Java with the ability to work with data compressed in a wide variety of formats including GZIP and ZIP as well as Java ARchives (JARs)—which are nothing more than platform-independent ZIP archives.

Note

You do not need to use this package to use JARs in your Java programs, but this package is compatible with the JAR file format. For more information on JARs, please see JavaSoft's JAR page at http://java.sun.com/products/jdk/1.1/docs/guide/jar.

The actual implementations for the classes in this package are merely stream filters that either compress or uncompress data going through a specified input/output stream using a particular compression format. This package also contains several supporting classes facilitating the ability to implement a checksum algorithm to verify the integrity of the data.

Class Adler32

public synchronized java.util.zip.Adler32 extends java.lang.Object implements java.util.zip.Checksum

The Adler32 class is used to compute the checksum on a compression/decompression stream using the ADLER-32 algorithm.

Syntax & Usage

Java 1.1 offers two algorithms for performing checksum calculations: cyclic redundancy check-32 bit precision (CRC-32) and ADLER-32. The first one, CRC-32, is very reliable but takes a long time to calculate. The ADLER-32 checksum is not as reliable as CRC-32 but can be computed much faster. Nonetheless, both classes for these algorithms, Adler32 and CRC32, implement the Checksum interface and therefore use the same set of methods (with different implementations on the back end), making their use transparent from a programmer's point of view.

For more information, please see "Class CRC32," later in this chapter. For an example of checksums being computed, please see the next section, "Class CheckedInputStream."

Fields

None

Constructors

Modifiers	Constructor
public	Adler32()

Methods

Modifiers	Return Type	Method
public	long	getValue()
public	void	reset()
public	void	update(byte[])
public native	void	update(byte[], int, int)
public	void	update(int)

See Also

java.lang.Object • java.util.zip.CheckedInputStream • java.util.zip.CheckedOutputStream • java.util.zip.Checksum • java.util.zip.CRC32

Class CheckedInputStream

public synchronized java.util.zip.CheckedInputStream extends java.io.FilterInputStream

The CheckedInputStream class is a FilterInputStream subclass that is used to automatically update the checksum on data coming in from a given input stream. Note that the actual data passing through this filter do not change.

Syntax & Usage Working with this class is like working with a typical input stream filter except that in the constructor you need to specify the checksum algorithm you wish to use, and when the program has finished reading data from the stream, you need to call the getChecksum() method to retrieve the checksum value for these data.

Java 1.1 offers the CRC32 or Adler32 checksums (please see the sections for those classes, elsewhere in this chapter, for more information). But you can use any object (of your own design) that has implemented the Checksum interface. The following example method shows how to use this class:

```
static public long getCheckSum(
   InputStream stream)
{
   CheckedInputStream chStream = new
      CheckedInputStream(stream,
      new Adler32());
   try
   {
      // Read stream and update checksum
      while (chStream.read() != -1);
   }
   catch (IOException e)
   {
      System.out.println(
      "IOException: "+e.getMessage());
      return -1;
   }
   Checksum chSum = chStream.getChecksum();
   // Return the checksum
   return chSum.getValue();
}
```

This example creates an instance of the CheckedInputStream class using the specified InputStream and Adler32 instance. Until the end of stream is reached, it reads bytes from the input stream and automatically updates the checksum. Finally, this example retrieves and returns the checksum value using the getChecksum() method.

Fields None

Constructors

Modifiers	Constructor
public	CheckedInputStream(InputStream, Checksum)

Methods

Modifiers	Return Type	Method
public	Checksum	getChecksum()
public	int	read()
public	int	read(byte[], int, int)
public	long	skip(long)

See Also java.io.FilterInputStream • java.util.zip.Adler32 • java.util.zip.CheckedOutputStream • java.util.zip.CRC32

Class CheckedOutputStream

public synchronized java.util.zip.CheckedOutputStream extends java.io.FilterOutputStream

The CheckedOutputStream class is a FilterOutputStream subclass that is used to automatically update the checksum on data going out through a given output stream. Note that the actual data passing through this filter do not change.

Syntax & Usage Working with this class is like working with a typical output stream filter except that in the constructor you need to specify the checksum algorithm you wish to use, and when the program has finished sending data to the stream, you need to call the getChecksum() method to retrieve the checksum value for these data.

Java 1.1 offers the CRC32 or Adler32 checksums (please see the sections for those classes, elsewhere in this chapter, for more information). But you can use any object (of your own design) that has implemented the Checksum interface. The following example method shows how to use CheckedInputStream class:

```
static public long computeCheckSum(
  OutputStream stream, byte[] data)
{
  CheckedOutputStream chStream = new
    CheckedOutputStream(stream, new CRC32());
  try
  {
    // Write data and update checksum
    chStream.write(data, 0, data.length);
  }
  catch (IOException e)
  {
    System.out.println(
    "IOException: "+e.getMessage());
    return -1;
  }
  Checksum chSum = chStream.getChecksum();
  // Return the checksum
  return chSum.getValue();
}
```

This example creates an instance of the CheckedOutputStream class using the specified OutputStream and CRC32 instance. It then writes the given array of data to the output stream, which automatically updates the checksum. Finally, it retrieves and returns the checksum value using the getChecksum() method.

Fields None

Constructors

Modifiers	Constructor
public	CheckedOutputStream(OutputStream, Checksum)

Methods

Modifiers	Return Type	Method
public	Checksum	getChecksum()
public	void	write(byte[], int, int)
public	void	write(int)

See Also java.io.FilterOutputStream • java.util.zip.Adler32 • java.util.zip.CheckedInputStream • java.util.zip.CRC32

Interface Checksum

public abstract interface java.util.zip.Checksum

The Checksum interface is implemented by any class needing to be used to verify the integrity of some data.

Syntax & Usage It is up to the actual class to implement the specific checksum algorithm. However, in order for it to be used in Java, it must implement this interface, providing for the following methods:

- **getValue().** This method returns the computed checksum value.
- **reset().** This method resets the checksum engine.
- **update(byte[], int, int).** This method processes a given array of bytes and updates the checksum correspondingly.
- **update(int).** This method processes the byte specified, updating the checksum correspondingly.

Seldom do you need to write your own Checksum implementation; instead, use one of the two provided in this package: Adler32 or CRC32. Please see the sections for those classes, elsewhere in this chapter, for more information.

Fields None

Constructors None

Methods

Modifiers	Return Type	Method
public abstract	long	getValue()
public abstract	void	reset()
public abstract	void	update(byte[], int, int)
public abstract	void	update(int)

See Also java.util.zip.Adler32 • java.util.zip.CRC32

Class CRC32

public synchronized java.util.zip.CRC32 extends java.lang.Object implements java.util.zip.Checksum

The CRC32 class is used to compute the checksum on a compression/decompression stream using the CRC-32 algorithm.

Syntax & Usage Java 1.1 offers two algorithms for performing checksum calculations: CRC-32 and ADLER-32. The first one, CRC-32, is very reliable but takes a long time to calculate. An ADLER-32 checksum is not as reliable as CRC-32 but can be computed much faster. Nonetheless, both classes for these algorithms, Adler32 and CRC32, implement the Checksum interface and therefore use the same set of methods (with different implementations on the back end), making their use transparent from a programmer's point of view.

For more information, please see "Class Adler32," earlier in this chapter. For an example of checksums being computed, please see the sections for the CheckedOutputStream and ZipInputStream classes, elsewhere in this chapter.

Fields None

Constructors

Modifiers	Constructor
public	CRC32()

Methods

Modifiers	Return Type	Method
public	long	getValue()
public	void	reset()
public	void	update(byte[])
public native	void	update(byte[], int, int)
public	void	update(int)

See Also java.lang.Object • java.util.zip.CheckedOutputStream • java.util.zip.Checksum • java.util.zip.CRC32 • java.util.zip.ZipInputStream

Class DataFormatException

public synchronized java.util.zip.DataFormatException extends java.lang.Exception

DataFormatException is thrown any time there is an error formatting the data for a given compression/decompression operation.

Syntax & Usage This exception can be thrown by any of the overloaded inflate() methods in the Inflater class when the format for the data to be inflated is not valid. Please see "Class Inflater," later in this chapter, for more information.

Fields None

Constructors

Modifiers	Constructor
public	DataFormatException()
public	DataFormatException(String)

Methods None

See Also java.lang.Exception • java.util.zip.Inflater • java.util.zip.ZipException

Class Deflater

public synchronized java.util.zip.Deflater extends java.lang.Object

The Deflater class is used to perform compression of some given binary data based on the ZLIB compression library.

Note

The ZLIB compression library was written as a freely distributed technology to compress/decompress data without regard to the processor, operating system, or format of the data and with complete regard to data integrity. It also is flexible internally wherein it can use a variety of compression algorithms. For more information on this library, please go to http://www.cdrom.com/pub/info/infozip/pub/zlib.

Syntax & Usage Usually you do not use this class directly; instead, you use the ZipOutputStream class. The following example method uses this class to compress data read from the specified InputStream instance and then writes the compressed data to the specified OutputStream instance:

```
static public void deflateStream(
   InputStream in,
   OutputStream out)
{
   byte buffIn[] = new byte[1024];
   byte buffOut[] = new byte[1024];
   Deflater deflater = new Deflater(
      Deflater.DEFAULT_COMPRESSION);

   try
   {
      while (true)
      {
         // Read portion of input
         int nIn = in.read(
            buffIn, 0, buffIn.length);
         if (nIn <= 0)
            break;
         deflater.setInput(buffIn, 0, nIn);

         // Process current of input
         while (true)
         {
            int nOut = deflater.
               deflate(buffOut);
            if (nOut > 0)
               out.write(
                  buffOut, 0, nOut);
            if (deflater.needsInput())
               break;
         }
      }
   }
   catch (Exception e)
   {
      System.out.println(
         "Exception: "+e.getMessage());
   }
   deflater.end();
}
```

This example creates two buffers (one for input and the other for output) and an instance of the Deflater class specifying the default compression option. It then reads bytes from the specified input stream and passes them to the Deflater instance using the setInput() method. The deflate() method performs the actual deflating and sends the compressed bytes to the output buffer to write them to the specified output stream.

Fields

Modifiers	Type	Field
public static final	int	BEST_COMPRESSION
public static final	int	BEST_SPEED
public static final	int	DEFAULT_COMPRESSION
public static final	int	DEFAULT_STRATEGY
public static final	int	DEFLATED
public static final	int	FILTERED
public static final	int	HUFFMAN_ONLY
public static final	int	NO_COMPRESSION

Constructors

Modifiers	Constructor
public	Deflater()
public	Deflater(int)
public	Deflater(int, boolean)

Methods

Modifiers	Return Type	Method
public	int	deflate(byte[])
public native synchronized	int	deflate(byte[], int, int)
public native synchronized	void	end()
protected	void	finalize()
public synchronized	void	finish()
public synchronized	boolean	finished()
public native synchronized	int	getAdler()
public native synchronized	int	getTotalIn()
public native synchronized	int	getTotalOut()
public	boolean	needsInput()
public native synchronized	void	reset()
public	void	setDictionary(byte[])
public native synchronized	void	setDictionary(byte[], int, int)
public	void	setInput(byte[])
public synchronized	void	setInput(byte[], int, int)
public synchronized	void	setLevel(int)
public synchronized	void	setStrategy(int)

See Also java.io.InputStream • java.io.OutputStream • java.lang.Object • java.util.zip.DeflaterOutputStream • java.util.zip.Inflater • java.util.zip.InflaterInputStream • java.util.zip.ZipOutputStream

Class DeflaterOutputStream

public synchronized java.util.zip.DeflaterOutputStream extends java.io.FilterOutputStream

The DeflaterOutputStream class is a FilterOutputStream subclass that compresses the data contained in a given output stream using the "deflate" compression format.

Syntax & Usage You seldom use this class directly, but instead you use one of its subclasses, defined in these packages:

- GZIPOutputStream
- ZipOutputStream

For more information on these two classes, please see the appropriate sections, later in this chapter.

Fields

Modifiers	Type	Field
protected	byte[]	buf
protected	Deflater	def

Constructors

Modifiers	Constructor
public	DeflaterOutputStream(OutputStream)
public	DeflaterOutputStream(OutputStream, Deflater)
public	DeflaterOutputStream(OutputStream, Deflater, int)

Methods

Modifiers	Return Type	Method
public	void	close()
protected	void	deflate()
public	void	finish()
public	void	write(byte[], int, int)
public	void	write(int)

See Also java.io.FilterOutputStream • java.util.zip.Deflater • java.util.zip.GZIPOutputStream • java.util.zip.InflaterInputStream • java.util.zip.ZIPOutputStream

Class GZIPInputStream

public synchronized java.util.zip.GZIPInputStream extends java.util.zip.InflaterInputStream

The GZIPInputStream is used to perform decompression using the GZIP format on the data coming from a given input stream.

Note

GZIP is a freely available compression utility used in UNIX environments. (There are GZIP utilities available for other environments, including MS-DOS and OS/2, that let you compress/decompress files.) A "gzipped" file will show a .gz extension. GZIP also can uncompress files formerly compressed using the ***compress*** *tool in UNIX. (These files can be recognized by their .Z extension.)*

Syntax & Usage This class contains two constructors: One constructor lets you specify an InputStream and uses the default buffer size of 512 bytes. The second lets you specify both the InputStream and the buffer size. The following example method reads compressed data from the specified InputStream instance and writes the decompressed data to the specified OutputStream instance:

```
static public void unZip(
  InputStream compressed,
  OutputStream decompressed)
{
  byte buffer[] = new byte[1024];
  try
  {
    GZIPInputStream stream = new
      GZIPInputStream(compressed, 1024);
    while (true)
    {
      // Read portion of input
      int n = stream.read(buffer, 0,
        buffer.length);
      if (n <= 0)
        break;
      decompressed.write(buffer, 0, n);
    }
```

```
        stream.close();
    }
    catch (Exception e)
    {
        System.out.println(
            "Exception: "+e.getMessage());
    }
}
```

This creates an instance of this class using the specified InputStream object. Until no more data are available, it reads the buffer and decompresses the bytes, writing them to the specified OutputStream object.

Fields

Modifiers	Type	Field
protected	CRC32	crc
protected	boolean	eos
public static final	int	GZIP_MAGIC

Constructors

Modifiers	Constructor
public	GZIPInputStream(InputStream)
public	GZIPInputStream(InputStream, int)

Methods

Modifiers	Return Type	Method
public	void	close()
public	int	read(byte[], int, int)

See Also java.util.zip.GZIPOutputStream • java.util.InflaterInputStream

Class GZIPOutputStream

public synchronized java.util.zip.GZIPOutputStream extends java.util.zip.DeflaterOutputStream

The GZIPOutputStream is used to perform compression using the GZIP format on data going out via a given output stream.

Note

GZIP is a freely available compression utility used in UNIX environments. (There are GZIP utilities available for other environments, including MS-DOS and OS/2, that let you compress/decompress files.) A "gzipped" file will show a .gz extension. GZIP also can uncompress files formerly compressed using the ***compress*** *tool in UNIX. (These files can be recognized by their .Z extensions.)*

Syntax & Usage This class contains two constructors: One constructor lets you specify an OutputStream object and uses the default buffer size of 512 bytes. The second lets you specify both the OutputStream and the buffer size. The following example method reads uncompressed bytes from the specified InputStream instance and writes the compressed bytes to the specified OutputStream instance:

```
static public void zip(
   OutputStream compressed,
   InputStream uncompressed)
{
   byte buffer[] = new byte[1024];
   try
   {
      GZIPOutputStream stream = new
         GZIPOutputStream(compressed, 1024);
      while (true)
      {
         // Read portion of input
         int n = uncompressed.read(buffer, 0,
            buffer.length);
         if (n <= 0)
            break;
         stream.write(buffer, 0, n);
      }
      stream.close();
   }
   catch (Exception e)
   {
      System.out.println(
         "Exception: "+e.getMessage());
   }
}
```

This example creates an instance of this class using the specified OutputStream object. Until the end of stream is reached, it reads the uncompressed bytes, compresses them, and writes to the specified OutputStream object.

Fields

Modifiers	Type	Field
protected	CRC32	crc

Constructors

Modifiers	Constructor
public	GZIPOutputStream(OutputStream)
public	GZIPOutputStream(OutputStream, int)

Methods

Modifiers	Return Type	Method
public	void	close()
public	void	finish()
public synchronized	void	write(byte[], int, int)

See Also java.util.zip.DeflaterOutputStream • java.util.zip.GZIPInputStream

Class Inflater

public synchronized java.util.zip.Inflater extends java.lang.Object

The Inflater class is used to perform decompression of some given binary data based on the ZLIB compression library.

Note

The ZLIB compression library was written as a freely distributed technology to compress/decompress data without regard to the processor, operating system, or format of the data and with complete regard to data integrity. It also is flexible internally wherein it can use a variety of compression algorithms. For more information on this library, please go to http://www.cdrom.com/pub/info/infozip/pub/zlib.

Syntax & Usage You seldom use this class directly; instead, you use the ZipInputStream class. The following example method uses this class to decompress data read from the specified InputStream instance and writes the decompressed data to the specified OutputStream instance:

```
static public void inflateStream(
   InputStream in,
   OutputStream out)
{
   byte buffIn[] = new byte[1024];
   byte buffOut[] = new byte[1024];
   Inflater inflater = new Inflater();

   try
   {
      while (true)
      {
         // Read portion of input
         int nIn = in.read(
            buffIn, 0, buffIn.length);
         if (nIn <= 0)
            break;
         inflater.setInput(buffIn, 0, nIn);

         // Process current of input
         while (true)
         {
            int nOut = inflater.
               inflate(buffOut);
            if (nOut > 0)
               out.write(
                  buffOut, 0, nOut);
            if (deflater.needsInput())
               break;
         }
      }
   }
   catch (Exception e)
   {
      System.out.println(
         "Exception: "+e.getMessage());
   }
   deflater.end();
}
```

This example creates two buffers (one for input and the other for output) and an instance of this class. It then reads bytes from the specified input stream and passes them to the Inflater instance using the setInput() method. The inflate() method performs the actual inflating and fills the decompressed bytes into the output buffer to write them to the specified output stream.

Fields None

Constructors

Modifiers	Constructor
public	Inflater()
public	Inflater(boolean)

Methods

Modifiers	Return Type	Method
public native synchronized	void	end()
protected	void	finalize()
public synchronized	boolean	finished()
public native synchronized	int	getAdler()
public synchronized	int	getRemaining()
public native synchronized	int	getTotalIn()
public native synchronized	int	getTotalOut()
public	int	inflate(byte[])
public native synchronized	int	inflate(byte[], int, int)
public synchronized	boolean	needsDictionary()
public synchronized	boolean	needsInput()
public native synchronized	void	reset()
public	void	setDictionary(byte[])
public native synchronized	void	setDictionary(byte[], int, int)
public	void	setInput(byte[])
public synchronized	void	setInput(byte[], int, int)

See Also java.io.InputStream • java.io.OutputStream • java.lang.Object • java.util.zip.Deflater • java.util.zip.DeflaterOutputStream • java.util.zip.InflaterInputStream • java.util.zip.ZipInputStream

Class InflaterInputStream

public synchronized java.util.zip.InflaterInputStream extends java.io.FilterInputStream

The InflaterInputStream class is a FilterInputStream subclass that decompresses data contained in a given input stream using the "deflate" compression format.

Syntax & Usage You seldom use this class directly; instead, you use one of its subclasses, defined in these packages:

- GZIPInputStream
- ZipInputStream

For more information on these two classes, please see the appropriate sections, elsewhere in this chapter.

Fields

Modifiers	Type	Field
protected	byte[]	buf
protected	Inflater	inf
protected	int	len

Constructors

Modifiers	Constructor
public	InflaterInputStream(InputStream)
public	InflaterInputStream(InputStream, Inflater)
public	InflaterInputStream(InputStream, Inflater, int)

Methods

Modifiers	Return Type	Method
protected	void	fill()
public	int	read()
public	int	read(byte[], int, int)
public	long	skip(long)

See Also java.io.FilterInputStream • java.util.zip.DeflaterOutputStream • java.util.zip.GZIPInputStream • java.util.zip.Inflater • java.util.zip.ZIPInputStream

Class ZipEntry

public synchronized java.util.zip.ZipEntry extends java.lang.Object implements java.util.zip.ZipConstants

The ZipEntry class represents an entry contained in a given ZIP archive. An entry can be a compressed/uncompressed file or a directory recursively containing more entries.

Syntax & Usage

This class provides a set of methods to obtain/set information about a specific entry.

> **Note**
>
> *This class implements the ZipConstants interface. This interface contains various ZIP-based constants. The reason it is not documented in this book or in JavaSoft's online documentation is because it is not* ***public****.*

For more information and/or for examples of this class being used, please see the sections for the ZipFile, ZipInputStream, and ZipOutputStream classes, later in this chapter.

Fields

Modifiers	Type	Field
public static final	int	DEFLATED
public static final	int	STORED

Constructors

Modifiers	Constructor
public	ZipEntry(String)

Methods

Modifiers	Return Type	Method
public	String	getComment()
public	long	getCompressedSize()
public	long	getCrc()
public	byte[]	getExtra()
public	int	getMethod()
public	String	getName()
public	long	getSize()
public	long	getTime()
public	boolean	isDirectory()
public	void	setComment(String)
public	void	setCrc(long)
public	void	setExtra(byte[])
public	void	setMethod(int)
public	void	setSize(long)
public	void	setTime(long)
public	String	toString()

See Also

java.lang.Object • java.util.zip.ZipFile • java.util.ZipInputStream • java.util.ZipOutputStream

Class ZipException

public synchronized java.util.zip.ZipException extends java.io.IOException

ZipException is thrown any time there is an error during a given ZIP operation.

Syntax & Usage This exception can be thrown by numerous methods in this package belonging to various ZIP-related classes. For examples of where this exception can be caught, go to the sections for the ZipFile, ZipInputStream, and ZipOutputStream classes, later in this chapter.

Fields None

Constructors

Modifiers	Constructor
public	ZipException()
public	ZipException(String)

Methods None

See Also java.io.IOException • java.util.zip.DataFormatException • java.util.zip.ZipFile • java.util.zip.ZipInputStream • java.util.zip.ZipOutputStream

Class ZipFile

public synchronized java.util.zip.ZipFile extends java.lang.Object implements java.util.zip.ZipConstants

The ZipFile class is used to encapsulate a given ZIP archive.

Syntax & Usage Using this class, you can access entries (compressed and uncompressed) stored in a given ZIP archive.

Note

This class implements the ZipConstants interface. This interface contains various ZIP-based constants. The reason it is not documented in this book or in JavaSoft's online documentation is because it is not ***public****.*

The following example shows the usage of ZipFile and ZipEntry classes by displaying the contents of the specified ZIP archive in the specified List object:

```
// Display archive contents
static public void displayZip(
   String zipFileName, List list)
{
   try
   {
      ZipFile zipFile = new
         ZipFile(zipFileName);
      list.removeAll();
      Enumeration en = zipFile.entries();
      while (en.hasMoreElements())
      {
         ZipEntry zipEntr =
            (ZipEntry)en.nextElement();
         list.addItem(zipEntr.getName()+
            " "+zipEntr.getSize());
      }
      zipFile.close();
   }
   catch (ZipException e)
   {
      System.out.println(
         "ZipException: "+e.getMessage());
      return;
   }
   catch (Exception e)
   {
      System.out.println(
         "Exception: "+e.getMessage());
      return;
   }
}
```

This takes the specified ZIP archive and fills the specified java.awt.List instance with the entries stored in that archive. To do this, it retrieves an Enumeration object of all the entries stored in the archive. For each entry, the code also adds a line displaying the entry's name and size. Note that the ZipException exception can be thrown.

Fields None

Constructors

Modifiers	Constructor
public	ZipFile(File)
public	ZipFile(String)

Methods

Modifiers	Return Type	Method
public	void	close()
public	Enumeration	entries()
public	ZipEntry	getEntry(String)
public	InputStream	getInputStream(ZipEntry)
public	String	getName()

See Also java.awt.List • java.lang.Object • java.util.Enumeration • java.util.zip.ZipEntry • java.util.ZipInputStream • java.util.ZipOutputStream

Class ZipInputStream

public synchronized java.util.zip.ZipInputStream extends java.util.zip.InflaterInputStream implements java.util.zip.ZipConstants

The ZipInputStream class is used to extract ZIPped data coming from a given input stream.

Note

ZIP is a compression technology from PKWARE that gives you the ability to create archives (a ZIP archive can be identified by its .zip extension) containing files or directories wherein the files/subdirectories can be saved recursively as part of the archive.

Syntax & Usage This class contains only one constructor, letting you specify an InputStream.

Note

This class implements the ZipConstants interface. This interface contains various ZIP-based constants. The reason it is not documented in this book or in JavaSoft's online documentation is because it is not ***public****.*

The following example method uses a ZipInputStream instance to extract the specified compressed file from the specified archive storing it in the specified output name:

```
// Extract file from archive
static public void extractZipFile(
   String zipName,
   String fileName, String outputName)
{
   byte buffer[] = new byte[1024];
   try
   {
      // Open archive file
      FileInputStream stream =
         new FileInputStream(
         zipName);
      ZipInputStream zipStream = new
         ZipInputStream(stream);

      // Find archive entry
      ZipEntry zipExtract = null;
      while (true)
      {
         zipExtract = zipStream.
            getNextEntry();
         if (zipExtract == null)
            break;
         if (zipExtract.getName().
            equals(fileName))
            break;
         zipStream.closeEntry();
      }
      if (zipExtract == null ||
         !zipExtract.getName().
         equals(fileName))
      {
         stream.close();
         System.out.println(
         "Can't find requested entry");
         return;
      }
```

```
            // Create output file
            FileOutputStream output =
               new FileOutputStream(
               outputName);

            // Check stored CRC
            long crcReq = zipExtract.getCrc();
            CRC32 crc = new CRC32();

            // Read input & write to output
            while (true)
            {
               int nRead = zipStream.read(
                  buffer, 0, buffer.length);
               if (nRead <= 0)
                  break;
               output.write(buffer, 0, nRead);
               crc.update(buffer, 0, nRead);
            }

            // Close all
            output.close();
            zipStream.closeEntry();
            stream.close();

            // Check CRC value, if available
            if (crcReq != -1 && crc.getValue()
               != crcReq)
            {
               System.out.println(
               "CRC Error then extracting file");
               return;
            }
         }
         catch (ZipException e)
         {
            System.out.println(
               "ZipException: "+e.getMessage());
            return;
         }
         catch (Exception e)
         {
            System.out.println(
               "Exception: "+e.getMessage());
            return;
         }

         System.out.println("File "+fileName+
            " has been extracted as "+outputName);
      }
```

This example takes three String parameters representing the compressed entry name (zipName), the archive name (fileName) to which the zipName entry belongs, and the resulting decompressed filename (outputName). The method starts by creating a FileInputStream object and a ZipInputStream object (passing it the FileInputStream object). Then the code looks for the specified entry (zipName) by sequentially going through all the entries contained in the archive (using the getNextEntry() method). If the requested entry is not found, the program prints a warning message and returns.

If the requested entry is found, a FileOutputStream instance is opened to the file specified in outputName. If available, the getCrc() method retrieves the CRC value from the archive, thereby creating a CRC32 instance to verify integrity of decompressed data (please see the "Class CRC32," earlier in the chapter, for more information). Then in a **while** loop, the code reads the data buffer from the ZipInputStream object (which automatically extracts the data contained therein), writing these now-unzipped data to the output stream and updating the CRC value.

Finally, the code closes both streams and retrieves the computed CRC value using the getValue() method from the CRC32 class. If the original CRC is available (i.e., it doesn't equal -1) but is not equal to the computed CRC, an error message is printed.

Note that ZipException can be thrown and must be handled (or rethrown) in this method. If everything runs successfully and no exceptions are thrown, the code displays a confirmatory message that the specified file (zipName) has been extracted successfully to the specified output file (outputName).

Fields None

Constructors

Modifiers	Constructor
public	ZipInputStream(InputStream)

Methods

Modifiers	Return Type	Method
public	void	close()
public	void	closeEntry()
public	ZipEntry	getNextEntry()
public	int	read(byte[], int, int)
public	long	skip(long)

See Also java.util.zip.InflaterInputStream • java.util.zip.ZipEntry • java.util.zip.ZipException • java.util.zip.ZipFile • java.util.zip.ZipOutputStream

Class ZipOutputStream

public synchronized java.util.zip.ZipOutputStream extends java.util.zip.DeflaterOutputStream implements java.util.zip.ZipConstants

The ZipOutputStream class is used to compress data (using the ZIP format) going through a given output stream.

Note

ZIP is a compression technology from PKWARE that gives you the ability to create archives (a ZIP archive can be identified by its .zip extension) containing files or directories wherein the files/subdirectories can be saved recursively as part of the archive.

Syntax & Usage This class contains only one constructor, letting you specify an InputStream.

Note

This class implements the ZipConstants interface. This interface contains various ZIP-based constants. The reason it is not documented in this book or in JavaSoft's online documentation is because it is not ***public****.*

The following example method uses a ZipOutputStream instance to add the specified compressed file entry to the specified archive:

```
// Add a new file to archive
static public void writeZipFile(
   String zipName,
   String fileName)
{
   byte buffer[] = new byte[1024];
   try
   {
      // Open archive file
      FileOutputStream stream =
         new FileOutputStream(zipName);
      ZipOutputStream zipStream = new
         ZipOutputStream(stream);
```

```
            // Create zip entry
            ZipEntry zipPut = new ZipEntry(fileName);
            zipStream.putNextEntry(zipPut);

            // Open input file
            FileInputStream inputStream =
               new FileInputStream(fileName);

            // Read input & write to output
            while (true)
            {
               int nRead = inputStream.read(
                  buffer, 0, buffer.length);
               if (nRead <= 0)
                  break;
               zipStream.write(buffer, 0, nRead);
            }

            // Close all
            inputStream.close();
            zipStream.closeEntry();
            stream.close();
         }
         catch (ZipException e)
         {
            System.out.println(
               "ZipException: "+e.getMessage());
            return;
         }
         catch (Exception e)
         {
            System.out.println(
               "Exception: "+e.getMessage());
            return;
         }

         System.out.println("File "+fileName+
            " has been added to "+zipName);
      }
```

This example starts by taking two String parameters. The first parameter (zipName) represents the name of the uncompressed file, and the second parameter (fileName) represents the name of the archive to which the file entry in zipName is to be added. The method starts by opening the archive with a FileOutputStream instance. After that, a ZipOutputStream instance is created specifying the newly created FileOutputStream object in its constructor. Then a ZipEntry object is created for zipName and, using the putNextEntry() method from this class, the code creates an entry for the newly created ZipEntry object in the archive.

At this point, the code can start writing. To do this, it opens a FileInputStream object and as long as data are available, reads the data buffer from the FileInputStream instance and writes it to the ZipOutputStream object, which automatically zips the data going thorough it.

Finally, this example closes both streams. Note that ZipException has to be caught. If everything runs smoothly and no exceptions were thrown, it prints a confirmatory message that the specified entry was added successfully to the specified archive.

Fields

Modifiers	Type	Field
public static final	int	DEFLATED
public static final	int	STORED

Constructors

Modifiers	Constructor
public	ZipOutputStream(OutputStream)

Methods

Modifiers	Return Type	Method
public	void	close()
public	void	closeEntry()
public	void	finish()
public	void	putNextEntry(ZipEntry)
public	void	setComment(String)
public	void	setLevel(int)
public	void	setMethod(int)
public synchronized	void	write(byte[], int, int)

See Also java.util.zip.DeflaterOutputStream • java.util.zip.ZipEntry • java.util.zip.ZipException • java.util.zip.ZipFile • java.util.zip.ZipInputStream

The sun.tools.debug Package

24

The sun.tools.debug package contains a rather obscure set of classes that are used to implement a real-time Java debugger. The classes in this package were used in the actual implementation of the jdb.exe command line debugger, which is part of the Java Development Kit (JDK). These classes have also been implemented in various third-party Java Integrated Development Environments (IDEs). Needless to say, unless you have the full intention of writing your own debugger, you will not need to use this package.

Interface DebuggerCallback

public abstract interface sun.tools.debug.DebuggerCallback

The DebuggerCallback interface is the only **public** interface in this package. It is used to define methods that help notify the debugger of various actions (usually debugging related) that are occurring in the program being debugged.

Syntax & Usage This interface must be implemented (by an object of your own design) to use the debugging features contained in this package.

> **Note**
>
> *You need an instance of DebuggerCallback to construct an object of the RemoteDebugger class. Please see "Class RemoteDebugger," later in this chapter, for details.*

Fields None

Constructors None

Methods

Modifiers	Return Type	Method
public abstract	void	breakpointEvent(RemoteThread)
public abstract	void	exceptionEvent(RemoteThread, String)
public abstract	void	printToConsole(String)
public abstract	void	quitEvent()
public abstract	void	threadDeathEvent(RemoteThread)

See Also sun.tools.debug.RemoteDebugger

Class NoSessionException

public synchronized sun.tools.debug.NoSessionException extends java.lang.Exception

The NoSessionException exception is thrown any time there is an attempt to use a debugging session that is no longer available.

Syntax & Usage This exception often is thrown when a session is closed.

Fields None

Constructors

Modifiers	Constructor
public	NoSessionException()
public	NoSessionException(String)

Methods None

See Also java.lang.Exception • sun.tools.debug.NoSuchLineNumberException

Class NoSuchLineNumberException

public synchronized sun.tools.debug.NoSuchLineNumberException extends java.lang.Exception

The NoSuchLineNumberException exception is thrown any time during a debugging session when a specified source code line number is invalid.

Syntax & Usage An "invalid" line number is usually one that does not contain any code. This exception can be thrown by the two overloaded getMethodLineNumber() methods in the RemoteClass class (see that class for more information).

Fields None

Constructors

Modifiers	Constructor
public	NoSuchLineNumberException()
public	NoSuchLineNumberException(String)

Methods None

See Also java.lang.Exception • sun.tools.debug.RemoteClass • sun.tools.debug.NoSessionException

Class RemoteArray

public synchronized sun.tools.debug.RemoteArray extends sun.tools.debug.RemoteObject

The RemoteArray class is used for the debugging of Java arrays.

Syntax & Usage

It is no coincidence that this class extends the RemoteObject class because arrays in Java are actually objects. This class is a special breed of the RemoteObject class, tailored for the debugging of arrays. It provides functionality to retrieve information about an array's size and any elements contained therein.

The following example method displays the contents of the array specified by its name (arrayName) in the specified RemoteObject object (ro):

```
static public void displayArray(
  RemoteObject ro, String arrayName)
{
  try
  {
    RemoteValue rv =
      ro.getFieldValue(arrayName);
    if (rv instanceof RemoteArray)
    {
      RemoteArray ra = (RemoteArray)rv;
      for (int k=0; k<ra.getSize(); k++)
      {
         RemoteValue element =
          ra.getElement(k);
         System.out.println(
          k+"\t"+ra.toString());
      }
    }
  }
  catch(Exception e)
  {
    System.err.println("Error: "
      +e.getMessage());
  }
}
```

This retrieves a RemoteValue object for the array specified in arrayName using the ro.getFieldValue() method. This RemoteValue object then is checked to see if it represents an array (using the **instanceof** operator). If this is **true**, the code retrieves the array's size using the getSize() method from this class and prints all the array's elements to the standard output.

Fields None

Constructors None

Methods

Modifiers	Return Type	Method
public	String	arrayTypeName(int)
public	String	description()
public final	RemoteValue	getElement(int)
public final	RemoteValue[]	getElements()
public final	RemoteValue[]	getElements(int, int)
public final	int	getElementType()
public final	int	getSize()
public	String	toString()
public	String	typeName()

See Also sun.tools.debug.RemoteObject • sun.tools.debug.RemoteValue

Class RemoteBoolean

public synchronized sun.tools.debug.RemoteBoolean extends sun.tools.debug.RemoteValue

The RemoteBoolean class is used for the debugging of Java **boolean** fields.

Syntax & Usage This RemoteValue subclass provides functionality to get a given **boolean** field's current value. The following example displays the value for the specified **boolean** (name) in the given RemoteObject object (ro):

```
static public void displayBoolean(
   RemoteObject ro, String name)
{
   try
   {
      RemoteValue rv =
         ro.getFieldValue(name);
      if (rv instanceof RemoteBoolean)
      {
         RemoteBoolean rb =
            (RemoteBoolean)rv;
          System.out.println(
            "Boolean "+name+"="
            +rb.get());
      }
```

```
    }
    catch(Exception e)
    {
      System.err.println("Error: "
        +e.getMessage());
    }
}
```

This retrieves a RemoteValue object for the **boolean** specified in name using the ro.getFieldValue() method. This RemoteValue object then is checked to see if it represents a **boolean** (using the **instanceof** operator). If this is **true**, the code prints the field's name, then prints the field's value using the get() method from this class.

Fields None

Constructors None

Methods

Modifiers	Return Type	Method
public	boolean	get()
public	String	toString()
public	String	typeName()

See Also java.lang.Boolean • sun.tools.debug.RemoteObject • sun.tools.debug.RemoteValue

Class RemoteByte

public synchronized sun.tools.debug.RemoteByte extends sun.tools.debug.RemoteValue

The RemoteByte class is used for the debugging of Java **byte** fields.

Syntax & Usage This class provides the functionality to get a given **byte** field's current value. The usage of this class is very similar to the usage of other sub-classes of RemoteValue (see "Class RemoteValue," later in this chapter, for more information). Please see the previous section, "Class RemoteBoolean," for a comparable example.

Fields None

Constructors None

Methods

Modifiers	Return Type	Method
public	byte	get()
public	String	toString()
public	String	typeName()

See Also java.lang.Byte • sun.tools.debug.RemoteBoolean • sun.tools.debug.RemoteValue

Class RemoteChar

public synchronized sun.tools.debug.RemoteChar extends sun.tools.debug.RemoteValue

The RemoteChar class is used for the debugging of Java **char** fields.

Syntax & Usage This class provides the functionality to get a given **char** field's current value. The usage of this class is very similar to the usage of other subclasses of RemoteValue (see "Class RemoteValue," later in this chapter, for more information). Please see "Class RemoteBoolean," earlier in this chapter, for a comparable example.

Fields None

Constructors None

Methods

Modifiers	Return Type	Method
public	char	get()
public	String	toString()
public	String	typeName()

See Also java.lang.Character • sun.tools.debug.RemoteBoolean • sun.tools.debug.RemoteValue

Class RemoteClass

public synchronized sun.tools.debug.RemoteClass extends sun.tools.debug.RemoteObject

The RemoteClass class is used to debug a Java class definition.

Syntax & Usage

Since this class does not have any constructors, you can get a reference to a RemoteClass instance using one of the following methods:

- **RemoteDebugger.findClass(String).** This method is used to get a RemoteClass instance representing a class as specified by its name.
- **RemoteDebugger.listClasses().** This method is used to retrieve an array of RemoteClass objects representing all available classes.
- **RemoteObject.getClass().** This method is used to get a RemoteClass object representing the class for this remote object.

As soon as you have a RemoteClass instance, you then can use the plethora of methods in this class to manage breakpoints, access class definitions and implementations, and even gather information about the parent class. Consider the following:

```
static public void setBreakpoint(
  DebuggerCallback callback, String host,
  String name, int lineno)
{
  try
  {
    RemoteDebugger rd = new
      RemoteDebugger(host, callback,
      true);
    RemoteClass rc = rd.findClass(name);
    if (rc != null)
      rc.setBreakpointLine(lineno);
  }
  catch(Exception e)
  {
    System.err.println("Error: "
      +e.getMessage());
  }
}
```

This example creates an instance of the RemoteDebugger class using the specified host and DebuggerCallback object. Then it retrieves a reference to the RemoteClass instance using the findClass() method from the RemoteDebugger class. If this succeeds, the code sets the breakpoint to the specified line of the class's source code using the setBreakpointLine() method from this class (which in turn invokes the breakpointEvent() method in the DebuggerCallback object; see the first section in this chapter for more information).

Fields None

Constructors None

Methods

Modifiers	Return Type	Method
public	void	catchExceptions()
public	String	clearBreakpoint(int)
public	String	clearBreakpointLine(int)
public	String	clearBreakpointMethod(RemoteField)
public	String	description()
public	RemoteObject	getClassLoader()
public	RemoteField	getField(int)
public	RemoteField	getField(String)
public	RemoteField[]	getFields()
public	RemoteValue	getFieldValue(int)
public	RemoteValue	getFieldValue(String)
public	RemoteField	getInstanceField(int)
public	RemoteField[]	getInstanceFields()
public	RemoteClass[]	getInterfaces()
public	int[]	getLineNumbers()
public	RemoteField	getMethod(String)
public	int	getMethodLineNumber(int)
public	int	getMethodLineNumber(String)
public	String[]	getMethodNames()
public	RemoteField[]	getMethods()
public	String	getName()
public	InputStream	getSourceFile()
public	String	getSourceFileName()
public	RemoteField[]	getStaticFields()
public	RemoteClass	getSuperclass()
public	void	ignoreExceptions()
public	boolean	isInterface()
public	String	setBreakpointLine(int)
public	String	setBreakpointMethod(RemoteField)
public	String	toString()
public	String	typeName()

See Also java.lang.Class • sun.tools.debug.DebuggerCallback • sun.tools.debug.RemoteDebugger • sun.tools.debug.RemoteObject

Class RemoteDebugger

public synchronized sun.tools.debug.RemoteDebugger extends java.lang.Object

The RemoteDebugger class is used to represent the "connection" between a debugger and the program being debugged.

Syntax & Usage Before you can actually use this class, you need to have an implementation (of your own design) of the DebuggerCallback interface wherein you can use instances of that class as a parameter in the constructor for this class (please see "Interface DebuggerCallback," the first section in this chapter, for more information).

Once you have a RemoteDebugger instance, you now have a handle to a given Java program, including the ability to query information about it and its hosting Java virtual machine (VM). You also have the ability to perform various debugging-related actions on the program and the program's hosting Java VM. Consider the following example method, which uses this class to instantiate a class contained in the Java program being debugged:

```
static public void remoteRun(
   DebuggerCallback callback, String host,
   String name, String arg)
{
   try
   {
      RemoteDebugger rd = new
      RemoteDebugger(host, callback, true);
      String argv[] = new String[] {name, arg};
      RemoteThreadGroup thread =
         rd.run(argv.length, argv);
   }
   catch(Exception e)
   {
      System.err.println("Error: "
         +e.getMessage());
   }
}
```

This creates an instance of the RemoteDebugger class using the specified host name and DebuggerCallback object. Then it calls the run() method from this class to execute the class specified in the method's name parameter, passing any parameters that may be used by that class's constructor (as specified by the arg parameter of this method).

Fields None

Constructors

Modifiers	Constructor
public	RemoteDebugger(String, DebuggerCallback, boolean)
public	RemoteDebugger(String, String, DebuggerCallback, boolean)

Methods

Modifiers	Return Type	Method
public	void	addSystemThread()
public	void	addSystemThread(Thread)
public	void	close()
public	RemoteClass	findClass(String)
public	int	freeMemory()
public	void	gc(RemoteObject[])
public	RemoteObject	get(Integer)
public	String[]	getExceptionCatchList()
public	String	getSourcePath()
public	void	itrace(boolean)
public	String[]	listBreakpoints()
public	RemoteClass[]	listClasses()
public	RemoteThreadGroup[]	listThreadGroups(RemoteThreadGroup)
public	RemoteThreadGroup	run(int, String[])
public	void	setSourcePath(String)
public	int	totalMemory()
public	void	trace(boolean)

See Also java.lang.Object • java.lang.Runnable • sun.tools.debug.DebuggerCallback • sun.tools.debug.RemoteThreadGroup

Class RemoteDouble

public synchronized sun.tools.debug.RemoteDouble extends sun.tools.debug.RemoteValue

The RemoteDouble class is used for the debugging of Java **double** fields.

Syntax & Usage

This class provides the functionality to get a given **double** field's current value. The usage of this class is very similar to the usage of other subclasses of RemoteValue (see the section for that class, later in this chapter, for more information). Please see "Class RemoteBoolean," earlier in this chapter, for a comparable example.

Fields None

Constructors None

Methods

Modifiers	Return Type	Method
public	double	get()
public	String	toString()
public	String	typeName()

See Also java.lang.Double • sun.tools.debug.RemoteBoolean • sun.tools.debug.RemoteValue

Class RemoteField

public synchronized sun.tools.debug.RemoteField extends sun.tools.debug.Field implements sun.tools.debug.AgentConstants

The RemoteField class is used to query information about a variable or method in a given class or object.

Syntax & Usage This class lets you retrieve information about the instance (or **static**) variables and methods in a given RemoteClass object or RemoteObject object (please see the sections for those classes, elsewhere in this chapter, for more information).

> **Note**
>
> *This class extends a non-**public** Field class; it is not documented because it is not **public**. This class also implements the undocumented AgentConstants interface, which contains constants used internally by this class.*

The following example method prints the contents of the specified remote field:

```
static public void displayField(
  RemoteField rf)
{
  System.out.println("Modifiers:\t"+
    rf.getModifiers());
```

```
    System.out.println("Name:\t"+
      rf.getName());
    System.out.println("Type:\t"+
      rf.getTypedName());
}
```

This example uses the getModifiers(), getName(), and getTypedName() methods (all from this class) to display information about the specified RemoteField instance.

Fields None

Constructors None

Methods

Modifiers	Return Type	Method
public	String	getModifiers()
public	String	getName()
public	Type	getType()
public	String	getTypedName()
public	boolean	isStatic()
public	String	toString()

See Also sun.tools.debug.RemoteClass • sun.tools.debug.RemoteObject

Class RemoteFloat

public synchronized sun.tools.debug.RemoteFloat extends sun.tools.debug.RemoteValue

The RemoteFloat class is used for the debugging of Java **float** fields.

Syntax & Usage This class provides the functionality to get a given **float** field's current value. The usage of this class is very similar to the usage of other subclasses of RemoteValue (see the section for that class, later in this chapter, for more information). Please see "Class RemoteBoolean," earlier in this chapter, for a comparable example.

Fields None

Constructors None

Methods

Modifiers	Return Type	Method
public	float	get()
public	String	toString()
public	String	typeName()

See Also java.lang.Float • sun.tools.debug.RemoteBoolean • sun.tools.debug.RemoteValue

Class RemoteInt

public synchronized sun.tools.debug.RemoteInt extends sun.tools.debug.RemoteValue

The RemoteInt class is used for the debugging of Java **int** fields.

Syntax & Usage This class provides the functionality to get a given **int** field's current value. The usage of this class is very similar to the usage of other subclasses of RemoteValue (see the section for that class, later in this chapter, for more information). Please see "Class RemoteBoolean," earlier in this chapter, for a comparable example.

Fields None

Constructors

Modifiers	Constructor
public	RemoteInt(int)

Methods

Modifiers	Return Type	Method
public	int	get()
public	String	toString()
public	String	typeName()

See Also java.lang.Integer • sun.tools.debug.RemoteBoolean • sun.tools.debug.RemoteValue

Class RemoteLong

public synchronized sun.tools.debug.RemoteLong extends sun.tools.debug.RemoteValue

The RemoteLong class is used for the debugging of Java **long** fields.

Syntax & Usage This class provides the functionality to get a given **long** field's current value. The usage of this class is very similar to the usage of other subclasses of RemoteValue (see the section for that class, later in this chapter, for more information). Please see "Class RemoteBoolean," earlier in this chapter, for a comparable example.

Fields None

Constructors None

Methods

Modifiers	Return Type	Method
public	long	get()
public	String	toString()
public	String	typeName()

See Also java.lang.Long • sun.tools.debug.RemoteBoolean • sun.tools.debug.RemoteValue

Class RemoteObject

public synchronized sun.tools.debug.RemoteObject extends sun.tools.debug.RemoteValue

The RemoteObject class is used for the debugging of Java objects.

Syntax & Usage This class provides a number of methods to access and/or modify a given object including its class definition and current field values.

Note

The instances of this class are not garbage collected automatically. Rather, you need to invoke the garbage collector manually to clean up, using one of the overloaded gc() methods from the RemoteDebugger class.

The following example method displays the contents of the specified RemoteObject instance:

```
static public void displayObject(
   RemoteObject ro)
{
   try
   {
      System.out.println("Class:\t"+
         ro.getClazz().toString());
      RemoteField[] fields = ro.getFields();
      for (int k=0; k<fields.length; k++)
      {
         RemoteValue rv =
            ro.getFieldValue(k);
         System.out.println(
            k+"\t"+fields[k].getName()+
            "\t"+rv.toString());
      }
   }
   catch (Exception e)
   {
      System.err.println("Exception: "
         +e.getMessage());
   }
}
```

This example requests and displays the name of the actual class for the specified RemoteObject object (ro) using the getClazz() method. Then this example obtains an array containing all the object's fields using the getFields() method. The actual value of every field is then requested using the getFieldValue() method in a **for** loop. Finally, all information about the fields and their values are displayed in a tabular format.

Fields None

Constructors None

Methods

Modifiers	Return Type	Method
public	String	description()
protected	void	finalize()
public final	RemoteClass	getClazz()
public	RemoteField	getField(int)
public	RemoteField	getField(String)
public	RemoteField[]	getFields()
public	RemoteValue	getFieldValue(int)
public	RemoteValue	getFieldValue(String)
public final	int	getId()
public	void	setField(int, boolean)
public	void	setField(int, char)
public	void	setField(int, double)
public	void	setField(int, float)
public	void	setField(int, int)
public	void	setField(int, long)
public	void	setField(int, RemoteObject)
public	void	setField(String, boolean)
public	void	setField(String, char)
public	void	setField(String, double)
public	void	setField(String, float)
public	void	setField(String, int)
public	void	setField(String, long)
public	void	setField(String, RemoteObject)
public	String	toString()
public	String	typeName()

See Also sun.tools.debug.RemoteDebugger • sun.tools.debug.RemoteValue

Class RemoteShort

public synchronized sun.tools.debug.RemoteShort extends sun.tools.debug.RemoteValue

The RemoteShort class is used for the debugging of Java **short** fields.

Syntax & Usage This class provides the functionality to get a given **short** field's current value. The usage of this class is very similar to the usage of other subclasses of RemoteValue (see the section for that class, later in this chapter, for more information). Please see "Class RemoteBoolean," earlier in this chapter, for a comparable example.

Fields None

Constructors None

Methods

Modifiers	Return Type	Method
public	short	get()
public	String	toString()
public	String	typeName()

See Also sun.tools.debug. • sun.tools.debug.RemoteDebugger • sun.tools.debug.RemoteValue

Class RemoteStackFrame

public synchronized sun.tools.debug.RemoteStackFrame extends sun.tools.debug.StackFrame

The RemoteStackFrame class is used to debug a stack frame of a given thread (that is currently suspended).

Syntax & Usage During a debugging session, there are points at which a given thread in the program being debugged is halted from execution (via a breakpoint, or a call to its suspend() or stop() method) wherein a programmer can peer in and see various real-time data about the thread. This class is used to represent the stack of a given thread (which is represented as a RemoteThread object) that is currently halted. The following example method displays the contents of the stack frame in the specified RemoteThread instance:

```
static public void displayStack(
  RemoteThread rt)
{
  try
  {
    RemoteStackFrame rs =
      rt.getCurrentFrame();
```

```
        RemoteStackVariable[] rv =
          rs.getLocalVariables();
        for (int k=0; k<rv.length; k++)
        {
          System.out.println(
            k+"\t"+rv[k].getName()+"\t"
            +rv[k].getValue().toString());
        }
      }
      catch (Exception e)
      {
        System.err.println("Exception: "
          +e.getMessage());
      }
    }
```

This example takes the specified RemoteThread instance and obtains a RemoteStackFrame object from it, using the getCurrentFrame() method from the RemoteThread class. Then this example obtains an array of RemoteStackVariable objects (containing the values inside the stack frame), using the getLocalVariables() method also from the RemoteThread class. The name and value of each variable in the stack are then requested, using the getName() and getValue() methods, respectively (both of these methods are from the RemoteStackVariable class). Finally, all this information is coagulated and displayed in a tabular format.

Fields None

Constructors None

Methods

Modifiers	Return Type	Method
public	int	getLineNumber()
public	RemoteStackVariable	getLocalVariable(String)
public	RemoteStackVariable[]	getLocalVariables()
public	String	getMethodName()
public	int	getPC()
public	RemoteClass	getRemoteClass()

See Also sun.tools.debug.RemoteStackVariables • sun.tools.debug.RemoteThread • sun.tools.debug.StackFrame

Class RemoteStackVariable

public synchronized sun.tools.debug.RemoteStackVariable extends sun.tools.debug.LocalVariable implements sun.tools.debug.AgentConstants

The RemoteStackVariable class is used to access the actual values of a given remote stack frame for some thread that is being debugged.

Note

*This class extends the **private** class LocalVariable; it is not documented because it is not **public**. This class also implements the undocumented AgentConstants interface, which contains constants used internally by this class.*

Syntax & Usage The class is used to access the actual values of a given RemoteStackFrame object. To use this class, you need to already have a RemoteStackFrame instance (please see the section for that class, earlier in this chapter, for details). Then you can call the getStackVariable() (or getStackVariables()) method from that class to retrieve an instance (or an array of instances) of this class, representing the actual stack value(s). For an example of this class in action, please see "Class RemoteStackFrame," earlier in this chapter.

Fields None

Constructors None

Methods

Modifiers	Return Type	Method
public	String	getName()
public	Type	getType()
public	RemoteValue	getValue()
public	boolean	inScope()
public	boolean	methodArgument()

See Also sun.tools.debug.RemoteStackFrame

Class RemoteString

public synchronized sun.tools.debug.RemoteString extends sun.tools.debug.RemoteObject

The RemoteString class is used for the debugging of Java String objects.

Syntax & Usage As you know, Java has defined String objects to be unique among typical Java objects. It is a sort of object hybrid containing several features that usually are exclusive only to primitive data types. In light of this uniqueness, this class extends the RemoteObject class but facilitates the debugging capabilities of only a typical primitive data type. Specifically, this class provides the functionality to get a given String object's current value. The following example method displays the value of the String specified by its name in the specified RemoteObject object:

```
static public void displayString(
   RemoteObject ro, String name)
{
   try
   {
      RemoteValue rv =
         ro.getFieldValue(name);
      if (rv instanceof RemoteString)
      {
         RemoteString rs =
            (RemoteString)rv;
          System.out.println(
            "String "+name+"="
            +rs.toString());
      }
   }
   catch(Exception e)
   {
      System.err.println("Error: "
         +e.getMessage());
   }
}
```

This example retrieves the RemoteValue object from the specified remote object using the getFieldValue() method from that class. If this value represents a String, then the code prints the String object's name and value.

Fields None

Constructors None

Methods

Modifiers	Return Type	Method
public	String	description()
public	String	toString()
public	String	typeName()

See Also java.lang.String • sun.tools.debug.RemoteObject • sun.tools.debug.RemoteValue

Class RemoteThread

public synchronized sun.tools.debug.RemoteThread extends sun.tools.debug.RemoteObject

The RemoteThread class is used to debug a given thread of execution in the program being debugged.

Syntax & Usage This class provides a complete set of tools to perform all kinds of debugging operations on a given thread. These operations include accessing the thread's stack frame (please see "Class RemoteStackFrame," earlier in this chapter, for more information) and any values contained therein, managing the thread's execution, and/or performing various stepping operations with this thread. Note that before you can use this class the target thread must have been halted in some way (i.e., stopping a breakpoint, having its suspend() or stop() method called, etc.).

Fields None

Constructors None

Methods

Modifiers	Return Type	Method
public	void	cont()
public	void	down(int)
public	RemoteStackFrame[]	dumpStack()
public	RemoteStackFrame	getCurrentFrame()
public	int	getCurrentFrameIndex()
public	String	getName()
public	RemoteStackVariable	getStackVariable(String)
public	RemoteStackVariable[]	getStackVariables()

Modifiers	Return Type	Method
public	String	getStatus()
public	boolean	isSuspended()
public	void	next()
public	void	resetCurrentFrameIndex()
public	void	resume()
public	void	setCurrentFrameIndex(int)
public	void	step(boolean)
public	void	stop()
public	void	suspend()
public	void	up(int)

See Also java.lang.Thread • sun.tools.debug.RemoteObject • sun.tools.debug.RemoteStackFrame • sun.tools.debug.RemoteThreadGroup

Class RemoteThreadGroup

public synchronized sun.tools.debug.RemoteThreadGroup extends sun.tools.debug.RemoteObject

The RemoteThreadGroup class is used to debug a given thread group that is executing in the Java program being debugged.

Syntax & Usage The listThreads() method from this class returns an array of threads (and/or subthread groups) housed in the RemoteThreadGroup instance. This allows you to then debug each thread (and/or subthread group) in the specified thread group. Please see the previous section, "Class RemoteThread," for more information.

Fields None

Constructors None

Methods

Modifiers	Return Type	Method
public	String	getName()
public	RemoteThread[]	listThreads(boolean)
public	void	stop()

See Also java.lang.ThreadGroup • sun.tools.debug.RemoteObject • sun.tools.debug.RemoteThread

Class RemoteValue

public abstract synchronized sun.tools.debug.RemoteValue extends java.lang.Object implements sun.tools.debug.AgentConstants

The RemoteValue class is an **abstract** class that defines the functionality for retrieving a copy of the value for some type (i.e., primitive data type, object type, and so on).

Syntax & Usage

This class provides the general functionality for the debugging of remote values and is the root class for the following subclasses:

- RemoteBoolean
- RemoteByte
- RemoteChar
- RemoteDouble
- RemoteFloat
- RemoteInt
- RemoteLong
- RemoteObject
- RemoteArray
- RemoteClass
- RemoteString
- RemoteThread
- RemoteThreadGroup
- RemoteShort

Usually, you do not need to work with this class; rather, you work with its subclasses (as shown in the list). For more information on the subclasses in this list, please see the appropriate sections, earlier in this chapter.

Note

This class implements the undocumented AgentConstants interface, which contains constants used internally by this class.

Fields None

Constructors None

Methods

Modifiers	Return Type	Method
public	String	description()
public static	int	fromHex(String)
public final	int	getType()
public final	boolean	isObject()
public final	boolean	isString()
public static	String	toHex(int)
public abstract	String	typeName()

See Also java.lang.Object • sun.tools.debug.RemoteArray • sun.tools.debug.RemoteBoolean • sun.tools.debug.RemoteByte • sun.tools.debug.RemoteChar • sun.tools.debug.RemoteClass • sun.tools.debug.RemoteDouble • sun.tools.debug.RemoteFloat • sun.tools.debug.RemoteInt • sun.tools.debug.RemoteLong • sun.tools.debug.RemoteObject • sun.tools.debug.RemoteShort • sun.tools.debug.RemoteString • sun.tools.debug.RemoteThread • sun.tools.debug.RemoteThreadGroup

Class StackFrame

public synchronized sun.tools.debug.StackFrame extends java.lang.Object

The StackFrame class is used to represent the stack frame for a given thread (that is currently halted).

Syntax & Usage This class is very simple and is the root class for the RemoteStackFrame class (for more information, please see the section for that class, earlier in this chapter). This class facilitates a no parameter constructor and one method, toString(), which returns a String representation for the given StackFrame instance.

Fields None

Constructors

Modifiers	Constructor
public	StackFrame()

Methods

Modifiers	Return Type	Method
public	String	toString()

See Also java.lang.Object • sun.tools.debug.RemoteStackFrame

The sunw.io Package

25

This tiny package contains only one interface. This package is closely related to the sunw.util package (which is also very small). Both are used to facilitate the ability for Java beans developed in the JDK 1.0.2 to execute properly using the JDK 1.1.

Interface Serializable

public interface sunw.io.Serializable extends java.io.Serializable

The Serializable interface extends the java.io.Serializable interface and acts as a "placeholder" for those Java beans that will look for Serializable here (i.e., those developed in the JDK 1.0.2).

Syntax & Usage This class is included in the JDK 1.1 for backwards compatibility only. Do not use this class.

Fields None

Constructors None

Methods None

See Also java.io.Serializable

The sunw.util Package

26

This tiny package contains only two members: one class and one interface. This package is closely related to the sunw.io package (which is also very small). Both are used to facilitate the ability for Java beans developed in the JDK 1.0.2 to execute properly in the JDK 1.1.

Interface EventListener

public interface sunw.util.EventListener implements java.util.EventListener

The EventListener interface extends the java.util.EventListener interface and acts as a "placeholder" for those Java beans that look for EventListener here (i.e., those developed in the JDK 1.0.2).

Syntax & Usage This interface is included in the JDK 1.1 for backward compatibility only. Do not use this interface.

Fields None

Constructors None

Methods None

See Also java.util.EventListener

Class EventObject

public synchronized sunw.util.EventObject extends java.util.EventObject

The EventObject class extends the java.util.EventObject class and acts as a "placeholder" for those Java beans that look for EventObject here (i.e., those developed in the JDK 1.0.2).

Syntax & Usage This class is included in the JDK 1.1 for backward compatibility only. Do not use this class.

Fields None

Constructors

Modifiers	Constructor
public	EventObject(Object)

Methods None

See Also java.util.EventObject

Appendix A

About the Companion CD-ROM

The Companion CD-ROM included with your copy of *Java 1.1 Programmer's Reference* contains the entire book in hypertext, plus author example files. The hypertext version of the book is in a directory called Book.

CD Directory Structure

The Companion CD-ROM contains a UNIX directory and a PC directory. Each of these directories has two subdirectories: Resource and Book. The Resource subdirectory contains author example files and the Book subdirectory contains the entire book in HTML format.

Macintosh users will see a Resource folder and a Book folder after double-clicking on the CD-ROM icon. To find out more about the CD-ROM and its contents, please open the README.HTM file in your favorite browser. You will see a small menu offering several links.

Notes About UNIX files

The UNIX files on this Companion CD-ROM are in the UNIX directory in .TAR format. To decompress and install them, copy [filename].tar to a local directory. Then, at the UNIX prompt, type **tar xvf [filename].tar**.

Listing of Author Example Files

BignumTest	An applet that demonstrates the functionality of the BigDecimal class.
ListTest	An applet example that demonstrates the use of inner classes.ListA supporting class for ListTest.
ClipTest	An application that shows an example of using clipboard functionality in Java.
EventTest	An applet that demonstrates the new Java delegation-based event notification system.
PopupTest	An applet activated by a right mouse click that lets you specify a background color for the applet via a popup menu.
PrintTest	An appletcation (can be run as either an applet or application) that exemplifies printing capabilities in Java.
ScrollTest	An applet that demonstrates the ScrollPane container new to the AWT 1.1.System.
ColorTest	An application that gives an example of specifying system colors for your Java applet.
TabTest	An applet that demonstrates tabbing capabilities in Java.
ReflectionTest	An appletcation that uses the Reflection API to both instance a frame and introspect information about the frame during run-time.
NativeColor	An application that uses the JNI interface to call a native method that brings up the Windows common color dialog box, letting you specify a background color for your Java program.
JarTest	An appletcation archive extractor similar to WinZip or PKUNZIP written entirely in Java.
PrintTest.jar.sig	A signed version of the PrintTest appletcation that can be signed digitally and run as an applet without invoking a security exception. Please refer to the book for more information.
InternlAppl	An appletcation that contains locales for several countries, demonstrating the international API.
JDBCTest	A simple Java program that executes an SQL query on a sample Microsoft Access database.

RMI Weather	A client/server Java program that creates a pseudo weather forecast for several cities. The forecast can be retrieved via an RMI method call from the server and displayed on the client. Includes the following files: Weather.java, WeatherServer.java, WeatherClient.java, index.html, compapp.bat, compstub.bat, and run.bat.MyServerAn application that demonstrates the use of extended socket classes. When executing, be sure to start this application first.
MyClient	An application that demonstrates the use of extended socket classes.
BeanScale	A JavaBean component that facilitates basic scaling functionality.
BeansTest	An applet that demonstrates the BeanScale bean.
EXTRASAppletTag	An applet that gives an example of inter-applet communication.
Currency	An application that uses internet connection, HTML parsing, and object serialization, first to download real-time exchange rates, and then to plug them into an exchange rate calculator.
SerialTest	A simple address book program that uses object serialization to save each address entry to disk. SerialTest also contains the SerList.java supporting file for SerialTest.

Technical Support

Technical support is available for installation-related problems only. The technical support office is open from 8:00 A.M. to 6:00 P.M. Monday through Friday and can be reached via the following methods:

- Phone: (919) 544-9404 extension 81
- Faxback Answer System: (919) 544-9404 extension 85
- E-mail: help@vmedia.com
- FAX: (919) 544-9472
- World Wide Web: **http://www.vmedia.com/support**
- America Online: keyword *Ventana*

Limits of Liability & Disclaimer of Warranty

Glossary

The purpose of this glossary is to aid you in understanding obscure and difficult terms that appear in the text of this book. The glossary has been designed to complement the material in this book with embedded cross-references and external references back to the book. Note that each definition is theoretical from the context of Java (and not necessarily from computer science in general).

abstract A keyword used to modify a class and/or method. Anything declared abstract contains no implementation (methods are appended with a semicolon) wherein it is up to a subclass to implement the functionality. *See also* **class**; **implements**; **method**; **subclass**.

Abstract Window Toolkit (AWT) The name given by JavaSoft to its architecturally neutral graphical user interface (GUI) and graphics-building environment. The AWT underwent considerable improvements in Java 1.1 and is loosely referred to as the AWT 1.1 to distinguish it from its previous version. *See also* **graphical user interface**. *Reference* java.awt.*

Access Control List (ACL) Defines a database of permissions (using set algebra) to calculate if a given principle (which can belong to one or more groups) has permission to access a specific resource. *Reference* java.security.acl.*

action event An event resulting from some sort of semantic action. Most notably, a command button click precipitates this type of event. *See also* **event**. *Reference* java.awt.event.ActionEvent

adjustment event An event resulting from a change in some given scale of values. Most notably, this event is precipitated when the value for a given scrollbar or scrollpane changes. *See also* **event**. *Reference* java.awt.event.AdjustmentEvent

appletcation A loosely used term to indicate a Java program that can be executed as either an applet or an application. This is not a new program definition but merely a programming technique.

authenticate To verify the validity of a user or the integrity of some data. *See also* **certificate**; **key**; **private key**; **public key**. *Reference* java.security.*

AWT *See* **Abstract Window Toolkit**.

bean A reusable component (usually visual) that is neutral from a component architecture standpoint. *Reference* java.beans.*

boolean A primitive type that can be represented as one of two values: true or false. *See also* **false**; **true**. *Reference* java.lang.Boolean

break A keyword used as Java's solution to its absence of goto functionality. You can use break to jump outside of the innermost loop. You also can perform labeled breaks that jump to the specified label. Note that break also is used in switch statements. *See also* **continue**; **switch**.

by reference When a given type is passed somewhere, only a reference to the actual value of the source is passed. Thus, any changes made to the destination value directly affect the source. Note that all Java objects are passed by reference. *See also* **by value**; **reference type**.

byte A primitive type that is an 8-bit signed integer, giving it a range of –128 to +127. *See also* **primitive type**. *Reference* java.lang.Boolean

by value When a given type is passed somewhere, the actual value of the source is copied to the destination. Thus, if changes are made to the destination value, the source value remains unaffected and vice versa. Note that Java primitive types are passed by value. *See also* **by reference**; **primitive type**.

byvalue A keyword that has been defined for reservation purposes only.

case A keyword used to define a numerical value in a given switch statement. *See also* **default**; **switch**.

cast 1. To convert from one type to another. There are two forms of casting: implicit and explicit. Implicit casting lets you cast from one type to another by merely assigning the two types to each other. Explicit casting is the same as implicit except you must put the name of the type to which you are casting (in parentheses) in front of the type from which you are casting. There are two ways to cast in Java: between primitive types and between reference (i.e., object) types. Casting between primitive and reference types is strictly prohibited. Performing primitive type casts is always explicit, and you must be wary of data truncation, which can occur when casting from a larger type to a smaller one. Reference type casting is a bit more complex. First, casting between reference types can be done only in ancestor-to-descendent (and vice versa) or same-class relationships; all others precipitate a compile-time error. Implicit reference casts can be performed in a subclass-to-superclass situation. However, all superclass-to-subclass casts must be done explicitly, and the former must be an instance of the latter; otherwise, a run-time cast exception is thrown. *See also* **primitive type**; **reference type**. 2. A keyword that has been defined for reservation purposes only. *Reference* java.lang.ClassCastException

catch A Java keyword used in exception handling in conjunction with try. A catch statement specifies an exception and a block of code. If, during the execution of the try statement, that exception (or any of its descendants) is thrown, the block of code defined for catch will be fired. *See also* **finally**; **try**. *Reference* java.lang.Exception

certificate *See* **digital certificate**.

char A primitive type representing a 16-bit Unicode value. *See also* **primitive type**; **Unicode**. *Reference* java.lang.Character

class 1. The actual implementation for the framework of an object that can contain constructors, methods, and fields. 2. A keyword used to declare a class. *See also* **class Field**; **class Method**; **constructor**; **field**; **method**. *Reference* java.lang.Class

class Field A field that has been declared static. *See also* **static**. *Reference* java.lang.reflect.Field

class Method A method that has been declared static. *See also* **static**. *Reference* java.lang.reflect.Method

class signature The opening line of code for a given class consisting of its modifiers (if any), name, the superclass it extends, and any interfaces that it implements. *See also* **class**; **method signature**.

clone To create a copy of a given object. *Reference* java.lang.Cloneable

component 1. A widget or container in the Abstract Window Toolkit. This loosely used term originated because all widgets/containers extend the java.awt.Component class. When an event originates from a component, the event sometimes is referred to as a component event. Along these lines, the classes for components sometimes are referred to as component-based classes. *See also* **container**; **widget**. 2. A reusable piece of software. *See also* **bean**. *Reference* java.awt.Component

component architecture The environment and/or proprietary design that is used to create a software component. For example, a Java bean component is neutral from this standpoint because it can be bridged to other component technologies. *See also* **bean**; **component**. *Reference* java.beans

const A keyword that has been defined for reservation purposes only.

constructor A method that is invoked to instantiate a class. All constructors must be defined without a return type and must have the same name as the class they are supposed to construct. *See also* **instance**; **method**; **new**; **return type**.

container A holding tank (usually having some sort of visual boundaries) for components in your graphical user interface. A window (or frame) is a good example of a typical container. Some containers (e.g., panels) can hold not only other components but also other containers. *See also* **component**; **layout**; **widget**. *Reference* java.awt.Container

continue A keyword used as Java's solution to its absence of goto functionality. You can use continue to immediately iterate the innermost loop. You also can perform labeled continues that jump to the specified label and iterate the loop that is currently in scope at that label. *See also* **break**.

customizer A customizer is a wizard-like tool used for editing properties in more sophisticated bean components. Customizers almost always have a visual presence and sometimes coagulate one or more property editors for their bean components. *See also* **bean**; **component**; **descriptor**; **property editor**. *Reference* java.beans.Customizer

daemon thread Background processes (also called user threads) that have a perpetual existence facilitating some basic service. In a Java program, when all of its nondaemon threads have finished, the program is finished. *See also* **thread**. *Reference* java.lang.Thread

default A keyword used to define a default value in a given switch statement. The default option always will be selected if there is no match to any of the available cases. *See also* **case**; **switch**.

delegation model The new event-handling model for Java 1.1 wherein events are delegated to listeners that have registered themselves to the given event source. Also, events themselves are represented as a hierarchy of classes rather than one class containing an ID for each event type. *See also* **event**; **listener**; **register a listener**. *Reference* java.awt.event.*

delimiter A character (or characters) that is specified the breakpoint to be looked for during the tokenizing of some text. *See also* **tokenizing**.

deprecated Used to reference a class, method, or field indicating that using this class/method/field is no longer recommended. *See also* **class**; **field**; **method**.

descriptor Used in Java beans to describe a class that facilitates information about its corresponding bean component. *See also* **bean**; **component**; **customizer**; **introspection**. *Reference* java.beans.FeatureDescriptor

design pattern A process that defines a specific naming convention for some given set of classes and/or methods. For example, design patterns are used in Java beans to define the methods to access a given bean property (among other things). These methods use get*XXX*() and set*XXX*(), where *XXX* is the name of the property. *See also* **bean**.

digital certificate Issued by a certificate authority (CA) and used to attest to the identity of some approved entity. Effectively, it is a way to digitally sign that entity's public key, thereby attesting that the public key does in fact correspond to that entity. *See also* **digital signature**; **key**; **private key**; **public key**. *Reference:* java.security.Certificate

digital signature A form of public key encryption that was introduced by Diffie and Hellman in 1976 and used to verify the integrity and origin of some data (note that it is not used for confidentiality). *See also* **certificate**; **key**; **public key**. *Reference* java.security.Signature

distributed garbage collector The distributed garbage collector (dgc) is used in conjunction with Remote Method Invocation (RMI) to manage the destruction of remote objects. *See also* **garbage collector**; **Remote Method Invocation**. *Reference* java.rmi.*

do A Java keyword used in conjunction with while to create a do-while loop. In this type of loop, the block of code is always executed first; then the evaluation is performed. *See also* **while**.

double A primitive type that is a 64-bit floating point data type, giving it a range of +/-1.79769313486231570E+308 to +/-4.94065645841246544e-324 and the ability to hold 15 significant digits. Note that this data type conforms to IEEE 754 format. *See also* **float**; **primitive type**. *Reference* java.lang.Double

else A Java keyword used in conjunction with an if conditional to define a block of code to be executed in the event that the if conditional returns false. You also can define else-if conditionals in cases in which, if the original if conditional returns false, the first else-if conditional will be tested and so on. Note that the use of else is an optional part in constructing an if conditional. *See also* **if**.

encryption Making some data unintelligible except to those who have the correct decryption process. *See also* **key**; **private key**; **public key**.

engine class A type of class that performs calculations for a given calculation-intensive operation.

error Signifies an unexpected and abnormal issue during program execution. *See also* **exception**. *Reference* java.lang.Error

event Some sort of occurrence, action, or happening that usually is initiated by the user. For instance, a mouse click, a button click, key clicks, and similar actions generate events. Other programs and the operating system also can initiate events. *See also* **event mask**. *Reference* java.util.EventObject

event mask A way to filter events so that only events of a particular type will be processed further. *See also* **event**. *Reference* java.awt.AWTEvent

exception An exception signifies an illegal, invalid, or unexpected issue during program execution. Since exceptions are almost always assumed to be anticipated, you need to provide exception handling as appropriate. *See also* **catch**; **error**; **finally**; **try**. *Reference* java.lang.Exception

extends A Java keyword used in class or interface declarations to specify the superclass that this class or interface is to inherit. *See also* **inheritance**.

false A reserved word that represents the opposite of true. *See also* **boolean**; **true**.

fdlibm Stands for "freely distributable math library" (or something similar). *Reference* java.lang.Math

field A variable.

final A Java keyword used as a modifier for classes, methods, and fields indicating that the given class cannot be subclassed, the given method cannot be overridden, and the given field is to be treated as a constant. *See also* **class**; **method**; **static**; **subclass**; **superclass**.

finally A Java keyword used as an optional part of an exception-handling statement to specify a block of code that will be executed regardless of whether an exception is thrown. Usually any cleanup code will go here. *See also* **catch**; **exception**; **try**.

float A primitive type that is a 32-bit floating-point data type, giving it a range +/-3.40282347E+38 to +/-1.4023984E-45 and the ability to hold seven significant digits. Note that this data type conforms to IEEE 754 format. *See also* **double**; **primitive type**. *Reference* java.lang.Float

focus event An event relating to the gaining/losing of focus. *See also* **event**. *Reference* java.awt.event.FocusAdapter

for A Java keyword used to create a for loop. In every for loop there is an initialization statement called once when the loop starts. Then the loop will continue to cycle between executing a specified block of code, each time calling an incrementing or decrementing expression, and retesting a conditional expression. Note that for loops can be designed to loop forever. *See also* **continue**.

garbage collector A process (borrowed from Smalltalk) of identifying and getting rid of objects that are no longer being referenced and therefore no longer being used. This is performed internally by the Java virtual machine (VM). *See also* **distributed garbage collector**; **virtual machine**.

goto A keyword that has been defined for reservation purposes only. *See also* **break**; **continue**.

graphical user interface (GUI) Relates to and/or specifies the visual part of a program. *See also* **Abstract Window Toolkit**.

GUI *See* **graphical user interface**.

Hashtable An elementary data structure used to hold and quickly retrieve objects based on a key/value association. *See also* **key**; **stack**; **value**.

if A Java keyword used to create an if conditional. In an if conditional are a specified boolean expression and a block of code. In situations in which the expression is true, the corresponding block of code will be executed. In situations in which the expression is false, the block of code is skipped over. *See also* **boolean**; **else**; **false**; **true**.

implements A Java keyword used in class declarations to specify one (or more) interfaces that this class is to implement. The implementing class must then provide for all methods in the interface(s) it is implementing—unless the class is declared abstract. *See also* **abstract**; **class**; **interface**.

import A Java keyword used at (or near) the beginning of a source code file before any class definitions to make the specified class (or package) available to the class(es) in this file. *See also* **class**; **package**.

inheritance An object-oriented programming (OOP) term in which the nonprivate features and attributes of a given superclass are made available to its subclass(es). *See also* **extends**; **object-oriented programming**; **subclass**; **superclass**.

inner class A concept pioneered in the Beta language that is a new addition to Java 1.1. Inner classes give you the ability to define a class inside another class or define a class anonymously inside a given expression (among other things). *See also* **class**.

instance An object-oriented programming (OOP) term used to denote an object, for example, "myA is an instance of class A." Instance is also used to specify nonstatic fields and methods. *See also* **object-oriented programming**; **static**.

instanceof A Java keyword used to check whether a given object is an instance of a given class. *See also* **cast**.

int A primitive type that is a 32-bit signed integer, giving it a range of –2,147,483,648 to +2,147,483,647. *Reference* java.lang.Integer

interface A Java keyword used in a class declaration to define an interface. An interface is used as a way to generically define constants and methods wherein the actual implementation for these methods is done by the class (or classes) implementing this interface. By default, interfaces are defined abstract. Fields in a given interface are defined automatically as static and final. Methods in a given interface are automatically abstract and public. Note that interfaces can extend other interfaces. *See also* **class**; **final**; **field**; **method**; **public**; **static**.

introspection The internal gathering of information about the various attributes and other information. In Java Beans, bean components facilitate descriptors, which introspect the available properties (among other things) about their corresponding bean. Also, reflection lets a Java program introspect real-time data about itself. *See also* **bean**; **component**; **descriptor**; **reflection**. *Reference* java.beans.Introspector

item event An event resulting from a selection/unselection of some choice. Most notably, this event precipitates when a given checkbox is checked/ unchecked. *See also* **event**. *Reference* java.awt.ItemSelectable

Java Database Connectivity (JDBC) A set of application programming interfaces (APIs) that facilitates the framework to let Java talk to a Structured Query Language (SQL) database. The JDBC API was first introduced as an add-on package to the JDK 1.0x and later became part of the standard API for the JDK 1.1x. *See also* **Java Development Kit**; **Structured Query Language**. *Reference* java.sql.*

Java Development Kit (JDK) Contains a set of command-line tools with which to develop Java programs. For more information, see http:// www.javasoft.com. Sometimes referred to as the Java Developer's Kit.

JDBC *See* **Java Database Connectivity**.

JDK *See* **Java Development Kit**.

JIT *See* **Just In Time**.

Just In Time (JIT) A compiler that facilitates the conversion of Java bytecodes to native code on the fly. Usually there is about a tenfold increase in performance between JIT and non-JIT compilers. *Reference* java.lang.Compiler

key 1. In security, a special value used to encrypt and/or decrypt a given piece of data. 2. In dictionary-based data structures a key represents an object which identifies a value. *See also* **encryption**; **private key**; **public key**. *Reference* java.security.Key

keyboard event An event resulting from a key (or keys) being pressed by the user. *See also* **event**. *Reference* java.awt.event.KeyAdapter

layout A type of class that is part of the Abstract Window Toolkit and whose job it is to manage components in a given container using some particular format. Synonymous with "layout manager." *See also* **Abstract Window Toolkit**; **component**. *Reference* java.awt.LayoutManager

listener An object (implementing a Listener interface) that is designated to receive notification if an event is spawned from the object to which it is registered to listen. *See also* **delegation model**; **event**; **register a listener**. *Reference* java.util.EventListener

long A primitive type that is a 64-bit signed integer, giving it a range of –9,223,372,036,854,775,808 to +9,223,372,036,854,775,807. *See also* **primitive type**. *Reference* java.lang.Long

marshal To coagulate parameters (originating from different memory locations) to an array of bytes so they can be sent over a given stream. The term used for the reverse process is "unmarshal." Marshaling is used in Remote Method Invocation to send/receive parameters to/from a given remote call. *See also* **Remote Method Invocation**. *Reference* java.rmi.MarshalException

message digest An algorithm (also known as a "one-way hash function") that can take an arbitrarily sized data input and produce a fixed-length output. Message digests are used in creating the digital fingerprints in a digital signature. *See also* **encryption**; **key**; **private key**; **public key**. *Reference* java.security.MessageDigest

method A function. *See also* **class**; **class Method**; **field**.

method signature The opening line of code for a given method consisting of its modifiers (if any), return type, name, and parameters (if any). *See also* **class signature**; **method**.

model view controller A way for a program to internally listen to parts of itself and respond accordingly based on externally invoked changes to the program. *Reference* java.util.Observer

mouse event An event resulting from a user's mouse. Events can be spawned with the clicking of one of the mouse buttons, its current location, and any of its movements. *See also* **event**. *Reference* java.awt.event.MouseEvent

native A Java keyword used to declare a native method. *See also* **native method**.

native method A method whose implementation is provided natively via some given library. For security reasons, native methods cannot be used by untrusted applets. *See also* **native**.

new A Java keyword that is used to construct instances of a given class or a given array. *See also* **class**; **constructor**.

null A Java keyword used to represent that a given variable is currently undefined. Please do not assume that this is synonymous with zero. Technically speaking, zero is a defined value. *Reference* java.lang.NullPointerException

object An instance of a given class. *See also* **class**; **constructor**; **instance**.

object exportation A Remote Method Invocation process in which a given remote object is made available for receiving remote calls. *See also* **Remote Method Invocation**. *Reference* java.rmi.server.UnicastRemoteObject

object-oriented programming (OOP) A way to organize programs into a collection of objects using inheritance and other related OOP technologies. Note that Java is an object-oriented language. *See also* **inheritance**.

object serialization A process of encoding/decoding an object to an array of bytes so that it can be transmitted over a given input/output stream. When an object has been encoded, it is said to be serialized, and when it has just been decoded, it is said to be deserialized. *See also* **transient**. *Reference* java.io.ObjectInputStream

one-byte pushback Sending a given byte back to the buffer or to the stream so another process can read it. This operation is often used in parsing solutions. The same as one-character pushback except that it is used in conjunction with character streams as opposed to byte streams. *Reference* java.io.PushbackInputStream

OOP *See* **object-oriented programming**.

overload When several methods of the same name vary in return type and/or input parameters. Note that the actual mapping between method calls and the appropriate overloaded method is handled automatically by the compiler.

override When a method in a subclass is defined with the same method signature as that of a method in a superclass. The newer method will replace the older and is said to have "overridden" or "shadowed" it. Note that the superclass method still can be accessed with a super and/or a direct reference. *See also* **method**; **super**.

package A Java keyword used at the beginning of a source code file to make the class(es) defined here a member of the specified package. *See also* **class**; **import**.

packet In Transmission Control Protocol/Internet Protocol (TCP/IP), represents a unit of data in the form of bytes. Depending on the type of TCP/IP protocol used, a packet can be a completely self-contained message or part of a series. *See also* **Transmission Control Protocol**; **Transmission Control Protocol/Internet Protocol**; **User Datagram Protocol**.

paint event An event that is used internally by the Abstract Window Toolkit to ensure that a given Java graphical user interface is painted/updated properly. *See also* **Abstract Window Toolkit**; **event**; **graphical user interface**.

permissions A computer security term used to denote the accessibility (either read, write, or both) to some resource. *See also* **Access Control List**. *Reference* java.security.acl.*

primitive type Corresponding to one of Java's nonobject data types. These types—boolean, char, byte, short, int, long, float, and double—are built into the Java language and as a result are passed by value rather than by reference. *See also* **by reference**; **by value**.

principal In computer security, an entity (i.e., a person, organization, department, etc.) that can be referenced with a name. *See also* **Access Control List**. *Reference* java.security.Principal

private A Java keyword that is an access modifier used in methods and fields. This modifier imposes the highest level of restrictions wherein the method/field is available only to the class in which it is defined. *See also* **class**; **method**; **protected**; **public**.

private key A key that can decrypt only a given piece of data formerly encrypted with the corresponding public key. *See also* **encryption**; **key**; **public key**.

property editor An object (usually visual) used to read and/or edit the value for a given data type (primitive or object). Property editors are used to give users access to properties of a corresponding data type for a given bean component. *See also* **bean**; **component**; **customizer**; **primitive type**.

protected A Java keyword that is an access modifier used on fields and methods. This modifier allows access, by the declaring class, by subclasses, or by any other classes in the package to which the declaring class belongs. *See also* **class**; **method**; **package**; **private**; **public**.

public A Java keyword that is an access modifier used on classes, interfaces, fields, and methods. This modifier is the least restrictive, granting accessibility from any class. *See also* **class**; **method**; **private**; **protected**.

public key A key that can encrypt only a given piece of data. *See also* **encryption**; **key**; **private key**.

reference type Objects are sometimes referred to as reference types because in Java all objects are passed by reference. *See also* **by reference**; **object**.

reflection The overall concept of reflection is to perform introspection on some object during real time. *See also* **introspection**; **object**. *Reference* java.lang.reflect.*

register a listener The process of assigning a listener to a given source object (usually a component) for which it will "listen" for any events originating from that source. *See also* **component**; **delegation model**; **event**; **listener**.

Remote Method Invocation (RMI) Denotes a set of application programming interfaces that facilitate the support for Java to call methods from remote Java virtual machines. *See also* **object exportation**; **object serialization**; **remote object**. *Reference* java.rmi.*

remote object An object that has been designed to be accessed remotely using Remote Method Invocation. *See also* **Remote Method Invocation**. *Reference* java.rmi.server.*

return A Java keyword used in methods and constructors to return execution back to the caller. When using return in methods that have a return type defined, a corresponding return value (or expression) must be appended to the keyword. If return is called inside an exception-handling statement, the finally code will be executed. *See also* **constructor**; **finally**; **method**; **return type**.

return type The data type specified as the returning value for a given method. *See also* **method**; **primitive type**; **reference type**.

RMI *See* **Remote Method Invocation**.

sandbox A term used to denote the restricted environment to which all untrusted applets are confined. In the sandbox, an applet cannot access the file system direct, make arbitrary network connections, or call native methods (among other things). *See also* **untrusted applet**.

short A primitive type that is an 8-bit signed integer, giving it a range of –32,768 to 32,767. *See also* **primitive type**. *Reference* java.lang.Short

signed applet Used to denote a Java applet that has been digitally signed, giving it the ability to have its origin and integrity verified by a given client. Once verified, the applet will be granted trusted status, giving it freedom from the sandbox. *See also* **certificate**; **digital signature**; **key**; **sandbox**.

skeleton A Remote Method Invocation term for a "server-side proxy" that is generated by the rmic compiler for a given remote object. A skeleton is used to receive and dispatch remote calls, unmarshal any parameters, and marshal the results between the remote reference layer and the actual remote object. *See also* **marshal**; **Remote Method Invocation**; **stub**. *Reference* java.rmi.server.Skeleton

socket The endpoints in a Transmission Control Protocol connection. *See also* **Transmission Control Protocol**; **Transmission Control Protocol/Internet Protocol**; **User Datagram Protocol**. *Reference* java.net.Socket

SQL *See* **Structured Query Language**.

stack A stack is an elementary data structure used to hold data temporarily by a Last In First Out (LIFO) policy. *Reference* java.util.Stack

static A Java keyword that is a modifier used to designate a field or method to the class rather than a given instance. In this way, you can create constants from fields and "global" methods that can be accessed without having to instantiate the class of which the method/field is a member. *See also* **class Field**; **class Method**; **instance**.

Structured Query Language (SQL) A database language that lets you manipulate information contained in a Relational Database Management System (RDMS). Because SQL is fairly uniform across all the major databases and is easy to use, it has rapidly become the accepted standard in the industry. *See also* **Java Database Connectivity**.

SQL92 A term used to reference the current standard for SQL that was introduced in 1992. *See also* **SQL**.

stack A stack is an elementary data structure used to temporarily hold data in a Last In First Out (LIFO) policy. *Reference* java.util.Stack

static A Java keyword that is a modifier used to designate a field or method to the class rather than a given instance. In this way you can create constants from fields and "global" methods that can be accessed without having to instance the class the method/field is a member of. *See also* **class Field**; **class Method**; **instance**.

stub A Remote Method Invocation term for a "client-side proxy" that is generated by the rmic compiler. A stub is used to receive and initiate remote calls, marshal any parameters, and unmarshal the results between the client object and the remote reference layer. *See also* **marshal**; **Remote Method Invocation**; **skeleton**. *Reference* java.rmi.server.RemoteStub

subclass A term used to denote a class is a descendent of another class. Technically speaking, all classes extend from another class. Even those classes that don't explicitly have the extends clause implicitly extend java.lang.Object (the root class in Java). The term "subclass" is used for situations in which you wish to make apparent that this class extends another. *See also* **extends**; **superclass**.

super A Java keyword used to reference nonstatic methods and/or variables of the parent class that may be hidden by the current class. This keyword, when called like a method (i.e., super(), super(a, b, c,)), also can be used to call the parent class's constructor. *See also* **this**.

superclass A term used to denote a class that is extended by another class (or classes) in some way. *See also* **extends**; **subclass**.

switch A Java keyword used to create a switch statement. A switch statement is used to evaluate an integral expression and select a case based on results of that expression. Unless a break is specified in each case, the program will continue to execute into the following cases until it reaches the end of the switch statement or comes across a break. Note that, optionally, you can add a default selection, which will be chosen in the event that there is no matching case for the given expression. *See also* **break**; **default**.

synchronized A Java keyword used to avoid concurrency conflicts. You can specify this as a modifier in a nonstatic method or a class or as a statement for a block of code, in which case only one thread can execute the synchronized item at a time. *See also* **static**; **thread**.

TCP *See* **Transmission Control Protocol**.

TCP/IP *See* **Transmission Control Protocol/Internet Protocol**.

this A Java keyword used to reference the current object inside a class definition, bypassing the need for an instance variable. You also can use a this reference in the first line of a class's constructor to reference another of the class's constructors. *See also* **super**.

thread A given stream of execution. Since Java is a multithreaded environment, more than one thread can be executing in a given program at the same time. While this can sometimes lead to concurrency issues, having multiple threads executing can make your program more responsive. *See also* **daemon thread**; **synchronized**. *Reference* java.lang.Thread

throw A Java keyword used to throw a given exception object. *See also* **catch**; **finally**; **throws**; **try**. *Reference* java.lang.Exception

throws A Java keyword used to declare all exceptions that a given method can throw. It is then up to the program calling that method to catch or rethrow these exceptions. Note that Error (and its derivatives) as well as RuntimeException (and its derivatives) do not need to be declared (or caught for that matter) in a given method. *Reference* java.lang.Exception

tokenizing The process of chopping up some given textual information into pieces (known as tokens) based on any specified delimiter(s). *See* **delimiter**.

transaction processing Transaction processing deals with contingency SQL queries. The most common examples are financial transactions in which money must be accounted for either by committing the SQL query if everything is processed successfully or rolling everything back to its original state. *See also* **JDBC**; **SQL**.

transient A Java keyword used as a modifier for fields in a class stating that the specified field is not a persistent part of the given class instance. In object serialization, any transient fields are ignored. *See also* **object serialization**.

Transmission Control Protocol (TCP) Part of the TCP/IP suite. TCP implements a continuous and connection-oriented session, facilitating a more reliable form of communication than its User Datagram Protocol counterpart. TCP resequences received packets and, if any are found to be lost, it has them resent. However, the cost of all this is added overhead. *See also* **packet**; **Transmission Control Protocol/Internet Protocol**; **User Datagram Protocol**.

Transmission Control Protocol/Internet Protocol (TCP/IP) A suite of protocols developed by the Department of Defense, making big improvements in fault tolerance and heterogeneous communication. First implemented in the early Internet, TCP/IP is now the standard for networking on the Net and in Java. *See also* **Transmission Control Protocol**; **User Datagram Protocol**. *Reference* java.util.Socket

true A reserved word that represents the opposite of false. *See also* **boolean**; **false**.

trusted applet An applet that has been digitally signed, thereby granting it freedom from the sandbox. It is still ultimately up to the user to decide what and how much freedom the applet can have. *See also* **sandbox**; **signed applet**; **untrusted applet**.

try A Java keyword used to declare an exception-handling statement. Any code specified in the try block will be "tried" and, if an exception is thrown, it should be caught in the corresponding catch block. *See also* **catch**; **finally**; **throw**; **throws**.

UDP *See* **User Datagram Protocol**.

Unicode Unicode is a 16-bit character code set. Unlike the older ANSI/ASCII standards used in C/C++ that are 8 bits in length (and therefore can contain only a total of 255 characters), Unicode can contain 65,536. Unicode contains symbols for just about every major dialect in the world and is the code set used in Java.

unmarshal *See* **marshal**.

unsigned applet *See* **untrusted applet**.

untrusted applet An applet that is not digitally signed and therefore must be verified and restricted to the sandbox. *See also* **digital signature**; **sandbox**; **trusted applet**.

User Datagram Protocol (UDP) Part of the Transmission Control Protocol/Internet Protocol (TCP/IP) suite facilitating a connectionless session wherein each packet is sent on its own. While this is more efficient (and quite useful for sending data to multiple hosts), it is not as reliable as its TCP counterpart. *See also* **packet**; **Transmission Control Protocol**; **Transmission Control Protocol/Internet Protocol**. *Reference* java.net.DatagramPacket

value In dictionary-based data structures, values are the actual objects being stored and referenced by a corresponding key. *See also* **Hashtable**; **key**.

virtual machine (VM) The run-time environment, also referred to as the "Java virtual machine," on top of which Java programs sit to execute. Its primary duties include loading, verifying, and interpreting a compiled Java program. In lay terms, the VM could be considered the bridge between Java's platform-independent environment and the given native environment on which the Java program is running.

VM *See* **virtual machine**.

void A Java keyword used in methods to specify that no value will be returning. *See also* **method**; **return type**.

volatile A Java keyword used as a modifier for fields, specifying that this field may be accessed in an asynchronous fashion and therefore should not be optimized. *See also* **field**.

while A Java keyword used to create a while loop. In this type of loop, the evaluation is always performed first; then the specified block of code is executed. *See also* **do**.

widget A term used to denote an elementary graphical user interface component in the Abstract Window Toolkit. *See also* **Abstract Window Toolkit**; **component**; **graphical user interface**.

window event An event resulting from some sort of window action. For example, minimizing, maximizing, opening, and closing a given window in Java can spawn such events. *See also* **event**. *Reference* java.awt.event.WindowAdapter

The Comprehensive Guide to Visual Basic 5

$49.99, 600 pages, illustrated, part #: 1-56604-484-7

From the author of Ventana's bestselling *Visual Guide to Visual Basic for Windows*! Command and syntax descriptions feature real-world examples. Thoroughly covers new features, uses, backward compatibility and much more. The CD-ROM features a complete, searchable text version of the book including all code.

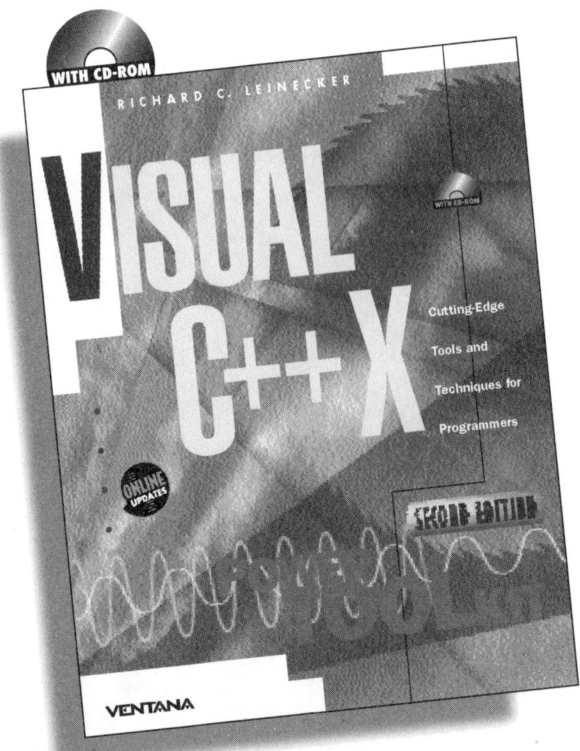

Visual C++ X Power Toolkit, Second Edition

$49.99, 800 pages, part #: 1-56604-528-2

Completely updated to cover all new features in the latest version of Visual C++ — including graphics, animation, sound, connectivity and more. Class libraries, tutorials and techniques offer programmers a professional edge. The CD-ROM features fully compiled class libraries, demo programs and complete standards files for all major picture formats.

Net Security: Your Digital Doberman

$29.99, 312 pages, illustrated, part #: 1-56604-506-1

Doing business on the Internet can be safe . . . if you know the risks and take appropriate steps. This thorough overview helps you put a virtual Web watchdog on the job—to protect both your company and your customers from hackers, electronic shoplifters and disgruntled employees. Easy-to-follow explanations help you understand complex security technologies, with proven technologies for safe Net transactions. Tips, checklists and action plans cover digital dollars, pilfer-proof "storefronts," protecting privacy and handling breaches.

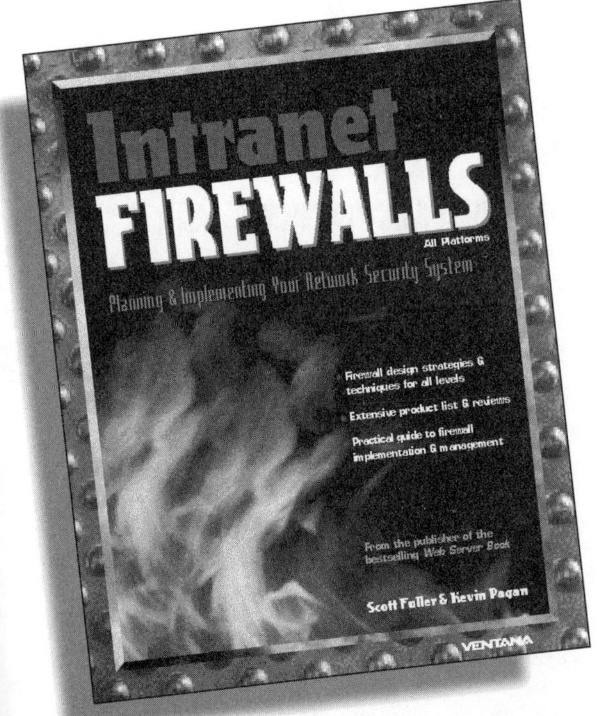

Intranet Firewalls

$34.99, 360 pages, illustrated, part #: 1-56604-506-1

Protect your network by controlling access—inside and outside your company—to proprietary files. This practical, hands-on guide takes you from intranet and firewall basics through creating and launching your firewall. Professional advice helps you assess your security needs and choose the best system for you. Includes tips for avoiding costly mistakes, firewall technologies, in-depth reviews and uses for popular firewall software, advanced theory of firewall design strategies and implementation, and more.

Java Programming for the Internet

$49.95, 816 pages, illustrated, part #: 1-56604-355-7

Master the programming language of choice for Internet applications. Expand the scope of your online development with this comprehensive, step-by-step guide to creating Java applets. The CD-ROM features Java Developers Kit, source code for all the applets, samples and programs from the book, and much more.

The Visual Basic Programmer's Guide to Java

$39.99, 450 pages, part #: 1-56604-527-4

At last—a Java book that speaks your language! Use your understanding of Visual Basic as a foundation for learning Java and object-oriented programming. This unique guide not only relates Java features to what you already know—it also highlights the areas in which Java excels over Visual Basic, to build an understanding of its appropriate use. The CD-ROM features comparative examples written in Java & Visual Basic, code for projects created in the book and more

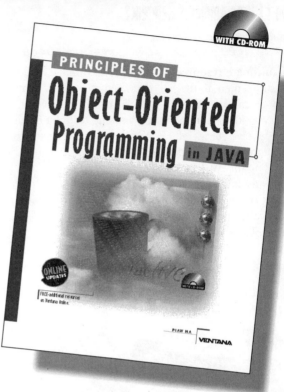

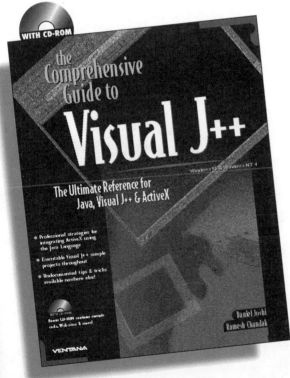

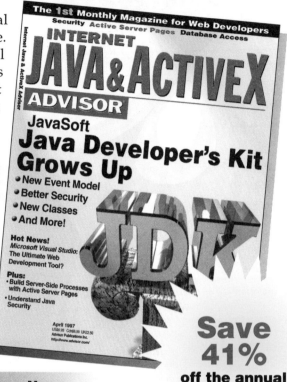